Family
Encyclopedia

Titles in this series

HUTCHINSON

Family
Encyclopedia

BROCKHAMPTON PRESS
LONDON

Copyright © Helicon Publishing Ltd 1995
All rights reserved

Helicon Publishing Ltd
42 Hythe Bridge Street
Oxford OX1 2EP

Printed and bound in Great Britain by
Mackays of Chatham Plc,
Chatham, Kent

This edition published 1997 by
Brockhampton Press Ltd
20 Bloomsbury Street
London WC1B 3QA
(*a member of the Hodder Headline PLC Group*)

ISBN 1-86019-565-2

British Cataloguing in Publication Data

A catalogue record for this book is available
from the British Library

Contents

Managing editor
Denise Dresner

Editors
Sue Croft
Catherine Thompson

Production
Tony Ballsdon

Contributors
Christine Avery PhD
John Ayto MA
Paul Bahn
Anne Baker
Tallis Barker
Nigel Davis MSc
Ian D Derbyshire PhD
J Denis Derbyshire PhD, FBIM
Michael Dewar
Dougal Dixon BSc, MSc
Nigel Dudley
Ingrid von Essen
Peter Fleming PhD
Lawrence Garner BA
Wendy Grossman
Michael Hitchcock PhD
Peter Lafferty MSc
Graham Ley MPhil
Carol Lister PhD, FSS

Tom McArthur PhD
David Munro PhD
Chris Murray
Joanna O'Brien
Robert Paisley PhD
Martin Palmer
Paulette Pratt
Tim Pulleine
Chris Rhys
Ian Ridpath FRAS
Adrian Room MA
Julian Rowe PhD
Jack Schofield BA, MA
Joe Staines
Catherine Thompson
Norman Vance, PhD
Stephen Webster BSc, MPhil
John Wells

Preface

This handy mini-encyclopedia is packed with thousands of articles in a single alphabetical listing, so you can quickly find what you're looking for. The material is derived from the continually updated database of *The Hutchinson Encyclopedia*, rated the most authoritative and accessible encyclopedia on the market.

The Pocket Encyclopedia covers a similar range of subject areas to its parent volume, including history, science, the arts, sport, technology, religion, and countries of the world. In selecting entries to include, every effort has been made to strike a balance between core reference articles (such as *Charlemagne, neutrino, psychology*); topical articles (such as *CD-ROM, Tony Blair, Human Genome Project*); and international articles (such as *Gujarat, Deng Xiaoping, Haute-Normandie*). Most entries consist of a succinct paragraph, but further information is given where needed, for example on the origins of the human species, the theory of relativity, the history of agriculture.

Tables
A number of tables can be found at the back of the book – conversion tables, Nobel prizes, Academy Awards, sovereigns of the UK, signs of the zodiac, birthstones and anniversaries, and more.

Arrangement of entries
Entries are ordered alphabetically, as if there were no spaces between words, thus

> Korean
> Korea, North
> Korean War
> Korea, South

Words beginning 'Mc' and 'Mac' are treated as if they begin 'Mac'; 'St' and 'Saint' are both treated as if they were spelt 'Saint'.

Cross-references

The text includes hundreds of cross-references to related topics, shown by a ◊ symbol in front of the reference. Cross-references are also used for common alternative spellings (thus 'Mohammed' will direct you to Muhammad) and for the full entries of common abbreviations and acronyms (such as DNA and NATO).

Chinese names

Pinyin, the preferred system for transcribing Chinese names of people and places, is generally used: thus, there is an entry at Mao Zedong, not Mao Tse-tung. Exceptions are made for a few names that are more familiar in their former (Wade-Giles) form, such as Chiang Kai-shek.

Your comments

Part of the success and continual improvement of our encyclopedias is due to feedback from our readers. All letters are gratefully received and acknowledged, whether in regard to corrections, suggestions for new entries, or general comments.

A

abacus ancient calculating device made up of a frame of parallel wires on which beads are strung. The method of calculating with a handful of stones on a 'flat surface' (Latin *abacus*) was familiar to the Greeks and Romans, and used by earlier peoples, possibly even in ancient Babylon; it survives in the more sophisticated bead-frame form of the Russian *schoty* and the Japanese *soroban*.

abdomen in vertebrates, the part of the body below the ◊thorax, containing the digestive organs; in insects and other arthropods, it is the hind part of the body. In mammals, the abdomen is separated from the thorax by the diaphragm, a sheet of muscular tissue; in arthropods, commonly by a narrow constriction.

Aberdeen city and seaport on the east coast of Scotland, administrative headquarters of Grampian Region; population (1991) 204,900. There are shore-based maintenance and service depots for the North Sea oil rigs. Aberdeen is Scotland's third-largest city and its biggest resort.

Abidja'n port and former capital (until 1983) of the Republic of Ivory Coast, W Africa; population (1982) 1,850,000. Yamoussoukro became the new capital 1983, but was not internationally recognized as such until 1992.

abiotic factor a nonorganic variable within the ecosystem, affecting the life of organisms. Examples include temperature, light, and soil structure. Abiotic factors can be harmful to the environment, as when sulphur dioxide emissions from power stations produce acid rain.

Abkhazia autonomous republic in Georgia, situated on the Black Sea; *capital* Sukhumi; *area* 8,600 sq km/3,320 sq mi; *population* (1989) 526,000.

abolitionism in UK and US history, a movement culminating in the late 18th and early 19th centuries that aimed first to end the slave trade, and then to abolish the institution of ◊slavery and emancipate slaves.

aborigine any indigenous inhabitant of a region or country. The word often refers to the original peoples of areas colonized by Europeans, and especially to ◊Australian Aborigines.

abortion ending of a pregnancy before the fetus is developed sufficiently to survive outside the uterus. Loss of a fetus at a later gestational age is termed premature stillbirth. Abortion may be accidental (miscarriage) or deliberate (termination of pregnancy).

Abraham In the Old Testament, founder of the Jewish nation. In his early life he was called Abram. God promised him heirs and land for his people in

Canaan (Israel), renamed him Abraham ('father of many nations'), and tested his faith by a command (later retracted) to sacrifice his son Isaac.

Abruzzi mountainous region of S central Italy, comprising the provinces of L'Aquila, Chieti, Pescara, and Teramo; area 10,800 sq km/4,169 sq mi; population (1990) 1,272,000; capital L'Aquila. Gran Sasso d'Italia, 2,914 m/9,564 ft, is the highest point of the ▷Apennines.

absolute value or *modulus* in mathematics, the value, or magnitude, of a number irrespective of its sign. The absolute value of a number n is written $|n|$ (or sometimes as mod n), and is defined as the positive square root of n^2. For example, the numbers -5 and 5 have the same absolute value:

$$|5| = |-5| = 5$$

absorption in science, the taking up of one substance by another, such as a liquid by a solid (ink by blotting paper) or a gas by a liquid (ammonia by water). In biology, absorption describes the passing of nutrients or medication into and through tissues such as intestinal walls and blood vessels.

abstract art nonrepresentational art. Ornamental art without figurative representation occurs in most cultures. The modern abstract movement in sculpture and painting emerged in Europe and North America between 1910 and 1920. Two approaches produce different abstract styles: images that have been 'abstracted' from nature to the point where they no longer reflect a conventional reality, and nonobjective, or 'pure', art forms, without any reference to reality.

Abu Dhabi sheikdom in SW Asia, on the Persian Gulf, capital of the ▷United Arab Emirates; area 67,350 sq km/ 26,000 sq mi; population (1982 est) 516,000. Formerly under British protection, it is now the provisional capital of the United Arab Emirates.

Abuja capital of Nigeria (formally designated as such 1982, although not officially recognized until 1992); population (1991) 378,700 (federal capital territory). Shaped like a crescent, the city was designed by Japanese architect Kenzo Tange; it began construction 1976 as a replacement for Lagos.

abyssal zone dark ocean region 2,000–6,000 m/6,500–19,500 ft deep; temperature 4°C/39°F. Three- quarters of the area of the deep-ocean floor lies in the abyssal zone, which is too far from the surface for photosynthesis to take place. Some fish and crustaceans living there are blind or have their own light sources. The region above is the bathyal zone; the region below, the hadal zone.

abzyme in biotechnology, an artificially created antibody that can be used like an enzyme to accelerate reactions.

AC in physics, abbreviation for ▷*alternating current.*

acacia any of a large group of shrubs and trees of the genus *Acacia* of the legume family Leguminosae. Acacias include the thorn trees of the African savanna and the gum arabic tree *A. senegal* of N Africa, and several North American species of the SW USA and Mexico. Acacias are found in warm regions of the world, particularly Australia.

Academy Award annual award in many categories, given since 1927 by the

American Academy of Motion Picture Arts and Sciences (founded by Louis B Mayer of Metro-Goldwyn-Mayer 1927). Arguably the film community's most prestigious accolade, the award is a gold-plated statuette, which has been nick-named 'Oscar' since 1931. *(See table on page 559.)*

Acapulco or *Acapulco de Juarez* port and holiday resort in S Mexico; population (1990) 592,200. Acapulco was Mexico's major Pacific coast port until about 1815.

acceleration rate of change of the velocity of a moving body. It is usually measured in metres per second per second (m s^{-2}) or feet per second per second (ft s^{-2}). Because velocity is a ◊vector quantity (possessing both magnitude and direction) a body travelling at constant speed may be said to be accelerating if its direction of motion changes. According to Newton's second law of motion, a body will accelerate only if it is acted upon by an unbalanced, or resultant, ◊force.

accelerator in physics, a device to bring charged particles (such as protons and electrons) up to high speeds and energies, at which they can be of use in industry, medicine, and pure physics. At low energies, accelerated particles can be used to produce the image on a television screen and generate X-rays (by means of a ◊cathode-ray tube), destroy tumour cells, or kill bacteria. When high-energy particles collide with other particles, the fragments formed reveal the nature of the fundamental forces of nature.

Accra capital and port of Ghana; population (1984) 964,800. The port trades in cacao, gold, and timber. Osu (Christiansborg) Castle is the presidential residence.

Achilles Greek hero of Homer's *Iliad*. He was the son of Peleus, king of the Myrmidons in Thessaly, and of the sea nymph Thetis, who rendered him invulnerable, except for the heel by which she held him, by dipping him in the river Styx. Achilles killed ◊Hector at the climax of the *Iliad*, and according to subsequent Greek legends was himself killed by ◊Paris, who shot a poisoned arrow into Achilles' heel.

acid compound that, in solution in an ionizing solvent (usually water), gives rise to hydrogen ions (H^{+} or protons). In modern chemistry, acids are defined as substances that are proton donors and accept electrons to form ◊ionic bonds. Acids react with ◊bases to form salts, and they act as solvents. Strong acids are corrosive; dilute acids have a sour or sharp taste, although in some organic acids this may be partially masked by other flavour characteristics.

acid rain acidic precipitation thought to be caused principally by the release into the atmosphere of sulphur dioxide (SO$_2$) and oxides of nitrogen. Sulphur dioxide is formed by the burning of fossil fuels, such as coal, that contain high quantities of sulphur; nitrogen oxides are contributed from various industrial activities and from car exhaust fumes.

acoustics in general, the experimental and theoretical science of sound and its transmission; in particular, that branch of the science that has to do with the phenomena of sound in a particular space such as a room or theatre. In architecture, the sound-reflecting character of a room.

acquired immune deficiency syndrome full name for the disease ◊AIDS.

acrylic fibre synthetic fibre often used as a substitute for wool. It was first developed 1947 but not produced in great volumes until the 1950s. It is manufactured as a filament, then cut into short staple lengths similar to wool hairs, and spun into yarn.

actinide any of a series of 15 radioactive metallic chemical elements with atomic numbers 89 (actinium) to 103 (lawrencium). Elements 89 to 95 occur in nature; the rest of the series are synthesized elements only.

Actium, Battle of naval battle in which Octavian defeated the combined fleets of ◊Mark Antony and ◊Cleopatra 31 BC to become the undisputed ruler of the Roman world, as emperor Augustus. The site is at Akri, a promontory in W Greece.

act of Congress in the USA, a bill or resolution passed by both houses of Congress, the Senate and the House of Representatives, which becomes law with the signature of the president. The UK equivalent is an act of Parliament.

act of Parliament in Britain, a change in the law originating in Parliament and called a statute. Before an act receives the royal assent and becomes law it is a *bill*. The US equivalent is an act of Congress.

acupuncture in alternative medicine, system of inserting long, thin metal needles into the body at predetermined points to relieve pain, as an anaesthetic in surgery, and to assist healing. The needles are rotated manually or electrically. The method, developed in ancient China and increasingly popular in the West, is thought to work by somehow stimulating the brain's own painkillers, the ◊endorphins.

Adam Family of Scottish architects and designers. *William Adam* (1689–1748) was the leading Scottish architect of his day, and his son *Robert Adam* (1728–1792) is considered one of the greatest British architects of the late 18th century, responsible for transforming the prevailing Palladian fashion in architecture to a Neo-Classical style.

Adam in the Old Testament, the first human. Formed by God from dust and given the breath of life, Adam was placed in the Garden of Eden, where ◊Eve was created from his rib and given to him as a companion. Because she tempted him, he tasted the forbidden fruit of the Tree of Knowledge of Good and Evil, for which trespass they were expelled from the Garden.

Adams Gerry (Gerard) 1948– . Northern Ireland politician, president of Provisional Sinn Féin (the political wing of the ◊Irish Republican Army (IRA) from 1978. He was elected member of Parliament for Belfast West 1983 but declined to take up his Westminster seat, stating that he did not believe in the British government. After he announced an IRA ceasefire 1994, the British government lifted the ban on his public appearances and freedom to travel to the UK (in force since 1988).

adaptation in biology, any change in the structure or function of an organism that allows it to survive and reproduce more effectively in its environment. In ◊evolution, adaptation is thought to occur as a result of random variation in the genetic make-up of organisms coupled with ▷natural selection. Species become extinct when they are no longer adapted to their environment – for instance, if the climate suddenly becomes colder.

adder European venomous snake, the common ▷viper *Vipera berus*. Growing to about 60 cm/24 in in length, it has a thick body, triangular head, a characteristic V-shaped mark on its head and, often, zigzag markings along the back. It feeds on small mammals and lizards.

addiction state of dependence caused by habitual use of drugs, alcohol, or other substances. It is characterized by uncontrolled craving, tolerance, and symptoms of withdrawal when access is denied. Habitual use produces changes in body chemistry and treatment must be geared to a gradual reduction in dosage.

Addis Ababa or *Adis Abeba* capital of Ethiopia; population (1984) 1,413,000. It was founded 1887 by Menelik, chief of Shoa, who ascended the throne of Ethiopia 1889. It is the headquarters of the Organization of African Unity.

additive in food, any natural or artificial chemical added to prolong the shelf life of processed foods (salt or nitrates), alter the colour or flavour of food, or improve its food value (vitamins or minerals). Many chemical additives are used and they are subject to regulation, since individuals may be affected by constant exposure even to traces of certain additives and may suffer side effects ranging from headaches and hyperactivity to cancer. Within the European Union, approved additives are given an official E number.

Adelaide capital and industrial city of South Australia; population (1990) 1,049,100. Founded 1836, Adelaide was named after William IV's queen.

Aden (Arabic *'Adan*) main port and commercial centre of Yemen, commanding the entrance to the Red Sea; population (1984) 318,000. A British territory from 1839, Aden became part of independent South Yemen 1967; it was the capital of South Yemen until 1990.

Adenauer Konrad 1876–1967. German Christian Democrat politician, chancellor of West Germany 1949–63. With the French president Charles de Gaulle he achieved the postwar reconciliation of France and Germany and strongly supported all measures designed to strengthen the Western bloc in Europe.

adenoids masses of lymphoid tissue, similar to ▷tonsils, located in the upper part of the throat, behind the nose. They are part of a child's natural defences against the entry of germs but usually shrink and disappear by the age of ten.

adiabatic in physics, a process that occurs without loss or gain of heat, especially the expansion or contraction of a gas in which a change takes place in the pressure or volume, although no heat is allowed to enter or leave.

Adi Granth or *Guru Granth Sahib* the holy book of ▷Sikhism.

adolescence in the human life cycle, the period between the beginning of puberty and adulthood.

Adonis in Greek mythology, a beautiful youth loved by the goddess ▷Aphrodite. He was killed while boar-hunting but was allowed to return from the underworld for six months every year to rejoin her. The anemone sprang from his blood.

adrenal gland or *suprarenal gland* triangular gland situated on top of the kidney. The adrenals are soft and yellow, and consist of two parts: the cortex and medulla. The *cortex* (outer part) secretes various steroid hormones, controls salt and water metabolism, and regulates the use of carbohydrates, proteins, and fats. The *medulla* (inner part) secretes the hormones adrenaline and noradrenaline which, during times of stress, cause the heart to beat faster and harder, increase blood flow to the heart and muscle cells, and dilate airways in the lungs, thereby delivering more oxygen to cells throughout the body and in general preparing the body for 'fight or flight'.

adrenaline or *epinephrine* hormone secreted by the medulla of the ◊adrenal glands.

Adriatic Sea large arm of the Mediterranean Sea, lying NW to SE between the Italian and the Balkan peninsulas. The western shore is Italian; the eastern includes Croatia, Montenegro, and Albania, with a small strip of coastline owned by Slovenia. Bosnia has 20 km of coastline, but no port. The sea is about 805 km/500 mi long, and its area is 135,250 sq km/52,220 sq mi.

Adventist person who believes that Jesus will return to make a second appearance on Earth. Expectation of the Second Coming of Christ is found in New Testament writings generally. Adventist views are held by the Seventh-Day Adventists, Christadelphians, Jehovah's Witnesses, and the Four Square Gospel Alliance.

Aegean Sea branch of the Mediterranean between Greece and Turkey; the Dardanelles connect it with the Sea of Marmara. The numerous islands in the Aegean Sea include Crete, the Cyclades, the Sporades, and the Dodecanese.

Aeneas in classical mythology, a Trojan prince who became the ancestral hero of the Romans. According to ◊Homer, he was the son of Anchises and the goddess Aphrodite. Virgil's epic poem the *Aeneid* is based on his mythical escape from Troy.

aerial or *antenna* in radio and television broadcasting, a conducting device that radiates or receives electromagnetic waves. The design of an aerial depends principally on the wavelength of the signal.

aerobic in biology, descriptive of those living organisms that require oxygen (usually dissolved in water) for the efficient release of energy contained in food molecules, such as glucose. They include almost all living organisms (plants as well as animals) with the exception of certain bacteria, yeasts, and internal parasites.

aerobics (Greek 'air' and 'life') exercises to improve the performance of the heart and lungs. A strenuous application of movement to raise the heart rate to 120 beats per minute or more for sessions of 5–20 minutes' duration, 3–5 times per week.

aerodynamics branch of fluid physics that studies the forces exerted by air or other gases in motion – for example, the airflow around bodies (such as land vehicles, bullets, rockets, and aircraft) moving at speed through the atmosphere. For maximum efficiency, the aim is usually to design the shape of an object to produce a streamlined flow, with a minimum of turbulence in the moving air.

aeroplane (US *airplane*) powered heavier-than-air craft supported in flight by fixed wings. Aeroplanes are propelled by the thrust of a jet engine or airscrew (propeller). They must be designed aerodynamically, since streamlining ensures maximum flight efficiency. The Wright brothers flew the first powered plane (a biplane) in Kitty Hawk, North Carolina, USA, 1903. For the history of aircraft and aviation, see ▷flight.

aerosol particles of liquid or solid suspended in a gas. Fog is a common natural example. Aerosol cans contain a substance such as scent or cleaner packed under pressure with a device for releasing it as a fine spray. Most aerosols used chlorofluorocarbons (CFCs) as propellants until these were found to cause destruction of the ▷ozone layer in the stratosphere. The international community has agreed to phase out the use of CFCs.

Aeschylus *c.* 525–*c.* 456 BC. Athenian dramatist. He developed Greek tragedy by introducing the second actor, enabling dialogue and dramatic action to occur independently of the chorus. Aeschylus composed some 90 plays between 500 and 456 BC, of which seven complete tragedies survive in his name: *Persians* 472 BC, *Seven Against Thebes* 467, *Suppliants* 463, the *Oresteia* trilogy (*Agamemnon*, *Libation-Bearers*, and *Eumenides*) 458, and *Prometheus Bound*.

Aesop by tradition, a writer of Greek fables. According to the historian Herodotus, he lived in the mid-6th century BC and was a slave. The fables, which are ascribed to him, were collected at a later date and are anecdotal stories using animal characters to illustrate moral or satirical points.

Aesthetic Movement English artistic movement of the late 19th century, dedicated to the doctrine of 'art for art's sake' – that is, art as a self-sufficient entity concerned solely with beauty and not with any moral or social purpose. Associated with the movement were the artists Aubrey Beardsley and James McNeill Whistler and the writers Walter Pater and Oscar Wilde.

affirmative action government policy of positive discrimination that favours members of minority ethnic groups and women in such areas as employment and education, designed to counter the effects of long-term discrimination against them. In Europe, Sweden, Belgium, the Netherlands, and Italy actively promote affirmative action through legal and financial incentives.

Afghanistan Republic of (*Jamhuria Afghanistan*); *area* 652,090 sq km/ 251,707 sq mi; *capital* Kabul; *environment* an estimated 95% of the urban population is without access to sanitation services; *features* Hindu Kush mountain range (Khyber and Salang passes, Wakhan salient and Panjshir Valley), Amu Darya (Oxus) River, Helmand River, Lake Saberi; *political system* emergent democracy; *population* (1993 est) 17,400,000 (more than 5 million became refugees after 1979); growth rate 0.6% p.a.; *languages* Pushtu, Dari (Persian); *religion* Muslim (80% Sunni, 20% Shi'ite).

Africa second largest of the continents, three times the area of Europe; *area* 30,097,000 sq km/11,620,451 sq mi; *largest cities* (population over 1 million) Cairo, Algiers, Lagos, Kinshasa,

Abidjan, Cape Town, Nairobi, Casablanca, El Gîza, Addis Ababa, Luanda, Dar es Salaam, Ibadan, Douala, Mogadishu; *features* Great Rift Valley, containing most of the great lakes of E Africa (except Lake Victoria); Atlas Mountains in the NW; Drakensberg mountain range in the SE; Sahara Desert (world's largest desert) in the N; Namib, Kalahari, and Great Karoo deserts in the S; Nile, Zaïre, Niger, Zambezi, Limpopo, Volta, and Orange rivers; *population* (1988) 610 million, rising to an estimated 900 million by 2000.

African National Congress (ANC) South African political party, founded 1912 as a multiracial nationalist organization with the aim of extending the franchise to the whole population and ending all racial discrimination. Nelson ◊Mandela became the party's president 1991. It was banned by the government from 1960 to Jan 1990. Talks between the ANC and the South African government 1991–93 culminated in a nonracial constitution. In the country's first multiracial elections April 1994, the ANC won a sweeping victory, and Mandela was elected president of South Africa.

Afrikaans an official language of the Republic of South Africa and Namibia. Spoken mainly by Afrikaners – descendants of Dutch and other 17th-century colonists – it is a variant of Dutch, modified by circumstance and the influence of German, French, and other immigrant as well as local languages. It became a standardized written language about 1875.

Afro-Asiatic language any of a family of languages spoken throughout the world. There are two main branches, the languages of N Africa and the languages originating in Syria, Mesopotamia, Palestine, and Arabia, but now found

from Morocco in the west to the Persian Gulf in the east.

Agamemnon Greek hero of the Trojan wars, son of Atreus, king of Mycenae, and brother of Menelaus. He sacrificed his daughter Iphigenia in order to secure favourable winds for the Greek expedition against Troy and after a ten years' siege sacked the city, receiving Priam's daughter Cassandra as a prize. On his return home, he and Cassandra were murdered by his wife Clytemnestra and her lover, Aegisthus.

Agincourt, Battle of battle of the Hundred Years' War in which Henry V of England defeated the French on 25 Oct 1415, mainly through the overwhelming superiority of the English longbow. Henry gained France and the French princess, Catherine of Valois, as his wife. The village of Agincourt (modern *Azincourt*) is south of Calais, in N France.

Agricola Gnaeus Julius AD 37–93. Roman general and politician. Born in Provence, he became consul AD 77, and then governor of Britain AD 78–85. He extended Roman rule to the Firth of Forth in Scotland and sailed round the north of Scotland, proving Britain an island.

agricultural revolution sweeping changes that took place in British agriculture over the period 1750–1850 in response to the increased demand for food from a rapidly expanding population. Recent research has shown these changes to be only part of a much larger, ongoing process of development.

agriculture the practice of farming, including the cultivation of the soil (for raising crops) and the raising of domesticated animals. Crops are for human nourishment, animal fodder, or commodities such as cotton and sisal. Animals are raised for wool, milk, leather, dung (as fuel), or meat. The units for managing agricultural production vary from small holdings and individually owned farms to corporate-run farms and collective farms run by entire communities.

history Agriculture developed in the Middle East and Egypt at least 10,000 years ago. Farming communities soon became the base for society in China, India, Europe, Mexico, and Peru, then spread throughout the world. Reorganization along more scientific and productive lines took place in Europe in the 18th century in response to dramatic population growth. Mechanization made considerable progress in the USA and Europe during the 19th century. After World War II, there was an explosive growth in the use of agricultural chemicals: herbicides, insecticides, fungicides, and fertilizers.

In the 1960s there was development of high-yielding species, especially in the *green revolution* of the Third World, and the industrialized countries began intensive farming of cattle, poultry, and pigs. In the 1980s, hybridization by genetic engineering methods and pest control by the use of chemicals were developed. However, there was also a reaction against some forms of intensive agriculture because of the pollution and habitat destruction caused. One result of this was a growth of alternative methods, including organic agriculture.

Ahmedabad or *Ahmadabad* capital of Gujarat, India; population (1981) 2,515,195. It is a cotton-manufacturing centre, and has many sacred buildings of the Hindu, Muslim, and Jain faiths.

aid, development money given or lent on concessional terms to developing countries or spent on maintaining agencies for this purpose. The ◊World Bank is the largest dispenser of aid. All industrialized United Nations member countries devote a proportion of their gross national product to aid.

AIDS (acronym for *acquired immune deficiency syndrome*) the gravest of the sexually transmitted diseases, or STDs. It is caused by the human immunodeficiency virus (HIV), now known to be a ◊retrovirus, an organism first identified 1983. HIV is transmitted in body fluids, mainly blood and genital secretions. The estimated incubation period between infection with HIV and the onset of AIDS is about 10 years. The effect of the virus in those who become ill is the devastation of the immune system, leaving the victim susceptible to diseases that would not otherwise develop. By mid-1994 it was estimated by the World Health Organization that around 4 million AIDS cases had occurred worldwide, representing a 60% increase over the estimated 2.5 million cases as of July 1993.

aircraft carrier ocean-going naval vessel with a broad, flat-topped deck for launching and landing military aircraft; an effort to provide a floating military base for warplanes too far from home for refuelling, repairing, reconnaissance, escorting, and various attack and defence operations.

air sac in birds, a thin-walled extension of the lungs. There are nine of these and they extend into the abdomen and bones, effectively increasing lung capacity. In mammals, it is another name for the alveoli in the lungs, and in some insects, for widenings of the trachea.

Ajax Greek hero in Homer's *Iliad*. Son of Telamon, king of Salamis, he was second only to Achilles among the Greek heroes in the Trojan War. According to subsequent Greek legends, Ajax went mad with jealousy when ▷Agamemnon awarded the armour of the dead Achilles to ▷Odysseus. He later committed suicide in shame.

Akihito 1933– Emperor of Japan from 1989, succeeding his father Hirohito (Showa). His reign is called the Heisei ('achievement of universal peace') era.

Alabama state in southern USA; *area* 134,700 sq km/51,994 sq mi; *capital* Montgomery; *features* rivers: Alabama, Tennessee; Appalachian mountains; George Washington Carver Museum at the Tuskegee Institute; White House of the Confederacy at Montgomery; George C Marshall Space Flight Center at Huntsville; *population* (1990) 4,040,600

Alaska largest state of the USA, on the northwest extremity of North America, separated from the lower 48 states by British Columbia; territories include Aleutian Islands; *total area* 1,530,700 sq km/591,004 sq mi; *capital* Juneau; *features* Yukon River; Rocky Mountains; Valley of Ten Thousand Smokes; Arctic Wild Life Range; *population* (1990) 550,000; including 9% American Indians, Aleuts, and Inuits.

Albania (Republic of (*Republika e Shqipërisë*) *area* 28,748 sq km/11,097 sq mi; *capital* Tiranë; *features* Dinaric Alps, with wild boar and wolves; *political system* emergent democracy; *population* (1993 est) 3,400,000; growth rate 1.9% p.a.; *languages* Albanian, Greek; *religion* Muslim about 50%, Orthodox 18%, Roman Catholic 13%.

albatross large seabird, genus *Diomedea*, with long narrow wings adapted for gliding and a wingspan of up to 3 m/10 ft, mainly found in the southern hemisphere. It belongs to the order Procellariiformes, the same group as petrels and shearwaters.

Albert Prince Consort 1819–1861. Husband of British Queen ▷Victoria from 1840. Albert was the second son of the Duke of Saxe Coburg-Gotha and first cousin to Queen Victoria. He became his wife's chief adviser and planned the Great Exhibition 1851, promoting the industrial products of Britain and Europe. He died of typhoid.

Alberta province of W Canada; *area* 661,200 sq km/255,223 sq mi; *capital* Edmonton; *features* Banff, Elk Island, Jasper, Waterton Lake, and Wood Buffalo national parks; extensive dinosaur finds near Drumheller; *population* (1991) 2,501,400.

albinism rare hereditary condition in which the body has no tyrosinase, one of the enzymes that form the pigment melanin, normally found in the skin, hair, and eyes. As a result, the hair is white and the skin and eyes are pink. The skin and eyes are abnormally sensitive to light, and vision is often impaired. The condition can occur among all human and animal groups.

albumin or *albumen* any of a group of sulphur-containing ▷proteins. The best known is in the form of egg white; others occur in milk, and as a major component of serum. They are soluble in water and dilute salt solutions, and are coagulated by heat.

alcohol any member of a group of organic chemical compounds characterized by the presence of one or more aliphatic OH (hydroxyl) groups in the molecule, and which form ▷esters with acids. The main uses of alcohols are as solvents for gums, resins, lacquers, and varnishes; in the making of dyes; for essential oils in perfumery; and for medical substances in pharmacy. Alcohol (ethanol) is produced naturally in the ▷fermentation process and is consumed as part of alcoholic beverages.

Aleutian Islands volcanic island chain in the N Pacific, stretching 1,200 mi/1,900 km SW of Alaska, of which it forms part; population 6,000 Aleuts (most of whom belong to the Orthodox Church, plus a large US defence establishment). The islands are mountainous, barren, and treeless, with only about 25 days of sunshine recorded annually.

Alexander the Great 356–323 BC. King of Macedon from 336 BC and conqueror of the large Persian empire. As commander of the vast Macedonian army he conquered Greece 336, defeated the Persian king Darius in Asia Minor 333, then moved on to Egypt, where he founded Alexandria. He defeated the Persians again in Assyria 331, then advanced further east to reach the Indus. He conquered the Punjab before diminished troops forced his retreat.

Alexandria or *El Iskandariya* city, chief port, and second-largest city of Egypt, situated between the Mediterranean and Lake Maryut; population (1986) 5,000,000. It is linked by canal with the Nile and is an industrial city. Founded 331 BC by Alexander the Great, Alexandria was the capital of Egypt for over 1,000 years and the chief culural centre of the Western world. The vast Library of Alexandria was founded by Ptolemy I 330 BC.

alfalfa or *lucerne* perennial tall herbaceous plant *Medicago sativa* of the pea family Leguminosae. It is native to Eurasia and bears spikes of small purple flowers in late summer. It is now a major fodder crop, generally processed into hay, meal, or silage.

Alfred *the Great* c. 848–c. 900. King of Wessex from 871. He defended England against Danish invasion, founded the first English navy, and put into operation a legal code. He encouraged the translation of works from Latin (some he translated himself), and promoted the development of the Anglo-Saxon Chronicle.

algae (singular *alga*) diverse group of plants (including those commonly called seaweeds) that shows great variety of form, ranging from single-celled forms to multicellular seaweeds of considerable size and complexity.

algebra system of arithmetic applying to any set of non-numerical symbols (usually letters), and the axioms and rules by which they are combined or operated upon; sometimes known as *generalized arithmetic*.

Algeria Democratic and Popular Republic of (*al- Jumhuriya al-Jazairiya ad-Dimuqratiya ash-Shabiya*); **area** 2,381,741 sq km/919,352 sq mi; **capital** Algiers (al-Jazair); **features** Atlas mountains, Barbary Coast, Chott Melrhir depression, Hoggar mountains; **political system** military rule; **population** (1993) 26,600,000 (83% Arab, 17% Berber); growth rate 3.0% p.a. **languages** Arabic (official); Berber, French **religion** Sunni Muslim (state religion).

Algiers (Arabic *al-Jazair*; French *Alger*) capital of Algeria, situated on the narrow coastal plain between the Atlas

algorithm **12**

Mountains and the Mediterranean; population (1984) 2,442,300.

algorithm procedure or series of steps that can be used to solve a problem. In computer science, it describes the logical sequence of operations to be performed by a program.

Ali *c.* 598–660. 4th caliph of Islam. He was born in Mecca, the son of Abu Talib, uncle to the prophet Muhammad, who gave him his daughter Fatima in marriage. On Muhammad's death 632, Ali had a claim to succeed him, but this was not conceded until 656. After a stormy reign, he was assassinated. Around Ali's name the controversy has raged between the Sunni and the Shi'ites (see ▷Islam), the former denying his right to the caliphate and the latter supporting it.

Ali Muhammad. Adopted name of Cassius Marcellus Clay, Jr, 1942– . US boxer. Olympic light-heavyweight champion 1960, he went on to become world professional heavyweight champion 1964, and was the only man to regain the title twice. He was known for his fast footwork and extrovert nature.

alimentary canal in animals, the tube through which food passes; it extends from the mouth to the anus. It is a complex organ, adapted for digestion. In human adults, it is about 9 m/30 ft long, consisting of the mouth cavity, pharynx, oesophagus, stomach, and the small and large intestines.

alkali in chemistry, a compound classed as a ▷base that is soluble in water. Alkalis neutralize acids and are soapy to the touch. The hydroxides of metals are alkalis: those of sodium (sodium hydroxide, NaOH) and of potassium (potassium hydroxide, KOH) being

chemically powerful; both were derived from the ashes of plants.

alkali metal any of a group of six metallic elements with similar chemical bonding properties: lithium, sodium, potassium, rubidium, caesium, and francium. They form a linked group in the ▷periodic table of the elements. They are univalent (have a valency of one) and of very low density (lithium, sodium, and potassium float on water); in general they are reactive, soft, low-melting-point metals. Because of their reactivity they are only found as compounds in nature.

alkaline-earth metal any of a group of six metallic elements with similar bonding properties: beryllium, magnesium, calcium, strontium, barium, and radium. They form a linked group in the ▷periodic table of the elements. They are strongly basic, bivalent (have a valency of two), and occur in nature only in compounds.

alkane member of a group of ▷hydrocarbons having the general formula C_nH_{2n+2}, commonly known as *paraffins*. Lighter alkanes, such as methane, ethane, propane, and butane, are colourless gases; heavier ones are liquids or solids.

alkene member of the group of ▷hydrocarbons having the general formula C_nH_{2n}, formerly known as *olefins*. Lighter alkenes, such as ethene and propene, are gases, obtained from the cracking of oil fractions.

alkyne member of the group of ▷hydrocarbons with the general formula C_nH_{2n-2}, formerly known as the *acetylenes*. They are unsaturated compounds, characterized by one or more triple bonds between adjacent carbon atoms.

allele one of two or more alternative forms of a ▷gene at a given position (locus) on a chromosome, caused by a difference in the ▷DNA. Blue and brown eyes in humans are determined by different alleles of the gene for eye colour.

Allen Woody. Adopted name of Allen Stewart Konigsberg 1935– . US film writer, director, and actor. He is known for his cynical, witty, often self- deprecating parody and offbeat humour. His film *Annie Hall* 1977 won him three Academy Awards.

allergy special sensitivity of the body that makes it react with an exaggerated response of the natural immune defence mechanism to the introduction of an otherwise harmless foreign substance (*allergen*).

Allies, the in World War I, the 23 countries allied against the Central Powers (Germany, Austria-Hungary, Turkey, and Bulgaria), including France, Italy, Russia, the UK, Australia and other Commonwealth nations, and, in the latter part of the war, the USA; and in World War II, the 49 countries allied against the Axis Powers (Germany, Italy, and Japan), including France, the UK, Australia and other Commonwealth nations, the USA, and the USSR.

allotropy property whereby an element can exist in two or more forms (allotropes), each possessing different physical properties but the same state of matter (gas, liquid, or solid). The allotropes of carbon are diamond and graphite.

alloy metal blended with some other metallic or nonmetallic substance to give it special qualities, such as resistance to corrosion, greater hardness, or tensile strength. Useful alloys include bronze, brass, cupronickel, duralumin, German silver, gunmetal, pewter, solder, steel, and stainless steel.

Alma-Ata formerly (until 1921) *Vernyi* capital of Kazakhstan; population (1991) 1,151,300.

alphabet set of conventional symbols used for writing, based on a correlation between individual symbols and spoken sounds, so called from *alpha* (α) and *beta* (β), the names of the first two letters of the classical Greek alphabet. The earliest known alphabet is from Palestine, about 1700 BC. Alphabetic writing now takes many forms – for example, the Hebrew *aleph- beth* and the Arabic script, both written from right to left; the Devanagari script of the Hindus, in which the symbols 'hang' from a line common to all the symbols; and the Greek alphabet, with the first clearly delineated vowel symbols.

Alps mountain chain, the barrier between N Italy and France, Germany and Austria, and extending along the Adriatic coast into Slovenia, Croatia, Bosnia-Herzegovina, Yugoslavia, and N Albania; *peaks* include *Mont Blanc*, the highest at 4,809 m/15,777 ft, first climbed by Jacques Balmat and Michel Paccard 1786; *Matterhorn* in the Pennine Alps, 4,479 m/14,694 ft, first climbed by Edward Whymper 1865; *Eiger* in the Bernese Alps/Oberland, 3,970 m/13,030 ft, with a near-vertical rock wall on the north face, first climbed 1858; *Jungfrau*, 4,166 m/13,673 ft; and *Finsteraarhorn* 4,275 m/14,027 ft.

Alsace-Lorraine area of NE France, lying west of the river Rhine. It forms the French regions of Alsace and Lorraine. The German dialect spoken does not have equal rights with French, and there is autonomist sentiment.

alternating current (AC) electric current that flows for an interval of time in one direction and then in the opposite direction, that is, a current that flows in alternately reversed directions through or around a circuit. Electric energy is usually generated as alternating current in a power station, and alternating currents may be used for both power and lighting.

altimeter instrument used in aircraft that measures altitude, or height above sea level. The common type is a form of aneroid ▷barometer, which works by sensing the differences in air pressure at different altitudes. The ▷radar altimeter measures the height of the aircraft above the ground, measuring the time it takes for radio pulses emitted by the aircraft to be reflected. Radar altimeters are essential features of automatic and blind-landing systems.

aluminium lightweight, silver-white, ductile and malleable, metallic element, symbol Al, atomic number 13, relative atomic mass 26.9815. It is the third most abundant element (and the most abundant metal) in the Earth's crust, of which it makes up about 8.1% by mass. It is an excellent conductor of electricity and oxidizes easily, the layer of oxide on its surface making it highly resistant to tarnish.

Alzheimer's disease common manifestation of ▷dementia, thought to afflict one in 20 people over 65. After heart disease, cancer, and stroke it is the most common cause of death in the Western world. Attacking the brain's 'grey

matter', it is a disease of mental processes rather than physical function, characterized by memory loss and progressive intellectual impairment.

Amal radical Lebanese ▷Shi'ite military force, established by Musa Sadr in the 1970s; its headquarters are in Borj al-Barajneh. The movement split into extremist and moderate groups 1982, but both sides agreed on the aim of increasing Shi'ite political representation in Lebanon.

amalgam any alloy of mercury with other metals. Most metals will form amalgams, except iron and platinum. Amalgam is used in dentistry for filling teeth, and usually contains copper, silver, and zinc as the main alloying ingredients.

Amazon South American river, the world's second longest, 6,570 km/4,080 mi, and the largest in volume of water. Its main headstreams, the Marañón and the Ucayali, rise in central Peru and unite to flow E across Brazil for about 4,000 km/2,500 mi. It has 48,280 km/30,000 mi of navigable waterways, draining 7,000,000 sq km/2,750,000 sq mi, nearly half the South American landmass. It reaches the Atlantic on the equator, its estuary 80 km/50 mi wide, discharging a volume of water so immense that 64 km/40 mi out to sea, fresh water remains at the surface. *The Amazon basin* covers 7.5 million sq km/ 3 million sq mi, of which 5 million sq km/2 million sq mi is tropical forest containing 30% of all known plant and animal species. The wettest region on Earth, the average rainfall 2.54 m/8.3 ft a year.

Amazon in Greek mythology, a member of a group of female warriors living near the Black Sea, who cut off their right breasts to use the bow more easily. Their queen, Penthesilea, was killed by Achilles at the siege of Troy. The term Amazon has come to mean a large, strong woman.

amber fossilized resin from coniferous trees of the Middle Tertiary period. It is often washed ashore on the Baltic coast with plant and animal specimens preserved in it; many extinct species have been found preserved in this way. It ranges in colour from red to yellow, and is used to make jewellery.

America western hemisphere of the Earth, containing the continents of ◊North America and ◊South America, with ◊Central America in between. This great landmass extends from the Arctic to the Antarctic, from beyond 75° N to past 55° S. The area is about 42,000,000 sq km/16,000,000 sq mi, and the estimated population is over 500 million. Politically, it consists of 36 nations and US, British, French, and Dutch dependencies.

American Indian one of the aboriginal peoples of the Americas. Columbus named them Indians 1492 because he believed he had found not the New World, but a new route to India. The Asian ancestors of the Indians are thought to have entered North America by the land bridge, Beringia, exposed by the lowered sea level between Siberia and Alaska during the last ice age, 60,000–35,000 BC.

American Revolution or *American War of Independence* revolt 1775–83 of the British North American colonies that resulted in the establishment of the United States of America. Caused by colonial opposition to British economic exploitation and the unwillingness of the colonists to pay for a standing army, it was also fuelled by the colonists' anti-monarchist sentiment and a desire to participate in the policies affecting them.

amethyst variety of ◊quartz, SiO_2, coloured violet by the presence of small quantities of impurities such as manganese or iron; used as a semiprecious stone. Amethysts are found chiefly in the Ural Mountains, India, the USA, Uruguay, and Brazil.

Amhara member of an ethnic group comprising approximately 25% of the population of Ethiopia; 13 million (1987). The Amhara are traditionally farmers. They speak Amharic, a language of the Semitic branch of the Afro-Asiatic family. Most are members of the Ethiopian Christian Church.

Amin (Dada) Idi 1926– . Ugandan politician, president 1971–79. He led the coup that deposed Milton Obote 1971, expelled the Asian community 1972, and exercised a reign of terror over his people. He fled to Libya when insurgent Ugandan and Tanzanian troops invaded the country 1979.

amine any of a class of organic chemical compounds in which one or more of the hydrogen atoms of ammonia (NH_3) have been replaced by other groups of atoms.

amino acid water-soluble organic ◊molecule, mainly composed of carbon, oxygen, hydrogen, and nitrogen, containing both a basic amino group (NH_2) and an acidic carboxyl (COOH) group. When two or more amino acids are joined together, they are known as ◊peptides; ◊proteins are made up of interacting polypeptides (peptide chains consisting of more than three amino acids) and are folded or twisted in characteristic shapes.

Amis Kingsley 1922– . English novelist and poet. He was associated early on with the Angry Young Men group of writers. His sharply ironic works frequently debunk pretentious mediocrity; his first novel, the best-selling *Lucky Jim* 1954, is a comic portrayal of life in a provincial university. His later novels include *The Alteration* 1976, which imagines a 20th-century society dominated by the Catholic Church. He is the father of writer Martin Amis.

Amis Martin 1949– . English novelist. His works are characterized by their acerbic black humour and include *The Rachel Papers* 1973, a memoir of adolescence told through flashbacks, *Dead Babies* 1975, which addresses decadence and sadism, *Money* 1984, *London Fields* 1989, and *Time's Arrow* 1991.

Amman capital and chief industrial centre of Jordan; population (1986) 1,160,000. It is a major communications centre, linking historic trade routes across the Middle East.

ammeter instrument that measures electric current, usually in ◊amperes.

ammonia NH_3 colourless pungent-smelling gas, lighter than air and very soluble in water. It is made on an industrial scale by the ◊Haber process, and used mainly to produce nitrogenous fertilizers, some explosives, and nitric acid.

amnesia loss or impairment of memory. As a clinical condition it may be caused by disease or injury to the brain, by some drugs, or by shock; in some cases it may be a symptom of an emotional disorder.

Amnesty International human-rights organization established in the UK 1961 to campaign for the release of prisoners of conscience worldwide; fair trials for all political prisoners; an end to the death penalty, torture, and other inhuman treatment of all prisoners; and the cessation of extrajudicial executions and 'disappearances'. It is politically and economically unaligned. The organization was awarded the Nobel Prize for Peace 1977.

amniocentesis sampling the amniotic fluid surrounding a fetus in the womb for diagnostic purposes. It is used to detect Down's syndrome and other genetic abnormalities.

amoeba (plural *amoebae*) one of the simplest living animals, consisting of a single cell and belonging to the ◊protozoa group. The body consists of colourless protoplasm. Its activities are controlled by the nucleus, and it feeds by flowing round and engulfing organic debris. It reproduces by ◊binary fission.

ampere SI unit (abbreviation amp, symbol A) of electrical current. Electrical current is measured in a similar way to water current, in terms of an amount per unit time; one ampere represents a flow of about 6.28×10^{18} ◊electrons per second, or a rate of flow of charge of one coulomb per second.

amphetamine or *speed* powerful synthetic ◊stimulant. After their introduction in the 1940s, amphetamines were frequently prescribed by doctors as an appetite suppressant for weight loss; as an antidepressant, to induce euphoria; and as a stimulant, to increase alertness.

Since the 1970s the use of amphetamines has been restricted because of severe side effects and addiction.

amphibian member of the vertebrate class Amphibia, which generally spend their larval (tadpole) stage in fresh water, transferring to land at maturity (after ⊳metamorphosis) and generally returning to water to breed. Like fish and reptiles, they continue to grow throughout life, and cannot maintain a temperature greatly differing from that of their environment. The class includes caecilians (wormlike in appearance), salamanders, frogs, and toads.

amplifier electronic device that magnifies the strength of a signal, such as a radio signal. The ratio of output signal strength to input signal strength is called the *gain* of the amplifier. As well as achieving high gain, an amplifier should be free from distortion and able to operate over a range of frequencies.

Amritsar industrial city in the Punjab, India; population (1981) 595,000. In 1919 it was the scene of the *Amritsar massacre* when thousands were killed by troops under British control. It is the holy city of ⊳Sikhism, with the Guru Nanak University (named after the first Sikh guru) and the Golden Temple.

Amsterdam capital of the Netherlands; population (1990) 695,100. Canals cut through the city link it with the North Sea and the Rhine, and as a Dutch port it is second only to Rotterdam.

Amundsen Roald 1872–1928. Norwegian explorer who in 1903–06 became the first person to navigate the Northwest Passage. Beaten to the North Pole by US explorer Robert Peary 1910, he reached the South Pole ahead of Captain Scott 1911.

Anabaptist member of any of various 16th-century radical Protestant sects. They believed in adult rather than child baptism, and sought to establish utopian communities. Anabaptist groups spread rapidly in N Europe, particularly in Germany, and were widely persecuted.

anabolic steroid any ⊳hormone of the ⊳steroid group that stimulates tissue growth. Its use in medicine is limited to the treatment of some anaemias and breast cancers; it may help to break up blood clots. Side effects include aggressive behaviour, masculinization in women, and, in children, reduced height. Frequently administered to athletes to promote muscle growth, the use of anabolic steroids is now generally banned by major sporting organizations.

anaemia condition caused by a shortage of haemoglobin, the oxygen-carrying component of red blood cells. The main symptoms are fatigue, pallor, breathlessness, palpitations, and poor resistance to infection. Treatment depends on the cause.

anaerobic (of living organisms) not requiring oxygen for the release of energy from food molecules such as glucose. Anaerobic organisms include many bacteria, yeasts, and internal parasites.

anaesthetic drug that produces loss of sensation or consciousness; the resulting state is *anaesthesia*, in which the patient is insensitive to stimuli.

analgesic agent for relieving pain. ⊳Opiates alter the perception or appreciation of pain and are effective in controlling 'deep' visceral (internal) pain. Non-opiates, such as ⊳aspirin, paracetamol, and NSAIDs (nonsteroidal anti-inflammatory drugs), relieve musculoskeletal pain and reduce inflammation in soft tissues.

analogue (of a quantity or device) changing continuously; by contrast a digital quantity or device varies in series of distinct steps. For example, an analogue clock measures time by means of a continuous movement of hands around a dial, whereas a digital clock measures time with a numerical display that changes in a series of discrete steps.

anarchism political belief that society should have no government, laws, police, or other authority, but should be a free association of all its members. It does not mean 'without order'; most theories of anarchism imply an order of a very strict and symmetrical kind, but they maintain that such order can be achieved by cooperation. Anarchism is essentially a pacifist movement.

Anatolia (Turkish *Anadolu*) Asian part of Turkey, consisting of a mountainous peninsula with the Black Sea to the N, the Aegean Sea to the W, and the Mediterranean Sea to the S.

ANC abbreviation for ▷*African National Congress,* a South African political party and former nationalist organization.

Anchorage port and largest city of Alaska, USA, at the head of Cook Inlet; population (1990) 226,340. Established 1918, Anchorage is an important centre of administration, communication, and commerce.

Andalusia (Spanish *Andalucia*) fertile autonomous region of S Spain, including the provinces of Almería, Cádiz, Córdoba, Granada, Huelva, Jaén, Málaga, and Seville; area 87,300 sq km/33,698 sq mi; population (1986) 6,876,000. Málaga, Cádiz, and Algeciras are the chief ports and industrial centres. The *Costa del Sol* on the south coast has many tourist resorts, including Marbella and Torremolinos.

Andersen Hans Christian 1805–1875. Danish writer of fairy tales. Well-known examples include 'The Ugly Duckling', 'The Snow Queen', 'The Little Mermaid', and 'The Emperor's New Clothes'. Their inventiveness, sensitivity, and strong sense of wonder have given these stories perennial and universal appeal; they have been translated into many languages.

Andes great mountain system or *cordillera* that forms the western fringe of South America, extending through some 67° of latitude and the republics of Colombia, Venezuela, Ecuador, Peru, Bolivia, Chile, and Argentina. The mountains exceed 3,600 m/ 12,000 ft for half their length of 6,500 km/4,000 mi.

Andhra Pradesh state in E central India; *area* 276,700 sq km/106,845 sq mi; *capital* Hyderabad; *population* (1991) 66,304,900; *languages* Telugu, Urdu, Tamil.

Andorra Principality of (*Principat d'Andorra*); *area* 468 sq km/181 sq mi; *capital* Andorra-la-Vella; *features* the E Pyrenees, Valira River; *political system* co-principality; *population* (1993) 59,000 (30% Andorrans, 61% Spanish, 6% French); *languages* Catalan (official); Spanish, French; *religion* Roman Catholic.

Andrea del Sarto (Andrea d'Agnola di Francesco) 1486–1530. Italian Renaissance painter. He was one of the finest portraitists and religious painters of his time. His frescoes in Florence, such as the *Birth of the Virgin* 1514 (Sta Annunziata), rank among the greatest of the Renaissance.

Andrew (full name Andrew Albert Christian Edward) 1960– . Prince of the UK, Duke of York, second son of Queen Elizabeth II. He married Sarah Ferguson 1986; their children are Princess Beatrice, born 1988, and Princess Eugenie, born 1990. The couple separated 1992.

Andrew, St New Testament apostle. According to tradition, he went with John to Ephesus, preached in Scythia, and was martyred at Patras on an X-shaped cross (*St Andrew's cross*). He is the patron saint of Scotland. Feast day 30 Nov.

Angel Falls highest waterfalls in the world, on the river Caroni in the tropical rainforest of Bolivar Region, Venezuela; total height 978 m/3,210 ft. They were named after the aviator and prospector James Angel who flew over the falls and crash-landed nearby 1935.

Angelico Fra (Guido di Pietro) *c.* 1400–1455. Italian painter. He was a monk, active in Florence, painting religious scenes. His series of frescoes at the monastery of San Marco, Florence, was begun after 1436. He also produced several altarpieces in a style characterized by a delicacy of line and colour.

angina or *angina pectoris* severe pain in the chest due to impaired blood supply to the heart muscle because a coronary artery is narrowed. Faintness and difficulty in breathing accompany the pain. Treatment is by drugs or bypass surgery.

angiosperm flowering plant in which the seeds are enclosed within an ovary, which ripens to a fruit. Angiosperms are divided into monocotyledons (single seed leaf in the embryo) and dicotyledons (two seed leaves in the embryo). They include the majority of flowers, herbs, grasses, and trees except conifers.

angle in mathematics, the amount of turn or rotation; it may be defined by a pair of rays (half-lines) that share a common endpoint but do not lie on the same line. Angles are measured in ◊degrees (°) or ◊radians (rads) – a complete turn or circle being 360° or 2π rads. Angles are classified generally by their degree measures: *acute angles* are less than 90°; *right angles* are exactly 90° (a quarter turn); *obtuse angles* are greater than 90° but less than 180°; *reflex angles* are greater than 180° but less than 360°.

Anglican Communion family of Christian churches including the Church of England, the US Episcopal Church, and those holding the same essential doctrines, that is the Lambeth Quadrilateral 1888 Holy Scripture as the basis of all doctrine, the Nicene and Apostles' Creeds, Holy Baptism and Holy Communion, and the historic episcopate.

Anglo-Saxon one of the several Germanic invaders (Angles, Saxons, and Jutes) who conquered much of Britain between the 5th and 7th centuries. The Norman invasion 1066 brought Anglo-Saxon rule to an end.

Angola People's Republic of (*República Popular de Angola*); *area* 1,246,700 sq km/481,226 sq mi; *capital* and chief port Luanda; *features* Cuanza, Cuito, Cubango, and Cunene rivers; Cabinda enclave; *political system* socialist republic; *population* (1993) 10,770,000 (largest ethnic group Ovimbundu); growth rate 2.5% p.a.; *languages* Portuguese (official); Bantu dialects; *religions*

Roman Catholic 68%, Protestant 20%, animist 12%.

angstrom unit (symbol Å) of length equal to 10^{-10} metre or one-ten-millionth of a millimetre, used for atomic measurements and the wavelengths of electromagnetic radiation. It is named after the Swedish scientist A J Ångström.

Anguilla island in the E Caribbean; *area* 160 sq km/62 sq mi; *capital* The Valley; *population* (1988) 7,000; *languages* English, Creole.

Anhui or *Anhwei* province of E China, watered by the Chang Jiang (Yangtze River); *area* 139,900 sq km/54,000 sq mi; *capital* Hefei; *population* (1990) 56,181,000.

animal or *metazoan* member of the kingdom Animalia, one of the major categories of living things, the science of which is *zoology*. Animals are all ◊heterotrophs (they obtain their energy from organic substances produced by other organisms); they have eukaryotic cells (the genetic material is contained within a distinct nucleus) bounded by a thin cell membrane rather than the thick cell wall of plants. Most animals are capable of moving around for at least part of their life cycle.

anion ion carrying a negative charge. During electrolysis, anions in the electrolyte move towards the anode (positive electrode).

Ankara formerly *Angora* capital of Turkey; population (1990) 2,559,500. It replaced Istanbul (then in Allied occupation) as capital 1923.

Annamese member of the majority ethnic group in Vietnam, comprising 90% of the population. The Annamese language is distinct from Vietnamese, though it has been influenced by Chinese and has loan words from Khmer. Their religion combines elements of Buddhism, Confucianism, and Taoism, as well as ancestor worship.

Anne 1665–1714. Queen of Great Britain and Ireland 1702–14. She was the second daughter of James, Duke of York, who became James II, and Anne Hyde. She succeeded William III 1702. Events of her reign include the War of the Spanish Succession, Marlborough's victories at Blenheim, Ramillies, Oudenarde, and Malplaquet, and the union of the English and Scottish parliaments 1707. Anne was succeeded by George I.

Anne (full name Anne Elizabeth Alice Louise) 1950– . Princess of the UK, second child of Queen Elizabeth II, declared Princess Royal 1987. Married to Mark Phillips 1973–92, they had two children: are Peter, born 1977, and Zara, born 1981. She married Commander Timothy Lawrence 1994.

annelid any segmented worm of the phylum Annelida. Annelids include earthworms, leeches, and marine worms such as lugworms.

anode in chemistry, the positive electrode of an electrolytic ◊cell, towards which negative particles (anions), usually in solution, are attracted. See ◊electrolysis.

anodizing process that increases the resistance to ◊corrosion of a metal, such as aluminium, by building up a protective oxide layer on the surface.

anorexia lack of desire to eat, especially the pathological condition of *anorexia nervosa*, most often found in adolescent girls and young women, who may be obsessed with the desire to lose weight. Compulsive eating, or ▷bulimia, and distortions of body image often accompany anorexia.

ant insect belonging to the family Formicidae, and to the same order (Hymenoptera) as bees and wasps. Ants are characterized by a conspicuous 'waist' and elbowed antennae. About 10,000 different species are known; all are social in habit, and all construct nests of various kinds.

Antananarivo formerly *Tananarive* capital of Madagascar, on the interior plateau, with a rail link to Tamatave; population (1986) 703,000.

Antarctica continent surrounding the South Pole, arbitrarily defined as the region lying S of the Antarctic Circle. Occupying 10% of the world's surface, Antarctica contains 90% of the world's ice and 70% of its fresh water; *area* 13,900,000 sq km/5,400,000 sq mi; *features* Mount Erebus on Ross Island is the world's southernmost active volcano; the Ross Ice Shelf is formed by several glaciers coalescing in the Ross Sea; *population* no permanent residents; population limited to scientific research stations with maximum population of 3,000 during the summer months.

antelope any of numerous kinds of even-toed, hoofed mammals belonging to the cow family, Bovidae. Most antelopes are lightly built and good runners. They are grazers or browsers, and chew the cud. They range in size from the dikdiks and duikers, only 30 cm/1 ft high, to the eland, which can be 1.8 m/6 ft at the shoulder.

antenna in zoology, an appendage ('feeler') on the head. Insects, centipedes, and millipedes each have one pair of antennae but there are two pairs in

crustaceans, such as shrimps. In insects, the antennae are involved with the senses of smell and touch.

anthracite hard, dense, shiny variety of ▷coal, containing over 90% carbon and a low percentage of ash and impurities, which causes it to burn without flame, smoke, or smell.

anthropology study of humankind, which developed following 19th-century evolutionary theory to investigate the human species, past and present, physically, socially, and culturally. The four subdisciplines are physical anthropology, linguistics, cultural anthropology, and archaeology.

antibiotic drug that kills or inhibits the growth of bacteria and fungi. It is derived from living organisms such as fungi or bacteria.

antibody protein molecule produced in the blood by ▷lymphocytes in response to the presence of foreign or invading substances (▷antigens); such substances include the proteins carried on the surface of infecting microorganisms.

anticyclone area of high atmospheric pressure caused by descending air, which becomes warm and dry. Winds radiate from a calm centre, taking a clockwise direction in the northern hemisphere and an anticlockwise direction in the southern hemisphere. Anticyclones are characterized by clear weather and the absence of rain and violent winds.

antigen any substance that causes the production of ▷antibodies by the body's immune system. Common antigens include the proteins carried on the surface of bacteria, viruses, and pollen grains.

Antigua and Barbuda State of; *area* Antigua 280 sq km/108 sq mi, Barbuda 161 sq km/62 sq mi, plus Redonda 1 sq km/0.4 sq mi; *capital* and chief port St John's; *features* Antigua is the largest of the Leeward Islands; Redonda is an uninhabited island of volcanic rock rising to 305 m/1,000 ft; *political system* liberal democracy; *population* (1993 est) 77,000; growth rate 1.3% p.a.; *language* English; *religion* Christian (mostly Anglican).

antihistamine any substance that counteracts the effects of ◊histamine. Antihistamines may occur naturally or they may be synthesized.

Antilles group of West Indian islands, divided N– S into the *Greater Antilles* (Cuba, Jamaica, Haiti – Dominican Republic, Puerto Rico) and *Lesser Antilles*, subdivided into the Leeward Islands (Virgin Islands, St Christopher–Nevis, Antigua and Barbuda, Anguilla, Montserrat, and Guadeloupe) and the Windward Islands (Dominica, Martinique, St Lucia, St Vincent and the Grenadines, Barbados, and Grenada).

antimatter in physics, a form of matter in which most of the attributes (such as electrical charge, magnetic moment, and spin) of ◊elementary particles are reversed. Such particles (◊antiparticles) can be created in particle accelerators, such as those at ◊CERN in Geneva, Switzerland, and at Fermilab in the USA.

Antioch ancient capital of the Greek kingdom of Syria, founded 300 BC by ◊Seleucus I in memory of his father Antiochus, and famed for its splendour and luxury. Under the Romans it was an early centre of Christianity. It was captured by the Arabs 637. In 1098 Antioch was taken by the crusaders, who held it until 1268. The site is now occupied by the Turkish town of Antakya.

antioxidant any substance that prevents deterioration by oxidation in fats, oils, paints, plastics, and rubbers. When used as food ◊additives, antioxidants prevent fats and oils from becoming rancid when exposed to air, and thus extend their shelf life.

antiparticle in nuclear physics, a particle corresponding in mass and properties to a given ◊elementary particle but with the opposite electrical charge, magnetic properties, or coupling to other fundamental forces. For example, an electron carries a negative charge whereas its antiparticle, the positron, carries a positive one. When a particle and its antiparticle collide, they destroy each other, their total energy being converted to lighter particles and/or photons. A substance consisting entirely of antiparticles is known as ◊antimatter.

antipope rival claimant to the elected pope for the leadership of the Roman Catholic Church, for instance in the Great Schism 1378–1417 when there were rival popes in Rome and Avignon.

anti-Semitism literally, prejudice against Semitic people (see ◊Semite), but in practice it has meant prejudice or discrimination against, and persecution of, the Jews as an ethnic group. Anti-Semitism was a tenet of Hitler's Germany, and in the Holocaust 1933–45 about 6 million Jews died in concentration camps and in local extermination ◊pogroms, such as the siege of the Warsaw ghetto. It is a form of ◊racism.

antiseptic any substance that kills or inhibits the growth of microorganisms.

The use of antiseptics was pioneered by Joseph ◊Lister.

antler 'horn' of a deer, often branched, and made of bone rather than horn. Antlers, unlike true horns, are shed and regrown each year.

Antonine Wall Roman line of fortification built AD 142 during the reign of Roman emperor Antoninus Pius (AD 86–161). It was the Roman Empire's northwest frontier, between the Clyde and Forth rivers, Scotland. It was defended until c. 200.

Antrim county of Northern Ireland; *area* 2,830 sq km/1,092 sq mi; *features* Giant's Causeway of natural hexagonal basalt columns on the N coast; peat bogs. *population* (1981) 642,000.

Antwerp (Flemish *Antwerpen*, French *Anvers*) port in Belgium on the river Scheldt, capital of the province of Antwerp; population (1991) 467,500. One of the world's busiest ports. The home of the artist Rubens is preserved, and many of his works are in the Gothic cathedral.

apartheid racial-segregation policy of the government of South Africa, legislated 1948 when the Afrikaner National Party gained power. It deprived non-whites – classified as Bantu (black), coloured (mixed), or Indian – of the full rights of citizenship granted to whites. In 1991 President de Klerk repealed the key elements of apartheid legislation, including restrictions on political activity and racial segregation, and by 1994 apartheid had ceased to exist.

ape ◊primate of the family Pongidae, closely related to humans, including gibbon, orang-utan, chimpanzee, and gorilla.

Apennines chain of mountains stretching the length of the Italian peninsula. A continuation of the Maritime Alps, from Genoa it swings across the peninsula to Ancona on the east coast, and then back to the west coast and into the 'toe' of Italy. The system is continued over the Strait of Messina along the N Sicilian coast, then across the Mediterranean Sea in a series of islands to the Atlas Mountains of N Africa. The highest peak is Gran Sasso d'Italia at 2,914 m/9,560 ft.

aphid any of the family of small insects, Aphididae, in the order Homoptera, that live by sucking sap from plants. There are many species, often adapted to particular plants.

Aphrodite in Greek mythology, the goddess of love (Roman Venus, Phoenician Astarte, Babylonian Ishtar); said to be either a daughter of Zeus (in Homer) or sprung from the foam of the sea (in Hesiod). She was the unfaithful wife of Hephaestus, the god of fire, and the mother of Eros.

Apia capital and port of Western ◊Samoa, on the north coast of Upolu Island, in the W Pacific; population (1981) 33,000. It was the final home of the writer Robert Louis Stevenson 1888–94.

Apocrypha appendix to the Old Testament of the Bible, not included in the final Hebrew canon but recognized by Roman Catholics. There are also disputed New Testament texts known as Apocrypha.

Apollinaire Guillaume. Pen name of Guillaume Apollinaire de Kostrowitsky 1880–1918. French poet of aristocratic Polish descent. His experimental poems, such as *Alcools/Alcohols* 1913 and *Calligrammes/Word Pictures* 1918, show him as a representative of the Cubist and Futurist movements.

Apollo in Greek and Roman mythology, the god of sun, music, poetry, prophecy, agriculture, and pastoral life, and leader of the Muses. He was the twin child of Zeus and Leto.

apostle in the New Testament, any of the chosen 12 disciples sent out by Jesus after his resurrection to preach the Gospel. In the earliest days of Christianity the term was extended to include some who had never known Jesus in the flesh, notably St Paul.

Appalachians mountain system of E North America, stretching about 2,400 km/1,500 mi from Alabama to Québec, composed of ancient eroded rocks and rounded peaks. The chain includes the Allegheny, Catskill, and Blue Ridge mountains, the latter having the highest peak, Mount Mitchell, 2,045 m/6,712 ft.

appendicitis inflammation of the appendix, a small, blind extension of the bowel in the lower right abdomen. In an acute attack, the pus-filled appendix may burst, causing a potentially lethal spread of infection (peritonitis). Treatment is by removal (appendicectomy).

apple fruit of *Malus pumila*, a tree of the family Rosaceae. There are several hundred varieties of cultivated apples, grown all over the world, which may be divided into eating, cooking, and cider apples. All are derived from the wild crab apple.

Aqaba, Gulf of gulf extending for 160 km/100 mi between the Negev and the Red Sea; its coastline is uninhabited except at its head, where the frontiers of Israel, Egypt, Jordan, and Saudi Arabia converge. The two ports of Eilat (Israeli 'Elath') and Aqaba, Jordan's only port, are situated here.

aqualung or *scuba* underwater breathing apparatus worn by divers, developed in the early 1940s by French diver Jacques Cousteau. Compressed-air cylinders strapped to the diver's back are regulated by a valve system and by a mouth tube to provide air to the diver at the same pressure as that of the surrounding water (which increases with the depth).

aqueduct any artificial channel or conduit for water, often an elevated structure of stone, wood, or iron built for conducting water across a valley.

aquifer any rock formation containing water. The rock of an aquifer must be porous and permeable (full of interconnected holes) so that it can absorb water. Aquifers are an important source of fresh water in many arid areas of the world.

Aquinas St Thomas *c.* 1226–1274. Neapolitan philosopher and theologian, the greatest figure of the school of ▷scholasticism. A Dominican monk, known as the 'Angelic Doctor', his Summa contra Gentiles/Against the Errors of the Infidels 1259–64 is the most influential of his completed works. In 1879 his works were recognized as the basis of Catholic theology.

Aquitaine region of SW France; capital Bordeaux; area 41,300 sq km/15,942 sq mi; population (1986) 2,718,000. It comprises the *départements* of Dordogne, Gironde, Landes, Lot-et-Garonne, and Pyrénées-Atlantiques. Red wines (Margaux, St Julien) are produced in the Médoc district, bordering the Gironde. Aquitaine was an English possession 1152–1452.

Arab any of a Semitic people native to the Arabian peninsula, but now settled throughout North Africa and the nations of the Middle East.

Arabia peninsula between the Persian Gulf and the Red Sea, in SW Asia; area 2,600,000 sq km/1,000,000 sq mi. The peninsula contains the world's richest oil and gas reserves. It comprises the states of Bahrain, Kuwait, Oman, Qatar, Saudi Arabia, the United Arab Emirates, and Yemen.

Arabian Sea northwestern branch of the ◊Indian Ocean.

Arabic major Semitic language of the Hamito-Semitic family of W Asia and North Africa, originating among the Arabs of the Arabian peninsula. It is spoken today by about 120 million people in the Middle East and N Africa. Arabic script is written from right to left.

Arabic numerals or *Hindu-Arabic numerals* the symbols 0, 1, 2, 3, 4, 5, 6, 7, 8, 9, early forms of which were in use among the Arabs before being adopted by the peoples of Europe during the Middle Ages in place of ◊Roman numerals. The symbols appear to have originated in India and probably reached Europe by way of Spain.

arachnid or *arachnoid* type of arthropod, including spiders, scorpions, and mites. They differ from insects in possessing only two main body regions, the cephalothorax and the abdomen, and in having eight legs.

Arafat Yassir 1929– . Palestinian nationalist politician, cofounder of al-◊Fatah 1957 and president of the ◊Palestine Liberation Organization (PLO) from 1969. In Sept 1993 he reached a historic peace accord of mutual recognition with Israel, under which the Gaza Strip and Jericho were transferred to PLO control. In July 1994 he returned to the former occupied territories as head of an embryonic Palestinian state. He was awarded the 1994 Nobel Prize for Peace jointly with Israeli president Yitzhak Rabin and foreign minister Shimon Peres.

Aragon autonomous region of NE Spain including the provinces of Huesca, Teruel, and Zaragoza; area 47,700 sq km/18,412 sq mi; population (1986) 1,215,000. Its capital is Zaragoza. Aragón was an independent kingdom 1035–1479.

Aral Sea inland sea divided between Kazakhstan and Uzbekistan, the world's fourth largest lake; former area 62,000 sq km/24,000 sq mi, but decreasing. Water from its tributaries, the Amu Darya and Syr Darya, has been diverted for irrigation and city use, and the sea is disappearing, with long-term consequences for the climate.

Aramaic Semitic language of the Hamito-Semitic family of W Asia, the everyday language of Palestine 2,000 years ago, during the Roman occupation and the time of Jesus.

Arawak member of an indigenous American people of the Caribbean and NE Amazon Basin. Arawaks lived mainly by shifting cultivation in tropical forests. They were driven out of many West Indian islands by another American Indian people, the Caribs, shortly before the arrival of the Spanish in the 16th century.

arc in geometry, a section of a curved line or circle. A circle has three types of arc: a *semicircle*, which is exactly half of the circle; *minor arcs*, which are less than the semicircle; and *major arcs*, which are greater than the semicircle.

Archaean or *Archaeozoic* the earliest eon of geological time; the first part of the Precambrian, from the formation of Earth up to about 2,500 million years ago. It was a time when no life existed, and with every new discovery of ancient life its upper boundary is being pushed further back.

archaeology study of prehistory and history, based on the examination of physical remains. Principal activities include preliminary field (or site) surveys, excavation (where necessary), and the classification, dating, and interpretation of finds. Since 1958 ▷radiocarbon dating has been used to establish the age of archaeological strata and associated materials.

archery use of the bow and arrow, originally in hunting and warfare, now as a competitive sport. The world governing body is the Fédération Internationale de Tir à l'Arc (FITA) founded 1931.

Archimedes *c.* 287–212 BC. Greek mathematician who made major discoveries in geometry, hydrostatics, and mechanics. He formulated a law of fluid displacement (Archimedes' principle), and is credited with the invention of the Archimedes screw, a cylindrical device for raising water.

Archimedes' principle in physics, law stating that an object totally or partly submerged in a fluid displaces a volume of fluid that weighs the same as

the apparent loss in weight of the object (which, in turn, equals the upwards force, or upthrust, experienced by that object). It was discovered by the Greek mathematician Archimedes.

architecture art of designing structures. The term covers the design of the visual appearance of structures; their internal arrangements of space; selection of external and internal building materials; design or selection of natural and artificial lighting systems, as well as mechanical, electrical, and plumbing systems; and design or selection of decorations and furnishings. Architectural style may emerge from evolution of techniques and styles particular to a culture in a given time period with or without identifiable individuals as architects, or may be attributed to specific individuals or groups of architects working together on a project.

Arctic, the that part of the northern hemisphere surrounding the North Pole; arbitrarily defined as the region lying N of the Arctic Circle (66° 32′N) or N of the tree line. There is no Arctic continent; the greater part of the region comprises the Arctic Ocean, the world's smallest ocean. Arctic climate, fauna, and flora extend over the islands and northern edges of continental land masses that surround it (Svalbard, Iceland, Greenland, Siberia, Scandinavia, Alaska, and Canada); *area* 36,000,000 sq km/14,000,000 sq mi; *features* pack-ice floating on the Arctic Ocean occupies almost the entire region between the North Pole and the coasts of North America and Eurasia, covering an area that ranges in diameter from 3,000 km/1,900 mi to 4,000 km/2,500 mi; the *Arctic Ocean*, surrounding the North Pole, has an *area* of 14,000,000 sq km/5,400,000 sq mi.

Ardennes wooded plateau in NE France, SE Belgium, and N Luxembourg, cut through by the river Meuse; also a *département* of ▷Champagne-Ardenne. There was heavy fighting here in World Wars I and II.

Ares in Greek mythology, the god of war, equivalent to the Roman ▷Mars. The son of Zeus and Hera, he was worshipped chiefly in Thrace.

Argentina Republic of (*República Argentina*); *area* 2,780,092 sq km/ 1,073,116 sq mi; *capital* Buenos Aires; *environment* an estimated 20,000 sq km/ 7,700 sq mi of land has been swamped with salt water; *features* Andes mountains, with Aconcagua the highest peak in the W hemisphere; Iguaçú Falls; *political system* democratic federal republic; *population* (1993 est) 33,500,000 (mainly of Spanish or Italian origin, only about 30,000 American Indians surviving); growth rate 1.5% p.a; *languages* Spanish (official); English, Italian, German, French; *religion* Roman Catholic (state-supported).

argon colourless, odourless, nonmetallic, gaseous element, symbol Ar, atomic number 18, relative atomic mass 39.948. It is grouped with the ▷inert gases, since it was long believed not to react with other substances, but observations now indicate that it can be made to combine with boron fluoride to form compounds.

Argonauts in Greek mythology, the band of heroes who accompanied ▷Jason when he set sail in the *Argo* to find the ▷Golden Fleece.

Aristide Jean-Bertrand 1953– . President of Haiti Dec 1990–Oct 1991 and from Oct 1994. A left-wing Catholic priest opposed to the right-wing regime of the Duvalier family, he represented a loose coalition of peasants, trade unionists, and clerics. He was deposed by the military Sept 1991 and took refuge in the USA, returning in Sept 1994 after US intervention caused the military to step down.

Aristophanes *c.* 448–380 BC. Greek comedy dramatist. Of his 11 extant plays (of a total of over 40), the early comedies are remarkable for their satire, such as his portrayal of the new learning of Socrates in *The Clouds* 423 BC and the power of women in *Lysistrata* 411. The chorus plays a prominent role, frequently giving the play its title, as in *The Wasps* 422, *The Birds* 414, and *The Frogs* 405.

Aristotle 384–322 BC. Greek philosopher who advocated reason and moderation. He maintained that sense experience is our only source of knowledge, and that by reasoning we can discover the essences of things, that is, their distinguishing qualities. In his works on ethics and politics, he suggested that human happiness consists in living in conformity with nature. Of Aristotle's works some 22 treatises survive, dealing with logic, metaphysics, physics, astronomy, meteorology, biology, psychology, ethics, politics, and literary criticism.

arithmetic branch of mathematics concerned with the study of numbers and their properties. The fundamental operations of arithmetic are addition, subtraction, multiplication, and division. Raising to powers (for example, squaring or cubing a number), the extraction of roots (for example, square roots), percentages, fractions, and ratios are developed from these operations.

arithmetic progression or *arithmetic sequence* sequence of numbers or terms that have a common difference between any one term and the next in the sequence. For example, 2, 7, 12, 17, 22, 27, ... is an arithmetic sequence with a common difference of 5.

Arizona state in southwestern USA; *area* 294,100 sq km/113,500 sq mi; *capital* Phoenix; *features* Grand Canyon National Park, 6–29 km/4–18 mi wide, up to 1.7 km/1.1 mi deep, and 350 km/217 mi long; Organ Pipe Cactus National Monument Park; Painted Desert, which includes the Petrified Forest of fossil trees; old London Bridge (transported 1971 to Lake Havasu City); *population* (1990) 3,665,000, including 4.5% American Indians, who by treaty own 25% of the state.

Arkansas state in S central USA; *area* 137,800 sq km/53,191 sq mi; *capital* Little Rock; *features* Hot Springs National Park; *population* (1990) 2,350,700.

Arkwright Richard 1732–1792. English inventor and manufacturing pioneer who developed a machine for spinning cotton (he called it a 'spinning frame') 1768. He set up a water- powered spinning factory 1771 and installed steam power in another factory 1790.

Armada fleet sent by Philip II of Spain against England 1588. See ⊳Spanish Armada.

armadillo mammal of the family Dasypodidae, with an armour of bony plates on its back. Some 20 species live between Texas and Patagonia and range in size from the fairy armadillo at 13 cm/5 in to the giant armadillo, 1.5 m/4.5 ft long. Armadillos feed on insects, snakes, fruit, and carrion.

Armageddon in the New Testament (Revelation 16), the site of the final battle between the nations that will end the world; it has been identified with Megiddo in Israel.

Armagh county of Northern Ireland; *area* 1,250 sq km/483 sq mi; *towns and cities* Armagh (county town), Lurgan, Portadown, Keady; *features* smallest county of Northern Ireland; flat in the N, with many bogs; low hills in the S; *population* (1981) 119,000.

Armenia Republic of; *area* 29,800 sq km/11,500 sq mi; *capital* Yerevan; *features* State Academia Theatre of Opera and Ballet; Yerevan Film Studio; *political system* emergent democracy; *population* (1993 est) 3,500,000 (90% Armenian, 5% Azeri, 2% Russian, 2% Kurd); *language* Armenian; *religion* traditionally Armenian Christian.

Armenian member of the largest ethnic group inhabiting Armenia. There are Armenian minorities in Azerbaijan, as well as in Turkey and Iran. Christianity was introduced to the ancient Armenian kingdom in the 3rd century. There are 4–5 million speakers of the *Armenian* language, which belongs to the Indo-European family of languages.

armistice cessation of hostilities while awaiting a peace settlement. 'The Armistice' refers specifically to the end of World War I between Germany and the Allies 11 Nov 1918.

Armstrong Louis ('Satchmo') 1901–1971. US jazz cornet and trumpet player and singer. His Chicago recordings in the 1920s with the Hot Five and Hot Seven brought him recognition for his warm and pure trumpet tone, his skill at improvisation, and his quirky, gravelly voice.

Armstrong Neil Alden 1930– . US astronaut. In 1969, he became the first person to set foot on the Moon, and said, 'That's one small step for a man, one giant leap for mankind.'

Arnold Matthew 1822–1888. English poet and critic. His poems, characterized by their elegiac mood and pastoral themes, include *The Forsaken Merman* 1849, *Thyrsis* 1867, *Dover Beach* 1867, and *The Scholar Gypsy* 1853. Arnold's critical works include his highly influential *Culture and Anarchy* 1869, which attacks 19th-century philistinism.

aromatic compound organic chemical compound in which some of the bonding electrons are delocalized (shared among several atoms within the molecule and not localized in the vicinity of the atoms involved in bonding). The commonest aromatic compounds have ring structures, the atoms comprising the ring being either all carbon or containing one or more different atoms (usually nitrogen, sulphur, or oxygen). Typical examples are benzene (C_6H_6) and pyridine (C_6H_5N).

Arp Hans or Jean 1887–1966. French abstract painter and sculptor. He was one of the founders of the ◊Dada movement 1916, and was later associated with the Surrealists. Using chance and automatism, Arp developed an abstract scuplture whose sensuous form suggests organic shapes.

arsenic brittle, greyish-white, semimetallic element (a metalloid), symbol As, atomic number 33, relative atomic mass 74.92. It occurs in many ores and is widely distributed, being present in minute quantities in the soil, the sea, and the human body. In larger quantities, it is poisonous. It is used in making semiconductors, alloys, and solders.

Art Deco style in the decorative arts which influenced design and architecture. It emerged in Europe in the 1920s and continued through the 1930s, becoming particularly popular in the USA and France. A self-consciously modern style, it is characterized by angular, geometrical patterns and bright colours, and by the use of materials such as enamel, chrome, glass, and plastic.

Artemis in Greek mythology, the goddess of chastity, the young of all creatures, the Moon, and the hunt (Roman Diana). She is the twin sister of ◊Apollo and was worshipped at cult centres throughout the Greek world, one of the largest of which was at Ephesus.

arteriosclerosis hardening of the arteries, with thickening and loss of elasticity. It is associated with smoking, aging, and a diet high in saturated fats.

artery vessel that carries blood from the heart to the rest of the body. It is built to withstand considerable pressure, having thick walls which contain smooth muscle fibres. During contraction of the heart muscle, arteries expand in diameter to allow for the sudden increase in pressure that occurs; the resulting ◊pulse or pressure wave can be felt at the wrist.

arthritis inflammation of the joints, with pain, swelling, and restricted motion. Many conditions may cause arthritis, including gout, infection, and trauma to the joint.

arthropod member of the phylum Arthropoda; an invertebrate animal with jointed legs and a segmented body with a horny or chitinous casing (exoskeleton), which is shed periodically and replaced as the animal grows. Included are arachnids such as spiders and mites, as well as crustaceans, millipedes, centipedes, and insects.

Arthur legendary British king and hero in stories of Camelot and the quest for the ◊Holy Grail. Arthur is said to have been born in Tintagel, Cornwall, and buried in Glastonbury, Somerset. He may have been a Romano-Celtic leader against pagan Saxon invaders.

artificial intelligence (AI) branch of science concerned with creating computer programs that can perform actions comparable with those of an intelligent human. Current AI research covers such areas as planning (for robot behaviour), language understanding, pattern recognition, and knowledge representation.

artillery collective term for military firearms too heavy to be carried. Artillery can be mounted on tracks, wheels, ships or aeroplanes and includes cannons and rocket launchers.

Art Nouveau in the visual arts and architecture, a decorative style of about 1890–1910 making use of sinuous lines reminiscent of unfolding tendrils, stylized flowers and foliage, and flame shapes. Examples of Art Nouveau can be seen in the UK, in the illustrations of Aubrey Beardsley; in France, in the art glass of René Lalique and the posters of Alphonse Mucha; and in the USA, in the lamps and metalwork of Louis Comfort Tiffany.

Aruba island in the Caribbean, the westernmost of the Lesser Antilles; an overseas part of the Netherlands; *area* 193 sq km/75 sq mi; *population* (1989) 62,400.

Arunachal Pradesh state of India, in the Himalayas on the borders of Tibet and Myanmar; *area* 83,600 sq km/

32,270 sq mi; *capital* Itanagar; *population* (1991) 858,400; *languages* 50 different dialects.

Aryan languages 19th-century name for the ◊Indo-European languages; the languages of the Aryan peoples of India. The name Aryan is no longer used by language scholars because of its association with the Nazi concept of white supremacy.

asbestos any of several related minerals of fibrous structure that offer great heat resistance because of their nonflammability and poor conductivity. Commercial asbestos is generally either made from serpentine ('white' asbestos) or from sodium iron silicate ('blue' asbestos). Asbestos usage is now strictly controlled; exposure to its dust can cause cancer.

Ascension British island of volcanic origin in the S Atlantic, a dependency of St Helena since 1922; population (1982) 1,625. The chief settlement is Georgetown.

ASCII (acronym for *American standard code for information interchange*) in computing, a coding system in which numbers are assigned to letters, digits, and punctuation symbols. Although computers work in binary number code, ASCII numbers are usually quoted as decimal or ◊hexadecimal numbers. For example, the decimal number 45 (binary 0101101) represents a hyphen, and 65 (binary 1000001) a capital A. The first 32 codes are used for control functions, such as carriage return and backspace.

ascorbic acid $C_6H_8O_6$ or *vitamin C* a relatively simple organic acid found in citrus fruits and vegetables. It is soluble in water and destroyed by prolonged boiling, so soaking or overcooking of vegetables reduces their vitamin C content. Lack of ascorbic acid results in scurvy.

asexual reproduction in biology, reproduction that does not involve the manufacture and fusion of sex cells, nor the necessity for two parents. The process carries a clear advantage in that there is no need to search for a mate nor to develop complex pollinating mechanisms; every asexual organism can reproduce on its own. Asexual reproduction can therefore lead to a rapid population build- up.

ash any tree of the worldwide genus *Fraxinus*, belonging to the olive family Oleaceae, with winged fruits. The ⬦*mountain ash* or *rowan* belongs to the family Rosaceae.

Ashcroft Peggy 1907–1991. English actress. Her Shakespearean roles included Desdemona in *Othello* and Juliet in *Romeo and Juliet* 1935 (with Laurence Olivier and John Gielgud), and she appeared in the British TV play *Caught on a Train* 1980, the series *The Jewel in the Crown* 1984, and the film *A Passage to India* 1985.

Ashdown Paddy (Jeremy John Durham) 1941– . English politician, leader of the merged Social and Liberal Democrats from 1988. A member of the Diplomatic Service 1971–76, he became a Liberal member of Parliament 1983. His constituency is Yeovil, Somerset.

Ashes, the cricket trophy theoretically held by the winning team in the England–Australia test series.

Ashgabat formerly *Ashkhabad* capital of Turkmenistan; population (1989) 402,000. The spelling was changed 1992 to reflect the Turkmen origin of the name. The spectacular natural setting has been used by the film-making industry.

Ashkenazi (plural *Ashkenazim*) Jew of German or E European descent, as opposed to a Sephardi, of Spanish, Portuguese, or N African descent.

Ashton Frederick 1904–1988. English choreographer and dancer. He was director of the Royal Ballet, London, 1963– –70. He studied with Marie Rambert before joining the Sadler's Wells (now Royal) Ballet 1935 as chief choreographer. His choreography is marked by a soft, pliant, classical lyricism. Ashton's long association with Margot Fonteyn produced her famous roles.

Ash Wednesday first day of Lent, the period in the Christian calendar leading up to Easter; in the Roman Catholic Church the foreheads of the congregation are marked with a cross in ash, as a sign of penitence.

Asia largest of the continents, occupying one-third of the total land surface of the world; *area* 44,000,000 sq km/ 17,000,000 sq mi; *largest cities* (population over 5 million) Tokyo, Shanghai, Osaka, Beijing, Seoul, Calcutta, Bombay, Jakarta, Bangkok, Tehran, Hong Kong, Delhi, Tianjin, Karachi; *features* Mount Everest, at 8,872 m/29,118 ft is the world's highest mountain; Dead Sea at –394 m/–1,293 ft is the world's lowest point below sea level; lakes (over 18,000 sq km/7,000 sq mi) include Caspian Sea (the largest lake in the world), Aral Sea, Baikal (largest freshwater lake in Eurasia); deserts include the Gobi, Takla Makan, Syrian Desert, Arabian Desert, Negev; *population* (1988) 496 million (excluding Turkey and the ex-Soviet republics); annual growth rate 0.3%.

Asmara or *Asmera* capital of Eritrea; 64 km/40 mi SW of Massawa on the Red Sea; population (1984) 275,385. It has a naval school. In 1974 unrest here precipitated the end of the Ethiopian Empire.

asphyxia suffocation; a lack of oxygen that produces a potentially lethal build-up of carbon dioxide waste in the tissues.

aspirin acetylsalicylic acid, a popular pain-relieving drug (⊳analgesic) developed in the late 19th century as a household remedy for aches and pains. It relieves pain and reduces inflammation and fever. It is derived from the white willow tree *Salix alba*.

Asquith Herbert Henry, 1st Earl of Oxford and Asquith 1852–1928. British Liberal politician, prime minister 1908–16. As chancellor of the Exchequer he introduced old-age pensions 1908. He limited the powers of the House of Lords and attempted to give Ireland Home Rule.

Assad Hafez al 1930– . Syrian Ba'athist politician, president from 1971. He became prime minister after a bloodless military coup 1970, and the following year was the first president to be elected by popular vote. Having suppressed dissent, he was re-elected 1978 and 1985. He is a Shia (Alawite) Muslim.

Assam state of NE India; *area* 78,400 sq km/30,262 sq mi; *capital* Dispur; *population* (1991) 24,294,600, including 12 million Assamese (Hindus), 5 million Bengalis (chiefly Muslim immigrants from Bangladesh), Nepalis, and 2 million indigenous people (Christian and traditional religions); *language* Assamese.

Assyria empire in the Middle East *c.* 2500–612 BC, in N Mesopotamia (now Iraq); early capital Ashur, later Nineveh. It was initially subject to Sumer and intermittently to Babylon. The Assyrians adopted largely the Sumerian religion and structure of society. At its greatest extent the empire included Egypt and stretched from the E Mediterranean coast to the head of the Persian Gulf.

Astaire Fred. Adopted name of Frederick Austerlitz 1899–1987. US dancer, actor, singer, and choreographer. He starred in numerous films, including *Top Hat* 1935, *Easter Parade* 1948, and *Funny Face* 1957, many containing inventive sequences which he designed and choreographed himself. He made ten classic films with the most popular of his dancing partners, Ginger Rogers.

asteroid or *minor planet* any of many thousands of small bodies, composed of rock and iron, that orbit the Sun. Most lie in a belt between the orbits of Mars and Jupiter, and are thought to be fragments left over from the formation of the ⊳Solar System. About 100,000 may exist, but their total mass is only a few hundredths the mass of the Moon.

asthma chronic condition characterized by difficulty in breathing due to spasm of the bronchi (air passages) in the lungs. Attacks may be provoked by allergy, infection, and stress. The incidence of asthma is increasing; air pollution and occupational hazard are thought to be factors. Treatment is with bronchodilators to relax the bronchial muscles and thereby ease the breathing, and in severe cases by inhaled ⊳steroids that reduce inflammation of the bronchi.

astigmatism aberration occurring in the lens of the eye. With astigmatic eyesight, the vertical and horizontal cannot be in focus at the same time; correction is by the use of a cylindrical lens that reduces the overall focal length of one plane so that both planes are seen in sharp focus.

astrology study of the relative position of the planets and stars in the unproven belief that they influence events on Earth. The astrologer casts a horoscope based on the time and place of the subject's birth. Practised since ancient times, Western astrology is based on the 12 signs of the zodiac while Chinese astrology is based on a 60-year cycle and lunar calendar.

astronomical unit unit (symbol AU) equal to the mean distance of the Earth from the Sun: 149,597,870 km/ 92,955,800 mi. It is used to describe planetary distances. Light travels this distance in approximately 8.3 minutes.

astronomy science of the celestial bodies: the Sun, the Moon, and the planets; the stars and galaxies; and all other objects in the universe. It is concerned with their positions, motions, distances, and physical conditions and with their origins and evolution. Astronomy thus divides into fields such as astrophysics, celestial mechanics, and cosmology.

astrophysics study of the physical nature of stars, galaxies, and the universe. It began with the development of spectroscopy in the 19th century, which allowed astronomers to analyse the composition of stars from their light. Astrophysicists view the universe as a vast natural laboratory in which they can study matter under conditions of temperature, pressure, and density that are unattainable on Earth.

Asunción capital and port of Paraguay, on the Paraguay River; population (1984) 729,000. Founded 1537, it was the first Spanish settlement in the La Plata region.

Aswan winter resort in Upper Egypt; population (1985) 183,000. It is near the *Aswan High Dam*, built 1960–70, which keeps the level of the Nile constant throughout the year without flooding.

asylum, political in international law, refuge granted in another country to a person who, for political reasons, cannot return to his or her own country without putting himself or herself in danger. A person seeking asylum is a type of ▷refugee.

Atatürk (Turkish 'Father of the Turks') (Mustafa Kemal Atatürk) Name assumed 1934 by Mustafa Kemal Pasha 1881–1938. Turkish politician and general, first president of Turkey from 1923. After World War I he established a provisional rebel government and in 1921–22 expelled the Greeks who were occupying Turkey. He was the founder of the modern republic, which he ruled as virtual dictator.

atavism (Latin *atavus* 'ancestor') in ▷genetics, the reappearance of a characteristic not apparent in the immediately preceding generations; in psychology, the manifestation of primitive forms of behaviour.

Athens (Greek *Athinai*) capital city of Greece and of ancient Attica; population (1981) 885,000, metropolitan area (1991) 3,096,800. It is built around the rocky hills of the Acropolis 169 m/555 ft and the Areopagus 112 m/368 ft, and is overlooked from the NE by the hill of Lycabettus. It has less green space than any other European capital (4%) and severe air and noise pollution.

athletics competitive track and field events consisting of running, throwing, and jumping disciplines. *Running events* range from sprint races (100 metres) and hurdles to the marathon (26 miles 385 yards). *Jumping events* are the high jump, long jump, and – for men only – the triple jump and pole vault. *Throwing events* are javelin, discus, shot put, and – for men only – hammer throw.

Atlanta capital and largest city of Georgia, USA; population (1990) 394,000, metropolitan area 2,010,000. It was founded 1837 and was partly destroyed by General Sherman 1864. In 1990 it was chosen as the host city for the 1996 summer Olympic Games.

Atlantic, Battle of the continuous battle fought in the Atlantic Ocean during World War II by the sea and air forces of the Allies and Germany, to control the supply routes to the UK. The Allies destroyed nearly 800 U-boats during the war and at least 2,200 convoys of 75,000 merchant ships crossed the Atlantic, protected by US naval forces. Before the US entry into the war 1941, destroyers were supplied to the British under the Lend-Lease Act 1941.

Atlantic Ocean ocean lying between Europe and Africa to the E and the Americas to the W, probably named after *Atlantis*, the island continent of Greek legend (although the structure of the sea bottom rules out its ever having existed there); area of basin 81,500,000 sq km/31,500,000 sq mi; including the Arctic Ocean and Antarctic seas, 106,200,000 sq km/41,000,000 sq mi. The average depth is 3 km/2 mi; greatest depth the Milwaukee Depth in the Puerto Rico Trench 8,648 m/28,374 ft.

The *Mid-Atlantic Ridge*, of which the Azores, Ascension, St Helena, and Tristan da Cunha form part, divides it from N to S. Lava welling up from this central area annually increases the distance between South America and Africa. The N Atlantic is the saltiest of the main oceans and has the largest tidal range.

Atlas in Greek mythology, one of the ◊Titans who revolted against the gods; as a punishment, he was compelled to support the heavens on his head and shoulders. Growing weary, he asked Perseus to turn him into stone, and he was transformed into Mount Atlas.

Atlas Mountains mountain system of NW Africa, stretching 2,400 km/1,500 mi from the Atlantic coast of Morocco to the Gulf of Gabes, Tunisia, and lying between the Mediterranean on the N and the Sahara on the S. The highest peak is Mount Toubkal 4,167 m/13,670 ft.

atmosphere mixture of gases that surrounds the Earth, prevented from escaping by the pull of the Earth's gravity. Atmospheric pressure decreases with height in the atmosphere. In its lowest layer, the atmosphere consists of nitrogen (78%) and oxygen (21%), both in molecular form (two atoms bounded together). The other 1% is largely argon, with very small quantities of other gases, including water vapour and carbon dioxide.

atom smallest unit of matter that can take part in a chemical reaction, and which cannot be broken down chemically into anything simpler. An atom is made up of protons and neutrons in a central nucleus surrounded by electrons (see ◊atomic structure). The atoms of the various elements differ in atomic number, relative atomic mass, and chemical behaviour.

atom bomb bomb deriving its explosive force from nuclear fission (see ◊nuclear energy) as a result of a neutron chain reaction, developed in the 1940s in the USA into a usable weapon.

atomic mass unit or *dalton unit* (symbol amu or u) unit of mass that is used to measure the relative mass of atoms and molecules. It is equal to one-twelfth of the mass of a carbon-12 atom, which is equivalent to the mass of a proton or 1.66×10^{-27} kg. The ◊relative atomic mass of an atom has no units; thus oxygen-16 has an atomic mass of 16 daltons but a relative atomic mass of 16.

atomic number or *proton number* the number (symbol Z) of protons in the nucleus of an atom. It is equal to the positive charge on the nucleus. In a neutral atom, it is also equal to the number of electrons surrounding the nucleus. The 109 elements are arranged in the ◊periodic table of the elements according to their atomic number.

atomic structure internal structure of an ◊atom. The core of the atom is the *nucleus*, a dense body only one ten-thousandth the diameter of the atom itself. The simplest nucleus, that of hydrogen, comprises a single stable positively charged particle, the *proton*. Nuclei of other elements contain more protons and additional particles, called *neutrons*, of about the same mass as the proton but with no electrical charge. Each element has its own characteristic nucleus with a unique number of protons, the atomic number. The number of neutrons may vary. Where atoms of a single element have different numbers of neutrons, they are called ◊isotopes.

In a neutral atom, the nucleus is surrounded by the same number of electrons as it contains protons. According to ◊quantum theory, the position of an electron is uncertain; it may be found at any point. The region of space in which an electron is most likely to be found is called an orbital. The chemical properties of an element are determined by the ease with which its atoms can gain or lose electrons from its outer orbitals.

atonement in Christian theology, the doctrine that Jesus suffered on the cross to bring about reconciliation and forgiveness between God and humanity.

Atonement, Day of Jewish holy day (*Yom Kippur*) held on the tenth day of Tishri (Sept–Oct), the first month of the Jewish year. It is a day of fasting, penitence, and cleansing from sin, ending the Ten Days of Penitence that follow *Rosh Hashanah*, the Jewish New Year.

ATP abbreviation for *adenosine triphosphate*, a nucleotide molecule found in all cells. It can yield large amounts of energy, and is used to drive the thousands of biological processes needed to sustain life, growth, movement, and reproduction. Green plants use light energy to manufacture ATP as part of the process of ◊photosynthesis. In animals, ATP is formed by the breakdown of glucose molecules, usually obtained from the carbohydrate component of a diet, in a series of reactions termed ◊respiration.

Attenborough Richard 1923– . English director, actor, and producer. He made his screen acting debut in *In Which We Serve* 1942. He co-produced the socially-conscious *The Angry Silence* 1960, and directed *Oh! What a Lovely War* 1969. His epic biography of *Gandhi*

1982 won eight Academy Awards. He is the brother of naturalist *David Attenborough* (1926–   ).

Attica (Greek *Attiki*) region of Greece comprising Athens and the district around it; area 3,381 sq km/1,305 sq mi. It is renowned for its language, art, and philosophical thought in Classical times. It is a prefecture of modern Greece with Athens as its capital.

Attila *c.* 406–453. King of the Huns in an area from the Alps to the Caspian Sea from 434, known to later Christian history as the 'Scourge of God'. He twice attacked the Eastern Roman Empire to increase the quantity of tribute paid to him, 441–443 and 447–449, and then attacked the Western Roman Empire 450–452.

Attlee Clement (Richard), 1st Earl 1883–1967. British Labour politician. In the coalition government during World War II he was Lord Privy Seal 1940–42, dominions secretary 1942–43, and Lord President of the Council 1943–45, as well as deputy prime minister from 1942. As prime minister 1945–51 he introduced a sweeping programme of nationalization and a whole new system of social services.

Attorney General in the UK, principal law officer of the crown and head of the English Bar; the post is one of great political importance. In the USA, it is the chief law officer of the government and head of the Department of Justice.

Auckland largest city in New Zealand, situated in N North Island; population (1991) 315,900. It fills the isthmus that separates its two harbours (Waitemata and Manukau), and its suburbs spread N across the Harbour Bridge. It is the country's chief port and leading industrial centre.

Auden W(ystan) H(ugh) 1907–1973. English-born US poet. He wrote some of his most original poetry, such as *Look, Stranger!* 1936, leading the influential left-wing literary group that included Louis MacNeice, Stephen Spender, and Cecil Day Lewis. Moving to the USA 1939, he became a US citizen 1946, and adopted a more conservative and Christian viewpoint, for example in *The Age of Anxiety* 1947.

Augustine of Hippo, St 354–430. One of the early Christian leaders and writers known as the Fathers of the Church. He was converted to Christianity by Ambrose in Milan and became bishop of Hippo (modern Annaba, Algeria) 396. Among Augustine's many writings are his *Confessions*, a spiritual autobiography, and *De Civitate Dei/The City of God*, vindicating the Christian church and divine providence in 22 books.

Augustine, St first archbishop of Canterbury, England. He was sent from Rome to convert England to Christianity by Pope Gregory I. He landed at Ebbsfleet in Kent 597 and soon after baptized Ethelbert, King of Kent, along with many of his subjects. He was consecrated bishop of the English at Arles in the same year, and appointed archbishop 601, establishing his see at Canterbury. Feast day 26 May.

Augustus 63 BC–AD 14. Title of Octavian (Gaius Julius Caesar Octavianus), first of the Roman emperors. He joined forces with Mark Antony and Lepidus in the Second Triumvirate. Following Mark Antony's liaison with the Egyptian queen Cleopatra, Augustus defeated her troops at Actium 31 BC. As emperor (from 27 BC) he reformed the government of the empire, the army, and Rome's public services and was a patron of the arts.

aurora coloured light in the night sky near the Earth's magnetic poles, called *aurora borealis* ('northern lights') in the northern hemisphere and *aurora australis* in the southern hemisphere. Auroras are caused at heights of over 100 km/60 mi by a fast stream of charged particles from solar flares and low-density 'holes' in the Sun's corona. These are guided by the Earth's magnetic field towards the north and south magnetic poles, where they enter the upper atmosphere and bombard the gases in the atmosphere, causing them to emit visible light.

Auschwitz (Polish *Oswiecim*) town near Kraków in Poland, site of a notorious ▷concentration camp used by the Nazis in World War II to exterminate Jews and other political and social minorities.

Austen Jane 1775–1817. English novelist. Her *Sense and Sensibility* was published 1811, *Pride and Prejudice* 1813, *Mansfield Park* 1814, *Emma* 1816, *Northanger Abbey* and *Persuasion* 1818, all anonymously. With wit and precision, she revealed her characters' absurdities in relation to high standards of integrity and appropriateness.

Austerlitz, Battle of battle on 2 Dec 1805, in which the French forces of Emperor Napoleon defeated those of Alexander I of Russia and Francis II of Austria at a small town in the Czech Republic (formerly in Austria), 19 km/12 mi E of Brno.

Australasia loosely applied geographical term, usually meaning Australia, New Zealand, and neighbouring islands.

Australia Commonwealth of; *area* 7,682,300 sq km/2,966,136 sq mi; *capital* Canberra; *features* Ayers Rock; Arnhem Land; Gulf of Carpentaria; Cape York Peninsula; Great Australian Bight; unique animal species include the kangaroo, koala, platypus, wombat, Tasmanian devil, and spiny anteater; of 800 species of bird, the budgerigar, cassowary, emu, kookaburra, lyre bird, and black swan are also unique. *head of state* Elizabeth II from 1952, represented by governor general William George Hayden from 1989; *head of government* Paul Keating from 1991; *political system* federal constitutional monarchy; *population* (1993 est) 17,800,000; growth rate 1.5% p.a.; *languages* English, Aboriginal languages; *religions* Anglican 26%, other Protestant 17%, Roman Catholic 26%.

Australian Aborigine any of the 500 groups of indigenous inhabitants of the continent of Australia, who migrated to the region from S Asia about 40,000 years ago. Originally hunters and gatherers, they lived throughout the continent in small kin-based groups. In recent years, a movement for the recognition of Aborigine rights has campaigned against racial discrimination in housing, education, wages, and medical facilities.

Australian Antarctic Territory islands and territories south of 60° S, between 160° E and 45° E longitude, excluding Adélie Land; area 6,044,000 sq km/2,332,984 sq mi of land and 75,800 sq km/29,259 sq mi of ice shelf. The population on the Antarctic continent is limited to research personnel.

Australian Capital Territory territory ceded to Australia by New South Wales 1911 to provide the site of ▷Canberra, with its port at Jervis Bay, ceded 1915; area 2,400 sq km/926 sq mi; population (1987) 261,000.

Austria Republic of (*Republik Österreich*); *area* 83,500 sq km/32,374 sq mi; *capital* Vienna; *environment* Hainburg, the largest primeval forest left in Europe, under threat from a dam project (suspended 1990); *features* Austrian Alps; river Danube; *head of state* Thomas Klestil from 1992; *head of government* Franz Vranitzky from 1986; *political system* democratic federal republic; *population* (1993 est) 7,900,000; growth rate 0.1% p.a.; *language* German; *religions* Roman Catholic 85%, Protestant 6%;

Austro-Hungarian Empire Dual Monarchy 1867–1918 established by the Habsburg Franz Joseph between his empire of Austria and his kingdom of Hungary (including territory that became Czechoslovakia as well as parts of Poland, the Ukraine, Romania, Yugoslavia, and Italy). Charles ruled as king-emperor 1916–18; the empire collapsed 1918 with the end of World War I.

autism rare disorder, generally present from birth, characterized by a withdrawn state, a failure to develop normally in language or social behaviour, and an emotional attachment to things rather than people. Although autistic children may, rarely, show signs of high intelligence (in music or with numbers, for example) most have impaired intellect. Autism is thought to involve a number of factors, possibly including an inherent abnormality of the child's brain. Special education may bring about some improvement.

autoimmunity in medicine, condition where the body's immune responses are mobilized not against 'foreign' matter, such as invading germs, but against the body itself. Diseases considered to be of autoimmune origin include rheumatoid arthritis and lupus erythematosus.

autonomic nervous system in mammals, the part of the nervous system that controls those functions not controlled voluntarily, including the heart rate, activity of the intestines, and the production of sweat. There are two divisions of the autonomic nervous system. The *sympathetic* system responds to stress, when it speeds the heart rate, increases blood pressure and generally prepares the body for action. The *parasympathetic* system is more important when the body is at rest, since it slows the heart rate, decreases blood pressure, and stimulates the digestive system.

autotroph any living organism that synthesizes organic substances from inorganic molecules by using light or chemical energy. Autotrophs are the *primary producers* in all food chains since the materials they synthesize and store are the energy sources of all other organisms. All green plants and many planktonic organisms are autotrophs, using sunlight to convert carbon dioxide and water into sugars by ▷photosynthesis.

Auvergne ancient province of central France and modern region comprising the *départements* of Allier, Cantal, Haute-Loire, and Puy-de-Dôme; *area* 26,000 sq km/10,036 sq mi; *population* (1986) 1,334,000; *capital* Clermont-Ferrand.

auxin plant ▷hormone that promotes stem and root growth in plants. Auxins influence many aspects of plant growth and development, including cell enlargement, inhibition of development of axillary buds, ▷tropisms, and the initiation of roots.

Avebury Europe's largest stone circle (diameter 412 m/1,352 ft), in Wiltshire, England, probably constructed in the Neolithic period 3,500 years ago.

aviation term used to describe both the science of powered *flight* and also aerial navigation by means of an aeroplane.

Avignon city in Provence, France, capital of Vaucluse *département*, on the river Rhône NW of Marseilles; population (1990) 89,400. An important Gallic and Roman city, it has a 12th-century bridge (only half still standing), a 13th-century cathedral, 14th-century walls, and a palace built during the residence here of the popes.

avocado tree *Persea americana* of the laurel family, native to Central America. Its dark-green, thick-skinned, pear-shaped fruit has buttery-textured flesh and is used in salads.

Avogadro's hypothesis in chemistry, the law stating that equal volumes of all gases, when at the same temperature and pressure, have the same numbers of molecules. It was first propounded by Amedeo Avogadro.

Avon county of SW England, formed 1974 from the city and county of Bristol and parts of NE Somerset and SW Gloucestershire; *area* 1,340 sq km/517 sq mi; *towns and cities* Bristol (administrative headquarters), Bath, Weston-super-Mare, Avonmouth; *features* low-lying basin bordered by Cotswold Hills in NE, Mendip Hills in S; river Avon flows west into Severn estuary; *population* (1991) 932,600.

axis (plural *axes*) in geometry, one of the reference lines by which a point on a graph may be located. The horizontal axis is usually referred to as the x-axis, and the vertical axis as the y-axis. The term is also used to refer to the imaginary line about which an object may be said to be symmetrical (*axis of symmetry*) – for example, the diagonal of a square – or the line about which an object may revolve (*axis of rotation*).

ayatollah honorific title awarded to Shi'ite Muslims in Iran by popular consent, as, for example, to Ayatollah Ruhollah ▷Khomeini.

Ayckbourn Alan 1939– . English dramatist. His prolific output, characterized by comic dialogue and experiments in dramatic structure, includes *The Norman Conquests* (a trilogy) 1974, *A Woman in Mind* 1986, *Henceforward* 1987, and *Man of the Moment* 1988.

Ayers Rock vast ovate mass of pinkish rock in Northern Territory, Australia; 335 m/1,110 ft high and 9 km/6 mi around. For the Aboriginals, whose paintings decorate its caves, it has magical significance.

Azerbaijan Republic of; *area* 86,600 sq km/33,400 sq mi; *capital* Baku; *features* Caspian Sea; the country ranges from semidesert to the Caucasus Mountains; *political system* emergent democracy; *population* (1993 est) 7,200,000 (83% Azeri, 6% Russian, 6% Armenian); *language* Turkic; *religion* traditionally Shi'ite Muslim.

Azores group of nine islands in the N Atlantic, belonging to Portugal; area 2,247 sq km/867 sq mi; population (1987) 254,000. They are outlying peaks of the Mid-Atlantic Ridge and are volcanic in origin. The capital is Ponta Delgada on the main island, San Miguel.

AZT drug used in the treatment of AIDS; see ▷zidovudine.

Aztec member of a Mexican American Indian people that migrated south into the valley of Mexico in the 12th century, and in the 14th century built their capital, Tenochtitlán, on the site of present-day Mexico City. After the conquistador Cortés landed 1519,

Montezuma II (reigned from 1502) was killed and Tenochtitlán subsequently destroyed. The ancient Aztecs are known for their architecture, jewellery (gold, jade, and turquoise), sculpture, and textiles. Their form of writing combined hieroglyphs and pictographs, and they used a complex calendar that combined a sacred period of 260 days with the solar year of 365 days. The Aztec state was a theocracy with farmers, artisans, and merchants taxed to support the priestly aristocracy. Tribute was collected from a federation of conquered nearby states.

B

Babbage Charles 1792–1871. English mathematician who devised a precursor of the computer. He designed an analytical engine, a general-purpose mechanical computing device for performing different calculations according to a program input on punched cards (an idea borrowed from the Jacquard loom). This device was never built, but it embodied many of the principles on which present digital computers are based.

Babylon capital of ancient Babylonia, on the bank of the lower Euphrates River. The site is now in Iraq, 88 km/55 mi S of Baghdad and 8 km/5 mi N of Hilla, which is built chiefly of bricks from the ruins of Babylon. The Hanging Gardens of Babylon, one of the ▷Seven Wonders of the World, were probably erected on a vaulted stone base, the only stone construction in the mud-brick city. They formed a series of terraces, irrigated by a hydraulic system.

Bacall Lauren. Stage name of Betty Joan Perske 1924– . US actress. She became an overnight star when cast by Howard Hawks opposite Humphrey Bogart in *To Have and Have Not* 1944. She and Bogart married 1945 and starred together in *The Big Sleep* 1946.

Bacchus in Greek and Roman mythology, the god of fertility (see ▷Dionysus) and of wine; his rites (the *Bacchanalia*) were orgiastic.

Bach Johann Sebastian 1685–1750. German composer. A master of counterpoint, his music epitomizes the Baroque polyphonic style. His orchestral music includes the six *Brandenburg Concertos* 1721, other concertos for keyboard instrument and violin, four orchestral suites, sonatas for various instruments, six violin partitas, and six unaccompanied cello suites. Bach's keyboard music, for clavier and organ, his fugues, and his choral music are of equal importance. He also wrote chamber music and songs.

backgammon board game for two players, often used in gambling. It was known in Mesopotamia, Greece, and Rome and in medieval England.

background radiation radiation that is always present in the environment. By far the greater proportion (87%) of it is emitted from natural sources. Alpha and beta particles, and gamma radiation are radiated by the traces of radioactive minerals that occur naturally in the environment and even in the human body, and by radioactive gases such as radon and thoron, which are found in soil and may seep upwards into buildings. Radiation from space (▷cosmic radiation) also contributes to the background level.

Bacon Francis 1909–1992. Irish painter. Self-taught, he practised abstract art, then developed a stark

Bacon

Expressionist style characterized by distorted, blurred figures enclosed in loosely defined space. One of his best-known works is *Study after Velázquez's Portrait of Pope Innocent X* 1953 (Museum of Modern Art, New York).

Bacon Roger 1214–1292. English philosopher, scientist, and a teacher at Oxford University. He was interested in alchemy, the biological and physical sciences, and magic. Many discoveries have been credited to him, including the magnifying lens. He foresaw the extensive use of gunpowder and mechanical cars, boats, and planes.

Bacon Francis 1561–1626. English politician, philosopher, and essayist. He became Lord Chancellor 1618, and the same year spent four days in the Tower of London for bribe-taking. His works include *Essays* 1597, *The Advancement of Learning* 1605, the *Novum Organum* 1620, and *The New Atlantis* 1626, describing his utopia.

bacteria (singular *bacterium*) microscopic single-celled organisms lacking a nucleus. Bacteria are widespread, present in soil, air, and water, and as parasites on and in other living things. Some parasitic bacteria cause disease by producing toxins, but others are harmless and may even benefit their hosts. It is thought that 1–10% of the world's bacteria have been identified.

bacteriophage virus that attacks ◊bacteria. Such viruses are now of use in genetic engineering.

Baden-Powell Robert Stephenson Smyth, 1st Baron Baden-Powell 1857–1941. British general, founder of the Scout Association. He fought in defence of Mafeking (now Mafikeng) during the Second South African War.

After 1907 he devoted his time to developing the Scout movement, which rapidly spread throughout the world.

Baden-Württemberg administrative region (German *Land*) of Germany; *area* 35,800 sq km/13,819 sq mi; *capital* Stuttgart; *population* (1988) 9,390,000.

badminton racket game similar to lawn ◊tennis but played on a smaller court and with a shuttlecock (a half sphere of cork or plastic with a feather or nylon skirt) instead of a ball. The object of the game is to prevent the opponent from being able to return the shuttlecock.

Baghdad historic city and capital of Iraq, on the river Tigris; population (1985) 4,649,000. During the Gulf War 1991, the UN coalition forces bombed it in repeated air raids and destroyed much of the city.

Baha'i religion founded in the 19th century from a Muslim splinter group, Babism, by the Persian Baha'ullah. His message was that all great religious leaders are manifestations of the unknowable God and all scriptures are sacred. There is no priesthood: all Baha'is are expected to teach, and to work towards world unification.

Bahamas Commonwealth of the; *area* 13,864 sq km/5,352 sq mi; *capital* Nassau on New Providence; *features* desert islands: only 30 are inhabited; Blue Holes of Andros, the world's longest and deepest submarine caves; the Exumas are a narrow spine of 365 islands; *principal islands* Andros, Grand Bahama, Great Abaco, Eleuthera, New Providence, Berry Islands, Biminis, Great Inagua, Acklins, Exumas, Mayaguana, Crooked Island, Long Island, Cat

Island, Rum Cay, Watling (San Salvador) Island; *political system* constitutional monarchy; *population* (1993 est) 270,000; growth rate 1.8% p.a.; *languages* English and some Creole; *religions* 29% Baptist, 23% Anglican, 22% Roman Catholic.

Bahrain State of (*Dawlat al Bahrayn*); *area* 688 sq km/266 sq mi; *capital* Manama on the largest island (also called Bahrain); *environment* a wildlife park on Bahrain preserves the endangered oryx; most of the south of the island is preserved for the ruling family's falconry; *features* causeway linking Bahrain to mainland Saudi Arabia; Sitra island is a communications centre for the lower Persian Gulf and has a satellite-tracking station; *political system* absolute emirate; *population* (1993) 538,000 (two-thirds are nationals); growth rate 4.4% p.a.; *languages* Arabic (official); Farsi, English, Urdu; *religion* 85% Muslim (Shi'ite 60%, Sunni 40%).

Baird John Logie 1888–1946. Scottish electrical engineer who pioneered television. In 1925 he gave the first public demonstration of television and in 1926 pioneered fibre optics, radar, and 'noctovision', a system for seeing at night by using infrared rays.

Baku capital city of the Republic of Azerbaijan, industrial port on the Caspian Sea; population (1987) 1,741,000. It is a major oil centre and is linked by pipelines with Batumi on the Black Sea. In Jan 1990 there were violent clashes between the Azeri majority and the Armenian minority.

Balaclava, Battle of in the Crimean War, an engagement on 25 Oct 1854, near a town in Ukraine, 10 km/6 mi SE of Sevastopol. It was the scene of the ill-timed *Charge of the Light Brigade* of

British cavalry against the Russian entrenched artillery. Of the 673 soldiers who took part, there were 272 casualties. *Balaclava helmets* were knitted hoods worn here by soldiers in the bitter weather.

balance apparatus for weighing or measuring mass. The various types include the *beam balance* consisting of a centrally pivoted lever with pans hanging from each end, and the *spring balance*, in which the object to be weighed stretches (or compresses) a vertical coil spring fitted with a pointer that indicates the weight on a scale. Kitchen and bathroom scales are balances.

balance of payments in economics, an account of a country's debit and credit transactions with other countries. Items are divided into the *current account*, which includes both visible trade (imports and exports of goods) and invisible trade (services such as transport, tourism, interest, and dividends), and the *capital account*, which includes investment in and out of the country, international grants, and loans. Deficits or surpluses on these accounts are brought into balance by buying and selling reserves of foreign currencies.

balance of power in politics, the theory that the best way of ensuring international order is to have power so distributed among states that no single state is able to achieve a dominant position. The term, which may also refer more simply to the actual distribution of power, is one of the most enduring concepts in international relations.

Balanchine George 1904–1983. Russian-born US choreographer. After leaving the USSR 1924, he worked with ◊Diaghilev in France. Moving to the

USA 1933, he became the most influential 20th-century choreographer of ballet in the country, starting the New York City Ballet 1948. His ballets are usually plotless and are performed in practice clothes to modern music.

Baldwin James 1924–1987. US writer and civil- rights activist. He portrayed with vivid intensity the suffering and despair of black Americans in contemporary society. After his first novel, *Go Tell It On The Mountain* 1953, set in Harlem, and *Giovanni's Room* 1956, about a homosexual relationship in Paris, his writing became more politically indignant with *Another Country* 1962 and *The Fire Next Time* 1963, a collection of essays.

Baldwin Stanley, 1st Earl Baldwin of Bewdley 1867–1947. British Conservative politician, prime minister 1923–24, 1924–29, and 1935–37; he weathered the general strike 1926, secured complete adult suffrage 1928, and handled the abdication crisis of Edward VIII 1936, but failed to prepare Britain for World War II.

Balearic Islands (Spanish *Baleares*) group of Mediterranean islands forming an autonomous region of Spain, including Majorca, Minorca, Ibiza, Cabrera, and Formentera; *area* 5,000 sq km/ 1,930 sq mi; *capital* Palma de Mallorca; *population* (1986) 755,000.

Balfour Declaration letter, dated 2 Nov 1917, from the British foreign secretary A J Balfour to Lord Rothschild (chair, British Zionist Federation) stating: 'HM government view with favour the establishment in Palestine of a national home for the Jewish people.' It helped form the basis for the foundation of Israel 1948.

Bali island of Indonesia, E of Java, one of the Sunda Islands; *area* 5,800 sq km/ 2,240 sq mi; *capital* Denpasar; *features* Balinese dancing, music, drama; around one million tourists a year; *population* (1989) 2,787,000.

Balkans peninsula of SE Europe, stretching into the Mediterranean Sea between the Adriatic and Aegean seas, comprising Albania, Bosnia-Herzegovina, Bulgaria, Croatia, Greece, Romania, Slovenia, the part of Turkey in Europe, and Yugoslavia. It is joined to the rest of Europe by an isthmus 1,200 km/750 mi wide between Rijeka on the W and the mouth of the Danube on the Black Sea to the E.

Balkan Wars two wars 1912–13 and 1913 (preceding World War I) which resulted in the expulsion by the Balkan states of Ottoman Turkey from Europe, except for a small area around Istanbul.

Balladur Edouard 1929– . French Conservative politician, prime minister from 1993. During his first year of 'cohabitation' with socialist president, François Mitterrand, he demonstrated his strong support of the European Union and of close relations between France and Germany.

ballet theatrical representation in dance form in which music also plays a major part in telling a story or conveying a mood. From Italy, ballet was brought by Catherine de' Medici to France in the form of a spectacle combining singing, dancing, and declamation. In the 20th century Russian ballet has had a vital influence on the classical tradition in the West, and ballet developed further in the USA through the work of George Balanchine and the American Ballet Theater, and in the UK through the influence of Marie Rambert.

ballistics study of the motion and impact of projectiles such as bullets, bombs, and missiles. For projectiles from a gun, relevant exterior factors include temperature, barometric pressure, and wind strength; and for nuclear missiles these extend to such factors as the speed at which the Earth turns.

balloon lighter-than-air craft that consists of a gasbag filled with gas lighter than the surrounding air and an attached basket, or gondola, for carrying passengers and/or instruments. In 1783, the first successful human ascent was in Paris, in a hot-air balloon designed by the Montgolfier brothers Joseph Michel and Jacques Etienne. In 1785, a hydrogen-filled balloon designed by French physicist Jacques Charles travelled across the English Channel.

ballot the process of voting in an election. In political elections in democracies ballots are usually secret: voters indicate their choice of candidate on a voting slip that is placed in a sealed ballot box. *Ballot rigging* is a term used to describe elections that are fraudulent because of interference with the voting process or the counting of votes.

Baltic Sea large shallow arm of the North Sea, extending NE from the narrow Skagerrak and Kattegat, between Sweden and Denmark, to the Gulf of Bothnia between Sweden and Finland. Its coastline is 8,000 km/5,000 mi long, and its area, including the gulfs of Riga, Finland, and Bothnia, is 422,300 sq km/163,000 sq mi. Its shoreline is shared by Denmark, Germany, Poland, the Baltic States, Russia, Finland, and Sweden.

Baltic States collective name for the states of ◊Estonia, ◊Latvia, and ◊Lithuania, former constituent republics of the USSR (from 1940). They regained independence Sept 1991.

Baltimore industrial port and largest city in Maryland, USA, on the western shore of Chesapeake Bay, NE of Washington DC; population (1990) 736,000.

Balzac Honoré de 1799–1850. French writer. One of the major novelists of the 19th century. His first success was *Les Chouans/The Chouans*, inspired by Walter Scott, which began the long series of novels *La Comédie humaine/The Human Comedy*, including *Eugénie Grandet* 1833, *Le Père Goriot* 1834, and *Cousine Bette* 1846. He also wrote the Rabelaisian *Contes drolatiques/Ribald Tales* 1833.

Bamako capital and port of Mali on the river Niger; population (1976) 400,000.

bamboo any of numerous plants of the subgroup Bambuseae within the grass family Gramineae, mainly found in tropical and subtropical regions. Some species grow as tall as 36 m/120 ft.

banana any of several treelike tropical plants of the genus *Musa*, family Musaceae, which grow up to 8 m/25 ft high. The edible banana is the fruit of a sterile hybrid form.

Banda Hastings Kamuzu 1902– . Malawi politician, president 1966–94. He led his country's independence movement and was prime minister of Nyasaland (now Malawi) from 1963. He became Malawi's first president 1966 and was named president for life 1971; his rule was authoritarian.

Bandar Seri Begawan formerly (until 1970) *Brunei Town* capital and largest town of Brunei, 14 km/9 mi from the mouth of the Brunei River; population (1987 est) 56,300.

Bangkok capital and port of Thailand, on the river Chao Phraya; population (1990) 6,019,000. It is the headquarters of the Southeast Asia Treaty Organization.

Bangladesh People's Republic of (Gana Prajatantri Bangladesh) (formerly *East Pakistan*); *area* 144,000 sq km/55,585 sq mi; *capital* Dhaka (formerly Dacca); *environment* deforestation on the slopes of the Himalayas increases the threat of flooding in the coastal lowlands of Bangladesh, which are also subject to devastating monsoon storms. Increased salinity has destroyed fisheries, contaminated drinking water, and damaged forests; *political system* emergent democratic republic; *population* (1993) 118,700,000; growth rate 2.17% p.a.; just over 1 million people live in small ethnic groups in the tropical Chittagong Hill Tracts, Mymensingh, and Sylhet districts; *language* Bangla (Bengali); *religions* Sunni Muslim 85%, Hindu 14%.

Bangui capital and port of the Central African Republic, on the river Ubangi; population (1988) 597,000.

Banjul capital and chief port of Gambia, on an island at the mouth of the river Gambia; population (1983) 44,536. Established 1816 as a settlement for freed slaves, it was known as Bathurst until 1973.

Bannister Roger Gilbert 1929- . English track and field athlete, the first person to run a mile in under four minutes. He achieved this feat at Oxford, England, on 6 May 1954, in a time of 3 min 59.4 sec.

Bannockburn, Battle of battle on 24 June 1314 in which ◊Robert (I) the Bruce of Scotland defeated the English under Edward II, who had come to relieve the besieged Stirling Castle. Named after the town of Bannockburn, S of Stirling, central Scotland.

Banting Frederick Grant 1891–1941. Canadian physician who discovered a technique for isolating the hormone insulin 1921 when, experimentally, he and his colleague Charles Best tied off the ducts of the ◊pancreas to determine the function of its cells. This led to the treatment of diabetes. Banting and John J R Macleod (1876–1935), his mentor, shared the 1923 Nobel Prize for Medicine, and Banting divided his prize with Best.

Bantu group of related languages belonging to the Niger-Congo family, spoken widely over the greater part of Africa south of the Sahara, including Swahili, Xhosa, and Zulu. Meaning 'people' in Zulu, the word Bantu itself illustrates a characteristic use of prefixes: *mu-ntu* 'man', *ba-ntu* 'people'.

banyan tropical Asian fig tree *Ficus benghalensis*, family Moraceae. It produces aerial roots that grow down from its spreading branches, forming supporting pillars that have the appearance of separate trunks.

baptism immersion in or sprinkling with water as a religious rite of initiation. It was practised long before the beginning of Christianity. In the Christian baptism ceremony, sponsors or godparents make vows on behalf of the child, which are renewed by the child at confirmation. It is one of the seven sacraments. The *amrit* ceremony in Sikhism is sometimes referred to as baptism.

Baptist member of any of several Protestant and evangelical Christian sects that practise baptism by immersion only upon profession of faith. Baptists seek their authority in the Bible. They originated among English Dissenters who took refuge in the Netherlands in the early 17th century, and spread by emigration and missionary activity.

Barbados; *area* 430 sq km/166 sq mi; *capital* Bridgetown; *features* highest point Mount Hillaby 340 m/1,115 ft; *political system* constitutional monarchy; *population* (1993 est) 265,000; growth rate 0.5% p.a.; *languages* English and Bajan (Barbadian English dialect); *religions* 70% Anglican, 9% Methodist, 4% Roman Catholic.

barbiturate hypnosedative drug, commonly known as a 'sleeping pill', consisting of any salt or ester of barbituric acid $C_4H_4O_3N_2$. It works by depressing brain activity. Most barbiturates, being highly addictive, are no longer prescribed and are listed as controlled substances.

Barcelona capital, industrial city, and port of Catalonia, NE Spain; population (1991) 1,653,200. It was prominent in the overthrow of the monarchy 1931 and was the last city of the republic to surrender to Franco 1939. In 1992 the city hosted the Olympic Games.

Bardot Brigitte 1934– . French film actress. A celebrated sex symbol of the 1960s, she did much to popularize French cinema internationally. Her films include *Et Dieu créa la femme/And God Created Woman* 1950, *Viva Maria* 1965, and *Shalako* 1968.

Barebones Parliament English assembly called by Oliver ▷Cromwell to replace the 'Rump Parliament' July 1653. Consisting of 140 members nominated by the army, it derived its name from 'Praise-God' Barbon, one of the members. Its attempts to abolish tithes, patronage, and the court of chancery, and to codify the law, led to the resignation of the moderates and its dissolution Dec 1653.

barium soft, silver-white, metallic element, symbol Ba, atomic number 56, relative atomic mass 137.33. It is one of the alkaline-earth metals, found in nature as barium carbonate and barium sulphate.

bark protective outer layer on the stems and roots of woody plants, composed mainly of dead cells. To allow for expansion of the stem, the bark is continually added to from within, and the outer surface often becomes cracked or is shed as scales. Trees deposit a variety of chemicals in their bark, including poisons. Many of these chemical substances have economic value because they can be used in the manufacture of drugs. Quinine, derived from the bark of the *Cinchona* tree, is used to fight malarial infections; curare, an anaesthetic used in medicine, comes from the *Strychnus toxifera* tree in the Amazonian rainforest.

barley cereal belonging to the grass family (Gramineae). It resembles wheat but is more tolerant of cold and draughts. Cultivated barley *Hordeum vulgare* comprises three main varieties –six-rowed, four-rowed, and two-rowed.

bar mitzvah in Judaism, initiation of a boy, which takes place at the age of 13, into the adult Jewish community; less common is the *bat mitzvah* or *bat* for girls aged 12. The child reads a passage from the Torah in the synagogue on the Sabbath and is subsequently regarded as a full member of the congregation.

barnacle marine crustacean of the subclass Cirripedia. The larval form is free-swimming, but when mature, it fixes itself by the head to rock or floating wood. The animal then remains attached, enclosed in a shell through which the cirri (modified legs) protrude to sweep food into the mouth.

Barnardo Thomas John 1845–1905. British philanthropist, who was known as Dr Barnardo, although not medically qualified. He opened the first of a series of homes for destitute children 1867 in Stepney, E London.

barometer instrument that measures atmospheric pressure as an indication of weather. Most often used are the *mercury barometer* and the *aneroid barometer*.

Baroque in the visual arts, architecture, and music, a style flourishing in Europe 1600–1750, broadly characterized as expressive, flamboyant, and dynamic. Playing a central role in the crusading work of the Catholic Counter-Reformation, the Baroque used elaborate effects to appeal directly to the emotions. Many masterpieces of the Baroque emerged in churches and palaces in Rome, but the style soon spread throughout Europe, changing in character as it did so.

Barrett Browning Elizabeth 1806–1861. English poet. In 1844 she published *Poems* (including 'The Cry of the Children'), which led to her friendship with and secret marriage to Robert Browning 1846. The *Sonnets from the Portuguese* published 1847 were written during their courtship. Later works include *Casa Guidi Windows* 1851 and the poetic novel *Aurora Leigh* 1857.

Barrie J(ames) M(atthew) 1860–1937. Scottish dramatist and novelist. His work includes *The Admirable Crichton* 1902 and the children's fantasy *Peter Pan* 1904.

barrow burial mound, usually composed of earth but sometimes of stones, examples of which are found in many parts of the world. The two main types are *long*, dating from the New Stone Age, or Neolithic, and *round*, dating from the later Mesolithic peoples of the early Bronze Age.

Barry Charles 1795–1860. English architect. He designed the Neo-Gothic Houses of Parliament at Westminster, London, 1840–60, in collaboration with Augustus ◊Pugin.

Bartók Béla 1881–1945. Hungarian composer. His works combine folk elements with mathematical concepts of tonal and rhythmic proportion. His large output includes six string quartets, a *Divertimento* for string orchestra 1939, concertos for piano, violin, and viola, the *Concerto for Orchestra* 1942–45, and a one-act opera *Duke Bluebeard's Castle* 1918.

baryon in nuclear physics, a heavy subatomic particle made up of three indivisible elementary particles called quarks. The baryons form a subclass of the ◊hadrons and comprise the nucleons (protons and neutrons) and hyperons.

Baryshnikov Mikhail 1948– . Latvian-born dancer, now based in the USA. He joined the Kirov Ballet 1967 and, after defecting from the Soviet Union 1974, joined the American Ballet Theater (ABT) as principal dancer, partnering Gelsey Kirkland. He left to join the New York City Ballet 1978–80, but rejoined ABT as director 1980–90.

basal metabolic rate (BMR) minimum amount of energy needed by the body to maintain life. It is measured when the subject is awake but resting, and includes the energy required to keep the heart beating, sustain breathing, repair tissues, and keep the brain and nerves functioning. Measuring the subject's consumption of oxygen gives an accurate value for BMR, because oxygen is needed to release energy from food.

basalt commonest volcanic ◊igneous rock, and the principal rock type on the ocean floor; it is basic, that is, it contains relatively little silica: about 50%. It is usually dark grey but can also be green, brown, or black.

base in mathematics, the number of different single-digit symbols used in a particular number system. In our usual (decimal) counting system of numbers (with symbols 0, 1, 2, 3, 4, 5, 6, 7, 8, 9) the base is 10. In the ◊binary number system, which has only the symbols 1 and 0, the base is two.

base in chemistry, a substance that accepts protons, such as the hydroxide ion (OH⁻) and ammonia (NH₃). Bases react with acids to give a salt. Those that dissolve in water are called ◊alkalis.

baseball national summer game of the USA, derived in the 19th century from the English game of rounders. Baseball is a bat-and-ball game played between two teams, each of nine players, on a pitch ('field') marked out in the form of a diamond, with a base at each corner. The ball is struck with a cylindrical bat, and the players try to score ('make a run') by circuiting the bases. A 'home run' is a circuit on one hit.

Basel or *Basle* (French *Bâle*) financial, commercial, and industrial city in Switzerland; population (1990) 171,000. In 1501 it joined the Swiss confederation and later developed as a centre for the Reformation.

base pair in biochemistry, the linkage of two base (purine or pyrimidine) molecules in ◊DNA. They are found in nucleotides, and form the basis of the genetic code.

Bashkir autonomous republic of Russia, with the Ural Mountains on the east; *area* 143,600 sq km/55,430 sq mi; *capital* Ufa; *population* (1982) 3,876,000; *languages* Russian, Bashkir (about 25%).

Basie Count (William) 1904–1984. US jazz band leader and pianist. He developed the big-band sound and a simplified, swinging style of music. He led impressive groups of musicians in a career spanning more than 50 years. Basie's compositions include 'One O'Clock Jump' and 'Jumpin' at the Woodside'.

basilica Roman public building; a large roofed hall flanked by columns, generally with an aisle on each side, used for judicial or other public business. The earliest known basilica, at Pompeii, dates from the 2nd century BC. This architectural form was adopted by the early Christians for their churches.

basketball ball game between two teams of five players on an indoor enclosed court. The object is, via a series of passing moves, to throw the large inflated ball through a circular hoop and net positioned at each end of the court, 3.05 m/10 ft above the ground. The first world championship for men was held in 1950, and in 1953 for women. They are now held every four years.

Basque member of a people inhabiting the ▷Basque Country of central N Spain and the extreme SW of France. The Basques are a pre-Indo-European people who largely maintained their independence until the 19th century. During the Spanish Civil War 1936–39, they were on the republican side defeated by Franco. Their language (*Euskara*) is unrelated to any other language. From 1968 Basque separatist movements have engaged in guerrilla activity in their campaign to secure a united Basque state.

Basque Country (Basque *Euskal Herria*) homeland of the Basque people in the W Pyrenees, divided by the Franco-Spanish border. The Spanish Basque Country (Spanish *País Vasco*) is an autonomous region (created 1979) of central N Spain, comprising the provinces of Vizcaya, Alava, and Guipúzcoa (Basque *Bizkaia*, *Araba*, and *Gipuzkoa*); area 7,300 sq km/2,818 sq mi; population (1988) 2,176,790. The French Basque Country (French *Pays Basque*) comprises the *département* of Pyrénées-Atlantiques, including the arrondissements of Labourd, Basse-Navarre, and Soule (Basque *Lapurdi*, *Nafarroa Beherea*, and *Zuberoa*); area 7,633 sq km/4770 sq mi; population (1981) 555,700. To Basque nationalists *Euskal Herria* also includes the autonomous Spanish province of Navarre.

Basra (Arabic *al-Basrah*) principal port in Iraq, in the Shatt-al-Arab delta, 97 km/60 mi from the Persian Gulf, founded in the 7th century; population (1977) 1.5 million (1991) 850,000. Aerial bombing during the 1991 Gulf War destroyed bridges, factories, power stations, water-treatment plants, sewage-treatment plants, and the port. A Shi'ite rebellion March 1991 was crushed by the Iraqi army, causing further death and destruction.

bass long-bodied scaly sea fish *Morone labrax* found in the N Atlantic and Mediterranean. They grow to 1 m/3 ft, and are often seen in shoals.

Basse-Normandie or *Lower Normandy* coastal region of NW France lying between Haute-Normandie and Brittany (Bretagne). It includes the *départements* of Calvados, Manche, and Orne; area 17,600 sq km/6,794 sq mi; population (1986) 1,373,000. Its capital is Caen.

Basseterre capital and port of St Christopher–Nevis, in the Leeward Islands; population (1980) 14,000.

bassoon double-reed woodwind instrument in B flat, the bass of the oboe family. It doubles back on itself in a tube about 2.5 m/7.5 ft long and has a rich and deep tone. The bassoon concert repertoire extends from the early Baroque via Vivaldi, Mozart, and Dukas to Stockhausen.

Bastille castle of St Antoine, built about 1370 as part of the fortifications of Paris. It was made a state prison by Cardinal ▷Richelieu and was stormed by the mob that set the French Revolution in motion 14 July 1789. Only seven prisoners were found in the castle when it was stormed; the governor and most of the garrison were killed, and the Bastille was razed.

bat flying mammal in which the forelimbs are developed as wings capable of rapid and sustained flight. There are two main groups of bats: *megabats*, or *flying foxes*, which eat fruit, and *microbats*, which mainly eat insects. Although by no means blind, many microbats rely largely on echolocation for navigation and finding prey, sending out pulses of high-pitched sound and listening for the echo. Bats are nocturnal, and those native to temperate countries hibernate in winter.

Bath historic city in Avon, England; population (1991) 78,700. *features* hot springs; the ruins of the baths after which it is named, as well as a great temple, are the finest Roman remains in Britain. There is much 18th- century architecture, notably the Royal Crescent by John Wood.

battery any energy-storage device allowing release of electricity on demand. It is made up of one or more electrical ▷cells. Primary-cell batteries are disposable; secondary-cell batteries, or accumulators, are rechargeable. Primary-cell batteries are an extremely uneconomical form of energy, since they produce only 2% of the power used in their manufacture.

Baudelaire Charles Pierre 1821–1867. French poet. He combined rhythmical and musical perfection with a morbid romanticism and eroticism, finding beauty in decadence and evil. His first and best-known book of verse was *Les Fleurs du mal/Flowers of Evil* 1857. He also published studies of Balzac and Flaubert. He was one of the major figures in the development of ▷Symbolism.

Baudouin 1930–1993. King of the Belgians 1951–93, succeeding his father, Leopold III. During his reign he held together a country divided by religion and language, while presiding over the dismemberment of Belgium's imperial past. In 1960 he married Fabiola de Mora y Aragón (1928–), member of a

Spanish noble family. He was succeeded by his brother, Alberto, 1993.

Bauhaus German school of architecture and design founded 1919 at Weimar in Germany by the architect Walter ▷Gropius in an attempt to fuse art, design, architecture, and crafts into a unified whole. Moved to Dessau under political pressure 1925 (where it was housed in a building designed by Gropius), the school was closed by the Nazis 1933. Among the artists associated with the Bauhaus were the painters Klee and Kandinsky and the architect Mies van der Rohe.

bauxite principal ore of ▷aluminium, consisting of a mixture of hydrated aluminium oxides and hydroxides, generally contaminated with compounds of iron, which give it a red colour. It is formed by the chemical weathering of rocks in tropical climates.

Bavaria (German *Bayern*) administrative region (German *Land*) of Germany; *area* 70,600 sq km/27,252 sq mi; *capital* Munich; *features* largest of the German *Länder*; forms the Danube basin; festivals at Bayreuth and Oberammergau; *population* (1988) 11,000,000; *religion* 70% Roman Catholic, 26% Protestant.

Bay of Pigs inlet on the S coast of Cuba about 145 km/90 mi SW of Havana. It was the site of an unsuccessful invasion attempt by 1,500 US-sponsored Cuban exiles 17–20 April 1961; 1,173 were taken prisoner.

bean any seed of numerous leguminous plants. Beans are rich in nitrogenous or protein matter and are grown both for human consumption and as food for cattle and horses.

bear large mammal with a heavily built body, short powerful limbs, and a very short tail. Bears breed once a year, producing one to four cubs. In northern regions they hibernate, and the young are born in the winter den. They are found mainly in North America and N Asia. The skin of the polar bear is black to conserve 80–90% of the solar energy trapped and channelled down the hollow hairs of its fur.

Beardsley Aubrey (Vincent) 1872–1898. English illustrator and leading member of the ▷Aesthetic Movement. His meticulously executed black-and-white drawings show the influence of Japanese prints and French Rococo, and also display elements of ▷Art Nouveau. His work was often charged with being grotesque and decadent.

Beat Generation or *Beat movement* US social and literary movement of the 1950s and early 1960s that sought personal liberation largely through Eastern mysticism, drugs, and music (particularly jazz); members of the movement were called 'beatniks'. Writers associated with the movement, were Jack ▷Kerouac (credited with coining the term), Allen Ginsberg, and William ▷Burroughs.

Beatles, the English pop group 1960–70. The members, all born in Liverpool, were John Lennon (1940–80, rhythm guitar, vocals), Paul McCartney (1942– , bass, vocals), George Harrison (1943– , lead guitar, vocals), and Ringo Starr (formerly Richard Starkey, 1940– , drums). Using songs written largely by Lennon and McCartney, the Beatles dominated rock music and pop culture in the 1960s.

Beaton Cecil 1904–1980. English photographer. His elegant and sophisticated fashion pictures and society portraits often employed exotic props and settings. He adopted a more simple style for his wartime photographs of bomb-damaged London. He also worked as a stage and film designer, notably for the musicals *Gigi* 1959 and *My Fair Lady* 1965.

Beatrix 1938– . Queen of the Netherlands. The eldest daughter of Queen Juliana, she succeeded to the throne on her mother's abdication 1980. In 1966 she married West German diplomat Claus von Amsberg (1926–), who was created Prince of the Netherlands. Her heir is Prince Willem Alexander (1967–).

Beaufort scale system of recording wind velocity, devised by Francis Beaufort 1806. It is a numerical scale ranging from 0 to 17, calm being indicated by 0 and a hurricane by 12; 13–17 indicate degrees of hurricane force.

Beauvoir Simone de 1908–1986. French socialist, feminist, and writer who taught philosophy at the Sorbonne university in Paris 1931–43. Her book *Le Deuxième sexe/The Second Sex* 1949 became a seminal work for many feminists.

Becket St Thomas à 1118–1170. English priest and politician. He was chancellor to Henry II 1155–62, when he was appointed archbishop of Canterbury. The interests of the church soon conflicted with those of the crown and Becket was assassinated; he was canonized 1172.

Beckett Samuel 1906–1989. Irish novelist and dramatist. He wrote in both French and English. His play *En attendant Godot*, in which life is taken to be meaningless, was first performed in Paris 1952 and, as *Waiting for Godot*, in London 1955 and New York 1956. The genre, tinged with a grave humour, is taken to further extremes in *Fin de Partie/Endgame* 1957 and *Happy Days* 1961. Nobel Prize for Literature 1969.

becquerel SI unit (symbol Bq) of ⊳radioactivity, equal to one radioactive disintegration (change in the nucleus of an atom when a particle or ray is given off) per second. It is named after French physicist Henri Becquerel (1852–1908)

Bede *c.* 673–735. English theologian and historian, known as *the Venerable Bede*, active in Durham and Northumbria. He wrote many scientific, theological, and historical works. His *Historia Ecclesiastica Gentis Anglorum/Ecclesiastical History of the English People* 731 is a seminal source for early English history.

Bedfordshire county of S central England; *area* 1,240 sq km/479 sq mi; *towns and cities* Bedford (administrative headquarters), Luton, Dunstable; *features* low lying with Chiltern Hills in the SW; Whipsnade Zoo 1931, near Dunstable; Woburn Abbey, seat of the duke of Bedford; *population* (1991) 514,200.

Bedouin Arab of any of the nomadic peoples occupying the desert regions of Arabia and N Africa, now becoming increasingly settled. Their traditional trade was the rearing of horses and camels.

bee four-winged insect of the superfamily Apoidea in the order Hymenoptera, usually with a sting. There are over 12,000 species, of which fewer than 1 in 20 are social in habit. The *hive bee* or *honey bee* *Apis mellifera* establishes perennial colonies of about ·80,000, the majority being infertile females (workers), with a few larger fertile males

(drones), and a single very large fertile female (the queen). Worker bees live for no more than a few weeks, while a drone may live a few months, and a queen several years.

beech any tree of the genera *Fagus* and *Nothofagus*, family Fagaceae. The common beech *F. sylvaticus*, found in European forests, has a smooth grey trunk and edible nuts, or 'mast', which are used as animal feed or processed for oil. The timber is used in furniture.

Beecham Thomas 1879–1961. English conductor and impresario. He established the Royal Philharmonic Orchestra 1946 and fostered the works of composers such as Delius, Sibelius, and Richard Strauss.

Beethoven Ludwig van 1770–1827. German composer and pianist. His mastery of musical expression in every genre made him the dominant influence on 19th-century music. Beethoven's repertoire includes concert overtures; the opera *Fidelio* 1805, revised 1814; five piano concertos and two for violin (one unfinished); 32 piano sonatas, including the *Moonlight* 1801 and *Appassionata* 1804–05; 17 string quartets; the Mass in D (*Missa solemnis*) 1824; and nine symphonies, as well as many youthful works. He was hampered by deafness 1801, but continued to compose.

beetle common name of insects in the order Coleoptera (Greek 'sheath-winged') with leathery forewings folding down in a protective sheath over the membranous hindwings, which are those used for flight. They pass through a complete metamorphosis. Comprising more than 50% of the animal kingdom, beetles number some 370,000 named species, with many not yet described.

Begin Menachem 1913–1992. Israeli politician. He was leader of the extremist Irgun Zvai Leumi organization in Palestine from 1942 and prime minister of Israel 1977–83, as head of the right-wing Likud party. In 1978 Begin shared a Nobel Peace Prize with President Sadat of Egypt for work on the Camp David Agreements for a Middle East peace settlement.

Behan Brendan 1923–1964. Irish dramatist. His early experience of prison and knowledge of the workings of the ◊IRA (recounted in his autobiography *Borstal Boy* 1958) provided him with two recurrent themes in his plays. *The Quare Fellow* 1954 was followed by the tragicomedy *The Hostage* 1958, first written in Gaelic.

behaviour therapy in psychology, the application of behavioural principles, derived from learning theories, to the treatment of clinical conditions such as phobias, obsessions, and emotional problems which are regarded as patterns of behaviour that therapy can enable the patient to unlearn. For example, in treating a phobia the person is taken into the feared situation in gradual steps, a process called *systematic desensitization*.

Behn Aphra 1640–1689. English novelist and playwright, the first woman in England to earn her living as a writer. Her writings were criticized for their explicitness; they frequently present events from a woman's point of view. Her novel *Oroonoko* 1688 is an attack on slavery.

Beiderbecke Bix (Leon Bismarck) 1903–1931. US jazz cornetist, composer, and pianist. A romantic soloist with the bands of King Oliver, Louis Armstrong, and Paul Whiteman, Beiderbecke was the first acknowledged white jazz innovator. He was influenced by the classical composers Debussy, Ravel, and Stravinsky.

Beijing or *Peking* capital of China; part of its northeast border is formed by the Great Wall of China; population (1989) 6,800,000. The municipality of Beijing has an area of 17,800 sq km/6,871 sq mi and a population (1990) of 10,819,000.

Beirut or *Beyrouth* capital and port of ◊Lebanon, devastated by civil war in the 1970s and 1980s, when it was occupied by armies of neighbouring countries; population (1993) 1.2 million.

Belarus Republic of; *area* 207,600 sq km/80,100 sq mi; *capital* Minsk (Mensk); *environment* large areas contaminated by fallout from Chernobyl; *features* Belovezhskaya Pushcha (scenic forest reserve); *political system* emergent democracy; *population* (1993 est) 10,400,000 (77% Byelorussian 'Eastern Slavs', 13% Russian, 4% Polish, 1% Jewish); *languages* Byelorussian, Russian; *religions* Roman Catholic, Russian Orthodox, with Baptist and Muslim minorities.

Belau, Republic of formerly *Palau* country in Micronesia (independence achieved 1994); *area* 500 sq km/193 sq mi; *capital* Koror; *features* 26 larger islands (eight inhabited) and about 300 islets; *population* (1990) 15,100.

Belfast city and industrial port in County Antrim and County Down, Northern Ireland, at the mouth of the river Lagan on Belfast Lough; the capital of Northern Ireland since 1920; population (1985) 300,000 (Protestants form the majority in E Belfast, Catholics in the W). It is the county town of County

Antrim. From 1968–94 the city was heavily damaged by civil disturbances.

Belgium Kingdom of (French *Royaume de Belgique*, Flemish *Koninkrijk België*); *area* 30,510 sq km/11,784 sq mi; *capital* Brussels; *environment* a 1989 government report judged the drinking water in Flanders to be 'seriously substandard' and more than half the rivers and canals in that region to be seriously polluted; *features* Ardennes Forest; rivers Scheldt and Meuse; *head of state* King Albert from 1993; *head of government* Jean-Luc Dehaene from 1992; *political system* federal constitutional monarchy; *population* (1993 est) 10,050,000 (comprising Flemings and Walloons); growth rate 0.1% p.a.; *languages* in the N (Flanders) Flemish (a Dutch dialect, known as *Vlaams*) 55%; in the S (Wallonia) Walloon (a French dialect) 32%; bilingual 11%; German (E border) 0.6%; all are official; *religion* Roman Catholic 75%.

Belgrade (Serbo-Croatian *Beograd*) capital of Yugoslavia and Serbia, and Danube river port linked with the port of Bar on the Adriatic Sea; population (1991) 1,087,900.

Belize (formerly *British Honduras*); *area* 22,963 sq km/8,864 sq mi; *capital* Belmopan; *environment* an extensive system of national parks and reserves protects large areas of tropical forest, coastal mangrove, and offshore islands. Forestry has been replaced by agriculture and ecotourism, which are now the most important sectors of the economy; *features* world's second longest barrier reef; Maya ruins; *political system* constitutional monarchy; *population* (1993) 230,000 (including Mayan minority in the interior); growth rate 2.5% p.a.; *languages* English (official); Spanish (widely spoken), native Creole dialects; *religions* Roman Catholic 60%, Protestant 35%.

Bell Alexander Graham 1847–1922. Scottish-born US scientist and inventor of the telephone. He patented his invention 1876, and later experimented with a type of phonograph and, in aeronautics, invented the tricycle undercarriage.

Bellini family of Italian Renaissance painters. Jacopo and his sons Gentile and Giovanni were founders of the Venetian School in the 15th and early 16th centuries.

Bellini Vincenzo 1801–1835. Italian composer of operas. He collaborated with the tenor Giovanni Battista Rubini (1794–1854) to develop a new simplicity of melodic expression in romantic evocations of classic themes, as in *La Sonnambula/The Sleepwalker* and *Norma*, both 1831.

Bellow Saul 1915– . Canadian-born US novelist. His first novel, *Dangling Man* 1944, displayed elements of ▷existentialism. In *The Adventures of Augie March* 1953 and *Henderson the Rain King* 1959, he created confident and comic picaresque heroes, before *Herzog* 1964, which pitches a comic but distressed scholar into a world of darkening humanism. Later works include *Mr Sammler's Planet* 1970, *Humboldt's Gift* 1975, and *More Die of Heartbreak* 1987. Nobel Prize for Literature 1976.

Belmopan capital of ▷Belize from 1970; population (1991) 4,000. It replaced Belize City as the administrative centre of the country.

Benedict, St *c.* 480–*c.* 547. Founder of Christian monasticism in the West and of the Benedictine order. He founded the monastery of Monte Cassino, Italy. Here he wrote out his rule for monastic life and was visited shortly before his death by the Ostrogothic king Totila, whom he converted to the Christian faith. His feast day is 11 July.

Bengal, Bay of part of the Indian Ocean lying between the east coast of India and the west coast of Myanmar (Burma) and the Malay Peninsula. The Irrawaddy, Ganges, and Brahmaputra rivers flow into the bay. The principal islands are to be found in the Andaman and Nicobar groups.

Bengali person of Bengali culture from Bangladesh and India (W Bengal, Tripura). There are 80–150 million speakers of *Bengali*, an Indo-Iranian language belonging to the Indo-European family. It is the official language of Bangladesh and of the Indian state of West Bengal. Bengalis in Bangladesh are predominantly Muslim, whereas those in India are mainly Hindu.

Ben-Gurion David. Adopted name of David Gruen 1886–1973. Israeli statesman and socialist politician, one of the founders of the state of Israel, the country's first prime minister 1948–53, and again 1955–63.

Benin People's Republic of (*République Populaire du Bénin*); *area* 112,622 sq km/43,472 sq mi; *capital* Porto Novo (official), Cotonou (de facto); *features* coastal lagoons with fishing villages on stilts; Niger River in NE; *political system* socialist pluralist republic; *population* (1993) 5,010,000; growth rate 3% p.a.; *languages* French (official); Fon 47% and Yoruba 9% in south; six major tribal languages in north; *religions* animist 65%, Christian 17%, Muslim 13%.

Ben Nevis highest mountain in the British Isles (1,343 m/4,406 ft), in the Grampian Mountains, Scotland.

Bentham Jeremy 1748–1832. English philosopher, legal and social reformer, and founder of ◊utilitarianism. The essence of his moral philosophy as in his Principles of Morals and Legislation (published 1789) is that the object of all legislation should be 'the greatest happiness for the greatest number'.

Benz Karl Friedrich 1844–1929. German automobile engineer who produced the world's first petrol- driven motor vehicle. He built his first model engine 1878 and the petrol- driven car 1885.

benzene C_6H_6 clear liquid hydrocarbon of characteristic odour, occurring in coal tar. It is used as a solvent and in the synthesis of many chemicals.

benzodiazepine any of a group of mood-altering drugs (tranquillizers), for example Librium and Valium. They are addictive and interfere with the process by which information is transmitted between brain cells, and various side effects arise from continued use. They were originally developed as muscle relaxants, and then excessively prescribed in the West as anxiety-relieving drugs.

Beowulf Anglo-Saxon poem (composed *c.* 700), the only complete surviving example of Germanic folk epic. It exists in a single manuscript copied in England about 1000 in the Cottonian collection of the British Museum.

Berber member of a non-Semitic Caucasoid people of North Africa who since prehistoric times inhabited the Mediterranean coastlands from Egypt to the Atlantic. Their language, present-day Berber (a member of the Afro-Asiatic language family), is spoken by about one-third of Algerians and nearly two-thirds of Moroccans.

Berg Alban 1885–1935. Austrian composer. He studied under Arnold Schoenberg and developed a personal twelve-tone idiom of great emotional and stylistic versatility. His relatively small output includes two operas: *Wozzeck* 1920, a grim story of working-class life, and the unfinished *Lulu* 1929–35; and chamber music incorporating coded references to friends and family.

Bergman Ingmar 1918– . Swedish stage producer and film director. His work typically deals with complex moral, psychological, and metaphysical problems, often strongly tinged with pessimism. His films include *Wild Strawberries* 1957, *The Seventh Seal* 1957, *Persona* 1966, *Autumn Sonata* 1978 and *Fanny and Alexander* 1982.

Bergman Ingrid 1917–1982. Swedish-born actress. She went to Hollywood to appear in David Selznick's *Intermezzo* 1939 and later appeared in *Casablanca* 1942, *For Whom the Bell Tolls* 1943, and *Gaslight* 1944 (Academy Award). She projected a combination of radiance, refined beauty, and fortitude.

Berkshire or *Royal Berkshire* county of S central England; *area* 1,260 sq km/486 sq mi; *towns and cities* Reading (administrative headquarters), Eton, Slough, Maidenhead, Ascot, Bracknell, Newbury, Windsor, Wokingham; *features* Inkpen Beacon, 297 m/975 ft; Bagshot Heath; Ridgeway Path; Windsor Castle; Eton College; Royal Military Academy at Sandhurst; atomic-weapons research establishment at Aldermaston; *population* (1991) 734,200.

Berlin industrial city and capital of the Federal Republic of Germany; population (1990) 3,102,500. After the division of Germany 1949, Bonn became the provisional capital of West Germany. The *Berlin Wall* divided the city from 1961 until it was dismantled 1989. Following reunification East and West Berlin were once more reunited as the 16th *Land* (state) of the Federal Republic.

Berlin Irving. Adopted name of Israel Baline 1888–1989. Russian-born US songwriter. His songs include such hits as 'Alexander's Ragtime Band' 1911, 'Always' 1925, 'God Bless America' 1917 (published 1939), and 'White Christmas' 1942, and the musicals *Top Hat* 1935, *Annie Get Your Gun* 1946, and *Call Me Madam* 1950. He also provided songs for films like *Blue Skies* 1946 and *Easter Parade* 1948.

Berlioz (Louis) Hector 1803–1869. French Romantic composer. The founder of modern orchestration. He wrote symphonic works, such as *Symphonie fantastique* 1830–31 and *Roméo et Juliette* 1839; dramatic cantatas including *La Damnation de Faust* 1846 and *L'Enfance du Christ* 1854; sacred music; and three operas: *Benvenuto Cellini* 1838, *Les Troyens* 1856–58, and *Béatrice et Bénédict* 1862.

Bermuda British colony in the NW Atlantic Ocean; *area* 54 sq km/21 sq mi; *capital* and chief port Hamilton; *features* consists of about 150 small islands, of which 20 are inhabited, linked by bridges and causeways; Britain's oldest colony; *population* (1988) 58,100; *language* English; *religion* Christian.

Bern (French *Berne*) capital of Switzerland and of Bern canton, in W Switzerland on the Aare River; population

(1990) 134,600; canton 945,600. It joined the Swiss confederation 1353 and became the capital 1848.

Bernhardt Sarah. Stage name of Rosine Bernard 1845–1923. French actress. She dominated the stage in her day, frequently performing at the Comédie-Française in Paris. She excelled in tragic roles, including Cordelia in Shakespeare's *King Lear* and the male roles of Hamlet and of Napoleon's son in Edmond Rostand's *L'Aiglon*.

Bernini Gianlorenzo (Giovanni Lorenzo) 1598–1680. Italian sculptor, architect, and painter. He was a leading figure in the development of the Baroque style. His work in Rome includes the colonnaded piazza in front of St Peter's Basilica 1656. His sculpture includes *The Ecstasy of St Theresa* 1645–52 (Sta Maria della Vittoria, Rome).

Bernoulli's principle law stating that the speed of a fluid varies inversely with pressure, an increase in speed producing a decrease in pressure (such as a drop in hydraulic pressure as the fluid speeds up flowing through a constriction in a pipe) and vice versa. The principle also explains the pressure differences on each surface of an aerofoil, which gives lift to the wing of an aircraft. The principle was named after Swiss mathematician and physicist Daniel Bernoulli.

Bernstein Leonard 1918–1990. US composer, conductor, and pianist. His works established a vogue for realistic, contemporary themes, including symphonies such as *The Age of Anxiety* 1949, ballets such as *Fancy Free* 1944, and scores for musicals such as *West Side Story* 1957, and *Mass* 1971 in memory of President J F Kennedy.

Bertolucci Bernardo 1940– . Italian film director. His work combines political and historical perspectives with an elegant and lyrical visual appeal. His films include *Last Tango in Paris* 1972, *The Last Emperor* 1987 (Academy Award), and *The Sheltering Sky* 1990.

Berzelius Jöns Jakob 1779–1848. Swedish chemist who accurately determined more than 2,000 relative atomic and molecular masses. He devised (1813–14) the system of chemical symbols and formulae now in use and proposed oxygen as a reference standard for atomic masses. His discoveries include the elements cerium (1804), selenium (1817), and thorium (1828); he was the first to prepare silicon in its amorphous form and to isolate zirconium.

beta-blocker any of a class of drugs that block impulses that stimulate certain nerve endings (beta receptors) serving the heart muscle. This reduces the heart rate and the force of contraction, which in turn reduces the amount of oxygen (and therefore the blood supply) required by the heart. Beta-blockers may be useful in the treatment of angina, arrhythmia (abnormal heart rhythms), raised blood pressure, and following heart attacks.

beta decay the disintegration of the nucleus of an atom to produce a beta particle, or high-speed electron, and an electron-antineutrino. During beta decay, a neutron in the nucleus changes into a proton, thereby increasing the atomic number by one while the mass number stays the same. The mass lost in the change is converted into kinetic (movement) energy of the beta particle.

beta particle electron ejected with great velocity from a radioactive atom that is undergoing spontaneous disintegration. Beta particles do not exist in the nucleus but are created on disintegration, beta decay, when a neutron converts to a proton to emit an electron.

Bethlehem (Hebrew *Beit-Lahm*) town on the west bank of the river Jordan, S of Jerusalem; population (1980) 14,000. It was occupied by Israel 1967. In the Bible it is mentioned as the birthplace of King David and Jesus.

Betjeman John 1906–1984. English poet and essayist. He was the originator of a peculiarly English light verse, nostalgic, and delighting in Victorian and Edwardian architecture. His *Collected Poems* appeared 1968 and a verse autobiography, *Summoned by Bells*, 1960. He became poet laureate 1972.

Bevan Aneurin (Nye) 1897–1960. British Labour politician. A miner at 13, he became a member of Parliament for Ebbw Vale 1929. As minister of health 1945–51, he inaugurated the National Health Service (NHS); he was minister of labour Jan–April 1951, when he resigned (with Harold Wilson) on the introduction of NHS charges and led a Bevanite faction against the government. He became deputy leader of the Labour party 1959.

Bhagavad-Gītā religious and philosophical Sanskrit poem, dating from around 300 BC, forming an episode in the sixth book of the *Mahābhārata*, one of the two great Hindu epics. It is the supreme religious work of Hinduism.

Bhopal industrial city and capital of Madhya Pradesh, central India; population (1981) 672,000. Nearby Bhimbetka Caves, discovered 1973, have the world's largest collection of prehistoric paintings, about 10,000 years old. In 1984 some 2,600 people died from an escape of the poisonous gas methyl isocyanate from a factory owned by US company Union Carbide; another 300,000 suffer from long-term health problems.

Bhutan Kingdom of (*Druk-yul*); *area* 46,500 sq km/17,954 sq mi; *capital* Thimbu (Thimphu); *features* Gangkar Punsum (7,529 m/24,700 ft) is one of the world's highest unclimbed peaks; *political system* absolute monarchy; *population* (1993 est) 1,700,000; growth rate 2% p.a. (75% Ngalops and Sharchops, 25% Nepalese); *languages* Dzongkha (official, a Tibetan dialect), Sharchop, Bumthap, Nepali, and English; *religions* 75% Lamaistic Buddhist (state religion), 25% Hindu.

Bhutto Benazir 1953– . Pakistani politician, leader of the Pakistan People's Party (PPP) from 1984 (in exile until 1986), prime minister of Pakistan 1988–90 (when the opposition manoeuvred her from office and charged her with corruption) and again from 1993.

Bhutto Zulfikar Ali 1928–1979. Pakistani politician, president 1971–73; prime minister from 1973 until the 1977 military coup led by General ◊Zia ulHaq. In 1978 Bhutto was sentenced to death for conspiring to murder a political opponent and was hanged the following year. He was the father of Benazir Bhutto.

Bible the sacred book of the Jewish and Christian religions. The Hebrew Bible, recognized by both Jews and Christians, is called the ◊*Old Testament* by Christians. The ◊*New Testament* comprises books recognized by the Christian church from the 4th century as canonical. The Roman Catholic Bible also includes the ◊*Apocrypha.*

Big Bang in astronomy, the hypothetical 'explosive' event that marked the origin of the universe as we know it. At the time of the Big Bang, the entire universe was squeezed into a hot, superdense state. The Big Bang explosion threw this compacted material outwards, producing the expanding universe (see ◊red shift). The cause of the Big Bang is unknown; observations of the current rate of expansion of the universe suggest that it took place about 10–20 billion years ago. The Big Bang theory began modern ◊cosmology.

Bihar or *Behar* state of NE India; *area* 173,900 sq km/67,125 sq mi; *capital* Patna; *features* river Ganges in the N, Rajmahal Hills in the S; *languages* Hindi, Bihari; *population* (1991) 86,338,900.

Bihari member of a N Indian people, also living in Bangladesh, Nepal, and Pakistan, and numbering over 40 million. The Bihari are mainly Muslim. The Bihari language is related to Hindi and has several widely varying dialects. It belongs to the Indic branch of the Indo-European family. Many Bihari were massacred during the formation of Bangladesh, which they opposed.

bile brownish alkaline fluid produced by the liver. Bile is stored in the gall bladder and is intermittently released into the duodenum (small intestine) to aid digestion. Bile consists of bile salts, bile pigments, cholesterol, and lecithin. *Bile salts* assist in the breakdown and absorption of fats; *bile pigments* are the breakdown products of old red blood cells that are passed into the gut to be eliminated with the faeces.

billiards indoor game played, normally by two players, with tapered poles (cues) and composition balls (one red, two white) on a rectangular table covered with a green, feltlike cloth (baize). The table has six pockets, one at each corner and in each of the long sides at the middle. Scoring strokes are made by potting the red ball, potting the opponent's ball, or potting another ball off one of these two. The cannon (when the cue ball hits the two other balls on the table) is another scoring stroke.

Bill of Rights in the USA, the first ten amendments to the US Constitution, incorporated 1791: *1* guarantees freedom of worship, of speech, of the press, of assembly, and to petition the government; *2* grants the right to keep and bear arms; *3* prohibits billeting of soldiers in private homes in peacetime; *4* forbids unreasonable search and seizure; *5* guarantees none be 'deprived of life, liberty or property without due process of law' or compelled in any criminal case to be a witness against himself or herself; *6* grants the right to speedy trial, to call witnesses, and to have defence counsel; *7* grants the right to trial by jury of one's peers; *8* prevents the infliction of excessive bail or fines, or 'cruel and unusual punishment'; *9, 10* provide a safeguard to the states and people for all rights not specifically delegated to the central government.

Bill of Rights in Britain, act of Parliament 1689 which established it as the primary governing body of the country. It embodied the Declarations of Rights listing the conditions on which William and Mary were offered the throne. The bill limited royal prerogative regarding legislation, executive power, money levies, courts, and the army and stipulated Parliament's consent to many government functions.

binary fission in biology, a form of ▷asexual reproduction, whereby a single-celled organism, such as the amoeba, divides into two smaller 'daughter' cells. It can also occur in a few simple multicellular organisms, such as sea anemones, producing two smaller sea anemones of equal size.

binary number system system of numbers to ▷base two, using combinations of the digits 1 and 0. Codes based on binary numbers are used to represent instructions and data in all modern digital computers, the values of the binary digits (contracted to 'bits') being stored or transmitted as, for example, open/closed switches, magnetized/unmagnetized discs and tapes, and high/low voltages in circuits.

binary star pair of stars moving in orbit around their common centre of mass. Observations show that most stars are binary, or even multiple –for example, the nearest star system to the Sun, Alpha Centauri.

biochemistry science concerned with the chemistry of living organisms: the structure and reactions of proteins (such as enzymes), nucleic acids, carbohydrates, and lipids.

biodegradable capable of being broken down by living organisms, principally bacteria and fungi. In biodegradable substances, such as food and sewage, the natural processes of decay lead to compaction and liquefaction, and to the release of nutrients that are then recycled by the ecosystem.

biodiversity (contraction of *biological diversity*) measure of the variety of the Earth's animal, plant, and microbial species; of genetic differences within species; and of the ecosystems that support those species. Its maintenance is important for ecological stability and as a resource for research into, for example, new drugs and crops. Research suggests that biodiversity is far greater than previously realized, especially among smaller organisms – for instance, it is thought that there are 30–40 million insects, of which only a million have so far been identified. In the 20th century, the destruction of habitats is believed to have resulted in the most severe and rapid loss of diversity in the history of the planet.

bioengineering the application of engineering to biology and medicine. Common applications include the design and use of artificial limbs, joints, and organs, including hip joints and heart valves.

biological control control of pests such as insects and fungi through biological means, rather than the use of chemicals. This can include breeding resistant crop strains; inducing sterility in the pest; infecting the pest species with disease organisms; or introducing the pest's natural predator.

biology science of life. Biology includes all the life sciences – for example, anatomy and physiology (the study of the structure of living things), cytology, zoology (the study of animals) and botany (the study of plants), ecology (the study of habitats and the interaction of living species), animal behaviour, embryology, and taxonomy, and plant breeding. Increasingly this century biologists have concentrated on molecular structures: biochemistry, biophysics, and genetics (the study of inheritance and variation).

bionics design and development of electronic or mechanical artificial systems that imitate those of living things. The bionic arm, for example, is an artificial limb (◊prosthesis) that uses electronics to amplify minute electrical signals generated in body muscles to work electric motors, which operate the joints of the fingers and wrist.

biosphere the narrow zone that supports life on our planet. It is limited to the waters of the Earth, a fraction of its crust, and the lower regions of the atmosphere.

biotechnology industrial use of living organisms to manufacture food, drugs, or other products. The brewing and baking industries have long relied on the yeast microorganism for ◊fermentation purposes, while the dairy industry employs a range of bacteria and fungi to convert milk into cheeses and yoghurts. ◊Enzymes, whether extracted from cells or produced artificially, are central to most biotechnological applications.

birch any tree of the genus *Betula*, including about 40 species found in cool temperate parts of the northern hemisphere. Birches grow rapidly, and their hard, beautiful wood is used for veneers and cabinet work.

bird backboned animal of the class Aves, the biggest group of land vertebrates, characterized by warm blood, feathers, wings, breathing through lungs, and egg-laying by the female. There are nearly 8,500 species of birds.

Birmingham industrial city in the West Midlands, second largest city of the UK; population (1991) 961,000, metropolitan area 2,632,000. It is an important manufacturing and commercial centre.

Birmingham commercial and industrial city; largest city in Alabama, USA; population (1990) 266,000.

birth control another name for ◊family planning; see also ◊contraceptive.

Biscay, Bay of bay of the Atlantic Ocean between N Spain and W France, known for rough seas and exceptionally high tides.

Bishkek (formerly *Pishpek* until 1926, and *Frunze* 1926–92) capital of Kyrgyzstan; population (1987) 632,000.

Bismarck Otto Eduard Leopold, Prince von 1815–1898. German politician, prime minister of Prussia 1862–90 and chancellor of the German Empire 1871–90. He pursued an aggressively expansionist policy, waging wars against Denmark 1863–64, Austria 1866, and France 1870–71, which brought about the unification of Germany.

Bissau capital and chief port of Guinea-Bissau, on an island at the mouth of the Geba River; population (1988) 125,000. Originally a fortified slave-trading centre, Bissau became a free port 1869.

bit (contraction of *bi*nary digi*t*) in computing, a single binary digit, either 0 or 1. A bit is the smallest unit of data stored in a computer; all other data must be coded into a pattern of individual bits. A ◊byte represents sufficient computer memory to store a single character of data, and usually contains eight bits.

bitumen impure mixture of hydrocarbons, including such deposits as petroleum, asphalt, and natural gas, although sometimes the term is restricted to a soft kind of pitch resembling asphalt.

bivalve marine or freshwater mollusc whose body is enclosed between two shells hinged together by a ligament on the dorsal side of the body.

Bizet Georges (Alexandre César Léopold) 1838–1875. French composer of operas. Among his works are *Les Pêcheurs de perles/The Pearl Fishers* 1863 and *La Jolie Fille de Perth/The Fair Maid of Perth* 1866. He also wrote the concert overture *Patrie* and incidental music to Alphonse Daudet's play *L'Arlésienne*. His operatic masterpiece *Carmen* was produced a few months before his death 1875.

Black Death name originating in the 19th century to describe the great epidemic of bubonic plague that ravaged Europe in the 14th century, killing between one-third and half of the population. The cause of the plague was the bacterium *Yersinia pestis*, transmitted by fleas borne by migrating Asian black rats.

Black Forest (German *Schwarzwald*) mountainous region of coniferous forest in Baden-Württemberg, W Germany. Bounded to the W and S by the Rhine, which separates it from the Vosges, it has an area of 4,660 sq km/1,800 sq mi and rises to 1,493 m/4,905 ft in the Feldberg. Parts of the forest have recently been affected by ◊acid rain.

black hole object in space whose gravity is so great that nothing can escape from it, not even light. Thought to form when massive stars shrink at the ends of their lives, a black hole sucks in more matter, including other stars, from the space around it. Matter that falls into a black hole is squeezed to infinite density at the centre of the hole. Black holes can be detected because gas falling towards them becomes so hot that it emits X-rays.

Black National State area in the Republic of South Africa set aside, from 1971 to 1994, for development towards self-government by black Africans, in accordance with ◊apartheid. Before 1980 these areas were known as *black homelands* or *bantustans*. Under the non-racial constitution, April 1994, they became part of the republic's provincial structure, with guaranteed legislative and executive power.

Black Sea (Russian *Chernoye More*) inland sea in SE Europe, linked with the seas of Azov and Marmara, and via the Dardanelles strait with the Mediterranean. Uranium deposits beneath it are among the world's largest. About 90% of the water is polluted, mainly by agricultural fertilizers.

bladder hollow elastic-walled organ which stores the urine produced in the kidneys. It is present in the ◊urinary systems of some fishes, most amphibians, some reptiles, and all mammals. Urine enters the bladder through two ureters, one leading from each kidney, and leaves it through the urethra.

Blair Tony (Anthony Charles Lynton) 1953– . British politician, leader of the Labour Party from 1994. A centrist in the manner of his predecessor John ◊Smith, he won by a large majority in the first fully democratic elections to the post July 1994, becoming the party's youngest leader.

Blake William 1757–1827. English poet, artist, engraver, and visionary. He was one of the most important figures of English Romanticism. His lyrics, as in *Songs of Innocence* 1789 and *Songs of Experience* 1794, express spiritual wisdom in radiant imagery and symbolism. In prophetic books like *The Marriage of Heaven and Hell* 1790 and *Milton* 1804, Blake created a vast personal mythology. He also created a new composite art form in engraving and hand-colouring his own works.

blast furnace smelting furnace used to extract metals from their ores, chiefly pig iron from iron ore. The temperature is raised by the injection of an air blast.

bleaching decolorization of coloured materials. The two main types of bleaching agent are the *oxidizing bleaches*, which bring about the ▷oxidation of pigments and include the ultraviolet rays in sunshine, hydrogen peroxide, and chlorine in household bleaches, and the *reducing bleaches*, which bring about ▷reduction and include sulphur dioxide.

Blériot Louis 1872–1936. French aviator who, in a 24-horsepower monoplane of his own construction, made the first flight across the English Channel on 25 July 1909.

Bligh William 1754–1817. English sailor who accompanied Captain James ▷Cook 1772–74, and in 1787 commanded HMS *Bounty* on an expedition to the Pacific. On the return voyage the crew mutinied 1789, and Bligh was cast adrift in a boat with 18 men, but eventually reached land. As governor of New South Wales 1805, he again provoked a mutiny 1808 (the Rum Rebellion). He returned to Britain, and was made an admiral 1811.

Bloemfontein capital of the Orange Free State and judicial capital of the Republic of South Africa; population (1985) 204,000. Founded 1846.

blood fluid circulating in the arteries, veins, and capillaries of vertebrate animals; the term also refers to the corresponding fluid in those invertebrates that possess a closed ▷circulatory system. Blood carries nutrients and oxygen to each body cell and removes waste products, such as carbon dioxide. It is also important in the immune response and, in many animals, in the distribution of heat throughout the body.

blood clotting complex series of events (known as the blood clotting cascade) that prevents excessive bleeding after injury. It is triggered by ▷vitamin K. The result is the formation of a meshwork of protein fibres (fibrin) and trapped blood cells over the cut blood vessels.

blood pressure pressure, or tension, of the blood against the inner walls of blood vessels, especially the arteries, due to the muscular pumping activity of the heart. Abnormally high blood pressure (▷hypertension) may be associated with various conditions or arise with no obvious cause; abnormally low blood pressure (hypotension) occurs in ▷shock and after excessive fluid or blood loss from any cause.

blood transfusion see ▷transfusion.

blood vessel tube that conducts blood either away from or towards the heart in multicellular animals. Freshly oxygenated blood is carried in the arteries – major vessels which give way to the arterioles (small arteries) and finally capillaries; deoxygenated blood is returned to the heart by way of capillaries, then venules (small veins) and veins.

Bloomsbury Group intellectual circle of writers and artists based in

Bloomsbury, London during the 1920s. It centred on the house of publisher Leonard Woolf (1880–1969) and his wife, novelist Virginia ◊Woolf, and included the artists Duncan ◊Grant and Vanessa Bell, the biographer Lytton ◊Strachey, art critics Roger Fry and Clive Bell and the economist Maynard ◊Keynes. The group was typically modernist and their artistic contributions innovative.

blue-green algae or *cyanobacteria* single- celled, primitive organisms that resemble bacteria in their internal cell organization, sometimes joined together in colonies or filaments. Blue-green algae are among the oldest known living organisms and, with bacteria, belong to the kingdom Monera; remains have been found in rocks up to 3.5 billion years old. They are widely distributed in aquatic habitats, on the damp surfaces of rocks and trees, and in the soil.

Blue Mountains part of the ◊Great Dividing Range, New South Wales, Australia, ranging 600–1,100 m/ 2,000–3,600 ft and blocking Sydney from the interior until the crossing 1813 by surveyor William Lawson, Gregory Blaxland, and William Wentworth.

Blue Nile (Arabic *Bahr el Azraq*) river rising in the mountains of Ethiopia. Flowing W then N for 2,000 km/1,250 mi, it eventually meets the White Nile at Khartoum. The river is dammed at Roseires where a hydroelectric scheme produces 70% of Sudan's electricity.

blues African-American music that originated in the work songs and Negro spirituals of the rural American South in the late 19th century. It is characterized by a 12-bar, or occasionally 16-bar, construction and melancholy lyrics which relate tales of woe or unhappy love. The guitar is the dominant instrument; harmonica and piano are also common.

blue shift in astronomy, a manifestation of the ◊Doppler effect in which an object appears bluer when it is moving towards the observer or the observer is moving towards it (blue light is of a higher frequency than other colours in the spectrum). The blue shift is the opposite of the ◊red shift.

Blyton Enid 1897–1968. English writer of children's books. She created the character Noddy and the adventures of the 'Famous Five' and 'Secret Seven'.

Boat Race annual UK ◊rowing race between the crews of Oxford and Cambridge universities. It is held during the Easter vacation over a 6.8 km/4.25 mi course on the river Thames between Putney and Mortlake, SW London.

bobsleighing or *bobsledding* sport of racing steel-bodied, steerable toboggans, crewed by two or four people, down mountain ice chutes at speeds of up to 130 kph/80 mph. It was introduced as an Olympic event 1924 and world championships have been held every year since 1931.

Boccaccio Giovanni 1313–1375. Italian writer and poet. He is chiefly known for the collection of tales called the *Decameron* 1348–53. Equally at home with tragic and comic narrative, he laid the foundations for the Humanism of the Renaissance and raised vernacular literature to the status enjoyed by the ancient classics.

Boer War the second of the ◊South African Wars 1899–1902, waged between Dutch settlers in South Africa (Boers) and the British.

Boethius Anicius Manilus Severinus AD 480–524. Roman philosopher. While imprisoned by the emperor Theodoric the Great, he wrote treatises on music and mathematics and *De Consolatione Philosophiae/The Consolation of Philosophy*, a dialogue in prose. It was translated into European languages during the Middle Ages.

bog type of wetland where decomposition is slowed down and dead plant matter accumulates as ▷peat. Bogs develop under conditions of low temperature, high acidity, low nutrient supply, stagnant water, and oxygen deficiency. Typical bog plants are sphagnum moss, rushes, and cotton grass; insectivorous plants such as sundews and bladderworts are common in bogs (insect prey make up for the lack of nutrients).

Bogarde Dirk. Stage name of Derek van den Bogaerde 1921– . English actor and writer. He appeared in comedies and adventure films such as *Doctor in the House* 1954 and *Campbell's Kingdom* 1957, before acquiring international recognition for complex roles, for example in Joseph Losey's *The Servant* 1963. He has also written novels and an autobiography, *A Postilion Struck by Lightning* 1977.

Bogart Humphrey 1899–1957. US film actor. He achieved fame as the gangster in *The Petrified Forest* 1936. He became an international cult figure as the tough, romantic 'loner' in such films as *The Maltese Falcon* 1941 and *Casablanca* 1942, a status resurrected in the 1960s and still celebrated today. He won an Academy Award for his role in *The African Queen* 1952.

Bogotá capital of Colombia, South America; 2,640 m/8,660 ft above sea level on the edge of the plateau of the E Cordillera; population (1985) 4,185,000. It was founded 1538.

Bohr Niels Henrik David 1885–1962. Danish physicist. His theoretic work produced a new model of atomic structure, now called the Bohr model, and helped establish the validity of ▷quantum theory.

boiling point for any given liquid, the temperature at which the application of heat raises the temperature of the liquid no further, but converts it into vapour.

Boleyn Anne 1507–1536. Queen of England 1533–36. Henry VIII broke with the pope (see ▷Reformation) in order to divorce his first wife and marry Anne. She was married to him 1533 and gave birth to the future Queen Elizabeth I in the same year. Accused of adultery, she was beheaded.

Bolger Jim (James) Brendan 1935– . New Zealand politician, prime minister from 1990. He retained power in the 1993 general election, with a majority of one, and in 1944 was forced into a coalition with Labour.

Bolivar Simón 1783–1830. South American nationalist, leader of revolutionary armies, known as *the Liberator*. He fought the Spanish colonial forces in several uprisings and eventually liberated his native Venezuela 1821, Colombia and Ecuador 1822, Peru 1824, and Bolivia (formerly Upper Peru) 1825.

Bolivia Republic of (*República de Bolivia*); *area* 1,098,581 sq km/424,052 sq mi; *capital* La Paz (seat of government), Sucre (legal capital and seat of judiciary; *features* Andes, Titicaca lake (the world's highest navigable lake, 3,800 m/12,500 ft); *political system* emergent democratic republic; *population* (1993 est) 8,010,000; (Quechua 25%, Aymara 17%, mestizo (mixed) 30%, European 14%); growth rate 2.7% p.a.; *languages* Spanish, Aymara, Quechua (all official); *religion* Roman Catholic 95% (state-recognized).

Böll Heinrich 1917–1985. German writer and poet. A radical Catholic and anti-Nazi, he attacked Germany's political past and his works satirized West German society, for example *Billard um Halbzehn/Billiards at Half-Past Nine* 1959 and *Gruppenbild mit Dame/Group Portrait with Lady* 1971. Nobel Prize for Literature 1972.

Bologna industrial city and capital of Emilia- Romagna, Italy, 80 km/50 mi N of Florence; population (1988) 427,000. It was the site of an Etruscan town, later of a Roman colony, and became a republic in the 12th century. It came under papal rule 1506 and was united with Italy 1860.

Bolshevik member of the majority of the Russian Social Democratic Party who split from the ◊Mensheviks 1903. The Bolsheviks, under ◊Lenin, advocated the destruction of capitalist political and economic institutions, and the setting-up of a socialist state with power in the hands of the workers. The Bolsheviks set the ◊Russian Revolution 1917 in motion. They changed their name to the Russian Communist Party 1918.

Boltzmann constant in physics, the constant (symbol k) that relates the kinetic energy (energy of motion) of a gas atom or molecule to temperature. Its value is 1.380662×10^{-23} joules per Kelvin.

Bombay industrial port, commercial centre, and capital of Maharashtra, W

India; population (1981) 8,227,000. It is the centre of the Hindi film industry.

Bonaparte Corsican family of Italian origin that gave rise to the Napoleonic dynasty, including ◊Napoleon I, Napoleon II and ◊Napoleon III.

bond in chemistry, the result of the forces of attraction that hold together atoms of an element or elements to form a molecule. The principal types of bonding are ◊ionic, ◊covalent, metallic, and intermolecular (such as hydrogen bonding).

Bond Edward 1935– . English dramatist. His early work aroused controversy because of the savagery of some of his imagery, for example, the brutal stoning of a baby by bored youths in *Saved* 1965. Other works include *Early Morning* 1968, *Lear* 1972, a reworking of Shakespeare's play; *Bingo* 1973, an account of Shakespeare's last days; and *The War Plays* 1985.

bone hard connective tissue comprising the ◊skeleton of most vertebrate animals. Bone is composed of a network of collagen fibres impregnated with mineral salts (largely calcium phosphate and calcium carbonate), a combination that gives it great density and strength, comparable in some cases with that of reinforced concrete. Enclosed within this solid matrix are bone cells, blood vessels, and nerves. The interior of the long bones of the limbs consists of a spongy matrix filled with a soft marrow that produces blood cells.

bone marrow substance found inside the cavity of bones. In early life it produces red blood cells but later on lipids (fat) accumulate and its colour changes from red to yellow.

Bonn industrial city in the Federal Republic of Germany, 18 km/15 mi SSE of Cologne, on the left bank of the Rhine; population (1988) 292,000. It was the seat of government of West Germany 1949–90 and of the Federal Republic of Germany from 1990. A proposed move back to Berlin was shelved by the Bundesrat (upper chamber of parliament) 1991.

Bonnard Pierre 1867–1947. French painter, designer, and graphic artist. He specialized in intimate domestic scenes and landscapes, his paintings shimmering with colour and light. Originally exploring the decorative arts, he became most widely known for his series of nudes, for example, *Nude in the Bath* 1938 (Petit Palais, Paris).

Bonnie Prince Charlie 1720–1788. Scottish name for ◊Charles Edward Stuart, pretender to the throne.

Boole George 1815–1864. English mathematician whose work *The Mathematical Analysis of Logic* 1847 established the basis of modern mathematical logic, and whose *Boolean algebra* can be used in designing computers.

Bophuthatswana Republic of; former self-governing ◊Black National State within South Africa, independent from 1977 (although not recognized by the United Nations) until 1994 when it was incorporated into South Africa; *area* 40,330 sq km/15,571 sq mi; *capital* Mmbatho or Sun City, a casino resort; *population* (1985) 1,627,000; *languages* Setswana, English; *religion* Christian.

Bordeaux port on the river Garonne, capital of Aquitaine, SW France, a centre for the wine trade; population (1990) 213,300. Bordeaux was under the English crown for three centuries until 1453. In 1870, 1914, and 1940 the French government was moved here because of German invasion.

Borders region of Scotland; *area* 4,700 sq km/1,815 sq mi; *towns and cities* Newtown St Boswells (administrative headquarters), Hawick, Jedburgh; *features* Lammermuir, Moorfoot, and Pentland hills; home of novelist Walter Scott at Abbotsford; Dryburgh Abbey, burial place of Field Marshal Haig and Scott; *population* (1991) 103,900.

Borges Jorge Luis 1899–1986. Argentine poet and short-story writer. He was an exponent of magic realism. In 1961 he became director of the National Library, Buenos Aires, and was professor of English literature at the university there. He is known for his fantastic and paradoxical work *Ficciones/Fictions* 1944.

Borgia Cesare 1476–1507. Italian general, illegitimate son of Pope Alexander VI (1431–1503). Made a cardinal at 17 by his father, he resigned to become captain- general of the papacy. Ruthless and treacherous in war, he was an able ruler (the model for Machiavelli's *The Prince*), but his power crumbled on the death of his father.

Borgia Lucrezia 1480–1519. Duchess of Ferrara from 1501, the illegitimate daughter of Pope Alexander VI (1431–1503) and sister of Cesare Borgia. She was married at 12 and 13, and again at 18, to further her father's ambitions. Her final marriage was to the Duke of Este, the son and heir of the Duke of Ferrara. She made the court a centre of culture and was a patron of authors and artists such as Ariosto and Titian.

Borneo third-largest island in the world, one of the Sunda Islands in the

W Pacific; area 754,000 sq km/290,000 sq mi. It comprises the Malaysian territories of *Sabah* and *Sarawak*; ▷*Brunei;* and, occupying by far the largest part, the Indonesian territory of *Kalimantan*. It is mountainous and densely forested. In coastal areas the people of Borneo are mainly of Malaysian origin, with a few Chinese, and the interior is inhabited by the indigenous Dyaks. It was formerly under both Dutch and British colonial influence until Sarawak was formed 1841.

Bosch Hieronymus (Jerome) *c.* 1450–1516. Early Dutch painter. His fantastic visions of weird and hellish creatures, as shown in *The Garden of Earthly Delights* about 1505–10 (Prado, Madrid), show astonishing imagination and a complex imagery, creating cruel caricatures of human sinfulness.

Bosnia-Herzegovina Republic of; *area* 51,129 sq km/19,745 sq mi; *capital* Sarajevo; *features* part of the Dinaric Alps, limestone gorges *political system* emergent democracy; *population* (1993 est) 4,400,000 including 44% Muslims, 33% Serbs, 17% Croats; a complex patchwork of ethnically mixed communities; *language* Serbian variant of Serbo-Croatian; *religions* Sunni Muslim, Serbian Orthodox, Roman Catholic.

boson in physics, an elementary particle whose spin can only take values that are whole numbers or zero. Bosons may be classified as ▷gauge bosons (carriers of the four fundamental forces) or ▷mesons. All elementary particles are either bosons or ▷fermions.

Bosporus (Turkish *Karadeniz Boğazı*) strait 27 km/17 mi long, joining the Black Sea with the Sea of Marmara and forming part of the water division between Europe and Asia; its name may be derived from the Greek legend of Io. Istanbul stands on its west side. The *Bosporus Bridge* 1973, 1,621 m/5,320 ft, links Istanbul and Anatolia (the Asian part of Turkey). In 1988 a second bridge across the straits was opened, linking Asia and Europe.

Boston industrial and commercial centre, capital of Massachusetts, USA; population (1990) 574,300; metropolitan area 4,171,600. It is a publishing centre and industrial port on Massachusetts Bay, but the economy is dominated by financial and health services and government.

Boswell James 1740–1795. Scottish biographer and diarist. He was a member of Samuel ▷Johnson's London Literary Club and the two men travelled to Scotland together 1773, as recorded in Boswell's *Journal of the Tour to the Hebrides* 1785. Boswell's ability to record Johnson's pithy conversation verbatim makes his *Life of Samuel Johnson* 1791 a classic of English biography.

Bosworth, Battle of last battle of the Wars of the ▷Roses, fought on 22 Aug 1485. Richard III, the Yorkist king, was defeated and slain by Henry of Richmond, who became Henry VII. The battlefield is near the village of Market Bosworth, 19 km/12 mi W of Leicester, England.

botany the study of plants. It is subdivided into a number of specialized studies, such as the identification and classification of plants (taxonomy), their external formation (plant morphology), their internal arrangement (plant anatomy), their microscopic examination (plant histology), their functioning and life history (plant physiology), and their distribution over the Earth's surface in relation to their surroundings (plant ecology). Palaeobotany concerns the study of fossil plants, while economic botany deals with the utility of plants. Horticulture, agriculture, and forestry are branches of botany.

Botany Bay inlet on the east coast of Australia, 8 km/5 mi S of Sydney, New South Wales. Chosen 1787 as the site for a penal colony, it proved unsuitable. Sydney now stands on the site of the former settlement. The name Botany Bay continued to be popularly used for any convict settlement in Australia.

Botha P(ieter) W(illem) 1916– . South African politician, prime minister from 1978–89. Botha initiated a modification of ▷apartheid, which later slowed in the face of Afrikaner (Boer) opposition. In 1984 he became the first executive state president. In 1989 he suffered a stroke and resigned. He was succeeded by F W de Klerk.

Botswana Republic of; *area* 582,000 sq km/225,000 sq mi; *capital* Gaborone; *environment* the Okavango Swamp is threatened by plans to develop the area for mining and agriculture; *features* Kalahari Desert in SW; Okavango Swamp in N, remarkable for its wildlife; Makgadikgadi salt pans in E; diamonds mined at Orapa and Jwaneng in partnership with De Beers of South Africa; *political system* democratic republic; *population* (1993 est) 1,400,000 (Bamangwato 80%, Bangwaketse 20%); growth rate 3.5% p.a.; *languages* English (official), Setswana (national); *religions* Christian 50%, animist 50%.

Botticelli Sandro 1445–1510. Florentine painter. He depicted religious and mythological subjects. He was patronized by the ruling ▷Medici family and deeply influenced by their Neo-Platonic circle. It was for the Medicis that he painted *Primavera* 1478 and *The Birth of Venus* about 1482–84 (both in the Uffizi, Florence). He later developed a harshly expressive and emotional style, as seen in his *Mystic Nativity* 1500 (National Gallery, London).

Boudicca Queen of the Iceni (native Britons), often referred to by the Latin form *Boadicea*. On the death of her husband, King Prasutagus, AD 60, the territory of the Iceni was violently annexed. Boudicca was scourged and her daughters raped. Raising the whole of SE England in revolt, she burned Londinium (London), Verulamium (St Albans), and Camulodunum (Colchester). Suetonius Paulinus defeated the British between London and Chester; they were virtually annihilated and Boudicca poisoned herself.

Boulez Pierre 1925– . French composer and conductor. He is the founder and director of IRCAM, a music research studio in Paris opened 1977. His music, strictly serial and expressionistic in style, includes the cantatas *Le Visage nuptial* 1946–52 and *Le Marteau sans maître* 1955, both to texts by René Char; *Pli selon pli* 1962 for soprano and orchestra; and *Répons* 1981 for soloists, orchestra, tapes, and computer-generated sounds.

Bourbon dynasty French royal house (succeeding that of Valois), beginning with Henry IV and ending with Louis XVI, with a brief revival under Louis XVIII, Charles X, and Louis Philippe. The Bourbons also ruled Spain almost uninterruptedly from Philip V to Alfonso XIII and were restored in 1975 (▷Juan Carlos); at one point they also ruled Naples and several Italian duchies.

The Grand Duke of Luxembourg is also a Bourbon by male descent.

Boutros-Ghali Boutros 1922– . Egyptian diplomat and politician, deputy prime minister 1991–92, secretary general of the United Nations (UN) from 1992. He has encountered a succession of challenges in conflict areas such as Bosnia-Herzegovina, Somalia, Haiti, and Rwanda, with which he has dealt with varying success.

Bowie David. Stage name of David Jones 1947– . English pop singer, songwriter, and actor. His career has been a series of image changes. His hits include 'Jean Genie' 1973, 'Rebel, Rebel' 1974, 'Golden Years' 1975, and 'Underground' 1986. He has acted in plays and films, including Nicolas Roeg's *The Man Who Fell to Earth* 1976.

bowls outdoor and indoor game popular in Commonwealth countries. It has been played in Britain since the 13th century and was popularized by Francis Drake, who is reputed to have played bowls on Plymouth Hoe as the Spanish Armada approached 1588.

boxing fighting with gloved fists, almost entirely a male sport. The sport dates from the 18th century, when fights were fought with bare knuckles and untimed rounds. Each round ended with a knockdown. Fighting with gloves became the accepted form in the latter part of the 19th century after the formulation of the Queensberry Rules 1867.

Boyle's law law stating that the volume of a given mass of gas at a constant temperature is inversely proportional to its pressure. For example, if the pressure of a gas doubles, its volume will be reduced by a half, and vice versa. The law was discovered in 1662 by Irish physicist and chemist Robert Boyle.

brachiopod or *lamp shell* any member of the phylum Brachiopoda, marine invertebrates with two shells, resembling but totally unrelated to bivalves. There are about 300 living species; they were much more numerous in past geological ages. They are suspension feeders, ingesting minute food particles from water. A single internal organ, the lophophore, handles feeding, aspiration, and excretion.

Bradbury Malcolm 1932– . English novelist and critic. His writings include comic and satiric portrayals of academic life. His major work is *The History Man* 1975, set in a provincial English university. Other works include *Rates of Exchange* 1983.

Bradford industrial city in West Yorkshire, England, 14 km/9 mi W of Leeds; population (1991) 457,300. It is the main city for wool textile in the UK.

Braganza the royal house of Portugal whose members reigned 1640–1910; another branch were emperors of Brazil 1822–89.

Brahe Tycho 1546–1601. Danish astronomer who made accurate observations of the planets from which the German astronomer and mathematician Johann ▷Kepler proved that planets orbit the Sun in ellipses. His discovery and report of the 1572 supernova brought him recognition, and his observations of the comet of 1577 proved that it moved on an orbit among the planets, thus disproving the Greek view that comets were in the Earth's atmosphere.

Brahma in Hinduism, the creator of the cosmos, who forms with Vishnu and

Siva the Trimurti, or three aspects of the absolute spirit.

Brahms Johannes 1833–1897. German composer, pianist, and conductor. Considered one of the greatest composers of symphonic music and of songs, his works include four symphonies, lieder (songs), concertos for piano and for violin, chamber music, sonatas, and the choral *Ein Deutsches Requiem/A German Requiem* 1868. He performed and conducted his own works.

brain in higher animals, a mass of interconnected ▷nerve cells forming the anterior part of the ▷central nervous system, whose activities it coordinates and controls. In ▷vertebrates, the brain is contained by the skull. At the base of the brainstem, the *medulla oblongata* contains centres for the control of respiration, heartbeat rate and strength, and blood pressure. Overlying this is the *cerebellum*, which is concerned with coordinating complex muscular processes such as maintaining posture and moving limbs. The cerebral hemispheres (*cerebrum*) are paired outgrowths of the front end of the forebrain, in early vertebrates mainly concerned with the senses, but in higher vertebrates greatly developed and involved in the integration of all sensory input and motor output, and in thought, emotions, memory, and behaviour.

Brancusi Constantin 1876–1957. Romanian sculptor. He is a seminal figure in 20th-century art. Active in Paris from 1904, he was a pioneer of abstract scultpure, developing increasingly simplified representations of natural, or organic, forms, for example the *Sleeping Muse* 1910 (Musée National d'Art Moderne, Paris), a sculpted head that gradually comes to resemble an egg.

Brando Marlon 1924– . US actor. His powerful stage presence, mumbling speech, and use of Method acting earned him a place as a distinctive actor. He won best-actor Academy Awards for *On the Waterfront* 1954 and *The Godfather* 1972.

Brandt Willy. Adopted name of Karl Herbert Frahm 1913–1992. German socialist politician, federal chancellor (premier) of West Germany 1969–74. As mayor of West Berlin 1957–66, Brandt became internationally known during the Berlin Wall crisis 1961. Nobel Peace Prize 1971.

Braque Georges 1882–1963. French painter. With Picasso, he founded the Cubist movement around 1907–10. His early work was influenced by Fauvism in its use of pure, bright colour, but from 1907 he developed a geometric style and during the next few years he and Picasso worked very closely developing Cubism.

Brasilia capital of Brazil from 1960, 1,000 m/3,000 ft above sea level; population (1991) 1,841,000. It was designed by Lucio Costa (1902–1963), with Oscar Niemeyer as chief architect, as a completely new city to bring life to the interior.

brass metal ▷alloy of copper and zinc, with not more than 5% or 6% of other metals. The zinc content ranges from 20% to 45%, and the colour of brass varies accordingly from coppery to whitish yellow. Brasses are characterized by the ease with which they may be shaped and machined; they are strong and ductile, resist many forms of corrosion, and are used for electrical fittings, ammunition cases, screws, household fittings, and ornaments.

brass instrument any of a class of musical instruments made of brass or other metal, including trumpets, bugles, trombones, and horns. The function of a reed is served by the lips, shaped and tensed by the mouthpiece, acting as a valve releasing periodic pulses of pressurized air into the tube. Orchestral brass instruments are derived from signalling instruments that in their natural or valveless form produce a directionally focused range of tones from the harmonic series by overblowing to as high as the 16th harmonic. They are powerful and efficient generators, and produce tones of great depth and resonance.

Bratislava (German ***Pressburg***) industrial port and capital of the Slovak Republic, on the river Danube; population (1991) 441,500. It was the capital of Hungary 1526–1784 and capital of Slovakia (within Czechoslovakia) until 1993.

Brazil Federative Republic of (*República Federativa do Brasil*); ***area*** 8,511,965 sq km/3,285,618 sq mi; ***capital*** Brasília; ***environment*** Brazil has one-third of the world's tropical rainforest. It contains 55,000 species of flowering plants (the greatest variety in the world) and 20% of all the world's bird species. In the 1980s 7% of the Amazon rainforest was destroyed for cultivation and grazing; ***features*** Mount Roraima, Xingu National Park; Amazon delta; Rio harbour; ***political system*** democratic federal republic; ***population*** (1993 est) 159,100,000 (including 200,000 Indians, mostly living on reservations); growth rate 2.2% p.a.; ***languages*** Portuguese (official); 120 Indian languages; ***religions*** Roman Catholic 89%; Indian faiths.

Brazzaville capital of the Congo, industrial port on the river Zaïre, opposite Kinshasa; population (1984) 595,000. There is a cathedral 1892 and the Pasteur Institute 1908. It stands on Pool Malebo (Stanley Pool).

breathing in terrestrial animals, the muscular movements whereby air is taken into the lungs and then expelled, a form of ▷gas exchange. Breathing is sometimes referred to as external respiration, for true respiration is a cellular (internal) process.

Brecht Bertolt 1898–1956. German dramatist and poet. He was one of the most influential figures in 20th- century drama. He aimed to destroy the 'suspension of disbelief' usual in the theatre and encourage audiences to develop an active and critical attitude to a play's subject. He adapted John Gay's *The Beggar's Opera* as *Die Dreigroschenoper/The Threepenny Opera* 1928, set to music by Kurt Weill. Later plays include *Der kaukasische Kreidekreis/The Caucasian Chalk Circle* 1949.

Bremen administrative region (German *Land*) of Germany, consisting of the cities of Bremen and Bremerhaven; area 400 sq km/154 sq mi; population (1988) 652,000.

Brest naval base and industrial port on ***Rade de Brest*** (Brest Roads), a great bay at the western extremity of Brittany, France; population (1983) 201,000. Occupied as a U-boat base by the Germans 1940–44, the city was destroyed by Allied bombing and rebuilt.

Breton André 1896–1966. French writer and poet. He was among the leaders of the ▷Dada art movement. *Les Champs magnétiques/Magnetic Fields* 1921, an experiment in automatic writing, was one of the products of the movement. He was also a founder of

◊Surrealism, publishing *Le Manifeste de surréalisme/Surrealist Manifesto* 1924. Other works include *Najda* 1928, the story of his love affair with a medium.

brewing making of beer, ale, or other alcoholic beverage from malt and ◊barley by steeping (mashing), boiling, and fermenting. Mashing the barley releases its sugars. Yeast is then added, which contains the enzymes needed to convert the sugars into ethanol (alcohol) and carbon dioxide. Hops are added to give a bitter taste.

Brezhnev Leonid Ilyich 1906–1982. Soviet leader. A protégé of Stalin and Khrushchev, he came to power (after he and Kosygin forced Khrushchev to resign) as general secretary of the Soviet Communist Party (CPSU) 1964–82 and was president 1977–82. Domestically he was conservative; abroad the USSR was established as a military and political superpower during the Brezhnev era, extending its influence in Africa and Asia.

bridge structure that provides a continuous path or road over water, valleys, ravines, or above other roads. The basic designs and composites of these are based on the way they bear the weight of the structure and its load. *Beam*, or *girder*, bridges are supported at each end by the ground with the weight thrusting downwards. *Cantilever* bridges are a complex form of girder. *Arch* bridges thrust outwards but downwards at their ends; they are in compression. *Suspension* bridges use cables under tension to pull inwards against anchorages on either side of the span, so that the roadway hangs from the main cables by the network of vertical cables. The *cablestayed* bridge relies on diagonal cables connected directly between the bridge deck and supporting towers at each end.

Some bridges are too low to allow traffic to pass beneath easily, so they are designed with movable parts, like swing and draw bridges.

bridge card game derived from whist. First played among members of the Indian Civil Service about 1900, bridge was brought to England in 1903 and played at the Portland Club in 1908. It is played in two forms: auction bridge and contract bridge.

Bridgetown port and capital of Barbados; population (1987) 8,000. Sugar is exported through the nearby deepwater port. Bridgetown was founded 1628.

Brighton seaside resort on the E Sussex coast, England; population (1991) 143,600. It has Regency architecture and the Royal Pavilion 1782 in Oriental style. There are two piers and an aquarium.

Brisbane industrial port, capital of Queensland, E Australia, near the mouth of Brisbane River, dredged to carry ocean-going ships; population (1990) 1,301,700.

Bristol industrial port and administrative headquarters of Avon, SW England; population (1991) 376,100. The old docks have been redeveloped for housing, industry, yachting facilities, and the National Lifeboat Museum. There is a new city centre, with Brunel's Temple Meads railway station at its focus, and a weir across the Avon nearby to improve the waterside environment.

Britain island off the NW coast of Europe, one of the British Isles. It comprises England, Scotland, and Wales (together officially known as ◊Great Britain), and is part of the ◊United Kingdom. The name is derived from the

Roman name Britannia, which in turn is derived from the ancient Celtic name of the inhabitants, *Bryttas*.

Britain, ancient period in the British Isles (excluding Ireland) extending through prehistory to the Roman occupation (1st century AD). Settled agricultural life evolved in Britain during the 3rd millennium BC. Neolithic society reached its peak in southern England, where it was capable of producing the great stone circles of Avebury and Stonehenge early in the 2nd millennium BC. It was succeeded in central southern Britain by the Early Bronze Age Wessex culture, with strong trade links across Europe. The Iron Age culture of the Celts was predominant in the last few centuries BC, and the Belgae (of mixed Germanic and Celtic stock) were partially Romanized in the century between the first Roman invasion of Britain under Julius Caesar (54 BC) and the Roman conquest (AD 43).

Britain, Battle of World War II air battle between German and British air forces over Britain lasting 10 July–31 Oct 1940.

British Columbia province of Canada on the Pacific Ocean; *area* 947,800 sq km/365,851 sq mi; *capital* Victoria; *population* (1991) 3,185,900.

British Empire various territories all over the world conquered or colonized by Britain from about 1600, most now independent or ruled by other powers. The British ◊Commonwealth is composed of former and remaining territories of the British Empire.

British Isles group of islands off the northwest coast of Europe, consisting of Great Britain (England, Wales, and Scotland), Ireland, the Channel Islands, the Orkney and Shetland islands, the Isle of Man, and many other islands that are included in various counties, such as the Isle of Wight, Scilly Isles, Lundy Island, and the Inner and Outer Hebrides. The islands are divided from Europe by the North Sea, Strait of Dover, and the English Channel, and face the Atlantic to the W.

Brittany (French *Bretagne*, Breton *Breiz*) region of NW France in the Breton peninsula between the Bay of Biscay and the English Channel; area 27,200 sq km/10,499 sq mi; capital Rennes; population (1987) 2,767,000. A farming region, it includes the *départements* of Côtes-du-Nord, Finistère, Ille-et-Vilaine, and Morbihan.

Britten (Edward) Benjamin 1913–1976. English composer. He often wrote for the individual voice; for example, the role in the opera *Peter Grimes* 1945, based on verses by George Crabbe, was created for his life companion Peter Pears (1910–1986). Among his many works are; the chamber opera *The Rape of Lucretia* 1946; *Billy Budd* 1951; *A Midsummer Night's Dream* 1960; and *Death in Venice* 1973.

Brodsky Joseph 1940– . Russian poet. He emigrated to the USA 1972. His work, often dealing with themes of exile, is admired for its wit and economy of language, particularly in its use of understatement. Many of his earlier poems, written in Russian, have been translated into English (*A Part of Speech* 1980). He became US poet laureate 1991. Nobel Prize for Literature 1987.

bronchitis inflammation of the bronchi (air passages) of the lungs, usually caused initially by a viral infection, such as a cold or flu. It is aggravated by environmental pollutants, especially smoking, and results in a persistent cough, irritated mucus-secreting glands, and large amounts of sputum.

Brontë three English novelists, daughters of a Yorkshire parson. *Charlotte* (1816–1855), notably with *Jane Eyre* 1847 and *Villette* 1853, reshaped autobiographical material into vivid narrative. *Emily* (1818–1848) in *Wuthering Heights* 1847 expressed the intensity and nature mysticism which also pervades her poetry (*Poems* 1846). The more modest talent of *Anne* (1820–1849) produced *Agnes Grey* 1847 and *The Tenant of Wildfell Hall* 1848.

bronze alloy of copper and tin, yellow or brown in colour. It is harder than pure copper, more suitable for casting, and also resists ◊corrosion. Bronze may contain as much as 25% tin, together with small amounts of other metals, mainly lead.

Bronze Age stage of prehistory and early history when copper and bronze became the first metals worked extensively and used for tools and weapons. It developed out of the Stone Age, preceded the Iron Age, and may be dated 5000–1200 BC in the Middle East and about 2000–500 BC in Europe. Recent discoveries in Thailand suggest that the Far East, rather than the Middle East, was the cradle of the Bronze Age.

Brooke Rupert (Chawner) 1887–1915. English poet. He stands as a symbol of the World War I 'lost generation'. His five war sonnets, the best known of which is 'The Patriot', were published posthumously. Other notable works include 'Grantchester' and 'The Great Lover'.

Brown Ford Madox 1821–1893. English painter. He was associated with the ◊Pre-Raphaelite Brotherhood. His pictures, which include *The Last of England* 1855 (City Art Gallery, Birmingham) and *Work* 1852–65 (City Art Gallery, Manchester), are characterized by their abundance of realistic detail and their use of symbolism.

Brown John 1800–1859. US slavery abolitionist. On 16 Oct 1859, he seized the government arsenal at Harper's Ferry in W Virginia, in order to distribute weapons to runaway slaves who Brown hoped would then form their own republic. On 18 Oct the arsenal was stormed by US Marines under Col Robert E Lee. Brown was tried and hanged on 2 Dec, becoming a martyr and the hero of the song 'John Brown's Body'.

Browning Robert 1812–1889. English poet. He was married to Elizabeth ◊Barrett Browning. His work is characterized by the use of dramatic monologue and an interest in obscure literary and historical figures. It includes the play *Pippa Passes* 1841 and the poems 'The Pied Piper of Hamelin' 1842, 'My Last Duchess' 1842, 'Home Thoughts from Abroad' 1845, and 'Rabbi Ben Ezra' 1864.

Brueghel or *Bruegel* family of Flemish painters. *Pieter Brueghel the Elder* (c. 1525–1569) was one of the greatest artists of his time. His pictures of peasant life helped to establish genre painting and he also popularized works illustrating proverbs, such as *The Blind leading the Blind* 1568 (Museo di Capodimonte, Naples). One of his best-known works is *Hunters in the Snow* 1565 (Kunsthistorisches Museum, Vienna).

Brundtland Gro Harlem 1939– . Norwegian Labour politician. Environment minister 1974–76, briefly prime minister 1981, and re-elected 1986, 1990, and 1993. She chaired the World Commission on Environment and Development which produced the Brundtland Report, published as *Our Common Future* 1987 and which popularized the phrase 'sustainable development'.

Brunei Islamic Sultanate of (*Negara Brunei Darussalam*); *area* 5,765 sq km/ 2,225 sq mi; *capital* Bandar Seri Begawan; *features* Temburong, Tutong, and Belait rivers; Mount Pagon (1,850 m/6,070 ft); *political system* absolute monarchy; *population* (1993 est) 280,000 (65% Malay, 20% Chinese – few Chinese granted citizenship); growth rate 12% p.a.; *languages* Malay (official), Chinese (Hokkien), English; *religion* 60% Muslim (official).

Brunel Isambard Kingdom 1806–1859. British engineer and inventor. In 1833 he became engineer to the Great Western Railway, which adopted the 2.1 m/7 ft gauge on his advice. He built the Clifton Suspension Bridge over the river Avon at Bristol and the Saltash Bridge over the river Tamar near Plymouth. His shipbuilding designs include the *Great Western* 1838, the first steamship to cross the Atlantic regularly; the *Great Britain* 1845, the first large iron ship to have a screw propeller; and the *Great Eastern* 1858, which laid the first transatlantic telegraph cable.

Brunelleschi Filippo 1377–1446. Italian Renaissance architect. The first and one of the greatest of the Renaissance architects, he pioneered the scientific use of perspective. He was responsible for the construction of the dome of Florence Cathedral (completed 1436), a feat deemed impossible by many of his contemporaries.

Brussels (Flemish *Brussel*, French *Bruxelles*) capital of Belgium, industrial city; population (1987) 974,000 (80% French-speaking, the suburbs Flemish-speaking). It is the headquarters of the European Union and since 1967 of the international secretariat of ▷NATO.

Brutus Marcus Junius *c.* 78–42 BC. Roman senator and general, against ▷Caesar in the civil war. Pardoned by Caesar and raised to high office, he nevertheless plotted Caesar's assassination. Brutus committed suicide on his defeat by ▷Mark Antony, Caesar's lieutenant, at Philippi 42 BC.

bryophyte member of the Bryophyta, a division of the plant kingdom containing three classes: the Hepaticae (liverwort), Musci (▷moss), and Anthocerotae (hornwort). Bryophytes are generally small, low-growing, terrestrial plants with no vascular (water-conducting) system as in higher plants. Their life cycle shows a marked alternation of generations. Bryophytes chiefly occur in damp habitats and require water for the dispersal of the male gametes (antherozoids).

bubonic plague epidemic disease of the Middle Ages; see ▷plague and ▷Black Death.

Bucharest (Romanian *Bucureşti*) capital and largest city of Romania; population (1985) 1,976,000; conurbation district has an area of 1,520 sq km/587 sq mi and a population of 2,273,000. Originally a citadel built by Vlad the Impaler to stop the advance of the Ottoman invasion in the 14th century, Bucharest became the capital of the princes of Wallachia 1698 and of Romania 1861. Savage fighting took place in the city during Romania's 1989 revolution.

Buckinghamshire county of SE central England; *area* 1,880 sq km/726 sq mi; *towns and cities* Aylesbury (administrative headquarters), Buckingham, High Wycombe, Beaconsfield, Olney, Milton Keynes; *features* Chiltern Hills; Chequers (country seat of the prime minister); Bletchley Park, home of World War II code-breaking activities, now Britain's electronic surveillance centre; homes of the poets William Cowper at Olney and John Milton at Chalfont St Giles, and of the Tory prime minister Benjamin Disraeli at Hughenden; *population* (1991) 632,500

buckminsterfullerene form of carbon, made up of molecules (buckyballs) consisting of 60 carbon atoms arranged in 12 pentagons and 20 hexagons to form a perfect sphere. It was named after US architect and engineer Richard Buckminster Fuller because of its structural similarity to the geodesic dome that he designed.

bud undeveloped shoot usually enclosed by protective scales; inside is a very short stem and numerous undeveloped leaves, or flower parts, or both. Terminal buds are found at the tips of shoots, while axillary buds develop in the axils of the leaves, often remaining dormant unless the terminal bud is removed or damaged. Adventitious buds may be produced anywhere on the plant, their formation sometimes stimulated by an injury, such as that caused by pruning.

Budapest capital of Hungary, industrial city on the river Danube; population (1989) 2,115,000. Buda, on the right bank of the Danube, became the Hungarian capital 1867 and was joined with Pest, on the left bank, 1872.

Buddha 'enlightened one', title of Prince *Gautama Siddhártha c.* 563–483 BC. Religious leader, founder of Buddhism, born at Lumbini in Nepal. At the age of 29 he left his wife and son and a life of luxury, to escape from the material burdens of existence. After six years of austerity he realized that asceticism, like overindulgence, was futile, and chose the middle way of meditation. He became enlightened under a bo, or bodhi, tree near Buddh Gaya in Bihar, India. He began teaching at Varanasi, and founded the Sangha, or order of monks. He spent the rest of his life travelling around N India, and died at Kusinagara in Uttar Pradesh.

Buddhism one of the great world religions, which originated in India about 500 BC. It derives from the teaching of the Buddha, who is regarded as one of a series of such enlightened beings; there are no gods. The chief doctrine is that of *karma*, good or evil deeds meeting an appropriate reward or punishment either in this life or (through reincarnation) a long succession of lives. The main divisions in Buddhism are *Theravãda* (or Hinayãna) in SE Asia and *Mahãyãna* in N Asia; *Lamaism* in Tibet and *Zen* in Japan are among the many Mahãyãna sects. Its symbol is the lotus. There are over 247.5 million Buddhists worldwide.

Buenos Aires capital and industrial city of Argentina, on the south bank of the Rio de la Plata; population (1991) 2,961,000, metropolitan area 7,950,400. It was founded 1536, and became the capital 1853.

bug in computing, an error in a program. It can be an error in the logical structure of a program or a syntax error, such as a spelling mistake. Some bugs cause a program to fail immediately; others remain dormant, causing problems only when a particular combination of events occurs.

bug in entomology, an insect belonging to the order Hemiptera. All these have two pairs of wings with forewings partly thickened. They also have piercing mouthparts adapted for sucking the juices of plants or animals, the 'beak' being tucked under the body when not in use.

Bujumbura capital of Burundi; population (1986) 272,600. Formerly called *Usumbura* (until 1962), it was founded 1899 by German colonists. The university was established 1960.

Bulawayo industrial city and railway junction in Zimbabwe; population (1982) 415,000. It lies at an altitude of 1,355 m/4,450 ft on the river Matsheumlope, a tributary of the Zambezi. Bulawayo developed with the exploitation of gold mines in the neighbourhood.

bulb underground bud with fleshy leaves containing a reserve food supply and with roots growing from its base. Bulbs function in vegetative reproduction and are characteristic of many monocotyledonous plants such as the daffodil, snowdrop, and onion. Bulbs are grown on a commercial scale in temperate countries, such as England and the Netherlands.

Bulgaria Republic of (*Republika Bulgaria*); *area* 110,912 sq km/42,812 sq mi; *capital* Sofia; *environment* pollution has virtually eliminated all species of fish once caught in the Black Sea. Traffic pollution in Sofia is twice the medically accepted level; *features* Black Sea coast;

Balkan and Rhodope mountains; Danube River in N; *political system* emergent democratic republic; *population* (1993 est) 9,020,000 (including 900,000–1,500,000 ethnic Turks, concentrated in S and NE); growth rate 0.1% p.a.; *languages* Bulgarian, Turkish; *religions* Eastern Orthodox Christian 90%, Sunni Muslim 10%.

Bulgarian member of an ethnic group living mainly in Bulgaria. There are 8–8.5 million speakers of Bulgarian, a Slavic language belonging to the Indo-European family. The Bulgarians use the Cyrillic alphabet.

bulimia condition of continuous, uncontrolled overeating. Considered a manifestion of stress or depression, this eating disorder is found chiefly in young women. However, it may also arise as a result of brain damage or disease. When compensated for by forced vomiting or overdoses of laxatives, the condition is called *bulimia nervosa*. It is sometimes associated with ▷anorexia.

bullfighting the national sport of Spain (where there are more than 400 bullrings), which is also popular in Mexico, Portugal, and much of Latin America. It involves the ritualized taunting of a bull in a large circular stadium, until its eventual death at the hands of the matador. Originally popular in Greece and Rome, it was introduced into Spain by the Moors in the 11th century.

Bunker Hill, Battle of the first significant engagement in the ▷American Revolution, 17 June 1775, near a small hill in Charlestown (now part of Boston), Massachusetts, USA; the battle actually took place on Breed's Hill. Although the colonists were defeated they were able to retreat to Boston and suffered fewer casualties than the British.

Bunsen burner gas burner used in laboratories, consisting of a vertical metal tube through which a fine jet of fuel gas is directed. Air is drawn in through airholes near the base of the tube and the mixture is ignited and burns at the tube's upper opening.

Buñuel Luis 1900–1983. Spanish Surrealist film director (see ▷Surrealism). He collaborated with Salvador Dali on *Un chien andalou* 1928 and *L'Age d'or/The Golden Age* 1930, and established his solo career with *Los olvidados/The Young and the Damned* 1950. His works are often anticlerical, with black humour and erotic imagery.

Bunyan John 1628–1688. English author. A Baptist, he was imprisoned in Bedford 1660–72 for unlicensed preaching and wrote *Grace Abounding* 1666, which describes his early spiritual life. During a second jail sentence 1675 he started to write *The Pilgrim's Progress*, the first part of which was published 1678. The fervour and imagination of this allegorical story of Christian's spiritual quest has ensured its continued popularity.

Burgess Anthony. Pen name of Anthony John Burgess Wilson 1917–1993. English novelist, critic, and composer. Burgess wrote some 60 books as well as screenplays, television scripts, and reviews. His prolific work includes *A Clockwork Orange* 1962 and *Earthly Powers* 1980.

Burgundy (French *Bourgogne*) modern region and former duchy of France that includes the *départements* of Côte-d'Or, Nièvre, Sâone- et- Loire, and Yonne; area 31,600 sq km/12,198 sq mi; population (1986) 1,607,000. Its capital is Dijon.

Burke Edmund 1729–1797. British Whig politician and political theorist, born in Dublin, Ireland. In Parliament from 1765, he opposed the government's attempts to coerce the American colonists, for example in *Thoughts on the Present Discontents* 1770, and supported the emancipation of Ireland, but denounced the French Revolution, for example in *Reflections on the Revolution in France* 1790.

Burkina Faso The People's Democratic Republic of (formerly *Upper Volta*); *area* 274,122 sq km/105,811 sq mi; *capital* Ouagadougou; *environment* tropical savanna subject to overgrazing and deforestation; *features* linked by rail to Abidjan in Ivory Coast, Burkina Faso's only outlet to the sea; *political system* transitional; *population* (1993 est) 9,810,000; growth rate 2.4% p.a.; *languages* French (official); about 50 native Sudanic languages spoken by 90% of population; *religions* animist 53%, Sunni Muslim 36%, Roman Catholic 11%.

Burma former name (to 1989) of ▷Myanmar.

Burman member of the largest ethnic group in Myanmar (formerly Burma). The Burmans, speakers of a Sino-Tibetan language, migrated from the hills of Tibet, settling in the areas around Mandalay by the 11th century AD .

Burne-Jones Edward Coley 1833–1898. English painter. In 1856 he was apprenticed to the Pre-Raphaelite painter and poet Dante Gabriel ▷Rossetti, who remained a dominant influence. He also designed tapestries and stained glass in association with William ◊Morris. His work influenced both ◊Symbolism and ◊Art Nouveau.

Burns Robert 1759–1796. Scottish poet. He used the Scots dialect at a time when it was not considered suitably 'elevated' for literature. Burns's first volume, *Poems, Chiefly in the Scottish Dialect*, appeared 1786. In addition to his poetry, Burns wrote or adapted many songs, including 'Auld Lang Syne'.

Burroughs Edgar Rice 1875–1950. US novelist. He wrote *Tarzan of the Apes* 1914, the story of an aristocratic child lost in the jungle and reared by apes, and followed it with over 20 more books about the Tarzan character. He also wrote a series of novels about life on Mars.

Burroughs William S(eward) 1914–   . US writer. His work is noted for its experimental methods, black humour, explicit homo-eroticism, and apocalyptic vision. He and Allen Ginsberg and Jack Kerouac became leading members of the ◊Beat Generation. His first novel, *Junkie* 1953, documented his heroin addiction and expatriation to Mexico, where in 1951, he accidentally killed his common-law wife. He settled in Tangier 1954 and wrote his celebrated anti-novel *Naked Lunch* 1959.

Burton Richard Francis 1821–1890. British explorer and translator (he knew 35 oriental languages). He travelled mainly in the Middle East and NE Africa, often disguised as a Muslim; made two attempts to find the source of the Nile, 1855 and 1857–58 (on the second, with John Speke, he reached Lake Tanganyika); and wrote many travel books. He translated oriental erotica and the *Arabian Nights* 1885–88.

Burton Richard. Stage name of Richard Jenkins 1925–1984. Welsh stage and screen actor. He had a rich, dramatic voice but his career was dogged by an often poor choice of roles. Films in which he appeared with his wife, Elizabeth Taylor, include *Cleopatra* 1962 and *Who's Afraid of Virginia Woolf?* 1966. Among his later films are *Equus* 1977 and *Nineteen Eighty-Four* 1984.

Burundi Republic of (*Republika y'Uburundi*); *area* 27,834 sq km/10,744 sq mi; *capital* Bujumbura; *features* Lake Tanganyika, Great Rift Valley; *political system* emergent democratic republic; *population* (1993 est) 5,970,000 (15% are the Nilotic Tutsi, still holding most of the land and political power, 1% are Pygmy Twa, and the remainder Bantu Hutu); growth rate 2.8% p.a.; *languages* Kirundi (a Bantu language) and French (both official), Kiswahili; *religions* Roman Catholic 62%, Protestant 5%, Muslim 1%, animist 32%.

Bush George 1924–   . 41st president of the USA 1989–93, a Republican. He was director of the Central Intelligence Agency (CIA) 1976–81 and US vice president 1981–89. His success in the 1991 Gulf War against Iraq boosted his waning popularity, but he was later defeated in the 1992 presidential elections by Democrat Bill Clinton.

butane C_4H_{10} one of two gaseous alkanes (paraffin hydrocarbons) having the same formula but differing in structure. Normal butane is derived from natural gas; isobutane is a by-product of petroleum manufacture. Liquefied under pressure, it is used as a fuel for industrial and domestic purposes (for example, in portable cookers).

Buthelezi Chief Gatsha 1928– . South African Zulu leader and politician, president of the Zulu-based ◊Inkatha Freedom Party (IFP), which he founded as a paramilitary organization for attaining a nonracial democratic society in 1975. In May 1994 he was appointed home affairs minister in the country's first post-apartheid government.

Butler Samuel 1835–1902. English author. He made his name 1872 with a satiric attack on contemporary utopianism, *Erewhon* (*nowhere* reversed), but is now remembered for his autobiographical *The Way of All Flesh* written 1872–85 and published 1903.

buttercup plant of the genus *Ranunculus* of the buttercup family with divided leaves and yellow flowers.

butterfly insect belonging, like moths, to the order Lepidoptera, in which the wings are covered with tiny scales, often brightly coloured. There are some 15,000 species of butterfly, many of which are under threat throughout the world because of the destruction of habitat.

Byelorussian or *Belorussian* 'White Russian' native of Belarus. Byelorussian, a Balto-Slavic language belonging to the Indo-European family, is spoken by about 10 million people, including some in Poland. It is written in the Cyrillic script. Byelorussian literature dates to the 11th century AD.

Byron George Gordon, 6th Baron Byron 1788–1824. English poet. He became the symbol of Romanticism and political liberalism throughout Europe in the 19th century. His reputation was established with the first two cantos of *Childe Harold* 1812. Later works include, most notably, the satirical *Don Juan* 1819–24. He left England 1816, spending most of his later life in Italy.

byte sufficient computer memory to store a single character of data. The character is stored in the byte of memory as a pattern of ◊bits (binary digits), using a code such as ◊ASCII. A byte usually contains eight bits – for example, the capital letter F can be stored as the bit pattern 01000110.

Byzantine Empire the *Eastern Roman Empire* 395–1453, with its capital at Constantinople (formerly Byzantium, modern Istanbul). In AD 395 the Roman Empire was divided into eastern and western halves. In 1453 the Turks captured Constantinople and founded the Ottoman Empire.

Byzantium (modern Istanbul) ancient Greek city on the Bosporus, founded as a colony of the Greek city of Megara on an important strategic site at the entrance to the Black Sea in about 660 BC. In AD 330 the capital of the Eastern Roman Empire (or Byzantine Empire) was transferred there by Constantine the Great, who renamed it ◊Constantinople.

C

cabbage plant *Brassica oleracea* of the cress family Cruciferae, allied to the turnip and wild mustard, or charlock. It is a table vegetable, cultivated as early as 2000 BC, and the numerous commercial varieties include kale, Brussels sprouts, common cabbage, savoy, cauliflower, sprouting broccoli, and kohlrabi.

cabinet in politics, the group of ministers holding a country's highest executive offices who decide government policy. In Britain the cabinet system originated under the Stuarts. Under William III it became customary for the king to select his ministers from the party with a parliamentary majority. The US cabinet, unlike the British, does not initiate legislation, and its members, appointed by the president, must not be members of ▷Congress.

cable television distribution of broadcast signals through cable relay systems. Narrow-band systems were originally used to deliver services to areas with poor regular reception; systems with wider bands, using coaxial and fibreoptic cable, are increasingly used for distribution and development of home- based interactive services.

Caboto Giovanni or *John Cabot* 1450–1498. Italian navigator. Commissioned, with his three sons, by Henry VII of England to discover unknown lands, he arrived at Cape Breton Island on 24 June 1497, thus becoming the first European to reach the North American mainland (he thought he was in NE Asia). In 1498 he sailed again, touching Greenland, and probably died on the voyage.

cactus (plural *cacti*) plant of the family Cactaceae, although the term is commonly applied to many different succulent and prickly plants. True cacti have a woody axis (central core) overlaid with an enlarged fleshy stem, which assumes various forms and is usually covered with spines (actually reduced leaves). They all have special adaptations to growing in dry areas.

CAD (acronym for *computer-aided design*) the use of computers in creating and editing design drawings. CAD also allows such things as automatic testing of designs and multiple or animated three-dimensional views of designs. CAD systems are widely used in architecture, electronics, and engineering, for example in the motor-vehicle industry, where cars designed with the assistance of computers are now commonplace.

Cadiz Spanish city and naval base, capital and seaport of the province of Cadiz, standing on Cadiz Bay, an inlet of the Atlantic, 103 km/64 mi S of Seville; population (1991) 156,600. After the discovery of the Americas 1492, Cadiz became one of Europe's most vital trade ports. The English adventurer Francis

◊Drake burned a Spanish fleet here 1587 to prevent the sailing of the ◊Armada.

Caesar Gaius Julius 100–44 BC. Roman statesman and general. He formed with Pompey and Crassus the First Triumvirate 60 BC. He conquered Gaul 58–50 and invaded Britain 55 and 54. He fought against Pompey 49–48, defeating him at Pharsalus. After a period in Egypt Caesar returned to Rome as dictator from 46. He was assassinated by conspirators on the Ides of March 44.

Caesarean section surgical operation to deliver a baby by way of an incision in the mother's abdominal and uterine walls. It may be recommended for almost any obstetric complication implying a threat to mother or baby.

caffeine alkaloid organic substance found in tea, coffee, and kola nuts; it stimulates the heart and central nervous system. When isolated, it is a bitter crystalline compound, $C_8H_{10}N_4O_2$. Too much caffeine (more than six average cups of tea or coffee a day) can be detrimental to health.

Cage John 1912–1992. US composer. His interest in Indian classical music led him to the view that the purpose of music was to change the way people listen. From 1948 he experimented with instruments, graphics, and methods of random selection in an effort to generate a music of pure incident. His ideas and collected writings, including *Silence* 1961 and *For the Birds* 1981, have profoundly influenced late 20th-century aesthetics.

Cairo capital of Egypt, on the east bank of the river Nile 13 km/8 mi above the apex of the delta and 160 km/100 mi from the Mediterranean; the largest city in Africa and in the Middle East; population (1985) 6,205,000; metropolitan area (1987) 13,300,000. An earthquake in a suburb of the city Oct 1992 left over 500 dead.

calcium soft, silvery-white metallic element, symbol Ca, atomic number 20, relative atomic mass 40.08. It is one of the ◊alkaline-earth metals. It is the fifth most abundant element (the third most abur.dant metal) in the Earth's crust. It is found mainly as its carbonate $CaCO_3$, which occurs in a fairly pure condition as chalk and limestone. Calcium is an essential component of bones, teeth, shells, milk, and leaves, and it forms 1.5% of the human body by mass.

calcium carbonate $CaCO_3$ white solid, found in nature as limestone, marble, and chalk. It is a valuable resource, used in the making of iron, steel, cement, glass, slaked lime, bleaching powder, sodium carbonate and bicarbonate, and many other industrially useful substances.

calculus branch of mathematics that permits the manipulation of continuously varying quantities, used in practical problems involving such matters as changing speeds, problems of flight, varying stresses in the framework of a bridge, and alternating current theory. *Integral calculus* deals with the method of summation or adding together the effects of continuously varying quantities. *Differential calculus* deals in a similar way with rates of change. Many of its applications arose from the study of the gradients of the tangents to curves.

Calcutta largest city of India, on the river Hooghly, the westernmost mouth of the river Ganges, some 130 km/80 mi N of the Bay of Bengal. It is the capital of West Bengal; population (1981) 9,166,000. It is chiefly a commercial and industrial centre. Calcutta was the seat of government of British India 1773–1912. There is severe air pollution.

Calgary city in Alberta, Canada, on the Bow River, in the foothills of the Rocky Mountains; at 1,048 m/3,440 ft it is one of the highest Canadian cities; population (1986) 671,000. It is the centre of a large agricultural region and is the oil and financial centre of Alberta and W Canada. The 1988 Winter Olympic Games were held here.

California Pacific-coast state of the USA; *area* 411,100 sq km/158,685 sq mi; *capital* Sacramento; *features* California Institute of Technology (Caltech); Stanford University, which has the Hoover Institute and is the powerhouse of Silicon Valley; Paul Getty art museum at Malibu; Hollywood; *population* (1990) 29,760,000 (69.9% white; 25.8% Hispanic; 9.6% Asian and Pacific islander, including many Vietnamese, 7.4% black; 0.8% American Indian).

Callaghan (Leonard) James, Baron Callaghan 1912– . British Labour politician. As Chancellor of the Exchequer 1964–67, he introduced corporation and capital-gains taxes, and resigned following devaluation. He was home secretary 1967–70 and prime minister 1976–79 in a period of increasing economic stress.

Callas Maria. Adopted name of Maria Kalogeropoulos 1923–1977. US lyric soprano. She was born in New York of Greek parents. With a voice of fine range and a gift for dramatic expression, she excelled in operas including *Norma, La Sonnambula, Madame Butterfly, Aida, Tosca*, and *Medea*.

calorie c.g.s. unit of heat, now replaced by the joule (one calorie is approximately 4.2 joules). It is the heat required to raise the temperature of one gram of water by 1°C. In dietetics, the Calorie or kilocalorie is equal to 1,000 calories.

Calvin John (also known as *Cauvin* or *Chauvin*) 1509–1564. French-born Swiss Protestant church reformer and theologian. He was a leader of the Reformation in Geneva and set up a strict religious community there. His theological system is known as Calvinism, and his church government as ▷Presbyterianism. Calvin wrote (in Latin) *Institutes of the Christian Religion* 1536 and commentaries on the New Testament and much of the Old Testament.

Calvinism Christian doctrine as interpreted by John Calvin and adopted in Scotland, parts of Switzerland, and the Netherlands; by the ▷Puritans in England and New England, USA; and by the subsequent Congregational and Presbyterian churches in the USA. Its central doctrine is predestination, under which certain souls (the elect) are predestined by God through the sacrifice of Jesus to salvation, and the rest to damnation.

calyx collective term for the ▷sepals of a flower, forming the outermost whorl of the perianth. It surrounds the other flower parts and protects them while in bud. In some flowers, for example, the campions *Silene*, the sepals are fused along their sides, forming a tubular calyx.

cambium in botany, a layer of actively dividing cells (lateral meristem), found within stems and roots, that gives rise to secondary growth in perennial plants, causing an increase in girth. There are two main types of cambium: *vascular* *cambium*, which gives rise to secondary ◊xylem and ◊phloem tissues, and *cork cambium* (or phellogen), which gives rise to secondary cortex and cork tissues (see ◊bark).

Cambodia State of; (formerly *Khmer Republic* 1970–76, *Democratic Kampuchea* 1976–79; *People's Republic of Kampuchea* 1979–89); *area* 181,035 sq km/ 69,880 sq mi; *capital* Phnom Penh; *environment* infrastructure destroyed during the war, which left 4– 7 million land mines; *features* ruins of ancient capital Angkor; Lake Tonle Sap; *political system* limited constitutional monarchy; *population* (1993) 12,000,000; growth rate 2.2% p.a.; *languages* Khmer (official), French; *religion* Theravāda Buddhist 95%.

Cambrian period of geological time 570–510 million years ago; the first period of the Palaeozoic era. All invertebrate animal life appeared, and marine algae were widespread. The earliest fossils with hard shells, such as trilobites, date from this period.

Cambridge city in England, on the river Cam (a river sometimes called by its earlier name, Granta), 80 km/50 mi N of London; population (1991) 91,900; administrative headquarters of Cambridgeshire. The city is centred on Cambridge University (founded 12th century), some of whose outstanding buildings, including Kings College Chapel, back onto the river.

Cambridgeshire county of E England; *area* 3,410 sq km/1,316 sq mi; *towns and cities* Cambridge (administrative headquarters), Ely, Huntingdon, Peterborough; *population* (1991) 645,100.

camera apparatus used in ◊photography, consisting of a lens system set in a light-proof box inside of which a sensitized film or plate can be placed. The lens collects rays of light reflected from the subject and brings them together as a sharp image on the film; it has marked numbers known as apertures, or f-stops, that reduce or increase the amount of light. Apertures also control depth of field. A shutter controls the amount of time light has to affect the film. There are small-, medium-, and large-format cameras; the format refers to the size of recorded image and the dimensions of the print obtained.

Cameroon Republic of (*République du Cameroun*); *area* 475,440 sq km/ 183,638 sq mi; *capital* Yaoundé; *environment* the Korup National Park preserves 1,300 sq km/500 sq mi of Africa's fast-disappearing tropical rainforest; nearly 100 potentially useful chemical substances are produced naturally by the plants of this forest; *features* Mount Cameroon 4,070 m/13,358 ft, an active volcano on the coast, W of the Adamawa Mountains; *political system* emergent democratic republic; *population* (1993 est) 12,800,000; growth rate 2.7% p.a.; *languages* French and English in pidgin variations (official) – there are 163 indigenous peoples with their own African languages; *religions* Roman Catholic 35%, animist 25%, Muslim 22%, Protestant 18%.

camouflage colours or structures that allow an animal to blend with its surroundings to avoid detection by other animals. Camouflage can take the form of matching the background colour, of countershading (darker on top, lighter below, to counteract natural shadows), or of irregular patterns that break up the outline of the animal's body. More elaborate camouflage involves closely resembling a feature of the natural environment, as with the stick insect; this is closely akin to mimicry.

Campania agricultural region (wheat, citrus, wine, vegetables, tobacco) of S Italy, including the volcano ▷Vesuvius; area 13,600 sq km/5,250 sq mi; population (1990) 5,853,900. The capital is Naples. There are ancient sites at Pompeii, Herculaneum, and Paestum.

Camus Albert 1913–1960. Algerian-born French writer. A journalist in France, he was active in the Resistance during World War II. His novels, which owe much to ▷existentialism, include *L'Etranger/The Outsider* 1942, *La Peste/The Plague* 1948, and *L'Homme révolté/The Rebel* 1952. Nobel Prize for Literature 1957.

Canaan ancient region between the Mediterranean and the Dead Sea, called in the Bible the 'Promised Land' of the Israelites. It was occupied as early as the 3rd millennium BC by the Canaanites, a Semitic-speaking people who were known to the Greeks of the 1st millennium BC as Phoenicians. The capital was Ebla (now Tell Mardikh, Syria).

Canada *area* 9,970,610 sq km/3,849,674 sq mi; *capital* Ottawa; *environment* nine rivers in Nova Scotia are now too acid to support salmon or trout reproduction; *features* St Lawrence Seaway, Mackenzie River; Great Lakes; Arctic Archipelago; Rocky Mountains; Great Plains or Prairies; Canadian Shield; Niagara Falls; *head of state* Elizabeth II from 1952, represented by governor general Ramon John Hnatyshyn from 1990; *head of government* Jean Chretien from 1993; *political system* federal constitutional monarchy; *population* (1993 est) 28,100,000 – including 300,000 North American Indians; some 300,000 Métis (people of

mixed race) and 32,000 (1991) Inuit. Growth rate 1.1% p.a.; *languages* English, French (both official; about 70% speak English, 20% French, and the rest are bilingual); there are also North American Indian languages and the Inuit Inuktitut; *religion* Roman Catholic 46%, Protestant 35%.

canal artificial waterway constructed for drainage, irrigation, or navigation. *Irrigation canals* carry water for irrigation from rivers, reservoirs, or wells, and are designed to maintain an even flow of water over the whole length. *Navigation and ship canals* are constructed at one level between ▷locks, and frequently link with rivers or sea inlets to form a waterway system.

Canary Islands (Spanish *Canarias*) group of volcanic islands 100 km/60 mi off the NW coast of Africa, forming the Spanish provinces of Las Palmas and Santa Cruz de Tenerife; area 7,300 sq km/2,818 sq mi; population (1986) 1,615,000. *features* The chief centres are Santa Cruz on Tenerife and Las Palmas on Gran Canaria. The province of Santa Cruz comprises Tenerife, Palma, Gomera, and Hierro; the province of Las Palmas comprises Gran Canaria, Lanzarote, and Fuerteventura. There are also six uninhabited islets. The Northern Hemisphere Observatory (1981) is on La Palma.

Canberra capital of Australia (since 1908), situated in the Australian Capital Territory, enclosed within New South Wales, on a tributary of the Murrumbidgee River; area (Australian Capital Territory including the port at Jervis Bay) 2,432 sq km/939 sq mi; population (1988) 297,300.

cancer group of diseases characterized by abnormal proliferation of cells.

Cancer (malignant) cells are usually degenerate, capable only of reproducing themselves (tumour formation). Malignant cells tend to spread from their site of origin by travelling through the bloodstream or lymphatic system.

cannabis dried leaves and female flowers (marijuana) and resin (hashish) of certain varieties of hemp *Cannabis sativa*, which are smoked or swallowed to produce a range of effects, including euphoria and altered perception.

canon law rules and regulations of the Christian church, especially the Greek Orthodox, Roman Catholic, and Anglican churches. Its origin is sought in the declarations of Jesus and the apostles. In 1983 Pope John Paul II issued a new canon law code reducing offences carrying automatic excommunication, extending the grounds for annulment of marriage, removing the ban on marriage with non-Catholics, and banning trade union and political activity by priests.

Canterbury historic cathedral city in Kent, England, on the river Stour, 100 km/62 mi SE of London; population (1981) 39,000. In 597 King Ethelbert welcomed Augustine's mission to England here, and the city has since been the metropolis of the Anglican Communion and seat of the archbishop of Canterbury.

Canterbury, archbishop of primate of all England, archbishop of the Church of England (Anglican), and first peer of the realm, ranking next to royalty. He crowns the sovereign, has a seat in the House of Lords, and is a member of the Privy Council. He is appointed by the prime minister. George Carey is the current archbishop of Canterbury (from 1991).

cantilever beam or structure that is fixed at one end only, though it may be supported at some point along its length; for example, a diving board. The cantilever principle, widely used in construction engineering, eliminates the need for a second main support at the free end of the beam, allowing for more elegant structures and reducing the amount of materials required. Many large-span bridges have been built on the cantilever principle.

Canute c. 995–1035. King of England from 1016, Denmark from 1018, and Norway from 1028. Having invaded England 1013 with his father, Sweyn, king of Denmark, he was acclaimed king on his father's death 1014 by his ▷Viking army. Canute defeated ▷Edmund (II) Ironside at Assandun, Essex, 1016, and became king of all England on Edmund's death. He succeeded his brother Harold as king of Denmark 1018, invaded Scotland about 1027, and conquered Norway 1028. He was succeeded by his illegitimate son Harold I.

Cape Horn southernmost point of South America, in the Chilean part of the archipelago of Tierra del Fuego; notorious for gales and heavy seas. It was named 1616 by Dutch explorer Willem Schouten (1580–1625) after his birthplace (Hoorn).

Cape of Good Hope South African headland forming a peninsula between Table Bay and False Bay, Cape Town. The first European to sail around it was Bartholomew Diaz 1488. Formerly named Cape of Storms, it was given its present name by King John II of Portugal.

Cape Province (Afrikaans *Kaapprovinsie*) largest province of the Republic of South Africa, named after the Cape of Good Hope; *area* 641,379 sq km/ 247,638 sq mi; *capital* Cape Town; *population* (1985) 5,041,000; officially including 44% coloured; 31% black; 25% white; 0.6% Asian.

Cape Town (Afrikaans *Kaapstad*) port and oldest city (founded 1652) in South Africa, situated in the SW on Table Bay; population (1985) 776,617. It is the legislative capital of the Republic of South Africa and capital of Cape Province.

Cape Verde Republic of (*República de Cabo Verde*); *area* 4,033 sq km/1,557 sq mi; *capital* Praia; *features* strategic importance guaranteed by its domination of western shipping lanes; Sal, Boa Vista, and Maio lack water supplies but have fine beaches; *political system* socialist pluralist state; *population* (1993) 350,000 (including 100,000 Angolan refugees); growth rate 1.9% p.a.; *language* Creole dialect of Portuguese; *religion* Roman Catholic 80%;

capitalism economic system in which the principal means of production, distribution, and exchange are in private (individual or corporate) hands and competitively operated for profit. A *mixed economy* combines the private enterprise of capitalism and a degree of state monopoly, as in nationalized industries.

capital punishment punishment by death. Capital punishment is retained in 92 countries and territories (1990), including the USA (37 states), China, and Islamic countries. It was abolished in the UK 1965 for all crimes except treason. Methods of execution include electrocution, lethal gas, hanging, shooting, lethal injection, garrotting, and decapitation.

capsicum any pepper plant of the genus *Capsicum* of the nightshade family Solanaceae, native to Central and South America. The differing species produce green to red fruits that vary in size. The small ones are used whole to give the hot flavour of chilli, or ground to produce cayenne pepper; the large pointed or squarish pods, known as sweet peppers, are mild-flavoured and used as a vegetable.

car small, driver-guided, passenger-carrying motor vehicle; originally the automated version of the horse-drawn carriage, meant to convey people and their goods over streets and roads. Over 50 million motor cars are produced each year worldwide. Most are four-wheeled and have water-cooled, piston-type internal-combustion engines fuelled by petrol or diesel. Variations have existed for decades that use ingenious and often nonpolluting power plants, but the motor industry long ago settled on this general formula for the consumer market. Experimental and sports models are usually streamlined, energy-efficient, and hand-built.

carat unit for measuring the mass of precious stones; it is equal to 0.2 g/0.00705 oz, and is part of the troy system of weights. It is also the unit of purity in gold (US karat). Pure gold is 24-carat; 22-carat (the purest used in jewellery) is 22 parts gold and two parts alloy (to give greater strength).

Caravaggio Michelangelo Merisi da 1573–1610. Italian early Baroque painter. He was active in Rome 1592–1606, then in Naples, and finally in Malta. He created a forceful style, using contrasts of light and shade, dramatic foreshortening, and a meticulous attention to detail.

carbohydrate chemical compound composed of carbon, hydrogen, and oxygen, with the basic formula $C_m(H_2O)_n$, and related compounds with the same basic structure but modified functional groups. As sugar and starch, carbohydrates form a major energy-providing part of the human diet.

carbon nonmetallic element, symbol C, atomic number 6, relative atomic mass 12.011. It occurs on its own as diamond, graphite, and as fullerenes (the allotropes), as compounds in carbonaceous rocks such as chalk and limestone, as carbon dioxide in the atmosphere, as hydrocarbons in petroleum, coal, and natural gas, and as a constituent of all organic substances.

carbonate CO_3^{2-} ion formed when carbon dioxide dissolves in water; any salt formed by this ion and another chemical element, usually a metal.

carbon cycle sequence by which ◊carbon circulates and is recycled through the natural world. The carbon element from carbon dioxide, released into the atmosphere by living things as a result of ◊respiration, is taken up by plants during ◊photosynthesis and converted into carbohydrates; the oxygen component is released back into the atmosphere. Some of this carbon becomes locked up in coal and petroleum and other sediments. The simplest link in the carbon cycle occurs when an animal eats a plant and carbon is transferred from, say, a leaf cell to the animal body. Today, the carbon cycle is in danger of being disrupted by the increased consumption and burning of fossil fuels, and the burning of large tracts of tropical forests, as a result of which levels of carbon dioxide are

building up in the atmosphere and probably contributing to the ◊greenhouse effect.

carbon dioxide CO_2 colourless, odourless gas, slightly soluble in water and denser than air. It is formed by the complete oxidation of carbon.

Carboniferous period of geological time 363–290 million years ago, the fifth period of the Palaeozoic era. In the USA it is divided into two periods: the Mississippian (lower) and the Pennsylvanian (upper). Typical of the lower-Carboniferous rocks are shallow-water ◊limestones, while upper-Carboniferous rocks have ◊delta deposits with ◊coal (hence the name). Amphibians were abundant, and reptiles evolved during this period.

carbon monoxide CO colourless, odourless gas formed when carbon is oxidized in a limited supply of air. It is a poisonous constituent of car exhaust fumes, forming a stable compound with haemoglobin in the blood, thus preventing the haemoglobin from transporting oxygen to the body tissues.

carcinogen any agent that increases the chance of a cell becoming cancerous (see ◊cancer), including various chemical compounds, some viruses, X-rays, and other forms of ionizing radiation.

carcinoma malignant ◊tumour arising from the skin, the glandular tissues, or the mucous membranes that line the gut and lungs.

Cardiff (Welsh *Caerdydd*) seaport and capital of Wales (from 1955) and administrative headquarters of South and Mid Glamorgan, at the mouth of the Taff, Rhymney, and Ely rivers; population (1991) 270,100.

cardinal in the Roman Catholic church, the highest rank next to the pope. Cardinals act as an advisory body to the pope and elect him. Their red hat is the badge of office. The number of cardinals has varied; there were 151 in 1989.

cardinal number in mathematics, one of the series of numbers 0, 1, 2, 3, 4, ... Cardinal numbers relate to quantity, whereas ordinal numbers (first, second, third, fourth, ...) relate to order.

Carey George Leonard 1935– . 103rd archbishop of Canterbury from 1991. A product of a liberal evangelical background, he was appointed bishop of Bath and Wells 1987.

Caribbean Sea western part of the Atlantic Ocean between the southern coast of North America and the northern coasts of South America. Central America is to the W and the West Indies are the islands within the sea, which is about 2,740 km/1,700 mi long and 650–1,500 km/400–900 mi wide. It is from here that the ◊Gulf Stream turns towards Europe.

Carlow county of the Republic of Ireland, in the province of Leinster; county town Carlow; area 900 sq km/347 sq mi; population (1991) 40,900. Mostly flat except for mountains in the S, the land is fertile, and well suited to dairy farming.

Carlyle Thomas 1795–1881. Scottish essayist and social historian. His works include *Sartor Resartus* 1833–34, describing his loss of Christian belief; *The French Revolution* 1837; the pamphlet *Chartism* 1839, attacking the doctrine of *laissez-faire*, *Past and Present* 1843, the notable *Letters and Speeches of Cromwell* 1845, and the miniature life of his friend John Sterling 1851.

carnivore mammal of the order Carnivora. Although its name describes the flesh-eating ancestry of the order, it includes pandas, which are herbivorous, and civet cats that eat fruit.

Carpathian Mountains central European mountain system, forming a semicircle through Slovakia–Poland–Ukraine–Moldova–Romania, 1,450 km/900 mi long. The central *Tatra Mountains* on the Slovak–Polish frontier include the highest peak, Gerlachovka, 2,663 m/8,737 ft.

carpel female reproductive unit in flowering plants (◊angiosperms). It usually comprises an ◊ovary containing one or more ovules, the stalk or style, and a stigma at its top which receives the pollen. A flower may have one or more carpels, and they may be separate or fused together. Collectively the carpels of a flower are known as the gynoecium.

Carreras José 1947– . Spanish operatic tenor. His comprehensive repertoire includes Handel's Samson and whose recordings include *West Side Story* 1984 under Leonard Bernstein. His vocal presence, charmingly insinuating rather than forceful, is favoured for Italian and French romantic roles.

Carroll Lewis. Pen name of Charles Lutwidge Dodgson 1832–1898. English author. He is best known for the children's classics *Alice's Adventures in Wonderland* 1865 and its sequel *Through the Looking-Glass* 1872. Among later works was the mock-heroic 'nonsense' poem *The Hunting of the Snark* 1876.

carrot hardy European biennial *Daucus carota* of the family Umbelliferae. Cultivated since the 16th century for its edible root, it has a high sugar content and also contains carotene, which is converted by the human liver to vitamin A.

Carthage ancient Phoenician port in N Africa founded by colonists from Tyre in the late 9th century BC; it lay 16 km/10 mi N of Tunis, Tunisia. A leading trading centre, it was in conflict with Greece from the 6th century BC, and then with Rome, and was destroyed by Roman forces 146 BC at the end of the ▷Punic Wars. About 45 BC, Roman colonists settled in Carthage, and it became the wealthy capital of the province of Africa. After its capture by the Vandals AD 439 it was little more than a pirate stronghold. From 533 it formed part of the Byzantine Empire until its final destruction by Arabs 698, during their conquest in the name of Islam.

Cartier-Bresson Henri 1908– . French photographer. He is considered one of the greatest photographic artists. His documentary work was shot in black and white, using a small-format Leica camera. His work is remarkable for its tightly structured composition and his ability to capture the decisive moment. He was a founder member of the Magnum photographic agency.

cartilage flexible bluish-white connective tissue made up of the protein collagen. In cartilaginous fish it forms the skeleton; in other vertebrates it forms the greater part of the embryonic skeleton, and is replaced by ▷bone in the course of development, except in areas of wear such as bone endings, and the discs between the backbones. It also forms structural tissue in the larynx, nose, and external ear of mammals.

Casablanca (Arabic *Dar el-Beida*) port, commercial and industrial centre on the Atlantic coast of Morocco; population (1982) 2,139,000. The Great Hassan II Mosque, completed 1989, is the world's largest; it is built on a platform (40,000 sq m/430,000 sq ft) jutting out over the Atlantic, with walls 60 m/200 ft high, topped by a hydraulic sliding roof, and a minaret 175 m/574 ft high.

cash crop crop grown solely for sale rather than for the farmer's own use, for example, coffee, cotton, or sugar beet. Many Third World countries grow cash crops to meet their debt repayments rather than grow food for their own people. The price for these crops depends on financial interests, such as those of the multinational companies and the International Monetary Fund.

Caspian Sea world's largest inland sea, divided between Iran, Azerbaijan, Russia, Kazakhstan, and Turkmenistan; area about 400,000 sq km/155,000 sq mi, with a maximum depth of 1,000 m/3,250 ft. The chief ports are Astrakhan and Baku. Drainage in the N and damming of the Volga and Ural rivers for hydroelectric power left the sea approximately 28 m/90 ft below sea level. In June 1991 opening of sluices in the dams caused the water level to rise dramatically, threatening towns and industrial areas.

Cassius (Gaius Cassius Longinus) Roman soldier, one of the conspirators who killed Julius ▷Caesar 44 BC. He fought with Pompey against Caesar, and was pardoned after the battle of Pharsalus 48, but became a leader in the conspiracy of 44. After Caesar's death he joined Brutus, and committed suicide after their defeat at Philippi 42.

caste stratification of Hindu society into four main groups: *Brahmans* (priests), *Kshatriyas* (nobles and warriors), *Vaisyas* (traders and farmers), and

Sudras (servants); plus a fifth group, *Harijan* (untouchables). No upward or downward mobility exists, as in classed societies. The system dates from ancient times, and there are more than 3,000 subdivisions.

Castile kingdom founded in the 10th century, occupying the central plateau of Spain. Its union with Aragon 1479, based on the marriage of Ferdinand and Isabella, effected the foundation of the Spanish state, which at the time was occupied and ruled by the ◊Moors. The area now forms the regions of Castilla–León and Castilla–La Mancha.

cast iron cheap but invaluable constructional material, most commonly used for car engine blocks. Cast iron is partly refined pig (crude) ◊iron, which is very fluid when molten and highly suitable for shaping by casting; it contains too many impurities (for example, carbon) to be readily shaped in any other way. Solid cast iron is heavy and can absorb great shock but is very brittle.

Castries port and capital of St Lucia, on the northwest coast of the island in the Caribbean; population (1988) 53,000.

Castro (Ruz) Fidel 1927– . Cuban communist politician, prime minister 1959–76 and president from 1976. He led two unsuccessful coups against the right-wing Batista regime and led the revolution that overthrew the dictator 1959. He raised the standard of living for most Cubans but dealt harshly with dissenters. From 1990, deprived of the support of the USSR and experiencing the long-term effects of a US trade embargo, Castro faced increasing pressure for reform.

cat small, domesticated, carnivorous mammal *Felis catus*, often kept as a pet or for catching small pests such as rodents. Found in many colour variants, it may have short, long, or no hair, but the general shape and size is constant. All cats walk on the pads of their toes, and have retractile claws. They have strong limbs, large eyes, and acute hearing. The canine teeth are long and well-developed, as are the shearing teeth in the side of the mouth.

Catalan member of the Romance branch of the Indo- European language family, an Iberian language closely related to Provençal in France. It is spoken in Catalonia in NE Spain, the Balearic Islands, Andorra, and a corner of SW France.

Catalonia (Spanish *Cataluña*, Catalan *Catalunya*) autonomous region of NE Spain; area 31,900 sq km/12,313 sq mi; population (1986) 5,977,000. It includes Barcelona (the capital), Gerona, Lérida, and Tarragona.

catalyst substance that alters the speed of, or makes possible, a chemical or biochemical reaction but remains unchanged at the end of the reaction. ◊Enzymes are natural biochemical catalysts. In practice most catalysts are used to speed up reactions.

catalytic converter device fitted to the exhaust system of a motor vehicle in order to reduce toxic emissions from the engine. It converts harmful exhaust products to relatively harmless ones by passing the exhaust gases over a mixture of catalysts.

cataract eye disease in which the crystalline lens or its capsule becomes cloudy, causing blindness.

catastrophe theory mathematical theory developed by René Thom in 1972, in which he showed that the growth of an organism proceeds by a series of gradual changes that are triggered by, and in turn trigger, large-scale changes or 'catastrophic' jumps. It also has applications in engineering – for example, the gradual strain on the structure of a bridge that can eventually result in a sudden collapse – and has been extended to economic and psychological events.

cathedral principal church of a bishop or archbishop, containing his throne which is usually situated on the south side of the choir. A cathedral is governed by a dean and chapter.

Catherine (II) the Great 1729–1796. Empress of Russia from 1762, and daughter of the German prince of Anhalt-Zerbst. Married to Tsar Peter III from 1745, she ruled alone after he was murdered in 1762. She extended Russia's boundaries to include territory gained from wars with the Turks 1768–74, 1787–92, and from the partitions of Poland 1772, 1793, and 1795, and established hegemony over the Black Sea.

Catherine de' Medici 1519–1589. French queen consort of Henry II, whom she married 1533; daughter of Lorenzo de' Medici, Duke of Urbino; and mother of Francis II, Charles IX, and Henry III. She became regent 1560–63 for Charles IX and remained in power until his death 1574.

Catherine of Aragon 1485–1536. First queen of Henry VIII of England, 1509–33, and mother of Mary I. Catherine had married Henry's elder brother Prince Arthur 1501 and on his death 1502 was betrothed to Henry, marrying him on his accession. She failed to produce a male heir and Henry divorced her without papal approval, thus creating the basis for the English ◊Reformation.

cathode in chemistry, the negative electrode of an electrolytic ◊cell, towards which positive particles (cations), usually in solution, are attracted. See ◊electrolysis.

cathode-ray tube vacuum tube in which a beam of electrons is produced and focused onto a fluorescent screen. It is an essential component of television receivers, computer visual display units, and oscilloscopes.

CAT scan or *CT scan* (acronym for *computerized axial tomography*) sophisticated method of X-ray imaging. Quick and noninvasive, CAT scanning is used in medicine as an aid to diagnosis, helping to pinpoint problem areas without the need for exploratory surgery. It is also used in archaeology to investigate mummies.

Catullus Gaius Valerius *c.* 84–54 BC. Roman lyric poet. He wrote in a variety of metres and forms, from short narratives and hymns to epigrams. Born in Verona, N Italy, he moved with ease through the literary and political society of late republican Rome. His love affair with the woman he called Lesbia provided the inspiration for many of his poems.

Caucasus series of mountain ranges between the Caspian and Black seas, in the republics of Russia, Georgia, Armenia, and Azerbaijan; 1,200 km/750 mi long. The highest peak is Elbruz, 5,633 m/18,480 ft.

cavalier horseman of noble birth, but mainly used to describe a male supporter of Charles I in the English Civil War (Cavalier), typically with courtly dress and long hair (as distinct from a Roundhead); also a supporter of Charles II after the Restoration.

Cavour Camillo Benso di, Count 1810–1861. Italian nationalist politician, a leading figure in the Italian ⟩*Risorgimento*. As prime minister of Piedmont 1852–59 and 1860–61, he enlisted the support of Britain and France for the concept of a united Italy, achieved 1861; after expelling the Austrians 1859, he assisted Garibaldi in liberating southern Italy 1860.

Caxton William *c.* 1422–1491. The first English printer. He learned the art of printing in Cologne, Germany, 1471 and set up a press in Belgium where he produced the first book printed in English, his own version of a French romance, *Recuyell of the Historyes of Troye* 1474. Returning to England 1476, he established himself in London, where he produced the first book printed in England, *Dictes or Sayengis of the Philosophres* 1477.

Cayenne capital and chief port of French Guiana, on Cayenne Island, NE South America, at the mouth of the river Cayenne; population (1990) 41,700.

Cayman Islands British island group in the West Indies; *area* 260 sq km/100 sq mi; *features* comprises three low-lying islands: Grand Cayman, Cayman Brac, and Little Cayman; *population* (1988) 22,000; *language* English.

CD-ROM (abbreviation for *compact-disc read-only memory*) computer storage device developed from the technology of the audio ⟩compact disc. It consists of a plastic-coated metal disc, on which binary digital information is etched in the form of microscopic pits. This can then be read optically by passing a light beam over the disc. CD-ROMs typically hold about 550 ⟩megabytes of data, and are used in distributing large amounts of text and graphics, such as encyclopedias, catalogues, and technical manuals.

Ceauşescu Nicolae 1918–1989. Romanian politician, leader of the Romanian Communist Party (RCP), in power 1965–89. With his wife *Elena*, he governed in a severely repressive manner, zealously implementing schemes that impoverished the nation. The Ceauşescus were overthrown in a bloody revolutionary coup Dec 1989 and executed.

Cebu chief city and port of the island of Cebu in the Philippines; population (1990) 610,400; area of the island 5,086 sq km/1,964 sq mi. The oldest city of the Philippines, Cebu was founded as San Miguel 1565 and became the capital of the Spanish Philippines.

cell in biology, a discrete, membrane-bound portion of living matter, the smallest unit capable of an independent existence. All living organisms consist of one or more cells, with the exception of ⟩viruses. Bacteria, protozoa, and many other microorganisms consist of single cells, whereas a human is made up of billions of cells. Essential features of a cell are the membrane, which encloses it and restricts the flow of substances in and out; the jellylike material within, the ⟩cytoplasm; the ⟩ribosomes, which carry out protein synthesis; and the ⟩DNA, which forms the hereditary material.

cell, electrical or *voltaic cell* or *galvanic cell* device in which chemical energy is converted into electrical energy; the popular name is ▷'battery', but this actually refers to a collection of cells in one unit. The reactive chemicals of a *primary cell* cannot be replenished, whereas *secondary cells* – such as storage batteries – are rechargeable: their chemical reactions can be reversed and the original condition restored by applying an electric current. It is dangerous to attempt to recharge a primary cell.

Cellini Benvenuto 1500–1571. Italian sculptor and goldsmith. Among his works are a graceful bronze *Perseus* 1545–54 (Loggia dei Lanzi, Florence) and a celebrated gold salt cellar made for Francis I of France 1540–43 (Kunsthistorisches Museum, Vienna), topped by nude reclining figures.

cello common abbreviation for *violoncello*, tenor member of the ▷violin family and fourth member of the string quartet. Its solo potential was recognized by J S Bach, and a concerto repertoire extends from Haydn and Boccherini to Dvořák, Elgar, Britten, Ligeti, and Lukas Foss.

cellular phone or *cellphone* mobile radio telephone, one of a network connected to the telephone system by a computer-controlled communication system. Service areas are divided into small 'cells', about 5 km/3 mi across, each with a separate low-power transmitter.

celluloid transparent or translucent, highly flammable, plastic material (a thermoplastic) made from cellulose nitrate and camphor. It was once used for toilet articles, novelties, and photographic film, but has now been replaced by the nonflammable substance cellulose acetate.

cellulose complex ▷carbohydrate composed of long chains of glucose units. It is the principal constituent of the cell wall of higher plants, and a vital ingredient in the diet of many ▷herbivores. Molecules of cellulose are organized into long, unbranched microfibrils that give support to the cell wall. No mammal produces the enzyme (cellulase) necessary for digesting cellulose; mammals such as rabbits and cows are only able to digest grass because the bacteria present in their gut manufacture the appropriate enzyme.

Celsius scale of temperature, previously called centigrade, in which the range from freezing to boiling of water is divided into 100 degrees, freezing point being 0 degrees and boiling point 100 degrees.

Celt member of an Indo-European people that originated in Alpine Europe and spread to the Iberian peninsula and beyond. They were ironworkers and farmers. In the 1st century BC they were defeated by the Roman Empire and by Germanic tribes and confined largely to Britain, Ireland, and N France.

Celtic languages branch of the Indo-European family, divided into two groups: the *Brythonic* or *P-Celtic* (Welsh, Cornish, Breton, and Gaulish) and the *Goidelic* or *Q-Celtic* (Irish, Scottish, and Manx Gaelic). Celtic languages once stretched from the Black Sea to Britain, but have been in decline for centuries, limited to the so-called 'Celtic fringe' of western Europe.

Cenozoic or *Caenozoic* era of geological time that began 65 million years ago and is still in process. It is divided into the Tertiary and Quaternary periods. The Cenozoic marks the emergence of mammals as a dominant group, including humans, and the formation of the mountain chains of the Himalayas and the Alps.

centigrade former name for the ⏵Celsius temperature scale.

Central region of Scotland; *area* 2,600 sq km/1,004 sq mi; *features* Stirling Castle; field of Bannockburn; Loch Lomond; the Trossachs; *population* (1991) 267,500.

Central African Republic (*République Centrafricaine*); *area* 622,436 sq km/240,260 sq mi; *capital* Bangui; *environment* an estimated 87% of the urban population is without access to safe drinking water; *features* Kotto and Mbali river falls; the Oubangui River rises 6 m/20 ft at Bangui during the wet season (June–Nov); *political system* emergent democratic republic; *population* (1993 est) 3,200,000 (more than 80 ethnic groups); growth rate 2.3% p.a.; *languages* Sangho (national), French (official), Arabic, Hunsa, and Swahili; *religions* Protestant 25%, Roman Catholic 25%, Muslim 10%, animist 10%.

Central America the part of the Americas that links Mexico with the Isthmus of Panama, comprising Belize, Costa Rica, El Salvador, Guatemala, Honduras, Nicaragua, and Panama. It is also an isthmus, crossed by mountains that form part of the Cordilleras, rising to a maximum height of 4,220 m/13,845 ft. There are numerous active volcanoes. Central America is about 523,000 sq km/200,000 sq mi in area and has a population (1980) estimated at 22,700,000, mostly Indians or mestizos (of mixed white-Indian ancestry).

Central Asian Republics group of five republics: ⏵Kazakhstan, ⏵Kyrgyzstan, ⏵Tajikistan, ⏵Turkmenistan, and ⏵Uzbekistan. They were part of the Soviet Union until their independence was recognized 1991. They comprise a large part of the geographical region of Turkestan and are the home of large numbers of Muslims.

Central Intelligence Agency (CIA) US intelligence organization established 1947. It has actively intervened overseas, generally to undermine left-wing regimes or to protect US financial interests; for example, in the Congo (now Zaire) and Nicaragua. From 1980 all covert activity by the CIA had by law to be reported to Congress, preferably beforehand, and to be authorized by the president. Robert James Woolsey became CIA director 1993. In 1994 the CIA's estimated budget was around $3.1 billion.

Central Lowlands one of the three geographical divisions of Scotland, occupying the fertile and densely populated plain that lies between two geological fault lines, which run nearly parallel NE–SW across Scotland from Stonehaven to Dumbarton and from Dunbar to Girvan.

central nervous system (CNS) the brain and spinal cord, as distinct from other components of the ⏵nervous system. The CNS integrates all nervous function.

central processing unit (CPU) main component of a computer, the part that executes individual program instructions and controls the operation of other parts. It is sometimes called the central processor or, when contained on a single integrated circuit, a microprocessor.

centrifugal force useful concept in physics, based on an apparent (but not real) force. It may be regarded as a force that acts radially outward from a spinning or orbiting object, thus balancing the ▷centripetal force (which is real). For an object of mass m moving with a velocity v in a circle of radius r, the centrifugal force F equals mv^2/r (outward).

centripetal force force that acts radially inward on an object moving in a curved path. For example, with a weight whirled in a circle at the end of a length of string, the centripetal force is the tension in the string. For an object of mass m moving with a velocity v in a circle of radius r, the centripetal force F equals mv^2/r (inward). The reaction to this force is the ▷centrifugal force.

cephalopod any predatory marine mollusc of the class Cephalopoda, with the mouth and head surrounded by tentacles. Cephalopods are the most intelligent, the fastest- moving, and the largest of all animals without backbones, and there are remarkable luminescent forms which swim or drift at great depths. They have the most highly developed nervous and sensory systems of all invertebrates, the eye in some closely paralleling that found in vertebrates. Examples include octopus, squid, and cuttlefish.

ceramics objects made from clay, hardened into a permanent form by baking (firing) at very high temperatures in a kiln. Ceramics are used for building construction and decoration (bricks, tiles), for specialist industrial uses (linings for furnaces used to manufacture steel, fuel elements in nuclear reactors, and so on), and for plates and vessels used in the home. Different types of clay and different methods and temperatures of firing create a variety of results. Ceramics may be cast in a mould or hand-built out of slabs of clay, coiled, or thrown on a wheel. Technically, the main categories are earthenware, stoneware, and hard- and softpaste porcelain (see under ▷pottery and porcelain).

cereal grass grown for its edible, nutrient-rich, starchy seeds. The term refers primarily to wheat, oats, rye, and barley, but may also refer to maize (corn), millet, and rice. Cereals contain about 75% complex carbohydrates and 10% protein, plus fats and fibre (roughage). They store well. If all the world's cereal crop were consumed as whole-grain products directly by humans, everyone could obtain adequate protein and carbohydrate; however, a large proportion of cereal production in affluent nations is used as animal feed to boost the production of meat, dairy products, and eggs.

Cervantes Saavedra, Miguel de 1547–1616. Spanish novelist, playwright, and poet. His masterpiece *Don Quixote* (in full *El ingenioso hidalgo Don Quixote de la Mancha*) was published 1605. In 1613, his *Novelas ejemplares/Exemplary Novels* appeared, followed by *Viaje del Parnaso/The Voyage to Parnassus* 1614. His second part of *Don Quixote* appeared 1615.

cervical smear removal of a small sample of tissue from the cervix (neck of the womb) to screen for changes implying a likelihood of cancer.

Cézanne Paul 1839–1906. French Post-Impressionist painter. He was a leading figure in the development of modern art. He broke away from the Impressionists' concern with the ever-changing effects of light to develop a style that tried to capture the structure of natural forms, whether in landscapes, still lifes, or portraits. *Cardplayers* about 1890–95 (Louvre, Paris) is typical of his work.

c.g.s. system system of units based on the centimetre, gram, and second, as units of length, mass, and time respectively. It has been replaced for scientific work by the ◊SI units to avoid inconsistencies in definition of the thermal calorie and electrical quantities.

Chad Republic of (*République du Tchad*); *area* 1,284,000 sq km/495,624 sq mi; *capital* Ndjamena (formerly Fort Lamy); *political system* emergent democratic republic; *population* (1993) 6,290,000; growth rate 2.3% p.a. Nomadic tribes move N–S seasonally in search of water; *languages* French, Arabic (both official), over 100 African languages spoken; *religions* Muslim 44% (N), Christian 33%, animist 23% (S).

Chadwick James 1891–1974. British physicist. In 1932 he discovered the particle in the nucleus of an atom that became known as the neutron because it has no electric charge. He received the Nobel Prize for Physics 1935.

Chagall Marc 1887–1985. Russian-born French painter and designer. Much of his highly coloured, fantastic imagery was inspired by village life and Jewish and Russian folk traditions. He designed stained glass, mosaics (for Israel's Knesset in the 1960s), the ceiling of the Paris Opera House 1964, tapestries, and stage sets. He is often seen as a precursor of Surrealism, as in *I and the Village* 1911 (Museum of Modern Art, New York).

chain reaction in nuclear physics, a fission reaction that is maintained because neutrons released by the splitting of some atomic nuclei themselves go on to split others, releasing even more neutrons. Such a reaction can be controlled (as in a nuclear reactor) by using moderators to absorb excess neutrons. Uncontrolled, a chain reaction produces a nuclear explosion (as in an atom bomb).

chalk soft, fine-grained, whitish rock composed of calcium carbonate, $CaCO_3$, extensively quarried for use in cement, lime, and mortar, and in the manufacture of cosmetics and toothpaste. *Blackboard chalk* in fact consists of gypsum (calcium sulphate, $CaSO_4$).

Chamberlain (Arthur) Neville 1869–1940. British Conservative politician, son of Liberal MP Joseph Chamberlain (1836–1914) and brother of Austen Chamberlain. He was prime minister 1937–40; his policy of appeasement toward the fascist dictators Mussolini and Hitler (with whom he concluded the ◊Munich Agreement 1938) failed to prevent the outbreak of World War II. He resigned 1940 following the defeat of the British forces in Norway.

Chamberlain (Joseph) Austen 1863–1937. British conservative politician; as foreign secretary 1924–29 he negotiated the Pact of Locarno, for which he won the Nobel Peace Prize 1925. He was the elder son of Liberal MP Joseph Chamberlain (1836–1914).

chamber music music intended for performance in a small room or chamber, rather than in the concert hall, and usually written for instrumental combinations, played with one instrument to a part, as in the string quartet.

Chamorro Violeta Barrios de *c.* 1939– . President of Nicaragua from 1990. With strong US support, she was elected to be the candidate for the National Opposition Union (UNO) 1989, winning the presidency from David Ortega Saavedra Feb 1990 and thus ending the period of ▷Sandinista rule.

Champagne-Ardenne region of NE France; area 25,600 sq km/9,882 sq mi; population (1986) 1,353,000. Its capital is Reims, and it comprises the *départements* of Ardennes, Aube, Marne, and Haute-Marne. It has sheep and dairy farming and vineyards.

Chancery in the UK, a division of the High Court that deals with such matters as the administration of the estates of deceased persons, the execution of trusts, the enforcement of sales of land, and foreclosure of mortgages. Before reorganization of the court system 1875, it administered the rules of equity as distinct from ▷common law.

Chandigarh city of N India, in the foothills of the Himalayas; population (1981) 421,000. It is also a union territory; area 114 sq km/44 sq mi; population (1991) 640,725. Planned by the architect Le Corbusier, the city was inaugurated 1953 to replace Lahore (capital of British Punjab), which went to Pakistan under partition 1947. Since 1966, when Chandigarh became a Union Territory, it has been the capital city of both Haryana and Punjab, until a new capital is built for the former.

Chandler Raymond 1888–1959. US novelist. He turned the pulp detective mystery form into a successful genre of literature and created the quintessential private eye in the tough but chivalric loner, Philip Marlowe. Marlowe is the narrator of such books as *The Big Sleep* 1939 (filmed 1946), *Farewell My Lovely* 1940 (filmed 1944), and *The Long Goodbye* 1954 (filmed 1975).

Chang Jiang or *Yangtze Kiang* longest river of China, flowing about 6,300 km/3,900 mi from Tibet to the Yellow Sea. It is a main commercial waterway.

Channel Islands group of islands in the English Channel, off the northwest coast of France; they are a possession of the British crown. They comprise the islands of Jersey, Guernsey, Alderney, Great and Little Sark, with the lesser Herm, Brechou, Jethou, and Lihou.

Channel Tunnel tunnel built beneath the ▷English Channel, linking Britain with mainland Europe. It comprises twin rail tunnels, 50 km/31 mi long and 7.3 m/24 ft in diameter, located 40 m/130 ft beneath the seabed. Specially designed shuttle trains carrying cars and lorries will run between terminals at Folkestone, Kent, and Sangatte, W of Calais, France. Work began 1986, and the French and English sections were linked Dec 1990. It was officially opened 6 May 1994.

chaos theory or *chaology* branch of mathematics used to deal with chaotic systems – for example, an engineered structure, such as an oil platform, that is subjected to irregular, unpredictable wave stress.

Chaplin Charlie (Charles Spencer) 1889–1977. English film actor and director. He made his reputation as a tramp with a smudge moustache, bowler hat, and twirling cane in silent comedies from the mid-1910s, including *The Rink* 1916, *The Kid* 1920, and *The Gold Rush* 1925. His later films combine dialogue with mime and music, as in *The Great Dictator* 1940 and *Limelight* 1952.

charcoal black, porous form of ◊carbon, produced by heating wood or other organic materials in the absence of air. It is used as a fuel in the smelting of metals such as copper and zinc, and by artists for making black line drawings.

Chardin Jean-Baptiste-Siméon 1699–1779. French painter. He took as his subjects naturalistic still lifes and quiet domestic scenes that recall the Dutch tradition. His work is a complete contrast to that of his contemporaries, the Rococo painters.

charge-coupled device (CCD) device for forming images electronically, using a layer of silicon that releases electrons when struck by incoming light. The electrons are stored in ◊pixels and read off into a computer at the end of the exposure. CCDs have now almost entirely replaced photographic film for applications such as astrophotography where extreme sensitivity to light is paramount.

Charlemagne (Charles [I] the Great) 742–814. King of the Franks from 768 and Holy Roman emperor from 800. By inheritance (his father was ◊Pepin the Short) and extensive campaigns of conquest, he united most of W Europe by 804, when after 30 years of war the Saxons came under his control. He reformed the legal, judicial, and military systems; established schools; and promoted Christianity, commerce, agriculture, arts, and literature. In his capital, Aachen, scholars gathered from all over Europe.

Charles (full name Charles Philip Arthur George) 1948– . Prince of the UK, heir to the British throne, and Prince of Wales since 1958 (invested 1969). He is the first-born child of Queen Elizabeth II and the Duke of Edinburgh. He studied at Trinity College, Cambridge, 1967–70, before serving in the Royal Air Force and Royal Navy. The first royal heir since 1659 to have an English wife, he married Lady Diana Spencer, daughter of the 8th Earl Spencer, 1981. They have two sons and heirs, William (1982–) and Henry (1984–). Amid much publicity, Charles and Diana separated 1992.

Charles I 1600–1649. King of Great Britain and Ireland from 1625, son of James I of England (James VI of Scotland). He accepted the petition of right 1628 but then dissolved Parliament and ruled without a parliament 1629–40. After the collapse of the Short and Long Parliaments of 1640, Charles declared war on Parliament 1642 but surrendered 1646 and was beheaded 1649. He was the father of Charles II.

Charles II 1630–1685. King of Great Britain and Ireland from 1660, when Parliament accepted the restoration of the monarchy after the collapse of Cromwell's Commonwealth; son of Charles I. His plans to restore Catholicism in Britain led to war with the Netherlands 1672–74 in support of Louis XIV of France and a break with Parliament, which he dissolved 1681. He was succeeded by James II.

Charles V 1500–1558. Holy Roman emperor 1519–56. Son of Philip of Burgundy and Joanna of Castile, he inherited vast possessions, which led to rivalry from Francis I of France, whose alliance with the Ottoman Empire brought Vienna under siege 1529 and 1532. Charles was also in conflict with the Protestants in Germany until the

Treaty of Passau 1552, which allowed the Lutherans religious liberty.

Charles Edward Stuart the *Young Pretender* or *Bonnie Prince Charlie* 1720–88. British prince, grandson of James II and son of James, the Old Pretender. In the Jacobite rebellion 1745 Charles won the support of the Scottish Highlanders; his army invaded England to claim the throne, but was routed at Culloden 1746. Charles went into exile.

Charlotte Amalie capital, tourist resort, and free port of the US Virgin Islands, on the island of St Thomas; population (1980) 11,756. Boatbuilding and rum distilling are among the economic activities. It was founded 1672 by the Danish West India Company.

Chartism radical British democratic movement, mainly of the working classes, which flourished around 1838–48. It derived its name from the People's Charter, a six-point programme comprising universal male suffrage, equal electoral districts, secret ballot, annual parliaments, and abolition of the property qualification for, and payment of, members of Parliament.

Chateaubriand François René, vicomte de 1768–1848. French writer. He was a founder of Romanticism. In exile from the French Revolution 1794–99, he wrote *Atala* 1801 (based on his encounters with North American Indians) and the autobiographical *René*, which formed part of *Le Génie du Christianisme/The Genius of Christianity* 1802. He later wrote *Mémoires d'outre tombe/Memoirs from Beyond the Tomb* 1848–50.

Chaucer Geoffrey *c.* 1340–1400. English poet. *The Canterbury Tales*, a collection of stories told by a group of

pilgrims on their way to Canterbury, reveals his knowledge of human nature and his stylistic variety, from urbane and ironic to simple and bawdy. Early allegorical poems, including *The Book of the Duchess*, were influenced by French poems like the *Roman de la Rose*. His *Troilus and Criseyde* is a substantial narrative poem about the tragic betrayal of an idealized courtly love.

Checheno-Ingush autonomous republic in S Russia, on the northern slopes of the Caucasus Mountains; *area 19,000 km/7,350 sq mi*; *capital* Grozny; *population* (1986) 1,230,000 including 53% Chechens, 12% Ingushes. In 1994 thousands were killed when Russian troops were sent in by President Yeltsin to quell demands for secession.

cheetah large wild cat *Acinonyx jubatus* native to Africa, Arabia, and SW Asia, but now rare in some areas. Yellowish with black spots, it has a slim lithe build. It is up to 1 m/3 ft tall at the shoulder, and up to 1.5 m/5 ft long. It can reach 110 kph/70 mph, but tires after about 400 yards. Cheetahs live in open country where they hunt small antelopes, hares, and birds.

Chekhov Anton (Pavlovich) 1860–1904. Russian dramatist and writer of short stories. His plays concentrate on the creation of atmosphere and delineation of internal development, rather than external action. His first play, *Ivanov* 1887, was a failure, as was *The Seagull* 1896 until revived by Stanislavsky 1898 at the Moscow Art Theatre, for which Chekhov went on to write his finest plays: *Uncle Vanya* 1897, *The Three Sisters* 1901, and *The Cherry Orchard* 1904.

chemical warfare use in war of gaseous, liquid, or solid substances intended to have a toxic effect on humans, animals, or plants. Together with biological warfare, it was banned by the Geneva Protocol 1925 and the United Nations in 1989 also voted for a ban. In Jan 1993, over 120 nations, including the USA and Russia, signed a treaty outlawing the manufacture, stockpiling, and use of chemical weapons.

chemistry science concerned with the composition of matter (gas, liquid, or solid) and of the changes that take place in it under certain conditions.

chemosynthesis method of making ▷protoplasm (contents of a cell) using the energy from chemical reactions, in contrast to the use of light energy employed for the same purpose in ▷photosynthesis. The process is used by certain bacteria, which can synthesize organic compounds from carbon dioxide and water using the energy from special methods of ▷respiration.

chemotherapy any medical treatment with chemicals. It usually refers to treatment of cancer with cytotoxic and other drugs. The term was coined by the German bacteriologist Paul Ehrlich for the use of synthetic chemicals against infectious diseases.

Chernobyl town in central Ukraine; site of a nuclear power station. In April 1986 two huge explosions destroyed a central reactor at the station. In the immediate vicinity of Chernobyl, 31 people died (all firemen or workers at the plant) and 135,000 were permanently evacuated because of the serious dangers to health caused by the nuclear fallout. It has been estimated that there will be an additional 20–40,000 deaths from cancer in the next 60 years as a result of long-term exposure to radiation.

Chesapeake Bay largest of the inlets on the Atlantic coast of the USA, bordered by Maryland and Virginia. It is about 320 km/200 mi in length and 6–64 km/4–40 mi in width.

Cheshire county of NW England; *area* 2,320 sq km/896 sq mi; *towns and cities* Chester (administrative headquarters), Warrington, Crewe, Widnes, Macclesfield, Congleton; *features* Pennines in the E; salt mines and geologically rich former copper workings at Alderley Edge; Little Moreton Hall; discovery of Lindow Man, the first 'bogman' to be found in mainland Britain, dating from around 500 BC; *population* (1991) 956,600.

chess board game originating as early as the 2nd century AD. Two players use 16 pieces each, on a board of 64 squares of alternating colour, to try to force the opponent into a position where the main piece (the king) is threatened and cannot move to another position without remaining threatened.

Chesterton G(ilbert) K(eith) 1874–1936. English novelist, essayist, and poet. He wrote numerous short stories featuring a Catholic priest, Father Brown, who solves crimes by drawing on his knowledge of human nature. Other novels include the fantastic *The Napoleon of Notting Hill* 1904 and *The Man Who Was Thursday* 1908, a deeply emotional allegory about the problem of evil.

chestnut tree of the genus *Castanea*, belonging to the beech family Fagaceae. The Spanish or sweet chestnut *C. sativa* produces edible nuts inside husks; its timber is also valuable. Horse chestnuts are quite distinct, belonging to the genus *Aesculus*, family Hippocastanaceae.

Chetnik member of a Serbian nationalist group that operated underground during the German occupation of Yugoslavia in World War II. Led by Col Draza Mihailovič (1893–1946), the Chetniks initially received aid from the Allies, but this was later transferred to the communist partisans led by Tito. The term has also popularly been applied to Serb militia forces in the 1991–92 Yugoslav civil war.

Chiang Kai-shek (Pinyin *Jiang Jie Shi*) 1887–1975. Chinese nationalist ▷Guomindang (Kuomintang) general and politician, president of China 1928–31 and 1943–49, and of Taiwan from 1949, where he set up a US-supported right-wing government on his expulsion from the mainland by the communist forces.

Chicago financial and industrial city in Illinois, USA, on Lake Michigan. It is the third largest US city; population (1990) 2,783,700, metropolitan area 8,065,000.

chicken domestic fowl; see under ▷poultry.

chickenpox or *varicella* common, usually mild disease, caused by a virus of the ▷herpes group and transmitted by airborne droplets. Chickenpox chiefly attacks children under the age of ten. The incubation period is two to three weeks. One attack normally gives immunity for life.

chickpea annual plant *Cicer arietinum*, family Leguminosae, which is grown for food in India and the Middle East. Its short, hairy pods contain edible pealike seeds.

Chile Republic of (República de Chile); *area* 756,950 sq km/292,257 sq mi; *capital* Santiago; *features* Atacama Desert is one of the driest regions in the world; *political system* emergent democratic republic; *population* (1993) 13,440,000 (the majority are of European origin or are mestizos, of mixed American Indian and Spanish descent); growth rate 1.6% p.a.; *language* Spanish; *religion* Roman Catholic 89%.

chilli (North American *chili*) pod, or powder made from the pod, of a variety of ▷capsicum, *Capsicum frutescens*, a hot, red pepper. It is widely used in cooking. Capsaicin is the hot ingredient of chilli. It causes a burning sensation in the mouth by triggering nerve branches in the eyes, nose, tongue and mouth. Capsaicin has no intrinsic flavour as it does not activate taste buds. It is claimed that people may actually become physically addicted to capsaicin.

Chiluba Frederick 1943– . Zambian politician and trade unionist, president from 1991. In 1993 he was forced to declare a state of emergency, following the discovery of documents suggesting an impending coup. He later carried out a major reorganization of his cabinet but failed to silence his critics.

chimera or *chimaera* in Greek mythology, a fire-breathing animal with a lion's head, a goat's body, and a tail in the form of a snake; hence any apparent hybrid of two or more creatures. The chimera was killed by the hero Bellerophon on the winged horse Pegasus.

chimpanzee highly intelligent African ape *Pan troglodytes* that lives mainly in rain forests but sometimes in wooded savanna. Chimpanzees are covered in thin but long black body hair, except for the face, hands, and feet, which may have pink or black skin. They normally walk on all fours, supporting the front of the body on the knuckles of the fingers, but can stand or walk upright for a short distance. They can grow to 1.4 m/4.5 ft tall, and weigh up to 50 kg/110 lb. They are strong and climb well, but spend time on the ground, living in loose social groups. The bulk of the diet is fruit, with some leaves, insects, and occasional meat. Chimpanzees can use 'tools', fashioning twigs to extract termites from their nests.

China People's Republic of (*Zhonghua Renmin Gonghe Guo*); *area* 9,596,960 sq km/3,599,975 sq mi; *capital* Beijing (Peking); *features* Great Wall of China; Gezhouba Dam; Ming Tombs; Terracotta Warriors (Xi'ain); Gobi Desert; world's most populous country; *head of state* Jiang Zemin from 1993; *head of government* Li Peng from 1987; *political system* communist republic; *political party* Chinese Communist Party (CCP), Marxist-Leninist-Maoist; *population* (1993 est) 1,185,000,000 (the majority are Han or ethnic Chinese; the 67 million of other ethnic groups, including Tibetan, Uigur, and Zhuang, live in border areas). Growth rate 1.2% p.a. *languages* Chinese, including Mandarin (official), Cantonese, and other dialects; *religions* officially atheist, but traditionally Taoist, Confucianist, and Buddhist; Muslim 13 million; Catholic 3–6 million (divided between the 'patriotic' church established 1958 and the 'loyal' church subject to Rome); Protestant 3 million.

China Sea area of the Pacific Ocean bordered by China, Vietnam, Borneo, the Philippines, and Japan. Various groups of small islands and shoals, including the Paracels, 500 km/300 mi E of Vietnam, have been disputed by China and other powers because they lie in oil-rich areas.

Chinese native to or an inhabitant of China and Taiwan, or a person of Chinese descent. The Chinese comprise more than 25% of the world's population. The *Chinese language* (Mandarin) is the largest member of the Sino-Tibetan family and is spoken in China, Taiwan, Hong Kong, and Singapore. Its written form uses thousands of ideographic symbols. *Putonghua* ('common speech'), is based on the educated dialect known as Mandarin Chinese and is promoted in China as the national spoken and written language.

Chinese Revolution series of great political upheavals in China 1911–49 that eventually led to Communist Party rule and the establishment of the People's Republic of China under Mao Zedong. In 1912, a nationalist revolt overthrew the imperial Manchu dynasty. Led by Sun Yat-sen 1923–25 and by Chiang Kai-shek 1925–49, the nationalists, or Guomindang, were increasing challenged by the growing communist movement. The 10,000 km/6,000 mi *Long March* to the NW by the communists 1934–35 to escape from attacks by the Guomindang forces resulted in Mao Zedong's emergence as communist leader and the expulsion of the Guomindang to Taiwan 1949.

chip or *silicon chip* another name for an ◊integrated circuit, a complete electronic circuit on a slice of silicon (or other semiconductor) crystal only a few millimetres square.

Chippendale Thomas *c.* 1718–1779. English furniture designer. He set up his workshop in St Martin's Lane, London, 1753. His book *The Gentleman and Cabinet Maker's Director* 1754, was a significant contribution to furniture design. Although many of his most characteristic designs are Rococo, he also employed Louis XVI, Chinese, Gothic, and Neo- Classical styles. He worked mainly in mahogany.

Chişinău (Russian *Kishinev*) capital of Moldova, situated in a rich agricultural area; population (1989) 565,000. It is a commercial and cultural centre.

Chissano Joaquim 1939– . Mozambique nationalist politician, president from 1986; foreign minister 1975–86. In Oct 1992 Chissano signed a peace accord with the leader of the rebel Mozambique National Resistance (MNR) party, bringing to an end 16 years of civil war, and in 1994 won the first free presidential elections.

chitin complex long-chain compound, or ◊polymer; a nitrogenous derivative of glucose. Chitin is widely found in invertebrates. It forms the exoskeleton of insects and other arthropods. It combines with protein to form a covering that can be hard and tough, as in beetles, or soft and flexible, as in caterpillars and other insect larvae. It is insoluble in water and resistant to acids, alkalis, and many organic solvents. In crustaceans such as crabs, it is impregnated with calcium carbonate for extra strength.

chloride Cl⁻ negative ion formed when hydrogen chloride dissolves in water, and any salt containing this ion, commonly formed by the action of hydrochloric acid (HCl) on various metals or by direct combination of a metal and chlorine. Sodium chloride (NaCl) is common table salt.

chlorine greenish-yellow, gaseous, non-metallic element with a pungent odour, symbol Cl, atomic number 17, relative atomic mass 35.453. It is a member of the ◊halogen group and is widely distributed, in combination with the ◊alkali metals, as chlorates or chlorides.

chlorofluorocarbon (CFC) synthetic chemical that is odourless, nontoxic, nonflammable, and chemically inert. Their stability and apparently harmless properties made CFCs popular as ◊aerosol cans, as refrigerants in refrigerators and air conditioners, and in the manufacture of foam packaging. They are partly responsible for the destruction of the ◊ozone layer. In June 1990 representatives of 93 nations, including the UK and the USA, agreed to phase out production of CFCs and various other ozone- depleting chemicals by the end of the 20th century.

chlorophyll green pigment present in most plants; it is responsible for the absorption of light energy during ◊photosynthesis.

cholera disease caused by infection with various strains of the bacillus *Vibrio cholerae*, transmitted in contaminated water and characterized by violent diarrhoea and vomiting. It is prevalent in many tropical areas.

cholesterol white, crystalline sterol found throughout the body, especially in fats, blood, nerve tissue, and bile; it is also provided in the diet by foods such as eggs, meat, and butter. A high level of cholesterol in the blood is thought to contribute to atherosclerosis (hardening of the arteries).

Chopin Frédéric (François) 1810–1849. Polish composer and pianist. He made his debut as a pianist at the age of eight. As a performer, Chopin revolutionized the technique of pianoforte-playing, turning the hands outward and favouring a light, responsive touch. His compositions for piano, which include two concertos and other works with orchestra, are characterized by great volatility of mood, and rhythmic fluidity.

chordate animal belonging to the phylum Chordata, which includes vertebrates, sea squirts, amphioxi, and others. All these animals, at some stage of their lives, have a supporting rod of tissue (notochord or backbone) running down their bodies.

Chou En-lai alternative transliteration of ▷Zhou Enlai.

Chretien Jean 1934– . French-Canadian politician, prime minister from 1993. He won the leadership of the Liberal Party 1990 and defeated Kim Campbell in the Oct 1993 election. He is a vigorous advocate of national unity.

Christ the ▷Messiah as prophesied in the Hebrew Bible, or Old Testament.

Christianity world religion derived from the teaching of Jesus in the first third of the 1st century, with a present-day membership of about one billion. Separated according to some differences in beliefs and practice, its main denominations are the ▷Roman Catholic, Eastern Orthodox, and ▷Protestant churches. Christians believe in one God with three aspects: God the Father, God the Son (Jesus), and God the Holy Spirit. God showed his love for the world by coming to Earth as Jesus, and suffering and dying in order to be reconciled with humanity. Christians believe that three days after his death by crucifixion Jesus was raised to life by God's power, appearing many times in bodily form to his followers, and that he is now alive in the world through the Holy Spirit. Christians believe that everlasting life in God's presence is promised to those who have faith in Jesus Christ and who live according to his teaching.

Christian Science or *the Church of Christ, Scientist* sect established in the USA by Mary Baker Eddy 1879. Christian Scientists believe that since God is good and is a spirit, matter and evil are not ultimately real. Consequently they refuse all medical treatment. The church has its own daily newspaper, the *Christian Science Monitor*.

Christie Agatha Mary Clarissa (born Miller) 1890–1976. English detective novelist. She created the characters Hercule Poirot and Miss Jane Marple and wrote more than 70 novels. A number of her books have been filmed, for example *Murder on the Orient Express* 1975. Her play *The Mousetrap*, which opened in London 1952, is the longest continuously running show in the world.

Christie Linford 1960– . Jamaican-born English sprinter who, with his win in the 1993 World Championships, became the first track athlete ever to hold World, Olympic, European, and Commonwealth titles simultaneously.

Christmas Christian religious holiday, observed throughout the Western world on Dec 25 and traditionally marked by feasting and gift-giving. In the Christian church, it is the day on which the birth of Jesus is celebrated, although the actual birth date is unknown. Many of its customs have a non-Christian origin and were adapted from celebrations of the winter ▷solstice.

Christopher, St third century AD. Patron saint of travellers. His feast day, 25 July, was dropped from the Roman Catholic liturgical calendar 1969.

chromatography technique for separating or analysing a mixture of gases, liquids, or dissolved substances. This is brought about by means of two immiscible substances, one of which (*the mobile phase*) transports the sample mixture through the other (*the stationary phase*). The mobile phase may be a gas or a liquid; the stationary phase may be a liquid or a solid, and may be in a column, on paper, or in a thin layer on a glass or plastic support. The components of the mixture are absorbed or impeded by the stationary phase to different extents and therefore become separated. The technique is used for both qualitative and quantitive analyses in biology and chemistry.

chromium hard, brittle, grey-white, metallic element, symbol Cr, atomic number 24, relative atomic mass 51.996. It takes a high polish, has a high melting point, and is very resistant to corrosion. It is used in chromium electroplating, in the manufacture of stainless steel and other alloys, and as a catalyst. Its compounds are used for tanning leather and for alums. In human nutrition it is a vital trace element. In nature, it occurs chiefly as chrome iron ore or chromite ($FeCr_2O_4$). Kazakhstan, Zimbabwe, and Brazil are sources.

chromosome structure in a cell nucleus that carries the ◊genes. Each chromosome consists of one very long strand of DNA, coiled and folded to produce a compact body. The point on a chromosome where a particular gene occurs is known as its locus. Most higher organisms have two copies of each chromosome (they are ◊diploid) but some have only one (they are ◊haploid). There are 46 chromosomes in a normal human cell.

Chuang member of the largest minority group in China, numbering about 15 million. They live in S China, where they cultivate rice fields. Their religion includes elements of ancestor worship. The Chuang language belongs to the Tai family.

Churchill Winston (Leonard Spencer) 1874–1956. British Conservative politician, prime minister 1940–45 and 1951–55. In Parliament from 1900, as a Liberal until 1923, he held a number of ministerial offices, including First Lord of the Admiralty 1911–15 and chancellor of the Exchequer 1924–29. Absent from the cabinet in the 1930s, he returned Sept 1939 to lead a coalition government 1940–45, negotiatiing with Allied leaders in World War II to achieve the unconditional surrender of Germany 1945; he led a Conservative government 1951–55.

Church of England established form of Christianity in England, a member of the Anglican Communion. It was dissociated from the Roman Catholic Church 1534. In Nov 1992 the General Synod of the Church of England and the Anglican church in Australia voted in favour of the ordination of women.

Church of Scotland established form of Christianity in Scotland, first recognized by the state 1560. It is based on the Protestant doctrines of the reformer Calvin and governed on Presbyterian lines. After 1690, those who adhered to episcopacy (government of the Church by bishops) formed the Episcopal Church of Scotland, an autonomous church in communion with the Church of England. In 1843, there was a split in the Church of Scotland (the Disruption), in which almost a third of its ministers and members left and formed the Free Church of Scotland.

CIA abbreviation for the US ◊*Central Intelligence Agency.*

Cicero Marcus Tullius 106–43 BC. Roman orator, writer, and politician. His speeches and philosophical and rhetorical works are models of Latin prose, and his letters provide a picture of contemporary Roman life. As consul 63 BC he exposed the Roman politician Catiline's conspiracy in four major orations.

cinema 20th-century form of art and entertainment consisting of 'moving pictures' in either black and white or colour, projected onto a screen. Cinema borrows from the other arts, such as music, drama, and literature, but is entirely dependent for its origins on technological developments, including the technology of action photography, projection, sound reproduction, and film processing and printing (see ▷photography).

cinnamon dried inner bark of a tree *Cinnamomum zeylanicum* of the laurel family, grown in India and Sri Lanka. The bark is ground to make the spice used in curries and confectionery. Oil of cinnamon is obtained from waste bark and is used as flavouring in food and medicine.

Cinque Ports group of ports in S England, originally five, Sandwich, Dover, Hythe, Romney, and Hastings, later including Rye, Winchelsea, and others. Probably founded in Roman times, they rose to importance after the Norman conquest and until the end of the 15th century were bound to supply the ships and men necessary against invasion.

circle perfectly round shape, the path of a point that moves so as to keep a constant distance from a fixed point (the centre). Each circle has a *radius* (the distance from any point on the circle to the centre), a *circumference* (the boundary of the circle), *diameters* (straight lines crossing the circle through the centre), *chords* (lines joining two points on the circumference), *tangents* (lines that touch the circumference at one point only), *sectors* (regions inside the circle between two radii), and *segments* (regions between a chord and the circumference).

circuit in physics or electrical engineering, an arrangement of electrical components through which a current can flow. There are two basic circuits, series and parallel. In a series circuit, the components are connected end to end so that the current flows through all components one after the other. In a parallel circuit, components are connected side by side so that part of the current passes through each component. A circuit diagram shows in graphical form how components are connected together, using standard symbols for the components.

circulatory system system of vessels in an animal's body that transports essential substances (blood or other circulatory fluid) to and from the different parts of the body. Except for simple animals such as sponges and coelenterates (jellyfishes, sea anemones, corals), all animals have a circulatory system.

circumcision surgical removal of all or part of the foreskin (prepuce) of the penis, usually performed on the newborn; it is practised among Jews and Muslims. In some societies in Africa and the Middle East, female circumcision or clitoridectomy (removal of the labia minora and/or clitoris) is practised on adolescents as well as babies; it is illegal in the West.

circumference in geometry, the curved line that encloses a curved plane figure, for example a ▷circle or an ellipse. Its length varies according to the nature of the curve, and may be ascertained by the appropriate formula. The circumference of a circle is πd or $2\pi r$, where d is the diameter of the circle, r is its radius, and π is the constant pi, approximately equal to 3.1416.

cirrhosis any degenerative disease in an organ of the body, especially the liver, characterized by excessive development of connective tissue, causing scarring and painful swelling. Cirrhosis of the liver may be caused by an infection such as viral hepatitis, chronic obstruction of the common bile duct, chronic alcoholism or drug use, blood disorder, heart failure, or malnutrition. However, often no cause is apparent. If cirrhosis is diagnosed early, it can be arrested by treating the cause; otherwise it will progress to coma and death.

CIS abbreviation for ◊**Commonwealth of Independent States**, established 1992 by 11 former Soviet republics.

Ciskei Republic of; self-governing ◊Black National State within South Africa, independent from 1981, but not recognized by the United Nations (under the nonracial constitution adopted by South Africa 1993, homelands were to progressively disappear); *area* 7,700 sq km/2,974 sq mi; *capital* Bisho; *features* one of the two homelands of the Xhosa people created by South Africa (the other is Transkei); *population* (1985) 925,000; *language* Xhosa.

citric acid HOOCCH$_2$C(OH)(COOH)CH$_2$-COOH organic acid widely distributed in the plant kingdom; it is found in high concentrations in citrus fruits and has a sharp, sour taste. At one time it was commercially prepared from concentrated lemon juice, but now the main source is the fermentation of sugar with certain moulds.

citrus any tree or shrub of the genus *Citrus*, family Rutaceae. Citruses are found in Asia and other warm parts of the world. They are evergreen and aromatic, and several species – the orange, lemon, lime, citron, and grapefruit – are cultivated for fruit.

civil engineering branch of engineering that is concerned with the construction of roads, bridges, aqueducts, waterworks, tunnels, canals, irrigation works, and harbours.

civil law legal system based on ◊Roman law. It is one of the two main European legal systems, ◊English (common) law being the other. Civil law may also mean the law relating to matters other than criminal law, such as ◊contract and tort.

civil rights rights of the individual citizen. In many countries they are specified (as in the US Bill of Rights) and guaranteed by law to ensure equal treatment for all citizens. In the USA, the civil-rights movement has struggled since the end of World War II to obtain rights for former slaves and their descendants, both through legislation and in practice, and has some successes, for example the Civil Rights Act 1964 and the Voting Rights Act 1965. However, race relations remain a problem in practice. Other civil-rights movements have included the women's movement and equality for homosexuals.

Civil War, American also called the *War Between the States* war 1861–65 between the Southern or Confederate States of America and the Northern or Union States. The former wished to maintain certain 'states' rights', in particular the right to determine state law on the institution of slavery, and claimed the right to secede from the Union; the latter fought primarily to maintain the Union, with slave emancipation (proclaimed 1863) a secondary issue.

Civil War, English the conflict between King ▷Charles I and the Royalists (Cavaliers) on one side and the Parliamentarians (also called Roundheads) under Oliver ▷Cromwell on the other. Their differences centred on the king's unconstitutional acts but became a struggle over the relative powers of crown and Parliament. Hostilities began 1642 and a series of Royalist defeats (Marston Moor 1644, Naseby 1645) culminated in Charles's capture 1647 and execution 1649. The war continued until the final defeat of Royalist forces at Worcester 1651. Cromwell became Protector (ruler) from 1651 until his death 1658.

Civil War, Spanish war 1936–39 precipitated by a military revolt led by General Franco against the Republican government. Inferior military capability led to the gradual defeat of the Republicans by 1939, and the establishment of Franco's dictatorship.

Clare county on the west coast of the Republic of Ireland, in the province of Munster; county town Ennis; area 3,190 sq km/1,231 sq mi; population (1991) 90,800.

clarinet any of a family of single-reed woodwind instruments of cylindrical bore. The instrument has a range of tone from the dark low register rising to brilliance, and has a capacity for sustained dynamic control. The ability of the clarinet both to blend and to contrast with other instruments make it popular for chamber music, as a solo instrument, and as a jazz instrument.

Clarke Arthur C(harles) 1917– . English science-fiction and nonfiction writer, who originated the plan for a system of communications satellites in geostationary orbit 1945. His works include *Childhood's End* 1953, the short story 'The Sentinel' 1968 (filmed by Stanley Kubrick as *2001: A Space Odyssey*), and *2010: Odyssey Two* 1982.

Clarke Kenneth (Harry) 1940– . British Conservative politician. A cabinet minister from 1985, he held the posts of education secretary 1990–92 and home secretary 1992–93. He succeeded Norman Lamont as chancellor of the Exchequer May 1993.

class in biological classification, a group of related ▷orders. For example, all mammals belong to the class Mammalia and all birds to the class Aves. Among plants, all class names end in 'idae' (such as Asteridae) and among fungi in 'mycetes'; there are no equivalent conventions among animals. Related classes are grouped together in a ▷phylum.

Classicism in art, music, and literature, a style that emphasizes the qualities traditionally considered characteristic of ancient Greek and Roman art, that is, reason, balance, objectivity, restraint, and strict adherence to form. The term Classicism (also ▷Neo-Classicism) is often used to characterize the culture of 18th-century Europe, and contrasted with 19th-century Romanticism.

classification in biology, the arrangement of organisms into a hierarchy of groups on the basis of their similarities in biochemical, anatomical, or physiological characters. The basic grouping is a ▷species, several of which may constitute a ▷genus, which in turn are grouped into families, and so on up through orders, classes, phyla (in plants, sometimes called divisions), to kingdoms.

Claudius (Tiberius Claudius Drusus Nero Germanicus) 10 BC–AD 54. Nephew of Tiberius, made Roman emperor by his troops AD 41, after the murder of his nephew ▷Caligula. Claudius was a scholar, historian, and able administrator. During his reign the Roman empire was considerably extended, and in 43 he took part in the invasion of Britain.

clavichord small domestic keyboard instrument of delicate tone developed in the 16th century. Notes are sounded by a metal blade striking the string. The sound is clear and precise, and a form of vibrato (bebung) is possible by varying finger pressure on the key.

clay very fine-grained ▷sedimentary deposit that has undergone a greater or lesser degree of consolidation. When moistened it is plastic, and it hardens on heating, which renders it impermeable. It may be white, grey, red, yellow, blue, or black, depending on its composition. Clay minerals consist largely of hydrous silicates of aluminium and magnesium together with iron, potassium, sodium, and organic substances. The crystals of clay minerals have a layered structure, capable of holding water, and are responsible for its plastic properties. According to international classification, in mechanical analysis of soil, clay has a grain size of less than 0.002 mm/0.00008 in.

clef in music, a symbol prefixed to a five-line stave indicating the pitch range to which the written notes apply. Introduced as a visual aid in plainchant notation, it is based on the letter G (treble clef), establishing middle C (C4) as a prime reference pitch, G4 a fifth higher for higher voices, and F3 a fifth lower for lower voices.

Cleopatra c. 68–30 BC. Queen of Egypt 51–48 and 47–30 BC. The Roman general Julius Caesar restored her to the throne from which she had been ousted. They became lovers and she went with him to Rome. After Caesar's assassination 44 BC she resumed her position as queen of Egypt. In 41 BC she was joined there by Mark Antony, one of Rome's rulers. In 31 BC Rome declared war on Egypt and scored a decisive victory in the naval Battle of Actium off the W coast of Greece. Cleopatra and Antony fled and committed suicide.

Cleveland county of NE England, formed 1974 from parts of Durham and NE Yorkshire; *area* 580 sq km/224 sq mi; *towns and cities* Middlesbrough (administrative headquarters), Stockton on Tees, Billingham, Hartlepool; *features* Cleveland Hills; river Tees, with Seal Sands wildfowl refuge at its mouth; North Yorkshire Moors National Park; Teesside, the industrial area at the mouth of the Tees; *population* (1987) 555,300.

client-server architecture in computing, a system in which the mechanics of looking after data are separated from the programs that use the data. For example, the 'server' might be a central database, typically located on a large computer that is reserved for this purpose. The 'client' would be an ordinary program that requests data from the server as needed.

climate weather conditions at a particular place over a period of time. Climate encompasses all the meteorological elements and the factors that influence them. The primary factors that determine the variations of climate over the surface of the Earth are: (a) the effect of latitude and the tilt of the Earth's axis to the plane of the orbit about the Sun (66.5°); (b) the large-scale movements of different wind belts over the Earth's surface; (c) the temperature difference between land and sea; (d) contours of the ground; and (e) location of the area in relation to ocean currents.

clinical psychology discipline dealing with the understanding and treatment of health problems, particularly mental disorders. The main problems dealt with include anxiety, phobias, depression, obsessions, sexual and marital problems, drug and alcohol dependence, childhood behavioural problems, psychoses (such as schizophrenia), mental disability, and brain disease (such as dementia) and damage.

Clinton Bill (William Jefferson) 1946– . 42nd president of the USA from 1993, a Democrat. He served as governor of Arkansas 1979-81 and 1983-93, establishing a liberal and progressive reputation. As president, he sought to implement a *New Democrat* programme, combining social reform with economic conservatism as a means of bringing the country out of recession. He passed the North American Free Trade Agreement (NAFTA) and wide-ranging anticrime bills.

clone an exact replica. In genetics, any one of a group of genetically identical cells or organisms. An identical ◊twin is a clone; so, too, are bacteria living in the same colony. The term clone has also been adopted by computer technology to describe a (nonexistent) device that mimics an actual one to enable certain software programs to run correctly.

closed shop a place of work, such as a factory or an office, where all workers within a section must belong to a single officially recognized trade union. Trade unions favour closed shops because 100% union membership gives them greater industrial power. Management may find it convenient to deal with workers as a group. In the USA the closed shop was made illegal 1947. The closed shop was condemned by the European Court of Human Rights 1981.

cloud water vapour condensed into minute water particles that float in masses in the atmosphere. Clouds, like fogs or mists, which occur at lower levels, are formed by the cooling of air containing water vapour, which generally condenses around tiny dust particles.

cloud chamber apparatus for tracking ionized particles. It consists of a vessel fitted with a piston and filled with air or other gas, saturated with water vapour. When the volume of the vessel is suddenly expanded by moving the piston outwards, the vapour cools and a cloud of tiny droplets forms on any nuclei, dust, or ions present. As fast-moving ionizing particles collide with the air or gas molecules, they show as visible tracks.

clutch any device for disconnecting rotating shafts, used especially in a car's transmission system. In a car with a manual gearbox, the driver depresses the clutch when changing gear, thus disconnecting the engine from the gearbox.

Clwyd county of N Wales, created 1974; *area* 2,420 sq km/934 sq mi; *towns and cities* Mold (administrative headquarters), Flint, Denbigh, Wrexham;

seaside resorts: Colwyn Bay, Rhyl, Prestatyn; *features* Clwydian range of mountains with Offa's Dyke along the main ridge; Chirk, Denbigh, Flint, and Rhuddlan castles; *population* (1991) 408,100; *languages* English, 18% Welsh-speaking.

coal black or blackish mineral substance formed from the compaction of ancient plant matter in tropical swamp conditions. It is used as a fuel and in the chemical industry. Coal is classified according to the proportion of carbon it contains. The main types are ▷**anthracite** (shiny, with about 90% carbon), *bituminous coal* (shiny and dull patches, about 75% carbon), and *lignite* (woody, grading into peat, about 50% carbon). Coal burning is one of the main causes of ▷acid rain.

cobalt hard, lustrous, grey, metallic element, symbol Co, atomic number 27, relative atomic mass 58.933. It is found in various ores and occasionally as a free metal, sometimes in metallic meteorite fragments. It is used in the preparation of magnetic, wear-resistant, and high-strength alloys; its compounds are used in inks, paints, and varnishes.

cocaine alkaloid $C_{17}H_{21}NO_4$ extracted from the leaves of the coca tree. It has limited medical application, mainly as a local anaesthetic agent that is readily absorbed by mucous membranes (lining tissues) of the nose and throat. It is both toxic and addictive. Its use as a stimulant is illegal. ▷Crack is a derivative of cocaine.

Cockcroft John Douglas 1897–1967. British physicist. In 1932 he and the Irish physicist Ernest Walton succeeded in splitting the nucleus of an atom for the first time. In 1951 they were jointly awarded a Nobel prize.

cocoa and chocolate food products made from the cacao (or cocoa) bean, fruit of a tropical tree *Theobroma cacao*, now cultivated mainly in Africa. Chocolate as a drink was introduced to Europe from the New World by the Spanish in the 16th century; eating-chocolate was first produced in the late 18th century.

coconut fruit of the coconut palm *Cocos nucifera* of the family Arecaceae, which grows throughout the lowland tropics. The fruit has a large outer husk of fibres, which is split off and used for coconut matting and ropes. Inside this is the nut exported to temperate countries. Its hard shell contains white flesh and coconut milk, both of which are nourishing and palatable.

Cocos Islands or *Keeling Islands* group of 27 small coral islands in the Indian Ocean, about 2,770 km/1,720 mi NW of Perth, Australia; area 14 sq km/5.5 sq mi; population (1986) 616. They are owned by Australia.

Cocteau Jean 1889–1963. French poet, dramatist, and film director. A leading figure in European Modernism, he worked with Picasso, Diaghilev, and Stravinsky. He produced many volumes of poetry, ballets such as *Le Boeuf sur le toit/The Ox on the Roof* 1920, plays, for example, *Orphée/Orpheus* 1926, and a mature novel of bourgeois French life, *Les Enfants terribles/Children of the Game* 1929, which he made into a film 1950.

codeine opium derivative that provides analgesia in mild to moderate pain. It also suppresses the cough centre of the brain. It is an alkaloid, derived from morphine but less toxic and addictive.

coelenterate any freshwater or marine organism of the phylum Coelenterata, having a body wall composed of two layers of cells. They also possess stinging cells. Examples are jellyfish, hydra, and coral.

coffee drink made from the roasted and ground beanlike seeds found inside the red berries of any of several species of shrubs of the genus *Coffea*, originally native to Ethiopia and now cultivated throughout the tropics. It contains a stimulant, ▷caffeine. The world's largest producers are Brazil, Colombia, and the Côte d'Ivoire. Coffee drinking began in Arab regions in the 14th century and became common in Europe 300 years later.

coke clean, light fuel produced when coal is strongly heated in an airtight oven. Coke contains 90% carbon and makes a useful domestic and industrial fuel (used, for example in the iron and steel industries and in the production of town gas).

cold-blooded of animals, dependent on the surrounding temperature; see ▷*poikilothermy*.

Cold War ideological, political, and economic tensions 1945–90 between the USSR and Eastern Europe on the one hand and the USA and Western Europe on the other. It intensified at times of conflict anywhere in the world. Arms-reduction agreements between the USA and USSR in the late 1980s, and a diminution of Soviet influence in Eastern Europe, led to a reassessment of positions, and the 'war' officially ended 1990.

Coleridge Samuel Taylor 1772–1834. English poet. He was one of the founders of the Romantic movement. A friend of Southey and Wordsworth, he collaborated with the latter on *Lyrical Ballads* 1798. His poems include 'The Rime of the Ancient Mariner', 'Christabel', and 'Kubla Khan'; critical works include *Biographia Literaria* 1817.

colitis inflammation of the colon (large intestine) with diarrhoea (often bloody). It is usually due to infection or some types of bacterial dysentery.

collagen protein that is the main constituent of connective tissue. Collagen is present in skin, cartilage, tendons, and ligaments. Bones are made up of collagen, with the mineral calcium phosphate providing increased rigidity.

colloid substance composed of extremely small particles of one material (the dispersed phase) evenly and stably distributed in another material (the continuous phase). The size of the dispersed particles (1–1,000 nanometres across) is less than that of particles in suspension but greater than that of molecules in true solution. Colloids involving gases include *aerosols* (dispersions of liquid or solid particles in a gas, as in fog or smoke) and *foams* (dispersions of gases in liquids). Those involving liquids include *emulsions* (in which both the dispersed and the continuous phases are liquids) and *sols* (solid particles dispersed in a liquid). Sols in which both phases contribute to a molecular three-dimensional network have a jellylike form and are known as *gels*; gelatin, starch 'solution', and silica gel are common examples.

Cologne (German *Köln*) industrial and commercial port in North Rhine–Westphalia, Germany, on the left bank of the Rhine, 35 km/22 mi SE of Düsseldorf; population (1988) 914,000. To the N is the Ruhr coalfield.

Colombia Republic of (*República de Colombia*); *area* 1,141,748 sq km/ 440,715 sq mi; *capital* Santa Fé de Bogotá; *features* Zipaquira salt mine and underground cathedral; Lake Guatavita, source of the legend of 'El Dorado'; *political system* democratic republic; *population* (1993 est) 34,900,800 (mestizo 68%, white 20%, American Indian 1%); growth rate 2.2% p.a.; *language* Spanish; *religion* Roman Catholic 95%.

Colombo capital and principal seaport of Sri Lanka, on the west coast near the mouth of the Kelani River; population (1990) 615,000, Greater Colombo about 1,000,000. It trades in tea, rubber, and cacao. It has iron-and steelworks and an oil refinery.

Colón second largest city in Panama, at the Caribbean end of the Panama Canal; population (1990) 140,900. It has a special economic zone (created 1948) used by foreign companies to avoid taxes on completed products in their home countries.

Colorado river in North America, rising in the Rocky Mountains and flowing 2,333 km/1,450 mi to the Gulf of California through Colorado, Utah, Arizona (including the Grand Canyon), and N Mexico. The many dams along its course, including Hoover and Glen Canyon, provide power and irrigation water, but have destroyed wildlife and scenery. To the W of the river in SE California is the *Colorado Desert*, an arid area of 5,000 sq km/2,000 sq mi.

Colorado state of the W central USA; nicknamed Centennial State; *area* 269,700 sq km/104,104 sq mi; *capital* Denver; *features* Rocky Mountain National Park; Pikes Peak; prehistoric cliff dwellings of the Mesa Verde National Park; 'ghost' mining towns; *population* (1990) 3,294,400.

Colosseum amphitheatre in ancient Rome, begun by the emperor Vespasian to replace the one destroyed by fire during the reign of Nero, and completed by his son Titus AD 80. It was 187 m/615 ft long and 49 m/160 ft high, and seated 50,000 people. Early Christians were martyred there by lions and gladiators. It could be flooded for mock sea battles.

colour quality or wavelength of light emitted or reflected from an object. Visible white light consists of electromagnetic radiation of various wavelengths, and if a beam is refracted through a prism, it can be spread out into a spectrum, in which the various colours correspond to different wavelengths. From long to short wavelengths (from about 700 to 400 nanometres) the colours are red, orange, yellow, green, blue, indigo, and violet.

Columba, St 521–597. Irish Christian abbot, missionary to Scotland. He was born in County Donegal of royal descent, and founded monasteries and churches in Ireland. In 563 he sailed with 12 companions to Iona, and built a monastery there that was to play a leading part in the conversion of Britain. Feast day 9 June.

Columbia, District of seat of the federal government of the USA, coextensive with the city of Washington, situated on the Potomac River; area 178 sq km/69 sq mi. It was ceded by Maryland as the national capital site 1790.

Columbus capital of Ohio, USA, on the rivers Scioto and Olentangy; population (1990) 632,900. It has coalfield and natural gas resources nearby.

Columbus Christopher (Spanish *Cristóbal Colón*) 1451–1506. Italian navigator and explorer. Believing that Asia could be reached by sailing westwards, he won the support of King Ferdinand and Queen Isabella of Spain, and set sail from Palos on 3 Aug 1492 in the *Santa Maria*. Land was sighted 12 Oct, probably Watling Island (now San Salvador Island), and he reached Cuba and Haiti, returning to Spain March 1493. His other vogages were: 1493–96 to Guadaloupe, Montserrat, Antigua, Puerto Rico, and Jamaica; 1498 to Trinidad and the mainland of South America; and 1502–1504 to Honduras and Nicaragua.

combustion burning, defined in chemical terms as the rapid combination of a substance with oxygen, accompanied by the evolution of heat and usually light. A slow-burning candle flame and the explosion of a mixture of petrol vapour and air are extreme examples of combustion.

comedy drama that aims to make its audience laugh, usually with a happy or amusing ending, as opposed to tragedy. The comic tradition has undergone many changes since its Greek roots; the earliest comedy developed in ancient Greece, in the topical and fantastic satires of Aristophanes. Great comic dramatists include Shakespeare, Molière, Carlo Goldoni, Pierre de Marivaux, George Bernard Shaw, and Oscar Wilde. Genres of comedy include pantomime, satire, farce, black comedy, and ▷commedia dell'arte.

comet small, icy body orbiting the Sun, usually on a highly elliptical path. A comet consists of a central nucleus a few kilometres across, and has been likened to a dirty snowball because it consists mostly of ice mixed with dust. As the comet approaches the Sun the nucleus heats up, releasing gas and dust which form a tenuous coma, up to 100,000 km/60,000 mi wide, around the nucleus. Gas and dust stream away from the coma to form one or more tails, which may extend for millions of kilometres.

commedia dell'arte popular form of Italian improvised comic drama in the 16th and 17th centuries, performed by trained troupes of actors and involving stock characters and situations. It exerted considerable influence on writers such as Molière and Carlo Goldoni, and on the genres of pantomime, harlequinade, and the Punch and Judy show.

commensalism in biology, a relationship between two ▷species whereby one (the commensal) benefits from the association, whereas the other neither benefits nor suffers. For example, certain species of millipede and silverfish inhabit the nests of army ants and live by scavenging on the refuse of their hosts, but without affecting the ants.

common law that part of the English law not embodied in legislation. It consists of rules of law based on common custom and usage and on judicial decisions. English common law became the basis of law in the USA and many other English-speaking countries.

Commonwealth Games multisport gathering of competitors from British Commonwealth countries, held every four years. The first meeting (known as the British Empire Games) was in Hamilton, Canada, Aug 1930.

Commonwealth of Independent States (CIS) successor body to the ▷Union of Soviet Socialist Republics, initially formed as a new commonwealth of Slav republics on 8 Dec 1991 by the presidents of the Russian Federation,

Belarus, and Ukraine. On 21 Dec, eight of the nine remaining non-Slav republics – Moldova, Tajikistan, Armenia, Azerbaijan, Turkmenistan, Kazakhstan, Kyrgyzstan, and Uzbekistan – joined the CIS. Georgia joined 1993.

Commonwealth, the (British) voluntary association of 51 countries and their dependencies that once formed part of the ▷British Empire and are now independent sovereign states. Additionally, there are some 20 territories that are not completely sovereign and remain dependencies of the UK or another of the fully sovereign members. Heads of government meet every two years. The Commonwealth has no charter or constitution, and is founded more on tradition and sentiment than on political or economic factors.

communication in biology, the signalling of information by one organism to another, usually with the intention of altering the recipient's behaviour. Signals used in communication may be *visual* (such as the human smile or the display of colourful plumage in birds), *auditory* (for example, the whines or barks of a dog), *olfactory* (such as the odours released by the scent glands of a deer), *electrical* (as in the pulses emitted by electric fish), or *tactile* (for example, the nuzzling of male and female elephants).

communications satellite relay station in space for sending telephone, television, telex, and other messages around the world. Messages are sent to and from the satellites via ground stations. Most communications satellites are in geostationary orbit, appearing to hang fixed over one point on the Earth's surface.

Communion, Holy in the Christian church, another name for the ▷Eucharist.

communism revolutionary socialism based on the theories of political philosophers Karl Marx and Friedrich Engels, emphasizing common ownership of the means of production and a planned economy. Politically, it seeks the overthrow of capitalism through a proletarian revolution. The first communist state was the USSR after the revolution of 1917. China emerged after 1961 as a rival to the USSR in world communist leadership. The late 1980s saw a movement for more individual freedoms in many communist countries, culminating in the demise of communist rule in Eastern European countries and Mongolia, and further state repression in China. The failed hard-line coup in the USSR against President Gorbachev 1991 saw the effective abandonment of communism there. Communism as the ideology of a nation state survives in only a handful of countries, notably China, Cuba, North Korea, Laos, and Vietnam.

Comoros Federal Islamic Republic of (*Jumhuriyat al-Qumur al-Itthādīyah al-Islāmīyah*); *area* 1,862 sq km/719 sq mi; *capital* Moroni; *features* active volcano on Njazidja; poor tropical soil; *political system* emergent democracy; *population* (1993 est) 510,000; growth rate 3.1% p.a.; *languages* Arabic (official), Comorian (Swahili and Arabic dialect), Makua, French; *religions* Muslim (official) 86%, Roman Catholic 14%.

compact disc (or *CD*) disc for storing digital information, about 12 cm/4.5 in across, mainly used for music, when it can have over an hour's playing time. Entirely different from a conventional LP (long-playing) gramophone record, the compact disc is made of aluminium with a transparent plastic coating; the metal disc underneath is etched by a ▷laser beam with microscopic pits that carry a digital code representing the sounds. During playback, a laser beam reads the code and produces signals that are changed into near-exact replicas of the original sounds.

compass any instrument for finding direction. The most commonly used is a magnetic compass, consisting of a thin piece of magnetic material with the north-seeking pole indicated, free to rotate on a pivot and mounted on a compass card on which the points of the compass are marked. When the compass is properly adjusted and used, the north-seeking pole will point to the magnetic north, from which true north can be found from tables of magnetic corrections.

compound chemical substance made up of two or more ▷elements bonded together, so that they cannot be separated by physical means. Compounds are held together by ionic or covalent bonds.

computer programmable electronic device that processes data and performs calculations and other symbol- manipulation tasks. There are three types: the *digital computer*, which manipulates information coded as binary numbers (see ▷binary number system); the *analogue computer*, which works with continuously varying quantities; and the *hybrid computer*, which has characteristics of both analogue and digital computers.

computer game or *video game* any computer-controlled game in which the computer (sometimes) opposes the human player. Computer games typically employ fast, animated graphics on

a ▷VDU (visual display unit), and synthesized sound.

computer graphics use of computers to display and manipulate information in pictorial form. Input may be achieved by scanning an image, by drawing with a mouse or stylus on a graphics tablet, or by drawing directly on the screen with a light pen.

computer program coded instructions for a computer; see ▷program.

computer simulation representation of a real-life situation in a computer program. For example, the program might simulate the flow of customers arriving at a bank. The user can alter variables, such as the number of cashiers on duty, and see the effect.

Comte Auguste 1798–1857. French philosopher regarded as the founder of sociology, a term he coined 1830. He sought to establish sociology as an intellectual discipline, using a scientific approach ('positivism') as the basis of a new science of social order and social development.

concave of a surface, curving inwards, or away from the eye. For example, a bowl appears concave when viewed from above. In geometry, a concave polygon is one that has an interior angle greater than 180°. Concave is the opposite of ▷convex.

concentration camp prison camp for civilians in wartime or under totalitarian rule. The first concentration camps were devised by the British during the Second Boer War in South Africa 1899 for the detention of Afrikaner women and children. Hundreds of concentration camps were set up in Nazi Germany and occupied Europe (1933–45) to imprison Jews and opponents of

Hitler. The most infamous camps in World War II were Auschwitz, Belsen, Dachau, Maidanek, Sobibor, and Treblinka. More than 6 million people, mostly Jews, died at these camps.

concerto composition, usually in three movements, for solo instrument (or instruments) and orchestra. It developed during the 18th century from the *concerto grosso* form for string orchestra, in which a group of solo instruments (concerto) is contrasted with a full orchestra (ripieno).

condensation conversion of a vapour to a liquid. This is frequently achieved by letting the vapour come into contact with a cold surface. It is an essential step in distillation processes, and is the process by which water vapour turns into fine water droplets to form ▷cloud.

conditioning in psychology, two major principles of behaviour modification. In *classical conditioning*, described by Ivan Pavlov, a new stimulus can evoke an automatic response by being repeatedly associated with a stimulus that naturally provokes that response. For example, the sound of a bell repeatedly associated with food will eventually trigger salivation, even if sounded without food being presented. In *operant conditioning*, the frequency of a voluntary response can be increased by following it with a reinforcer or reward.

condom or *sheath* or *prophylactic* barrier contraceptive, made of rubber, which fits over an erect penis and holds in the sperm produced by ejaculation. It is an effective means of preventing pregnancy if used carefully, preferably with a spermicide (a cream or jelly that kills the sperm cells). A condom with spermicide is 97% effective; one without spermicide is 85% effective as a contraceptive. Condoms also give protection against sexually transmitted diseases, including AIDS.

conductance ability of a material to carry an electrical current, usually given the symbol G. For a direct current, it is the reciprocal of ▷resistance: a conductor of resistance R has a conductance of $1/R$. For an alternating current, conductance is the resistance R divided by the impedance Z: $G = R/Z$. Conductance was formerly expressed in reciprocal ohms (or mhos); the SI unit is the siemens (S).

conductor any material that conducts heat or electricity (as opposed to an insulator, or nonconductor). A good conductor has a high electrical or heat conductivity, and is generally a substance rich in free electrons such as a metal. A poor conductor (such as the nonmetals glass and porcelain) has few free electrons. Carbon is exceptional in being nonmetallic and yet (in some of its forms) a relatively good conductor of heat and electricity.

cone in botany, the reproductive structure of the conifers and cycads; also known as a strobilus. It consists of a central axis surrounded by numerous, overlapping, scalelike, modified leaves (sporophylls) that bear the reproductive organs. Usually there are separate male and female cones, the former bearing pollen sacs containing pollen grains, and the larger female cones bearing the ovules that contain the ova or egg cells. The pollen is carried from male to female cones by the wind (anemophily). The seeds develop within the female cone and are released as the scales open in dry atmospheric conditions, which favour seed dispersal.

Confederacy in US history, popular name for the *Confederate States of America*, the government established by 7 (later 11) Southern states in Feb 1861 when they seceded from the Union, precipitating the American ▷Civil War. Richmond, Virginia, was the capital, and Jefferson Davis the president. The Confederacy fell after its army was defeated 1865 and General Robert E Lee surrendered.

confirmation rite practised by a number of Christian denominations, including Roman Catholic, Anglican, and Orthodox, in which a previously baptized person is admitted to full membership of the church. In Reform Judaism there is often a confirmation service several years after the bar or bat mitzvah (initiation into the congregation).

Confucianism body of beliefs and practices based on the Chinese classics and supported by the authority of the Chinese philosopher Confucius (551–479 BC). The origin of things is seen in the union of *yin* and *yang*, the passive and active principles. Human relationships follow the patriarchal pattern of authority, obedience, and mutual respect. For more than 2,000 years Chinese political government, social organization, and individual conduct were shaped by Confucian principles. In 1912, Confucian philosophy, as a basis for government, was dropped by the state.

congenital disease in medicine, a disease that is present at birth. It is not necessarily genetic in origin; for example, congenital herpes may be acquired by the baby as it passes through the mother's birth canal.

Congo Republic of (*République du Congo*); *area* 342,000 sq km/132,012 sq mi; *capital* Brazzaville; *environment* an estimated 93% of the rural population is without access to safe drinking water; *features* 70% of the population lives in Brazzaville, Pointe-Noire, or in towns along the railway linking these two places; *political system* emergent democracy; *population* (1993 est) 2,700,000 (chiefly Bantu); growth rate 2.6% p.a.; *languages* French (official); many African languages; *religions* animist 50%, Christian 48%, Muslim 2%.

Congress national legislature of the USA, consisting of the House of Representatives (435 members, apportioned to the states of the Union on the basis of population, and elected for two-year terms) and the Senate (100 senators, two for each state, elected for six years, one-third elected every two years). Both representatives and senators are elected by direct popular vote. Congress meets in Washington DC, in the Capitol Building. An ▷act of Congress is a bill passed by both houses.

Congreve William 1670–1729. English dramatist and poet. His first success was the comedy *The Old Bachelor* 1693, followed by *The Double Dealer* 1694, *Love for Love* 1695, the tragedy *The Mourning Bride* 1697, and *The Way of the World* 1700. His plays, which satirize the social affectations of the time, are characterized by elegant wit and wordplay, and complex plots.

congruent in geometry, having the same shape and size, as applied to two-dimensional or solid figures. With plane congruent figures, one figure will fit on top of the other exactly, though this may first require rotation and/or rotation of one of the figures.

conic section curve obtained when a conical surface is intersected by a plane. If the intersecting plane cuts both extensions of the cone, it yields a hyperbola; if it is parallel to the side of the cone, it produces a parabola. Other intersecting planes produce ▷circles or ellipses.

conifer tree or shrub of the order Coniferales, in the gymnosperm or naked-seed-bearing group of plants. They are often pyramidal in form, with leaves that are either scaled or made up of needles; most are evergreen. Conifers include pines, spruces, firs, yews, junipers, monkey puzzles, and larches.

conjunctivitis inflammation of the conjunctiva, the delicate membrane that lines the inside of the eyelids and covers the front of the eye. Symptoms include redness, swelling, and a watery or pus-filled discharge. It may be caused by infection, allergy, or other irritant.

Connacht province of the Republic of Ireland, comprising the counties of Galway, Leitrim, Mayo, Roscommon, and Sligo; area 17,130 sq km/6,612 sq mi; population (1991) 422,900. The chief towns are Galway, Roscommon, Castlebar, Sligo, and Carrick-on-Shannon. Mainly lowland, it is agricultural and stock-raising country, with poor land in the W.

Connecticut state in New England, USA; *area* 13,000 sq km/5,018 sq mi; *capital* Hartford; *features* Yale University; Mystic Seaport (reconstruction of 19th-century village, with restored ships); *population* (1990) 3,287,100.

Connery Sean 1930– . Scottish film actor. He was the first interpreter of James Bond in several films based on the novels of Ian Fleming. His films include *Dr No* 1962, *From Russia with Love* 1963, *Marnie* 1964, *Goldfinger* 1964, *Diamonds Are Forever* 1971, *A Bridge Too Far* 1977, *The Name of the Rose* 1986, and *The Untouchables* 1987 (Academy Award).

Conrad Joseph. Pen name of Teodor Jozef Conrad Korzeniowski 1857–1924. English novelist, born in the Ukraine of Polish parents. He joined the French merchant navy at the age of 17 and first learned English at 21. His greatest works include the novels *Lord Jim* 1900, *Nostromo* 1904, *The Secret Agent* 1907, and *Under Western Eyes* 1911, the short novel *Heart of Darkness* 1902 and the short story 'The Shadow Line' 1917.

conservation in the life sciences, action taken to protect and preserve the natural world, usually from pollution, overexploitation, and other harmful features of human activity. The late 1980s saw a great increase in public concern for the environment, with membership of conservation groups, such as ▷Friends of the Earth, the Sierra Club, and the Nature Conservancy rising sharply. Globally the most important issues include the depletion of atmospheric ozone by the action of chlorofluorocarbons (CFCs), the build-up of carbon dioxide in the atmosphere (thought to contribute to an intensification of the ▷greenhouse effect), and ▷deforestation.

conservatism approach to government favouring the maintenance of existing institutions and identified with a number of Western political parties, such as the British Conservative, US Republican, German Christian Democratic, and Australian Liberal parties. It tends to be explicitly nondoctrinaire and pragmatic but generally emphasizes free-enterprise capitalism, minimal government intervention in the economy, rigid law and order, and the importance of national traditions.

Conservative Party UK political party, one of the two historic British parties; the name replaced *Tory* in general use from 1830 onwards. Traditionally the party of landed interests, it broadened its political base under Benjamin Disraeli's leadership in the 19th century. The present Conservative Party's free-market capitalism is supported by the world of finance and the management of industry.

Constable John 1776–1837. English artist. He was one of the greatest landscape painters of the 19th century. He painted scenes of his native Suffolk, including *The Haywain* 1821 (in the National Gallery, London), as well as castles, cathedrals, landscapes, and coastal scenes in other parts of Britain.

Constantine the Great c. AD 280–337. First Christian emperor of Rome and founder of Constantinople. He defeated Maxentius, joint emperor of Rome AD 312, and in 313 formally recognized Christianity. As sole emperor of the west of the empire, he defeated Licinius, emperor of the east, to become ruler of the Roman world 324.

Constantinople former name (330–1453) of Istanbul, Turkey. It was named after the Roman emperor Constantine the Great when he enlarged the Greek city of Byzantium 328 and declared it the capital of the ◊Byzantine Empire 330. Held by the Crusaders 1204–61, it was recaptured by the Greeks until taken by the Turks 1453, becaming the capital of the ◊Ottoman Empire.

constellation one of the 88 areas into which the sky is divided for the purposes of identifying and naming celestial objects. The first constellations were simple, arbitrary patterns of stars in which early civilizations visualized gods, sacred beasts, and mythical heroes.

constitution body of fundamental laws of a state, laying down the system of government and defining the relations of the legislature, executive, and judiciary to each other and to the citizens. Since the French Revolution almost all countries (the UK is an exception) have adopted written constitutions; that of the USA (1787) is the oldest.

continent any one of the seven large land masses of the Earth, as distinct from the oceans. They are Asia, Africa, North America, South America, Europe, Australia, and Antarctica. Continents are constantly moving and evolving (see ◊plate tectonics). A continent does not end at the coastline; its boundary is the edge of the shallow continental shelf, which may extend several hundred kilometres out to sea.

continental drift in geology, the theory that, about 250–200 million years ago, the Earth consisted of a single large continent (Pangaea), which subsequently broke apart to form the continents known today. The theory was proposed 1912 by German meteorologist Alfred Wegener, but such vast continental movements could not be satisfactorily explained until the study of ◊plate tectonics in the 1960s.

Contra member of a Central American right-wing guerrilla force attempting to overthrow the democratically elected Nicaraguan Sandinista government 1979–90. The Contras, many of them mercenaries or former members of the deposed dictator Somoza's guard, operated mainly from bases outside Nicaragua, mostly in Honduras, with covert US funding, as revealed by the Irangate hearings 1986–87.

contraceptive any drug, device, or technique that prevents pregnancy. The contraceptive pill (the ◊Pill) contains female hormones that interfere with egg production or the first stage of pregnancy. The 'morning-after' pill can be taken up to 72 hours after unprotected intercourse. Barrier contraceptives include ◊condoms (sheaths) and ◊diaphragms, also called caps or Dutch caps; they prevent the sperm entering the cervix (neck of the womb). ◊Intrauterine devices, also known as IUDs or coils, cause a slight inflammation of the lining of the womb; this prevents the fertilized egg from becoming implanted.

contract legal agreement between two or more parties, where each party agrees to do something. For example, a contract of employment is a legal agreement between an employer and an employee and lays out the conditions of employment. Contracts need not necessarily be written; they can be verbal contracts. In consumer law, for example, a contract is established when a good is sold.

convection heat energy transfer that involves the movement of a fluid (gas or liquid). According to ◊kinetic theory, molecules of fluid in contact with the source of heat expand and tend to rise within the bulk of the fluid. Less energetic, cooler molecules sink to take their place, setting up convection currents. This is the principle of natural convection in many domestic hot-water systems and space heaters.

convex of a surface, curving outwards, or towards the eye. For example, the outer surface of a ball appears convex. In geometry, the term is used to describe any polygon possessing no interior angle greater than 180°. Convex is the opposite of ◊concave.

Cook James 1728–1779. British naval explorer. After surveying the St Lawrence 1759, he made three voyages: 1768–71 to Tahiti, New Zealand, and Australia; 1772–75 to the South Pacific; and 1776–79 to the South and North Pacific, attempting to find the Northwest Passage and charting the Siberian coast. He was killed in Hawaii.

Cook Islands group of six large and a number of smaller Polynesian islands 2,600 km/1,600 mi NE of Auckland, New Zealand; area 290 sq km/112 sq mi; population (1991) 19,000.

Cooper Gary 1901–1962. US film actor. He epitomized the lean, true-hearted American, slow of speech but capable of outdoing the 'bad guys'. His films include *Lives of a Bengal Lancer* 1935, *Mr Deeds Goes to Town* 1936, *Sergeant York* 1940 (Academy Award), and *High Noon* 1952 (Academy Award).

coordinate in geometry, a number that defines the position of a point relative to a point or axis (reference line). Cartesian coordinates define a point by its perpendicular distances from two or more axes drawn through a fixed point mutually at right angles to each other. Polar coordinates define a point in a plane by its distance from a fixed point and direction from a fixed line.

Copenhagen (Danish *København*) capital of Denmark, on the islands of Zealand and Amager; population (1990) 1,337,100 (including suburbs).

Copernicus Nicolaus 1473–1543. Polish astronomer who believed that the

Sun, not the Earth, is at the centre of the Solar System, thus defying the Christian church doctrine of the time. For 30 years he worked on the hypothesis that the rotation and the orbital motion of the Earth were responsible for the apparent movement of the heavenly bodies.

Copland Aaron 1900–1990. US composer. His early works, such as his piano concerto 1926, were in the jazz idiom but he gradually developed a gentler style with a regional flavour drawn from American folk music. Among his works are the ballets *Billy the Kid* 1939, *Rodeo* 1942, and *Appalachian Spring* 1944 (based on a poem by Hart Crane), and *Inscape for Orchestra* 1967.

copper orange-pink, very malleable and ductile, metallic element, symbol Cu (from Latin *cuprum*), atomic number 29, relative atomic mass 63.546. It is used for its durability, pliability, high thermal and electrical conductivity, and resistance to corrosion.

Copt descendant of those ancient Egyptians who adopted Christianity in the 1st century, refusing to convert to Islam after the Arab conquest. They now form a small minority (about 5%) of Egypt's population. *Coptic* is a member of the Hamito-Semitic language family. It is descended from the language of the ancient Egyptians and is the ritual language of the Coptic Christian church. It is mostly written in the Greek alphabet.

coral marine invertebrate of the class Anthozoa in the phylum Cnidaria, which also includes sea anemones and jellyfish. It has a skeleton of lime (calcium carbonate) extracted from the surrounding water. Corals exist in warm seas, at moderate depths with sufficient light. Some coral is valued for decoration or jewellery, for example, Mediterranean red coral *Corallum rubrum*.

Córdoba capital of Córdoba province, Spain, on the river Guadalquivir; population (1991) 309,200. It has many Moorish remains, including the mosque, now a cathedral, founded by 'Abd-ar-Rahman I 785, which is one of the largest Christian churches in the world. Córdoba was probably founded by the Carthaginians; it was held by the Moors 711–1236.

Corfu (Greek *Kérkyra*) northernmost and second largest of the Ionian islands of Greece, off the coast of Epirus in the Ionian Sea; area 1,072 sq km/414 sq mi; population (1981) 96,500. Its largest town is the port of Corfu (Kérkyra), population (1981) 33,560. Corfu was colonized by the Corinthians about 700 BC. Venice held it 1386–1797, Britain 1815–64.

Corinth (Greek *Kórinthos*) port in Greece, on the isthmus connecting the Peloponnese with the mainland; population (1981) 22,650. The rocky isthmus is bisected by the 6.5 km/4 mi Corinth canal, opened 1893. The site of the ancient city-state of Corinth lies 7 km/4.5 mi SW of the port.

Coriolis effect the effect of the Earth's rotation on the atmosphere and on all objects on the Earth's surface. In the northern hemisphere it causes moving objects and currents to be deflected to the right; in the southern hemisphere it causes deflection to the left. The effect is named after its discoverer, French mathematician Gaspard Coriolis (1792–1843).

cork light, waterproof outer layers of the bark of the stems and roots of almost all trees and shrubs. The cork oak *Quercus suber*, a native of S Europe and N Africa, is cultivated in Spain and Portugal; the exceptionally thick outer layers of its bark provide the cork that is used commercially.

Cork largest county of the Republic of Ireland, in the province of Munster; county town Cork; area 7,460 sq km/ 2,880 sq mi; population (1991) 409,800. Natural gas and oil fields are found off the S coast at Kinsale.

corm short, swollen, underground plant stem, surrounded by protective scale leaves, as seen in the genus *Crocus*. It stores food, provides a means of ◊vegetative reproduction, and acts as a perennating organ.

Corneille Pierre 1606–1684. French dramatist. His tragedies, such as *Horace* 1640, *Cinna* 1641, and *Oedipe* 1659 established the French classical dramatic tradition. His comedies, of which the first was *Mélite* performed 1629, gained him a brief period of favour with Cardinal Richelieu. His early masterpiece, *Le Cid* 1636, was attacked by the Academicians, although it received public acclaim.

Corn Laws in Britain, laws in force 1360–1846 regulating the export or import of cereals in order to maintain an adequate supply for consumers and a secure price for producers. The laws were repealed because they became an unwarranted tax on food and a hindrance to British exports.

cornucopia in Greek mythology, one of the horns of the goat Amaltheia, which was caused by Zeus to refill itself indefinitely with food and drink. In paintings, the cornucopia is depicted as a horn-shaped container spilling over with fruit and flowers.

Cornwall county in SW England including the Isles of ◊Scilly (Scillies); *area* (excluding Scillies) 3,550 sq km/ 1,370 sq mi; *towns and cities* Truro (administrative headquarters), Camborne, Launceston; resorts of Bude, Falmouth, Newquay, Penzance, St Ives; *features* Bodmin Moor; Land's End peninsula; St Michael's Mount; *population* (1991) 469,300.

corona faint halo of hot (about 2,000,000°C/3,600,000°F) and tenuous gas around the Sun, which boils from the surface. It is visible at solar ◊eclipses or through a *coronagraph*, an instrument that blocks light from the Sun's brilliant disc. Gas flows away from the corona to form the ◊solar wind.

coronary artery disease condition in which the fatty deposits of atherosclerosis form in the coronary arteries that supply the heart muscle, narrowing them and restricting the blood flow.

coroner official who investigates the deaths of persons who have died suddenly by acts of violence or under suspicious circumstances, by holding an inquest or ordering a postmortem examination (autopsy).

Corot Jean-Baptiste Camille 1796–1875. French painter. He created a distinctive landscape style using a soft focus and a low-key palette of browns, ochres, and greens, and painted outdoors. His early work, including Italian scenes of the 1820s, influenced the Barbizon School of painters.

corporal punishment physical punishment of wrongdoers – for example, by whipping. It is still used as a punishment for criminals in many countries, especially under Islamic law. Corporal punishment of children by parents is illegal in some countries, including Sweden, Finland, Denmark, and Norway.

Correggio Antonio Allegri da *c.* 1494–1534. Italian painter of the High Renaissance. His style followed the Classical grandeur of Leonardo da Vinci and Titian but anticipated the Baroque in its emphasis on movement, softer forms, and contrasts of light and shade.

corrosion the eating away and eventual destruction of metals and alloys by chemical attack. The rusting of ordinary iron and steel is the most common form of corrosion. Rusting takes place in moist air, when the iron combines with oxygen and water to form a brown-orange deposit of ⊳rust (hydrated iron oxide). The rate of corrosion is increased where the atmosphere is polluted with sulphur dioxide. Salty road and air conditions accelerate the rusting of car bodies.

Corsica (French *Corse*) island region of France, in the Mediterranean off the west coast of Italy, N of Sardinia; it comprises the *départements* of Haute Corse and Corse du Sud; *area* 8,700 sq km/3,358 sq mi; *capital* Ajaccio (port); *features* Corsica's mountain bandits were eradicated 1931, but the tradition of the vendetta or blood feud lingers; *government* a 61-member regional parliament with the power to scrutinize French National Assembly bills applicable to the island and propose amendments; *population* (1986) 249,000, including just under 50% native Corsicans; there are about 400,000 *émigrés*, mostly in Mexico and Central America, who return to retire; *languages* French (official); the majority speak Corsican, an Italian dialect.

Cortés Hernán (Ferdinand) 1485–1547. Spanish conquistador. He conquered the Aztec empire 1519–21, and secured Mexico for Spain.

corticosteroid any of several steroid hormones secreted by the cortex of the ⊳adrenal glands; also synthetic forms with similar properties. Corticosteroids have anti-inflammatory and immunosuppressive effects and may be used to treat a number of conditions, including rheumatoid arthritis, severe allergies, asthma, some skin diseases, and some cancers. Side effects can be serious, and therapy must be withdrawn very gradually.

cortisone natural corticosteroid produced by the ⊳adrenal gland, now synthesized for its anti-inflammatory qualities and used in the treatment of rheumatoid arthritis.

corundum native aluminium oxide, Al_2O_3, the hardest naturally occurring mineral known apart from diamond (corundum rates 9 on the Mohs' scale of hardness); lack of cleavage also increases its durability. Its crystals are barrel-shaped prisms of the trigonal system. Varieties of gem-quality corundum are *ruby* (red) and *sapphire* (any colour other than red, usually blue). Poorer-quality and synthetic corundum is used in industry, for example as an abrasive.

cosine in trigonometry, a function of an angle in a right-angled triangle found by dividing the length of the side adjacent to the angle by the length of the hypotenuse (the longest side). It is usually shortened to *cos*.

cosmic background radiation or *3° radiation* electromagnetic radiation left over from the original formation of the universe in the Big Bang around 15 billion years ago. It corresponds to an overall background temperature of 3K (−270°C/−454°F), or 3°C above absolute zero. In 1992 the Cosmic Background Explorer satellite, COBE, detected slight 'ripples' in the strength of the background radiation that are believed to mark the first stage in the formation of galaxies.

cosmic radiation streams of high-energy particles from outer space, consisting of protons, alpha particles, and light nuclei, which collide with atomic nuclei in the Earth's atmosphere, and produce secondary nuclear particles (chiefly ▷mesons, such as pions and muons) that shower the Earth.

cosmology study of the structure of the universe. Modern cosmology began in the 1920s with the discovery that the universe is expanding, which suggested that it began in an explosion, the ▷Big Bang. An alternative – now discarded – view, the ▷steady-state theory, claimed that the universe has no origin, but is expanding because new matter is being continually created.

Cossack people of S and SW Russia, Ukraine, and Poland, predominantly of Russian or Ukrainian origin, who took in escaped serfs and lived in independent communal settlements (military brotherhoods) from the 15th to the 19th century. Later they held land in return for military service in the cavalry under Russian and Polish rulers. After 1917, the various Cossack communities were incorporated into the Soviet administrative and collective system.

Costa Rica Republic of (*República de Costa Rica*); *area* 51,100 sq km/19,735 sq mi; *capital* San José; *environment* by

1983 only 17% of the forest remained; massive environmental destruction also caused incalculable loss to the gene pool. It is now one of the leading centres of conservation in Latin America; *features* Poas Volcano; Guayabo pre-Colombian ceremonial site; *political system* liberal democracy; *population* (1993 est) 3,300,000 (including 1,200 Guaymi Indians); growth rate 2.6% p.a.; *language* Spanish (official); *religion* Roman Catholic 95%.

cot death or *sudden infant death syndrome* (SIDS) death of an apparently healthy baby, almost always during sleep. It is most common in the winter months, and strikes more boys than girls. The cause is not known but risk factors that have been identified include prematurity, respiratory infection, overheating, and sleeping position.

cotton tropical and subtropical herbaceous plant of the genus *Gossypium* of the mallow family Malvaceae. Fibres surround the seeds inside the ripened fruits, or bolls, and these are spun into yarn for cloth.

cotyledon structure in the embryo of a seed plant that may form a 'leaf' after germination and is commonly known as a seed leaf. The number of cotyledons present in an embryo is an important character in the classification of flowering plants (▷angiosperms).

Council of Europe body constituted May 1949 in Strasbourg, France (still its headquarters), to achieve greater unity between European countries, to facilitate their economic and social progress, and to uphold the principles of parliamentary democracy and respect for human rights.

council tax method of raising revenue for local government in Britain. It replaced the unpopular community charge, or poll tax, from April 1993. The tax is based on property values but takes some account of the number of people occupying each property.

Counter-Reformation movement initiated by the Catholic church at the Council of Trent 1545–63 to counter the spread of the ▷Reformation. Extending into the 17th century, its dominant forces included the rise of the Jesuits as an educating and missionary group and the deployment of the Spanish Inquisition in other countries.

country and western or *country music* popular music of the white US South and West; it evolved from the folk music of the English, Irish, and Scottish settlers and has a strong blues influence. Characteristic instruments are slide guitar, mandolin, and fiddle. Lyrics typically extol family values and traditional sex roles, and often have a strong narrative element.

county administrative unit of a country or state. It was the name given by the Normans to Anglo-Saxon 'shires', and the boundaries of many present-day English counties date back to Saxon times. In the USA a county is a subdivision of a state; the power of counties differs widely among states.

Courbet Gustave 1819–1877. French artist. He was a portrait, genre, and landscape painter. Reacting against academic trends, both Classicist and Romantic, he became a major exponent of Realism, depicting contemporary life with an unflattering frankness as in his *Burial at Ornans* 1850 (Musée d'Orsay, Paris).

covalent bond chemical ▷bond produced when two atoms share one or more pairs of electrons (usually each atom contributes an electron). The bond is often represented by a single line drawn between the two atoms. Covalently bonded substances include hydrogen (H_2), water (H_2O), and most organic substances.

Coward Noël 1899–1973. English dramatist, actor, revue-writer, director, and composer. He epitomized the witty and sophisticated man of the theatre. From his first success with *The Young Idea* 1923, he wrote and appeared in plays and comedies on both sides of the Atlantic such as *Hay Fever* 1925, *Private Lives* 1930 *Blithe Spirit* 1941, and *A Song at Twilight* 1966.

crab any decapod (ten-legged) crustacean of the division Brachyura, with a broad, rather round, upper body shell (carapace) and a small ▷abdomen tucked beneath the body. Crabs are related to lobsters and crayfish. Mainly marine, some crabs live in fresh water or on land. They are alert carnivores and scavengers. They have a typical sideways walk, and strong pincers on the first pair of legs, the other four pairs being used for walking. Periodically, the outer shell is cast to allow for growth. The name 'crab' is sometimes used for similar arthropods, such as the horseshoe crab, which is neither a true crab nor a crustacean.

Crab nebula cloud of gas 6,000 light years from Earth, in the constellation Taurus. It is the remains of a star that exploded as a ▷supernova (observed as a brilliant point of light on Earth 1054). At its centre is a ▷pulsar that flashes 30 times a second. The name comes from its crablike shape.

crack street name for a chemical derivative (bicarbonate) of ▷cocaine in hard, crystalline lumps; it is heated and inhaled (smoked) as a stimulant. Crack was first used in San Francisco in the early 1980s, and is highly addictive.

Cranach Lucas 1472–1553. German painter, etcher, and woodcut artist. He was a leading figure in the German Renaissance. He painted many full-length nudes and precise and polished portraits, such as *Martin Luther* 1521 (Uffizi, Florence).

Cranmer Thomas 1489–1556. English cleric, archbishop of Canterbury from 1533. A Protestant convert, he helped to shape the doctrines of the Church of England under Edward VI. He was responsible for the issue of the Prayer Books of 1549 and 1552, and supported the succession of Lady Jane Grey 1553.

Crécy, Battle of first major battle of the Hundred Years' War 1346. Philip VI of France was defeated by Edward III of England at the village of Crécy-en-Ponthieu, now in Somme *département*, France, 18 km/11 mi NE of Abbeville.

creed in general, any system of belief; in the Christian church the verbal confessions of faith expressing the accepted doctrines of the church. The different forms are the Apostles' Creed, the ▷Nicene Creed, and the Athanasian Creed. The only creed recognized by the Orthodox Church is the Nicene Creed.

Creole in the West Indies and Spanish America, originally someone of European descent born in the New World; later someone of mixed European and African descent. In Louisiana and other states on the Gulf of Mexico, it applies either to someone of French or Spanish descent or (popularly) to someone of mixed French or Spanish and African descent.

Creole language refers to any pidgin language that has ceased to be simply a trade jargon in ports and markets and has become the mother tongue of a particular community. For example, Jamaican Creole, Haitian Creole, Krio in Sierra Leone, and Tok Pisin, now the official language of Papua New Guinea.

Cretaceous period of geological time 146–65 million years ago. It is the last period of the Mesozoic era, during which angiosperm (seed-bearing) plants evolved, and dinosaurs reached a peak before their almost complete extinction at the end of the period. Chalk is a typical rock type of the second half of the period.

Crete (Greek *Kriti*) largest Greek island in the E Mediterranean Sea, 100 km/62 mi SE of mainland Greece; *area* 8,378 sq km/3,234 sq mi; *capital* Khaniá (Canea); *population* (1991) 536,900; *language* Cretan dialect of Greek.

Crick Francis 1916– . British molecular biologist. From 1949 he researched the molecular structure of DNA, and the means whereby characteristics are transmitted from one generation to another. For this work he was awarded a Nobel prize (with Maurice Wilkins [1916–] and James ▷Watson) 1962.

cricket bat-and-ball game between two teams of 11 players each. played with a small solid ball and long flat-sided wooden bats, on a round or oval field, at the centre of which is a finely mown pitch, 20m/22 yd long. At each end of the pitch is a wicket made up of three upright wooden stumps, surmounted by two smaller sticks (bails). The object of the game is to score more runs than the opposing team. A run is normally scored by the batsman striking the ball and exchanging ends with his or her partner until the ball is returned by a fielder, or by hitting the ball to the boundary line for an automatic four or six runs.

Crimea northern peninsula on the Black Sea, an autonomous republic of ▷Ukraine; formerly a region (1954–91); *area* 27,000 sq km/10,425 sq mi; *capital* Simferopol; *features* mainly steppe, but southern coast is a holiday resort; home of the Black Sea fleet (ownership of which is disputed between Russia and Ukraine); *population* 2.5 million (70% Russian, despite return of 150,000 Tatars since 1989).

Crimean War war 1853–56 between Russia and the allied powers of England, France, Turkey, and Sardinia. The war arose from British and French mistrust of Russia's ambitions in the Balkans. It began with an allied Anglo-French expedition to the Crimea to attack the Russian Black Sea city of Sevastopol. The battles of the river Alma, Balaclava (including the charge of the Light Brigade), and Inkerman 1854 led to a year-long siege. The war was ended by the Treaty of Paris 1856.

criminal law body of law that defines the public wrongs (crimes) that are punishable by the state and establishes methods of prosecution and punishment. It is distinct from ▷civil law, which deals with legal relationships between individuals (including organizations), such as contract law.

critical mass in nuclear physics, the minimum mass of fissile material that can undergo a continuous ▷chain reaction. Below this mass, too many ▷neutrons escape from the surface for a chain reaction to carry on; above the critical

mass, the reaction may accelerate into a nuclear explosion.

Croatia Republic of; *area* 56,538 sq km/21,824 sq mi; *capital* Zagreb; *features* popular sea resorts along the extensive Adriatic coastline; *political system* emergent democracy; *population* (1993 est) 4,850,000 including 75% Croats, 12% Serbs, and 1% Slovenes; *language* Croatian variant of Serbo-Croatian; *religions* Roman Catholic (Croats); Orthodox Christian (Serbs).

crocodile large aquatic carnivorous reptile of the family Crocodiliae, related to alligators and caymans, but distinguished from them by a more pointed snout and a notch in the upper jaw into which the fourth tooth in the lower jaw fits. Crocodiles can grow up to 6 m/20 ft, and have long, powerful tails that propel them when swimming. They can live up to 100 years.

Cro-Magnon prehistoric human *Homo sapiens sapiens* believed to be ancestral to Europeans, the first skeletons of which were found 1868 in the Cro-Magnon cave near Les Eyzies, in the Dordogne region of France. They are thought to have superseded the Neanderthals in the Middle East, Africa, Europe, and Asia about 40,000 years ago. They hunted bison, reindeer, and horses.

Cromwell Oliver 1599–1658. English general and politician, Puritan leader of the Parliamentary side in the ▷Civil War. He raised cavalry forces (later called *Ironsides*) which aided the victories at Edgehill 1642 and ▷Marston Moor 1644, and organized the New Model Army, which he led (with General Fairfax) to victory at Naseby 1645. He declared Britain a republic ('the Commonwealth') 1649, following the execution of Charles I, and ruled as Lord Protector from 1653.

Cromwell Thomas, Earl of Essex *c.* 1485–1540. English politician who drafted the legislation making the Church of England independent of Rome. Originally in Lord Chancellor Wolsey's service, he became secretary to Henry VIII 1534 and the real director of government policy; he was executed for treason.

crow any of 35 species of the genus *Corvus*, family Corvidae, which also includes jays and magpies. Ravens belong to the same genus as crows. Crows are usually about 45 cm/1.5 ft long, black, with a strong bill feathered at the base, and omnivorous with a bias towards animal food.

crown colony any British colony that is under the direct legislative control of the crown and does not possess its own system of representative government. Crown colonies are administered by a crown-appointed governor or by elected or nominated legislative and executive councils with an official majority.

crown court in England and Wales, any of several courts that hear serious criminal cases referred from ▷magistrates' courts after committal proceedings. They replaced quarter sessions and assizes, which were abolished 1971. Appeals against conviction or sentence at magistrates' courts may be heard in crown courts. Appeal from a crown court is to the Court of Appeal.

crusade European war against non-Christians and heretics, sanctioned by the pope; in particular, the Crusades, a series of wars 1096–1291 undertaken by European rulers to recover Palestine from the Muslims. Motivated by religious zeal, the desire for land, and the trading ambitions of the major Italian cities, the Crusades were varied in their aims and effects.

crustacean one of the class of arthropods that includes crabs, lobsters, shrimps, woodlice, and barnacles. The external skeleton is made of protein and chitin hardened with lime. Each segment bears a pair of appendages that may be modified as sensory feelers (antennae), as mouthparts, or as swimming, walking, or grasping structures.

cryogenics science of very low temperatures (approaching absolute zero), including the production of very low temperatures and the exploitation of special properties associated with them, such as the disappearance of electrical resistance (▷superconductivity).

crystal substance with an orderly three-dimensional arrangement of its atoms or molecules, thereby creating an external surface of clearly defined smooth faces having characteristic angles between them. Examples are table salt and quartz.

crystallography the scientific study of crystals. In 1912 it was found that the shape and size of the repeating atomic patterns (unit cells) in a crystal could be determined by passing X-rays through a sample. This method, known as ▷X-ray diffraction, opened up an entirely new way of 'seeing' atoms. It has been found that many substances have a unit cell that exhibits all the symmetry of the whole crystal; in table salt (sodium chloride, NaCl), for instance, the unit cell is an exact cube.

Cuba Republic of (*República de Cuba*); *area* 110,860 sq km/42,820 sq mi; *capital* Havana; *features* 3,380 km/2,100 mi of coastline, with deep bays, sandy beaches, coral islands and reefs; more than 1,600 islands surround the Cuban mainland; *political system* communist republic; *population* (1993 est) 11,000,000; 37% are white of Spanish descent, 51% mulatto, and 11% are of African origin; growth rate 0.6% p.a.; *language* Spanish; *religions* Roman Catholic 85%; also Episcopalians and Methodists.

Cubism revolutionary movement in early 20th-century painting, pioneering abstract forms. Its founders, Georges Braque and Pablo Picasso, were admirers of Paul Cézanne and were inspired by his attempt to create a highly structured visual language. The movement attracted such artists as Juan Gris, Fernand Léger, and Robert Delaunay, and the sculptor Jacques Lipchitz. Its message was that a work of art exists in its own right rather than as a representation of the real world.

Cultural Revolution Chinese mass movement 1966–69 begun by Communist Party chair Mao Zedong, directed against the upper middle class – bureaucrats, artists, and academics – who were killed, imprisoned, humiliated, or 'resettled'. Intended to 'purify' Chinese communism, it was also an attempt by Mao to renew his political and ideological pre-eminence inside China. Half a million people are estimated to have been killed.

Cumbria county of NW England, created 1974 from Cumberland, Westmorland, and parts of NW Lancashire and NW Yorkshire; *area* 6,810 sq km/ 2,629 sq mi; *towns and cities* Carlisle (administrative headquarters), Barrow, Kendal, Whitehaven, Workington, Penrith; *features* Lake District National Park, including Scafell Pike 978 m/3,210 ft, the highest mountain in England; Helvellyn 950 m/3,118 ft; Lake Windermere, the largest lake in England, 17 km/10.5 mi long, 1.6 km/1 mi wide; nculear power stations: Calder Hall, the world's first nuclear power station, 1956, and Sellafield; *population* (1991) 483,100.

cuneiform ancient writing system formed of combinations of wedge-shaped strokes, usually impressed on clay. It was probably invented by the Sumerians, and was in use in Mesopotamia as early as the middle of the 4th millennium BC.

Cupid in Roman mythology, the god of love, identified with the Greek ▷Eros.

Curie Marie (born Sklodovska) 1867–1934. Polish scientist. In 1898 she reported the possible existence of a new, powerfully radioactive element in pitchblende ores. Her husband, Pierre (1859–1906), abandoned his own researches to assist her, and in the same year they announced the existence of polonium and radium. They isolated the pure elements 1902. Both scientists refused to take out a patent on their discovery and were jointly awarded the Davy Medal 1903 and the Nobel Prize for Physics 1903, with Henri Becquerel (1852–1908), and Marie was awarded the Nobel Prize for Chemistry 1911.

current flow of a body of water or air, or of heat, moving in a definite direction. Ocean currents are fast-flowing currents of seawater generated by the wind or by variations in water density between two areas. They are partly responsible for transferring heat from the equator to the poles and thereby evening out the global heat imbalance.

cybernetics science concerned with how systems organize, regulate, and reproduce themselves, and also how they evolve and learn. In the laboratory, inanimate objects are created that behave like living systems. Applications range from the creation of electronic artificial limbs to the running of the fully automated factory where decision making machines operate up to managerial level.

cyberspace the imaginary, interactive 'worlds' created by computers; often used interchangeably with 'virtual world' or ◊'virtual reality'. (See also ◊Internet.)

Cyclops in Greek mythology, one of a race of Sicilian giants, who had one eye in the middle of the forehead and lived as shepherds. ◊Odysseus blinded the Cyclops Polyphemus in Homer's *Odyssey*.

Cynic school of Greek philosophy (Cynicism), founded in Athens about 400 BC by Antisthenes, a disciple of Socrates, who advocated a stern and simple morality and a complete disregard of pleasure and comfort.

cypress any coniferous tree or shrub of the genera *Cupressus* and *Chamaecyparis*, family Cupressaceae. There are about 20 species, originating from temperate regions of the northern hemisphere. They have minute, scalelike leaves and cones made up of woody, wedge-shaped scales containing an aromatic resin.

Cyprus Greek *Republic of Cyprus* (*Kypriaki Dimokratia*) in the south, and *Turkish Republic of Northern Cyprus* (*Kibris Cumhuriyeti*) in the north; *area* 9,251 sq km/3,571 sq mi; *capital* Nicosia (divided between Greeks and Turks); *features* archaeological and historic sites; Mount Olympus 1,953 m/6,406 ft (highest peak); beaches; *political system* democratic divided republic; *population* (1994) 725,000 (Greek Cypriot 78%, Turkish Cypriot 18%); growth rate 1.2% p.a.; *languages* Greek and Turkish (official), English; *religions* Greek Orthodox 78%, Sunni Muslim 18%.

Cyrano de Bergerac Savinien 1619–1655. French writer. He joined a corps of guards at 19 and performed heroic feats which brought him fame. He is the hero of a classic play Edmond Rostand (1869–1918), in which his excessively long nose is used as a counterpoint to his chivalrous character.

cystic fibrosis hereditary disease involving defects of various tissues, including the sweat glands, the mucous glands of the bronchi (air passages), and the pancreas. The sufferer experiences repeated chest infections and digestive disorders and generally fails to thrive. In 1989 a gene for cystic fibrosis was identified facilitating the development of a screening test for carriers.

cystitis inflammation of the bladder, usually caused by bacterial infection, and resulting in frequent and painful urination. It is more common in women. Treatment is by antibiotics and copious fluids with vitamin C.

cytoplasm the part of the cell outside the ◊nucleus. Strictly speaking, this includes all the ◊organelles (mitochondria, chloroplasts, and so on), but often cytoplasm refers to the jellylike matter in which the organelles are embedded (correctly termed the cytosol).

Czech Republic (*Česká Republika*); *area* 78,864 sq km/30,461 sq mi; *capital* Prague; *environment* one of the most polluted areas of Europe; up to twenty times the permissible level of sulphur dioxide is released over Prague, where 75% of the drinking water fails to meet the country's health standards; *features* summer and winter resort areas in Western Carpathian, Bohemian, and Sudetic mountain ranges; *political system* emergent democracy; *population* (1993) 10,330,000 (with German and other minorities); growth rate 0.4% p.a.; *languages* Czech (official); *religions* Roman Catholic (75%), Protestant, Hussite, Orthodox.

D

Dada or *Dadaism* artistic and literary movement founded 1915 in Zürich, Switzerland, by the Romanian poet Tristan Tzara (1896–1963) and others in a spirit of rebellion and disillusionment during World War I. Other Dadaist groups were soon formed by the artists Marcel ◊Duchamp and ◊Man Ray in New York, Francis Picabia in Barcelona, and Kurt Schwitters in Germany. The Dadaists produced deliberately anti-aesthetic images and directly scorned established art.

Daguerre Louis Jacques Mande 1789–1851. French pioneer of photography. Together with Joseph Niépce, he is credited with the invention of photography (though others were reaching the same point simultaneously). In 1838 he invented the daguerreotype, a single image process superseded ten years later by Fox Talbot's negative/positive process.

Dahl Roald 1916–1990. British writer of Norwegian ancestry. He is celebrated for short stories with a twist, for example, *Tales of the Unexpected* 1979, and for children's books, including *Charlie and the Chocolate Factory* 1964. He also wrote the screenplay for the James Bond film *You Only Live Twice* 1967.

Daimler Gottlieb 1834–1900. German engineer who pioneered the modern car. In 1886 he produced his first motor vehicle and a motorbicycle. He later joined forces with Karl ◊Benz and was one of the pioneers of the high-speed four-stroke petrol engine.

Dakar capital and chief port (with artificial harbour) of Senegal; population (1984) 1,000,000. It is an industrial centre, and there is a university, established 1957.

Dalai Lama 14th incarnation 1935– . Spiritual and temporal head of the Tibetan state until 1959, when he went into exile in protest against Chinese annexation and oppression. His people have continued to demand his return.

Dali Salvador 1904–1989. Spanish painter and designer. In 1929 he joined the Surrealists and became notorious for his flamboyant eccentricity. Influenced by the psychoanalytic theories of Sigmund ◊Freud, he developed a repertoire of striking, hallucinatory images in superbly executed works, which he termed 'hand-painted dream photographs'. *The Persistence of Memory* 1931 (Museum of Modern Art, New York) is typical. By the late 1930s he had developed a more conventional style.

Dallas commercial city in Texas, USA; population (1990) 1,006,900, metropolitan area (with Fort Worth) 3,885,400. Dallas–Fort Worth Regional Airport (opened 1973) is one of the world's largest. John F ◊Kennedy was assassinated here 1963.

Dalton John 1766–1844. English chemist who proposed the theory of atoms, which he considered to be the smallest parts of matter. He produced the first list of relative atomic masses in *Absorption of Gases* 1805 and put forward the law of partial pressures of gases (Dalton's law).

dam structure built to hold back water in order to prevent flooding, to provide water for irrigation and storage, and to provide hydroelectric power. The biggest dams are of the earth-and rock-fill type, also called *embankment dams*.

Daman and Diu union territory of W India; area 112 sq km/43 sq mi; capital Daman; population (1991) 101,400. *Daman* has an area of 72 sq km/28 sq mi. The port and capital, Daman, is on the west coast, 160 km/100 mi N of Bombay. The economy is based on tourism and fishing. *Diu* is an island off the Kathiawar peninsula with an area of 40 sq km/15 sq mi. The main town is also called Diu.

Damascus (Arabic *Dimashq*) capital of Syria, on the river Barada, SE of Beirut; population (1981) 1,251,000. Said to be the oldest continuously inhabited city in the world, Damascus was an ancient city even in Old Testament times. Most notable of the old buildings is the Great Mosque, completed as a Christian church in the 5th century.

Dane person of Danish culture from Denmark and N Germany. There are approximately 5 million speakers of Danish (including some in the USA), a Germanic language belonging to the Indo-European family. The Danes are known for their seafaring culture, which dates back to the Viking age of expansion between the 8th and 10th centuries.

Danelaw 11th-century name for the area of N and E England settled by the Vikings in the 9th century. It occupied about half of England, from the river Tees to the river Thames. Within its bounds, Danish law, customs, and language prevailed. Its linguistic influence is still apparent.

Danish member of the North Germanic group of the Indo-European language family, spoken in Denmark and Greenland and related to Icelandic, Faroese, Norwegian, and Swedish. It has had a particularly strong influence on Norwegian. As one of the languages of the Vikings Old Danish had a strong influence on English.

Dante Alighieri 1265–1321. Italian poet. His masterpiece *La divina commedia/The Divine Comedy* 1307–21 is an epic account in three parts of his journey through Hell, Purgatory, and Paradise, during which he is guided part of the way by the poet Virgil; on a metaphorical level, the journey is also one of Dante's own spiritual development. Other works include the philosophical prose treatise *Convivio/The Banquet* 1306–08, the first major work of its kind to be written in Italian rather than Latin.

Danube (German *Donau*) second longest of European rivers, rising on the eastern slopes of the Black Forest, and flowing 2,858 km/1,776 mi across Europe to enter the Black Sea in Romania by a swampy delta.

Dar es Salaam chief seaport in Tanzania, on the Indian Ocean, and capital of Tanzania until its replacement by

◊Dodoma 1974; population (1985) 1,394,000.

Darwin capital and port in Northern Territory, Australia, in NW Arnhem Land; population (1986) 69,000. It serves the uranium mining site at Rum Jungle to the south. Destroyed 1974 by a cyclone, the city was rebuilt on the same site.

Darwin Charles Robert 1809–1882. English scientist who developed the modern theory of ◊evolution and proposed, with Alfred Russel Wallace, the principle of ◊natural selection. After research in South America and the Galápagos Islands as naturalist on HMS *Beagle* 1831–36, Darwin published *On the Origin of Species by Means of Natural Selection or the Preservation of Favoured Races in the Struggle for Life* 1859. This explained the evolutionary process through the principles of natural and sexual selection.

data facts, figures, and symbols, especially as stored in computers. The term is often used to mean raw, unprocessed facts, as distinct from information, to which a meaning or interpretation has been applied.

database in computing, a structured collection of data, which may be manipulated to select and sort desired items of information. For example, an accounting system might be built around a database containing details of customers and suppliers. In larger computers, the database makes data available to the various programs that need it, without the need for those programs to be aware of how the data are stored. The term is also sometimes used for simple record-keeping systems, such as mailing lists, in which there are facilities for searching, sorting, and producing records.

David *c.* 1060–970 BC. Second king of Israel. According to the Old Testament he played the harp for King Saul to banish Saul's melancholy; he later slew the Philistine giant Goliath with a sling and stone. After Saul's death David was anointed king at Hebron, took Jerusalem, and made it his capital.

David, St or *Dewi* patron saint of Wales, Christian abbot and bishop. According to legend he was the son of a prince of Dyfed and uncle of King Arthur; he was responsible for the adoption of the leek as the national emblem of Wales, but his own emblem is a dove. Feast day 1 March.

Davis Bette 1908–1989. US actress. She entered films 1930, and established a reputation as a forceful dramatic actress with *Of Human Bondage* 1934. Later films included *Dangerous* 1935 and *Jezebel* 1938, both winning her Academy Awards; *All About Eve* 1950; and *Whatever Happened to Baby Jane?* 1962.

Davis Miles (Dewey, Jr) 1926–1991. US jazz trumpeter, composer, and bandleader. He was one of the most influential and innovative figures in jazz. He pioneered bebop with Charlie Parker 1945, cool jazz in the 1950s, and jazz-rock fusion from the late 1960s. His albums include *Birth of the Cool* 1957 (recorded 1949 and 1950), *Sketches of Spain* 1959, *Bitches Brew* 1970, and *Tutu* 1985.

Davy Humphry 1778–1829. English chemist. He discovered, by electrolysis, the metallic elements sodium and potassium in 1807, and calcium, boron, magnesium, strontium, and barium in

1808. In addition, he established that chlorine is an element and proposed that hydrogen is present in all acids. He invented the 'safety lamp' for use in mines where methane was present, enabling miners to work in previously unsafe conditions.

Day-Lewis Cecil 1904–1972. Irish poet, British poet laureate 1968–1972. With W H Auden and Stephen Spender, he was one of the influential left-wing poets of the 1930s. He also wrote detective novels under the pseudonym *Nicholas Blake*.

D-day 6 June 1944, the day of the Allied invasion of Normandy under the command of General Eisenhower, with the aim of liberating Western Europe from German occupation. The Anglo-American invasion fleet landed on the Normandy beaches on the stretch of coast between the Orne River and St Marcouf. After overcoming fierce resistance the allies broke through the German defences; Paris was liberated on 25 Aug, and Brussels on 2 Sept.

DDT (abbreviation for *dichlorodiphenyl-trichloroethane*) $(ClC_6H_5)_2$-$CHCHCl_2$) insecticide discovered 1939 by Swiss chemist Paul Müller. It is useful in the control of insects that spread malaria, but resistant strains develop. DDT is highly toxic and persists in the environment and in living tissue. Its use is now banned in most countries, but it continues to be used on food plants in Latin America.

Dead Sea large lake, partly in Israel and partly in Jordan, lying 394 m/1,293 ft below sea level; area 1,020 sq km/394 sq mi. The chief river entering it is the Jordan; it has no outlet and the water is very salty.

Dead Sea Scrolls collection of ancient scrolls (rolls of writing) and fragments of scrolls found 1947–56 in caves on the W side of the Jordan, 12 km/7 mi S of Jericho and 2 km/1 mi from the N end of the Dead Sea, at Qumran. They include copies of Old Testament books a thousand years older than those previously known to be extant. The documents date mainly from about 150 BC–AD 68, when the monastic community that owned them, the Essenes, was destroyed by the Romans because of its support for a revolt against their rule.

Dean James (Byron) 1931–1955. US actor. Killed in a car accident after the public showing of his first film, *East of Eden* 1955, he posthumously became a cult hero with *Rebel Without a Cause* 1955 and *Giant* 1956.

Debussy (Achille-) Claude 1862–1918. French composer. He broke with German Romanticism and introduced new qualities of melody and harmony based on the whole-tone scale, evoking oriental music. His work includes *Prélude à l'après-midi d'un faune/Prelude to the Afternoon of a Faun* 1894, illustrating a poem by Mallarmé, and the opera *Pelléas et Mélisande* 1902.

decibel unit (symbol dB) of measure used originally to compare sound intensities and subsequently electrical or electronic power outputs; now also used to compare voltages. An increase of 10 dB is equivalent to a 10-fold increase in intensity or power, and a 20-fold increase in voltage. A whisper has an intensity of 20 dB; 140 dB (a jet aircraft taking off nearby) is the threshold of pain.

deciduous of trees and shrubs, that shed their leaves at the end of the growing season or during a dry season to reduce ◊transpiration, the loss of water by evaporation.

decimal number system or *denary number system* the most commonly used number system, to the base ten. Decimal numbers do not necessarily contain a decimal point; 563, 5.63, and −563 are all decimal numbers. Other systems are mainly used in computing and include the ◊binary number system, octal number system, and ◊hexadecimal number system.

Declaration of Independence historic US document stating the theory of government on which the USA was founded, based on the right 'to life, liberty, and the pursuit of happiness'. The statement was issued by the Continental Congress 4 July 1776, renouncing all allegiance to the British crown and ending the political connection with Britain.

Deconstruction in literary theory, a radical form of ◊structuralism, pioneered by the French philosopher Jacques Derrida (1930–), which views text as a 'decentred' play of structures, lacking any ultimately determinable meaning. Through analysis of the internal structure of a text, particularly its contradictions, Deconstructionists demonstrate the existence of subtext meanings – often not those that the author intended – and hence illustrate the impossibility of attributing fixed meaning to a work. Roland Barthes (1915–1980) laid the foundations of Deconstruction in his book *Mythologies* 1957.

Defoe Daniel 1660–1731. English writer. His *Robinson Crusoe* 1719, though purporting to be a factual account of shipwreck and solitary survival, was influential in the development of the novel. The fictional *Moll Flanders* 1722 and the partly factual *A Journal of the Plague Year* 1724 are still read for their concrete realism.

deforestation destruction of forest for timber, fuel, charcoal burning, and clearing for agriculture and extractive industries, such as mining, without planting new trees to replace those lost (reafforestation) or working on a cycle that allows the natural forest to regenerate. Deforestation causes fertile soil to be blown away or washed into rivers, leading to ◊soil erosion, drought, flooding, and loss of wildlife. It may also increase the carbon dioxide content of the atmosphere and intensify the ◊greenhouse effect, because there are fewer trees absorbing carbon dioxide from the air for photosynthesis.

Degas (Hilaire Germain) Edgar 1834–1917. French Impressionist painter and sculptor. He devoted himself to lively, informal studies (often using pastels) of ballet, horse racing, and young women working. From the 1890s he turned increasingly to sculpture, modelling figures in wax in a fluent, naturalistic style.

de Gaulle Charles André Joseph Marie 1890–1970. French general and first president of the Fifth Republic 1958–69. He organized the Free French troops fighting the Nazis 1940–44, was head of the provisional French government 1944–46, and leader of his own Gaullist party. In 1958 the national assembly asked him to form a government during France's economic recovery and to solve the crisis in Algeria. He became president at the end of 1958, having changed the constitution to provide for a presidential system, and served until 1969.

degree in mathematics, a unit (symbol °) of measurement of an angle or arc. A circle or complete rotation is divided into 360°. A degree may be subdivided into 60 minutes (symbol '), and each minute may be subdivided in turn into 60 seconds (symbol ").

deism belief in a supreme being; but the term usually refers to a movement of religious thought in the 17th and 18th centuries, characterized by the belief in a rational 'religion of nature' as opposed to the orthodox beliefs of Christianity. Deists believed that God is the source of natural law but does not intervene directly in the affairs of the world, and that the only religious duty of humanity is to be virtuous.

de Klerk F(rederik) W(illem) 1936– . South African National Party politician, president 1989–94. In Feb 1990 he ended the ban on the ◊African National Congress (ANC) opposition movement and released its effective leader, Nelson ◊Mandela, and by June 1991 had repealed all racially discriminating laws. After Mandela's victory in the first universal suffrage elections April 1994, de Klerk became second executive deputy president. Nobel Prize for Peace jointly with Nelson Mandela 1993.

Delacroix Eugène 1798–1863. French Romantic painter. His prolific output included religious and historical subjects and portraits of friends, among them the musicians Paganini and Chopin. Antagonistic to the French academic tradition, he evolved a highly coloured, fluid style, as in *The Death of Sardanapalus* 1829 (Louvre, Paris).

de la Mare Walter 1873–1956. English poet. He is known for his verse for children, such as *Songs of Childhood* 1902,

and the novels *The Three Royal Monkeys* 1910 for children and, for adults, *The Memoirs of a Midget* 1921. He excelled at creating a sense of eeriness and supernatural mystery.

Delaware state in northeastern USA; *area* 5,300 sq km/2,046 sq mi; *capital* Dover; *features* one of the most industrialized states; headquarters of the Dupont chemical firm; Rehoboth Beach; *population* (1990) 666,200.

Delhi capital of India, comprising the walled city of *Old Delhi* (built 1639), situated on the west bank of the river Jumna, and *New Delhi* to the S; population (1991) 8,375,000. The city was largely designed by English architect Edwin Lutyens and chosen to replace Calcutta as the seat of government 1912 (completed 1929; officially inaugurated 1931). Delhi is the administrative centre of the Union Territory of Delhi (area 1,500 sq km/579 sq mi; population (1991) 9,370,000) and India's largest commercial and communications centre.

Delors Jacques 1925– . French socialist politician, finance minister 1981–84. As president of the European Commission 1984–94 he generally enjoyed a high-profile, successful presidency, including overseeing final ratification and implementation of the ◊Maastricht Treaty on European union.

Delphi city of ancient Greece, situated in a rocky valley north of the gulf of Corinth, on the southern slopes of Mount Parnassus, site of a famous ◊oracle in the temple of Apollo. The site was supposed to be the centre of the Earth and was marked by a conical stone, the *omphelos*. The oracle was interpreted by priests from the inspired utterances of the Pythian priestess until

delta

it was closed down by the Roman emperor Theodosius I AD 390.

delta tract of land at a river's mouth, composed of silt deposited as the water slows on entering the sea. Familiar examples of large deltas are those of the Mississippi, Ganges and Brahmaputra, Rhône, Po, Danube, and Nile; the shape of the Nile delta is like the Greek letter *delta* Δ, and thus gave rise to the name.

dementia mental deterioration as a result of physical changes in the brain. It may be due to degenerative change, circulatory disease, infection, injury, or chronic poisoning. *Senile dementia*, a progressive loss of mental faculties such as memory and orientation, is typically a disease process of old age, and can be accompanied by ▷depression.

Demeter in Greek mythology, the goddess of agriculture (Roman Ceres), daughter of Kronos and Rhea, and mother of Persephone by Zeus. She was later identified with the Egyptian goddess ▷Isis.

democracy (Greek *demos* 'the community', *kratos* 'sovereign power') government by the people, usually through elected representatives. In the modern world, democracy has developed from the American and French revolutions. The two concepts underlying *liberal democracy* are the right to representative government and the right to individual freedom; in practice the features include representative institutions based on majority rule, through free elections and a choice of political parties; accountability of the government to the electorate; freedom of expression, assembly, and the individual, guaranteed by an independent judiciary; and limitations on the power of government.

Democratic Party one of the two main political parties of the USA. It tends to be the party of the working person, as opposed to the Republicans, the party of big business, but the divisions between the two are not clear cut. Its stronghold since the Civil War has traditionally been industrial urban centres and the Southern states.

demography study of the size, structure, dispersement, and development of human populations to establish reliable statistics on such factors as birth and death rates, marriages and divorces, life expectancy, and migration.

Demosthenes *c.* 384–322 BC. Athenian politician, famed for his oratory. From 351 BC he led the party that advocated resistance to the growing power of ▷Philip of Macedon, and in his *Philippics*, a series of speeches, incited the Athenians to war. This policy resulted in the defeat of Chaeronea 338, and the establishment of Macedonian supremacy. After the death of Alexander he organized a revolt; when it failed, he took poison to avoid capture by the Macedonians.

demotic script cursive (joined) writing derived from Egyptian hieratic script, itself a cursive form of ▷hieroglyphic. Demotic documents are known from the 6th century BC to about AD 470. It was written horizontally, from right to left.

Deng Xiaoping or *Teng Hsiao-ping* 1904– . Chinese political leader. A member of the Chinese Communist Party (CCP) from the 1920s, he took part in the Long March 1934–36. He was in the Politburo from 1955 until ousted in the Cultural Revolution 1966–69. Reinstated in the 1970s, he gradually took power and introduced a radical economic modernization programme. He retired from the Politburo 1987 and from his last official position March 1990, but remained influential behind the scenes.

Denmark Kingdom of (*Kongeriget Danmark*); *area* 43,075 sq km/16,627 sq mi; *capital* Copenhagen; *features* Kronborg Castle in Helsingør (Elsinore); Tivoli Gardens (Copenhagen); Legoland Park in Sillund; *head of state* Queen Margrethe II from 1972; *head of government* Poul Nyrup Rasmussen from 1993; *political system* liberal democracy; *population* (1993) 5,180,000; growth rate 0% p.a.; *languages* Danish (official); there is a German-speaking minority; *religion* Lutheran 97%.

density measure of the compactness of a substance; it is equal to its mass per unit volume and is measured in kg per cubic metre/lb per cubic foot. Density is a scalar quantity. The density D of a mass m occupying a volume V is given by the formula: $D = m/V$. Relative density is the ratio of the density of a substance to that of water at 4°C.

dentition type and number of teeth in a species. Different kinds of teeth have different functions; a grass- eating animal will have large molars for grinding its food, whereas a meat-eater will need powerful canines for catching and killing its prey. The teeth that are less useful may be reduced in size or missing altogether. An animal's dentition is represented diagramatically by a dental formula.

Denver city and capital of Colorado, USA, on the South Platte River, near the foothills of the Rocky Mountains; population (1990) 467,600, Denver–Boulder metropolitan area 1,848,300.

deoxyribonucleic acid full name of ◊DNA.

depression or *cyclone* or *low* in meteorology, a region of low atmospheric pressure. A depression forms as warm, moist air from the tropics mixes with cold, dry polar air, producing warm and cold boundaries (◊fronts) and unstable weather – low cloud and drizzle, showers, or fierce storms. The warm air, being less dense, rises above the cold air to produce the area of low pressure on the ground. Air spirals in towards the centre of the depression in an anticlockwise direction in the northern hemisphere, clockwise in the southern hemisphere, generating winds up to gale force.

depression emotional state characterized by sadness, unhappy thoughts, apathy, and dejection. Sadness is a normal response to major losses such as bereavement or unemployment. After childbirth, ◊postnatal depression is common. However, clinical depression, which is prolonged or unduly severe, often requires treatment, such as antidepressants cognitive therapy, or, in rare cases, electroconvulsive therapy (ECT), in which an electrical current is passed through the brain.

De Quincey Thomas 1785–1859. English author. His works include *Confessions of an English Opium- Eater* 1821 and the essays *On the Knocking at the Gate in Macbeth* 1823 and *On Murder Considered as One of the Fine Arts* 1827.

Derby blue riband of the English horseracing season. It is run over 2.4 km/1.5 mi at Epsom, Surrey, every June. It was established 1780 and named after the 12th Earl of Derby. The USA has an equivalent horse race, the *Kentucky Derby*.

Derbyshire county of N central England; *area* 2,630 sq km/1,015 sq mi; *features* Peak District National Park (including Kinder Scout 636 m/2,088 ft); Chatsworth Housel; *population* (1991) 928,600.

Derry county of Northern Ireland; *area* 2,070 sq km/799 sq mi; *towns and cities* Matlock (administrative headquarters), Derby, Chesterfield, Ilkeston; *features* rivers Foyle, Bann, and Roe; borders Lough Neagh; *population* (1981) 187,000.

Derry (Gaelic *doire* 'a place of oaks') historic city and port on the river Foyle, County Derry, Northern Ireland; population (1981) 89,100. It was known as Londonderry until 1984; *features* the Protestant cathedral of St Columba (1633); the Guildhall (rebuilt 1912).

Descartes René 1596–1650. French philosopher and mathematician. He believed that commonly accepted knowledge was doubtful because of the subjective nature of the senses, and attempted to rebuild human knowledge using as his foundation *cogito ergo sum* ('I think, therefore I am'). He also believed that the entire material universe could be explained in terms of mathematical physics, and founded coordinate geometry as a way of defining and manipulating geometrical shapes by means of algebraic expressions. Cartesian coordinates, the means by which points are represented in this system, are named after him. Descartes also established the science of optics, and helped to shape contemporary theories of astronomy and animal behaviour.

desert arid area without sufficient rainfall and, consequently, vegetation to support human life. The term includes the ice areas of the polar regions (known as cold deserts). Almost 33% of the Earth's land surface is desert, and this proportion is increasing. Deserts can be created by changes in climate, or by the human-aided process of desertification.

desertification creation of deserts by changes in climate, or by human-aided processes. Desertification can sometimes be reversed by special planting (marram grass, trees) and by the use of water-absorbent plastic grains, which, added to the soil, enable crops to be grown. The processes leading to desertification include overgrazing, destruction of forest belts, and exhaustion of the soil by intensive cultivation without restoration of fertility – all of which may be prompted by the pressures of an expanding population or by concentration in land ownership. About 135 million people are directly affected by desertification, mainly in Africa, the Indian subcontinent, and South America.

desktop publishing (DTP) use of microcomputers for small-scale typesetting and page makeup. DTP systems are capable of producing camera-ready pages (pages ready for photographing and printing), made up of text and graphics, with text set in different typefaces and sizes. The page can be previewed on the screen before final printing on a laser printer.

detergent surface-active cleansing agent. The common detergents are made from ⊳fats (hydrocarbons) and sulphuric acid, and their long-chain molecules have a type of structure similar to that of ⊳soap molecules: a salt group at one end attached to a long hydrocarbon 'tail'. They have the advantage over soap in that they do not produce scum by forming insoluble salts with the calcium and magnesium ions present in hard water.

determinism in philosophy, the view that denies human freedom of action. Everything is strictly governed by the principle of cause and effect, and human action is no exception. It is the opposite of free will, and rules out moral choice and responsibility.

Detroit city in Michigan, USA, situated on Detroit River; population (1990) 1,028,000, metropolitan area 4,665,200. It is an industrial centre with the headquarters of Ford, Chrysler, and General Motors, hence its nickname, Motown (from 'motor town'). During the 1960s and 1970s Detroit became associated with the 'Motown Sound' of rock and soul music.

de Valera Eámon 1882–1975. Irish nationalist politician, prime minister of the Irish Free State/Eire/Republic of Ireland 1932–48, 1951–54, and 1957–59, and president 1959–73. Repeatedly imprisoned, he participated in the Easter Rising 1916 and was leader of the nationalist ⟩Sinn Féin party 1917–26, when he formed the republican ⟩Fianna Fáil party; he directed negotiations with Britain 1921 but refused to accept the partition of Ireland until 1937.

de Valois Ninette. Stage name of Edris Stannus 1898–   . Irish choreographer, dancer, and teacher. In setting up the Vic-Wells Ballet 1931 (later the Royal Ballet and Royal Ballet School) she was, along with choreographer Frederick ⟩Ashton, one of the architects of British ballet. Among her works are *Job* 1931 and *Checkmate* 1937.

devaluation in economics, the lowering of the official value of a currency against other currencies, so that exports become cheaper and imports more expensive. Used when a country is badly in deficit in its balance of trade, it results in the goods the country produces being cheaper abroad, so that the economy is stimulated by increased foreign demand.

devil in Jewish, Christian, and Muslim theology, the supreme spirit of evil (*Beelzebub, Lucifer, Iblis*), or an evil spirit generally.

Devon or *Devonshire* county of SW England; *area* 6,720 sq km/2,594 sq mi; *towns and cities* Exeter (administrative headquarters), Plymouth; resorts: Paignton, Torquay, Teignmouth, and Ilfracombe; *features* National Parks: Dartmoor, Exmoor; Lundy bird sanctuary and marine nature reserve in the Bristol Channel; *population* (1991) 1,010,000.

Devonian period of geological time 408–360 million years ago, the fourth period of the Palaeozoic era. Many desert sandstones from North America and Europe date from this time. The first land plants flourished in the Devonian period, corals were abundant in the seas, amphibians evolved from air-breathing fish, and insects developed on land.

Dhaka or *Dacca* capital of Bangladesh from 1971, in Dhaka region, W of the river Meghna; population (1984) 3,600,000.

diabetes disease *diabetes mellitus* in which a disorder of the islets of Langerhans in the ⟩pancreas prevents the body producing the hormone ▷insulin, so that sugars cannot be used properly. Treatment is by strict dietary control and oral or injected insulin, depending on the type of diabetes.

Diaghilev Sergei Pavlovich 1872–1929. Russian ballet impresario. In 1909 he founded the Ballets Russes/Russian Ballet (headquarters in Monaco), which he directed for 20 years, introducing Russian ballet to the West and encouraging a dazzling array of dancers and choreographers, including Anna Pavlova, Vaslav Nijinsky, and George Balanchine among many others.

diamond generally colourless, transparent mineral, the hard crystalline form of carbon. It is regarded as a precious gemstone, and is the hardest substance known (10 on the ▷Mohs' scale). Industrial diamonds, which may be natural or synthetic, are used for cutting, grinding, and polishing.

Diana in Roman mythology, the goddess of chastity, hunting, and the Moon, daughter of Jupiter and twin of Apollo. Her Greek equivalent is the goddess ▷Artemis.

Diana Princess of Wales 1961– . The daughter of the 8th Earl Spencer, she married Prince Charles in St Paul's Cathedral, London 1981, the first English bride of a royal heir since 1659. She is descended from the only sovereigns from whom Prince Charles is not descended, Charles II and James II. She had two sons, William and Henry, before her separation from Charles 1992.

diaphragm thin muscular sheet separating the thorax from the abdomen in mammals. It is attached by way of the ribs at either side and the breastbone and backbone. Arching upwards against the heart and lungs the diaphragm is important in the mechanics of breathing. It contracts at each inhalation, moving downwards to increase the volume of the chest cavity, and relaxes at exhalation.

diarrhoea frequent or excessive action of the bowels so that the faeces are liquid or semiliquid. It is caused by intestinal irritants (including some drugs and poisons), infection with harmful organisms (as in dysentery, salmonella, or cholera), or allergies.

Diaspora dispersal of the Jews, initially from Palestine after the Babylonian conquest 586 BC, and then following the Roman sack of Jerusalem AD 70 and their crushing of the Jewish revolt of 135. The term has come to refer to all the Jews living outside Israel.

Diaz Bartolomeu *c.* 1450–1500. Portuguese explorer, the first European to reach the Cape of Good Hope 1488, and to establish a route around Africa. He drowned during an expedition with Pedro Cabral (1460–1526).

Dickens Charles 1812–1870. English novelist. He is enduringly popular for his memorable characters and his portrayal of the social evils of Victorian England. In 1836 he published the first number of the *Pickwick Papers*, followed by *Oliver Twist* 1838, the first of his 'reforming' novels; *Nicholas Nickleby* 1839; *Barnaby Rudge* 1841; *The Old Curiosity Shop* 1841; and *David Copperfield* 1849. Among his later books are *A Tale of Two Cities* 1859 and *Great Expectations* 1861.

Diderot Denis 1713–1784. French philosopher. He is closely associated with the Enlightenment, the European intellectual movement for social and scientific progress, and was editor of the enormously influential *Encyclopédie* 1751–80.

Dido Phoenician princess. The legendary founder of Carthage, N Africa, she committed suicide to avoid marrying a local prince. In the Latin epic *Aeneid*, Virgil represents her death as the result of her desertion by the Trojan hero ◊Aeneas.

diesel engine ◊internal-combustion engine that burns a lightweight fuel oil. The diesel engine operates by compressing air until it becomes sufficiently hot to ignite the fuel. It is a piston-in-cylinder engine, like the ◊petrol engine, but only air (rather than an air-and-fuel mixture) is taken into the cylinder on the first piston stroke (down). The piston moves up and compresses the air until it is at a very high temperature. The fuel oil is then injected into the hot air, where it burns, driving the piston down on its power stroke. For this reason the engine is called a compression-ignition engine.

diesel oil lightweight fuel oil used in diesel engines. Like petrol, it is a petroleum product. When used in vehicle engines, it is also known as *derv* – *d*iesel-*e*ngine *r*oad *v*ehicle.

Dietrich Marlene (Maria Magdalene) 1904–1992. German-born US actress and singer. She appeared with Emil Jannings in both the German and American versions of the film *Der Blaue Engel/The Blue Angel* 1930, directed by Josef von Sternberg. Her husky, sultry singing voice added to her appeal. Her other films include *Blonde Venus* 1932, and *Just a Gigolo* 1978.

diffraction the slight spreading of a light beam into a pattern of light and dark bands when it passes through a narrow slit or past the edge of an obstruction. A *diffraction grating* is a plate of glass or metal ruled with close, equidistant parallel lines used for separating a wave train such as a beam of incident light into its component frequencies (white light results in a spectrum).

diffusion spontaneous and random movement of molecules or particles in a fluid (gas or liquid) from a region in which they are at a high concentration to a region of lower concentration, until a uniform concentration is achieved throughout. No mechanical mixing or stirring is involved. For instance, if a drop of ink is added to water, its molecules will diffuse until their colour becomes evenly distributed throughout.

digestive system mouth, stomach, intestine, and associated glands of animals, which are responsible for digesting food. The food is broken down by physical and chemical means in the ◊stomach; digestion is completed, and most nutrients are absorbed in the small intestine; what remains is stored and concentrated into faeces in the large intestine. In birds, additional digestive organs are the crop and gizzard.

digital recording technique whereby the pressure of sound waves is sampled more than 30,000 times a second and the values converted by computer into precise numerical values. These are recorded and, during playback, are reconverted to sound waves.

dinosaur any of a group (sometimes considered as two separate orders) of extinct reptiles living between 230 million and 65 million years ago. Their closest living relations are crocodiles and birds. Many species of dinosaur evolved during the millions of years they were the dominant large land animals. Most were large (up to 27 m/90 ft), but some were as small as chickens. They disappeared 65 million years ago for reasons not fully understood, although many theories exist.

Diocletian (Gaius Aurelius Valerius Diocletianus) AD 245–313. Roman emperor 284–305, when he abdicated in favour of Galerius. He reorganized and subdivided the empire, with two joint and two subordinate emperors, and in 303 initiated severe persecution of Christians.

diode combination of a cold anode and a heated cathode (or the semiconductor equivalent, which incorporates a *p–n* junction). Either device allows the passage of direct current in one direction only, and so is commonly used in a ▷rectifier to convert alternating current (AC) to direct current (DC).

Diogenes *c.* 412–323 BC. Ascetic Greek philosopher of the ▷Cynic school. He believed in freedom and self-sufficiency for the individual, and that the virtuous life was the simple life; he did not believe in social mores. His writings do not survive.

Dionysus in Greek mythology, the god of wine (son of Semele and Zeus), and also of orgiastic excess. He was attended by women called maenads who were believed to be capable of tearing animals to pieces with their bare hands when under his influence. He was identified with the Roman ▷Bacchus, whose rites were less savage.

diphtheria acute infectious disease in which a membrane forms in the throat (threatening death by ▷asphyxia), along with the production of a powerful toxin that damages the heart and nerves. The organism responsible is a bacterium (*Corynebacterium diphtheriae*). It is treated with antitoxin and antibiotics. Its incidence has been reduced greatly by immunization.

diploid having two sets of ▷chromosomes in each cell. In sexually reproducing species, one set is derived from each parent, the ▷gametes, or sex cells, of each parent being ▷haploid (having only one set of chromosomes) due to ▷meiosis (reduction cell division).

Dirac Paul Adrien Maurice 1902–1984. British physicist who worked out a version of quantum mechanics consistent with special ▷relativity. The existence of the positron (positive electron) was one of its predictions. He shared the Nobel Prize for Physics 1933 with Austrian physicist Erwin Schrödinger (1887–1961).

direct current (DC) electric current that flows in one direction, and does not reverse its flow as ▷alternating current does. The electricity produced by a battery is direct current.

disc or *disk* in computing, a common medium for storing large volumes of data (an alternative is magnetic tape). A *magnetic disc* is rotated at high speed in a disc-drive unit as a read/write (playback or record) head passes over its surfaces to record or read the magnetic variations that encode the data. Recently, *optical discs*, such as ▷CD-ROM (compact-disc read-only memory) and WORM (write once, read many times), have been used to store computer data. Data are recorded on the disc surface as etched microscopic pits and are read by a laser-scanning device. Optical discs have an enormous capacity – about 550 megabytes (million Ɗbytes) on a compact disc, and thousands of megabytes on a full-size optical disc.

discrimination distinction made (social, economic, political, legal) between individuals or groups such that one has the power to treat the other unfavourably. *Negative discrimination*, often based on stereotype, includes anti-Semitism, apartheid, caste, racism, sexism, and slavery. *Positive discrimination*, or 'affirmative action', is sometimes practised in an attempt to counteract the effects of previous long-term discrimination.

discus circular disc thrown by athletes who rotate the body to gain momentum from within a circle 2.5 m/8 ft in diameter. The men's discus weighs 2 kg/4.4 lb and the women's 1 kg/2.2 lb. Discus throwing was a competition in ancient Greece at gymnastic contests, such as those of the Olympic Games. It is an event in the modern Olympics and athletics meetings.

Disney Walt(er Elias) 1901–1966. US filmmaker and animator, a pioneer of family entertainment. He established his own studio in Hollywood 1923, and his first Mickey Mouse cartoons (*Plane Crazy*, which was silent, and *Steamboat Willie*, which had sound) appeared 1928. The studio later made feature-length animated films, including *Snow White and the Seven Dwarfs* 1938, *Pinocchio* 1940, and *Dumbo* 1941. The first Disneyland theme park was opened in California 1955.

dispersion in optics, the splitting of white light into a spectrum; for example, when it passes through a prism or a diffraction grating. It occurs because the prism (or grating) bends each component wavelength to a slightly different extent. The natural dispersion of light through raindrops creates a rainbow.

Disraeli Benjamin, Earl of Beaconsfield 1804–1881. British Conservative politician and novelist. Elected to Parliament 1837, he was chancellor of the Exchequer 1852, 1858–59, and 1866–68, and prime minister 1868 and 1874–80. His imperialist policies brought India directly under the crown, and he was personally responsible for purchasing control of the Suez Canal. The central Conservative Party organization is his creation. His novels reflect an interest in social reform and include *Coningsby* 1844 and *Sybil* 1845.

divine right of kings Christian political doctrine that hereditary monarchy is the system approved by God, hereditary right cannot be forfeited, monarchs are accountable to God alone for their actions, and rebellion against the lawful sovereign is therefore blasphemous.

divorce legal dissolution of a lawful marriage. It is distinct from an annulment, which is a legal declaration that the marriage was invalid. The ease with which a divorce can be obtained in different countries varies considerably and is also affected by different religious practices.

Djibouti chief port and capital of the Republic of Djibouti, on a peninsula 240 km/149 mi SW of Aden and 565 km/351 mi NE of Addis Ababa; population (1988) 290,000.

Djibouti Republic of (*Jumhouriyya Djibouti*); *area* 23,200 sq km/8,955 sq mi; *capital* (and chief port) Djibouti; *features* terminus of railway link with Ethiopia; Lac Assal salt lake is the second lowest point on Earth (-144 m/-471 ft); *political system* authoritarian nationalism; *population* (1993 est) 410,000; *languages* French (official), Somali, Afar, Arabic; *religion* Sunni Muslim.

DNA (*deoxyribonucleic acid*) complex giant molecule that contains, in chemically coded form, all the information needed to build, control, and maintain a living organism. DNA is a ladderlike double-stranded nucleic acid that forms the basis of genetic inheritance in all organisms, except for a few viruses that have only ▷RNA. In organisms other than bacteria it is organized into ▷chromosomes and contained in the cell nucleus.

dodo extinct bird *Raphus cucullatus* formerly found on the island of Mauritius, but exterminated before the end of the 17th century. Although related to the pigeons, it was larger than a turkey, with a bulky body and very short wings and tail. Flightless and trusting, it was easy prey to humans.

Dodoma capital (replacing Dar es Salaam 1974) of Tanzania; 1,132 m/3,713 ft above sea level; population (1985) 85,000. It is a centre of communications, linked by rail with Dar es Salaam and Kigoma on Lake Tanganyika, and by road with Kenya to the N and Zambia and Malawi to the S.

Doe Samuel Kenyon 1950–1990. Liberian politician and soldier, head of state 1980–90. He seized power in a coup. In 1981 he made himself general and army commander in chief. In 1985 he was narrowly elected president, as leader of the newly formed National Democratic Party of Liberia. Having successfully put down an uprising April 1990, Doe was deposed and killed by rebel forces Sept

1990. His human-rights record was poor.

dog any carnivorous mammal of the family Canidae, including wild dogs, wolves, jackals, coyotes, and foxes. Specifically, the domestic dog *Canis familiaris*, the earliest animal descended from the wolf or jackal. Dogs were first domesticated over 10,000 years ago, and migrated with humans to all the continents. They have been selectively bred into many different varieties for use as working animals and pets.

doge chief magistrate in the ancient constitutions of Venice and Genoa. The first doge of Venice was appointed 697 with absolute power (modified 1297), and from his accession dates Venice's prominence in history. The last Venetian doge, Lodovico Manin, retired 1797 and the last Genoese doge 1804.

Doha (Arabic *Ad Dawḥah*) capital and chief port of Qatar; population (1986) 217,000. It is the centre of vocational training for all the Persian Gulf states.

doldrums area of low atmospheric pressure along the equator, in the intertropical convergence zone where the NE and SE trade winds converge. The doldrums are characterized by calm or very light winds, during which there may be sudden squalls and stormy weather. For this reason the areas are avoided as far as possible by sailing ships.

dolomite white mineral with a rhombohedral structure, calcium magnesium carbonate ($CaMg(CO_3)_2$). The term also applies to a type of limestone rock where the calcite content is replaced by the mineral dolomite. Dolomite rock may be white, grey, brown, or reddish in colour, commonly crystalline. It is used as a building material. The region of the Alps known as the Dolomites is a fine example of dolomite formation.

dolphin any of various highly intelligent aquatic mammals of the family Delphinidae, which also includes porpoises. There are about 60 species. The name 'dolphin' is generally applied to species having a beaklike snout and slender body, whereas the name 'porpoise' is reserved for the smaller species with a blunt snout and stocky body. Dolphins use sound (echolocation) to navigate, to find prey, and for communication. The common dolphin *Delphinus delphis* is found in all temperate and tropical seas. It is up to 2.5 m/8 ft long, and is dark above and white below, with bands of grey, white, and yellow on the sides. It has up to 100 teeth in its jaws, which make the 15 cm/6 in 'beak' protrude forward from the rounded head. Dolphins feed on fish and squid.

Domesday Book record of the survey of England carried out 1086 by officials of William the Conqueror in order to assess land tax and other dues, ascertain the value of the crown lands, and enable the king to estimate the power of his vassal barons. The name is derived from the belief that its judgement was as final as that of Doomsday.

Domingo Placido 1937– . Spanish lyric tenor. He specializes in Italian and French 19th-century operatic roles to which he brings a finely-tuned dramatic temperament. He has made many films including the 1988 version of Puccini's *Tosca* set in Rome, and the 1990 Zeffirelli production of Leoncavallo's *I Pagliacci/The Strolling Players*.

Dominica Commonwealth of; *area* 751 sq km/290 sq mi *capital* Roseau, with a deepwater port; *political system* liberal democracy; *population* (1993 est) 88,000 (mainly black African in origin, but with a small Carib reserve of some 500); growth rate 1.3% p.a.; *language* English (official), but the Dominican patois reflects earlier periods of French rule; *religion* Roman Catholic 80%.

Dominican Republic (*República Dominicana*); *area* 48,442 sq km/18,700 sq mi; *capital* Santo Domingo; *features* Pico Duarte 3,174 m/10,417 ft, highest point in Caribbean islands; Santo Domingo is the oldest European city in the western hemisphere; *political system* democratic republic; *population* (1993 est) 7,600,000; growth rate 2.3% p.a.; *religion* Roman Catholic 95%.

Donatello (Donato di Niccolo) *c.* 1386–1466. Italian sculptor of the early Renaissance. He was instrumental in reviving the Classical style, as in his graceful bronze statue of the youthful *David* about 1433 (Bargello, Florence) and his equestrian statue of the general *Gattamelata* 1447–50 (Piazza del Santo, Padua).

Donegal mountainous county in Ulster province in the NW of the Republic of Ireland, surrounded on three sides by the Atlantic Ocean; area 4,830 sq km/1,864 sq mi; county town Lifford; population (1991) 127,900. The market town and port of Donegal is at the head of Donegal Bay in the SW. The river Erne hydroelectric project (1952) involved the building of large power stations at Ballyshannon.

Donizetti Gaetano 1797–1848. Italian composer. He created more than 60 operas, including *Lucrezia Borgia* 1833, *Lucia di Lammermoor* 1835, *La Fille du régiment* 1840, *La Favorite* 1840, and *Don Pasquale* 1843. They show the influence of Rossini and Bellini, and are characterized by a flow of expressive melodies.

Don Juan character of Spanish legend, Don Juan Tenorio, supposed to have lived in the 14th century and notorious for his debauchery. Tirso de Molina, Molière, Mozart, Byron, and George Bernard Shaw have featured the legend in their works.

Donne John 1571–1631. English metaphysical poet. His work consists of love poems, religious poems, verse satires, and sermons, most of which were first published after his death. His religious poems show the same passion and ingenuity as his love poetry. A Roman Catholic in his youth, he converted to the Church of England and finally became dean of St Paul's Cathedral, where he is buried.

Doppler effect change in the observed frequency (or wavelength) of waves due to relative motion between the wave source and the observer. The Doppler effect is responsible for the perceived change in pitch of a siren as it approaches and then recedes, and for the ◊red shift of light from distant stars. It is named after the Austrian physicist Christian Doppler (1803–1853).

Doré Gustave 1832–1883. French artist. Chiefly known as a prolific illustrator, he was also active as a painter, etcher, and sculptor. He produced closely worked engravings of scenes from, for example, Rabelais, Dante, Cervantes, the Bible, Milton, and Edgar Allan Poe.

Dorian people of ancient Greece. They entered Greece from the N and took most of the Peloponnese from the

Achaeans, perhaps destroying the ◊Mycenaean civilization; this invasion appears to have been completed before 1000 BC. Their chief cities were Sparta, Argos, and Corinth.

Dorset county of SW England; *area* 2,650 sq km/1,023 sq mi; *towns and cities* Dorchester (administrative headquarters), Poole, Shaftesbury, Sherborne; resorts: Bournemouth, Lyme Regis, Weymouth; *features* Chesil Bank, a shingle bank along the coast 19 km/11 mi long; Corfe Castle; Dorset Downs; Canford Heath, the home of some of Britain's rarest breeding birds and reptiles; *population* (1991) 645,200.

DOS (acronym for *disc operating system*) computer ◊operating system specifically designed for use with disc storage; also used as an alternative name for a particular operating system, ◊MS-DOS.

Dostoevsky Fyodor Mihailovich 1821–1881. Russian novelist. His works are remarkable for their profound psychological insight. In 1849 he was sentenced to four years' hard labour in Siberia for printing socialist propaganda. *The House of the Dead* 1861 recalls his prison experiences, and were followed by his major works *Crime and Punishment* 1866, *The Idiot* 1868–69, and *The Brothers Karamazov* 1879–80.

double bass large bowed four-stringed (sometimes five-stringed) musical instrument, the bass of the violin family. It is descended from the bass viol or violone. Until 1950, after which it was increasingly superseded by the electric bass, it also provided bass support (plucked) for jazz and dance bands.

Douglas capital of the Isle of Man in the Irish Sea; population (1986) 20,400. It is a holiday resort and terminus of shipping routes to and from Fleetwood and Liverpool; banking and financial services are important to the local economy.

Douglas Kirk. Stage name of Issur Danielovitch Demsky 1916– . US film actor. Usually cast as a dynamic though often ill-fated hero, as in *Spartacus* 1960, he was a major star of the 1950s and 1960s in such films as *Ace in the Hole* 1951, *The Bad and the Beautiful* 1953, *Lust for Life* 1956, *The Vikings* 1958, *Seven Days in May* 1964, and *The War Wagon* 1967. He continues to act and produce. He is the father of actor Michael Douglas (1944–).

Douglas-Home Alec (Alexander Frederick), Baron Home of the Hirsel 1903– . British Conservative politician. He was foreign secretary 1960–63, and succeeded Harold Macmillan as prime minister 1963. He renounced his peerage (as 14th Earl of Home) to fight (and lose) the general election 1964, and resigned as party leader 1965. He was again foreign secretary 1970–74, when he received a life peerage.

Dounreay experimental nuclear reactor site on the north coast of Scotland, 12 km/7 mi W of Thurso. Development started 1974 and continued until a decision was made 1988 to decommission the site by 1994.

Dover, Strait of (French *Pas-de-Calais*) stretch of water separating England from France, and connecting the English Channel with the North Sea. It is about 35 km/22 mi long and 34 km/21 mi wide at its narrowest part. It is one of the world's busiest sea lanes.

Dow Jones Index (*Dow Jones Industrial 30 Share Index*) scale for measuring the average share price and percentage change of 30 major US industrial companies. It has been calculated and published since 1897 by the financial news publisher Dow Jones and Co.

Down county of SE Northern Ireland; *area* 2,470 sq km/953 sq mi; *towns and cities* Downpatrick (county town); *features* Mourne Mountains; Strangford sea lough; *population* (1981) 339,200.

Down's syndrome condition caused by a chromosomal abnormality (the presence of an extra copy of chromosome 21), which in humans produces mental retardation; a flattened face; coarse, straight hair; and a fold of skin at the inner edge of the eye (hence the former name 'mongolism'). The condition can be detected by prenatal testing.

Doyle Arthur Conan 1859–1930. Scottish writer. He created the detective Sherlock Holmes and his assistant Dr Watson, who first appeared in *A Study in Scarlet* 1887 and featured in a number of subsequent stories, including *The Hound of the Baskervilles* 1902.

D'Oyly Carte Richard 1844–1901. English producer of the Gilbert and Sullivan operas. They were performed at the Savoy Theatre, London, which he built. The D'Oyly Carte Opera Company, founded 1876, was disbanded 1982 following the ending of its monopoly on the Gilbert and Sullivan operas. The present company, founded 1988, moved to the Alexandra Theatre, Birmingham, 1991.

Drabble Margaret 1939– . English writer. Her novels include *The Millstone* 1965, *The Middle Ground* 1980,

The Radiant Way 1987, *A Natural Curiosity* 1989, and *The Gates of Ivory* 1991. She portrays contemporary life with toughness and sensitivity.

Drake Francis *c.* 1545–1596. English buccaneer and explorer. He was sponsored by Elizabeth I for an expedition to the Pacific, sailing round the world 1577–80 in the *Golden Hind*. This was the second circumnavigation of the globe (the first was by Portuguese explorer Ferdinand Magellan). Drake also helped to defeat the Spanish Armada 1588 as a vice admiral in the *Revenge*.

Dresden capital of the state of Saxony, Germany; population (1990) 520,000. It was devastated by Allied fire-bombing 1945. Dresden county has an area of 6,740 sq km/2,602 sq mi and a population of 1,772,000.

Dreyfus Alfred 1859–1935. French army officer, victim of miscarriage of justice, anti-Semitism, and cover-up. Employed in the War Ministry, in 1894 he was accused of betraying military secrets to Germany, court-martialled, and sent to the penal colony on Devil's Island, French Guiana. When his innocence was discovered 1896 the military establishment tried to conceal it, and the implications of the Dreyfus affair were passionately discussed in the press until he was exonerated in 1906.

drug any of a range of substances, natural or synthetic, administered to humans and animals as therapeutic agents: to diagnose, prevent or treat disease or to assist recovery from injury. Traditionally many drugs were obtained from plants or animals; some minerals also had medicinal value. Today, increasing numbers of drugs are synthesized in the laboratory.

drug misuse illegal use of drugs for nontherapeutic purposes. Drugs used illegally include: narcotics, such as heroin, morphine, and the synthetic opioids; barbiturates; amphetamines and related substances; ▷benzodiazepine tranquillizers; cocaine, LSD, and cannabis. *Designer drugs*, for example ecstasy, are usually modifications of the amphetamine molecule. Crack, a highly toxic derivative of cocaine, became available to drug users in the 1980s. Some athletes misuse drugs such as ▷anabolic steroids.

Druidism religion of the Celtic peoples of the pre-Christian British Isles and Gaul. The word is derived from Greek *drus* 'oak'. The Druids regarded this tree as sacred; one of their chief rites was the cutting of mistletoe from it with a golden sickle. They taught the immortality of the soul and a reincarnation doctrine, were experts in astronomy, and are thought to have offered human sacrifices.

drum any of a class of percussion instruments including *slit drums* made of wood, *steel drums* fabricated from oil drums, and a majority group of *skin drums* consisting of a shell or vessel of wood, metal, or earthenware across one or both ends of which is stretched a membrane of hide or plastic. Drums are among the oldest instruments known.

Druse or *Druze* religious sect in the Middle East. They are monotheists, preaching that the Fatimid caliph al-Hakim (996–1021) is God; their scriptures are drawn from the Bible, the Koran, and Sufi allegories. Druse militia groups form one of the three main factions involved in the Lebanese civil war (the others are Amal Shi'ite Muslims and Christian Maronites).

Dryden John 1631–1700. English poet and dramatist. He is noted for his satirical verse and for his use of the heroic couplet. His poetry includes the verse satire *Absalom and Achitophel* 1681, *Annus Mirabilis* 1667, and 'St Cecilia's Day' 1687. Plays include the heroic drama *The Conquest of Granada* 1670–71, the comedy *Marriage à la Mode* 1672, and *All for Love* 1678, a reworking of Shakespeare's *Antony and Cleopatra*.

DTP abbreviation for ▷*desktop publishing.*

Dubai one of the ▷United Arab Emirates.

Dublin county in the Republic of Ireland, in Leinster province, facing the Irish Sea; county town Dublin; area 920 sq km/355 sq mi; population (1986) 1,021,000. It is mostly level and lowlying, but rises in the S to 753 m/2,471 ft in Kippure, part of the Wicklow Mountains. The river Liffey enters Dublin Bay. Dublin, the capital of the Republic of Ireland, and Dún Laoghaire are the two major towns.

Dublin (Gaelic *Baile Atha Cliath*) capital and port on the east coast of the Republic of Ireland, at the mouth of the river Liffey, facing the Irish Sea; population (1991) 478,400, Greater Dublin, including Dún Laoghaire (1986 est) 921,000. It is the site of one of the world's largest breweries (Guinness).

Duchamp Marcel 1887–1968. French-born US artist. He achieved notoriety with his *Nude Descending a Staircase No 2* 1912 (Philadelphia Museum of Art), influenced by Cubism and Futurism. An active exponent of ▷Dada, he invented ready-mades, everyday items (for example, a bicycle wheel mounted on a kitchen stool) which he displayed as works of art.

Dufy Raoul 1877–1953. French painter and designer. Inspired by ▷Fauvism he developed a fluent, brightly coloured style in watercolour and oils, painting scenes of gaiety and leisure, such as horse racing, yachting, and life on the beach. He also designed tapestries, textiles, and ceramics.

Dukas Paul (Abraham) 1865–1935. French composer and teacher. His scrupulous orchestration and chromatically-enriched harmonies were admired by Debussy. His small output includes the opera *Ariane et Barbe- Bleue/Ariane and Bluebeard* 1907, the ballet *La Péri/The Peri* 1912, and the animated orchestral scherzo *L'Apprenti sorcier/The Sorcerer's Apprentice* 1897.

Dumas Alexandre 1802–1870. French author, known as Dumas *père* (the father). He is remembered for his historical romances, including *Les Trois Mousquetaires/The Three Musketeers* 1844 and its sequels. His play *Henri III et sa cour/Henry III and His Court* 1829 established French romantic historical drama. He was the father of Alexandre Dumas *fils* (1824–1895), author of *La Dame aux camélias/The Lady of the Camellias* 1852.

Dumfries and Galloway region of Scotland *area* 6,500 sq km/2,510 sq mi *towns and cities* Dumfries (administrative headquarters) *features* Solway Firth; Galloway Hills; Glen Trool National Park; Ruthwell Cross, a runic cross dating from about 800; Stranraer provides the shortest sea route to Ireland; *population* (1991) 147,800.

Duncan Isadora 1877–1927. US dancer. A pioneer of modern dance, she adopted an emotionally expressive free form, dancing barefoot and wearing a loose tunic, inspired by the ideal of Hellenic beauty. She danced solos accompanied to music by Beethoven and other great composers.

Dundee city and fishing port, administrative headquarters of Tayside, Scotland, on the north side of the Firth of Tay; population (1991) 165,900. It is an important shipping and rail centre.

dune mound or ridge of wind-drifted sand. Loose sand is blown and bounced along by the wind, up the windward side of a dune. The sand particles then fall to rest on the lee side, while more are blown up from the windward side. In this way a dune moves gradually downwind.

Durban principal port of Natal, South Africa, and second port of the republic; population (1985) 634,000, urban area 982,000.

Dürer Albrecht 1471–1528. German artist. He was the leading figure of the northern Renaissance. He was born in Nuremberg and travelled widely in Europe. Highly skilled in drawing and a keen student of nature, he perfected the technique of woodcut and engraving, producing woodcut series such as the *Apocalypse* 1498 and copperplate engravings such as *The Knight, Death, and the Devil* 1513 and *Melancholia* 1514. His paintings include altarpieces and meticulously observed portraits, including many self-portraits.

Durham county of NE England; *area* 2,440 sq km/942 sq mi; *towns and cities* Durham (administrative headquarters), Darlington, Peterlee, Newton Aycliffe;

features Pennine Hills; Beamish open-air industrial museum; *population* (1991) 593,400.

Durkheim Emile 1858–1917. French sociologist, one of the founders of modern sociology, who also influenced social anthropology. He worked to establish sociology as a respectable and scientific discipline, capable of diagnosing social ills and recommending possible cures.

Durrell Lawrence (George) 1912–1990. English novelist and poet. He lived mainly in the E Mediterranean, the setting of his novels, including the Alexandria Quartet: *Justine, Balthazar, Mountolive,* and *Clea* 1957–60; he also wrote travel books. His heady prose and bizarre characters reflect his exotic sources of inspiration. He was the brother of the naturalist Gerald Durrell.

Dushanbe formerly (1929–69) *Stalinabad* capital of Tajikistan, 160 km/100 mi N of the Afghan frontier; population (1987) 582,000. It is a road, rail, and air centre.

Düsseldorf industrial city of Germany, on the right bank of the river Rhine, 26 km/16 mi NW of Cologne, capital of North Rhine–Westphalia; population (1988) 561,000. It is a river port and the commercial and financial centre of the Ruhr area.

Dutch member of the Germanic branch of the Indo-European language family, often referred to by scholars as Netherlandic and taken to include the standard language and dialects of the Netherlands (excluding Frisian) as well as Flemish (in Belgium and N France) and, more remotely, its offshoot Afrikaans in South Africa.

Duvalier François 1907–1971. Rightwing president of Haiti 1957–71. Known as *Papa Doc*, he ruled as a dictator, intimidating and assassinating his opponents. He rigged the 1961 elections in his favour and in 1964 declared himself president for life. He was excommunicated by the Vatican for harassing the church, and was succeeded on his death by his son Jean-Claude Duvalier (*Baby Doc*) 1951–   , who was forced to flee to France 1986.

Dvořák Antonin (Leopold) 1841–1904. Czech composer. International recognition came with two sets of *Slavonic Dances* 1878 and 1886. He was director of the National Conservatory, New York, 1892–95. Works such as his *New World Symphony* 1893 reflect his interest in American folk themes. He wrote nine symphonies; tone poems; operas, including *Rusalka* 1900; large-scale choral works; the *Carnival* 1891–92 and other overtures; violin and cello concertos; chamber music; piano pieces; and songs. His Romantic music displays the influence of Czech folk music.

dye substance that, applied in solution to fabrics, imparts a colour resistant to washing. *Direct dyes* combine with the material of the fabric, yielding a coloured compound; *indirect dyes* require the presence of another substance (a mordant), with which the fabric must first be treated; *vat dyes* are colourless soluble substances that on exposure to air yield an insoluble coloured compound.

Dyfed county of SW Wales, created 1974; *area* 5,770 sq km/2,227 sq mi; *towns and cities* Carmarthen (administrative headquarters), Llanelli, Haverfordwest, Aberystwyth, Cardigan, Lampeter; *features* Pembrokeshire Coast National Park; part of the Brecon Beacons National Park; part of the Cambrian Mountains, including Plynlimon Fawr, 752 m/2,468 ft; *population* (1991) 343,500 *languages* English; 44% Welsh-speaking.

Dylan Bob. Adopted name of Robert Allen Zimmerman 1941–   . US singer and songwriter. His lyrics provided catchphrases for a generation and influenced innumerable songwriters. His early albums *Freewheelin'* 1963 and *The Times They Are A-Changin'* 1964, were associated with the US civil-rights movement and antiwar protest. Later albums, produced in an individualistic rock style, include *Highway 61 Revisited* 1965, *Blonde on Blonde* 1966, *Blood on the Tracks* 1975, and *The Bootleg Years* 1991. He toured in 1994–95.

dynamics or *kinetics* in mechanics, the mathematical and physical study of the behaviour of bodies under the action of forces that produce changes of motion in them.

dysentery infection of the large intestine causing abdominal cramps and painful ⭗diarrhoea with blood. There are two kinds of dysentery: *amoebic* (caused by a protozoan), common in the tropics, which may lead to liver damage; and *bacterial*, the kind most often seen in the temperate zones.

dyslexia malfunction in the brain's synthesis and interpretation of written information, popularly known as 'word blindness'. It results in poor ability in reading and writing, though the person may excel in other areas, for example in mathematics.

E

ear organ of hearing in animals. It responds to the vibrations that constitute sound, and these are translated into nerve signals and passed to the brain. A mammal's ear consists of three parts: outer ear, middle ear, and inner ear. The *outer ear* is a funnel that collects sound, directing it down a tube to the *ear drum* (tympanic membrane), which separates the outer and *middle ears*. Sounds vibrate this membrane, the mechanical movement of which is transferred to a smaller membrane leading to the *inner ear* by three small bones, the auditory ossicles. Vibrations of the inner ear membrane move fluid contained in the snail-shaped cochlea, which vibrates hair cells that stimulate the auditory nerve connected to the brain. Three fluid-filled canals of the inner ear detect changes of position; this mechanism, with other sensory inputs, is responsible for the sense of balance.

Earhart Amelia 1898–1937. US aviation pioneer and author, who in 1928 became the first woman to fly across the Atlantic. With copilot Frederick Noonan, she attempted a round-the-world flight 1937. Somewhere over the Pacific their plane disappeared.

Earth third planet from the Sun. It is almost spherical, flattened slightly at the poles, and is composed of three concentric layers: the core, the mantle, and the crust. About 70% of the surface (including the north and south polar icecaps) is covered with water. The Earth is surrounded by a life-supporting atmosphere and is the only planet on which life is known to exist. *mean distance from the Sun* 149,500,000 km/92,860,000 mi *equatorial diameter* 12,756 km/7,923 mi *circumference* 40,070 km/24,900 mi *rotation period* 23 hr 56 min 4.1 sec *atmosphere* nitrogen 78.09%; oxygen 20.95%; argon 0.93%; carbon dioxide 0.03%; and less than 0.0001% neon, helium, krypton, hydrogen, xenon, ozone, radon *surface* land surface 150,000,000 sq km/57,500,000 sq mi (greatest height above sea level 8,872 m/29,118 ft Mount Everest); water surface 361,000,000 sq km/139,400,000 sq mi (greatest depth 11,034 m/36,201 ft Mariana Trench in the Pacific). The interior is thought to be an inner core about 2,600 km/1,600 mi in diameter, of solid iron and nickel; an outer core about 2,250 km/1,400 mi thick, of molten iron and nickel; and a mantle of mostly solid rock about 2,900 km/1,800 mi thick, separated by the Mohorovičić discontinuity from the Earth's crust. The crust and the topmost layer of the mantle form about 12 major moving plates, some of which carry the continents. The plates are in constant, slow motion, called tectonic drift. *age* 4.6 billion years. The Earth was formed with the rest of the ◊Solar System by consolidation of interstellar dust. Life began 3.5–4 billion years ago.

earthquake shaking of the Earth's surface as a result of the sudden release of stresses built up in the Earth's crust. The study of earthquakes is called ▷seismology. Most earthquakes occur along faults (fractures or breaks) in the crust. ▷Plate tectonic movements generate the major proportion: as two plates move past each other they can become jammed and deformed, and a series of shock waves (seismic waves) occur when they spring free. Their force (magnitude) is measured on the ▷Richter scale, and their effect (intensity) on the Mercalli scale. The point at which an earthquake originates is the *seismic focus*; the point on the Earth's surface directly above this is the *epicentre*.

east one of the four cardinal points of the compass, indicating that part of the horizon where the Sun rises; when facing north, east is to the right.

East Anglia region of E England, formerly a Saxon kingdom, including Norfolk, Suffolk, and parts of Essex and Cambridgeshire; Norwich is the principal city. East Anglian ports such as Harwich and Felixstowe have developed as trade with the rest of Europe has increased.

Easter spring feast of the Christian church, commemorating the Resurrection of Jesus. It is a moveable feast, falling on the first Sunday following the full moon after the vernal equinox (21 March), that is, between 22 March and 25 April.

Easter Island or *Rapa Nui* Chilean island in the S Pacific Ocean, part of the Polynesian group, about 3,500 km/2,200 mi W of Chile; area about 166 sq km/64 sq mi; population (1985) 2,000. It was first reached by Europeans on Easter Sunday 1722. On it stand over 800 huge carved statues (moai) and the remains of boat-shaped stone houses, the work of Neolithic peoples of unknown origin. The chief centre is Hanga-Roa.

Easter Rising or *Easter Rebellion* in Irish history, a republican insurrection that began on Easter Monday, April 1916, in Dublin. It was inspired by the Irish Republican Brotherhood (IRB) in an unsuccessful attempt to overthrow British rule in Ireland. It was led by Patrick Pearce of the IRB and James Connolly of Sinn Féin.

East India Company (British) commercial company 1600–1858 chartered by Queen Elizabeth I and given a monopoly of trade between England and the Far East. In the 18th century, the company became, in effect, the ruler of a large part of India, and a form of dual control by the company and a committee responsible to Parliament in London was introduced by Pitt's India Act 1784. The India Act 1858 abolished the company.

East Sussex county of SE England, created 1974, formerly part of Sussex; *area* 1,800 sq km/695 sq mi; *towns and cities* Lewes (administrative headquarters), Newhaven (cross-channel port), Brighton, Eastbourne, Hastings, Bexhill, Winchelsea, Rye; *features* Beachy Head, highest headland on the south coast at 180 m/590 ft; the Weald (including Ashdown Forest); Herstmonceux castle, site of the Greenwich Royal Observatory 1958–90; Battle Abbey and site of the Battle of Hastings; *population* (1991) 690,400.

East Timor disputed territory on the island of ▷Timor in the Malay Archipelago; prior to 1975, it was a Portuguese colony for almost 460 years. The people of East Timor are known as Maubere; *area* 14,874 sq km/5,706 sq mi; *capital* Dili; *population* (1980) 555,000.

Eastwood Clint 1930– . US film actor and director. As the 'Man with No Name' in *A Fistful of Dollars* 1964 and *The Good, the Bad, and the Ugly* 1966, he started the vogue for 'spaghetti Westerns' (made in Italy or Spain).

ebony any of a group of hardwood trees of the ebony family Ebenaceae, especially some tropical persimmons of the genus *Diospyros*, native to Africa and Asia.

EC abbreviation for *European Community*, former name (to 1993) of the ▷European Union.

echinoderm marine invertebrate of the phylum Echinodermata ('spiny-skinned'), characterized by a five- radial symmetry. Echinoderms have a water-vascular system which transports substances around the body. They include starfishes (or sea stars), brittlestars, sea-lilies, sea-urchins, and sea-cucumbers. The skeleton is external, made of a series of limy plates, and echinoderms generally move by using tube-feet, small water-filled sacs that can be protruded or pulled back to the body.

echo repetition of a sound wave, or of a ▷radar or ▷sonar signal, by reflection from a surface. By accurately measuring the time taken for an echo to return to the transmitter, and by knowing the speed of a radar signal (the speed of light) or a sonar signal (the speed of sound in water), it is possible to calculate the range of the object causing the echo (▷echolocation).

echolocation or *biosonar* method used by certain animals, notably bats, whales and dolphins, to detect the positions of objects by using sound. The animal emits a stream of high-pitched sounds, generally at ultrasonic frequencies (beyond the range of human hearing), and listens for the returning echoes reflected off objects to determine their exact location.

eclipse passage of an astronomical body through the shadow of another. The term is usually employed for solar and lunar eclipses, which may be either partial or total, but also, for example, for eclipses by Jupiter of its satellites. An eclipse of a star by a body in the Solar System is called an occultation.

ecology study of the relationship among organisms and the environments in which they live, including all living and nonliving components. The term was coined by the biologist Ernst Haeckel 1866.

economics social science devoted to studying the production, distribution, and consumption of wealth. It consists of the disciplines of *microeconomics*, the study of individual producers, consumers, or markets, and *macroeconomics*, the study of whole economies or systems (in particular, areas such as taxation and public spending).

ecosystem in ▷ecology, an integrated unit consisting of the community of living organisms and the nonliving, or physical, environment in a particular area. The relationships among species in an ecosystem are usually complex and finely balanced, and removal of any one species may be disastrous.

ECU abbreviation for *European Currency Unit*, the official monetary unit of the European Union. It is based on the value of the different currencies used in the ▷European Monetary System (EMS).

Ecuador Republic of (*República del Ecuador*); *area* 270,670 sq km/104,479 sq mi; *capital* Quito; *environment* about 25,000 species became extinct 1965–90 as a result of environmental destruction; *features* Ecuador is crossed by the equator; Galápagos Islands; Cotopaxi is world's highest active volcano; rich wildlife in rainforest of Amazon basin; *political system* emergent democratic republic; *population* (1993 est) 10,980,000; (mestizo 55%, Indian 25%, European 10%, black African 10%); growth rate 2.9% p.a.; *languages* Spanish (official), Quechua, Jivaro, and other Indian languages; *religion* Roman Catholic 95%.

Eden Anthony, 1st Earl of Avon 1897–1977. British Conservative politician, foreign secretary 1935–38, 1940–45, and 1951–55; prime minister 1955–57, when he resigned after the failure of the Anglo-French military intervention in the ▷Suez Crisis.

Edinburgh capital of Scotland and administrative centre of the region of Lothian, near the southern shores of the Firth of Forth; population (1991) 418,900. A cultural centre, it holds a major annual festival of music and the arts. The university was established 1583.

Edinburgh, Duke of title of Prince ▷Philip of the UK.

Edison Thomas Alva 1847–1931. US scientist and inventor, with over 1,000 patents. In Menlo Park, New Jersey, 1876–87, he produced his most important inventions, including the electric light bulb 1879. He constructed a system of electric power distribution for consumers, the telephone transmitter, and the phonograph.

Edmonton capital of Alberta, Canada, on the North Saskatchewan River; population (1986) 576,200. Petroleum pipelines link Edmonton with Superior, Wisconsin, USA, and Vancouver, British Columbia.

Edmund (II) Ironside *c.* 989–1016. King of England 1016, the son of Ethelred II the Unready. He led the resistance to ▷Canute's invasion 1015, and on Ethelred's death 1016 was chosen king by the citizens of London, whereas the Witan (the king's council) elected Canute. Edmund was defeated by Canute at Assandun (Ashington), Essex, and they divided the kingdom between them; when Edmund died Canute ruled the whole kingdom.

Edward (full name Edward Antony Richard Louis) 1964– . Prince of the UK, third son of Queen Elizabeth II. He is seventh in line to the throne.

Edward VIII 1894–1972. King of Great Britain and Northern Ireland Jan–Dec 1936, when he renounced the throne to marry Wallis Warfield ▷Simpson. He was created Duke of Windsor and was governor of the Bahamas 1940–45, subsequently settling in France.

Edward the Confessor *c.* 1003–1066. King of England from 1042, the son of Ethelred II. He lived in Normandy until shortly before his accession. During his reign power was held by Earl Godwin and his son ▷Harold, while the king devoted himself to religion, including the rebuilding of Westminster Abbey (consecrated 1065), where he is buried. His childlessness led ultimately to the Norman Conquest 1066. He was canonized 1161.

egg in animals, the ovum, or female ◊gamete (reproductive cell). After fertilization by a sperm cell, it begins to divide to form an embryo. Eggs may be deposited by the female (ovipary) or they may develop within her body (vivipary and ◊ovovivipary). In the oviparous reptiles and birds, the egg is protected by a shell, and well supplied with nutrients in the form of yolk.

Egypt Arab Republic of (*Jumhuriyat Misr al-Arabiya*); *area* 1,001,450 sq km/ 386,990 sq mi; *capital* Cairo; *environment* the Aswan Dam (opened 1970) on the Nile has caused widespread salinization and an increase in waterborne diseases; coastal erosion; *features* Aswan High Dam and Lake Nasser; Sinai; remains of ancient Egypt (pyramids, Sphinx, Luxor, Karnak, Abu Simbel, El Faiyum); *political system* democratic republic; *population* (1993) 56,430,000; growth rate 2.4% p.a.; *languages* Arabic (official); ancient Egyptian survives to some extent in Coptic; *religions* Sunni Muslim 95%, Coptic Christian 5%.

Ehrlich Paul 1854–1915. German bacteriologist and immunologist who produced the first cure for ◊syphilis. He developed the arsenic compounds, in particular Salvarsan, that were used in the treatment of syphilis prior to the discovery of antibiotics. He shared the 1908 Nobel Prize for Medicine with Ilya Mechnikov (1845–1916) for his work on immunity.

Eiffel (Alexandre) Gustave 1832–1923. French engineer who constructed the *Eiffel Tower* for the 1889 Paris Exhibition. The tower, made of iron, is 320 m/1,050 ft high, and stands in the Champ de Mars, Paris.

Einstein Albert 1879–1955. German-born US physicist who formulated the theories of ◊relativity, and worked on radiation physics and thermodynamics. In 1905 he published the special theory of relativity, and in 1915 issued his general theory of relativity. He received the Nobel Prize for Physics 1921. His latest conception of the basic laws governing the universe was outlined in his ◊unified field theory, made public 1953.

Eisenhower Dwight David ('Ike') 1890–1969. 34th president of the USA 1953–60, a Republican. A general in World War II, he commanded the Allied forces in Italy 1943, then the Allied invasion of Europe, and from Oct 1944 all the Allied armies in the West. As president he promoted business interests at home and conducted the ◊Cold War abroad. His vice president was Richard Nixon.

elder in botany, small tree or shrub of the genus *Sambucus*, of the honeysuckle family (Caprifoliaceae), native to North America, Eurasia, and N Africa. Some are grown as ornamentals for their showy yellow or white flower clusters and their colorful black or scarlet berries.

electoral system see ◊vote.

electric charge property of some bodies that causes them to exert forces on each other. Two bodies both with positive or both with negative charges repel each other, whereas bodies with opposite or 'unlike' charges attract each other, since each is in the ◊electric field of the other. In atoms, ◊electrons possess a negative charge, and ◊protons an equal positive charge. The ◊SI unit of electric charge is the coulomb (symbol C).

electric current the flow of electrically charged particles through a conducting circuit due to the presence of a ⊳potential difference. The current at any point in a circuit is the amount of charge flowing per second; its SI unit is the ampere (coulomb per second).

electric field in physics, a region in which a particle possessing electric charge experiences a force owing to the presence of another electric charge. It is a type of ⊳electromagnetic field.

electricity all phenomena caused by ⊳electric charge, whether static or in motion. Electric charge is caused by an excess or deficit of electrons in the charged substance, and an electric current by the movement of electrons around a circuit. Substances may be electrical conductors, such as metals, which allow the passage of electricity through them, or insulators, such as rubber, which are extremely poor conductors. Substances with relatively poor conductivities that can be improved by the addition of heat or light are known as ⊳semiconductors.

electrode any terminal by which an electric current passes in or out of a conducting substance; for example, the anode or cathode in a battery or the carbons in an arc lamp. The terminals that emit and collect the flow of electrons in thermionic ⊳valves (electron tubes) are also called electrodes: for example, cathodes, plates, and grids.

electrolysis in chemistry, the production of chemical changes by passing an electric current through a solution or molten salt (the electrolyte), resulting in the migration of ions to the electrodes: positive ions (cations) to the negative electrode (cathode) and negative ions (anions) to the positive electrode (anode).

electromagnetic field in physics, the region in which a particle with an ⊳electric charge experiences a force. If it does so only when moving, it is in a pure *magnetic field*; if it does so when stationary, it is in an *electric field*. Both can be present simultaneously.

electromagnetic force one of the four fundamental ⊳forces of nature, the other three being gravity, the strong nuclear force, and the weak nuclear force. The ⊳elementary particle that is the carrier for the electromagnetic (em) force is the photon.

electromagnetic waves oscillating electric and magnetic fields travelling together through space at a speed of nearly 300,000 km/186,000 mi per second. The (limitless) range of possible wavelengths or ⊳frequencies of electromagnetic waves, which can be thought of as making up the *electromagnetic spectrum*, includes radio waves, infrared radiation, visible light, ultraviolet radiation, X-rays, and gamma rays.

electromotive force (emf) loosely, the voltage produced by an electric battery or generator or, more precisely, the energy supplied by a source of electric power in driving a unit charge around an electrical circuit. The unit is the ⊳volt.

electron stable, negatively charged ⊳elementary particle; it is a constituent of all atoms, and a member of the class of particles known as ⊳leptons. The electrons in each atom surround the nucleus in groupings called shells; in a neutral atom the number of electrons is equal to the number of protons in the nucleus. This electron structure is responsible for the chemical properties of the atom (see ⊳atomic structure).

electronic mail or *E-mail* ▷telecommunications system that enables the users of a computer network to send messages to other users. Telephone wires are used to send the signals from terminal to terminal.

electronics branch of science that deals with the emission of ▷electrons from conductors and ▷semiconductors, with the subsequent manipulation of these electrons, and with the construction of electronic devices. The first electronic device was the thermionic ▷valve, or vacuum tube, in which electrons moved in a vacuum, and led to such inventions as ▷radio, ▷television, ▷radar, and the digital ▷computer. Replacement of valves with the comparatively tiny and reliable transistor from 1948 revolutionized electronic development. Modern electronic devices are based on minute ▷integrated circuits (silicon chips), wafer-thin crystal slices holding tens of thousands of electronic components.

electron microscope instrument that produces a magnified image by using a beam of ▷electrons instead of light rays, as in an optical ▷microscope. An *electron lens* is an arrangement of electromagnetic coils that control and focus the beam. Electrons are not visible to the eye, so instead of an eyepiece there is a fluorescent screen or a photographic plate on which the electrons form an image. The wavelength of the electron beam is much shorter than that of light, so much greater magnification and resolution (ability to distinguish detail) can be achieved. The development of the electron microscope has made possible the observation of very minute organisms, viruses, and even large molecules.

element substance that cannot be split chemically into simpler substances. The atoms of a particular element all have the same number of protons in their nuclei (their atomic number). Elements are classified in the periodic table (see ▷periodic table of the elements). Of the 109 known elements, 95 are known to occur in nature (those with atomic numbers 1–95). Those from 96 to 109 do not occur in nature and are synthesized only, produced in particle accelerators. Eighty-one of the elements are stable; all the others, which include atomic numbers 43, 61, and from 84 up, are radioactive.

elementary particle in physics, a subatomic particle that is not made up of smaller particles, and so can be considered one of the fundamental units of matter. There are three groups of elementary particles: quarks, leptons, and gauge bosons.

elephant mammal belonging to either of two surviving species of the order Proboscidea: the Asian elephant *Elephas maximus* and the African elephant *Loxodonta africana*. Elephants can grow to 4 m/13 ft and weigh up to 8 tonnes; they have a thick, grey, wrinkled skin, a large head, a long trunk used to obtain food and water, and upper incisors or tusks, which grow to a considerable length. The African elephant has very large ears and a flattened forehead, and the Asian species has smaller ears and a convex forehead.

Elgar Edward (William) 1857–1934. English composer whose *Enigma Variations* 1899 brought him lasting fame. Although his celebrated oratorio *The Dream of Gerontius* 1900 (based on the written work by theologian John Henry Newman), was initially unpopular in Britain, it was well received at Düsseldorf 1902, leading to a surge of interest in his earlier works, including the *Pomp and Circumstance Marches* 1901.

Elijah in the Old Testament, a Hebrew prophet during the reigns of the Israelite kings Ahab and Ahaziah. He came from Gilead. He was said to have been carried up to heaven in a fiery chariot in a whirlwind. In Jewish belief, Elijah will return to Earth to herald the coming of the Messiah.

Eliot George. Pen name of Mary Ann Evans 1819–1880. English novelist. Her works include the pastoral *Adam Bede* 1859; *The Mill on the Floss* 1860, with its autobiographical elements; *Silas Marner* 1861, which contains elements of the folktale; and *Daniel Deronda* 1876. *Middlemarch*, published serially 1871–72, is considered her greatest novel.

Eliot T(homas) S(tearns) 1888–1965. US poet, playwright, and critic. He lived in London from 1915. His first volume of poetry, *Prufrock and Other Observations* 1917, introduced new verse forms and rhythms; further collections include *The Waste Land* 1922, *The Hollow Men* 1925, and *Old Possum's Book of Practical Cats* 1939. His plays include *Murder in the Cathedral* 1935 and *The Cocktail Party* 1949. His critical works include *The Sacred Wood* 1920. Nobel Prize for Literature 1948.

Elizabeth the *Queen Mother* 1900– . Wife of King George VI of England. She was born Lady Elizabeth Angela Marguerite Bowes-Lyon, and on 26 April 1923 she married Albert, Duke of York, who became King George VI in 1936. Their children are Queen Elizabeth II and Princess Margaret.

Elizabeth I 1533–1603. Queen of England 1558–1603, the daughter of Henry VIII and Anne Boleyn. Through her Religious Settlement of 1559 she enforced the Protestant religion by law. She had ◊Mary Queen of Scots, executed 1587. Her conflict with Roman Catholic Spain led to the defeat of the ◊Spanish Armada 1588. The Elizabethan age was expansionist in commerce and geographical exploration, and arts and literature flourished. She was succeeded by James I.

Elizabeth II 1926– . Queen of Great Britain and Northern Ireland from 1952, the elder daughter of George VI. She married her third cousin, Philip, the Duke of Edinburgh, 1947. They have four children: Charles, Anne, Andrew, and Edward.

Ellington Duke (Edward Kennedy) 1899–1974. US pianist. He became one of the leading figures in jazz over a 55-year period. Some of his most popular compositions include 'Mood Indigo', 'Sophisticated Lady', 'Solitude', and 'Black and Tan Fantasy'. He was one of the founders of big band jazz.

El Salvador Republic of (*República de El Salvador*); *area* 21,393 sq km/8,258 sq mi; *capital* San Salvador; *features* smallest and most densely populated Central American country; Mayan archaeological remains; *political system* emergent democracy; *population* (1993 est) 5,580,000 (mainly of mixed Spanish and Indian ancestry; 10% Indian); growth rate 2.9% p.a.; *languages* Spanish, Nahuatl; *religion* Roman Catholic 97%.

Elysium in Greek mythology, originally another name for the Islands of the Blessed, to which favoured heroes were sent by the gods to enjoy a life after death. It was later a region in ◊Hades.

Emancipation Proclamation in US history, President Lincoln's Civil War announcement, 22 Sept 1862, stating that from the beginning of 1863 all black slaves in states still engaged in rebellion against the federal government would be emancipated. Slaves in border states still remaining loyal to the Union were excluded.

embryo early developmental stage of an animal or a plant following fertilization of an ovum (egg cell), or activation of an ovum by ▷parthenogenesis. In humans, the term embryo describes the fertilized egg during its first seven weeks of existence; from the eighth week onwards it is referred to as a fetus.

Emerson Ralph Waldo 1803–1882. US philosopher, essayist, and poet. He settled in Concord, Massachusetts, which he made a centre of transcendentalism, and wrote *Nature* 1836, which states the movement's main principles emphasizing the value of self-reliance and the godlike nature of human souls. His two volumes of *Essays* (1841, 1844) made his reputation: 'Self-Reliance' and 'Compensation' in the earlier volume are among the best known.

emf in physics, abbreviation for ▷electromotive force.

empiricism (Greek *empeiria* 'experience' or 'experiment') in philosophy, the belief that all knowledge is ultimately derived from sense experience. It is frequently contrasted with ▷rationalism. It developed in the 17th and early 18th centuries through the work of John ▷Locke and David ▷Hume.

endangered species plant or animal species whose numbers are so few that it is at risk of becoming extinct. Officially designated endangered species are listed by the International Union for the Conservation of Nature. One-quarter of the world's plants are threatened with extinction by the year 2010; three-quarters of all bird species are declining or threatened with extinction; almost all species of cats and bears are declining in numbers; about 80 species of invertebrates are lost each day due to deforestation; half of Australia's mammals are threatened; 40% of mammals in France, the Netherlands, Germany, and Portugal are threatened; two-thirds of primate species are threatened; over 40% of reptile species are threatened. (See also ▷extinction.)

endocrine gland gland that secretes hormones into the bloodstream to regulate body processes. Endocrine glands are most highly developed in vertebrates, but are also found in other animals, notably insects. In humans the main endocrine glands are the pituitary, thyroid, parathyroid, adrenal, pancreas, ovary, and testis.

endorphin natural substance (a polypeptide) that modifies the action of nerve cells. Endorphins are produced by the pituitary gland and hypothalamus of vertebrates. They lower the perception of pain by reducing the transmission of signals between nerve cells. ▷Opiates act in a similar way to endorphins, but are not rapidly degraded by the body, as natural endorphins are, and thus have a long-lasting effect on pain perception and mood. Endorphin release is stimulated by exercise.

energy capacity for doing work. Potential energy (PE) is energy deriving from position; thus a stretched spring has elastic PE, and an object raised to a height above the Earth's surface, or the water in an elevated reservoir, has gravitational PE. A lump of coal and a tank of petrol, together with the oxygen needed for their combustion, have chemical energy. Other sorts of energy include electrical and nuclear energy, and light and sound. Moving bodies possess kinetic energy (KE). Energy can be converted from one form to another, but the total quantity stays the same (in accordance with the conservation of energy principle). For example, as an apple falls, it loses gravitational PE but gains KE.

energy, alternative energy from sources that are renewable and ecologically safe, as opposed to sources that are nonrenewable with toxic by- products, such as coal, oil, or gas (fossil fuels), and uranium (for nuclear power). The most important alternative energy source is flowing water, harnessed as ◊hydroelectric power. Other sources include the oceans' tides and waves and ◊wave power), wind (harnessed by windmills and wind turbines), the Sun (◊solar energy), and the heat trapped in the Earth's crust (◊geothermal energy).

Engels Friedrich 1820–1895. German social and political philosopher, a friend of, and collaborator with, Karl ◊Marx on *The Communist Manifesto* 1848 and other key works. His later interpretations of Marxism, and his own philosophical and historical studies such as *Origins of the Family, Private Property, and the State* 1884 (which linked patriarchy with the development of private property), developed such concepts as historical materialism.

engine device for converting stored energy into useful work or movement. Most engines use a fuel as their energy store. The fuel is burnt to produce heat energy – hence the name 'heat engine' – which is then converted into movement. Heat engines can be classified according to the fuel they use (◊petrol engine or ◊diesel engine), or according to whether the fuel is burnt inside (◊internal combustion engine) or outside (◊steam engine) the engine, or according to whether they produce a reciprocating or rotary motion (◊turbine or ◊Wankel engine).

engineering the application of science to the design, construction, and maintenance of works, machinery, roads, railways, bridges, harbour installations, engines, ships, aircraft and airports, spacecraft and space stations, and the generation, transmission, and use of electrical power. The main divisions of engineering are aerospace, chemical, civil, electrical, electronic, gas, marine, materials, mechanical, mining, production, radio, and structural.

England largest division of the United Kingdom; *area* 130,357 sq km/50,318 sq mi; *capital* London; *features* variability of climate and diversity of scenery; the second most densely populated country in Europe; *population* (1991) 47,055,200; *languages* English, with more than 100 minority languages; *religions* Christian, with the Church of England as the established church, 31,500,000; and various Protestant groups, of which the largest is the Methodist 1,400,000; Roman Catholic about 5,000,000; Muslim 900,000; Jewish 410,000; Sikh 175,000; Hindu 140,000.

English Channel stretch of water between England and France, leading in the W to the Atlantic Ocean, and in the E via the Strait of Dover to the North Sea; it is also known as *La Manche* (French 'the sleeve') from its shape. The ◊Channel Tunnel, officially opened 1994, runs between Folkestone, Kent, and Sangatte, W of Calais.

English member of the Germanic branch of the Indo-European language family. It is traditionally described as having passed through four major stages over about 1,500 years: *Old English* or *Anglo-Saxon* (c. 500–1050), rooted in the dialects of invading settlers (Jutes, Saxons, Angles, and Frisians); *Middle English* (c. 1050–1550), influenced by Norman French after the Conquest 1066 and by ecclesiastical Latin; *Early Modern English* (c. 1550–1700), including a standardization of the diverse influences of Middle English; and *Late Modern English* (c. 1700 onwards), in particular the development and spread of current Standard English. It is the most important international language of trade and technology.

English law one of the major European legal systems, ▷Roman law being the other. English law has spread to many other countries, including former English colonies such as the USA, Canada, Australia, and New Zealand.

Enlightenment European intellectual movement that reached its high point in the 18th century. Enlightenment thinkers were believers in social progress and in the liberating possibilities of rational and scientific knowledge. They were often critical of existing society and were hostile to religion, which they saw as keeping the human mind chained down by superstition.

entropy in ▷thermodynamics, a parameter representing the state of disorder of a system at the atomic, ionic, or molecular level; the greater the disorder, the higher the entropy. Thus the fast-moving disordered molecules of water vapour have higher entropy than those of more ordered liquid water, which in turn have more entropy than the molecules in solid crystalline ice.

environment in ecology, the sum of conditions affecting a particular organism, including physical surroundings, climate, and influences of other living organisms. See also ▷biosphere and ▷habitat.

enzyme biological ▷catalyst produced in cells, and capable of speeding up the chemical reactions necessary for life by converting one molecule (substrate) into another. Enzymes are not themselves destroyed by this process. They are large, complex ▷proteins, and are highly specific, each chemical reaction requiring its own particular enzyme. The enzyme fits into a 'slot' (active site) in the substrate molecule, forming an enzyme–substrate complex that lasts until the substrate is altered or split, after which the enzyme can fall away. The substrate may therefore be compared to a lock, and the enzyme to the key required to open it.

Eocene second epoch of the Tertiary period of geological time, 56.5–35.5 million years ago. Originally considered the earliest division of the Tertiary, the name means 'early recent', referring to the early forms of mammals evolving at the time, following the extinction of the dinosaurs.

Ephesus ancient Greek seaport in Asia Minor, a centre of the ▷Ionian Greeks, with a temple of Artemis destroyed by the Goths AD 262. Now in Turkey, it is one of the world's largest archaeological sites. St Paul visited the city and addressed a letter (▷epistle) to the Christians there.

Epicureanism system of philosophy that claims soundly based human happiness is the highest good, so that its rational pursuit should be adopted. It was named after the Greek philosopher

Epicurus. The most distinguished Roman Epicurean was ▷Lucretius.

epidermis outermost layer of ▷cells on an organism's body. In plants and many invertebrates such as insects, it consists of a single layer of cells. In vertebrates, it consists of several layers of cells.

epilepsy medical disorder characterized by a tendency to develop fits, which are convulsions or abnormal feelings caused by abnormal electrical discharges in the cerebral hemispheres of the ▷brain. Epilepsy can be controlled with a number of anticonvulsant drugs.

Epiphany festival of the Christian church, held 6 Jan, celebrating the coming of the Magi (the three Wise Men) to Bethlehem with gifts for the infant Jesus, and symbolizing the manifestation of Jesus to the world. It is the 12th day after Christmas, and marks the end of the Christmas festivities.

epistle in the New Testament, any of the 21 letters to individuals or to the members of various churches written by Christian leaders, including the 13 written by St ▷Paul. The term also describes a letter with a suggestion of pomposity and literary affectation, and a letter addressed to someone in the form of a poem, as in the epistles of ▷Horace and Alexander ▷Pope.

epoch subdivision of a geological period in the geological time scale. Epochs are sometimes given their own names (such as the Palaeocene, Eocene, Oligocene, Miocene, and Pliocene epochs comprising the Tertiary period), or they are referred to as the late, early, or middle portions of a given period (as the Late Cretaceous or the Middle Triassic epoch).

Epstein Jacob 1880–1959. American-born British sculptor. Initially influenced by Rodin, he turned to primitive forms after Brancusi and is chiefly known for his controversial muscular nude figures such as *Genesis* 1931 (Whitworth Art Gallery, Manchester). He was better appreciated as a portraitist (bust of Einstein, 1933), and in later years executed several monumental figures, notably the expressive bronze of *St Michael and the Devil* 1959 (Coventry Cathedral).

equator *terrestrial equator* or the great circle whose plane is perpendicular to the Earth's axis (the line joining the poles). Its length is 40,092 km/24,901.8 mi, divided into 360 degrees of longitude. The equator encircles the broadest part of the Earth, and represents 0° latitude. It divides the Earth into two halves, called the northern and the southern hemispheres.

Equatorial Guinea Republic of (*República de Guinea Ecuatorial*); *area* 28,051 sq km/10,828 sq mi; *capital* Malabo (Bioko); *features* volcanic mountains on Bioko; *political system* emergent democratic republic; *population* (1993 est) 390,000 (plus 110,000 estimated to live in exile abroad); growth rate 2.2% p.a.; *languages* Spanish (official); pidgin English is widely spoken; *religions* nominally Christian, mainly Catholic, but in 1978 Roman Catholicism was banned.

era any of the major divisions of geological time, each including several periods, but smaller than an eon. The currently recognized eras all fall within the Phanerozoic eon – or the vast span of time, starting about 570 million years ago, when fossils are found to become abundant. The eras in ascending order are the Palaeozoic, Mesozoic, and Cenozoic. We are living in the Recent epoch of the Quaternary period of the Cenozoic era.

Erasmus Desiderius *c.* 1466–1536. Dutch scholar and leading humanist of the Renaissance era, who taught and studied all over Europe and was a prolific writer. His pioneer translation of the Greek New Testament (with parallel Latin text) 1516 exposed the Vulgate as a second-hand document. Although opposed to dogmatism and abuse of church power, he remained impartial during Martin ◊Luther's conflict with the pope.

ergonomics study of the relationship between people and the furniture, tools, and machinery they use at work. The object is to improve work performance by removing sources of muscular stress and general fatigue: for example, by presenting data and control panels in easy-to-view form, making office furniture comfortable, and creating a generally pleasant environment.

Erie, Lake fourth largest of the Great Lakes of North America, connected to Lake Ontario by the Niagara River and bypassed by the Welland Canal; area 9,930 sq mi/25,720 sq km.

Eritrea State of; *area* 125,000 sq km/ 48,250 sq mi; *capital* Asmara; *features* Dahlak Islands; *political system* emergent democracy; *population* (1993 est) 3,500,000; *languages* Amharic (official), Tigrinya (official), Arabic, Afar, Bilen, Hidareb, Kunama, Nara, Rashaida, Saho, and Tigre; *religions* Muslim, Coptic Christian.

Eros in Greek mythology, boy-god of love, traditionally armed with bow and arrows. He was the son of ◊Aphrodite, and fell in love with Psyche. He is identified with the Roman Cupid.

erosion wearing away of the Earth's surface, caused by the breakdown and transportation of particles of rock or soil (by contrast, weathering does not involve transportation). Agents of erosion include the sea, rivers, glaciers, and wind. Water, consisting of sea waves and currents, rivers, and rain; ice, in the form of glaciers; and wind, hurling sand fragments against exposed rocks and moving dunes along, are the most potent forces of erosion. People also contribute to erosion by bad farming practices and the cutting down of forests, which can lead to the formation of dust bowls.

Eskimo member of a group of Asian, North American, and Greenland Arctic peoples who migrated east from Siberia about 2,000 years ago, exploiting the marine coastal environment and the tundra.

Esperanto language devised 1887 by Polish philologist Ludwig L Zamenhof (1859–1917) as an international auxiliary language. For its structure and vocabulary it draws on Latin, the Romance languages, English, and German.

Essen city in North Rhine–Westphalia, Germany; population (1988) 615,000. It is the administrative centre of the Ruhr region, situated between the rivers Emscher and Ruhr. Its 9th–14th-century minster is one of the oldest churches in Germany.

Essex county of SE England; *area* 3,670 sq km/1,417 sq mi; *features* former royal hunting ground of Epping Forest (controlled from 1882 by the City of London); the marshy coastal headland of the Naze; Stansted, London's third airport; *population* (1991) 1,528,600.

Essex Robert Devereux, 2nd Earl of Essex 1566–1601. English soldier and politician. He became a favourite with Queen Elizabeth I from 1587, but was executed because of his policies in Ireland.

ester organic compound formed by the reaction between an alcohol and an acid, with the elimination of water. Unlike ◊salts, esters are covalent compounds.

Estonia Republic of; *area* 45,000 sq km/17,000 sq mi; *capital* Tallinn; *environment* former Soviet army bases are contaminated by toxic chemicals, radioactive waste, and oil; cleanup cost estimated at £2.6 billion (1994); *features* Lake Peipus and Narva River forming boundary with Russian Federation; Baltic islands, the largest of which is Saaremaa Island; *political system* emergent democracy; *population* (1993 est) 1,620,000 (Estonian 62%, Russian 30%, Ukrainian 3%, Byelorussian 2%); *language* Estonian, allied to Finnish; *religion* traditionally Lutheran.

Estonian member of the largest ethnic group in Estonia. There are 1 million speakers of the *Estonian language*, a member of the Finno-Ugric branch of the Uralic family. Most live in Estonia.

ethanol common name *ethyl alcohol* C_2H_5OH alcohol found in beer, wine, cider, spirits, and other alcoholic drinks. When pure, it is a colourless liquid with a pleasant odour, miscible with water or ether; it burns in air with a pale blue flame. The vapour forms an explosive mixture with air and may be used in high-compression internal combustion engines. It is produced naturally by the fermentation of carbohydrates by yeast cells.

Ethelbert *c.* 552–616. King of Kent 560–616. He was defeated by the West Saxons 568 but later became ruler of England S of the river Humber. Ethelbert received the Christian missionary Augustine 597 and later converted to become the first Christian ruler of Anglo-Saxon England. He issued the first written code of laws known in England.

Ethelred (II) the Unready *c.* 968–1016. King of England from 978. He tried to buy off the Danish raiders by paying Danegeld. In 1002, he ordered the massacre of the Danish settlers, provoking an invasion by Sweyn I of Denmark. War with Sweyn and Sweyn's son, Canute, occupied the rest of Ethelred's reign. He was nicknamed the 'Unready' because of his apparent lack of foresight.

ether in chemistry, any of a series of organic chemical compounds having an oxygen atom linking the carbon atoms of two hydrocarbon radical groups (general formula R-O-R'); also the common name for ethoxyethane $C_2H_5OC_2H_5$ (also called diethyl ether).

ethics area of ◊philosophy concerned with human values, which studies the meanings of moral terms and theories of conduct and goodness; also called *moral philosophy*. It is one of the three main branches of contemporary philosophy.

Ethiopia People's Democratic Republic of (*Hebretesebawit Ityopia*, formerly known as *Abyssinia*); *area* 1,096,900 sq km/423,403 sq mi; *capital* Addis Ababa; *environment* more than

90% of the forests of the Ethiopian highlands have been destroyed since 1900; *features* Danakil and Ogaden deserts; ancient remains (in Aksum, Gondar, Lalibela, among others); only African country to retain its independence during the colonial period; *political system* transition to democratic socialist republic; *population* (1993) 51,980,000 (Oromo 40%, Amhara 25%, Tigré 12%, Sidamo 9%); growth rate 2.5% p.a.; *languages* Amharic (official), Tigrinya, Orominga, Arabic; *religions* Sunni Muslim 45%, Christian (Ethiopian Orthodox Church, which has had its own patriarch since 1976) 40%.

ethnic cleansing the forced expulsion of one ethnic group by another, particularly of Muslims by Serbs in ▷Bosnia-Herzegovina from 1992 as part of a policy of creating a Greater Serbia. The practice created nearly 700,000 refugees and was widely condemned by the international community.

ethyne common name *acetylene* CHCH colourless inflammable gas produced by mixing calcium carbide and water. It is the simplest member of the ▷alkyne series of hydrocarbons. It is used in the manufacture of the synthetic rubber neoprene, and in oxyacetylene welding and cutting.

Etna volcano on the east coast of Sicily, 3,323 m/10,906 ft, the highest in Europe. About 90 eruptions have been recorded since 1800 BC, yet because of the rich soil, the cultivated zone on the lower slopes is densely populated, including the coastal town of Catania. The most recent eruption was in Dec 1985.

Etruscan member of an ancient people inhabiting Etruria, Italy (modern-day Tuscany and part of Umbria) from the 8th to 4th centuries BC. The Etruscan dynasty of the Tarquins ruled Rome 616–509 BC. At the height of their civilization, in the 6th century BC, the Etruscans achieved great wealth and power from their maritime strength. They were driven out of Rome 509 BC and eventually dominated by the Romans.

EU abbreviation for ▷*European Union.*

eucalyptus any tree of the genus *Eucalyptus* of the myrtle family Myrtaceae, native to Australia and Tasmania, where they are commonly known as gum trees. About 90% of Australian timber belongs to the eucalyptus genus, which comprises about 500 species. The trees have dark hardwood timber which is used principally for heavy construction as in railway and bridge building. They are tall, aromatic, evergreen trees with pendant leaves and white, pink, or red flowers.

Eucharist chief Christian sacrament, in which bread is eaten and wine drunk in memory of the death of Jesus. Other names for it are the *Lord's Supper, Holy Communion*, and (among Roman Catholics, who believe that the bread and wine are transubstantiated, that is, converted to the body and blood of Christ) the *Mass*. The doctrine of transubstantiation was rejected by Protestant churches during the Reformation.

Euclid *c.* 330–*c.* 260 BC. Greek mathematician, who lived in Alexandria and wrote the *Stoicheia/Elements* in 13 books, of which nine deal with plane and solid geometry and four with number theory. His great achievement lay in the systematic arrangement of previous discoveries, based on axioms, definitions, and theorems.

eukaryote in biology, one of the two major groupings into which all organisms are divided. Included are all organisms, except bacteria and cyanobacteria (▷blue-green algae), which belong to the ▷prokaryote grouping.

Euphrates (Arabic *Furat*) river, rising in E Turkey, flowing through Syria and Iraq and joining the river Tigris above Basra to form the river Shatt-al-Arab, at the head of the Persian/Arabian Gulf; 3,600 km/2,240 mi in length. The ancient cities of Babylon, Eridu, and Ur were situated along its course.

Euripides *c.* 485–*c.* 406 BC. Athenian tragic dramatist. He is ranked with ▷Aeschylus and ▷Sophocles as one of the three great tragedians. He wrote about 90 plays, of which 18 and some long fragments survive. These include *Alcestis, Medea Hippolytus*, the satyr-drama *Cyclops, Electra, Trojan Women, Iphigenia in Tauris, Iphigenia in Aulis*, and *The Bacchae*.

Europe second-smallest continent, occupying 8% of the Earth's surface; *area* 10,400,000 sq km/4,000,000 sq mi; *largest cities* (population over 1.5 million) Athens, Barcelona, Berlin, Birmingham, Bucharest, Budapest, Hamburg, Istanbul, Kharkov, Kiev, Lisbon, London, Madrid, Manchester, Milan, Moscow, Paris, Rome, St Petersburg, Vienna, Warsaw; *features* Mount Elbruz 5,642 m/18,517 ft in the Caucasus Mountains is the highest peak in Europe; Mont Blanc 4,807 m/15,772 ft is the highest peak in the Alps; lakes (over 5,100 sq km/2,000 sq mi) include Ladoga, Onega, Vänern; rivers (over 800 km/500 mi) include the Volga, Danube, Dnieper Ural, Don, Pechora, Dniester, Rhine, Loire, Tagus, Ebro, Oder, Prut, Rhône; *population* (1985) 496 million (excluding Turkey and the ex-Soviet republics); annual growth rate 0.3%, projected population of 512 million by 2000.

European Community (EC) former name (to 1993) of the ▷European Union.

European Monetary System (EMS) attempt by the European Community (now the European Union) to bring financial cooperation and monetary stability to Europe. It was established 1979 in the wake of the 1974 oil crisis, which brought growing economic disruption to European economies because of floating exchange rates. Central to the EMS is the ▷Exchange Rate Mechanism (ERM), a voluntary system of semi-fixed exchange rates based on the European Currency Unit (ECU).

European Parliament the parliament of the European Union, which meets in Strasbourg to comment on the legislative proposals of the European Commission. Members are elected for a five-year term.

European Union (EU; formerly until 1993 *European Community*) political and economic alliance consisting of the European Coal and Steel Community (1952), European Economic Community (EEC, popularly called the Common Market, 1957), and the European Atomic Energy Commission (Euratom, 1957). The original members – Belgium, France, West Germany, Italy, Luxembourg, and the Netherlands – were joined by the UK, Denmark, and the Republic of Ireland 1973, Greece 1981, and Spain and Portugal 1986. East Germany was incorporated on German reunification 1990. Austria, Finland, Sweden became members 1995. On 1 Nov 1993 the ▷Maastricht Treaty on European union came into effect. A single market with free movement of goods and capital was established Jan 1993.

euthanasia in medicine, mercy killing of someone with a severe and incurable condition or illness. The Netherlands legalized voluntary euthanasia 1983, but is the only country to have done so.

eutrophication excessive enrichment of rivers, lakes, and shallow sea areas, primarily by nitrate fertilizers washed from the soil by rain, by phosphates from fertilizers, and from nutrients in municipal sewage, and by sewage itself. These encourage the growth of algae and bacteria which use up the oxygen in the water, thereby making it uninhabitable for fishes and other animal life.

Evans Edith 1888–1976. English character actress. She performed on the London stage and on Broadway. Her many imposing performances include the Nurse in *Romeo and Juliet* (first performed 1926); her film roles include Lady Bracknell in Wilde's comedy *The Importance of Being Earnest* 1952 and Betsy in the television version of *David Copperfield* 1969.

evaporation process in which a liquid turns to a vapour without its temperature reaching boiling point. A liquid left to stand in a saucer eventually evaporates because, at any time, a proportion of its molecules will be fast enough (have enough kinetic energy) to escape through the attractive intermolecular forces at the liquid surface into the atmosphere. The temperature of the liquid tends to fall because the evaporating molecules remove energy from the liquid. The rate of evaporation rises with increased temperature because as the mean kinetic energy of the liquid's molecules rises, so will the number possessing enough energy to escape.

Eve in the Old Testament, the first woman, wife of ◊Adam. She was tempted by Satan (in the form of a snake) to eat the fruit of the Tree of Knowledge of Good and Evil, and then tempted Adam to eat of the fruit as well, thus bringing about their expulsion from the Garden of Eden.

evening primrose any plant of the genus *Oenothera*, family Onagraceae. Some 50 species are native to North America, several of which now also grow in Europe. Some are cultivated for their oil, which is rich in gamma-linoleic acid (GLA). The body converts GLA into substances which resemble hormones, and evening primrose oil is beneficial in alleviating the symptoms of ◊premenstrual tension. It is also used in treating eczema and chronic fatigue syndrome.

Everest, Mount (Nepalese *Sagarmatha* 'head of the earth') world's highest mountain above sea level, in the Himalayas, on the China–Nepal frontier; height 8,872 m/29,118 ft (recently measured by satellite to this new height from the former official height of 8,848 m/29,028 ft). It was first climbed by New Zealand mountaineer Edmund Hillary and Sherpa Tenzing Norgay 1953. More than 360 climbers have reached the summit; over 100 have died during the ascent.

evergreen in botany, a plant such as pine, spruce, or holly, that bears its leaves all year round. Most ◊conifers are evergreen. Plants that shed their leaves in autumn or during a dry season are described as ◊deciduous.

evolution slow process of change from one form to another, as in the evolution of the universe from its formation in the ◊Big Bang to its present state, or in the evolution of life on Earth. Some

Christians and Muslims deny the theory of evolution as conflicting with the belief that God created all things. Darwin assigned the major role in evolutionary change to ◊natural selection acting on randomly occurring variations (now known to be produced by spontaneous changes or ◊mutations in the genetic material of organisms).

Exchange Rate Mechanism (ERM) voluntary system for controlling exchange rates within the European Union's ◊European Monetary System. The member currencies of the ERM are fixed against each other within a narrow band of fluctuation based on a central European Currency Unit (ECU) rate, but floating against nonmember countries. If a currency deviates significantly from the central ECU rate, the European Monetary Cooperation Fund and the central banks concerned intervene to stabilize the currency.

excommunication in religion, exclusion of an offender from the rights and privileges of the Roman Catholic Church; King John, Henry VIII, and Elizabeth I were all excommunicated.

existentialism branch of philosophy based on the concept of an absurd universe where humans have free will. Existentialists argue that humans are responsible for and the sole judge of their actions as they affect others, though no one else's existence is real to the individual. Usually traced back to Danish philosopher ◊Kierkegaard, its proponents included Martin Heidegger in Germany and Jean-Paul ◊Sartre in France.

Expressionism style of painting, sculpture, and literature that expresses inner emotions; in particular, a movement in early 20th-century art in northern and central Europe. Expressionists tended to distort or exaggerate natural appearance in order to create a reflection of an inner world; the Norwegian painter Edvard Munch's *Skriket/The Scream* 1893 (National Gallery, Oslo) is perhaps the most celebrated example of the genre.

extinction in biology, the complete disappearance of a species. In the past, extinctions are believed to have occurred because species were unable to adapt quickly enough to a naturally changing environment. Today, most extinctions are due to human activity, particularly through hunting and destruction of habitat. In the tropical rainforests at least three species are becoming extinct each hour – at least 27,000 species each year. Most of them disappear before they can be studied or even identified. See also ◊endangered species.

Eyck Jan van *c.* 1390–1441. Flemish painter of the early northern Renaissance. He was one of the first to work in oils. His paintings are technically brilliant and sumptuously rich in detail and colour. In his *Giovanni Arnolfini and his Wife* 1434 (National Gallery, London), the bride and groom appear in a domestic interior crammed with disguised symbols, a kind of pictorial marriage certificate.

eye the organ of vision. In the human eye, the light is focused by the combined action of the curved *cornea*, the internal fluids, and the *lens*. The insect eye is compound – made up of many separate facets – known as ommatidia, each of which collects light and directs it separately to a receptor to build up an image. Invertebrates have much simpler eyes, with no lenses. Among molluscs, cephalopods have complex eyes similar to those of vertebrates. The *human eye* is a roughly spherical structure contained in a body socket. Light enters it through the cornea, and passes through the circular opening (*pupil*) in the iris (the coloured part of the eye). The ciliary muscles act on the lens (the rounded transparent structure behind the iris) to change its shape, so that images of objects at different distances can be focused on the retina. This is at the back of the eye, and is packed with light-sensitive cells (rods and cones), connected to the brain by the optic nerve.

F

Fabergé Peter Carl 1846–1920. Russian goldsmith and jeweller. Among his masterpieces was a series of jewelled Easter eggs, the first of which was commissioned by Alexander III for the tsarina 1884.

Fabian Society UK socialist organization for research, discussion, and publication, founded in London 1884. Its name is derived from the Roman commander Fabius Maximus, and refers to the evolutionary methods by which it hopes to attain socialism by a succession of gradual reforms. Early members included the playwright George Bernard Shaw and Beatrice and Sidney Webb.

Fabius Laurent 1946– . French politician, leader of the Socialist Party (PS) 1992–93. As prime minister 1984–86, he introduced a liberal, free-market economic programme, but his career was damaged by the 1985 ◊Greenpeace sabotage scandal.

FA Cup abbreviation for *Football Association Cup*, the major annual soccer knockout competition in England and Wales, open to all member clubs of the British Football Association. First held 1871–72, it is the oldest football knockout competition.

Fagatogo capital of American ◊Samoa, situated on Pago Pago Harbour, Tutuila Island; population (1980) 30,124.

Fahd 1921– . King of Saudi Arabia from 1982, when he succeeded his half-brother Khalid. As head of government, he has been active in trying to bring about a solution to the Middle East conflicts.

Fahrenheit scale temperature scale invented 1714 by Gabriel Fahrenheit which was commonly used in English-speaking countries until the 1970s, after which the ◊Celsius scale was generally adopted, in line with the rest of the world. In the Fahrenheit scale, intervals are measured in degrees (°F); °F = (°C x ⅘) + 32.

Fairbanks Douglas, Sr. Stage name of Douglas Elton Ulman 1883–1939. US actor. He played acrobatic swashbuckling heroes in silent films such as *The Mark of Zorro* 1920, *The Three Musketeers* 1921, *Robin Hood* 1922, *The Thief of Bagdad* 1924, and *Don Quixote* 1925. In 1919 he founded United Artists with Charlie Chaplin and D W Griffith. He was the father of actor *Douglas Fairbanks Jr* 1909– , who appeared in the same type of film roles as his father.

Fairfax Thomas, 3rd Baron Fairfax of Cameron 1612–1671. English general, commander in chief of the Parliamentary army in the English Civil War. With Oliver Cromwell he formed the New Model Army and defeated Charles I at Naseby. He opposed the king's execution, resigned in protest 1650 against the invasion of Scotland, and participated in the restoration of Charles II after Cromwell's death.

Falkland Islands (Argentine *Islas Malvinas*) British crown colony in the S Atlantic; *area* 12,173 sq km/4,700 sq mi, made up of two main islands: East Falkland 6,760 sq km/2,610 sq mi, and West Falkland 5,413 sq km/2,090 sq mi; *capital* Stanley; new port facilities opened 1984, Mount Pleasant airport 1985; *features* in addition to the two main islands, there are about 200 small islands, all with wild scenery and rich bird life; *population* (1991) 2,100.

Falklands War war between Argentina and Britain over disputed sovereignty of the Falkland Islands initiated when Argentina invaded and occupied the islands 2 April 1982. A British task force was dispatched and, after a fierce conflict in which more than 1,000 Argentine and British lives were lost, the Argentine troops surrendered and the islands were returned to British rule 14–15 June 1982.

Falla Manuel de (full name Manuel Maria de Falla y Matheu) 1876–1946. Spanish composer. His opera *La vida breve/Brief Life* 1905 (performed 1913) was followed by the ballets *El amor bru-jo/Love the Magician* 1915 and *El sombrero de tres picos/The Three-Cornered Hat* 1919, and his most ambitious concert work, *Noches en los jardines de España/Nights in the Gardens of Spain* 1916.

Fallopian tube or *oviduct* in mammals, one of two tubes that carry eggs from the ovary to the uterus. An egg is fertilized by sperm in the Fallopian tubes, which are lined with cells whose cilia move the egg towards the uterus.

fallout harmful radioactive material released into the atmosphere in the debris of a nuclear explosion and descending to the surface of the Earth. Such material can enter the food chain, cause radiation sickness, and last for hundreds of thousands of years (see ◊half-life).

family in biological classification, a group of related genera (see ◊genus). Family names are not printed in italic (unlike genus and species names), and by convention they all have the ending -idae (animals) or -aceae (plants and fungi). For example, the genera of hummingbirds are grouped in the hummingbird family, Trochilidae. Related families are grouped together in an ◊order.

family planning spacing or preventing the birth of children. Access to family-planning services (see ◊contraceptive) is a significant factor in women's health as well as in limiting population growth. If all those women who wished to avoid further childbirth were able to do so, the number of births would be reduced by 27% in Africa, 33% in Asia, and 35% in Latin America; and the number of women who die during pregnancy or childbirth would be reduced by about 50%.

famine severe shortage of food affecting a large number of people. Almost 750 million people (equivalent to double the population of Europe) worldwide suffer from hunger and malnutrition. The *food availability deficit* (FAD) theory explains famines as being caused by insufficient food supplies. A more recent theory is that famines arise when one group in a society loses its opportunity to exchange its labour or possessions for food.

Faraday Michael 1791–1867. English chemist and physicist. In 1821 he began experimenting with electromagnetism, and ten years later discovered the induction of electric currents and made the first dynamo. He subsequently found that a magnetic field will rotate the plane of polarization of light. Faraday also investigated electrolysis.

Far East geographical term for all Asia east of the Indian subcontinent.

Faroe Islands or *Faeroe Islands* or *Faeroes* (Danish *Faerøerne* 'Sheep Islands') island group (18 out of 22 inhabited) in the N Atlantic, between the Shetland Islands and Iceland, forming an outlying part of ◊Denmark; *area* 1,399 sq km/540 sq mi; largest islands are Strømø, Østerø, Vagø, Suderø, Sandø, and Bordø; *capital* Thorshavn on Strømø, *population* (1986) 15,287; *population* (1986) 46,000; *languages* Faeroese, Danish.

Farsi or *Persian* language belonging to the Indo-Iranian branch of the Indo-European family, and the official language of Iran (formerly Persia). It is also spoken in Afghanistan, Iraq, and Tajikistan.

fascism political ideology that denies all rights to individuals in their relations with the state; specifically, the totalitarian nationalist movement founded in Italy 1919 by ◊Mussolini and followed by Hitler's Germany 1933. Fascism protected the existing social order by forcible suppression of the working-class movement and by providing scapegoats for popular anger such as outsiders who lived within the state: Jews, foreigners, or blacks; it also prepared the citizenry for the economic and psychological mobilization of war.

fast reactor or *fast breeder reactor* ◊nuclear reactor that makes use of fast neutrons to bring about fission. Unlike other reactors used by the nuclear-power industry, it has little or no moderator, to slow down neutrons. The reactor core is surrounded by a 'blanket' of uranium carbide. During operation, some of this uranium is converted into plutonium, which can be extracted and later used as fuel.

fat in the broadest sense, a mixture of ◊lipids –chiefly triglycerides (lipids containing three ◊fatty acid molecules linked to a molecule of glycerol). More specifically, the term refers to a lipid mixture that is solid at room temperature (20°C); lipid mixtures that are liquid at room temperature are called *oils*. The higher the proportion of saturated fatty acids in a mixture, the harder the fat.

Fatah, al- Palestinian nationalist organization, founded 1958 to bring about an independent state of Palestine. It was the first Palestinian resistance group, based 1968–70 in Jordan, then in Lebanon, and from 1982 in Tunisia. Also called the Palestine National Liberation Movement, it is the main component of the ◊Palestine Liberation Organization. Its leader is Yassir ◊Arafat.

Fates in Greek mythology, the three female figures who determined the destiny of human lives. They were envisaged as spinners: Clotho spun the thread of life, Lachesis twisted the thread, and Atropos cut it off. They are analogous to the Roman Parcae and Norse Norns.

fatty acid or *carboxylic acid* organic compound consisting of a hydrocarbon chain, up to 24 carbon atoms long, with a carboxyl group (–COOH) at one end.

The covalent bonds between the carbon atoms may be single or double; where a double bond occurs the carbon atoms concerned carry one instead of two hydrogen atoms. Chains with only single bonds have all the hydrogen they can carry, so they are said to be *saturated* with hydrogen. Chains with one or more double bonds are said to be *unsaturated* (see ◊polyunsaturate).

fatwa in Islamic law, an authoritative legal opinion on a point of doctrine. In 1989 a fatwa calling for the death of English novelist Salman ◊Rushdie was made by the Ayatollah ◊Khomeini of Iran, following publication of Rushdie's controversial and allegedly blasphemous book *The Satanic Verses*.

Faulkner William (Harrison) 1897–1962. US novelist. His works are noted for their difficult narrative styles and epic mapping of a quasi-imaginary Southern region, Yoknapatawpha County. His third and most celebrated novel, *The Sound and the Fury* 1929 begins with an especially complex stream-of- consciousness narrative. Nobel Prize for Literature 1949.

Faust legendary magician who sold his soul to the Devil. The historical Georg Faust appears to have been a wandering scholar and conjurer in Germany at the start of the 16th century. Goethe, Heine, Thomas Mann, and Paul Valéry all used the legend, and it inspired musical works by Schumann, Berlioz, Gounod, Boito, and Busoni.

Fauvism style of painting characterized by a bold use of vivid colours inspired by the work of van Gogh, Cézanne, and Gaugin. A short-lived but influential art movement, Fauvism originated in Paris 1905 with the founding of the Salon d'Automne by Henri ◊Matisse and others, when the critic Louis Vauxcelles, on seeing a piece of conventional sculpture, said it was like 'Donatello amid wild beasts' ('*Donatello chez les fauves*'). Rouault, Dufy, Marquet, Derain, and Signac were early Fauves.

Fawkes Guy 1570–1606. English conspirator in the ◊Gunpowder Plot to blow up King James I and the members of both Houses of Parliament. Fawkes, a Roman Catholic convert, was arrested in the cellar underneath the House 4 Nov 1605, tortured, and executed. The event is still commemorated in Britain and elsewhere every 5 Nov with bonfires, fireworks, and the burning of the 'guy', an effigy.

fax (common name for *facsimile transmission* or *telefax*) the transmission of images over a ◊telecommunications link, usually the telephone network. When placed on a fax machine, the original image is scanned by a transmitting device and converted into coded signals, which travel via the telephone lines to the receiving fax machine, where an image is created that is a copy of the original. Photographs as well as printed text and drawings can be sent. The standard transmission takes place at 4,800 or 9,600 bits of information per second.

feather rigid outgrowth of the outer layer of the skin of birds, made of the protein keratin. Feathers provide insulation and facilitate flight. There are several types, including long quill feathers on the wings and tail, fluffy down feathers for retaining body heat, and contour feathers covering the body. The colouring of feathers is often important in camouflage or in courtship and other displays. Feathers are replaced at least once a year.

Federal Bureau of Investigation (FBI) agency of the US Department of Justice that investigates violations of federal law not specifically assigned to other agencies, being particularly concerned with internal security. The FBI was established 1908 and built up a position of powerful autonomy during the autocratic directorship of J Edgar Hoover 1924–72. Louis Joseph Freeh, a former FBI agent and federal prosecutor, has been director since 1993.

federation political entity made up from a number of smaller units or states where the central government has powers over national issues such as foreign policy and defence, while the individual states retain a high degree of regional and local autonomy. Contemporary examples include the USA, Canada, Australia, India, and the Federal Republic of Germany.

feldspar one of a group of rock-forming minerals; the chief constituents of ⬦igneous rock. Feldspars all contain silicon, aluminium, and oxygen, linked together to form a framework; spaces within this structure are occupied by sodium, potassium, calcium, or occasionally barium, in various proportions. Feldspars form white, grey, or pink crystals and rank 6 on the ⬦Mohs' scale of hardness.

Fellini Federico 1920–1993. Italian film director and screenwriter. A major influence on modern cinema, his films combine dream and fantasy sequences with satire and autobiographical detail, including *La strada/The Street* 1954 (Academy Award), *Le notti di Cabiria/Nights of Cabiria* 1956 (Academy Award), *La dolce vita* 1960, *Otto e mezzo/8½* 1963 (Academy Award), *Roma/Fellini's Rome* 1972, *Amarcord* 1974 (Academy Award), and *Ginger e*

Fred/Ginger and Fred 1986. He was presented with a Special Academy Award for his life's work 1993.

fencing sport of fighting with swords including the *foil*, derived from the light weapon used in practice duels; the *épée*, a heavier weapon derived from the duelling sword proper; and the *sabre*, with a curved handle and narrow V-shaped blade. In sabre fighting, cuts count as well as thrusts. Masks and protective jackets are worn, and hits are registered electronically in competitions. Men's fencing has been part of every Olympic programme since 1896; women's fencing was included from 1924 but only using the foil.

Fenian movement Irish-American republican secret society, founded 1858 and named after the ancient Irish legendary warrior band of the Fianna. The collapse of the movement began when an attempt to establish an independent Irish republic by an uprising in Ireland 1867 failed, as did raids into Canada 1866 and 1870, and England 1867.

Fens, the level, low-lying tracts of land in E England, W and S of the Wash, about 115 km/70 mi N–S and 55 km/34 mi E–W. They fall within the counties of Lincolnshire, Cambridgeshire, and Norfolk, consisting of a huge area, formerly a bay of the North Sea, but now crossed by numerous drainage canals and forming some of the most productive agricultural land in Britain.

Ferdinand V 1452–1516. King of Castile from 1474, *Ferdinand II* of Aragon from 1479, and *Ferdinand III* of Naples from 1504; first king of all Spain. In 1469 he married his cousin Isabella I, who succeeded to the throne of Castile

1474; Ferdinand and Isabella catholicized Spain after 700 years of rule by the ◊Moors. Ferdinand inherited the throne of Aragon 1479, bringing it and Castile under a single government for the first time. The Inquisition was introduced by Ferdinand and Isabella 1480. They expelled the Jews, forced the final surrender of the Moors at Granada, and financed Columbus' expedition to the Americas, 1492.

Fermanagh county of Northern Ireland; *area* 1,680 sq km/648 sq mi; *features* in the centre is a broad trough of low-lying land, in which lie Upper and Lower Lough Erne; *population* (1991) 50,000.

fermentation the breakdown of sugars by bacteria and yeasts using a method of respiration without oxygen (◊anaerobic). Fermentation processes have long been utilized in baking bread, making beer and wine, and producing cheese, yoghurt, soy sauce, and many other foodstuffs.

Fermi Enrico 1901–1954. Italian-born US physicist who proved the existence of new radioactive elements produced by bombardment with neutrons, and discovered nuclear reactions produced by low-energy neutrons. His theoretical work included study of the weak nuclear force, one of the fundamental forces of nature, and (with Paul Dirac) of the quantum statistics of fermion particles. He was awarded a Nobel prize 1938.

fermion in physics, a subatomic particle whose spin can only take values that are half-integers, such as $\frac{1}{2}$ or $\frac{3}{2}$. Fermions may be classified as leptons, such as the electron, and baryons, such as the proton and neutron. All elementary particles are either fermions or ◊bosons.

fern plant of the class Filicales, related to horsetails and clubmosses. Ferns are spore-bearing, not flowering, plants, and most are perennial, spreading by low-growing roots. The leaves, known as fronds, vary widely in size and shape. Some taller types, such as tree-ferns, grow in the tropics. There are over 7,000 species.

fertilization in ◊sexual reproduction, the union of two ◊gametes (sex cells, often called egg and sperm) to produce a ◊zygote, which combines the genetic material contributed by each parent. In self-fertilization the male and female gametes come from the same plant; in cross-fertilization they come from different plants. Self-fertilization rarely occurs in animals; usually even ◊hermaphrodite animals cross-fertilize each other.

fertilizer substance containing some or all of a range of about 20 chemical elements necessary for healthy plant growth, used to compensate for the deficiencies of poor or depleted soil. Fertilizers may be *organic*, for example farmyard manure, composts, bonemeal, blood, and fishmeal; or *inorganic*, in the form of compounds, mainly of nitrogen, phosphate, and potash, which have been used on a very much increased scale since 1945.

fetus or *foetus* stage in mammalian ◊embryo development. The human embryo is usually termed a fetus after the eighth week of development, when the limbs and external features of the head are recognizable.

feudalism main form of social organization in medieval Europe. A system based primarily on land, it involved a hierarchy of authority, rights, and power that extended from the monarch downwards. An intricate network of duties and obligations linked royalty, nobility, lesser gentry, free tenants, villeins, and serfs. Feudalism was reinforced by a complex legal system and supported by the Christian church.

Fianna Fáil Republic of Ireland political party, founded by the Irish nationalist de Valera 1926. It has been the governing party in the Republic of Ireland 1932–48, 1951–54, 1957–73, 1977–81, 1982, and 1987–   (from 1993 in coalition with Labour). It aims at the establishment of a united and completely independent all-Ireland republic.

fibre, dietary or *roughage* plant material that cannot be digested by human digestive enzymes; it consists largely of cellulose, a carbohydrate found in plant cell walls. Fibre adds bulk to the gut contents, assisting the muscular contractions that force food along the intestine. A diet low in fibre causes constipation and is believed to increase the risk of developing diverticulitis, diabetes, gall-bladder disease, and cancer of the large bowel – conditions that are rare in nonindustrialized countries, where the diet contains a high proportion of unrefined cereals.

fibreglass glass that has been formed into fine fibres, either as long continuous filaments or as a fluffy, short-fibred glass wool. Fibreglass is heat- and fire-resistant and a good electrical insulator. It has applications in the field of fibre optics and as a strengthener for plastics in GRP (glass-reinforced plastics).

fibre optics branch of physics dealing with the transmission of light and images through glass or plastic fibres known as ⏍optical fibres.

field in physics, a region of space in which an object exerts a force on another separate object because of certain properties they both possess. For example, there is a force of attraction between any two objects that have mass when one is in the gravitational field of the other.

Fielding Henry 1707–1754. English novelist. His greatest work, *The History of Tom Jones, a Foundling* 1749 (which he described as 'a comic epic in prose'), realized for the first time in English the novel's potential for memorable characterization, coherent plotting, and perceptive analysis.

Fields W C. Stage name of William Claude Dukenfield 1879–1946. US actor and screenwriter. His distinctive speech and professed attitudes such as hatred of children and dogs gained him enormous popularity in such films as *David Copperfield* 1935, *My Little Chickadee* (co- written with Mae West) and *The Bank Dick* both 1940, and *Never Give a Sucker an Even Break* 1941.

Fife region of E Scotland; *area* 1,300 sq km/502 sq mi; *features* Lomond Hills in the NW (the only high land); Rosyth naval base and dockyard (used for nuclear submarine refits) on northern shore of the Firth of Forth; Tentsmuir, possibly the earliest settled site in Scotland; the ancient palace of the Stuarts was at Falkland, and eight Scottish kings are buried at Dunfermline; *population* (1991) 341,200.

fifth-generation computer anticipated new type of computer based on emerging microelectronic technologies with high computing speeds and ⏍parallel processing.   The development of very large-scale integration (VLSI) technology, which can put many more circuits on to an integrated circuit (chip) than is currently possible, and developments in computer hardware and software design may produce computers far more powerful than those in current use.

Fiji Republic of; *area* 18,333 sq km/ 7,078 sq mi; *capital* Suva; *features* almost all islands surrounded by coral reefs; high volcanic peaks; crossroads of air and sea services between N America and Australia; *political system* democratic republic. *population* (1993) 758,300 (46% Fijian, holding 80% of the land communally, and 49% Indian, introduced in the 19th century to work the sugar crop); growth rate 2.1% p.a.; *languages* English (official), Fijian, Hindi; *religions* Hindu 50%, Methodist 44%.

film, photographic strip of transparent material (usually cellulose acetate) coated with a light-sensitive emulsion, used in cameras to take pictures. The emulsion contains a mixture of light-sensitive silver halide salts (for example, bromide or iodide) in gelatin. When the emulsion is exposed to light, the silver salts are invisibly altered, giving a latent image, which is then made visible by the process of developing. Films differ in their sensitivities to light, this being indicated by their speeds. Colour film consists of several layers of emulsion, each of which records a different colour in the light falling on it.

filtration technique by which suspended solid particles in a fluid are removed by passing the mixture through a filter, usually porous paper, plastic, or cloth. The particles are retained by the filter to form a residue and the fluid passes through to make up the filtrate. For example, soot may be filtered from air, and suspended solids from water.

Fine Gael Republic of Ireland political party founded 1933 by W J Cosgrave and led by Alan Dukes from 1987. It is socially liberal but fiscally conservative.

Finland Republic of (*Suomen Tasavalta*); *area* 338,145 sq km/130,608 sq mi; *capital* Helsinki; *features* Helsinki is the most northerly national capital on the European continent; at the 70th parallel there is constant daylight for 73 days in summer and 51 days of uninterrupted night in winter; *political system* democratic republic; *population* (1993 est) 5,020,000; growth rate 0.5% p.a.; *languages* Finnish 93%, Swedish 6% (both official), small Saami- and Russian- speaking minorities; *religions* Lutheran 97%, Eastern Orthodox 1.2%.

Finn Mac Cumhaill legendary Irish hero, identified with a general who organized an Irish regular army in the 3rd century. James Macpherson (1736–96) featured him (as Fingal) and his followers in the verse of his popular epics 1762–63, which were supposedly written by a 3rd-century bard, Ossian. Although challenged by the critic Dr Johnson, the poems were influential in the Romantic movement.

Finno-Ugric group or family of more than 20 languages spoken by some 22 million people in scattered communities from Norway in the west to Siberia in the east and to the Carpathian mountains in the south. Members of the family include Finnish, Lapp, and Hungarian.

fir any ◊conifer of the genus *Abies* in the pine family Pinaceae. The true firs include the balsam fir of N North America and the Eurasian silver fir *A.*

alba. Douglas firs of the genus *Pseudotsuga* are native to W North America and the Far East.

First World War another name for ◊World War I, 1914–18.

fish aquatic vertebrate that uses gills for obtaining oxygen from fresh or sea water. There are three main groups, not closely related: the bony fishes or Osteichthyes (goldfish, cod, tuna); the cartilaginous fishes or Chondrichthyes (sharks, rays); and the jawless fishes or Agnatha (hagfishes, lampreys).

fission in physics, the splitting of a heavy atomic nucleus into two or more major fragments. It is accompanied by the emission of two or three neutrons and the release of large amounts of ◊nuclear energy.

Fitzgerald Ella 1918– . US jazz singer. She is recognized as one of the finest, most lyrical voices in jazz, both in solo work and with big bands. She is celebrated for her smooth interpretations of George and Ira Gershwin and Cole Porter songs.

Fitzgerald F(rancis) Scott (Key) 1896–1940. US novelist and short-story writer. His early autobiographical novel *This Side of Paradise* 1920 made him known in the postwar society of the East Coast, and *The Great Gatsby* 1925 epitomizes the Jazz Age.

fjord or *fiord* narrow sea inlet enclosed by high cliffs. Fjords are found in Norway, New Zealand, and western parts of Scotland. They are formed when an overdeepened U-shaped glacial valley is drowned by a rise in sea-level. At the mouth of the fjord there is a characteristic lip causing a shallowing of the water. This is due to reduced glacial erosion and the deposition of moraine at this point.

Flanders region of the Low Countries that in the 8th and 9th centuries extended from Calais to the Scheldt and is now covered by the Belgian provinces of Oost Vlaanderen and West Vlaanderen (East and West Flanders), the French *département* of Nord, and part of the Dutch province of Zeeland. The language is Flemish. East Flanders, capital Ghent, has an area of 3,000 sq km/1,158 sq mi and a population (1991) of 1,335,700. West Flanders, capital Bruges, has an area of 3,100 sq km/1,197 sq mi and a population (1991) of 1,106,800.

flatworm invertebrate of the phylum Platyhelminthes. Some are free-living, but many are parasitic (for example, tapeworms and flukes). The body is simple and bilaterally symmetrical, with one opening to the intestine. Many are hermaphroditic (with both male and female sex organs) and practise self-fertilization.

Flaubert Gustave 1821–1880. French writer. One of the major novelists of the 19th century, he was the author of *Madame Bovary* 1857, *Salammbô* 1862, *L'Education sentimentale/Sentimental Education* 1869, and *La Tentation de Saint Antoine/The Temptation of St Anthony* 1874. Flaubert also wrote the short stories *Trois Contes/Three Tales* 1877. His dedication to art resulted in a meticulous prose style, realistic detail, and psychological depth, which is often revealed through interior monologue.

flax any plant of the genus *Linum*, family Linaceae. The species *L. usitatissimum* is the cultivated strain; *linen* is produced from the fibre in its stems. The seeds yield *linseed oil*, used in paints and varnishes. The plant, of almost worldwide distribution, has a stem up to 60 cm/24 in high, small leaves, and bright blue flowers.

Fleming Alexander 1881–1955. Scottish bacteriologist who discovered the first antibiotic drug, ◊penicillin, in 1928. In 1922 he had discovered lysozyme, an antibacterial enzyme present in saliva, nasal secretions, and tears. While studying this, he found an unusual mould growing on a neglected culture dish, which he isolated and grew into a pure culture; this led to his discovery of penicillin. Nobel Prize for Physiology and Medicine with Howard W Florey and Ernst B Chain 1945.

flight or *aviation* method of transport in which aircraft carry people and goods through the air. People first took to the air in ◊balloons and began powered flight 1852 in airships, but the history of flying, both for civilian and military use, is dominated by the ◊aeroplane. The earliest planes were designed for ◊gliding; the advent of the petrol engine saw the first powered flight by the ◊Wright brothers 1903 in the USA. This inspired the development of aircraft throughout Europe. Biplanes were succeeded by monoplanes in the 1930s. The first jet plane was produced 1939, and after the end of World War II the development of jetliners brought about a continuous expansion in passenger air travel. In 1969 came the supersonic aircraft Concorde.

flint compact, hard, brittle mineral (a variety of chert), brown, black, or grey in colour, found in nodules in limestone or shale deposits. It consists of fine-grained silica, SiO_2 (usually ◊quartz), in cryptocrystalline form. Flint implements were widely used in prehistory.

floppy disc in computing, a storage device consisting of a light, flexible disc enclosed in a cardboard or plastic jacket. The disc is placed in a disc drive, where it rotates at high speed. Data are recorded magnetically on one or both surfaces.

Florence (Italian *Firenze*) capital of ◊Tuscany, N Italy, 88 km/55 mi from the mouth of the river Arno; population (1988) 421,000. Its art and architecture attract large numbers of tourists.

Florida southeasternmost state of the USA; mainly a peninsula jutting into the Atlantic, which it separates from the Gulf of Mexico; *area* 152,000 sq km/ 58,672 sq mi; *capital* Tallahassee; *population* (1990) 12,937,900, including 15% nonwhite; 10% Hispanic, (especially Cuban); *features* Palm Beach island resort; Florida Keys; John F Kennedy Space Center at Cape Canaveral; Disney World theme park.

flower the reproductive unit of an ◊angiosperm or flowering plant, typically consisting of four whorls of modified leaves: ◊sepals, petals, ◊stamens, and ◊carpels. These are borne on a central axis or receptacle. The many variations in size, colour, number, and arrangement of parts are closely related to the method of pollination. Flowers adapted for wind pollination typically have reduced or absent petals and sepals and long, feathery stigmas that hang outside the flower to trap airborne pollen. In contrast, the petals of insect-pollinated flowers are usually conspicuous and brightly coloured.

flowering plant term generally used for ◊angiosperms, which bear flowers with various parts, including sepals, petals, stamens, and carpels. Sometimes the term is used more broadly, to include both angiosperms and ◊gymnosperms, in which case the ◊cones of conifers and cycads are referred to as 'flowers'. Usually, however, the angiosperms and gymnosperms are referred to collectively as ◊seed plants, or spermatophytes.

fluoridation addition of small amounts of fluoride salts to drinking water by certain water authorities to help prevent tooth decay. Experiments in Britain, the USA, and elsewhere have indicated that a concentration of fluoride of 1 part per million in tap water retards the decay of children's teeth by more than 50%.

fluoride negative ion (Fl^-) formed when hydrogen fluoride dissolves in water; compound formed between fluorine and another element in which the fluorine is the more electronegative element.

fluorine pale yellow, gaseous, nonmetallic element, symbol F, atomic number 9, relative atomic mass 19. It is the first member of the halogen group of elements, and is pungent, poisonous, and highly reactive, uniting directly with nearly all the elements. It occurs naturally as the minerals fluorite (CaF_2) and cryolite (Na_3AlF_6). Hydrogen fluoride is used in etching glass, and the freons, which all contain fluorine, are widely used as refrigerants.

flute or *transverse flute* side-blown soprano woodwind instrument of considerable antiquity. The flute is difficult to master but capable of intricate melodies and expressive tonal shading. The player blows across an end hole, the air current being split by the opposite edge which causes pressure waves to form within the tube. The fingers are placed over holes in the tube to create different notes.

fly any insect of the order Diptera. A fly has a single pair of wings, antennae, and compound eyes; the hind wings have become modified into knoblike projections (halteres) used to maintain equilibrium in flight. There are over 90,000 species.

flying squirrel any of numerous species of squirrel, not closely related to the true squirrels. They are characterized by a membrane along the side of the body from forelimb to hindlimb (in some species running to neck and tail) which allows them to glide through the air. Several genera of flying squirrel are found in the Old World; the New World has the genus *Glaucomys*. Most species are E Asian.

Flynn Errol. Stage name of Leslie Thompson 1909–1959. Australian-born US film actor. He is renowned for his portrayal of swashbuckling heroes in such films as *Captain Blood* 1935, *Robin Hood* 1938, *The Charge of the Light Brigade* 1938, *The Private Lives of Elizabeth and Essex* 1939, *The Sea Hawk* 1940, and *The Master of Ballantrae* 1953.

fog cloud that collects at the surface of the Earth, composed of water vapour that has condensed on particles of dust in the atmosphere. Cloud and fog are both caused by the air temperature falling below dew point. The thickness of fog depends on the number of water particles it contains.

folklore the oral traditions and culture of a people, expressed in legends, riddles, songs, tales, and proverbs. The term was coined 1846 by W J Thoms

(1803–85), but the founder of the systematic study of the subject was Jakob ◊Grimm.

folk music body of traditional music, originally transmitted orally. Many folk songs originated as a rhythmic accompaniment to manual work or to mark a specific ritual. Folk song is usually melodic, not harmonic, and the modes used are distinctive of the country of origin.

Fonda Henry 1905–1982. US actor. His engaging style made him ideal in the role of the American pioneer and honourable man. His many films include *The Grapes of Wrath* 1940, *My Darling Clementine* 1946, *12 Angry Men* 1957, and *On Golden Pond* 1981, for which he won the Academy Award for best actor. He was the father of actress Jane Fonda (1937–) and actor and director Peter Fonda (1939–).

Fonteyn Margot. Stage name of Peggy (Margaret) Hookham 1919–1991. English ballet dancer. She made her debut with the Vic-Wells Ballet in *Nutcracker* 1934 and first appeared as Giselle 1937, eventually becoming prima ballerina of the Royal Ballet, London. Renowned for her perfect physique, clear line, musicality, and interpretive powers, she created many roles in Frederick ◊Ashton's ballets and formed a legendary partnership with Rudolf ◊Nureyev.

food anything eaten by human beings and other animals to sustain life and health. The building blocks of food are nutrients, and humans can utilize the following nutrients: *carbohydrates*, as starches found in bread, potatoes, and pasta; as simple sugars in sucrose and honey; as fibres in cereals, fruit, and vegetables; *proteins* as from nuts, fish,

meat, eggs, milk, and some vegetables; *fats* as found in most animal products (meat, lard, dairy products, fish), also in margarine, nuts and seeds, olives, and edible oils; *vitamins* are found in a wide variety of foods, except for vitamin B$_{12}$, which is mainly found in foods of animal origin; *minerals* are found in a wide variety of foods (for example, calcium from milk and broccoli, iodine from seafood, and iron from liver and green vegetables); *water* ubiquitous in nature; *alcohol* is found in fermented distilled beverages, from 40% in spirits to 0.01% in low-alcohol lagers and beers.

food chain in ecology, a sequence showing the feeding relationships between organisms in a particular ◊ecosystem. Each organism depends on the next lowest member of the chain for its food.

food poisoning any acute illness characterized by vomiting and diarrhoea and caused by eating food contaminated with harmful bacteria (for example, listeriosis), poisonous food (for example, certain mushrooms, puffer fish), or poisoned food (such as lead or arsenic introduced accidentally during processing). A frequent cause of food poisoning is ◊Salmonella bacteria.

Foot Michael 1913– . British Labour politician and writer. A leader of the left-wing Tribune Group, he was secretary of state for employment 1974–76, Lord President of the Council and leader of the House 1976–79, and succeeded James Callaghan as Labour Party leader 1980–83.

football, American contact sport similar to the English game of rugby, played between two teams of 11 players, with an inflated oval ball. Players are well padded for protection and wear protective helmets. The *Super Bowl*, first held in 1967, is now an annual meeting between the winners of the National and American Football Conferences.

football, association or *soccer* form of football originating in the UK, popular in Europe and Latin America. The modern game is played in the UK according to the rules laid down by the Football Association. Slight amendments to the rules take effect in certain competitions and overseas matches as laid down by the sport's world governing body, Fédération Internationale de Football Association (FIFA, 1904). FIFA organizes the competitions for the World Cup, held every four years since 1930.

force any influence that tends to change the state of rest or the uniform motion in a straight line of a body. The action of an unbalanced or resultant force results in the acceleration of a body in the direction of action of the force, or it may, if the body is unable to move freely, result in its deformation (see ◊Hooke's law). Force is a vector quantity, possessing both magnitude and direction; its SI unit is the newton.

forces, fundamental in physics, the four fundamental interactions believed to be at work in the physical universe. There are two long-range forces: *gravity*, which keeps the planets in orbit around the Sun, and acts between all particles that have mass; and the *electromagnetic force*, which stops solids from falling apart, and acts between all particles with ◊electric charge. There are two very short- range forces which operate only inside the atomic nucleus: the *weak nuclear force*, responsible for the reactions that fuel the Sun and for the emission of ◊beta particles from certain

nuclei; and the *strong nuclear force*, which binds together the protons and neutrons in the nuclei of atoms. The relative strengths of the four forces are: strong, 1; electromagnetic, 10^{-2}; weak, 10^{-6}; gravitational, 10^{-40}.

Ford Henry 1863–1947. US automobile manufacturer, who built his first car 1896 and founded the Ford Motor Company 1903. His Model T (1908–27) was the first car to be constructed solely by assembly-line methods and to be mass marketed; 15 million of these cars were made and sold.

Ford John. Adopted name of Sean O'Feeney 1895–1973. US film director. Active from the silent film era, he was one of the key creators of the 'Western', directing *The Iron Horse* 1924; *Stagecoach* 1939 became his masterpiece. He won Academy Awards for *The Informer* 1935, *The Grapes of Wrath* 1940, *How Green Was My Valley* 1941, and *The Quiet Man* 1952.

forensic science the use of scientific techniques to solve criminal cases. It embraces chemistry, physics, botany, zoology, and medicine and includes the identification of human bodies or traces. Traditional methods such as fingerprinting are still used, assisted by computers; in addition, blood analysis, forensic dentistry, voice and speech spectograms, and genetic fingerprinting are increasingly applied.

forestry the science of forest management. Recommended forestry practice aims at multipurpose crops, allowing the preservation of varied plant and animal species as well as human uses (lumbering, recreation). Forestry has often been confined to the planting of a single species, such as a rapid- growing conifer providing softwood for paper pulp and construction timber, for which world demand is greatest. In tropical countries, logging contributes to the destruction of ▷rainforests, causing global environmental problems. Small unplanned forests are ▷woodland. In the UK, Japan, and other countries, forestry practices have been criticized for concentration on softwood conifers to the neglect of native hardwood.

formula in chemistry, a representation of a molecule, radical, or ion, in which the component chemical elements are represented by their symbols. An *empirical formula* indicates the simplest ratio of the elements in a compound, without indicating how many of them there are or how they are combined. A *molecular formula* gives the number of each type of element present in one molecule. A *structural formula* shows the relative positions of the atoms and the bonds between them. For example, for ethanoic acid, the empirical formula is CH_2O, the molecular formula is $C_2H_4O_2$, and the structural formula is CH_3COOH.

Forster E(dward) M(organ) 1879–1970. English novelist. He was concerned with the interplay of personality and the conflict between convention and instinct. His novels include *A Room with a View* 1908, *Howards End* 1910, and *A Passage to India* 1924. He also wrote short stories, for example 'The Eternal Omnibus' 1914; criticism, including *Aspects of the Novel* 1927; and essays, including *Abinger Harvest* 1936.

Fort-de-France capital, chief commercial centre, and port of Martinique, West Indies, at the mouth of the Madame River; population (1990) 101,500. It trades in sugar, rum, and cacao.

fossil remains of an animal or plant preserved in rocks. Fossils may be formed by refrigeration (for example, Arctic mammoths in ice); carbonization (leaves in coal); formation of a cast (dinosaur or human footprints in mud); or mineralization of bones, more generally teeth or shells. The study of fossils is called ▷palaeontology.

fossil fuel fuel, such as coal, oil, and natural gas, formed from the fossilized remains of plants that lived hundreds of millions of years ago. Fossil fuels are a ▷nonrenewable resource and will eventually run out. Extraction of coal and oil causes considerable environmental pollution, and burning coal contributes to problems of ▷acid rain and the ▷greenhouse effect.

four-stroke cycle the engine-operating cycle of most petrol and ▷diesel engines. The 'stroke' is an upward or downward movement of a piston in a cylinder. In a petrol engine the cycle begins with the induction of a fuel mixture as the piston goes down on its first stroke. On the second stroke (up) the piston compresses the mixture in the top of the cylinder. An electric spark then ignites the mixture, and the gases produced force the piston down on its third, power, stroke. On the fourth stroke (up) the piston expels the burned gases from the cylinder into the exhaust.

Fox Charles James 1749–1806. English Whig politician, son of the 1st Baron Holland. He entered Parliament 1769 as a supporter of the court, but went over to the opposition 1774. As secretary of state 1782, leader of the opposition to Pitt, and foreign secretary 1806, he welcomed the French Revolution and brought about the abolition of the slave trade.

fractal an irregular shape or surface produced by a procedure of repeated subdivision. Generated on a computer screen, fractals are used in creating models for geographical or biological processes (for example, the creation of a coastline by erosion or accretion, or the growth of plants).

fraction in mathematics, a number that indicates one or more equal parts of a whole. Usually, the number of equal parts into which the unit is divided (denominator) is written below a horizontal line, and the number of parts comprising the fraction (numerator) is written above; thus ⅔ or ¾. Such fractions are called *vulgar* or *simple* fractions. The denominator can never be zero.

Fragonard Jean-Honoré 1732–1806. French painter. He was the leading exponent of the Rococo style (along with his master Boucher). His light-hearted subjects, often erotic, include *The Swing* about 1766 (Wallace Collection, London).

France French Republic (*République Française*); *area* (including Corsica) 543,965 sq km/209,970 sq mi; *capital* Paris; *features* Ardennes forest, Auvergne mountain region, Riviera, Mont Blanc (4,810 m/15,781 ft), caves of Dordogne with relics of early humans; largest W European nation; *head of state* Jacques Chirac from 1995; *head of government* Edouard Balladur from 1993; *political system* liberal democracy; *population* (1994) 57,800,000 (including 4,500,000 immigrants, chiefly from Portugal, Algeria, Morocco, and Tunisia); growth rate 0.3% p.a.; *language* French (regional languages include Basque, Breton, Catalan, and the Provençal dialect); *religion* Roman Catholic 90%, Protestant 2%, Muslim 1%.

France Anatole. Pen name of Anatole François Thibault 1844–1924. French writer. He is renowned for the wit, urbanity, and style of his works. His earliest novel was *Le Crime de Sylvestre Bonnard/The Crime of Sylvester Bonnard* 1881; later books include the autobiographical series beginning with *Le Livre de mon ami/My Friend's Book* 1885, the satiric *L'Ile des pingouins/Penguin Island* 1908, and *Les Dieux ont soif/The Gods Are Athirst* 1912. Nobel Prize for Literature 1921.

Franche-Comté region of E France; area 16,200 sq km/6,253 sq mi; population (1987) 1,086,000. Its capital is Besançon, and it includes the *départements* of Doubs, Jura, Haute Saône, and Territoire de Belfort.

Francis of Assisi, St 1182–1226. Italian founder of the Roman Catholic Franciscan order of friars 1209 and, with St Clare, of the Poor Clares 1212. In 1224 he is said to have undergone a mystical experience during which he received the *stigmata* (five wounds of Jesus). Many stories are told of his ability to charm wild animals, and he is the patron saint of ecologists. Feast day 4 Oct.

Franco Francisco (Paulino Hermenegildo Teódulo Bahamonde) 1892–1975. Spanish dictator from 1939. As a general, he led the insurgent Nationalists to victory in the Spanish ▷Civil War 1936–39, supported by Fascist Italy and Nazi Germany, and established a dictatorship. In 1942 Franco reinstated a Cortes (Spanish parliament), which in 1947 passed an act by which he became head of state for life.

Franco-Prussian War 1870–71. The Prussian chancellor Bismarck put forward a German candidate for the vacant

Spanish throne with the deliberate, and successful, intention of provoking the French emperor Napoleon III into declaring war. The Prussians defeated the French at Sedan, then besieged Paris. The Treaty of Frankfurt May 1871 gave Alsace, Lorraine, and a large French indemnity to Prussia. The war established Prussia, at the head of a newly established German empire, as Europe's leading power.

Frank member of a group of Germanic peoples prominent in Europe in the 3rd to 9th centuries. Believed to have originated in Pomerania on the Baltic Sea, they had settled on the Rhine by the 3rd century, spread into the Roman Empire by the 4th century, and gradually conquered most of Gaul, Italy, and Germany under the Merovingian and ◊Carolingian dynasties. The kingdom of the western Franks became France, the kingdom of the eastern Franks became Germany.

Frankfurt-am-Main city in Hessen, Germany, 72 km/45 mi NE of Mannheim, with an inland port on the river Main; population (1988) 592,000. It is a commercial and banking centre. An international book fair is held here annually.

Franklin Benjamin 1706–1790. US printer, publisher, author, scientist, and statesman. He proved that lightning is a form of electricity, distinguished between positive and negative electricity, and invented the lightning conductor. He was the first US ambassador to France 1776–85, and negotiated peace with Britain 1783. As a delegate to the Continental Congress from Pennsylvania 1785–88, he helped to draft the ◊Declaration of Independence and the US ◊Constitution.

Franz Joseph or *Francis Joseph* 1830–1916. Emperor of Austria-Hungary from 1848, when his uncle, Ferdinand I, abdicated. After the suppression of the 1848 revolution, Franz Joseph tried to establish an absolute monarchy but had to grant Austria a parliamentary constitution 1861 and Hungary equality with Austria 1867. He was defeated in the Italian War 1859 and the Prussian War 1866. In 1914 he made the assassination of his heir and nephew Franz Ferdinand the excuse for attacking Serbia, thus precipitating World War I.

Frederick (II) the Great 1712–1786. King of Prussia from 1740, when he succeeded his father Frederick William I. In that year he started the War of the Austrian Succession by his attack on Austria. In the peace of 1745 he secured Silesia. The struggle was renewed in the Seven Years' War 1756–63. He acquired West Prussia in the first partition of Poland 1772 and left Prussia as Germany's foremost state. He was an efficient and just ruler in the spirit of the Enlightenment and a patron of the arts.

freemasonry the beliefs and practices of a group of linked national organizations open to men over the age of 21, united by a common code of morals and certain traditional 'secrets'. Modern freemasonry began in 18th-century Europe. Freemasons do much charitable work, but have been criticized in recent years for their secrecy, their male exclusivity, and their alleged use of influence within and between organizations to further each other's interests.

free radical in chemistry, an atom or molecule that has an unpaired electron and is therefore highly reactive. Most free radicals are very short-lived. They are by-products of normal cell chemistry and rapidly oxidize other molecules they encounter. They are thought to do considerable damage. They are neutralized by protective enzymes.

Freetown capital of Sierra Leone, W Africa; population (1988) 470,000. It has a naval station and a harbour. It was founded as a settlement for freed slaves in the 1790s.

free will the doctrine that human beings are free to control their own actions, and that these actions are not fixed in advance by God or fate. Some Jewish and Christian theologians assert that God gave humanity free will to choose between good and evil; others that God has decided in advance the outcome of all human choices (◊predestination), as in Calvinism.

freezing change from liquid to solid state, as when water becomes ice. For a given substance, freezing occurs at a definite temperature, known as the *freezing point*, that is invariable under similar conditions of pressure, and the temperature remains at this point until all the liquid is frozen. The amount of heat per unit mass that has to be removed to freeze a substance is a constant for any given substance, and is known as the latent heat of fusion.

French Guiana (French *Guyane Française*) French overseas *département* from 1946, and administrative region from 1974, on the north coast of South America, bounded W by Surinam and E and S by Brazil; *area* 83,500 sq km/ 32,230 sq mi; *capital* Cayenne; *features* Eurospace rocket launch pad at Kourou; Iles du Salut, which include Devil's Island; *languages* 90% Creole, French, American Indian.

French member of the Romance branch of the Indo- European language family, spoken in France, Belgium, Luxembourg, Monaco, and Switzerland in Europe; also in Canada (principally in the province of Québec), various Caribbean and Pacific Islands (including overseas territories such as Martinique and French Guiana), and certain N and W African countries (for example, Mali and Senegal).

French Polynesia French Overseas Territory in the S Pacific, consisting of five archipelagos: Windward Islands, Leeward Islands (the two island groups comprising the ◊Society Islands), Tuamotu Archipelago (including Gambier Islands), Tubuai Islands, and Marquesas Islands *total area* 3,940 sq km/1,521 sq mi *capital* Papeete on Tahiti; *population* (1990) 199,100 *languages* Tahitian (official), French.

French Revolution the period 1789–1799 that saw the end of the French monarchy. Although the revolution began as an attempt to create a constitutional monarchy, by late 1792 demands for long-overdue reforms resulted in the proclamation of the First Republic. The violence of the revolution, attacks by other nations, and bitter factional struggles, riots, and counterrevolutionary uprisings consumed the republic. This helped bring the extremists to power, and the bloody Reign of Terror followed. French armies then succeeded in holding off their foreign enemies and one of the generals, ◊Napoleon, seized power 1799.

frequency in physics, the number of periodic oscillations, vibrations, or waves occurring per unit of time. The unit of frequency is the hertz (Hz), one hertz being equivalent to one cycle per second.

fresco mural painting technique using water-based paint on wet plaster. Some of the earliest frescoes (about 1750–1400 BC) were found in Knossos, Crete (now preserved in the Heraklion Museum). Fresco reached its finest expression in Italy from the 13th to the 17th centuries. Giotto, Masaccio, Michelangelo, and many other artists worked in the medium. In the 20th century the Mexican muralists Orozco and Rivera used fresco.

Freud Lucian 1922– . German-born British painter. He is one of the greatest contemporary figurative artists. He combines meticulous accuracy with a disquieting intensity, emphasizing the physicality of his subjects, whether nudes, still lifes, or interiors. His *Portrait of Francis Bacon* 1952 (Tate Gallery, London) is one of his best-known works. He is a grandson of Sigmund Freud.

Freud Sigmund 1865–1939. Austrian physician who pioneered the study of the unconscious mind. He developed the methods of free association and interpretation of dreams that are basic techniques of ◊psychoanalysis, and formulated the concepts of the id, ego, and superego. His books include *Die Traumdeutung/The Interpretation of Dreams* 1900, *Totem and Taboo* 1913, and *Das Unbehagen in der Kultur/Civilization and its Discontents* 1930.

friction in physics, the force that opposes the relative motion of two bodies in contact. The *coefficient of friction* is the ratio of the force required to achieve this relative motion to the force pressing the two bodies together.

Friedman Milton 1912– . US economist. The foremost exponent of ◊monetarism, he argued that a country's

economy, and hence inflation, can be controlled through its money supply, although most governments lack the 'political will' to control inflation by cutting government spending and thereby increasing unemployment. Nobel Prize for Economics 1976.

Friends of the Earth (FoE or FOE) environmental pressure group, established in the UK 1971, that aims to protect the environment and to promote rational and sustainable use of the Earth's resources.

Friends, Society of or *Quakers* Christian Protestant sect founded by George ◊Fox in England in the 17th century. They were persecuted for their nonviolent activism, and many emigrated to form communities elsewhere, for example in Pennsylvania and New England, USA. Their worship stresses meditation and the freedom of all to take an active part in the service (called a meeting, held in a meeting house); there are no priests or ministers.

frog any amphibian of the order Anura (Greek 'tailless'). There are some 24 different families of frog, containing more than 3,800 species. There are no clear rules for distinguishing between frogs and toads. Frogs usually have squat bodies, hind legs specialized for jumping, and webbed feet for swimming. Many use their long, extensible tongues to capture insects. They vary in size from the tiny North American little grass frog *Limnaoedus ocularis*, 12 mm/0.5 in long, to the giant aquatic frog *Telmatobius culeus*, 50 cm/20 in long, of Lake Titicaca, South America. Frogs are widespread, inhabiting all continents except Antarctica, and they have adapted to a range of environments including deserts, forests, grasslands, and even high altitudes, with some species in the Andes and Himalayas existing above 5,000 m/19,600 ft.

front in meteorology, the boundary between two air masses of different temperature or humidity. A *cold front* marks the line of advance of a cold air mass from below, as it displaces a warm air mass; a *warm front* marks the advance of a warm air mass as it rises up over a cold one. Frontal systems define the weather of the mid-latitudes, where warm tropical air is constantly meeting cold air from the poles.

Frost Robert (Lee) 1874–1963. US poet. His accessible, colloquial blank verse, often flavoured with New England speech patterns, is written with an individual voice and penetrating vision. His poems, include 'Mending Wall', 'The Road Not taken', and 'Stopping by Woods on a Snowy Evening'; they are collected in *A Boy's Will* 1913, *North of Boston* 1914, *New Hampshire* 1924, *Collected Poems* 1930, *A Further Range* 1936, and *A Witness Tree* 1942.

frostbite the freezing of skin or flesh, with formation of ice crystals leading to tissue damage. The treatment is slow warming of the affected area; for example, by skin-to-skin contact or with lukewarm water. Frostbitten parts are extremely vulnerable to infection, with the risk of gangrene.

fructose $C_6H_{12}O_6$ a sugar that occurs naturally in honey, the nectar of flowers, and many sweet fruits; it is commercially prepared from glucose.

fruit in botany, the ripened ovary in flowering plants that develops from one or more seeds or carpels and encloses one or more seeds. Its function is to protect the seeds during their development and to aid in their dispersal. Fruits are often edible, sweet, juicy, and colourful. When eaten they provide vitamins, minerals, and enzymes, but little protein.

fugue in music, a contrapuntal form with two or more subjects (principal melodies) for a number of parts, which enter in succession in direct imitation of each other or transposed to a higher or lower key, and may be combined in augmented form (larger note values). It represents the highest form of contrapuntal ingenuity in works such as J S Bach's *Das musikalische Opfer/The Musical Offering* 1747, on a theme of Frederick II of Prussia, and *Die Kunst der Fuge/The Art of the Fugue* published 1751, and Beethoven's *Grosse Fuge/Great Fugue* for string quartet 1825–26.

Fujiyama or *Mount Fuji* Japanese volcano and highest peak, on Honshu Island, near Tokyo; height 3,778 m/12,400 ft. Extinct since 1707, it has a ▷Shinto shrine and a weather station on its summit. Fuji has long been revered for its picturesque cone- shaped crater peak, and figures prominently in Japanese art, literature, and religion.

Fuller (Richard) Buckminster 1895–1983. US architect, engineer, and social philosopher. He embarked on an unorthodox career in an attempt to maximize energy resources through improved technology. In 1947 he invented the geodesic dome, a lightweight frame of triangular components linked by rods, independent of buttress or vault and capable of covering large-span areas.

fullerene form of carbon, discovered 1985, based on closed cages of carbon atoms. The molecules of the most symmetrical of the fullerenes are called

▷buckminsterfullerenes. They are perfect spheres made up of 60 carbon atoms linked together in 12 pentagons and 20 hexagons fitted together like those of a spherical football. Other fullerenes with 28, 32, 50, 70, and 76 carbon atoms have also been identified.

Functionalism in architecture and design, the principle of excluding everything that serves no practical purpose. Central to 20th-century ▷Modernism, the Functionalist ethic developed as a reaction against the 19th- century practice of imitating and combining earlier styles. Its finest achievements are in the realms of ▷Industrial architecture and office furnishings.

fundamentalism in religion, an emphasis on basic principles or articles of faith. *Christian fundamentalism* emerged in the USA just after World War I (as a reaction to theological modernism and the historical criticism of the Bible) and insisted on belief in the literal truth of everything in the Bible. *Islamic fundamentalism* insists on strict observance of Muslim Shari'a law.

fungus (plural *fungi*) any of a group of organisms in the kingdom Fungi. Fungi are not considered plants. They lack leaves and roots; they contain no chlorophyll and reproduce by spores. Moulds, yeasts, rusts, smuts, mildews, and mushrooms are all types of fungi.

fusion in physics, the fusing of the nuclei of light elements, such as hydrogen, into those of a heavier element, such as helium. The resultant loss in their combined mass is converted into energy. Stars and thermonuclear weapons work on the principle of nuclear fusion.

G

Gable (William) Clark 1901–1960. US actor. A star for more than 30 years in 90 films, he played romantic roles such as Rhett Butler in *Gone with the Wind* 1939. His other films include *It Happened One Night* 1934 (Academy Award), *Mutiny on the Bounty* 1935, and *The Misfits* 1961.

Gabon Gabonese Republic (*République Gabonaise*); *area* 267,667 sq km/ 103,319 sq mi; *capital* Libreville; *features* Schweitzer hospital at Lambaréné; Trans-Gabonais railway; *political system* emergent democracy; *population* (1993) 1,010,000 including 40 Bantu groups; growth rate 1.6% p.a.; *languages* French (official), Bantu; *religions* Christian 96% (Roman Catholic 65%), small Muslim minority 1%, animist 3%.

Gaborone capital of Botswana, mainly an administrative and government-service centre; population (1990) 341,100. The University of Botswana and Swaziland (1976) is here. The city developed after it replaced Mafikeng as the country's capital 1965.

Gaddafi alternative form of ⊳Khaddhafi, Libyan leader.

Gaelic member of the Celtic branch of the Indo-European language family, spoken in Ireland, Scotland, and (until 1974) the Isle of Man. It has been in decline for several centuries, discouraged until recently within the British state. There is a small Gaelic-speaking community in Nova Scotia, Canada.

Gagarin Yuri (Alexeyevich) 1934–1968. Soviet cosmonaut who in 1961 became the first human in space aboard the spacecraft *Vostok 1*.

Gaia hypothesis theory that the Earth's living and nonliving systems form an inseparable whole that is regulated and kept adapted for life by living organisms themselves. The planet therefore functions as a single organism, or a giant cell. Since life and environment are so closely linked, there is a need for humans to understand and maintain the physical environment and living things around them. The hypothesis was elaborated by British scientist James (Ephraim) Lovelock (1919–) and first published in 1968. It was not named 'Gaia' until some years later, at the suggestion of the writer William Golding.

Gainsborough Thomas 1727–1788. English landscape and portrait painter. In 1760 he settled in Bath and painted society portraits. In 1774 he went to London and became one of the original members of the Royal Academy. He was one of the first British artists to follow the Dutch example in painting realistic landscapes rather than imaginative Italianate scenery.

Galahad in Arthurian legend, one of the knights of the Round Table. Galahad succeeded in the quest for the ◊Holy Grail because of his virtue. He was the son of Lancelot of the Lake.

Galápagos Islands (official name *Archipiélago de Colón*) group of 15 islands in the Pacific, belonging to Ecuador; area 7,800 sq km/3,000 sq mi; population (1982) 6,120. The capital is San Cristóbal on the island of the same name. The islands are a nature reserve. Their unique fauna (including giant tortoises, iguanas, penguins, flightless cormorants, and Darwin's finches, which inspired Charles ◊Darwin to formulate the principle of evolution by natural selection) is under threat from introduced species.

galaxy congregation of millions or billions of stars, held together by gravity. *Spiral galaxies*, such as the ◊Milky Way, are flattened in shape, with a central bulge of old stars surrounded by a disc of younger stars, arranged in spiral arms like a Catherine wheel. *Barred spirals* are spiral galaxies that have a straight bar of stars across their centre, from the ends of which the spiral arms emerge. The arms of spiral galaxies contain gas and dust from which new stars are still forming. *Elliptical galaxies* contain old stars and very little gas. They include the most massive galaxies known, containing a trillion stars. At least some elliptical galaxies are thought to be formed by mergers between spiral galaxies. There are also irregular galaxies. Most galaxies occur in clusters, containing anything from a few to thousands of members.

Galen *c.* 130–*c.* 200. Greek physician whose ideas dominated Western medicine for almost 1,500 years. Central to his thinking were the theories of humours and the threefold circulation of the blood. He remained the highest medical authority until Andreas Vesalius and William Harvey exposed the fundamental errors of his system.

Galilee, Sea of alternative name for Lake Tiberias in N Israel.

Galileo properly Galileo Galilei 1564–1642. Italian mathematician, astronomer, and physicist. He developed the astronomical telescope and was the first to see sunspots, the four main satellites of Jupiter, mountains and craters on the Moon, and the appearance of Venus going through 'phases', thus proving it was orbiting the Sun. In mechanics, Galileo discovered that freely falling bodies, heavy or light, had the same, constant acceleration (although the story of his dropping cannonballs from the Leaning Tower of Pisa is questionable) and that a body moving on a perfectly smooth horizontal surface would neither speed up nor slow down.

gall bladder small muscular sac, part of the digestive system of most, but not all, vertebrates. In humans, it is situated on the underside of the liver and connected to the small intestine by the bile duct. It stores bile from the liver. *Gallstones* are pebblelike, insoluble accretions formed in the human gall bladder or bile ducts from cholesterol or calcium salts present in bile. Gallstones may be symptomless or they may cause pain, indigestion, or jaundice. They can be dissolved with medication or removed.

Gallipoli port in European Turkey, giving its name to the peninsula (ancient name *Chersonesus*) on which it stands. In World War I, at the instigation of Winston Churchill, an unsuccessful attempt was made Feb 1915–Jan 1916 by Allied troops (mostly those of Australia and New Zealand) to force their way through the Dardanelles and link up with Russia.

Galsworthy John 1867–1933. English novelist and dramatist. His work examines the social issues of the Victorian period. He wrote *The Forsyte Saga* 1922 and its sequel *A Modern Comedy* 1929. His other novels include *The Country House* 1907 and *Fraternity* 1909; plays include *The Silver Box* 1906. Nobel Prize 1932.

Galway county on the W coast of the Republic of Ireland, in the province of Connacht; county town Galway; area 5,940 sq km/2,293 sq mi; population (1991) 180,300. Towns include Ballinasloe, Tuam, Clifden, and Loughrea (near which deposits of lead, zinc, and copper were found 1959).

Gama Vasco da *c.* 1469–1524. Portuguese navigator who commanded an expedition in 1497 to discover the route to India around the Cape of Good Hope in modern South Africa. On Christmas Day 1497 he reached land, which he named Natal. He then crossed the Indian Ocean, arriving at Calicut May 1498, and returning to Portugal Sept 1499.

Gambia Republic of The; *area* 10,402 sq km/4,018 sq mi; *capital* Banjul; *features* smallest state in black Africa; stone circles; Karantaba obelisk marking spot where Mungo Park began his journey to the Niger River 1796; *political system* interim military republic; *population* (1993 est) 920,000; growth rate 1.9% p.a.; *languages* English (official), Mandinka, Fula and other native tongues; *religions* Muslim 90%, with animist and Christian minorities.

gamete cell that functions in sexual reproduction by merging with another gamete to form a ▷zygote. Examples of gametes include sperm and egg cells. In most organisms, the gametes are haploid (they contain half the number of chromosomes of the parent), owing to reduction division or ▷meiosis.

gamma radiation very high-frequency electromagnetic radiation, similar in nature to X-rays but of shorter wavelength, emitted by the nuclei of radioactive substances during decay or by the interactions of high-energy electrons with matter. Cosmic gamma rays have been identified as coming from pulsars, radio galaxies, and quasars, although they cannot penetrate the Earth's atmosphere.

Gandhi (Mohandas Karamchand Gandhi, given the honorific name of *Mahatma* [Sanskrit 'Great Soul']) 1869–1948. Indian nationalist leader. A pacifist, he led the struggle for Indian independence from the UK by advocating nonviolent noncooperation (*satyagraha*, defence of and by truth) from 1915. He was imprisoned several times by the British authorities and was influential in the nationalist Congress Party and in the independence negotiations 1947. He was assassinated by a Hindu nationalist in the violence that followed the partition of British India into India and Pakistan.

Gandhi Indira (born Nehru) 1917–1984. Indian politician, prime minister of India 1966–77 and 1980–84, and leader of the Congress Party 1966–77 and subsequently of the Congress (I) party. She was assassinated 1984 by members of her Sikh bodyguard, resentful of her use of troops to clear malcontents from the Sikh temple at ▷Amritsar. She was succeeded as prime minister by her son Rajiv Gandhi (1944–91) who was also assassinated.

Ganges (Hindi *Ganga*) major river of India and Bangladesh; length 2,510 km/1,560 mi. It is the most sacred river for Hindus.

Garbo Greta. Stage name of Greta Lovisa Gustafsson 1905–1990. Swedish-born US film actress. She went to the USA 1925, and her captivating beauty and leading role in *Flesh and the Devil* 1927 made her one of Hollywood's greatest stars. Her later films include *Mata Hari* 1931, *Grand Hotel* 1932, *Queen Christina* 1933, *Anna Karenina* 1935, *Camille* 1936, and *Ninotchka* 1939. She retired 1941.

Garcia Márquez Gabriel 1928– . Colombian novelist. His sweeping novel *Cien años de soledad/One Hundred Years of Solitude* 1967 (which tells the story of a family over a period of six generations) is an example of magic realism, a technique used to heighten the intensity of realistic portrayal of social and political issues by introducing grotesque or fanciful material. Nobel Prize for Literature 1982.

Garibaldi Giuseppe 1807–1882. Italian soldier who played a central role in the unification of Italy by conquering Sicily and Naples 1860. From 1834 a member of the nationalist Mazzini's Young Italy society, he was forced into exile until 1848 and again 1849–54. He fought against Austria 1848–49, 1859, and 1866, and led two unsuccessful expeditions to liberate Rome from papal rule in 1862 and 1867.

Garland Judy. Stage name of Frances Gumm 1922–1969. US singer and actress. Her performances are marked by a compelling intensity. Her films

include *The Wizard of Oz* 1939 (which featured the tune that was to become her theme song, 'Over the Rainbow'), *Babes in Arms* 1939, *Strike Up the Band* 1940, *Meet Me in St Louis* 1944, *Easter Parade* 1948, *A Star is Born* 1954, and *Judgment at Nuremberg* 1961.

garlic perennial plant *Allium sativum* of the lily family Liliaceae, with white flowers. The bulb, made of small segments, or cloves, is used in cookery, and its pungent essence has an active medical ingredient, allyl methyl trisulphide, which prevents blood clotting.

garnet group of silicate minerals with the formula $X_3Y_2(SiO_4)_3$, when X is calcium, magnesium, iron, or manganese, and Y is iron, aluminium, or chromium. Garnets are used as semiprecious gems (usually pink to deep red) and as abrasives. They occur in metamorphic rocks such as gneiss and schist.

Garrick David 1717–1779. English actor and theatre manager. From 1747 he became joint licensee of the Drury Lane Theatre with his own company, and instituted a number of significant theatrical conventions including concealed stage lighting and banishing spectators from the stage. He played Shakespearean characters such as Richard III, King Lear, Hamlet, and Benedick, and collaborated with George Colman (1732–1794) in writing the play *The Clandestine Marriage* 1766.

gas in physics, a form of matter, such as air, in which the molecules move randomly in otherwise empty space, filling any size or shape of container into which the gas is put.

gas exchange in biology, the exchange of gases between living organisms and the atmosphere, principally oxygen and carbon dioxide.

Gaskell 'Mrs' (Elizabeth Cleghorn, born Stevenson) 1810–1865. English novelist. Her most popular book, *Cranford* 1853, is the study of small, close-knit circle in a small town, modelled on Knutsford, Cheshire. Her other books, often dealing with social concerns, include *Mary Barton* 1848, *North and South* 1855, and *Sylvia's Lovers* 1863–64.

gastroenteritis inflammation of the stomach and intestines, giving rise to abdominal pain, vomiting, and diarrhoea. It may be caused by food or other poisoning, allergy, or infection. Dehydration may be severe and it is a particular risk in infants.

gastropod any member of a very large class (Gastropoda) of ◊molluscs. Gastropods are single- shelled (in a spiral or modified spiral form), have eyes on stalks, and move on a flattened, muscular foot. They have well- developed heads and rough, scraping tongues called radulae. Some are marine, some freshwater, and others land creatures, but all tend to inhabit damp places.

GATT acronym for ◊General Agreement on Tariffs and Trade.

gauge boson or *field particle* any of the particles that carry the four fundamental forces of nature (see ◊forces, fundamental). Gauge bosons are ◊elementary particles that cannot be subdivided, and include the photon, the graviton, the gluons, and the weakons.

Gauguin Paul 1848–1903. French Post-Impressionist painter. Going beyond the Impressionists' notion of reality, he sought a more direct experience of life in the rich colours of the South Sea islands and the magical rites of its people. His work, often heavily symbolic and decorative, is characterized by his sensuous use of pure colours. Among his paintings is *Le Christe jaune* 1889 (Albright-Knox Art Gallery, Buffalo, New York State).

Gaul member of the Celtic-speaking peoples who inhabited France and Belgium in Roman times; also their territory. Certain Gauls invaded Italy around 400 BC, sacked Rome 387 BC, and settled between the Alps and the Apennines; this district, known as Cisalpine Gaul, was conquered by Rome in about 225 BC.

Gawain in Arthurian legend, one of the knights of the Round Table who participated in the quest for the ◊Holy Grail. He is the hero of the 14th-century epic poem *Sir Gawayne and the Greene Knight*.

Gay John 1685–1732. English poet and dramatist. He wrote *Trivia* 1716, a verse picture of 18th- century London. His *The Beggar's Opera* 1728, a 'Newgate pastoral' using traditional songs and telling of the love of Polly for highwayman Captain Macheath, was an extraordinarily popular success. Its satiric political touches led to the banning of *Polly*, a sequel.

Gaza Strip strip of land on the Mediterranean sea, under Israeli administration; capital Gaza; area 363 sq km/140 sq mi; population (1989) 645,000 of which 446,000 are refugees.

gazelle any of a number of species of lightly built, fast-running antelopes found on the open plains of Africa and

S Asia, especially those of the genus *Gazella*.

gear toothed wheel that transmits the turning movement of one shaft to another shaft. Gear wheels may be used in pairs, or in threes if both shafts are to turn in the same direction. The gear ratio – the ratio of the number of teeth on the two wheels – determines the torque ratio, the turning force on the output shaft compared with the turning force on the input shaft.

Geiger counter any of a number of devices used for detecting nuclear radiation and/or measuring its intensity by counting the number of ionizing particles produced (see ▷radioactivity). It detects the momentary current that passes between ▷electrodes in a suitable gas when a nuclear particle or a radiation pulse causes the ionization of that gas. The electrodes are connected to electronic devices that enable the number of particles passing to be measured. The increased frequency of measured particles indicates the intensity of radiation. It is named after the German physicist Hans Geiger (1882–1945).

gel solid produced by the formation of a three-dimensional cage structure, commonly of linked large-molecular-mass polymers, in which a liquid is trapped. It is a form of ▷colloid. A gel may be a jellylike mass (pectin, gelatin) or have a more rigid structure (silica gel).

gem mineral valuable by virtue of its durability (hardness), rarity, and beauty, cut and polished for ornamental use, or engraved. Of 120 minerals known to have been used as gemstones, only about 25 are in common use in jewellery today; of these, the diamond, emerald, ruby, and sapphire are classified as precious, and all the others semiprecious, for example the topaz, amethyst, opal, and aquamarine.

gene unit of inherited material, encoded by a strand of ▷DNA, and transcribed by ▷RNA. In higher organisms, genes are located on the ▷chromosomes. The term 'gene', coined 1909 by the Danish geneticist Wilhelm Johannsen (1857–1927), refers to the inherited factor that consistently affects a particular character in an individual – for example, the gene for eye colour. Also termed a Mendelian gene, after Austrian biologist Gregor ▷Mendel, it occurs at a particular point or locus on a particular chromosome and may have several variants or ▷alleles, each specifying a particular form of that character – for example, the alleles for blue or brown eyes. Some alleles show dominance. These mask the effect of other alleles known as ▷recessive.

General Agreement on Tariffs and Trade (GATT) organization within the United Nations founded 1948 with the aim of encouraging free trade between nations through low tariffs, abolitions of quotas, and curbs on subsidies.

General Strike In British history, a nationwide strike called by the Trade Union Congress on 3 May 1926 in support of the miners' union. Elsewhere, general strikes have been used as a political weapon by anarchists and others.

genetic code the way in which instructions for building proteins, the basic structural molecules of living matter, are 'written' in the genetic material ▷DNA. This relationship between the sequence of bases (the subunits in a DNA molecule) and the sequence of ▷amino acids (the subunits of a protein molecule) is the basis of heredity. The code employs codons of three bases each; it is the same in almost all organisms, except for a few minor differences recently discovered in some protozoa.

genetic engineering deliberate manipulation of genetic material by biochemical techniques. It is often achieved by the introduction of new ◊DNA, usually by means of a virus or plasmid. This can be for pure research or to breed functionally specific plants, animals, or bacteria. These organisms with a foreign gene added are said to be transgenic (see ◊transgenic organism).

genetics study of inheritance and of the units of inheritance (◊genes). The founder of genetics was Austrian biologist Gregor ◊Mendel, whose experiments with plants, such as peas, showed that inheritance takes place by means of discrete 'particles', which later came to be called genes.

Geneva (French *Genève*) Swiss city, capital of Geneva canton, on the shore of Lake Geneva; population (1990) city 167,200; canton 376,000. It is a point of convergence of natural routes and is a cultural and commercial centre.

Geneva Convention international agreement 1864 regulating the treatment of those wounded in war, and later extended to cover the types of weapons allowed, the treatment of prisoners and the sick, and the protection of civilians in wartime. The rules were revised at conventions held 1906, 1929, and 1949, and by the 1977 Additional Protocols.

Geneva, Lake (French *Lac Léman*) largest of the central European lakes, between Switzerland and France; area 580 sq km/225 sq mi.

Genghis Khan *c.* ?1167–1227. Mongol conqueror, ruler of all Mongol peoples from 1206. He began the conquest of N China 1213, overran the empire of the shah of Khiva 1219–25, and invaded N India, while his lieutenants advanced as far as the Crimea. His empire ranged from the Yellow Sea to the Black Sea; it continued to expand after his death to extend from Hungary to Korea.

Genoa (Italian *Genova*) historic city in NW Italy, capital of Liguria; population (1989) 706,700. It is Italy's largest port.

genocide deliberate and systematic destruction of a national, racial, religious, or ethnic group defined by the exterminators as undesirable. The term is commonly applied to the policies of the Nazis during World War II (what they called the 'final solution' – the extermination of all 'undesirables' in occupied Europe, particularly the Jews). See ◊Holocaust.

genome the full complement of ◊genes carried by a single (haploid) set of ◊chromosomes. The term may be applied to the genetic information carried by an individual or to the range of genes found in a given species.

genotype the particular set of ◊alleles (variants of genes) possessed by a given organism. The term is usually used in conjunction with ◊phenotype, which is the product of the genotype and all environmental effects. See also ◊nature–nurture controversy.

Gentile da Fabriano *c.* 1370–1427. Italian painter of frescoes and altarpieces. He was one of the most important exponents of the International Gothic style. Gentile was active in Venice, Florence, Siena, Orvieto, and Rome and collaborated with the artists Pisanello and Jacopo Bellini. His *Adoration of the*

Magi 1423 (Uffizi, Florence) is typically rich in detail and colour.

genus (plural *genera*) group of ▷species with many characteristics in common. Thus all doglike species (including dogs, wolves, and jackals) belong to the genus *Canis* (Latin 'dog'). Species of the same genus are thought to be descended from a common ancestor species. Related genera are grouped into families.

geography the study of the Earth's surface; its topography, climate, and physical conditions, and how these factors affect people and society. It is usually divided into *physical geography*, dealing with landforms and climates, and *human geography*, dealing with the distribution and activities of peoples on Earth.

geological time time scale embracing the history of the Earth from its physical origin to the present day. Geological time is traditionally divided into eons (Phanerozoic, Proterozoic, and Archaean), which in turn are divided into eras, periods, epochs, ages, and finally chrons.

geology science of the Earth, its origin, composition, structure, and history. It is divided into several branches: *mineralogy* (the minerals of Earth), *petrology* (rocks), *stratigraphy* (the deposition of successive beds of sedimentary rocks), *palaeontology* (fossils), and *tectonics* (the deformation and movement of the Earth's crust).

geometry branch of mathematics concerned with the properties of space, usually in terms of plane (two-dimensional) and solid (three-dimensional) figures. The subject is usually divided into *pure geometry*, which embraces roughly the plane and solid geometry dealt with in

Euclid's *Elements*, and *analytical* or *coordinate geometry*, in which problems are solved using algebraic methods. A third, quite distinct, type includes the non-Euclidean geometries.

George VI 1895–1952. King of Great Britain from 1936, when he succeeded after the abdication of his brother Edward VIII, who had succeeded their father George V. Created Duke of York 1920, he married in 1923 Lady Elizabeth Bowes- Lyon (1900–   ), and their children are Elizabeth II and Princess Margaret. During World War II, he visited the Normandy and Italian battlefields.

George, St patron saint of England. The story of St George rescuing a woman by slaying a dragon, evidently derived from the Perseus legend, first appears in the 6th century. The cult of St George was introduced into W Europe by the Crusaders. Feast day 23 April.

Georgetown capital and port of Guyana, situated at the mouth of the Demerara River on the Caribbean coast; population (1983) 188,000. There is food processing and shrimp fishing.

Georgia state in SE USA; *area* 58,904 sq mi/152,600 sq km; *capital* Atlanta; *features* Okefenokee National Wildlife Refuge (656 sq mi/1,700 sq km), Sea Islands, historic Savannah; *population* (1990) 6,478,200.

Georgia Republic of; *area* 69,700 sq km/26,911 sq mi; *capital* Tbilisi; *features* holiday resorts and spas on the Black Sea; two autonomous republics, Abkhazia and Adzharia; one autonomous region, South Ossetia; *political system* emergent democracy; *population* (1993 est) 5,600,000 (Georgian 70%, Armenian 8%, Russian 8%, Azeri 6%,

Ossetian 3%, Abkhazian 2%); *language* Georgian; *religion* Georgian Church, independent of the Russian Orthodox Church since 1917.

geothermal energy energy extracted for heating and electricity generation from natural steam, hot water, or hot dry rocks in the Earth's crust. Water is pumped down through an injection well where it passes through joints in the hot rocks. It rises to the surface through a recovery well and may be converted to steam or run through a heat exchanger. Dry steam may be directed through turbines to produce electricity. It is an important source of energy in volcanically active areas such as Iceland and New Zealand.

Germanic branch of the Indo-European language family, divided into *East Germanic* (Gothic, now extinct), *North Germanic* (Danish, Faroese, Icelandic, Norwegian, Swedish), and *West Germanic* (Afrikaans, Dutch, English, Flemish, Frisian, German, Yiddish).

German measles or *rubella* mild, communicable virus disease, usually caught by children. It is marked by a sore throat, pinkish rash, and slight fever, and has an incubation period of two to three weeks. If a woman contracts it in the first three months of pregnancy, it may cause serious damage to the unborn child.

Germany Federal Republic of (*Bundesrepublik Deutschland*); *area* 357,041 sq km/137,853 sq mi; *capital* Berlin; *environment* acid rain causing *Waldsterben* (tree death) affects more than half the country's forests; industrial E Germany has the highest sulphurdioxide emissions in the world per head of population; *features* Black Forest, Harz Mountains, Erzgebirge (Ore Mountains), Bavarian Alps, Fichtelgebirge, Thüringer Forest; *political system* liberal democratic federal republic. *population* (1993 est) 80,800,000 (including nearly 5 million 'guest workers', *Gastarbeiter*, of whom 1,600,000 are Turks; the rest are Yugoslav, Italian, Greek, Spanish, and Portuguese); growth rate −0.7% p.a.; *languages* German, Sorbian; *religions* Protestant 42%, Roman Catholic 35%.

Germany, East (German Democratic Republic, GDR) country 1949–90, formed from the Soviet zone of occupation in the partition of Germany following World War II. East Germany became a sovereign state 1954, and was reunified with West Germany Oct 1990.

Germany, West (Federal Republic of Germany) country 1949–90, formed from the British, US, and French occupation zones in the partition of Germany following World War II; reunified with East Germany Oct 1990.

germination in botany, the initial stages of growth in a seed, spore, or pollen grain. Seeds germinate when they are exposed to favourable external conditions of moisture, light, and temperature, and when any factors causing dormancy have been removed.

Gershwin George 1898–1937. US composer. He wrote concert works including the tone poems *Rhapsody in Blue* 1924 and *An American in Paris* 1928, and popular musicals and songs, many with lyrics by his brother *Ira Gershwin* (1896–1983), including 'I Got Rhythm', ''S Wonderful', and 'Embraceable You'. His opera *Porgy and Bess* 1935 incorporated jazz rhythms and popular song styles in an operatic format.

gestalt concept of a unified whole that is greater than, or different from, the sum of its parts; that is, a complete structure whose nature is not explained simply by analysing its constituent elements. A chair, for example, will generally be recognized as a chair despite great variations between individual chairs in such attributes as size, shape, and colour. The term was first used in psychology in Germany about 1910. It has been adopted from German because there is no exact equivalent in English.

Gestapo (contraction of *Geheime Staatspolizei*) Nazi Germany's secret police, formed 1933, and under the direction of Heinrich ◊Himmler from 1934.

gestation in all mammals except the ◊monotremes (duck-billed platypus and spiny anteaters), the period from the time of implantation of the embryo in the uterus to birth. This period varies among species; in humans it is about 266 days, in elephants 18–22 months, in cats about 60 days, and in some species of marsupial (such as opossum) as short as 12 days.

Gettysburg site in Pennsylvania of a decisive battle of the American ◊Civil War 1863, won by the North. At its dedication as a national cemetry, President Lincoln delivered the *Gettysburg Address* 19 Nov, reiterating the principles of freedom, equality, and democracy embodied in the US Constitution.

geyser natural spring that intermittently discharges an explosive column of steam and hot water into the air due to the build-up of steam in underground chambers. One of the most remarkable geysers is Old Faithful, in Yellowstone National Park, Wyoming, USA. Geysers also occur in New Zealand and Iceland.

Ghana Republic of; *area* 238,305 sq km/91,986 sq mi; *capital* Accra; *environment* forested areas shrank from 8.2 million sq km/3.17 million sq mi at the beginning of the 20th century to 1.9 million sq km/730,000 sq mi by 1990; *features* world's largest artificial lake, Lake Volta; relics of traditional kingdom of Ashanti: 32,000 chiefs and kings; *political system* emergent democracy; *population* (1993 est) 16,700,000; growth rate 3.2% p.a.; *languages* English (official) and African languages; *religion* animist 38%, Muslim 30%, Christian 24%.

Ghent (Flemish *Gent*, French *Gand*) city and port in East Flanders, NW Belgium; population (1991) 230,200. The cathedral of St Bavon (12th–14th centuries) has paintings by van Eyck and Rubens.

Ghiberti Lorenzo 1378–1455. Italian sculptor and goldsmith. In 1402 he won the commission for a pair of gilded bronze doors for Florence's Baptistry. He produced a second pair (1425–52), the *Gates of Paradise*, one of the masterpieces of the early Italian Renaissance. They show a sophisticated use of composition and perspective, and the influence of Classical models.

Gibraltar British dependency, situated on a narrow rocky promontory in S Spain; *area* 6.5 sq km/2.5 sq mi; *features* strategic naval and air base, with NATO underground headquarters and communications centre; colony of Barbary apes; the frontier zone is adjoined by the Spanish port of La Linea; *population* (1988) 30,000.

Gibraltar, Strait of strait between N Africa and Spain, with the Rock of Gibraltar to the N north side and Jebel Musa to the S, the so-called Pillars of Hercules.

Gide André 1869–1951. French novelist, playwright, and critic. His work is largely autobiographical and concerned with the conflict between desire and conventional morality. It includes *L'Immoraliste/The Immoralist* 1902, *La Porte étroite/Strait Is the Gate* 1909, *Les Caves du Vatican/The Vatican Cellars* 1914, and *Les Faux-monnayeurs/The Counterfeiters* 1926. He was a cofounder of the influential literary periodical *Nouvelle Revue française* and kept an almost lifelong *Journal*. Nobel Prize for Literature 1947.

Gielgud John 1904– . English actor and director. He is renowned as one of the greatest Shakespearean actors of his time. He made his debut at the Old Vic 1921, and his numerous stage appearances ranged from roles in works by Chekhov and Sheridan to those of Alan Bennett, Harold Pinter, and David Storey. Gielgud's films include *Becket* 1964, *Oh! What a Lovely War* 1969, *Providence* 1977, *Chariots of Fire* 1980, *Arthur* 1981 (Academy Award), and *Prospero's Books* 1991.

gigabyte in computing, a measure of memory capacity, equal to 1,024 ▷megabytes. It is also used, less precisely, to mean 1,000 billion ▷bytes.

Gilbert W(illiam) S(chwenk) 1836–1911. English humorist and dramatist. He collaborated with composer Arthur ▷Sullivan, providing the libretti for their series of light comic operas from 1871 performed by the D'Oyly Carte Opera Company; they include *HMS Pinafore* 1878, *The Pirates of Penzance* 1879, and *The Mikado* 1885.

gill in biology, the main respiratory organ of most fishes and immature amphibians, and of many aquatic invertebrates. In all types, water passes over the gills, and oxygen diffuses across the gill membranes into the circulatory system, while carbon dioxide passes from the system out into the water. In aquatic insects, these gases diffuse into and out of air-filled canals called tracheae.

Gillespie Dizzy (John Birks) 1917–1993. US jazz trumpeter. With Charlie ▷Parker, he was the chief creator and exponent of the bebop style (*Groovin' High* is a CD re-issue of their seminal 78– rpm recordings). Gillespie influenced many modern jazz trumpeters, including Miles Davis.

ginger SE Asian reedlike perennial *Zingiber officinale*, family Zingiberaceae; the hot-tasting underground root is used as a condiment and in preserves.

ginseng plant *Panax ginseng*, family Araliaceae, with a thick, forked aromatic root used in alternative medicine as a tonic.

Giorgione da Castelfranco (Giorgio Barbarelli) *c*. 1475–1510. Italian Renaissance painter. He was active in Venice, and was probably trained by Giovanni Bellini. His work greatly influenced Titian and other Venetian painters. His subjects are imbued with a sense of mystery and treated with a soft technique, reminiscent of Leonardo da Vinci's later works, as in *The Tempest* 1504 (Academia, Venice).

Giotto di Bondone 1267–1337. Italian painter and architect. His influence on the development of painting in Europe was profound. He broke away from the conventions of ▷International Gothic and introduced a naturalistic style, painting saints as real people, lifelike and expressive; an enhanced sense of volume and space also characterizes his work. He painted cycles of frescoes in churches at Assisi, Florence, and Padua.

giraffe world's tallest mammal, *Giraffa camelopardalis*, belonging to the ruminant family Giraffidae. It stands over 5.5 m/18 ft tall, the neck accounting for nearly half this amount. The giraffe has two to four small, skin- covered, horn-like structures on its head and a long, tufted tail. The skin has a mottled appearance and is reddish brown and cream. Giraffes are found only in Africa, south of the Sahara Desert.

Girl Guide female member of the ▷Scout organization founded 1910 in the UK by Robert Baden-Powell and his sister Agnes. There are three branches: Brownie Guides (age 7–11); Guides (10–16); Ranger Guides (14–20); and Guiders (adult leaders). They are known as the World Association of Girl Guides and Girl Scouts in the USA.

Gîza, El or *al-Jîzah* site of the Great Pyramids and Sphinx; a suburb of ▷Cairo, Egypt; population (1983) 1,500,000.

glacier tongue of ice, originating in mountains in snowfields above the snowline, which moves slowly downhill and is constantly replenished from its source. The scenery produced by the erosive action of glaciers is characteristic and includes glacial troughs (U-shaped valleys), corries, and arêtes. In lowlands, the laying down of moraine (rocky debris once carried by glaciers) produces a variety of landscape features.

Gladstone William Ewart 1809–1898. British Liberal politician, repeatedly prime minister. He entered Parliament as a Tory in 1833 and held ministerial office, but left the party 1846 and after 1859 identified himself with the Liberals. He was chancellor of the Exchequer 1852–55 and 1859–66, and prime minister 1868–74, 1880–85, 1886, and 1892–94. He introduced elementary education 1870 and vote by secret ballot 1872.

Glamorgan (Welsh *Morgannwg*) three counties of S Wales: Mid Glamorgan, South Glamorgan, and West Glamorgan – created 1974 from the former county of Glamorganshire. All are on the Bristol Channel.

gland specialized organ of the body that manufactures and secretes enzymes, hormones, or other chemicals. In animals, glands vary in size from small (for example, tear glands) to large (for example, the pancreas), but in plants they are always small, and may consist of a single cell. Some glands discharge their products internally, ▷endocrine glands, and others, exocrine glands, externally. Lymph nodes are sometimes wrongly called glands.

glandular fever or *infectious mononucleosis* viral disease characterized at onset by fever and painfully swollen lymph nodes; there may also be digestive upset, sore throat, and skin rashes. Lassitude persists for months and even years, and recovery can be slow. It is caused by the Epstein-Barr virus.

Glasgow city and administrative headquarters of Strathclyde, Scotland; population (1991) 662,900.

glass transparent or translucent substance that is physically neither a solid nor a liquid. Although glass is easily shattered, it is one of the strongest substances known. It is made by fusing certain types of sand (silica); this fusion occurs naturally in volcanic glass (see ◊obsidian).

glaucoma condition in which pressure inside the eye (intraocular pressure) is raised abnormally as excess fluid accumulates. It occurs when the normal outflow of fluid within the chamber of the eye (aqueous humour) is interrupted. As pressure rises, the optic nerve suffers irreversible damage, leading to a reduction in the field of vision and, ultimately, loss of eyesight.

Glendower Owen *c.* 1359–*c.* 1416. (Welsh *Owain Glyndwr*) Welsh nationalist leader of a successful revolt against the English in N Wales, who defeated Henry IV in three campaigns 1400–02, although Wales was reconquered 1405–13. Glendower disappeared 1416.

gliding art of using air currents to fly unpowered aircraft. Technically, gliding involves the gradual loss of altitude; gliders designed for soaring flight (utilizing air rising up a cliff face or hill, warm air rising as a 'thermal' above sun-heated ground, and so on) are known as sailplanes. *Hang-gliding* was developed in the 1970s. The aeronaut, attached to a sail wing of nylon stretched on a aluminium frame, jumps into the air from a high place, and soars on the 'thermals'.

global warming projected imminent climate change attributed to the ◊greenhouse effect.

Gloucestershire county of SW England; *area* 2,640 sq km/1,019 sq mi; *towns and cities* Gloucester (administrative headquarters), Stroud, Cheltenham, Tewkesbury, Cirencester; *features* Cotswold Hills; Berkeley Castle,

where Edward II was murdered; Cotswold Farm Park, near Stow-on-the-Wold, which has rare and ancient breeds of farm animals; Tewkesbury Abbey; *population* (1991) 528,400.

glucose or *dextrose* or *grape-sugar* $C_6H_{12}O_6$ sugar present in the blood, and found also in honey and fruit juices. It is a source of energy for the body, being produced from other sugars and starches to form the 'energy currency' of many biochemical reactions also involving ◊ATP.

glue-sniffing or *solvent misuse* inhalation of the fumes from organic solvents of the type found in paints, lighter fuel, and glue, for their hallucinatory effects. As well as being addictive, solvents are dangerous for their effects on the user's liver, heart, and lungs.

gluon in physics, a ◊gauge boson that carries the ◊strong nuclear force, responsible for binding quarks together to form the strongly interacting subatomic particles known as ◊hadrons. There are eight kinds of gluon.

glycerol or *glycerine* or *propan-1,2,3-triol* $HOCH_2CH(OH)CH_2OH$ thick, colourless, odourless, sweetish liquid. It is obtained from vegetable and animal oils and fats (by treatment with acid, alkali, superheated steam, or an enzyme), or by fermentation of glucose, and is used in the manufacture of high explosives, in antifreeze solutions, to maintain moist conditions in fruits and tobacco, and in cosmetics.

gneiss coarse-grained ◊metamorphic rock, formed under conditions of increasing temperature and pressure, and often occurring in association with schists and granites. It has a foliated, laminated structure, consisting of thin bands of micas and/or amphiboles alternating with granular bands of quartz and feldspar. Gneisses are formed during regional metamorphism; *paragneisses* are derived from sedimentary rocks and *orthogneisses* from igneous rocks. Garnets are often found in gneiss.

Gnosticism esoteric cult of divine knowledge (a synthesis of Christianity, Greek philosophy, Hinduism, Buddhism, and the mystery cults of the Mediterranean), which flourished during the 2nd and 3rd centuries and was a rival to, and influence on, early Christianity. The medieval French Cathar heresy and the modern Mandean sect (in S Iraq) descend from Gnosticism.

Goa state of India; *area* 3,700 sq km/ 1,428 sq mi; *capital* Panaji; *population* (1991) 1,168,600; *features* Portuguese colonial architecture; church with remains of St Francis Xavier.

Gobi Desert Asian desert divided between the Mongolian People's Republic and Inner Mongolia, China; 800 km/500 mi N–S, and 1,600 km/1,000 mi E–W. It is rich in fossil remains of extinct species.

God the concept of a supreme being, a unique creative entity, basic to several monotheistic religions (for example Judaism, Christianity, Islam); in many polytheistic cultures (for example Norse, Roman, Greek), the term 'god' refers to a supernatural being who personifies the force behind an aspect of life (for example Neptune, Roman god of the sea).

Godthaab (Greenlandic *Nuuk*) capital and largest town of Greenland; population (1982) 9,700. It is a storage centre for oil and gas.

Goebbels (Paul) Josef 1897–1945. German Nazi leader. As minister of propaganda from 1933, he brought all cultural and educational activities under Nazi control and built up sympathetic movements abroad to carry on the 'war of nerves' against Hitler's intended victims. On the capture of Berlin by the Allies, he poisoned himself.

Goethe Johann Wolfgang von 1749–1832. German poet, novelist, and dramatist. He is generally considered the founder of modern German literature, and was the leader of the Romantic *'Sturm und Drang'* movement. His works include the autobiographical *Die Leiden des Jungen Werthers/The Sorrows of the Young Werther* 1774 and the poetic play ▷*Faust* 1808 and 1832, his masterpiece. A visit to Italy 1786–88 inspired the classical dramas *Iphigenie auf Tauris/Iphigenia in Tauris* 1787 and *Torquato Tasso* 1790.

Gogh Vincent van 1853–1890. Dutch Post-Impressionist painter. He tried various careers, including preaching, and began painting in thee 1880s, his early works often being sombre depictions of peasant life, such as *The Potato Eaters* 1885 (Van Gogh Museum, Amsterdam). Influenced by both the Impressionists and Japanese prints, he developed a freer style characterized by intense colour and expressive brushwork, as seen in his *Sunflowers* series 1888.

Gogol Nicolai Vasilyevich 1809–1852. Russian writer. His first success was a collection of stories, *Evenings on a Farm near Dikanka* 1831–32, followed by *Mirgorod* 1835. Later works include *Arabesques* 1835, the comedy play *The Inspector General* 1836, and the picaresque novel *Dead Souls* 1842, which satirizes Russian provincial society.

goitre enlargement of the thyroid gland seen as a swelling on the neck. It is most pronounced in simple goitre, which is caused by iodine deficiency. More common is toxic goitre or hyperthyroidism, caused by overactivity of the thyroid gland.

gold heavy, precious, yellow, metallic element; symbol Au, atomic number 79, relative atomic mass 197.0. It is unaffected by temperature changes and is highly resistant to acids. For manufacture, gold is alloyed with another strengthening metal (such as copper or silver), its purity being measured in ▷carats on a scale of 24.

Gold Coast former name for ▷Ghana, but historically the west coast of Africa from Cape Three Points to the Volta River, where alluvial gold is washed down. Portuguese and French navigators visited this coast in the 14th century, and a British trading settlement developed into the colony of the Gold Coast 1618. With its dependencies of Ashanti and Northern Territories plus the trusteeship territory of Togoland, it became Ghana 1957.

Golden Fleece in Greek legend, the fleece of the winged ram Chrysomallus, which hung on an oak tree at Colchis and was guarded by a dragon. It was stolen by ▷Jason and the Argonauts.

Golding William 1911–1993. English novelist. His work is often principally concerned with the fundamental corruption and evil inherent in human nature. His first book, *Lord of the Flies* 1954,

concerns the degeneration into savagery of a group of English schoolboys marooned on a Pacific island. *Pincher Martin* 1956 is a study of greed and self-delusion. Later novels include *The Spire* 1964 and *Darkness Visible* 1979. Nobel Prize for Literature 1983.

Goldsmith Oliver 1728–1774. Irish writer. His works include the novel *The Vicar of Wakefield* 1766; the poem 'The Deserted Village' 1770; and the play *She Stoops to Conquer* 1773. In 1761 Goldsmith met Samuel Johnson, and became a member of his 'club'.

gold standard system under which a country's currency is exchangeable for a fixed weight of gold on demand at the central bank. It was almost universally applied 1870–1914, but by 1937 no single country was on the full gold standard. Britain abandoned the gold standard 1931; the USA abandoned it 1971. Holdings of gold are still retained because it is an internationally recognized commodity, which cannot be legislated upon or manipulated by interested countries.

golf outdoor game in which a small rubber-cored ball is hit with a wooden- or iron-faced club into a series of holes using the least number of shots. On the first shot for each hole, the ball is hit from a tee, which elevates the ball slightly off the ground; subsequent strokes are played off the ground. Most courses have 18 holes and are approximately 5,500 m/6,000 yd in length.

gonorrhoea common sexually transmitted disease arising from infection with the bacterium *Neisseria gonorrhoeae*, which causes inflammation of the genito-urinary tract. After an incubation period of two to ten days, infected men experience pain while urinating and a discharge from the penis; infected women often have no external symptoms.

González Márquez Felipe 1942– . Spanish socialist politician, leader of the Socialist Workers' Party (PSOE), prime minister from 1982. His party was re-elected 1989 and 1993, but his popularity suffered from economic upheaval and allegations of corruption.

Gorbachev Mikhail Sergeyevich 1931– . Soviet president, in power 1985–91. He was a member of the Politburo from 1980. As general secretary of the Communist Party (CPSU) 1985–91, and president of the Supreme Soviet 1988–91, he introduced liberal reforms at home (*perestroika* and *glasnost*), proposed the introduction of multiparty democracy, and attempted to halt the arms race abroad. He became head of state 1989. Following an abortive coup attempt by hardliners Aug 1991, independence for the Baltic states, and accelerated moves towards independence in other republics, Gorbachev resigned Dec 1991. Nobel Peace Prize 1990.

Gore Al(bert) 1948– . US politician, vice president from 1993. A Democrat, he became a member of the House of Representatives 1977–79, and was elected senator for Tennessee 1985–92.

gorilla largest of the apes, *Gorilla gorilla*, found in the dense forests of West Africa and mountains of central Africa. The male stands about 1.8 m/6 ft, and weighs about 200 kg/450 lbs. Females are about half the size. The body is covered with blackish hair, silvered on the back in older males. Gorillas live in family groups and are vegetarian.

Gorky Maxim. Pen name of Alexei Peshkov 1868–1936. Russian writer. Born in Nizhni-Novgorod (named Gorky 1932–90 in his honour), he was exiled 1906–13 for his revolutionary principles. His works, which include the play *The Lower Depths* 1902 and the memoir *My Childhood* 1913–14, combine realism with optimistic faith in the potential of the industrial proletariat.

Gospel in the New Testament generally, the message of Christian salvation; in particular the four written accounts of the life of Jesus by Matthew, Mark, Luke, and John. Although the first three give approximately the same account or synopsis (thus giving rise to the name 'Synoptic Gospels'), their differences from John have raised problems for theologians.

Goth E Germanic people who settled near the Black Sea around AD 2nd century. The eastern *Ostrogoths* were conquered by the Huns 372, but under Theodoric the Great conquered Italy 488–93. They disappeared as a nation after Byzantine emperor Justinian I reconquered Italy 535–55. The western *Visigoths* migrated to Thrace. Under Alaric they raided Greece and Italy 395–410, sacked Rome, and established a kingdom in S France. Expelled from there by the Franks, they established a Spanish kingdom which lasted until the Moorish conquest of 711.

Gothic architecture style of architecture that flourished in Europe from the mid-12th century to the end of the 15th century. It is characterized by the vertical lines of tall pillars and spires, greater height in interior spaces, the pointed arch, rib vaulting, and the flying buttress.

Goya Francisco José de Goya y Lucientes 1746–1828. Spanish painter and engraver. He painted portraits of four successive kings of Spain; his series of etchings include the famous *Caprichos* 1797–98 and *The Disasters of War* 1810–14, both depicting the horrors of the French invasion of Spain. Among his later works are the 'Black Paintings' (Prado, Madrid), with such horrific images as *Saturn Devouring One of His Sons* about 1822.

Grace W(illiam) G(ilbert) 1848–1915. English cricketer. By profession a doctor, he became the best batsman in England. He began playing first-class cricket at the age of 16, scored 152 runs in his first test match, and scored the first triple century 1876. Throughout his career, which lasted nearly 45 years, he scored more than 54,000 runs.

Graces in Greek mythology, three goddesses (Aglaia, Euphrosyne, Thalia), daughters of Zeus and Hera, personifications of pleasure, charm, and beauty; the inspirers of the arts and the sciences.

grafting in medicine, the operation by which an organ or other living tissue is removed from one organism and transplanted into the same or a different organism. In horticulture, it is a technique widely used for propagating plants, especially woody species. A bud or shoot on one plant, termed the *scion*, is inserted into another, the *stock*, so that they continue growing together, the tissues combining at the point of union. In this way some of the advantages of both plants are obtained.

Grahame Kenneth 1859–1932. Scottish author. The early volumes of sketches of childhood, *The Golden Age* 1895 and *Dream Days* 1898, were followed by his masterpiece *The Wind in the Willows*

1908, an animal fantasy created for his young son, which was dramatized by A A Milne as *Toad of Toad Hall* 1929.

Grampian region of Scotland; *area* 8,600 sq km/3,320 sq mi; *features* part of the Grampian Mountains (the Cairngorm Mountains); valley of the river Spey, with its whisky distilleries; Balmoral Castle (royal residence); Braemar Highland Games in Aug; *population* (1991) 503,900.

Granada city in the Sierra Nevada in Andalusia, S Spain; population (1986) 281,000. The *Alhambra*, a fortified hilltop palace, was built in the 13th and 14th centuries by the Moorish kings.

Grand Canyon gorge of multicoloured rock strata cut by and containing the Colorado River, N Arizona, USA. It is 350 km/217 mi long, 6–29 km/4–18 mi wide, and reaches depths of over 1.7 km/1.1 mi. It was made a national park 1919. Millions of tourists visit the canyon each year.

grand slam in tennis, the four major tournaments: the Australian Open, the French Open, Wimbledon, and the US Open. In golf, it is also the four major tournaments: the US Open, the British Open, the Masters, and the PGA (Professional Golfers Association). In baseball, a grand slam is a home run with runners on all the bases. A grand slam in bridge is when all 13 tricks are won by one team.

grand unified theory (GUT) in physics, a sought-for theory that would combine the theory of the strong nuclear force (called quantum chromodynamics) with the theory of the weak nuclear and electromagnetic forces. The search for the grand unified theory is part of a larger programme seeking a ▷unified field theory, which would combine all the forces of nature (including gravity) within one framework.

granite coarse-grained ▷igneous rock, typically consisting of the minerals quartz, feldspar, and mica. It may be pink or grey, depending on the composition of the feldspar. Granites are chiefly used as building materials.

Grant Cary. Stage name of Archibald Leach 1904–1986. British-born actor, a US citizen from 1942. His witty, debonair personality made him a screen favourite for more than three decades. He was directed by Alfred ▷Hitchcock in *Suspicion* 1941, *Notorious* 1946, *To Catch a Thief* 1955, and *North by Northwest* 1959. He received a 1970 Academy Award for general excellence.

Grant Ulysses S(impson) 1822–1885. US Civil War general in chief for the Union and 18th president of the USA 1869–77. As a Republican president, he carried through a liberal ▷Reconstruction policy in the South. He failed to suppress extensive political corruption within his own party and cabinet, which tarnished the reputation of his second term.

graphical user interface (GUI) or *WIMP* in computing, a type of user interface in which programs and files appear as icons (small pictures), user options are selected from pull-down menus, and data are displayed in windows (rectangular areas), which the operator can manipulate in various ways. The operator uses a pointing device, typically a mouse, to make selections and initiate actions.

graphite blackish-grey, laminar, crystalline form of ▷carbon. It is used as a lubricant and as the active component of pencil lead.

grass plant of the large family Gramineae of monocotyledons, with about 9,000 species distributed worldwide except in the Arctic regions. The majority are perennial, with long, narrow leaves and jointed, hollow stems; hermaphroditic flowers are borne in spikelets; the fruits are grainlike. Included are bluegrass, wheat, rye, maize, sugarcane, and bamboo.

Grass Günter 1927– . German writer. The grotesque humour and socialist feeling of his novels *Die Blechtrommel/The Tin Drum* 1959 and *Der Butt/The Flounder* 1977 are also characteristic of many of his poems.

Graves Robert (Ranke) 1895–1985. English poet and author. He was severely wounded on the Somme in World War I, and his frank autobiography *Goodbye to All That* 1929 is one of the outstanding war books. Other works include the poems *Over the Brazier* 1916; two historical novels of imperial Rome, *I Claudius* and *Claudius the God*, both 1934; and books on myth – for example, *The White Goddess* 1948.

gravity force of attraction that arises between objects by virtue of their masses. On Earth, gravity is the force of attraction between any object in the Earth's gravitational field and the Earth itself. It is regarded as one of the four ▷fundamental forces of nature, the other three being the ▷electromagnetic force, the ▷strong nuclear force, and the weak nuclear force. The gravitational force is the weakest of the four forces, but it acts over great distances. The particle that is postulated as the carrier of the gravitational force is the graviton.

gray SI unit (symbol Gy) of absorbed radiation dose. It replaces the rad (1 Gy equals 100 rad), and is defined as the dose absorbed when one kilogram of matter absorbs one joule of ionizing radiation. Different types of radiation cause different amounts of damage for the same absorbed dose; the SI unit of *dose equivalent* is the ▷sievert.

Gray Thomas 1716–1771. English poet. His 'Elegy Written in a Country Churchyard' 1751 is one of the most quoted poems in English. Other poems include 'Ode on a Distant Prospect of Eton College', 'The Progress of Poesy', and 'The Bard'; these poems are now seen as the precursors of Romanticism.

Great Barrier Reef chain of coral reefs and islands about 2,000 km/1,250 mi long, off the E coast of Queensland, Australia, at a distance of 15–45 km/10–30 mi. It is believed to be the world's largest living organism and forms an immense natural breakwater, the coral rock forming a structure larger than all human-made structures on Earth combined. The formation of the reef is now thought to be a recent geological event.

Great Bear Lake lake on the Arctic Circle, in the Northwest Territories, Canada; area 31,800 sq km/12,275 sq mi.

Great Britain official name for ▷England, ▷Scotland, and ▷Wales, and the adjacent islands (except the Channel Islands and the Isle of Man) from 1603, when the English and Scottish crowns were united under James I of England (James VI of Scotland). With Northern ▷Ireland it forms the ▷United Kingdom.

Great Dividing Range E Australian mountain range, extending 3,700 km/2,300 mi N–S from Cape York Peninsula, Queensland, to Victoria. It includes the Carnarvon Range, Queensland, which has many Aboriginal cave paintings, the Blue Mountains in New South Wales, and the Australian Alps.

Great Lakes series of five freshwater lakes along the US–Canadian border: Lakes Superior, Michigan, Huron, Erie, and Ontario; total area 245,000 sq km/94,600 sq mi. Interconnecting canals make them navigable by large ships, and they are drained by the St Lawrence River. The whole forms the St Lawrence Seaway. They are said to contain 20% of the world's surface fresh water.

Great Plains semi-arid region to the E of the Rocky Mountains, USA, stretching as far as the 100th meridian of longitude through Oklahoma, Kansas, Nebraska, and the Dakotas. The plains, which cover one-fifth of the USA, extend from Texas in the S over 2,400 km/1,500 mi N to Canada. Ranching and wheat farming have resulted in over-use of water resources to such an extent that available farmland has been reduced by erosion.

Great Slave Lake lake in the Northwest Territories, Canada; area 28,450 sq km/10,980 sq mi. It is the deepest lake (615 m/2,020 ft) in North America.

Great Wall of China continuous defensive wall stretching from W Gansu to the Gulf of Liaodong (2,250 km/1,450 mi). It was built under the Qin dynasty from 214 BC to prevent incursions by the Turkish and Mongol peoples and extended westwards by the Han dynasty. Some 8 m/25 ft high, it consists of a brick-faced wall of earth and stone, has a series of square watchtowers, and has been carefully restored.

grebe any of 19 species of water birds belonging to the family Podicipedidae. The great crested grebe *Podiceps cristatus* is the largest of the Old World grebes. It lives in ponds and marshes in Eurasia, Africa, and Australia, feeding on fish. It grows to 50 cm/20 in long and has a white breast, with chestnut and black feathers on its back and head. The head and neck feathers form a crest, especially prominent during the breeding season.

Greco, El (Doménikos Theotokopoulos) 1541–1614. painter called 'the Greek' because he was born in Crete. He studied in Italy, worked in Rome from about 1570, and by 1577 had settled in Toledo, Spain. He painted elegant portraits and intensely emotional religious scenes with increasingly distorted figures and flickering light; for example, *The Burial of Count Orgaz* 1586 (church of San Tomé, Toledo).

Greece Hellenic Republic (*Elliniki Dimokratia*); *area* 131,957 sq km/ 50,935 sq mi; *capital* Athens; *environment* acid rain and other airborne pollutants are destroying the Classical buildings and ancient monuments of Athens; *features* Corinth canal; Mount Olympus; the Acropolis; many classical archaeological sites; the Aegean and Ionian Islands; *head of state* Constantine Karamanlis from 1990; *head of government* Andreas Papandreou from 1993; *political system* democratic republic; *population* (1993 est) 10,300,000; growth rate 0.3% p.a.; *language* Greek; *religion* Greek Orthodox 97%.

Greek architecture the architecture of ancient Greece is the base for virtually all architectural developments in Europe. The Greeks invented the entablature, which allowed roofs to be hipped (inverted V-shape), and perfected the design of arcades with support columns. There were three styles, or orders, of columns: Doric (with no base), Ionic (with scrolled capitals), and Corinthian (with acanthus-leafed capitals).

Greek member of the Indo-European language family, which has passed through at least five distinct phases since the 2nd millennium BC: *Ancient Greek* 14th–12th centuries BC; *Archaic Greek*, including Homeric epic language, until 800 BC; *Classical Greek* until 400 BC; *Hellenistic Greek*, the common language of Greece, Asia Minor, W Asia, and Egypt to the 4th century AD , and *Byzantine Greek*, used until the 15th century and still the ecclesiastical language of the Greek Orthodox Church. *Modern Greek* is principally divided into the general vernacular (*Demotic Greek*) and the language of education and literature (*Katharevousa*).

Greene (Henry) Graham 1904–1991. English writer. His novels of guilt, despair, and penitence are set in a world of urban seediness or political corruption in many parts of the world. They include *Brighton Rock* 1938, *The Power and the Glory* 1940, *The Heart of the Matter* 1948, *The Third Man* 1949, *The Honorary Consul* 1973, and *Monsignor Quixote* 1982.

greenhouse effect phenomenon of the Earth's atmosphere by which solar radiation, trapped by the Earth and re-emitted from the surface, is prevented from escaping by various gases in the air. The result is a rise in the Earth's temperature. The main greenhouse gases are carbon dioxide, methane, and ▷chlorofluorocarbons (CFCs). Fossil-fuel consumption and forest fires are the main causes of carbon- dioxide build-up; methane is a byproduct of agriculture (rice, cattle, sheep). Water vapour is another greenhouse gas.

Greenland (Greenlandic *Kalaalit Nunaat*) world's largest island, lying between the North Atlantic and Arctic Oceans east of North America; *area* 2,175,600 sq km/840,000 sq mi; *capital* Godthaab (Greenlandic *Nuuk*) on the W coast; *features* the whole of the interior is covered by a vast ice sheet; the island has an important role strategically and in civil aviation, and shares military responsibilities with the USA; *population* (1990) 55,500; Inuit (Ammassalik Eskimoan), Danish, and other European; *language* Greenlandic (Ammassalik Eskimoan).

Greenpeace international environmental pressure group, founded 1971, with a policy of nonviolent direct action backed by scientific research.

Greenwich Mean Time (GMT) local time on the zero line of longitude (the *Greenwich meridian*), which passes through the Old Royal Observatory at Greenwich, London. It was replaced 1986 by coordinated universal time (UTC), but continued to be used to measure longitudes and the world's standard time zone.

Gregorian chant any of a body of plainsong choral chants associated with Pope Gregory the Great (540–604), which became standard in the Roman Catholic Church.

Gregory (I) the Great (St Gregory) *c.* 540–604. Pope from 590 who asserted Rome's supremacy and exercised almost imperial powers. In 596 he sent St ▷Augustine to England. He introduced the choral *Gregorian chant* into the liturgy. Feast day 12 March.

Grenada *area* (including the Grenadines, notably Carriacou) 340 sq km/131 sq mi; *capital* St George's; *features* Grand-Anse beach; Annandale Falls; the Great Pool volcanic crater; *political system* emergent democracy; *population* (1993) 95,300 (84% of black African descent); growth rate –0.2% p.a.; *language* English (official); some French patois spoken; *religion* Roman Catholic 60%.

Grenadines chain of about 600 small islands in the Caribbean Sea, part of the group known as the Windward Islands. They are divided between ▷St Vincent and ▷Grenada.

Grey Lady Jane 1537–1554. Queen of England for nine days, 10–19 July 1553, the great-granddaughter of Henry VII. She was married 1553 to Lord Guildford Dudley (died 1554), son of the Duke of ▷Northumberland. Edward VI was persuaded by Northumberland to set aside the claims to the throne of his sisters Mary and Elizabeth. When Edward died on 9 July 1553, Jane reluctantly accepted the crown. However, on 19 July the Lord Mayor of London announced that Mary was queen. Grey was executed on Tower Green.

Grieg Edvard Hagerup 1843–1907. Norwegian nationalist composer. Much of his music is small-scale, particularly his songs, dances, sonatas, and piano works, strongly identifying with Norwegian folk music. Among his orchestral works are the *Piano Concerto in A Minor* 1869 and the incidental music for Ibsen's *Peer Gynt* 1876, commissioned by Ibsen and the Norwegian government.

Griffith D(avid) W(ark) 1875–1948. US film director. He was an influential figure in the development of cinema as an art. He made hundreds of 'one-reelers' 1908–13, in which he pioneered the techniques of masking, fade- out, flashback, crosscut, close-up, and long shot. *The Birth of a Nation* 1915, about the aftermath of the Civil War, was criticized as degrading to blacks.

Grimm brothers Jakob Ludwig Karl (1785–1863) and Wilhelm (1786–1859), philologists and collectors of German fairy tales such as 'Hansel and Gretel' and 'Rumpelstiltskin'. Joint compilers of an exhaustive dictionary of German, they saw the study of language and the collecting of folk tales as strands in a single enterprise.

Gromyko Andrei 1909–1989. President of the USSR 1985–88. As ambassador to the USA from 1943, he took part in the Tehran, Yalta, and Potsdam conferences; as United Nations representative 1946–49, he exercised the Soviet veto 26 times. He was foreign minister 1957–85. It was Gromyko who formally nominated Mikhail Gorbachev as Communist Party leader 1985.

Gropius Walter Adolf 1883–1969. German architect. He lived in the USA from 1937. He was an early exponent of the ▷International Style defined by glass curtain walls, cubic blocks, and unsupported corners, for example, the model factory and office building at the 1914 Cologne Werkbund exhibition, designed with Adolph Meyer. He was a founder-director of the ▷Bauhaus school in Weimar 1919–28.

gross domestic product (GDP) value of the output of all goods and services produced within a nation's borders, normally given as a total for the year. It thus includes the production of foreign-owned firms within the country, but excludes the income from domestically owned firms located abroad.

gross national product (GNP) the most commonly used measurement of the wealth of a country. GNP is defined as the total value of all goods and services produced by firms owned by the country concerned. It is measured as the gross domestic product plus income from abroad, minus income earned during the same period by foreign investors within the country.

ground water water collected underground in porous rock strata and soils; it emerges at the surface as springs and streams. The groundwater's upper level is called the *water table*. Sandy or other kinds of beds that are filled with groundwater are called *aquifers*. Recent estimates are that usable ground water amounts to more than 90% of all the fresh water on Earth; however, keeping such supplies free of pollutants entering the recharge areas is a critical environmental concern.

Grünewald (Mathias or Mathis Gothardt-Neithardt) *c.* 1475–1528. German painter. He was active in Mainz, Frankfurt, and Halle. He was court painter, architect, and engineer to the archbishop of Mainz 1508–14. His few surviving paintings show an intense involvement with religious subjects. His *Isenheim Altarpiece* 1515 (Unterlinden Museum, Colmar, France), with its tortured figure of Jesus, recalls medieval traditions.

Guadalcanal largest of the ▷Solomon Islands; area 6,500 sq km/2,510 sq mi; population (1987) 71,000. During

World War II it was the scene of a major battle for control of the area that was won by US forces after six months of fighting.

Guadeloupe island group in the Leeward Islands, West Indies, an overseas *département* of France; area 1,705 sq km/658 sq mi; population (1990) 387,000. The main islands are Basse-Terre (on which is the chief town of the same name) and Grande-Terre.

Guam largest of the ▷Mariana Islands in the W Pacific, an unincorporated territory of the USA; *area* 540 sq km/208 sq mi; *capital* Agaña; *features* major US air and naval base, much used in the Vietnam War; tropical, with much rain; *population* (1990) 133,200; *languages* English, Chamorro (basically Malay-Polynesian); *religion* 96% Roman Catholic.

Guatemala Republic of (República de Guatemala); *area* 108,889 sq km/42,031 sq mi; *capital* Guatemala City; *environment* between 1960 and 1980 nearly 57% of the country's forest was cleared for farming; *features* Mayan archaeological remains, including site at Tikal; *political system* democratic republic; *population* (1993 est) 10,000,000 (Mayaquiche Indians 54%, mestizos (mixed race) 42%); growth rate 2.8% p.a. (87% of under-fives suffer from malnutrition); *languages* Spanish (official); 40% speak 18 Indian languages; *religion* Roman Catholic 80%, Protestant 20%.

Guatemala City capital of Guatemala; population (1983) 1,300,000. It was founded 1776 when its predecessor (Antigua) was destroyed in an earthquake. It was severely damaged by another earthquake 1976.

guava tropical American tree *Psidium guajava* of the myrtle family Myrtaceae; the astringent yellow pear-shaped fruit is used to make guava jelly, or it can be stewed or canned. It has a high vitamin C content.

Guayaquil largest city and chief port and economic centre of ▷Ecuador; population (1986) 1,509,100. It was founded 1537 by the Spanish explorer Francisco de Orellana.

Guernsey second largest of the ▷Channel Islands; area 63 sq km/24.3 sq mi; population (1991) 58,900. The capital is St Peter Port. From 1975 it has been a major financial centre. Guernsey cattle, which are a distinctive pale fawn colour and give rich creamy milk, originated here.

Guevara Che (Ernesto) 1928–1967. Latin American revolutionary. He was born in Argentina and trained there as a doctor, but left his homeland 1953 because of his opposition to the right-wing president Perón. In effecting the Cuban revolution of 1959, he was second only to Castro and Castro's brother Raúl.

Guiana NE part of South America that includes ▷French Guiana, ▷Guyana, and ▷Surinam.

guild or *gild* medieval association, particularly of artisans or merchants, formed for mutual aid and protection and the pursuit of a common purpose, religious or economic. Guilds became politically powerful in Europe but after the 16th century their position was undermined by the growth of capitalism.

Guinea Republic of (*République de Guinée*); *area* 245,857 sq km/94,901 sq mi; *capital* Conakry; *environment* large amounts of toxic waste from industrialized countries have been dumped in Guinea; *features* Fouta Djallon, area of sandstone plateaus, cut by deep valleys; *political system* emergent democratic republic; *population* (1993 est) 7,700,000 (chief peoples are Fulani, Malinke, Susu); growth rate 2.3% p.a.; *languages* French (official), African languages; *religions* Muslim 85%, Christian 10%, local 5%.

Guinea-Bissau *Republic of* (*República da Guiné-Bissau*); *area* 36,125 sq km/ 13,944 sq mi; *capital* Bissau; *features* the archipelago of Bijagós; *political system* emergent democracy; *population* (1993 est) 1,050,000; growth rate 2.4% p.a.; *languages* Portuguese (official), Crioulo (Cape Verdean dialect of Portuguese), African languages; *religions* animism 54%, Muslim 38%, Christian 8%.

guitar six-stringed, or twelve-stringed, flat-bodied musical instrument, plucked or strummed with the fingers. The *Hawaiian guitar*, laid across the lap, uses a metal bar to produce a distinctive gliding tone; the solid-bodied *electric guitar*, developed in the 1950s by Les Paul and Leo Fender, mixes and amplifies vibrations from electromagnetic pickups at different points to produce a range of tone qualities.

Gujarat or *Gujerat* state of W India; *area* 196,000 sq km/75,656 sq mi; *capital* Ahmedabad; *features* heavily industrialized; includes most of the Rann of Kutch; the Gir Forest (the last home of the wild Asian lion); *languages* Gujarati (Gujerati), Hindi *population* (1991) 41,174,000.

Gujarati inhabitant of Gujarat on the NW coast of India. The Gujaratis number approximately 30 million. They are predominantly Hindu (90%), with

Muslim (8%) and Jain (2%) minorities. They speak their own Indo-European language, *Gujarati*, which has a long literary tradition, written in its own script which is a variant of the Devanagari script used for Sanskrit and Hindi.

Gulf States oil-rich countries sharing the coastline of the ◊Persian Gulf (Bahrain, Iran, Iraq, Kuwait, Oman, Qatar, Saudi Arabia, and the United Arab Emirates). In the USA, the term refers to those states bordering the Gulf of Mexico (Alabama, Florida, Louisiana, Mississippi, and Texas).

Gulf Stream warm ocean ◊current that flows north from the warm waters of the Gulf of Mexico. Part of the current is diverted east across the Atlantic, where it is known as the *North Atlantic Drift*, and warms what would otherwise be a colder climate in the British Isles and NW Europe.

Gulf War war 16 Jan–28 Feb 1991 between Iraq and a coalition of 28 nations led by the USA. (It is also another name for the Iran–Iraq War). The invasion and annexation of Kuwait by Iraq on 2 Aug 1990 provoked a build-up of US troops in Saudi Arabia, eventually totalling over 500,000. The UK subsequently deployed 42,000 troops, France 15,000, Egypt 20,000, and other nations smaller contingents. An air offensive lasting six weeks, in which 'smart' weapons came of age, destroyed about one-third of Iraqi equipment and inflicted massive casualties. A 100-hour ground war followed, which effectively destroyed the remnants of the 500,000-strong Iraqi army in or near Kuwait.

gum in botany, complex polysaccharides (carbohydrates) formed by many plants and trees, particularly by those from dry regions. They form four main groups: plant exudates (gum arabic); marine plant extracts (agar); seed extracts; and fruit and vegetable extracts. Some are made synthetically.

Gunpowder Plot in British history, the Catholic conspiracy to blow up James I and his parliament on 5 Nov 1605. It was discovered through an anonymous letter. Guy ◊Fawkes was found in the cellar beneath the Palace of Westminster, ready to fire a store of explosives. Several of the conspirators were killed, and Fawkes and seven others were executed.

Guomindang Chinese National People's Party, founded 1894 by Sun Yat-sen, which overthrew the Manchu Empire 1912. From 1927 the right wing, led by ◊Chiang Kai-shek, was in conflict with the left, led by Mao Zedong until the Communist victory 1949 (except for the period of the Japanese invasion 1937–45). It survives as the dominant political party of Taiwan, where it is still spelled *Kuomintang*.

Gutenberg Johann *c.* 1400–1468. German printer, the inventor of printing from movable metal type, based on the Chinese wood-block-type method (although Laurens Janszoon Coster (1370–1440) has a rival claim).

Guyana Cooperative Republic of; *area* 214,969 sq km/82,978 sq mi; *capital* (and port) Georgetown; *features* Mount Roraima; Kaietur National Park, including Kaietur Fall on the Potaro (tributary of Essequibo) 250 m/821 ft; *political system* democratic republic; *population* (1993 est) 800,000 (51% descendants of workers introduced from India to work the sugar plantations after the abolition of slavery, 30% black, 5% American Indian); growth rate 2% p.a.; *languages* English (official), Hindi, American Indian; *religions* Christian 57%, Hindu 33%, Sunni Muslim 9%.

Gwent county of S Wales, created 1974; *area* 1,380 sq km/533 sq mi; *towns and cities* Cwmbran (administrative headquarters), Abergavenny, Newport, Tredegar; *population* (1991) 442,200; *languages* English; 2.4% Welsh-speaking.

Gwynedd county of NW Wales, created 1974; *area* 3,870 sq km/1,494 sq mi; *towns and cities* Caernarvon (administrative headquarters), Bangor; *population* (1991) 235,450; *languages* English; 61% Welsh-speaking.

gymnastics physical exercises, originally for health and training. *Men's gymnastics* includes high bar, parallel bars, horse vault, rings, pommel horse, and floor exercises. *Women's gymnastics* includes asymmetrical bars, side horse vault, balance beam, and floor exercises. Also popular are *sports acrobatics*, performed by gymnasts in pairs, trios, or fours to music, where the emphasis is on dance, balance, and timing, and *rhythmic gymnastics*, choreographed to music and performed by individuals or six-girl teams, with small hand apparatus such as a ribbon, ball, or hoop.

gymnosperm in botany, any plant whose seeds are exposed, as opposed to the structurally more advanced ◊angiosperms, where they are inside an ovary. The group includes conifers and related plants such as cycads and ginkgos, whose seeds develop in ◊cones. Fossil gymnosperms have been found in rocks about 350 million years old.

H

Haarlem industrial city and capital of the province of North Holland, the Netherlands, 20 km/12 mi W of Amsterdam; population (1991) 149,500. At Velsea to the N a road-rail tunnel runs under the North Sea Canal, linking North and South Holland. Haarlem is renowned for flowering bulbs and has a 15th–16th- century cathedral and a Frans Hals museum.

Haber Fritz 1868–1934. German chemist whose conversion of atmospheric nitrogen to ammonia opened the way for the synthetic fertilizer industry. His study of the combustion of hydrocarbons led to the commercial 'cracking' or fractional distillation of natural oil (petroleum) into its components (for example, diesel, petrol, and paraffin). In electrochemistry, he was the first to demonstrate that oxidation and reduction take place at the electrodes; from this he developed a general electrochemical theory.

habitat localized ⊳environment in which an organism lives, and which provides for all (or almost all) of its needs. The diversity of habitats found within the Earth's ecosystem is enormous, and they are changing all the time. Many can be considered inorganic or physical, for example the Arctic ice cap, a cave, or a cliff face. Others are more complex, for instance a woodland or a forest floor. Some habitats are so precise that they are called *microhabitats*, such as the area under ⊳ stone where a particular type of insect lives. Most habitats provide a home for many species.

Habsburg or *Hapsburg* European royal family, former imperial house of Austria–Hungary. A Habsburg, Rudolf I, became king of Germany 1273 and began the family's control of Austria and Styria. They acquired a series of lands and titles, including that of Holy Roman emperor which they held 1273–91, 1298–1308, 1438–1740, and 1745–1806. The Habsburgs reached the zenith of their power under the emperor Charles V (1519–1556) who divided his lands, creating an Austrian Habsburg line (which ruled until 1918) and a Spanish line (which ruled to 1700).

hacking unauthorized access to a computer, either for fun or for malicious or fraudulent purposes. Hackers generally use microcomputers and telephone lines to obtain access. In computing, the term is used in a wider sense to mean using software for enjoyment or self-education, not necessarily involving unauthorized access.

Hades in Greek mythology, the underworld where spirits went after death, usually depicted as a cavern or pit underneath the Earth, the entrance of which was guarded by the three-headed dog Cerberus. It was presided over by the god Pluto or Hades (Roman Dis). Pluto was the brother of Zeus and married Persephone, daughter of Demeter and Zeus.

Hadrian (Publius Aelius Hadrianus) AD 76–138. Roman emperor from 117. Born in Spain, he was adopted by his relative, the emperor Trajan, whom he succeeded. He abandoned Trajan's conquests in Mesopotamia and adopted a defensive policy, which included the building of Hadrian's Wall in Britain.

Hadrian's Wall Roman fortification built AD 122–126 to mark England's northern boundary and abandoned about 383; its ruins run 185 km/115 mi from Wallsend on the river Tyne to Maryport, W Cumbria. In some parts, the wall was covered with a glistening, white coat of mortar. The fort at South Shields, Arbeia, built to defend the eastern end, is being reconstructed.

hadron in physics, a subatomic particle that experiences the strong nuclear force. Each is made up of two or three indivisible particles called ▷quarks. The hadrons are grouped into the ▷baryons (protons, neutrons, and hyperons) and the ▷mesons (particles with masses between those of electrons and protons).

haemoglobin protein used by all vertebrates and some invertebrates for oxygen transport because the two substances combine reversibly. In vertebrates it occurs in red blood cells (erythrocytes), giving them their colour.

haemophilia any of several inherited diseases in which normal blood clotting is impaired. The sufferer experiences prolonged bleeding from the slightest wound, as well as painful internal bleeding without apparent cause. The condition is mainly restricted to males, but females are carriers.

haemorrhage loss of blood from the circulatory system. It is 'manifest' when the blood can be seen, as when it flows from a wound, and 'occult' when the bleeding is internal, as from an ulcer or internal injury.

Hague, The (Dutch *'s-Gravenhage* or *Den Haag*) capital of the province of South Holland and seat of the Netherlands government, linked by canal with Rotterdam and Amsterdam; population (1991) 444,200.

Haile Selassie Ras (Prince) Tafari ('the Lion of Judah') 1892–1975. Emperor of Ethiopia 1930–74. He pleaded unsuccessfully to the League of Nations against the Italian conquest of his country 1935–36, and was then deposed and fled to the UK. He went to Egypt 1940 and raised an army which he led into Ethiopia Jan 1941 alongside British forces and was restored to the throne 5 May. He was deposed by a military coup 1974.

hair fine filament growing from mammalian skin. Each hair grows from a pit-shaped follicle embedded in the second layer of the skin, the dermis. It consists of dead cells impregnated with the protein keratin.

Haiti Republic of (*République d'Haïti*); *area* 27,750 sq km/10,712 sq mi; *capital* Port-au-Prince; *features* oldest black republic in the world; only French-speaking republic in the Americas; island of La Tortuga off N coast was formerly a pirate lair; *political system* transitional; *population* (1993 est) 6,600,000; growth rate 1.7% p.a.; one of highest population densities in the world; about 400,000 live in virtual slavery in the Dominican Republic; *languages* French (official, spoken by literate 10% minority), Creole (spoken by 90% black majority); *religion* Christian 95% of which 80% Roman Catholic, voodoo 4%.

halal conforming to the rules laid down by Islam. The term can be applied to all aspects of life, but usually refers to food permissible under Muslim dietary laws, including meat from animals that have been slaughtered in the correct ritual fashion.

half-life during ◊radioactive decay, the time in which the strength of a radioactive source decays to half its original value. In theory, the decay process is never complete and there is always some residual radioactivity. For this reason, the half-life of a radioactive isotope is measured, rather than the total decay time. It may vary from millionths of a second to billions of years.

Halifax capital of Nova Scotia, E Canada's main port; population (1986) 296,000. There are six military bases in Halifax and it is a major centre of oceanography. It was founded by British settlers 1749.

Halley Edmond 1656–1742. English astronomer who not only identified 1705 the comet that was later to be known by his name, but also compiled a star catalogue, detected the proper motion of stars using historical records, and began a line of research that – after his death – resulted in a reasonably accurate calculation of the astronomical unit.

Halley's comet comet that orbits the Sun about every 76 years, named after Edmond Halley who calculated its orbit. It is the brightest and most conspicuous

of the periodic comets. Recorded sightings go back over 2,000 years. It travels around the Sun in the opposite direction to the planets. Its orbit is inclined at almost 20° to the main plane of the Solar System and ranges between the orbits of Venus and Neptune. It is next due to appear 2061.

hallucinogen any substance that acts on the central nervous system to produce changes in perception and mood and often hallucinations. Hallucinogens include LSD, peyote, and mescaline. Their effects are unpredictable and they are illegal in most countries. Spiritual or religious experiences are common, hence the ritual use of hallucinogens in some cultures. They work by chemical interference with the normal action of neurotransmitters in the brain.

halogen any of a group of five nonmetallic elements with similar chemical bonding properties: fluorine, chlorine, bromine, iodine, and astatine. They form a linked group in the ◊periodic table of the elements, descending from fluorine, the most reactive, to astatine, the least reactive. They combine directly with most metals to form salts, such as common salt (NaCl). Each halogen has seven electrons in its valence shell, which accounts for the chemical similarities displayed by the group.

Hals Frans *c.* 1581–1666. Flemish-born painter of lively portraits. His work includes the *Laughing Cavalier* 1624 (Wallace Collection, London), and large groups of military companies, governors of charities, and others (many examples in the Frans Hals Museum, Haarlem, the Netherlands). In the 1620s he experimented with genre scenes.

Hamburg largest inland port of Europe, in Germany, on the river Elbe; population (1988) 1,571,000.

Hamburg administrative region (German *Land*) of Germany; *area* 760 sq km/293 sq mi; *capital* Hamburg; *features* the Hamburg Schauspielhaus is one of Germany's leading theatres; *population* (1990 est) 1,626,000; *religion* 74% Protestant, 8% Roman Catholic.

Hamilton capital (since 1815) of Bermuda, on Bermuda Island; population (1980) 1,617. It has a deep-sea harbour. Hamilton was founded 1612.

Hamilton Richard 1922– . English artist. He was a pioneer of Pop art. His collage *Just What Is It That Makes Today's Homes So Different, So Appealing?* 1956 (Kunsthalle, Tübingen, Germany) is often cited as the first Pop art work: its 1950s interior, inhabited by the bodybuilder Charles Atlas and a pin-up, is typically humorous, concerned with popular culture and contemporary kitsch.

hammer in track and field athletics, a throwing event in which only men compete. The hammer is a spherical weight attached to a chain with a handle. The competitor spins the hammer over his head to gain momentum, within the confines of a circle, and throws it as far as he can. The hammer weighs 7.26 kg/16 lb.

Hammerstein Oscar, II 1895–1960. US lyricist and librettist. He collaborated with Richard ◊Rodgers over a period of 16 years on some of the best-known American musicals, including *Oklahoma!* 1943, *Carousel* 1945, *South Pacific* 1949, *The King and I* 1951, and *The Sound of Music* 1959.

Hammett (Samuel) Dashiell 1894–1961. US crime novelist. He introduced the 'hard-boiled' detective character into fiction and attracted a host of imitators, with works including *The Maltese Falcon* 1930 (filmed 1941), *The Glass Key* 1931 (filmed 1942), and his most successful novel, the light-hearted *The Thin Man* 1932 (filmed 1934).

Hampshire county of S England; *area* 3,770 sq km/1,455 sq mi; *towns and cities* Winchester (administrative headquarters), Southampton, Portsmouth, Gosport; *features* New Forest, area 373 sq km/144 sq mi, a Saxon royal hunting ground; Hampshire Basin, with onshore and offshore oil; Danebury, 2,500-year-old Celtic hillfort; Beaulieu (including National Motor Museum); site of the Roman town of Silchester; Jane Austen's cottage 1809–17 is a museum; *population* (1991) 1,541,500.

Han member of the majority ethnic group in China, numbering about 990 million. The Hans speak a wide variety of dialects of the same monosyllabic language, a member of the Sino-Tibetan family. Their religion combines Buddhism, Taoism, Confucianism, and ancestor worship.

Handel Georg Friedrich 1685–1759. German composer, a British subject from 1726. His first opera, *Almira*, was performed in Hamburg 1705. In 1710 he was appointed kapellmeister to the elector of Hanover (the future George I of England). In 1712 he settled in England, where he established his popularity with such works as the *Water Music* 1717 (written for George I). His great choral works include the *Messiah* 1742 and the later oratorios *Samson* 1743, *Belshazzar* 1745, *Judas Maccabaeus* 1747, and *Jephtha* 1752.

Hannibal 247–182 BC. Carthaginian general from 221 BC, son of Hamilcar Barca. His siege of Saguntum (now Sagunto, near Valencia) precipitated the Second ▷Punic War with Rome. Following a campaign in Italy (after crossing the Alps in 218), Hannibal was the victor at Trasimene in 217 and Cannae in 216, but he failed to take Rome. In 203 he returned to Carthage to meet a Roman invasion but was defeated at Zama in 202 and exiled in 196 at Rome's insistence.

Hanoi capital of Vietnam, on the Red River; population (1989) 1,088,900. Central Hanoi has one of the highest population densities in the world: 1,300 people per hectare/3,250 per acre.

Hanover industrial city, capital of Lower Saxony, Germany; population (1988) 506,000.

Hanseatic League confederation of N European trading cities from the 12th century to 1669. At its height in the late 14th century the Hanseatic League included over 160 cities and towns, among them Lübeck, Hamburg, Cologne, Breslau, and Kraków. The basis of the league's power was its monopoly of the Baltic trade and its relations with Flanders and England.

haploid having a single set of ▷chromosomes in each cell. Most higher organisms are ▷diploid – that is, they have two sets – but their gametes (sex cells) are haploid. Some plants, such as mosses, liverworts, and many seaweeds, are haploid, and male honey bees are haploid because they develop from eggs that have not been fertilized. See also ▷meiosis.

Harare capital of Zimbabwe, on the Mashonaland plateau, about 1,525 m/5,000 ft above sea level; population (1982) 656,000. It is the centre of a rich farming area.

hard disc in computing, a storage device usually consisting of a rigid metal ▷disc coated with a magnetic material. Data are read from and written to the disc by means of a disc drive. The hard disc may be permanently fixed into the drive or in the form of a disc pack that can be removed and exchanged with a different pack. Hard discs vary from large units with capacities of more than 3,000 megabytes, intended for use with mainframe computers, to small units with capacities as low as 20 megabytes, intended for use with microcomputers.

Hardie (James) Keir 1856–1915. Scottish socialist, member of Parliament 1892–95 and 1900–15. He worked in the mines as a boy and in 1886 became secretary of the Scottish Miners' Federation. In 1888 he was the first Labour candidate to stand for Parliament; he entered Parliament independently as a Labour member 1892 and was a chief founder of the Independent Labour Party 1893.

hardness physical property of materials that governs their use. Methods of heat treatment can increase the hardness of metals. A scale of hardness was devised by German-Austrian mineralogist Friedrich ▷Mohs in the 1800s, based upon the hardness of certain minerals from soft talc (Mohs hardness 1) to diamond (10), the hardest of all materials.

hardware the mechanical, electrical, and electronic components of a computer system, as opposed to the various programs, which constitute ▷software.

Hardy Thomas 1840–1928. English novelist and poet. His novels, set in rural 'Wessex' (his native West Country), portray intense human relationships played out in a harshly indifferent natural world. They include *Far From the Madding Crowd* 1874, *The Return of the Native* 1878, *The Mayor of Casterbridge* 1886, *The Woodlanders* 1887, *Tess of the d'Urbervilles* 1891, and *Jude the Obscure* 1895. His poetry includes the *Wessex Poems* 1898.

Harlow Jean. Stage name of Harlean Carpenter 1911–1937. US film actress. She was the original 'platinum blonde' and the wisecracking sex symbol of the 1930s. Her films include *Hell's Angels* 1930, *Red Dust* 1932, *Platinum Blonde* 1932, *Dinner at Eight* 1933, *China Seas* 1935, and *Saratoga* 1937, during the filming of which she died (her part was completed by a double).

Harold II *c.* 1020–1066. King of England from Jan 1066 until his death the same year. In 1063 William of Normandy (◊William the Conqueror) tricked him into supporting his claim to the English throne. Harold was elected to succeed Edward the Confessor and William prepared to invade. Harold's treacherous brother Tostig (died 1066) joined the king of Norway, Harald Hardrada (1015–1066), in invading Northumbria. Harold killed them at Stamford Bridge 25 Sept. Three days later William landed at Pevensey, Sussex, and Harold was killed at the Battle of Hastings 14 Oct 1066.

harp plucked musical string instrument, with the strings stretched vertically within a wood and brass soundbox of triangular shape. The orchestral harp is the largest instrument of its type. It has up to 47 diatonically tuned strings, in the range B0–C7 (seven octaves), and seven double-action pedals to alter pitch. Composers for the harp include Mozart, Ravel, Salzedo, and Holliger.

harpsichord the largest and grandest of 18th-century keyboard string instruments, used in orchestras and as a solo instrument. The strings are plucked by 'jacks' made of leather or quill, and multiple keyboards offering variation in tone are common.

harrier bird of prey of the genus *Circus*, family Accipitridae. Harriers have long wings and legs, short beaks and soft plumage. They are found throughout the world.

Harrier the only truly successful vertical takeoff and landing fixed-wing aircraft, often called the *jump jet*. Built in Britain, it made its first flight 1966. It has a single jet engine and a set of swivelling nozzles. These deflect the jet exhaust vertically downwards for takeoff and landing, and to the rear for normal flight. Designed to fly from confined spaces with minimal ground support, it refuels in midair.

Haryana state of NW India; *area* 44,200 sq km/17,061 sq mi; *capital* Chandigarh; *features* part of the Ganges plain; a centre of Hinduism; *population* (1991) 16,317,700; *language* Hindi.

hashish drug made from the resin contained in the female flowering tops of hemp (◊cannabis).

Hasid or *Hassid, Chasid* (plural *Hasidim, Hassidim, Chasidim*) member of a sect of Orthodox Jews, originating in 18th-century Poland under the leadership of Israel Ba'al Shem Tov (*c.* 1700–1760). Hasidic teachings encourage prayer, piety, and 'serving the Lord with joy'. Many of their ideas are based on the ◊kabbala.

Hastings, Battle of battle 14 Oct 1066 at which William the Conqueror, Duke of Normandy, defeated Harold, King of England. The site is 10 km/6 mi inland from Hastings, at Senlac, Sussex; it is marked by Battle Abbey.

Haughey Charles 1925– . Irish Fianna Fáil politician of Ulster descent. Dismissed 1970 from Jack Lynch's cabinet for alleged complicity in IRA gun-running, he was afterwards acquitted. He was prime minister 1979–81, March–Nov 1982, and 1986–92, when he was replaced by Albert Reynolds.

Haute-Normandie or *Upper Normandy* coastal region of NW France lying between Basse-Normandie and Picardy and bisected by the river Seine; area 12,300 sq km/4,757 sq mi; population (1986) 1,693,000. It comprises the *départements* of Eure and Seine-Maritime; its capital is Rouen. Major ports include Dieppe and Fécamp. The area has many beech forests.

Havana capital and port of Cuba, on the northwest coast of the island; population (1989) 2,096,100. The palace of the Spanish governors and the stronghold of La Fuerza (1583) survive. Tourism, formerly a major source of revenue, ended when Fidel Castro came to power 1959.

Havel Václav 1936– . Czech dramatist and politician, president of Czechoslovakia 1989–92 and of the Czech Republic from 1993. He became widely known as a human- rights activist and was imprisoned 1979–83 and again 1989. As president of Czechoslovakia he sought to preserve a united republic, but resigned on the breakup of the federation 1992. In 1993 he became president of the newly independent Czech Republic.

Hawaii Pacific state of the USA; *area* [1]6,800 sq km/6,485 sq mi; *capital* Honolulu on Oahu; *features* a chain of some 20 volcanic islands, of which *Hawaii* is the largest, noted for Mauna Loa (4,170 m/13,686 ft), the world's largest active volcanic crater; *Maui*, the second largest of the islands; *Oahu*, the third largest, has Waikiki beach and the Pearl Harbor naval base; *population* (1990) 1,108,200 (34% European, 25% Japanese, 14% Filipino, 12% Hawaiian, 6% Chinese); *language* English; *religions* Christianity; Buddhist minority.

Hawking Stephen 1942– . English physicist who has researched ◊black holes and gravitational field theory. His books include *A Brief History of Time* 1988, in which he argues that our universe is only one small part of a 'superuniverse' that has existed for ever and comprises an infinite number of universes like our own.

Hawksmoor Nicholas 1661–1736. English architect. He was assistant to Christopher ◊Wren in designing various London churches and St Paul's Cathedral and joint architect with John ◊Vanbrugh of Castle Howard and Blenheim Palace.

hawthorn shrub or tree of the genus *Crataegus* of the rose family Rosaceae. Species are most abundant in E North America, but there are also many in Eurasia. All have alternate, toothed leaves and bear clusters of showy white, pink, or red flowers. Small applelike fruits can be red, orange, blue, or black. Hawthorns are popular as ornamentals.

Haydn Franz Joseph 1732–1809. Austrian composer. A teacher of Mozart and Beethoven, he was a major exponent of the classical sonata form in his numerous chamber and orchestral works (he wrote more than 100 symphonies). He also composed choral music, including the oratorios *The Creation* 1798 and *The Seasons* 1801. He was the first great master of the string quartet.

hay fever allergic reaction to pollen, causing sneezing, with inflammation of the nasal membranes and conjunctiva of the eyes. Symptoms are due to the release of ◊histamine. Treatment is by antihistamine drugs.

hazel shrub or tree of the genus *Corylus*, family Corylaceae, including the European common hazel or cob *C. avellana*, of which the filbert is the cultivated variety. North American species include the American hazel *C. americana*.

heart muscular organ that rhythmically contracts to force blood around the body of an animal with a circulatory system. Annelid worms and some other invertebrates have simple hearts consisting of thickened sections of main blood vessels that pulse regularly. An earthworm has ten such hearts. Vertebrates have one heart. A fish heart has two chambers – the thin-walled *atrium* (once called the auricle) that expands to receive blood, and the thick-walled *ventricle* that pumps it out. Amphibians and most reptiles have two atria and one ventricle; birds and mammals have two atria and two ventricles. The beating of the heart is controlled by the autonomic nervous system and an internal control centre or pacemaker, the sinoatrial node.

heart attack or *myocardial infarction* sudden onset of gripping central chest pain, often accompanied by sweating and vomiting, caused by death of a portion of the heart muscle following obstruction of a coronary artery by thrombosis (formation of a blood clot). Half of all heart attacks result in death within the first two hours, but in the remainder survival has improved following the widespread use of thrombolytic (clot-buster) drugs.

heat form of internal energy possessed by a substance by virtue of the kinetic energy in the motion of its molecules or atoms. Heat energy is transferred by conduction, convection, and radiation. It always flows from a region of higher ◊temperature (heat intensity) to one of lower temperature. Its effect on a substance may be simply to raise its temperature, or to cause it to expand, melt (if a solid), vaporize (if a liquid), or increase its pressure (if a confined gas).

heat capacity in physics, the quantity of heat required to raise the temperature of an object by one degree. The *specific heat capacity* of a substance is the heat capacity per unit of mass, measured in joules per kilogram per kelvin (J kg^{-1} K^{-1}).

Heath Edward (Richard George) 1916– . British Conservative politician, party leader 1965–75. As prime minister 1970–74 he took the UK into the European Community (now the European Union) but was brought down by economic and industrial relations crises at home. He was replaced as party leader by Margaret Thatcher 1975.

heather low-growing evergreen shrub of the heath family, common on sandy or acid soil. The common heather *Calluna vulgaris* is a carpet-forming shrub, growing up to 60 cm/24 in high and bearing pale pink-purple flowers. It is found over much of Europe and has been introduced to North America.

heat treatment in industry, the subjection of metals and alloys to controlled heating and cooling after fabrication to relieve internal stresses and improve their physical properties. Methods include annealing, quenching, and tempering.

Hebrew member of the Semitic people who lived in Palestine at the time of the Old Testament and who traced their ancestry to ▷Abraham. The *Hebrew language* is a member of the Hamito-Semitic language family, spoken in SW Asia by the ancient Hebrews, sustained for many centuries in the Diaspora as the liturgical language of Judaism, revived by the late-19th- century Haskala movement, and developed in the 20th century as Israeli Hebrew, the national language of the state of Israel. It is the original language of the Old Testament of the Bible.

Hebrew Bible the sacred writings of Judaism (some dating from as early as 1200 BC), called by Christians the ▷Old Testament. It includes the Torah (the first five books, ascribed to Moses), historical and prophetic books, and psalms, originally written in Hebrew and later translated into Greek (Pentateuch) and other languages.

Hebrides group of more than 500 islands (fewer than 100 inhabited) off W Scotland; total area 2,900 sq km/ 1,120 sq mi. The Hebrides were settled by Scandinavians during the 6th to 9th centuries and passed under Norwegian rule from about 890 to 1266.

Hector in Greek mythology, a Trojan prince, son of King Priam and husband of Andromache, who, in the siege of ▷Troy, was the foremost warrior on the Trojan side until he was killed by ▷Achilles.

hedgehog insectivorous mammal of the genus *Erinaceus*, native to Europe, Asia, and Africa. The body, including the tail, is 30 cm/1 ft long. It is greyish-brown in colour, has a piglike snout, and is covered with sharp spines. When alarmed it can roll itself into a ball. Hedgehogs feed on insects, slugs, and carrion. Long-eared hedgehogs and desert hedgehogs are placed in different genera.

hedonism ethical theory that pleasure or happiness of the individual is, or should be, the main goal in life. Hedonist sects in ancient Greece were the Cyrenaics and the Epicureans. Modern hedonistic philosophies, such as those of the British philosophers Jeremy Bentham and J S Mill, regard the happiness of society, rather than that of the individual, as the aim.

Hegel Georg Wilhelm Friedrich 1770–1831. German philosopher who conceived of consciousness and the external object as forming a unity in which neither factor can exist independently, mind and nature being two abstractions of one indivisible whole. He believed development took place through dialectic: thesis and antithesis (contradiction) and synthesis, the resolution of contradiction. He wrote *The Phenomenology of Spirit* 1807, *Encyclopaedia of the Philosophical Sciences* 1817, and *Philosophy of Right* 1821.

Heidegger Martin 1889–1976. German philosopher. In *Sein und Zeit/Being and Time* 1927 (translated 1962) he used the methods of Edmund Husserl's phenomenology to explore the structures of human existence. His later writings meditated on the fate of a world dominated by science and technology.

Heine Heinrich 1797–1856. German Romantic poet and journalist. He wrote *Reisebilder* 1826–31, blending travel writing and satire, and *Buch der Lieder/-Book of Songs* 1827. From 1831 he lived mainly in Paris, working as a correspondent for German newspapers and publishing *Neue Gedichte/New Poems* 1844. He excelled in both the Romantic lyric and satire.

Helen in Greek mythology, the daughter of Zeus and Leda, and the most beautiful of women. She married Menelaus, King of Sparta, but during his absence, was abducted by Paris, Prince of Troy. This precipitated the Trojan War. Afterwards she returned to Sparta with her husband.

helicopter powered aircraft that achieves both lift and propulsion by means of a rotary wing, or rotor, on top of the fuselage. It can take off and land vertically, move in any direction, or remain stationary in the air. It can be powered by piston or jet engine.

helium colourless, odourless, gaseous, nonmetallic element, symbol He, atomic number 2, relative atomic mass 4.0026. It is grouped with the ◊inert gases, is nonreactive, and forms no compounds. It is the second-most abundant element (after hydrogen) in the universe, and has the lowest boiling (−268.9°C/−452°F) and melting points (−272.2°C/−458°F) of all the elements.

Hellenic period (from *Hellas*, Greek name for Greece) classical period of ancient Greek civilization, from the first Olympic Games 776 BC until the death of Alexander the Great 323 BC.

Hellenistic period period in Greek civilization from the death of Alexander 323 BC until the accession of the Roman emperor Augustus 27 BC. Alexandria in Egypt was the centre of culture and commerce during this period, and Greek culture spread throughout the Mediterranean region and the near East.

Helsinki (Swedish *Helsingfors*) capital and port of Finland; population (1990) 492,400, metropolitan area 978,000. The homes of the architect Eliel Saarinen and the composer Jean Sibelius outside the city are museums.

hematite principal ore of iron, consisting mainly of iron(III) oxide, Fe_2O_3. It occurs as *specular hematite* (dark, metallic lustre), *kidney ore* (reddish radiating fibres terminating in smooth, rounded surfaces), and a red earthy deposit.

Hemingway Ernest (Miller) 1899–1961. US writer. War, bullfighting, and fishing are used symbolically in his work to represent honour, dignity, and primitivism – prominent themes in his short stories and novels, which include *A Farewell to Arms* 1929, *For Whom the Bell Tolls* 1941, and *The Old Man and the Sea* 1952. His deceptively simple writing styles attracted many imitators. Nobel Prize for Literature 1954.

henna small shrub *Lawsonia inermis* of the loosestrife family Lythraceae, found in Iran, India, Egypt, and N Africa. The leaves and young twigs are ground to a powder, mixed to a paste with hot water, and applied to fingernails and hair, giving an orange-red hue. The colour may then be changed to black by applying a preparation of indigo.

Henry V 1387–1422. King of England from 1413, son of Henry IV. Invading Normandy 1415 during the Hundred Years' War, he captured Harfleur and defeated the French at ▷Agincourt. He invaded again 1417–19, capturing Rouen, forcing the French into the Treaty of Troyes 1420, which gave Henry control of the French government. He married Catherine of Valois 1420 gaining recognition as heir to the French throne by his father-in-law Charles VI, but died before him. He was succeeded by his son Henry VI.

Henry VII 1457–1509. King of England from 1485, son of Edmund Tudor, Earl of Richmond (c. 1430–1456). He spent his early life in Brittany until 1485, when he landed in Britain to lead the rebellion against Richard III whom he defeated at ▷Bosworth. By his marriage to Elizabeth of York 1486, he united the houses of York and Lancaster, restoring order after the Wars of the ▷Roses by the ▷Star Chamber. He achieved independence from Parliament by amassing a private fortune through confiscations. He was succeeded by his son Henry VIII.

Henry VIII 1491–1547. King of England from 1509, when he succeeded his father Henry VII and married Catherine of Aragon, the widow of his brother. During the period 1513–29 Henry pursued an active foreign policy, largely under the guidance of his Lord Chancellor, Cardinal Wolsey who shared Henry's desire to make England stronger. Wolsey was replaced by Thomas More 1529 for failing to persuade the pope to grant Henry a divorce. After 1532 Henry broke with papal authority, proclaimed himself head of the church in England, dissolved the monasteries, and divorced Catherine. His subsequent wives were Anne Boleyn, Jane Seymour, Anne of Cleves, Catherine Howard, and Catherine Parr. He was succeeded by his son Edward VI.

hepatitis any inflammatory disease of the liver, usually caused by a virus. Other causes include alcohol, drugs, gallstones, ▷lupus erythematosus, and amoebic ▷dysentery. Symptoms include weakness, nausea, and jaundice.

Hepburn Audrey (Audrey Hepburn-Rushton) 1929–1993. British actress of Anglo-Dutch descent. She became a Hollywood star in *Roman Holiday* 1951, such films as *Funny Face* 1957, *My Fair Lady* 1964, and *Wait Until Dark* 1968.

Hepburn Katharine 1909– . US actress. She made feisty self-assurance her trademark, appearing in such films as *Morning Glory* 1933 (Academy Award), *The African Queen* 1951, *Guess Who's Coming to Dinner* 1967 (Academy Award), *Lion in Winter* 1968 (Academy Award), and *On Golden Pond* 1981 (Academy Award).

Hepworth Barbara 1903–1975. English sculptor. She developed a distinctive abstract style, creating hollowed forms of stone or wood with spaces bridged by wires or strings; many later works are in bronze.

Heracles in Greek mythology, a hero (Roman Hercules), son of Zeus and Alcmene, famed for strength. Driven mad by the goddess Hera, he murdered his first wife Megara and their children, and was himself poisoned by mistake by his second wife Deianira.

herbivore animal that feeds on green plants (or photosynthetic single- celled organisms) or their products, including seeds, fruit, and nectar. The most numerous type of herbivore is thought to be the zooplankton, tiny invertebrates in the surface waters of the oceans that feed on small photosynthetic algae. Herbivores are more numerous than other animals because their food is the most abundant. They form a vital link in the food chain between plants and carnivores.

Herculaneum ancient city of Italy between Naples and Pompeii. Along with Pompeii, it was buried when Vesuvius erupted AD 79. It was excavated from the 18th century onwards.

Hercules Roman form of ◊Heracles.

heredity in biology, the transmission of traits from parent to offspring. See also ◊genetics.

Hereford and Worcester county of W central England, created 1974 from the counties of Herefordshire and Worcestershire; *area* 3,930 sq km/1,517 sq mi; *towns and cities* Worcester (administrative headquarters), Hereford, Kidderminster, Evesham, Ross-on-Wye, Ledbury *features* Malvern Hills; Black Mountains; Vale of Evesham; spa baths at Droitwich; *population* (1991) 676,700.

hermaphrodite organism that has both male and female sex organs. Hermaphroditism is the norm in species such as earthworms and snails, and is common in flowering plants. Cross-fertilization is the rule among hermaphrodites, with the parents functioning as male and female simultaneously, or as one or the other sex at different stages in their development. Human hermaphrodites are extremely rare.

Hermes in Greek mythology, a god, son of Zeus and Maia; messenger of the gods. He wore winged sandals, a wide-brimmed hat, and carried a staff around which serpents coiled. Identified with the Roman Mercury and ancient Egyptian Thoth, he protected thieves, travellers, and merchants.

hernia or *rupture* protrusion of part of an internal organ through a weakness in the surrounding muscular wall, usually in the groin. The appearance is that of a rounded soft lump or swelling.

Herodotus *c.* 484–424 BC. Greek historian. After four years in Athens, he travelled widely in Egypt, Asia, and the Black Sea region of E Europe, before settling at Thurii in S Italy 443 BC. He wrote a nine-book history of the Greek-Persian struggle that culminated in the defeat of the Persian invasion attempts 490 and 480 BC.

Herod the Great 74–4 BC. King of the Roman province of Judaea, S Palestine, from 40 BC. With the aid of Mark Antony, he established his government in Jerusalem 37 BC. His last years were a reign of terror, and in the New Testament Matthew alleges that he ordered the slaughter of all the infants in Bethlehem to ensure the death of Jesus, whom he foresaw as a rival. He was the father of Herod Antipas.

heroin or *diamorphine* powerful ◊opiate analgesic, an acetyl derivative of ◊morphine. It is more addictive than morphine but causes less nausea. It has an important place in the control of severe pain in terminal illness, severe injuries, and heart attacks, but is widely used illegally.

herpes any of several infectious diseases caused by viruses of the herpes group. *Herpes simplex I* is the causative agent of a common inflammation, the cold sore. *Herpes simplex II* is responsible for genital herpes, a highly contagious, sexually transmitted disease characterized by painful blisters in the genital area. It can be transmitted in the birth canal from mother to newborn. *Herpes zoster* causes shingles; another herpes virus causes chickenpox.

Herschel William 1738–1822. German-born English astronomer. He was a skilled telescope maker, and pioneered the study of binary stars and nebulae. He discovered the planet Uranus 1781 and infrared solar rays 1801. He catalogued over 800 double stars, and found over 2,500 nebulae, catalogued by his sister Caroline Herschel; this work was continued by his son John Herschel. By studying the distribution of stars, William established the basic form of our Galaxy, the Milky Way.

Hertfordshire county of SE England; *area* 1,630 sq km/629 sq mi; *towns and cities* Hertford (administrative headquarters), St Albans, Watford, Hatfield, Hemel Hempstead, Bishop's Stortford; *features* part of the Chiltern Hills; Hatfield House; Brocket Hall (home of Palmerston and Melbourne); Berkhamsted Castle (Norman); *population* (1991) 975,800.

Hess (Walter Richard) Rudolf 1894–1987. German Nazi leader. Imprisoned with Hitler 1924–25, he became his private secretary, taking down *Mein Kampf* from Hitler's dictation. In 1933 he was appointed deputy *Führer* to Hitler, replaced by Goering Sept 1939. In May 1941 he flew to the UK on his own peace mission, but was held a prisoner of war until 1945, when he was tried at Nuremberg as a war criminal and sentenced to life imprisonment.

Hesse Hermann 1877–1962. German writer, a Swiss citizen from 1923. A conscientious objector in World War I

and a pacifist opponent of Hitler, he published short stories, poetry, and novels, including *Peter Camenzind* 1904, *Siddhartha* 1922, and *Steppenwolf* 1927. Later works, such as *Das Glasperlenspiel/The Glass Bead Game* 1943, show the influence of Indian mysticism and Jungian psychoanalysis. Nobel Prize for Literature 1946.

heterotroph any living organism that obtains its energy from organic substances produced by other organisms. All animals and fungi are heterotrophs, and they include herbivores, carnivores, and saprotrophs (those that feed on dead animal and plant material).

hexadecimal number system number system to the base 16, used in computing. In hex (as it is commonly known) the decimal numbers 0–15 are represented by the characters 0, 1, 2, 3, 4, 5, 6, 7, 8, 9, A, B, C, D, E, F. Hexadecimal numbers are easy to convert to the computer's internal binary code and are more compact than binary numbers.

hibernation state of dormancy in which certain animals spend the winter. It is associated with a dramatic reduction in all metabolic processes, including body temperature, breathing, and heart rate. It is a fallacy that animals sleep throughout the winter.

hieroglyphic Egyptian writing system of the mid-4th millennium BC–3rd century AD, which combines picture signs with those indicating letters. The direction of writing is normally from right to left, the signs facing the beginning of the line. It was deciphered 1822 by the French Egyptologist J F Champollion (1790–1832) with the aid of the *Rosetta Stone*, which has the same inscription carved in hieroglyphic, demotic, and Greek.

high jump field event in athletics in which competitors leap over a horizontal crossbar held between rigid uprights at least 3.66 m/12 ft apart. The bar is placed at increasingly higher levels. Elimination occurs after three consecutive failures to clear the bar.

Highland region of Scotland; *area* 26,100 sq km/10,077 sq mi; *towns and cites* Inverness (administrative headquarters), Thurso, Wick; *features* Grampian Mountains; Ben Nevis (highest peak in the UK); Loch Ness, Caledonian Canal; Dounreay (site of Atomic Energy Authority's first experimental fastbreeder reactor and a nuclear processing plant); *population* (1991) 204,000; *languages* English; 7.5% Gaelic-speaking.

Highlands one of the three geographical divisions of Scotland, lying to the N of a geological fault line that stretches from Stonehaven in the North Sea to Dumbarton on the Clyde. It is a mountainous region of hard rocks, shallow infertile soils, and high rainfall.

Hijrah or *Hegira* the trip from Mecca to Medina of the prophet Muhammad, which took place AD 622 as a result of the persecution of the prophet and his followers. The Muslim calendar dates from this event, and the day of the Hijrah is celebrated as the Muslim New Year.

Hillary Edmund Percival 1919– . New Zealand mountaineer. In 1953, with Nepalese Sherpa mountaineer Tenzing Norgay, he reached the summit of Mount Everest, the first to climb the world's highest peak. As a member of the Commonwealth Transantarctic Expedition 1957–58, he was the first person since Scott to reach the South Pole overland, on 3 Jan 1958.

Himachal Pra state of NW India; *area* 55,700 sq km/21,500 sq mi; *capital* Simla; *features* mainly agricultural state, one-third forested; *population* (1991) 5,111,000; mainly Hindu; *language* Pahari.

Himalayas vast mountain system of central Asia, extending from the Indian states of Kashmir in the W to Assam in the E, covering the S part of Tibet, Nepal, Sikkim, and Bhutan. It is the highest mountain range in the world. The two highest peaks are *Mount ◊Everest and Kangchenjunga.*

Himmler Heinrich 1900–1945. German Nazi leader, head of the ◊SS elite corps from 1929, the police and the ◊Gestapo secret police from 1936, and supervisor of the extermination of the Jews in E Europe. During World War II he replaced Goering as Hitler's second-in-command. He was captured May 1945 and committed suicide.

Hindenburg Paul Ludwig Hans von Beneckendorf und Hindenburg 1847–1934. German field marshal and right-wing politician. During World War I he was supreme commander and, with Ludendorff, practically directed Germany's policy until the end of the war. He was president of Germany 1925–33.

Hindi member of the Indo-Iranian branch of the Indo- European language family, the official language of the Republic of India, although resisted as such by the Dravidian-speaking states of the south. Hindi proper is used by some 30% of Indians, in such northern states as Uttar Pradesh and Madhya Pradesh.

Hinduism religion originating in N India about 4,000 years ago, which is superficially and in some of its forms polytheistic, but has a concept of the supreme spirit, Brahman, above the many divine manifestations. These include the triad of chief gods (the Trimurti): Brahma, Vishnu, and Siva (creator, preserver, and destroyer). Central to Hinduism are the beliefs in reincarnation and ⊳karma; the oldest scriptures are the *Vedas*.

Hindustan ('land of the Hindus') the whole of India, but more specifically the plain of the Ganges and Jumna rivers, or that part of India N of the Deccan.

Hindustani member of the Indo-Iranian branch of the Indo-European language family, closely related to Hindi and Urdu and originating in the bazaars of Delhi. It is a lingua franca in many parts of the Republic of India.

Hippocrates *c.* 460–*c.* 370 BC. Greek physician, often called the father of medicine. Important Hippocratic ideas include cleanliness (for patients and physicians), moderation in eating and drinking, letting nature take its course, and living where the air is good. He believed that health was the result of the 'humours' of the body being in balance; imbalance caused disease. These ideas were later adopted by ⊳Galen.

hippopotamus large herbivorous, even-toed hoofed mammal of the family Hippopotamidae. The common hippopotamus *Hippopotamus amphibius* is found in Africa. It averages over 4 m/13 ft long, 1.5 m/5 ft high, weighs about 4,500 kg/5 tons, and has a brown or slate-grey skin. It is an endangered species.

Hirohito (regnal era name *Shōwa*) 1901–1989. Emperor of Japan from 1926, when he succeeded his father Taishō (Yoshihito). After the defeat of Japan in World War II 1945, he was made a figurehead monarch by the US-backed 1946 constitution. He is believed to have played a reluctant role in General Tōjō's prewar expansion plans. He was succeeded by his son ⊳Akihito.

Hiroshima industrial city and port on the south coast of Honshu Island, Japan, destroyed by the first wartime use of an atomic bomb 6 Aug 1945. The city has largely been rebuilt since the war; population (1990) 1,085,700.

histamine inflammatory substance normally released in damaged tissues, which also accounts for many of the symptoms of ⊳allergy. Substances that neutralize its activity are known as ⊳antihistamines. Histamine was first described 1911 by British physiologist Henry Dale (1875–1968).

history record of the events of human societies. The earliest surviving historical records are the inscriptions denoting the achievements of Egyptian and Babylonian kings. As a literary form in the Western world, historical writing or *historiography* began with the Greek Herodotus in the 5th century BC, who was first to pass beyond the limits of a purely national outlook. Contemporary historians make extensive use of statistics, population figures, and primary records to justify historical arguments.

Hitchcock Alfred 1899–1980. English film director, a US citizen from 1955. A master of the suspense thriller, he was noted for his meticulously drawn storyboards that determined his camera angles and for his cameo 'walk-ons' in his own films. His *The Thirty-Nine Steps* 1935 and *The Lady Vanishes* 1939 are British suspense classics. He went to Hollywood 1940, where he made films such as *Rebecca* 1940, *Rear Window* 1954, *Vertigo* 1958, *Psycho* 1960, and *The Birds* 1963.

Hitler Adolf 1889–1945. German Nazi dictator, born in Austria. He was *Führer* (leader) of the Nazi Party from 1921 and author of *Mein Kampf/My Struggle* 1925–27. As chancellor of Germany from 1933 and head of state from 1934, he created a dictatorship by playing party and state institutions against each other. He reoccupied the Rhineland and formed an alliance with the Italian Fascist Mussolini 1936, annexed Austria 1938, and occupied the Sudetenland under the ◊Munich Agreement. The rest of Czechoslovakia was annexed March 1939. The Ribbentrop–Molotov pact (or Hitler–Stalin pact) was followed in Sept by the invasion of Poland and the declaration of war by Britain and France. He committed suicide as Berlin fell.

Hittite member of any of a succession of peoples who inhabited Anatolia and N Syria from the 3rd millennium to the 1st millennium BC. The city of Hattusas (now Boğazköy in central Turkey) became the capital of a strong kingdom which overthrew the Babylonian Empire. After a period of eclipse the Hittite New Empire became a great power (about 1400–1200 BC), which successfully waged war with Egypt. The Hittite language is an Indo-European language.

HIV (abbreviation for *human immunodeficiency virus*), the infectious agent that is believed to cause ◊AIDS. It was first discovered 1983 by Luc Montagnier of the Pasteur Institute in Paris, who called it lymphocyte-associated virus (LAV). Independently, US scientist Robert Gallo, of the National Cancer Institute in Bethesda, Maryland, claimed its discovery in 1984 and named it human T-lymphocytotrophic virus 3 (HTLV-III). As of mid-1994 it was estimated by the World Health Organization that over 16 million adults, and over one million children, had been infected with HIV since the beginning of the pandemic (late 1970s to early 1980s).

Hobbes Thomas 1588–1679. English political philosopher and the first thinker since Aristotle to attempt to develop a comprehensive theory of nature, including human behaviour. In *Leviathan* 1651, he advocates absolutist government as the only means of ensuring order and security; he saw this as deriving from the ◊social contract.

Ho Chi Minh adopted name of Nguyen Tat Thanh 1890–1969. North Vietnamese communist politician, premier and president 1954–69. He headed the communist Vietminh from 1941 and fought against the French during the ◊Indochina War 1946–54, becoming president and prime minister of the republic at the armistice. He relinquished the premiership 1955, but continued as president. Ho successfully led his country's fight against US-aided South Vietnam in the ◊Vietnam War 1954–75.

Ho Chi Minh City (until 1976 *Saigon*) chief port and industrial city of S Vietnam; population (1989) 3,169,100. Saigon was the capital of the Republic of Vietnam (South Vietnam) from 1954 to 1976, when it was renamed.

Hockney David 1937– . English painter, printmaker, and designer, resident in California. He developed an individual figurative style, as in his portrait *Mr and Mrs Clark and Percy* 1971 (Tate Gallery, London). His views of swimming pools reflect a preoccupation with surface pattern and effects of light.

Hogarth William 1697–1764. English painter and engraver. He produced portraits and moralizing genre scenes, such as the series of prints *A Rake's Progress* 1735. His portraits are remarkably direct and full of character, for example *Heads of Six of Hogarth's Servants* about 1750–55 (Tate Gallery, London). He published *A Harlot's Progress*, a series of six engravings, 1732.

Hokkaido formerly (until 1868) *Yezo* or *Ezo* northernmost of the four main islands of Japan, separated from Honshu to the S by Tsugaru Strait and from Sakhalin to the N by Soya Strait; area 83,500 sq km/32,231 sq mi; population (1986) 5,678,000, including 16,000 Ainus. The capital is Sapporo. Natural resources include coal, mercury, manganese, oil and natural gas, timber, and fisheries.

Holbein Hans, *the Younger* 1497/98–1543. German painter and woodcut artist, the son and pupil of Hans Holbein the Elder. As painter to Henry VIII he created a a series of graphic, perceptive portraits of the English court, the best-known being those of Henry VIII and of Thomas More. One of the finest graphic artists of his age, he executed a woodcut series *Dance of Death* about 1525, and designed title pages for Luther's New Testament and More's *Utopia*.

Holiday Billie. Stage name of Eleanora Gough McKay 1915–1959. US jazz singer, also known as 'Lady Day'. She made her debut in Harlem clubs and became known for her emotionally charged delivery and idiosyncratic phrasing; she brought a blues feel to performances with swing bands. Songs she made her own include 'Stormy Weather', 'Strange Fruit', and 'I Cover the Waterfront'.

holistic medicine umbrella term for an approach that virtually all alternative therapies profess, which considers the overall health and lifestyle profile of a patient, and treats specific ailments not primarily as conditions to be alleviated but rather as symptoms of more fundamental disease.

Holland popular name for the ◊Netherlands; also two provinces of the Netherlands, North Holland and South Holland.

Hollywood district in the city of Los Angeles, California; the centre of the US film industry from 1911. It is the home of film studios such as 20th Century Fox, MGM, Paramount, Columbia Pictures, United Artists, Disney, and Warner Brothers. Many film stars' homes are situated nearby in Beverly Hills and other communities adjacent to Hollywood.

Holocaust, the the annihilation of an estimated 6 million Jews by the Hitler regime 1933–45 in the numerous extermination and ◊concentration camps, most notably Auschwitz, Sobibor, Treblinka, and Maidanek in Poland, and Belsen, Buchenwald, and Dachau in Germany. An additional 10 million people died during imprisonment or were exterminated, among them were Ukrainian, Polish, and Russian civilians and prisoners of war, Romanies, socialists, homosexuals, and others (labelled 'defectives'). Victims were variously starved, tortured, experimented on, and worked to death. Millions were executed in gas chambers, shot, or hanged. It was euphemistically termed 'the final solution' (of the Jewish question).

Holocene epoch of geological time that began 10,000 years ago, the second and current epoch of the Quaternary period.

The glaciers retreated, the climate became warmer, and humans developed significantly.

holography method of producing three-dimensional (3-D) images by means of ◊laser light. Holography uses a photographic technique (involving the splitting of a laser beam into two beams) to produce a picture, or hologram, that contains 3-D information about the object photographed. Some holograms show meaningless patterns in ordinary light and produce a 3-D image only when laser light is projected through them, but reflection holograms produce images when ordinary light is reflected from them (as found on credit cards).

Holy Communion another name for the ◊Eucharist, a Christian sacrament.

Holy Grail in medieval Christian legend, the dish or cup used by Jesus at the Last Supper, supposed to have supernatural powers. Together with the spear with which he was wounded at the Crucifixion, it was an object of quest by King Arthur's knights in certain stories incorporated in the Arthurian legend.

Holy Roman Empire empire of ◊Charlemagne and his successors, and the German Empire 962–1806, both being regarded as the Christian (hence 'holy') revival of the Roman Empire. At its height it comprised much of western and central Europe.

Homer 8th century BC. According to ancient tradition, the author of the Greek narrative epics, the *Iliad* and the *Odyssey* 508. Little is known about the man, but modern research suggests that both poems should be assigned to the 8th century BC, with the *Odyssey* the later of the two. The predominant dialect in the poems indicates that Homer may have come from an Ionian Greek settlement, such as Smyrna or Chios, as was traditionally believed.

Home Rule, Irish movement to repeal the Act of ◊Union 1801 that joined Ireland to Britain and to establish an Irish parliament responsible for internal affairs. In 1870 Isaac Butt (1813–1879) formed the Home Rule Association and the movement was led in Parliament from 1880 by Charles ◊Parnell. After 1918 the demand for an independent Irish republic replaced that for home rule.

homoeopathy or *homeopathy* system of alternative medicine based on the principle that symptoms of disease are part of the body's self-healing processes, and on the practice of administering extremely diluted doses of natural substances found to produce in a healthy person the symptoms manifest in the illness being treated. Developed by German physician Samuel Hahnemann (1755–1843), the system is widely practised today as an alternative to allopathic (orthodox) medicine, and many controlled tests and achieved cures testify its efficacy.

homosexuality sexual preference for, or attraction to, persons of one's own sex; in women it is referred to as lesbianism. Both sexes use the term 'gay'. Men and women who are attracted to both sexes are referred to as bisexual. The extent to which homosexual behaviour is caused by biological or psychological factors is an area of disagreement among experts.

Honduras Republic of (*República de Honduras*); *area* 112,100 sq km/43,282 sq mi; *capital* Tegucigalpa; *features* archaeological sites; Mayan ruins at Copán; *political system* democratic republic; *population* (1993 est) 5,240,000 (mestizo, or mixed, 90%; Indians and Europeans 10%); growth rate 3.1% p.a.; *languages* Spanish (official), English, Indian languages; *religion* Roman Catholic 97%.

Honecker Erich 1912–1994. German communist politician, in power in East Germany 1973–89, elected chair of the council of state (head of state) 1976. He was a loyal ally of the USSR. In Oct 1989, following prodemocracy demonstrations, he was replaced as leader of the Socialist Unity Party (SED) and head of state by Egon Krenz and was expelled from the Communist Party.

honey sweet syrup produced by honey ▷bees from the nectar of flowers. It is stored in honeycombs and made in excess of their needs as food for the winter. Honey comprises various sugars, mainly laevulose and dextrose, with enzymes, colouring matter, acids, and pollen grains. It has antibacterial properties and was widely used in ancient Egypt, Greece, and Rome as a wound salve. It is still popular for sore throats, in hot drinks or in lozenges.

Hong Kong British crown colony SE of China, in the South China Sea, comprising Hong Kong Island; the Kowloon Peninsula; many other islands, of which the largest is Lantau; and the mainland New Territories. It is due to revert to Chinese control 1997; *area* 1,070 sq km/ 413 sq mi; *capital* Victoria (Hong Kong City); *features* one of the world's finest natural harbours; a world financial centre, its stock market has four exchanges; *population* (1986) 5,431,000; 57% Hong Kong Chinese, most of the remainder refugees from the mainland; *languages* English, Chinese; *religions* Confucianist, Buddhist, Taoist, with Muslim and Christian minorities.

Honiara port and capital of the Solomon Islands, on the northwest coast of Guadalcanal Island, on the river Mataniko; population (1985) 26,000.

Honolulu capital city and port of Hawaii, on the south coast of Oahu; population (1990) 365,300. It is a holiday resort, noted for its beauty and tropical vegetation, with some industry.

Honshu principal island of Japan. It lies between Hokkaido to the NE and Kyushu to the SW; area 231,100 sq km/ 89,205 sq mi, including 382 smaller islands; population (1990) 99,254,200. A chain of volcanic mountains runs along the island, which is subject to frequent earthquakes. The main cities are Tokyo, Yokohama, Osaka, Kobe, Nagoya, and Hiroshima.

Hooke Robert 1635–1703. English scientist and inventor, originator of *Hooke's law*, and considered the foremost mechanic of his time. His inventions included a telegraph system, the spirit level, marine barometer, and sea gauge. He coined the term 'cell' in biology.

Hooke's law law stating that the deformation of a body is proportional to the magnitude of the deforming force, provided that the body's elastic limit is not exceeded. If the elastic limit is not reached, the body will return to its original size once the force is removed. The law was discovered by Robert Hooke 1676.

Hoover J(ohn) Edgar 1895–1972. US director of the Federal Bureau of Investigation (FBI) from 1924. He built up a powerful network for the detection of organized crime. His drive against alleged communist activities after World War II, and his opposition to the

Kennedy administration and others brought much criticism over abuse of power.

Hopkins Gerard Manley 1844–1889. English poet and Jesuit priest. His work, which is marked by its originality of diction and rhythm and includes 'The Wreck of the Deutschland' and 'The Windhover', published posthumously 1918. His poetry is profoundly religious and records his struggle to gain faith and peace, but also shows freshness of feeling and delight in nature.

Hopper Edward 1882–1967. US painter and etcher. He was one of the foremost American Realists. His views of life in New England and New York in the 1930s and 1940s, painted in rich, dark colours, convey a brooding sense of emptiness and solitude, as in *Nighthawks* 1942 (Art Institute, Chicago).

hops female fruit-heads of the hop plant *Humulus lupulus*, family Cannabiaceae; these are dried and used as a tonic and in flavouring beer. In designated areas in Europe, no male hops may be grown, since seedless hops produced by the unpollinated female plant contain a greater proportion of the alpha acid that gives beer its bitter taste.

Horace 65–8 BC. Roman lyric poet and satirist. He became a leading poet under the patronage of Emperor Augustus. His works include *Satires* 35–30 BC; the four books of *Odes*, about 25–24 BC; *Epistles*, a series of verse letters; and an influential critical work, *Ars poetica*. They are distinguished by their style, wit, discretion, and patriotism.

hormone product of the ◊endocrine glands, concerned with control of body functions. The major glands are the thyroid, parathyroid, pituitary, adrenal, pancreas, ovary, and testis. Hormones bring about changes in the functions of various organs according to the body's requirements. The hypothalamus, which adjoins the pituitary gland, at the base of the brain, is a control centre for overall coordination of hormone secretion; the thyroid hormones determine the rate of general body chemistry; the adrenal hormones prepare the organism during stress for 'fight or flight'; and the sexual hormones such as oestrogen govern reproductive functions.

hormone-replacement therapy (HRT) use of ◊oestrogen and progesterone to help limit the unpleasant effects of the menopause in women. The treatment was first used in the 1970s.

horse hoofed, odd-toed, grazing mammal *Equus caballus* of the family Equidae, which also includes zebras and asses. The many breeds of domestic horse of Euro-Asian origin range in colour from white to grey, brown, and black. The yellow-brown Mongolian wild horse or Przewalski's horse *E. przewalskii*, named after its Polish 'discoverer' about 1880, is the only surviving species of wild horse.

horse racing sport of racing mounted or driven horses. Two forms in Britain are *flat racing*, for thoroughbred horses over a flat course, and *National Hunt racing*, in which the horses have to clear obstacles.

horticulture art and science of growing flowers, fruit, and vegetables. Horticulture is practised in gardens and orchards, along with millions of acres of land devoted to vegetable farming. Some areas, like California, have specialized in horticulture because they have the mild climate and light fertile soil most suited to these crops.

housefly fly of the genus *Musca*, found in and around dwellings, especially *M. domestica*, a common worldwide species. Houseflies are grey and have mouthparts adapted for drinking liquids and sucking moisture from food and manure.

House of Commons lower chamber of the UK ◊Parliament.

House of Lords upper chamber of the UK ◊Parliament.

House of Representatives lower house of the US ◊Congress, with 435 members elected at regular two-year intervals, every even year, in Nov.

Houston port in Texas, USA; linked by canal to the Gulf of Mexico; population (1990) 1,630,600. It is a major centre of the petroleum industry and of finance and commerce. It is also one of the busiest US ports.

hovercraft vehicle that rides on a cushion of high-pressure air, free from all contact with the surface beneath, invented by British engineer Christopher Cockerell 1959. Hovercraft need a smooth terrain when operating overland and are best adapted to use on waterways. They are useful in places where harbours have not been established.

Howard Catherine *c.* 1520–1542. Queen consort of ◊Henry VIII of England from 1540. In 1541 the archbishop of Canterbury, Thomas Cranmer, accused her of being unchaste before marriage to Henry and she was beheaded 1542 after Cranmer made further charges of adultery.

Howe Geoffrey 1926– . British Conservative politician. Under Edward Heath he was solicitor general 1970–72 and minister for trade 1972–74; as chancellor of the Exchequer 1979–83 under Margaret Thatcher, his monetarist policy reduced inflation at the cost of a rise in unemployment. He became foreign secretary 1983, and deputy prime minister and leader of the House of Commons 1989. He resigned 1990 in protest at Thatcher's opposition to greater integration in Europe.

Hubble Edwin Powell 1889–1953. US astronomer who discovered the existence of other ◊galaxies outside our own, and classified them according to their shape. His theory that the universe is expanding is now generally accepted.

Hubble Space Telescope telescope placed into orbit around the Earth, at an altitude of 610 km/380 mi, by the space shuttle *Discovery* in April 1990. The telescope's position in space means that light from distant galaxies is not obscured by the atmosphere, and it therefore performs at least ten times better than any ground-based instrument.

Hudson river of the NE USA; length 485 km/300 mi. It rises in the Adirondack Mountains and flows S, emptying into a bay of the Atlantic Ocean at New York City.

Hudson Henry *c.* 1565–*c.* 1611. English explorer. He made two unsuccessful attempts to find the Northeast Passage to China 1607–1608. In Sept 1609, commissioned by the Dutch East India Company, he reached New York Bay and sailed 240 km/150 mi up the river that now bears his name. In 1610, he sailed from London in the *Discovery* and entered what is now the Hudson Strait. He was turned adrift by a mutinous crew in what is now Hudson Bay.

Hudson Bay inland sea of NE Canada, linked with the Atlantic Ocean by *Hudson Strait* and with the Arctic Ocean by Foxe Channel; area 1,233,000 sq km/ 476,000 sq mi. It is named after Henry Hudson, who reached it 1610.

Hudson's Bay Company chartered company founded by Prince Rupert 1670 to trade in furs with North American Indians. In 1783 the rival North West Company was formed, but in 1851 this became amalgamated with the Hudson's Bay Company. It is still Canada's biggest fur company, but today also sells general merchandise through department stores and has oil and natural gas interests.

Hughes Ted 1930– . English poet, poet laureate from 1984. His work includes *The Hawk in the Rain* 1957, *Lupercal* 1960, *Wodwo* 1967, and *River* 1983, and is characterized by its harsh portrayal of the crueller aspects of nature. In 1956 he married the poet Sylvia ▷Plath.

Hugo Victor (Marie) 1802–1885. French poet, novelist, and dramatist. The *Odes et poésies diverses* appeared 1822, and his verse play *Hernani* 1830 established him as the leader of French Romanticism. More volumes of verse followed between his series of dramatic novels, which included *Notre-Dame de Paris* 1831, later filmed as *The Hunchback of Notre Dame* 1924, 1939, and *Les Misérables* 1862, adapted as a musical 1980.

Huguenot French Protestant in the 16th century; the term referred mainly to Calvinists. Severely persecuted under Francis I and Henry II, the Huguenots survived both an attempt to exterminate them (the *Massacre of St Bartholomew* 24 Aug 1572) and the religious wars of the next 30 years. In 1598 Henry IV (himself formerly a Huguenot) granted them toleration under the *Edict of Nantes*. Louis XIV revoked the edict 1685, attempting their forcible conversion, and 400,000 emigrated.

Hui member of one of the largest minority ethnic groups in China, numbering about 25 million. Members of the Hui live all over China, but are concentrated in the northern central region. They have been Muslims since the 10th century, for which they have suffered persecution both before and since the Communist revolution.

Hull officially *Kingston upon Hull* city and port on the north bank of the Humber estuary, England, where the river Hull flows into it, England; population (1991) 254,100. It is linked with the south bank of the estuary by the Humber Bridge.

Human Genome Project research scheme, begun 1988, to map the complete nucleotide sequence of human ▷DNA. There are approximately 80,000 different ▷genes in the human genome, and one gene may contain more than 2 million nucleotides. The knowledge gained is expected to help prevent or treat many crippling and lethal diseases, but there are potential ethical problems associated with knowledge of an individual's genetic make-up, and fears that it may lead to misuses in ▷genetic engineering.

humanism belief in the high potential of human nature rather than in religious or transcendental values. Humanism culminated as a cultural and literary force in 16th-century Renaissance Europe in line with the period's enthusiasm for classical literature and art, growing individualism, and the ideal of the all-round male who should be statesman and poet, scholar and warrior. ⊳Erasmus is a great exemplar of Renaissance humanism.

Human Rights, Universal Declaration of charter of civil and political rights drawn up by the United Nations 1948. They include the right to life, liberty, education, and equality before the law; to freedom of movement, religion, association, and information; and to a nationality. Under the European Convention of Human Rights 1950, the *European Commission of Human Rights* investigates complaints by states or individuals; its findings are examined by the *European Court of Human Rights*.

human species, origins of evolution of humans from ancestral ⊳primates. The African apes (gorilla and chimpanzee) are shown by anatomical and molecular comparisons to be the closest living relatives of humans. Humans are distinguished from apes by the size of their brain and jaw, their bipedalism, and their elaborate culture. Molecular studies put the date of the split between the human and African ape lines at 5–10 million years ago. There are only fragmentary remains of ape and *hominid* (of the human group) fossils from this period; the oldest known hominids, found in Ethiopia and Tanzania, date from 3.5 to 4 million years ago. These creatures are known as *Australopithecus afarensis*, and they walked upright. They were either direct ancestors or an offshoot of the line that led to modern humans. They may have been the ancestors of *Homo habilis* (considered by some to be a species of *Australopithecus*), who appeared about a million years later, had slightly larger bodies and brains, and were probably the first to use stone tools. *A. robustus* and *A. africanus*

also lived in Africa at the same time, but these are not generally considered to be our ancestors.

Humberside county of NE England, created 1974 out of N Lincolnshire and parts of the East and West Ridings of Yorkshire; *area* 3,510 sq km/1,355 sq mi; *towns and cities* Beverley (administrative headquarters), Grimsby, Scunthorpe, Goole, Cleethorpes; *features* Humber Bridge (1981), over the Humber Estuary, the longest single-span suspension bridge in the world; Isle of Axholme, where medieval open-field strip farming is still practised; *population* (1991) 858,000.

Hume David 1711–1776. Scottish philosopher. *A Treatise of Human Nature* 1739–40 is a central text of British empiricism. Hume denies the possibility of going beyond the subjective experiences of 'ideas' and 'impressions'. The effect of this position is to invalidate metaphysics.

humidity the quantity of water vapour in a given volume of the atmosphere (absolute humidity), or the ratio of the amount of water vapour in the atmosphere to the saturation value at the same temperature (relative humidity). At dew point the relative humidity is 100% and the air is said to be saturated. Condensation (the conversion of vapour to liquid) may then occur. Relative humidity is measured by various types of hygrometer.

hummingbird any of various birds of the family Trochilidae, found in the Americas. The name is derived from the sound produced by the rapid vibration of their wings. Hummingbirds are brilliantly coloured, and have long, needle-like bills and tongues to obtain nectar from flowers and capture insects. They are the only birds able to fly backwards. The Cuban bee hummingbird *Mellisuga helenae*, the world's smallest bird, is 5.5 cm/2 in long, and weighs less than 2.5 g/ 0.1 oz.

Hun member of any of a number of nomad Mongol peoples, first recorded historically in the 2nd century BC, raiding across the Great Wall into China. They entered Europe about AD 372, settled in what is now Hungary, and imposed their supremacy on the Ostrogoths and other Germanic peoples. Under Attila they attacked the Byzantine Empire, invaded Gaul, and threatened Rome. The *White Huns*, or Ephthalites, a kindred people, raided Persia and N India in the 5th and 6th centuries.

Hundred Years' War series of conflicts between England and France 1337–1453. Its origins lay with the English kings' possession of Gascony (SW France), which the French kings claimed as their fief, and with trade rivalries over Flanders. The conflicts were caused by fears of French intervention in Scotland, which the English were trying to subdue, and by the claim of England's Edward III (through his mother Isabel, daughter of Charles IV) to the crown of France.

Hungary Republic of (*Magyar Köztársaság*); *area* 93,032 sq km/35,910 sq mi; *capital* Budapest; *environment* an estimated 35%–40% of the population live in areas with officially 'inadmissible' air and water pollution. In Budapest lead levels have reached 30 times the maximum international standards *features* more than 500 thermal springs; Hortobágy National Park; Tokay wine area; *political system* emergent democratic republic; *population* (1993) 10,310,000 (Magyar 92%, Romany 3%, German 2.5%; Hungarian minority in Romania has caused some friction between the two countries); growth rate 0.2% p.a.; *language* Hungarian (or Magyar), one of the few languages of Europe with non-Indo-European origins; it is grouped with Finnish, Estonian, and others in the Finno-Ugric family; *religions* Roman Catholic 67% other Christian denominations 25%.

Hurd Douglas (Richard) 1930– . English Conservative politician, home secretary 1985–89, and foreign secretary from 1989. In Nov 1990 he was an unsuccessful candidate in the Tory leadership contest following Margaret Thatcher's unexpected resignation. He retained his post as foreign secretary under John Major.

hurricane revolving storm in tropical regions, called *typhoon* in the N Pacific. It originates at latitudes between 5° and 20° N or S of the equator, when the surface temperature of the ocean is above 27°C/80°F. A central calm area, called the eye, is surrounded by inwardly spiralling winds (anticlockwise in the northern hemisphere) of up to 320 kph/200 mph. A hurricane is accompanied by lightning and torrential rain, and can cause extensive damage. In meteorology, a hurricane is a wind of force 12 or more on the ⊳Beaufort scale. The most intense hurricane recorded in the Caribbean/Atlantic sector was Hurricane Gilbert in 1988, with sustained winds of 280 kph/175 mph and gusts of over 320 kph/200 mph.

Hussein Saddam 1937– . Iraqi politician, in power from 1968, president from 1979. He presided over the Iran-Iraq war 1980–88, and harshly repressed Kurdish rebels in N Iraq. He annexed Kuwait 1990 but was driven out by a

US-dominated coalition army Feb 1991. Savage repression of Kurds and Shi'ites led to charges of genocide and the United Nations established 'safe havens' in the N and 'no-fly zones' in the S. Infringement of the latter led to US air strikes Jan 1993.

Hussein ibn Talal 1935– . King of Jordan from 1952. By 1967 he had lost all his kingdom west of the river Jordan in the Arab-Israeli Wars, and in 1970 suppressed the ▷Palestine Liberation Organization acting as a guerrilla force against his rule on the remaining East Bank territories. In 1994 signed a peace agreement with Israel, ending a 46-year-old 'state of war' between the two countries.

Huston John 1906–1987. US film director, screenwriter, and actor. An impulsive and individualistic filmmaker, he often dealt with the themes of greed, treachery in human relationships, and the loner. His works as a director include *The Maltese Falcon* 1941 (his debut), *The Treasure of the Sierra Madre* 1948 (Academy Award), *The African Queen* 1951, and his last, *The Dead* 1987.

Hutu member of the majority ethnic group of both Burundi and Rwanda. Traditionally dominated by the Tutsi minority, there is a long history of violent conflict between the two groups. The 1994 civil in Rwanda, where the balance of power is more even, saw the massacre of several hundred thousand Tutsi by Hutu death squads. The Hutu language belongs to the Bantu branch of the Niger-Congo family.

Huxley Aldous (Leonard) 1894–1963. English writer. From the disillusionment and satirical eloquence of *Crome Yellow* 1921, *Antic Hay* 1923, and *Point*

Counter Point 1928, Huxley developed towards the Utopianism exemplified in *Island* 1962. The science fiction novel *Brave New World* 1932 shows human beings mass-produced in laboratories and rendered incapable of freedom by indoctrination and drugs.

Huygens Christiaan 1629–1695. Dutch mathematical physicist and astronomer who proposed the wave theory of light. He developed the pendulum clock, discovered polarization, and observed Saturn's rings.

hybrid offspring from a cross between individuals of two different species, or two inbred lines within a species. In most cases, hybrids between species are infertile and unable to reproduce sexually. In plants, however, doubling of the chromosomes can restore the fertility of such hybrids.

Hydra in Greek mythology, a huge monster with nine heads. If one were cut off, two would grow in its place. One of the 12 labours of ▷Heracles was to kill it.

hydra in zoology, any member of the family Hydridae, or freshwater polyps, of the phylum Cnidaria (coelenterates). The body is a double-layered tube (with six to ten hollow tentacles around the mouth), 1.25 cm/0.5 in long when extended, but capable of contracting to a small knob. Usually fixed to waterweed, hydras feed on minute animals that are caught and paralysed by stinging cells on the tentacles.

hydraulics field of study concerned with utilizing the properties of water and other liquids, in particular the way they flow and transmit pressure, and with the application of these properties in engineering. It applies the principles of hydrostatics and hydrodynamics.

hydrocarbon any of a class of chemical compounds containing only hydrogen and carbon (for example, the alkanes and alkenes). Hydrocarbons are obtained industrially principally from petroleum and coal tar.

hydroelectric power (HEP) electricity generated by moving water. In a typical HEP scheme, water stored in a reservoir, often created by damming a river, is piped into water ⊳turbines, coupled to electricity generators. In pumped storage plants, water flowing through the turbines is recycled. A tidal power station exploits the rise and fall of the tides. About one-fifth of the world's electricity comes from HEP.

hydrogen colourless, odourless, gaseous, nonmetallic element, symbol H, atomic number 1, relative atomic mass 1.00797. It is the lightest of all the elements and occurs on Earth chiefly in combination with oxygen as water. Hydrogen is the most abundant element in the universe, where it accounts for 93% of the total number of atoms and 76% of the total mass. It is a component of most stars, including the Sun, whose heat and light are produced through the nuclear-fusion process that converts hydrogen into helium. When subjected to a pressure 500,000 times greater than that of the Earth's atmosphere, hydrogen becomes a solid with metallic properties, as in one of the inner zones of Jupiter. Hydrogen's common and industrial uses include the hardening of oils and fats by hydrogenation, the creation of high-temperature flames for welding, and as rocket fuel. It has been proposed as a fuel for road vehicles.

hydrogen bomb bomb that works on the principle of nuclear ⊳fusion. Large-scale explosion results from the thermonuclear release of energy when hydrogen nuclei are fused to form helium nuclei. The first hydrogen bomb was exploded at Eniwetok Atoll in the Pacific Ocean by the USA 1952.

hydrogencarbonate or *bicarbonate* compound containing the ion HCO_3-, an acid salt of carbonic acid (solution of carbon dioxide in water). When heated or treated with dilute acids, it gives off carbon dioxide. The most important compounds are ⊳sodium hydrogencarbonate (bicarbonate of soda), and calcium hydrogencarbonate.

hydroponics cultivation of plants without soil, using specially prepared solutions of mineral salts. Beginning in the 1930s, large crops were grown by hydroponic methods, at first in California but since then in many other parts of the world.

hyena any of three species of carnivorous mammals in the family Hyaenidae, living in Africa and Asia. Hyenas have extremely powerful jaws. They are scavengers, although they will also attack and kill live prey.

hypertension abnormally high ⊳blood pressure due to a variety of causes, leading to excessive contraction of the smooth muscle cells of the walls of the arteries. It increases the risk of kidney disease, stroke, and heart attack.

hypertext system for viewing information (both text and pictures) on a computer screen in such a way that related items of information can easily be reached. For example, the program might display a map of a country; if the user clicks (with a mouse) on a particular city, the program will display some information about that city.

hypnosis artificially induced state of relaxation in which suggestibility is heightened. The subject may carry out orders after being awakened, and may be made insensitive to pain. Hypnosis is sometimes used to treat addictions to tobacco or overeating, or to assist amnesia victims.

hypotenuse the longest side of a right-angled triangle, opposite the right angle. It is of particular application in Pythagoras's theorem (the square of the hypotenuse equals the sum of the squares of the other two sides), and in trigonometry where the ratios ▷sine and ▷cosine are defined as the ratios opposite/hypotenuse and adjacent/hypotenuse respectively.

hypothermia condition in which the deep (core) temperature of the body falls below 35°C. If it is not discovered, coma and death ensue. Most at risk are the aged and babies (particularly if premature).

hysterectomy surgical removal of all or part of the uterus (womb). The operation is performed to treat fibroids (benign tumours growing in the uterus) or cancer; also to relieve heavy menstrual bleeding. A woman who has had a hysterectomy will no longer menstruate and cannot bear children.

I

Ibiza one of the ⬦Balearic Islands, a popular tourist resort; area 596 sq km/ 230 sq mi; population (1986) 45,000. The capital and port, also called Ibiza, has a cathedral.

Ibsen Henrik (Johan) 1828–1906. Norwegian dramatist and poet. His realistic and often controversial plays revolutionized European theatre. Driven into exile 1864–91 by opposition to the satirical *Love's Comedy* 1862, he wrote the verse dramas *Brand* 1866 and *Peer Gynt* 1867, followed by realistic plays dealing with social issues, including *Pillars of Society* 1877, *A Doll's House* 1879, *Ghosts* 1881, *An Enemy of the People* 1882, and *Hedda Gabler* 1891.

Icarus in Greek mythology, the son of Daedalus, who with his father escaped from the labyrinth in Crete by making wings of feathers fastened with wax. Icarus plunged to his death when he flew too near the Sun and the wax melted.

ice age any period of glaciation occurring in the Earth's history, but particularly that in the Pleistocene epoch, immediately preceding historic times. On the North American continent, ⬦glaciers reached as far south as the Great Lakes, and an ice sheet spread over N Europe, leaving its remains as far south as Switzerland.

ice hockey game played on ice between two teams of six, developed in Canada from hockey or bandy. A rubber disc (puck) is used in place of a ball. Players wear skates and protective clothing.

Iceland Republic of (*Lýðveldið Ísland*); *area* 103,000 sq km/39,758 sq mi; *capital* Reykjavik; *features* Thingvellir, where the oldest parliament in the world first met AD 930; shallow lake Mývatn (38 sq km/15 sq mi) in N; *political system* democratic republic; *population* (1993 est) 270,000; growth rate 0.8% p.a.; *language* Icelandic, the most archaic Scandinavian language; *religion* Evangelical Lutheran 95%.

Iceni ancient people of E England, who revolted against occupying Romans under ⬦Boudicca.

ice-skating see ⬦skating.

icon in the Greek or Eastern Orthodox church, a representation of Jesus, Mary, an angel, or a saint, in painting, low relief, or mosaic. The painted icons were traditionally done on wood. After the 17th century and mainly in Russia, a *riza*, or gold and silver covering that leaves only the face and hands visible (and may be adorned with jewels presented by the faithful in thanksgiving), was often added as protection.

icon in computing, a small picture on the computer screen, or ▷VDU, representing an object or function that the user may manipulate or otherwise use. It is a feature of ▷graphical user interface (GUI) systems. Icons make computers easier to use by allowing the user to point to and click with a ▷mouse on pictures, rather than type commands.

Idaho state of northwestern USA; *area* 216,500 sq km/83,569 sq mi; *capital* Boise; *features* Rocky Mountains; Snake River, which runs through Hell's Canyon (2,330 m/7,647 ft), the deepest in North America; *population* (1990) 1,006,700

igneous rock rock formed from cooling magma or lava, and solidifying from a molten state. Igneous rocks are classified according to their crystal size, texture, chemical composition, or method of formation. They are largely composed of silica (SiO_2) and they are classified by their silica content into groups: acid (over 66% silica), intermediate (55%–66%), basic (45%–55%), and ultrabasic (under 45%).

Ile-de-France region of N France; area 12,000 sq km/4,632 sq mi; population (1986) 10,251,000. It includes the French capital, Paris, and the towns of Versailles, Sèvres, and St-Cloud and comprises the *départements* of Essonne, Val-de-Marne, Val d'Oise, Ville de Paris, Seine-et- Marne, Hauts- de-Seine, Seine-Saint-Denis, and Yvelines. From here the early French kings extended their authority over the whole country.

Iliad Greek epic poem, product of an oral tradition; it was possibly written down by 700 BC and is attributed to ▷Homer. The title is derived from Ilion, the Greek name for Troy. Its subject is the wrath of the Greek hero Achilles at the loss of his concubine Briseis, and at the death of his friend Patroclus, during the Greek siege of Troy. The poems ends with the death of the Trojan hero Hector at the hands of Achilles.

Iliescu Ion 1930– . Romanian president from 1990. A former member of the Romanian Communist Party (PCR) and of Nicolae Ceauşescu's government, Iliescu swept into power on Ceauşescu's fall as head of the National Salvation Front.

Illinois midwest state of the USA; *area* 146,100 sq km/56,395 sq mi; *capital* Springfield; *features* Lake Michigan; rivers: Mississippi, Illinois, Ohio, Rock; the Art Institute and Field Museum, Chicago; *population* (1990) 11,430,600;

Illyria ancient name for the eastern coastal region on the Adriatic, N of the Gulf of Corinth, conquered by Philip of Macedon. It became a Roman province AD 9. The Albanians are the survivors of its ancient peoples.

imago sexually mature stage of an ▷insect.

IMF abbreviation for ▷*International Monetary Fund.*

Immaculate Conception in the Roman Catholic Church, the belief that the Virgin Mary was, by a special act of grace, preserved free from original sin from the moment she was conceived. This article of the Catholic faith was for centuries the subject of heated controversy, opposed by St Thomas Aquinas and other theologians, but generally accepted from about the 16th century. It became a dogma in 1854 under Pope Pius IX.

immunity the protection that organisms have against foreign microorganisms, such as bacteria and viruses, and against cancerous cells (see ♢cancer). The cells that provide this protection are called white blood cells, or leucocytes, and make up the immune system. They include neutrophils and macrophages, which can engulf invading organisms and other unwanted material, and natural killer cells that destroy cells infected by viruses and cancerous cells. Some of the most important immune cells are the B cells and T cells. Immune cells coordinate their activities by means of chemical messengers or lymphokines, including the antiviral messenger ♢interferon. The lymph nodes play a major role in organizing the immune response. *Immunization* confers immunity to infectious disease by artificial methods. The most widely used technique is vaccination.

Impressionism movement in painting that originated in France in the 1860s and dominated European and North American painting in the late 19th century. The Impressionists wanted to depict real life, to paint straight from nature, and to capture the changing effects of light. The term was first used abusively to describe Monet's painting *Impression: Sunrise* 1872 (Musée Marmottan, Paris); other Impressionists were Renoir and Sisley, and the style was adopted for periods by Cézanne, Manet, Degas, and others.

Inca member of an ancient Peruvian civilization of Quechua-speaking Indians that began in the Andean highlands about 1200; by the time of the Spanish Conquest in the 1530s, the Inca ruled from Ecuador in the north to Chile in the south.

incarnation assumption of living form (plant, animal, human) by a deity, for example the gods of Greece and Rome, Hinduism, and Christianity (Jesus as the second person of the Trinity).

incest sexual intercourse between persons thought to be too closely related to marry; the exact relationships that fall under the incest taboo vary widely from society to society. A biological explanation for the incest taboo is based on the necessity to avoid inbreeding.

Independence Day public holiday in the USA, commemorating the adoption of the ♢Declaration of Independence 4 July 1776.

India Republic of (Hindi *Bharat*); *area* 3,166,829 sq km/1,222,396 sq mi; *capital* Delhi; *environment* the controversial Narmada Valley Project is the world's largest combined hydroelectric irrigation scheme. In addition to displacing a million people, the damming of the holy Narmada River will submerge large areas of forest and farmland and create problems of waterlogging and salinization; *features* Taj Mahal monument; Golden Temple, Amritsar; archaeological sites and cave paintings (Ajanta); world's second most populous country; *political system* liberal democratic federal republic; *population* (1993 est) 903,000,000 (920 women to every 1,000 men); growth rate 2.0% p.a.; *languages* Hindi (widely spoken in N India), English, and 14 other official languages: Assamese, Bengali, Gujarati, Kannada, Kashmiri, Malayalam, Marathi, Oriya, Punjabi, Sanskrit, Sindhi, Tamil, Telugu, Urdu; *religions* Hindu 80%, Sunni Muslim 10%, Christian 2.5%, Sikh 2%.

Indiana state of the midwest USA; *area* 93,700 sq km/36,168 sq mi; *capital* Indianapolis; *features* Wyandotte Cavern; Indiana Dunes National Lakeshore; Lincoln Boyhood National Memorial; *population* (1990) 5,544,200.

Indianapolis capital and largest city of Indiana, on the White River; population (1990) 742,000. It is an industrial centre and venue of the 'Indianapolis 500' car race.

Indian languages traditionally, the languages of the subcontinent of India; since 1947, the languages of the Republic of India. These number some 200, depending on whether a variety is classified as a language or a dialect. They fall into five main groups, the two most widespread of which are the Indo-European languages (mainly in the north) and the Dravidian languages (mainly in the south).

Indian Mutiny or *Sepoy Rebellion* or *Mutiny* revolt 1857–58 of Indian soldiers (Sepoys) against the British in India. The uprising was confined to the north, from Bengal to the Punjab, and central India. It led to the end of rule by the British ▷East India Company and its replacement by direct British crown administration.

Indian Ocean ocean between Africa and Australia, with India to the N, and the southern boundary being an arbitrary line from Cape Agulhas to S Tasmania; area 73,500,000 sq km/28,371,000 sq mi; average depth 3,872 m/12,708 ft. The greatest depth is the Java Trench 7,725 m/25,353 ft.

indigo violet-blue vegetable dye obtained from plants of the genus *Indigofera*, family Leguminosae, but now replaced by a synthetic product. It was once a major export crop of India.

Indo-European languages family of languages that includes some of the world's major classical languages (Sanskrit and Pali in India, Zend Avestan in Iran, Greek and Latin in Europe), as well as several of the most widely spoken languages (English worldwide; Spanish in Iberia, Latin America, and elsewhere; and the Hindi group of languages in N India).

Indonesia Republic of (*Republik Indonesia*); *area* 1,919,443 sq km/740,905 sq mi; *capital* Jakarta; *environment* comparison of primary forest and 30-year-old secondary forest has shown that logging in Kalimantan has led to a 20% decline in tree species; *political system* authoritarian nationalist republic; *population* (1993) 187,800,000 (including 300 ethnic groups); growth rate 2% p.a.; *languages* Bahasa Indonesia (official), closely related to Malay; there are 583 regional languages and dialects; Javanese is the most widely spoken local language.

inductance in physics, a measure of the capability of an electronic circuit or circuit component to form a magnetic field or store magnetic energy when carrying a current. Its symbol is L, and its unit of measure is the henry.

inductor device included in an electrical circuit because of its inductance.

indulgence in the Roman Catholic church, the total or partial remission of temporal punishment for sins which remain to be expiated after penitence and confession have secured exemption from eternal punishment. The doctrine began as the commutation of church penances in exchange for suitable works of charity or money gifts to the church, and became a great source of church revenue, rousing Luther in 1517 to initiate the Reformation. The Council of Trent 1563 recommended moderate retention of indulgences, and they continue, notably in 'Holy Years'.

Industrial Revolution the sudden acceleration of technical and economic development that began in Britain in the second half of the 18th century. The traditional agrarian economy was replaced by one dominated by machinery and manufacturing, made possible through technical advances such as the steam engine. This transferred the balance of political power from the landowner to the industrial capitalist and created an urban working class. From 1830 to the early 20th century, the Industrial Revolution spread throughout Europe and the USA and to Japan and the various colonial empires.

industrial tribunal independent panel that rules on disputes between employers and employees or trade unions relating to statutory terms and conditions of employment. Employment issues brought before it include unfair dismissal, redundancy, equal opportunities, and discrimination at work. The panel is made up of a lawyer, a union representative, and a management representative.

industry the extraction and conversion of raw materials, the manufacture of goods, and the provision of services. Industry can be either low technology, unspecialized, and labour-intensive, as in Third World countries, or highly automated, mechanized, and specialized, using advanced technology, as in the industrialized countries. Major trends in industrial activity 1960–90 were the growth of electronic, robotic,

and microelectronic technologies, the expansion of the offshore oil industry, and the prominence of Japan and other Pacific-region countries in manufacturing and distributing electronics, computers, and motor vehicles.

Indus Valley civilization one of the four earliest ancient civilizations of the Old World (the other three being the ◊Sumerian civilization 3500 BC; ◊Egypt 3000 BC; and ◊China 2200 BC), developing in the NW of the Indian subcontinent about 2500 BC.

inert gas or *noble gas* any of a group of six elements (helium, neon, argon, krypton, xenon, and radon), so named because they were originally thought not to enter into any chemical reactions. This is now known to be incorrect: in 1962, xenon was made to combine with fluorine, and since then, compounds of argon, krypton, and radon with fluorine and/or oxygen have been described.

inertia in physics, the tendency of an object to remain in a state of rest or uniform motion until an external force is applied, as stated by Isaac Newton's first law of motion (see ◊Newton's laws of motion).

infinity mathematical quantity that is larger than any fixed assignable quantity; symbol ∞. By convention, the result of dividing any number by zero is regarded as infinity.

inflation in economics, a rise in the general level of prices. The many causes include cost-push inflation, which results from rising production costs. *Demand-pull inflation* occurs when overall demand exceeds supply. *Suppressed inflation* occurs in controlled economies and is reflected in rationing, shortages, and black market prices.

Deflation, a fall in the general level of prices, is the reverse of inflation. *Hyperinflation*, inflation of more than 50% in one month, has happened only 15 times this century.

information technology (IT) collective term for the various technologies involved in processing and transmitting information. They include computing, telecommunications, and microelectronics.

infrared radiation invisible electromagnetic radiation of wavelength between about 0.75 micrometres and 1 millimetre – that is, between the limit of the red end of the visible spectrum and the shortest microwaves. All bodies above the absolute zero of temperature absorb and radiate infrared radiation. Infrared radiation is used in medical photography and treatment, and in industry, astronomy, and criminology.

Ingres Jean-Auguste-Dominique 1780–1867. French painter. He was a student of David and a leading exponent of the Neo-Classical style. He studied and worked in Rome about 1807–20, where he began the *Odalisque* series of sensuous female nudes, then went to Florence, and returned to France 1824. His portraits painted in the 1840s–50s are meticulously detailed and highly polished.

Inkatha Freedom Party (IFP) South African political party, representing the nationalist aspirations of the country's largest ethnic group, the Zulus. It was founded as a paramilitary organization 1975 by its leader, Chief Gatsha ⊳Buthelezi. Fighting between Inkatha and the ⊳African National Congress during the early 1990s cost thousands of lives. In April 1994, after an initial violent boycott, Buthelezi agreed to register the IFP in the country's first multiracial elections.

Innsbruck capital of Tirol state, W Austria; population (1981) 117,000. It is a tourist and winter sports centre and a route junction for the Brenner Pass. The 1964 and 1976 Winter Olympics were held here.

Inns of Court four private legal societies in London, England: Lincoln's Inn, Gray's Inn, Inner Temple, and Middle Temple. All barristers (advocates in the English legal system) must belong to one of the Inns of Court. The main function of each Inn is the education, government, and protection of its members. Each is under the administration of a body of Benchers (judges and senior barristers).

inorganic chemistry branch of chemistry dealing with the chemical properties of the elements and their compounds, excluding the more complex covalent compounds of carbon, which are considered in ⊳organic chemistry.

insect any member of the class Insecta among the ⊳arthropods or jointed-legged animals. An insect's body is divided into head, thorax, and abdomen. The head bears a pair of feelers or antennae, and attached to the thorax are three pairs of legs and usually two pairs of wings. The scientific study of insects is termed entomology. More than 1 million species are known, and several thousand new ones are discovered every year. Insects vary in size from 0.02 cm/0.007 in to 35 cm/13.5 in in length. Throughout their history insects have proved remarkably resilient. Of the insect families alive 100 million years ago in the Cretaceous period, 84% are still living (compared with only 20% for four-legged vertebrate families).

insecticide any chemical pesticide used to kill insects. Among the most effective insecticides are synthetic organic chemicals such as ⚪DDT and dieldrin, which are chlorinated hydrocarbons. These chemicals, however, have proved persistent in the environment and are also poisonous to all animal life, including humans, and are consequently banned in many countries.

insectivore any animal whose diet is made up largely or exclusively of insects. In particular, the name is applied to mammals of the order Insectivora, which includes the shrews, hedgehogs, moles, and tenrecs.

insulin protein ⚪hormone, produced by specialized cells in the islets of Langerhans in the pancreas, that regulates the metabolism (rate of activity) of glucose, fats, and proteins. Insulin was discovered by Canadian physician Frederick ⚪Banting, who pioneered its use in treating ⚪diabetes.

integrated circuit (IC), popularly called *silicon chip*, a miniaturized electronic circuit produced on a single crystal, or chip, of a semiconducting material – usually silicon. It may contain many thousands of components and yet measure only 5 mm/0.2 in square and 1 mm/0.04 in thick. The IC is encapsulated within a plastic or ceramic case, and linked via gold wires to metal pins with which it is connected to a printed circuit board and the other components that make up such electronic devices as computers and calculators.

intelligence in military and political affairs, information, often secretly or illegally obtained, about other countries. *Counter-intelligence* is information on the activities of hostile agents. Much intelligence is gained by technical means, such as satellites and the electronic interception of data.

interference in physics, the phenomenon of two or more wave motions interacting and combining to produce a resultant wave of larger or smaller amplitude (depending on whether the combining waves are in or out of phase with each other).

interferon naturally occurring cellular protein that makes up part of the body's defences against viral disease. Three types (alpha, beta, and gamma) are produced by infected cells and enter the bloodstream and uninfected cells, making them immune to virus attack.

internal-combustion engine heat engine in which fuel is burned inside the engine, contrasting with an external combustion engine (such as the steam engine) in which fuel is burned in a separate unit. The ⚪diesel engine and ⚪petrol engine are both internal-combustion engines. Gas ⚪turbines and ⚪jet and ⚪rocket engines are sometimes also considered to be internal-combustion engines because they burn their fuel inside their combustion chambers.

International Court of Justice main judicial organ of the ⚪United Nations, in The Hague, the Netherlands. It hears international law disputes as well as playing an advisory role to UN organs. It was set up by the UN charter 1945 and superseded the World Court. There are 15 judges, each from a different member state.

International Date Line (IDL) imaginary line that approximately follows the 180° line of longitude. The date is put forward a day when crossing the line going west, and back a day when going east. The IDL was chosen at the International Meridian Conference 1884.

International Monetary Fund (IMF) specialized agency of the ▷United Nations, headquarters Washington DC, established 1944 and operational since 1947. It seeks to promote international monetary cooperation and the growth of world trade, and to smooth multilateral payment arrangements among member states. IMF standby loans are available to members in balance-of-payments difficulties usually on the basis that the country must agree to take certain corrective measures.

International Style or *International Modern* architectural style, whose output centred around the 1920s and 1930s, with distinct stylistic qualities: a dominance of geometric, especially rectilinear, forms and an emphasis on asymmetrical composition. An early and influential phase of the Modern Movement, it originated in Western Europe in the 1920s, finding its fullest expression in the 1930s, notably in the USA.

Internet global, on-line computer network connecting governments, companies, universities, and many other networks and users. The service offers ▷*electronic mail*, conferencing and chat services, as well as the ability to access remote computers and send and retrieve files. It began in 1984 and by late 1994 was estimated to have over 40 million users worldwide, with an estimated one million new users joining each month.

Interpol (acronym for *Inter*national Criminal *Pol*ice Organization) agency founded following the Second International Judicial Police Conference 1923 with its headquarters in Vienna, and reconstituted after World War II with its headquarters in Paris.

intestine in vertebrates, the digestive tract from the stomach outlet to the anus. The human *small intestine* is 6 m/20 ft long, 4 cm/1.5 in in diameter, and consists of the duodenum, jejunum, and ileum; the *large intestine* is 1.5 m/5 ft long, 6 cm/2.5 in in diameter, and includes the caecum, colon, and rectum. Both are muscular tubes comprising an inner lining that secretes alkaline digestive juice, a submucous coat containing fine blood vessels and nerves, a muscular coat, and a serous coat covering all, supported by a strong peritoneum, which carries the blood and lymph vessels, and the nerves.

Intifada Palestinian uprising; also the title of the involved *Liberation Army of Palestine*, a loosely organized group of adult and teenage Palestinians active 1987–93 in attacks on armed Israeli troops in the occupied territories of Palestine. Their campaign for self-determination included stone-throwing and petrol bombing.

intrauterine device (IUD) or *coil*, a contraceptive device that is inserted into the womb (uterus). It is a tiny plastic object, sometimes containing copper. By causing a mild inflammation of the lining of the uterus it prevents fertilized eggs from becoming implanted. They are generally very reliable, as long as they stay in place, with a success rate of about 98%.

Inuit people inhabiting the Arctic coasts of North America, the E islands of the

Canadian Arctic, and the ice- free coasts of Greenland. Inuktitut, their language, has about 60,000 speakers; it belongs to the Eskimo-Aleut group. The Inuit object to the name Eskimos ('eaters of raw meat') given them by the Algonquin Indians.

invertebrate animal without a backbone. The invertebrates comprise over 95% of the million or so existing animal species and include sponges, coelenterates, flatworms, nematodes, annelid worms, arthropods, molluscs, echinoderms, and primitive aquatic chordates, such as sea squirts and lancelets.

in vitro fertilization (IVF) ('fertilization in glass') allowing eggs and sperm to unite in a laboratory to form embryos. The embryos produced are then implanted into the womb of the otherwise infertile mother (an extension of artificial insemination). The first baby to be produced by this method was born 1978 in the UK.

iodine greyish-black nonmetallic element, symbol I, atomic number 53, relative atomic mass 126.9044. It is a member of the ◊halogen group. Its crystals give off, when heated, a violet vapour with an irritating odour resembling that of chlorine. It only occurs in combination with other elements. Its salts are known as iodides, which are found in sea water. As a mineral nutrient it is vital to the proper functioning of the thyroid gland, where it occurs in trace amounts as part of the hormone thyroxine. Absence of iodine from the diet leads to ◊goitre. Iodine is used in photography, in medicine as an antiseptic, and in making dyes.

ion atom, or group of atoms, that is either positively charged (cation) or negatively charged (anion), as a result of the loss or gain of electrons during chemical reactions or exposure to certain forms of radiation.

Ionesco Eugène 1912–1994. Romanian-born French dramatist. He was a leading exponent of the Theatre of the Absurd. Most of his plays are in one act and concern the futility of language as a means of communication. These include *La Cantatrice chauve/The Bald Prima Donna* 1950, and *La Leçon/The Lesson* 1951. Later full-length plays include *Rhinocéros* 1958 and *Le Roi se meurt/ Exit the King* 1961.

Ionian member of a Hellenic people from beyond the Black Sea who crossed the Balkans around 1980 BC and invaded Asia Minor. Driven back by the ◊Hittites, they settled all over mainland Greece, later being supplanted by the Achaeans.

ionic bond or *electrovalent bond* bond produced when atoms of one element donate electrons to atoms of another element, forming positively and negatively charged ◊ions respectively. The electrostatic attraction between the oppositely charged ions constitutes the bond. Sodium chloride (Na^+Cl^-) is a typical ionic compound.

ionosphere ionized layer of Earth's outer ◊atmosphere (60–1,000 km/ 38–620 mi) that contains sufficient free electrons to modify the way in which radio waves are propagated, for instance by reflecting them back to Earth. The ionosphere is thought to be produced by absorption of the Sun's ultraviolet radiation.

Iowa state of the midwest USA; *area* 145,800 sq km/56,279 sq mi; *capital* Des Moines; *features* Grant Wood Gallery, Davenport; Herbert Hoover birthplace, library, and museum near West Branch; 'Little Switzerland' region in the NE, overlooking the Mississippi River; *population* (1990) 2,776,800.

IRA abbreviation for ▷Irish Republican Army.

Iran Islamic Republic of (*Jomhori-e-Islami-e- Irân*; until 1935 *Persia*); *area* 1,648,000 sq km/636,128 sq mi; *capital* Tehran; *features* ruins of Persepolis; Mount Demavend 5,670 m/ 18,603 ft; *political system* authoritarian Islamic republic; *population* (1993 est) 61,660,000 (including minorities in Azerbaijan, Baluchistan, Khuzestan/Arabistan, and Kurdistan); growth rate 3.2% p.a.; *languages* Farsi (official), Kurdish, Turkish, Arabic, English, French; *religion* Shi'ite Muslim (official) 92%, Sunni Muslim 5%, Zoroastrian 2%, Jewish, Baha'i, and Christian 1%.

Iraq Republic of (*al Jumhouriya al 'Iraqia*); *area* 434,924 sq km/167,881 sq mi; *capital* Baghdad; *environment* a chemical-weapons plant covering an area of 65 sq km/25 sq mi, situated 80 km/50 mi NW of Baghdad, has been described by the UN as the largest toxic waste dump in the world; *features* reed architecture of the marsh Arabs; ancient sites of Eridu, Babylon, Nineveh, Ur, Ctesiphon; *political system* one-party socialist republic; *population* (1993) 19,410,000 (Arabs 77%, Kurds 19%, Turks 2%); growth rate 3.6% p.a.; *languages* Arabic (official); Kurdish, Assyrian, Armenian; *religion* Shi'ite Muslim 60%, Sunni Muslim 37%, Christian 3%.

Ireland one of the British Isles, lying to the W of Great Britain, from which it is separated by the Irish Sea. It comprises the provinces of Ulster, Leinster, Munster, and Connacht, and is divided into the Republic of ▷Ireland (which occupies the S, centre, and NW of the island) and Northern Ireland (which occupies the NE corner and forms part of the United Kingdom).

Ireland, Northern constituent part of the United Kingdom; *area* 13,460 sq km/5,196 sq mi; *capital* Belfast; *features* Mourne Mountains, Belfast Lough and Lough Neagh; Giant's Causeway; *population* (1991) 1,578,000; *language* English; 5.3% Irish-speaking; *religion* Protestant 51%, Roman Catholic 38%; *government* direct rule from the UK since 1972. Northern Ireland is entitled to send 12 members to the Westminster Parliament.

Ireland, Republic of (*Eire*); *area* 70,282 sq km/27,146 sq mi; *capital* Dublin; *features* Bog of Allen, source of domestic and national power; Macgillicuddy's Reeks, Wicklow Mountains; Lough Corrib, lakes of Killarney; Galway Bay and Aran Islands; *head of state* Mary Robinson from 1990; *head of government* John Bruton from 1994; *political system* democratic republic; *population* (1993 est) 3,600,000; growth rate 0.1% p.a.; *languages* Irish Gaelic and English (both official); *religion* Roman Catholic 94%.

iris in anatomy, the coloured muscular diaphragm that controls the size of the pupil in the vertebrate eye. It contains radial muscle that increases the pupil diameter and circular muscle that constricts the pupil diameter. Both types of muscle respond involuntarily to light intensity.

Irish Gaelic first official language of the Irish Republic, but much less widely used than the second official language, English. See ▷Gaelic.

Irish National Liberation Army (INLA) guerrilla organization committed to the end of British rule in Northern Ireland and the incorporation of Ulster into the Irish Republic. The INLA was a 1974 offshoot of the Irish Republican Army (IRA). Among the INLA's activities was the killing of British politician Airey Neave in 1979. It declared a cease- fire 1994, following similar action by the IRA.

Irish Republican Army (IRA) militant Irish nationalist organization whose aim is to create a united Irish socialist republic. The paramilitary wing of ◊Sinn Féin, it was founded 1919 by Michael Collins (1890–1922) and fought a successful war against Britain 1919–21. Declared illegal 1936, it began a bombing campaign against Britain 1939. Its activities intensified from 1968, as did the civil-rights disorders ('the Troubles') in Northern Ireland. In 1970 a breakaway group in the north became the *Provisional IRA*, and campaigned for the expulsion of the British from Northern Ireland. Peace talks held between Social Democratic Labour Party leader, John ◊Hume, and Sinn Féin leader, Gerry ◊Adams Sept 1993 led to a cessation of the IRA's military activities Sept 1994.

iron hard, malleable and ductile, silver-grey, metallic element, symbol Fe (from Latin *ferrum*), atomic number 26, relative atomic mass 55.847. It is the fourth most abundant element (the second most abundant metal, after aluminium) in the Earth's crust.

Iron Age developmental stage of human technology when weapons and tools were made from iron. Iron was produced in Thailand by about 1600 BC but was considered inferior in strength to bronze until about 1000 when metallurgical techniques improved and the alloy steel was produced by adding carbon during the smelting process.

Iron Curtain in Europe after World War II, the symbolic boundary between capitalist West and communist East during the ◊Cold War. The term was popularized by the UK prime minister Winston Churchill from 1945.

irrigation artificial water supply for dry agricultural areas by means of dams and channels. Drawbacks are that it tends to concentrate salts, ultimately causing soil infertility, and that rich river silt is retained at dams, to the impoverishment of the land and fisheries below them.

Irving Henry. Stage name of John Brodribb 1838–1905. English actor. He established his reputation from 1871, chiefly at the Lyceum Theatre in London, where he became manager 1878. He staged a series of successful Shakespearean productions, including *Romeo and Juliet* 1882, with himself and Ellen Terry (1847–1928) playing the leading roles. He was the first actor to be knighted, 1895.

Isherwood Christopher (William Bradshaw) 1904–1986. English novelist. He lived in Germany 1929–33 just before Hitler's rise to power, a period that inspired *Mr Norris Changes Trains* 1935 and *Goodbye to Berlin* 1939, creating the character of Sally Bowles (the basis of the musical *Cabaret* 1968).

Isis the principal goddess of ancient Egypt. She was the daughter of Geb and Nut (Earth and Sky), and as the sister-wife of Osiris searched for his body after his death at the hands of his brother, Set. Her son Horus then defeated and captured Set, but cut off his mother's head because she would not allow Set to be killed. She was later identified with Hathor. The cult of Isis ultimately spread to Greece and Rome.

Islam religion founded in the Arabian peninsula in the early 7th century AD. It emphasizes the oneness of God, his omnipotence, benificence, and inscrutability. The sacred book is the *Koran* of the prophet ▷Muhammad, the Prophet or Messenger of Allah. There are two main Muslim sects: ▷Sunni and ▷Shi'ite. Other schools include *Sufism*, a mystical movement originating in the 8th century.

Islamabad capital of Pakistan from 1967, in the Potwar district, at the foot of the Margala Hills and immediately NW of Rawalpindi; population (1981) 201,000. The city was designed by Constantinos Doxiadis in the 1960s. The Federal Capital Territory of Islamabad has an area of 907 sq km/350 sq mi and a population (1985) of 379,000.

isobar line drawn on maps and weather charts linking all places with the same atmospheric pressure (usually measured in millibars).

isomer chemical compound having the same molecular composition and mass as another, but with different physical or chemical properties owing to the different structural arrangement of its constituent atoms. For example, the organic compounds butane $(CH_3(CH_2)CH_3)$ and methyl propane $(CH_3CH(-CH_3)CH_3)$ are isomers, each possessing four carbon atoms and ten hydrogen atoms but differing in the way that these are arranged with respect to each other.

isotope one of two or more atoms that have the same atomic number (same number of protons), but which contain a different number of neutrons, thus differing in their atomic masses. They may be stable or radioactive, naturally occurring or synthesized. The term was coined by English chemist Frederick Soddy, pioneer researcher in atomic disintegration.

Israel State of (*Medinat Israel*); *area* 20,800 sq km/8,029 sq mi (as at 1949 armistice); *capital* Jerusalem (not recognized by the United Nations); *features* historic sites: Jerusalem, Bethlehem, Nazareth, Masada, Megiddo, Jericho; caves of the Dead Sea scrolls; *political system* democratic republic; *population* (1993) 5,300,000 (including 750,000 Arab Israeli citizens). Growth rate 1.8% p.a.; *languages* Hebrew and Arabic (official); English, Yiddish, European, and W Asian languages; *religion* Israel is a secular state, but the predominant faith is Judaism 83%; also Sunni Muslim, Christian, and Druse.

Istanbul city and chief seaport of Turkey; population (1990) 6,620,200. Founded as *Byzantium* about 660 BC, it was renamed *Constantinople* AD 330 and was the capital of the ▷Byzantine Empire until captured by the Turks 1453. As *Istamboul* it was capital of the Ottoman Empire until 1922.

Italy Republic of (*Repubblica Italiana*); *area* 301,300 sq km/116,332 sq mi; *capital* Rome; *environment* Milan has the highest recorded level of sulphur-dioxide pollution of any city in the world. The Po River, with pollution ten times higher than officially recommended levels, is estimated to discharge around 250 tonnes of arsenic into the sea each year; *features* continental Europe's only active volcanoes: Vesuvius, Etna, Stromboli; historic towns include Venice, Florence, Siena, Rome; Greek, Roman, Etruscan archaeological sites; *head of state* Oscar Luigi Scalfaro from 1992; *head of government* Lamberto Dini from 1995; *political system* democratic republic; *population* (1993 est) 58,100,000; growth rate 0.1% p.a.; *language* Italian; German, French, Slovene, and Albanian minorities; *religion* Roman Catholic 100% (state religion).

Ivan (IV) the Terrible 1530–1584. Grand duke of Muscovy from 1533; he assumed power 1544 and was crowned as first tsar of Russia 1547. He conquered Kazan 1552, Astrakhan 1556, and Siberia 1581. He reformed the legal code and local administration 1555 and established trade relations with England. In his last years he alternated between debauchery and religious austerities, executing thousands and, in rage, his own son.

IVF abbreviation for ▷*in vitro fertilization.*

ivory the hard white substance of which the teeth and tusks of certain mammals are composed. Among the most valuable are elephants' tusks, which are of unusual hardness and density. Ivory is used in carving and other decorative work, and is so valuable that poachers continue to illegally destroy the remaining wild elephant herds in Africa to obtain it.

Ivory Coast Republic of (*République de la Côte d'Ivoire*); *area* 322,463 sq km/ 124,471 sq mi; *capital* Yamoussoukro; *environment* an estimated 85% of the country's forest has been destroyed by humans; *features* Vridi canal, Kossou dam, Monts du Toura; *political system* emergent democratic republic; *population* (1993 est) 13,500,000; growth rate 3.3% p.a.; *languages* French (official), over 60 native dialects; *religions* animist 65%, Muslim 24%, Christian 11%.

Izetbegović Alija 1925– . Bosnia-Herzegovinan politician, president from 1990. A lifelong opponent of communism, he founded the Party of Democratic Action (PDA) 1990, ousting the communists in the multiparty elections that year. Adopting a moderate stance during the civil war in Bosnia-Herzegovina, he sought an honourable peace for his country in the face of ambitious demands from Serb and Croat political leaders. A former legal adviser, he was imprisoned for 'pan-Islamic activity' 1946–48 and 1983–88.

J

Jackson Glenda 1936– . English actress and politician, Labour member of Parliament from 1992. She has made many stage appearances for the Royal Shakespeare Company, including *Marat/Sade* 1966, Hedda in *Hedda Gabler* 1975, and Cleopatra in *Antony and Cleopatra* 1978. Her films include the Oscar-winning *Women in Love* 1969, *Sunday Bloody Sunday* 1971, and *A Touch of Class* 1973. On television she played Queen Elizabeth I in *Elizabeth R* 1971.

Jacobite in Britain, a supporter of the royal house of Stuart after the deposition of James II in 1688. They include the Scottish Highlanders, who rose unsuccessfully under John Claverhouse (1649–1689) in 1689; and those who rose in Scotland and N England under the leadership of ▷James Edward Stuart, the Old Pretender, in 1715, and followed his son ▷Charles Edward Stuart in an invasion of England that reached Derby in 1745–46. After the defeat at Culloden 1746, Jacobitism disappeared as a political force.

jade semiprecious stone consisting of either jadeite, $NaAlSi_2O_6$ (a pyroxene), or nephrite, $Ca_2(Mg,Fe)_5$-$Si_8O_{22}(OH,F)_2$ (an amphibole), ranging from colourless through shades of green to black according to the iron content. Jade ranks 5.5–6.5 on the Mohs' scale of hardness.

jaguar largest species of ▷cat *Panthera onca* in the Americas, formerly ranging from the southwestern USA to southern South America, but now extinct in most of North America. It can grow up to 2.5 m/8 ft long including the tail. The background colour of the fur varies from creamy white to brown or black, and is covered with black spots. The jaguar is usually solitary.

Jainism ancient Indian religion, sometimes regarded as an offshoot of Hinduism. Jains emphasize the importance of not injuring living beings, and sympathy and compassion for all forms of life. They believe in ▷karma but not in any deity. It is a monastic, ascetic religion. The two main sects are the Digambaras and the Swetambaras. Jainism practises the most extreme form of nonviolence (*ahimsā*) of all Indian sects, and influenced the philosophy of Mahatma Gandhi.

Jaipur capital of Rajasthan, India; population (1981) 1,005,000. It was formerly the capital of the state of Jaipur, which was merged with Rajasthan 1949.

Jakarta or *Djakarta* (formerly until 1949 *Batavia*) capital of Indonesia on the NW coast of Java; population (1980) 6,504,000. A canal links it with its port of Tanjung Priok. Jakarta was founded by Dutch traders 1619.

Jamaica *area* 10,957 sq km/4,230 sq mi; *capital* Kingston; *features* Blue Mountains (so called because of the haze over them) renowned for their coffee; partly undersea ruins of pirate city of Port Royal, destroyed by an earthquake 1692; *political system* constitutional monarchy; *population* (1993 est) 2,523,000 (African 76%, mixed 15%, Chinese, Caucasian, East Indian); growth rate 2.2% p.a.; *languages* English, Jamaican creole; *religions* Protestant 70%, Rastafarian.

James Henry 1843–1916. US novelist. He lived in Europe from 1875 becoming a naturalized British subject 1915. His novels deal with the social, moral, and aesthetic issues arising from the complex relationship of European to American culture. James was increasingly experimental, writing some of the essential works of early Modernism. His major novels include *The Portrait of a Lady* 1881, *The Bostonians* 1886, *What Maisie Knew* 1887, *The Ambassadors* 1903, and *The Golden Bowl* 1904.

James I 1566–1625. King of England from 1603 and Scotland (as *James VI*) from 1567. The son of Mary Queen of Scots and Lord Darnley, he succeeded on his mother's abdication from the Scottish throne, assumed power 1583, established a strong centralized authority, and in 1589 married Anne of Denmark (1574–1619). As successor to Elizabeth I in England, he alienated the Puritans by his High Church views and Parliament by his assertion of ▷divine right. He was generally unpopular because of his favourites, such as the Duke of Buckingham (1592–1628), and his schemes for an alliance with Spain. He was succeeded by his son Charles I.

James II 1633–1701. King of England and Scotland (as *James VII*) from 1685,

second son of Charles I. He succeeded Charles II. He married Anne Hyde 1659 (mother of Mary II and Anne) and Mary of Modena 1673 (mother of James Edward Stuart). He became a Catholic 1671, leading to attempts to exclude him from the succession, to the rebellions of Monmouth and Argyll, and to the Whig and Tory leaders' invitation to William of Orange to take the throne 1688. James fled to France, then led an uprising in Ireland 1689, but after defeat at the Battle of the Boyne 1690 remained in exile in France.

James Edward Stuart 1688–1766. British prince, known as the *Old Pretender* (for the ▷Jacobites, he was James III). Son of James II, he was born at St James's Palace and after the revolution of 1688 was taken to France. He landed in Scotland in 1715 to head a Jacobite rebellion but withdrew through lack of support. In his later years he settled in Rome.

Jammu and Kashmir state of N India; *area* 101,300 sq km/39,102 sq mi; *capital* Jammu (winter); Srinagar (summer); *towns and cities* Leh; *population* (1991) 7,718,700 (Indian-occupied territory).

Janáček Leoš 1854–1928. Czech composer. He became director of the Conservatoire at Brno 1919 and professor at the Prague Conservatoire 1920. His music, highly original and influenced by Moravian folk music, includes arrangements of folk songs, operas (*Jenůfa* 1904, *The Cunning Little Vixen* 1924), and the choral *Glagolitic Mass* 1926.

Janus in Roman mythology, the god of doorways and passageways, patron of the beginning of the day, month, and year, after whom January is named; he is represented as having two faces, one looking forwards and one back. In Roman ritual, the doors of Janus in the Forum were closed when peace was established.

Japan (*Nippon*); *area* 377,535 sq km/145,822 sq mi; *capital* Tokyo; *features* Mount Fuji, Mount Aso (volcanic), Japan Alps, Inland Sea archipelago; *head of state* (figurehead) Emperor Akihito (Heisei) from 1989; *head of government* Tomiichi Murayama from 1994; *political system* liberal democracy; *population* (1993 est) 124,900,000; growth rate 0.5% p.a.; *language* Japanese; *religions* Shinto, Buddhist (often combined), Christian; 30% claim a personal religious faith.

Jason in Greek mythology, the leader of the Argonauts who sailed in the *Argo* to Colchis in search of the ▷Golden Fleece. He eloped with ▷Medea, daughter of the king of Colchis, who had helped him achieve his goal, but later deserted her.

jaundice yellow discoloration of the skin and whites of the eyes caused by an excess of bile pigment in the bloodstream. Mild jaundice is common in newborns, but a serious form occurs in rhesus disease (see ▷rhesus factor).

Java or *Jawa* most important island of Indonesia, situated between Sumatra and Bali *area*; (with the island of Madura) 132,000 sq km/51,000 sq mi; *capital* Jakarta (also capital of Indonesia); *features* a chain of mountains, some of which are volcanic, runs along the centre, rising to 2,750 m/9,000 ft. The highest mountain, Semeru (3,676 m/12,060 ft), is in the E; *population* (with Madura; 1989) 107,513,800,

including people of Javanese, Sundanese, and Madurese origin, with differing languages; *religion* predominantly Muslim.

javelin spear used in athletics events. The men's javelin is about 260 cm/8.5 ft long, weighing 800 g/28 oz; the women's 230 cm/7.5 ft long, weighing 600 g/21 oz. It is thrown from a scratch line at the end of a run-up. The centre of gravity on the men's javelin was altered 1986 to reduce the vast distances (90 m/100 yd) that were being thrown.

jazz polyphonic syncopated music, characterized by solo virtuosic improvisation, which developed in the USA at the turn of the 20th century. Initially music for dancing, often with a vocalist, it had its roots in black American and other popular music. Developing from ▷blues and spirituals (religious folk songs) in the southern states, it first came to prominence in the early 20th century in New Orleans, St Louis, and Chicago, with a distinctive flavour in each city.

Jehovah's Witness member of a religious organization originating in the USA 1872 under Charles Taze Russell (1852–1916). Jehovah's Witnesses attach great importance to Christ's second coming, which Russell predicted would occur 1914, and which Witnesses still believe is imminent. All Witnesses are expected to take part in house-to-house preaching; there are no clergy in the organization.

jellyfish marine invertebrate of the phylum Cnidaria (coelenterates) with an umbrella-shaped body composed of a semi-transparent gelatinous substance, with a fringe of stinging tentacles. They feed on small animals that are paralyzed by stinging cells in the jellyfishes' tentacles.

Jerome, St *c.* 340–420. One of the early Christian leaders and scholars known as the Fathers of the Church. His Latin versions of the Old and New Testaments form the basis of the Roman Catholic Vulgate. He is usually depicted with a lion. Feast day 30 Sept.

Jersey largest of the ◊Channel Islands; capital St Helier; area 117 sq km/45 sq mi; population (1991) 58,900. It is governed by a lieutenant- governor representing the English crown and an assembly. Jersey cattle were originally bred here. Jersey gave its name to a woollen garment.

Jerusalem ancient city of Palestine, divided 1948 between Jordan and the new republic of Israel; area (pre-1967) 37.5 sq km/14.5 sq mi, (post-1967) 108 sq km/42 sq mi, including areas of the West Bank; population (1989) 500,000, about 350,000 Israelis and 150,000 Palestinians. In 1950 the western New City was proclaimed as the Israeli capital, and, having captured from Jordan the eastern Old City 1967, Israel affirmed 1980 that the united city was the country's capital; the United Nations does not recognize the claim..

Jesuit member of the largest and most influential Roman Catholic religious order (also known as the *Society of Jesus*) founded by Ignatius Loyola (1491–1556) 1534, with the aims of protecting Catholicism against the Reformation and carrying out missionary work. During the 16th and 17th centuries Jesuits were missionaries in Japan, China, Paraguay, and among the North American Indians. The order had (1991) about 29,000 members (15,000 priests plus students and lay members).

Jesuit schools and universities are renowned.

Jesus *c.* 4 BC–AD 29 or 30. Hebrew preacher on whose teachings Christianity was founded. According to the accounts of his life in the four Gospels, he was born in Bethlehem, Palestine, son of God and the Virgin Mary, and brought up by Mary and her husband Joseph as a carpenter in Nazareth. After adult baptism, he gathered 12 disciples, but his preaching antagonized the Roman authorities and he was executed by crucifixion. Three days later there came reports of his resurrection and, later, his ascension to heaven.

Jew follower of ◊Judaism, the Jewish religion. The term is also used to refer to those who claim descent from the ancient Hebrews, a Semitic people of the Middle East. Today, some may recognize their ethnic heritage but not practise the religious or cultural traditions. The term came into use in medieval Europe, based on the Latin name for Judeans, the people of Judah. Prejudice against Jews is termed ◊anti-Semitism.

Jiang Zemin 1926– . Chinese political leader, state president from 1993. He succeeded Zhao Ziyang as Communist Party leader after the Tiananmen Square massacre of 1989. Jiang is a cautious proponent of economic reform who has held with unswerving adherence to the party's 'political line'.

Jiddah or *Jedda* port in Hejaz, Saudi Arabia, on the E shore of the Red Sea; population (1986) 1,000,000.

Jinnah Muhammad Ali 1876–1948. Indian politician, Pakistan's first governor general from 1947. He was president of the Muslim League 1916, 1934–48, and by 1940 was advocating the need for a separate state of Pakistan; at the 1946 conferences in London he insisted on the partition of British India into Hindu and Muslim states.

Joan of Arc, St 1412–1431. French military leader. In 1429 at Chinon, NW France, she persuaded Charles VII that she had a divine mission to expel the occupying English and secure his coronation. She raised the siege of Orléans, defeated the English at Patay, and Charles was crowned in Reims. However, she failed to take Paris and was captured May 1430 by the Burgundians. She was found guilty of witchcraft and heresy and was burned to death at the stake in Rouen 30 May 1431. In 1920 she was canonized.

Johannesburg largest city of South Africa, situated on the Witwatersrand River in Transvaal; population (1985) 1,609,000. It is the centre of a large gold-mining industry.

John (I) Lackland 1167–1216. King of England from 1199 and acting king from 1189 during his brother Richard the Lion-Heart's absence on the third Crusade. He lost Normandy and almost all the other English possessions in France to Philip II of France by 1205. His repressive policies and excessive taxation brought him into conflict with his barons, and he was forced to seal the ◊Magna Carta 1215. Later repudiation of it led to the first Barons' War 1215–17, during which he died.

John of Gaunt 1340–1399. English nobleman and politician, born in Ghent, fourth son of Edward III, Duke of Lancaster from 1362. He distinguished himself during the Hundred Years' War. During Edward's last years, and the years before Richard II attained the age

of majority, he acted as head of government, and Parliament protested against his corrupt rule.

John Paul II (Karol Wojtyla) 1920– . Pope from 1978, the first non-Italian to be elected pope since 1522. He was born near Kraków, Poland. He has upheld the tradition of papal infallibility and has condemned contraception, women priests, married priests, and modern dress for monks and nuns – views that have aroused criticism from liberalizing elements in the church.

John, St New Testament apostle. Traditionally, he wrote the fourth Gospel and the Johannine Epistles (when he was bishop of Ephesus), and the Book of Revelation (while exiled to the Greek island of Patmos). His emblem is an eagle; his feast day 27 Dec.

Johnson Amy 1903–1941. English aviator. She made a solo flight from England to Australia 1930, in 9½ days, and in 1932 made the fastest ever solo flight from England to Cape Town, South Africa. Her plane disappeared over the English Channel in World War II while she was serving with the Air Transport Auxiliary.

Johnson Samuel, known as 'Dr Johnson', 1709–1784. English lexicographer, author, and critic. A brilliant conversationalist, he was the dominant figure in the literary circles of his day. His *Dictionary*, 1755, remained authoritative for over a century. In 1764 he founded the Literary Club, whose members included artist Joshua Reynolds, political philosopher Edmund Burke, dramatist Oliver Goldsmith, actor David Garrick, and James ◊Boswell, Johnson's biographer.

John the Baptist, St *c.* 12 BC–*c.* AD 27. In the New Testament, an itinerant preacher. After preparation in the wilderness, he proclaimed the coming of the Messiah and baptized Jesus in the river Jordan. He was later executed by Herod Antipas at the request of Salome, who demanded that his head be brought to her on a platter.

joint in any animal with a skeleton, a point of movement or articulation. In vertebrates, it is the point where two bones meet. Some joints allow no motion (the sutures of the skull), others allow a very small motion (the sacroiliac joints in the lower back), but most allow a relatively free motion. Of these, some allow a gliding motion (one vertebra of the spine on another), some have a hinge action (elbow and knee), and others allow motion in all directions (hip and shoulder joints) by means of a ball-and-socket arrangement. The ends of the bones at a moving joint are covered with cartilage for greater elasticity and smoothness, and enclosed in an envelope (capsule) of tough white fibrous tissue lined with a membrane which secretes a lubricating and cushioning synovial fluid. The joint is further strengthened by ligaments. In invertebrates with an exoskeleton, the joints are places where the exoskeleton is replaced by a more flexible outer covering, the arthrodial membrane, which allows the limb (or other body part) to bend at that point.

Jones Inigo 1573–*c.* 1652. English Classical architect. He introduced the Palladian style to England. He was employed by James I to design scenery for Ben Jonson's masques and appointed Surveyor of the King's Works 1615–42. He designed the Queen's House, Greenwich, 1616–35, and his English Renaissance masterpiece, the Banqueting House in Whitehall, London, 1619–22.

Jonson Ben(jamin) 1572–1637. English dramatist, poet, and critic. *Every Man in his Humour* 1598 established the English 'comedy of humours', in which each character embodies a 'humour', or vice, such as greed, lust, or avarice. This was followed by *Cynthia's Revels* 1600 and *Poetaster* 1601. His first extant tragedy is *Sejanus* 1603, with Burbage and Shakespeare as members of the original cast. The great comedies of his middle years include *Volpone, or The Fox* 1606, *The Alchemist* 1610, and *Bartholomew Fair* 1614.

Jordan Hashemite Kingdom of (*Al Mamlaka al Urduniya al Hashemiyah*); *area* 89,206 sq km/34,434 sq mi (West Bank 5,879 sq km/2,269 sq mi); *capital* Amman; *features* lowest point on Earth below sea level in the Dead Sea (−396 m/−1,299 ft); archaeological sites at Jerash and Petra; *political system* constitutional monarchy; *political parties* none; *population* (1993 est) 4,100,000; growth rate 3.6% p.a.; *languages* Arabic (official), English; *religions* Sunni Muslim 92%, Christian 8%.

Joseph in the New Testament, the husband of the Virgin Mary, a descendant of King David of the Tribe of Judah, and a carpenter by trade. Although Jesus was not the son of Joseph, Joseph was his legal father. According to Roman Catholic tradition, he had a family by a previous wife, and was an elderly man when he married Mary.

Josephine Marie Josèphe Rose Tascher de la Pagerie 1763–1814. As wife of ◊Napoleon Bonaparte, she was empress of France 1804–1809. Born on

Martinique, she married in 1779 Alexandre de Beauharnais, who played a part in the French Revolution, and in 1796 Napoleon, who divorced her 1809 because she had not produced children.

Joule James Prescott 1818–1889. English physicist whose work on the relations between electrical, mechanical, and chemical effects led to the discovery of the first law of ◊thermodynamics

Joyce James (Augustine Aloysius) 1882–1941. Irish writer. He revolutionized the form of the English novel with his 'stream of consciousness' technique. His works include *Dubliners* 1914 (short stories), *Portrait of the Artist as a Young Man* 1916, *Ulysses* 1922, and *Finnegans Wake* 1939.

Juan Carlos 1938– . King of Spain. The son of Don Juan, pretender to the Spanish throne, he married Princess Sofia in 1962, eldest daughter of King Paul of Greece. In 1969 he was nominated by ◊Franco to succeed on the restoration of the monarchy intended to follow Franco's death; his father was excluded because of his known liberal views. Juan Carlos became king 1975.

Judaism religion of the ancient Hebrews and their descendants the Jews, based, according to the Old Testament, on a covenant between God and Abraham about 2000 BC, and the renewal of the covenant with Moses about 1200 BC. It rests on the concept of one eternal invisible God, whose will is revealed in the *Torah* and who has a special relationship with the Jewish people. The *Torah* comprises the first five books of the Bible (the Pentateuch), which contains the history, laws, and guide to life for correct behaviour. Besides those living in Israel, there are large Jewish populations today in the USA, the former USSR (mostly Russia, Ukraine, Belarus, and Moldova), the UK and Commonwealth nations, and in Jewish communities throughout the world.

Judas Iscariot In the New Testament, the disciple who betrayed Jesus Christ. Judas was the treasurer of the group. At the last Passover supper, he arranged, for 30 pieces of silver, to point out Jesus to the chief priests so that they could arrest him. Afterward Judas was overcome with remorse and committed suicide.

judo form of wrestling of Japanese origin. The two combatants wear loose-fitting, belted jackets and trousers to facilitate holds, and falls are broken by a square mat; when one has established a painful hold that the other cannot break, the latter signifies surrender by slapping the ground with a free hand. Degrees of proficiency are indicated by the colour of the belt: for novices, white; after examination, brown (three degrees); and finally, black (nine degrees).

Juneau ice-free port and state capital of Alaska, USA, on Gastineau Channel in the S Alaska panhandle; population (1980) 19,528. Juneau is the commercial and distribution centre for the fur-trading and mining of the Panhandle region.

Jung Carl Gustav 1875–1961. Swiss psychiatrist who collaborated with Sigmund ◊Freud until their disagreement in 1912 over the importance of sexuality in causing psychological problems. Jung saw the unconscious as a source of spiritual insight and distinguished between introversion and extroversion. His books include *Modern Man in Search of a Soul* 1933.

Juno in Roman mythology, the principal goddess, identified with the Greek Hera. The wife of Jupiter and queen of heaven, she was concerned with all aspects of women's lives.

Jupiter or *Jove* in Roman mythology, the chief god, identified with the Greek ▷Zeus. He was god of the sky, associated with lightning and thunderbolts; protector in battle; and bestower of victory. The son of Saturn, he married his sister Juno, and reigned on Mount Olympus as lord of heaven. His most famous temple was on the Capitoline Hill in Rome.

Jurassic period of geological time 208–146 million years ago; the middle period of the Mesozoic era. Climates worldwide were equable, creating forests of conifers and ferns; dinosaurs were abundant, birds evolved, and limestones and iron ores were deposited.

jury body of lay people (usually 12) sworn to decide the facts of a case and reach a verdict in a court of law. Juries, used mainly in English-speaking countries, are implemented primarily in criminal cases, but also sometimes in civil cases; for example, inquests and libel trials.

Jute member of a Germanic people who originated in Jutland but later settled in Frankish territory. They occupied Kent, SE England, about 450, according to tradition under Hengist and Horsa, and conquered the Isle of Wight and the opposite coast of Hampshire in the early 6th century.

jute fibre obtained from two plants of the genus *Corchorus* of the linden family: *C. capsularis* and *C. olitorius*. Jute is used for sacks and sacking, upholstery, webbing, twine, and stage canvas.

K

K2 or *Chogori* second highest mountain above sea level, 8,611 m/28,261 ft, in the Karakoram range, in a disputed region of Pakistan. It was first climbed 1954 by an Italian expedition.

kabbala or *cabbala* (Hebrew 'tradition') ancient esoteric Jewish mystical tradition of philosophy containing strong elements of pantheism yet akin to neo-Platonism. Kabbalistic writing reached its peak between the 13th and 16th centuries. It is largely rejected by current Judaic thought as medieval superstition, but is basic to the Hasid sect.

Kabul capital of Afghanistan, 2,100 m/6,900 ft above sea level, on the river Kabul; population (1984) 1,179,300. It commands the strategic routes to Pakistan via the Khyber Pass. The city was captured by mujaheddin rebels 1992 and suffered heavy bombardment during subsequent fighting.

Kafka Franz 1883–1924. Czech novelist. He wrote in German. His three unfinished allegorical novels *Der Prozess/The Trial* 1925, *Der Schloss/ The Castle* 1926, and *Amerika/ America* 1927 were posthumously published despite his instructions that they should be destroyed. His short stories include 'Die Verwandlung/The Metamorphosis' 1915, in which a man turns into a huge insect. His vision of lonely individuals trapped in bureaucratic or legal labyrinths can be seen as a powerful metaphor for modern experience.

Kalahari Desert semi-desert area forming most of Botswana and extending into Namibia, Zimbabwe, and South Africa; area about 900,000 sq km/347,400 sq mi. The only permanent river, the Okavango, flows into a delta in the NW forming marshes rich in wildlife. Its inhabitants are the nomadic Kung.

Kampala capital of Uganda, on Lake Victoria; population (1983) 455,000. It is linked by rail with Mombasa.

Kandinsky Wassily 1866–1944. Russian painter. He was a pioneer of abstract art. He lived in Munich from 1896. He produced the series *Improvisations* and *Compositions* 1910–14, the first known examples of purely abstract work in 20th-century art. He was an originator of the *Blaue Reiter* movement 1911–12, a loose association of German Expressionist painters. From 1921 he taught at the ◊Bauhaus school of design. He moved to Paris 1933, becoming a French citizen 1939.

kangaroo any marsupial of the family Macropodidae found in Australia, Tasmania, and New Guinea. Kangaroos are plant-eaters and most live in groups. They are adapted to hopping, the vast majority of species having very large back legs and feet compared with the small forelimbs. The larger types can jump 9 m/30 ft at a single bound. Most are nocturnal. Species vary from small rat kangaroos, only 30 cm/1 ft long, through the medium-sized wallabies, to the large red and great grey kangaroos, which are the largest living marsupials. These may be 1.8 m/5.9 ft long with 1.1 m/3.5 ft tails.

Kanpur formerly *Cawnpore* capital of Kanpur district, Uttar Pradesh, India, SW of Lucknow, on the river Ganges; a commercial and industrial centre; population (1981) 1,688,000.

Kansas state in central USA; *area* 213,200 sq km/82,296 sq mi; *capital* Topeka; *features* Dodge City, once 'cowboy capital of the world'; Eisenhower Center, Abilene; Fort Larned and Fort Scott; Pony Express station, Hanover; Wichita Cowtown, a frontier-era reproduction; *population* (1990) 2,477,600.

Kansas City twin city in the USA at the confluence of the Missouri and Kansas rivers, partly in Kansas and partly in Missouri; population (1990) of Kansas City (Kansas) 149,800, Kansas City (Missouri) 435,100. It is a market and agricultural distribution centre and one of the chief livestock centres of the USA. Kansas City, Missouri, has car-assembly plants and Kansas City, Kansas, has the majority of offices.

Kant Immanuel 1724–1804. German philosopher who believed that knowledge is not merely an aggregate of sense impressions but is dependent on the conceptual apparatus of the human understanding, which is itself not derived from experience. In ethics, Kant argued that right action cannot be based on feelings or inclinations but conforms to a law given by reason, the *categorical imperative*.

Karachi largest city and chief seaport of Pakistan, and capital of Sind province, NW of the Indus delta; population (1981) 5,208,000. It was the capital of Pakistan 1947–59.

Karadžić Radovan 1945– . Montenegrin-born leader of the Bosnian Serbs, leader of the community's unofficial government from 1992. He cofounded the Serbian Democratic Party of Bosnia-Herzegovina (SDS-BH) 1990 and launched the siege of Sarajevo 1992, plunging the country into a prolonged and bloody civil war. Successive peace initiatives for the region failed due to his ambitious demands for Serbian territory.

Karajan Herbert von 1908–1989. Austrian conductor. He dominated European classical music performance after 1947. He was principal conductor of the Berlin Philharmonic Orchestra 1955–89, artistic director of the Vienna State Opera 1957–64, and of the Salzburg Festival 1956–60. A perfectionist, he cultivated an orchestral sound of notable smoothness and transparency. He had a special affinity with Mozart and Bruckner, although his repertoire extended from Bach to Schoenberg.

Karakoram mountain range in central Asia, divided among China, Pakistan, and India. Peaks include K2, Masharbrum, Gasharbrum, and Mustagh Tower. *Ladakh* subsidiary range is in NE Kashmir on the Tibetan border.

karate one of the ▷martial arts. Karate is a type of unarmed combat derived from *kempo*, a form of the Chinese

Shaolin boxing. It became popular in the West in the 1930s.

karma (Sanskrit 'fate') in Hinduism, the sum of a human being's actions, carried forward from one life to the next, resulting in an improved or worsened fate. Buddhism has a similar belief, except that no permanent personality is envisaged, the karma relating only to the physical and mental elements carried on from birth to birth, until the power holding them together disperses in the attainment of nirvana.

Karnataka formerly (until 1973) *Mysore* state in SW India; *area* 191,800 sq km/74,035 sq mi; *capital* Bangalore; *population* (1991) 44,817,400; *language* Kannada.

Kashmir Pakistan-occupied area, 30,445 sq mi/78,900 sq km, in the NW of the former state of Kashmir, now ⟡Jammu and Kashmir. Azad ('free') Kashmir in the W has its own legislative assembly based in Muzaffarabad while Gilgit and Baltistan regions to the N and E are governed directly by Pakistan. The Northern Areas are claimed by India and Pakistan; *population* 1,500,000; *features* W Himalayan peak Nanga Parbat 8,126 m/26,660 ft, Karakoram Pass, Indus River, Baltoro Glacier.

Katmandu or *Kathmandu* capital of Nepal; population (1981) 235,000. Founded in the 8th century on an ancient pilgrim and trade route from India to Tibet and China, it has a royal palace, Buddhist temples, and monasteries.

Kaunda Kenneth (David) 1924– . Zambian politician, president 1964–91. Imprisoned 1958–60 as founder of the Zambia African National Congress, he became in 1964 the first prime minister of Northern Rhodesia, then the first president of independent Zambia. In 1973 he introduced one-party rule. He lost the first multiparty elections, Nov 1991, to Frederick Chiluba.

Kazakhstan Republic of; *area* 2,717,300 sq km/1,049,150 sq mi; *capital* Alma-Ata; *features* Baikonur Cosmodrome (space launch site at Tyuratam, near Baikonur); *political system* emergent democracy; *population* (1993 est) 17,200,000 (Kazakh 40%, Russian 38%, German 6%, Ukrainian 5%); *language* Russian; Kazakh, related to Turkish; *religion* Sunni Muslim.

Keating Paul 1954– . Australian politician, Labor Party (ALP) leader and prime minister from 1991. He was treasurer and deputy leader of the ALP 1983–91. In 1993 he announced plans for Australia to become a federal republic by the year 2001, inciting a mixed reaction among Australians.

Keaton Buster (Joseph Frank) 1896–1966. US comedian, actor, and film director. After being a star in vaudeville, he became one of the great comedians of the silent film era, with an inimitable deadpan expression (the 'Great Stone Face') masking a sophisticated acting ability. His films include *One Week* 1920, *The Navigator* 1924, *The General* 1927, and *The Cameraman* 1928.

Keats John 1795–1821. English Romantic poet. He produced work of the highest quality and promise before dying at the age of 25. *Poems* 1817, *Endymion* 1818, the great odes (particularly 'Ode to a Nightingale' and 'Ode on a Grecian Urn' written 1819, published 1820), and the narratives 'Lamia', 'Isabella', and 'The Eve of St Agnes' 1820, show his lyrical richness and talent for drawing on both classical mythology and medieval lore.

kelp collective name for large brown seaweeds, such as those of the Fucaceae and Laminariaceae families. Kelp is also a term for the powdery ash of burned seaweeds, a source of iodine.

Kelvin William Thomson, 1st Baron Kelvin 1824–1907. Irish physicist who introduced the *kelvin scale*, the absolute scale of temperature. His work on the conservation of energy 1851 led to the second law of ▷thermodynamics.

kelvin scale temperature scale used by scientists. It begins at absolute zero (–273.15°C) and increases by the same degree intervals as the Celsius scale; that is, 0°C is the same as 273 K and 100°C is 373 K.

Kempis Thomas à. 1380–1471. Medieval German monk and religious writer; see ▷Thomas à Kempis.

Kennedy John F(itzgerald) 'Jack' 1917–1963. 35th president of the USA 1961–63, a Democrat; the first Roman Catholic and the youngest person to be elected president. His programme for reforms, called the *New Frontier*, was posthumously carried out by Lyndon Johnson. Kennedy created the Peace Corps, a volunteer organization providing aid overseas. He was assassinated while on a visit to Dallas, Texas, on 22 Nov 1963. Lee Harvey Oswald (1939–1963), who was within a few days shot dead by Jack Ruby (1911–1967), was named as the assassin.

Kennedy Robert (Francis) 1925–1968. US Democratic politician and lawyer. He was presidential campaign manager for his brother John F Kennedy, and as attorney general 1961–64 promoted the Civil Rights Act of 1964.

In 1968 he campaigned for the Democratic Party's presidential nomination, but during a campaign stop in California was assassinated by Sirhan Bissara Sirhan (1944–   ), a Jordanian.

Kent county of SE England, known as the 'garden of England'; *area* 3,730 sq km/1,440 sq mi; *towns and cities* Maidstone (administrative headquarters), Canterbury, Dover, Chatham, Rochester, Sheerness, Tunbridge Wells; resorts: Folkestone, Margate, Ramsgate; *features* the North Downs; Romney Marsh; the Isles of Grain, Sheppey, and Thanet; Leeds Castle; Hever Castle (where Henry VIII courted Anne Boleyn); Chartwell (Churchill's country home); *population* (1991) 1,508,900.

Kentucky state in S central USA; *area* 104,700 sq km/40,414 sq mi; *capital* Frankfort; *features* bluegrass country; horse racing at Louisville (Kentucky Derby); Mammoth Cave National Park; Abraham Lincoln's birthplace at Hodgenville; Fort Knox, US gold-bullion depository; *population* (1990) 3,365,300.

Kenya Republic of (*Jamhuri ya Kenya*) *area* 582,600 sq km/224,884 sq mi; *capital* Nairobi; *environment* the elephant faces extinction as a result of poaching; *features* Great Rift Valley, Mount Kenya, Lake Nakuru (salt lake with world's largest colony of flamingos), Malindini Marine Reserve, Olduvai Gorge; *political system* emergent democratic republic; *population* (1993 est) 27,900,000 (Kikuyu 21%, Luo 13%, Luhya 14%, Kelenjin 11%; Asian, Arab, European); growth rate 4.2% p.a.; *languages* Kiswahili (official), English; there are many local dialects; *religions* Protestant 38%, Roman Catholic 28%, indigenous beliefs 26%, Muslim 6%.

Kepler Johannes 1571–1630. German mathematician and astronomer. He formulated what are now called *Kepler's laws* of planetary motion: (1) the orbit of each planet is an ellipse with the Sun at one of the foci; (2) the radius vector of each planet sweeps out equal areas in equal times; (3) the squares of the periods of the planets are proportional to the cubes of their mean distances from the Sun.

Kerala state of SW India, formed 1956 from the former princely states of Travancore and Cochin; *area* 38,900 sq km/ 15,015 sq mi; *capital* Trivandrum; *features* most densely populated state of India; strong religious and caste divisions make it politically unstable; *population* (1991) 29,011,200; *languages* Kannada, Malayalam, Tamil.

keratin fibrous protein found in the ▷skin of vertebrates and also in hair, nails, claws, hooves, feathers, and the outer coating of horns.

kerosene thin oil obtained from the distillation of petroleum; a highly refined form is used in jet aircraft fuel. Kerosene is a mixture of hydrocarbons of the ▷paraffin series.

Kerouac Jack (Jean Louis) 1923–1969. US novelist. He named and epitomized the ▷Beat Generation of the 1950s. The first of his autobiographical, myth-making books, *The Town and the City* 1950, was followed by the *On the Road* 1957. Other works inspired by his interests in jazz and Buddhism include *The Dharma Bums* 1958, *Doctor Sax* 1959, and *Desolation Angels* 1965.

Kerry county of the Republic of Ireland, in the province of Munster; county town Tralee; area 4,700 sq km/1,814 sq mi; population (1991) 121,700. Low lying in the N, to the S are the highest mountains in Ireland, including Carrantuohill (part of Macgillycuddy's Reeks, the highest peak in Ireland at 1,041 m/3,417 ft. The western coastline is deeply indented and there are many rivers and lakes, notable of which are the Lakes of Killarney.

ketone member of the group of organic compounds containing the carbonyl group (C=O) bonded to two atoms of carbon (instead of one carbon and one hydrogen as in aldehydes). Ketones are liquids or low-melting- point solids, slightly soluble in water.

Keynes John Maynard, 1st Baron Keynes 1883–1946. English economist, whose *The General Theory of Employment, Interest, and Money* 1936 proposed the prevention of financial crises and unemployment by adjusting demand through government control of credit and currency. He is responsible for that part of economics now known as *macroeconomics*.

KGB secret police of the USSR, the *Komitet Gosudarstvennoy Bezopasnosti*/- Committee of State Security, which was in control of frontier and general security and the forced-labour system. KGB officers held key appointments in all fields of daily life, reporting to administration offices in every major town. The KGB was superseded by the Russian Federal Security Agency on the demise of the Soviet Union 1991.

Khaddhafi or *Gaddafi* or *Qaddafi*, Moamer al 1942– . Libyan revolutionary leader. Overthrowing King Idris 1969, he became virtual president of a republic, although he nominally gave up all except an ideological role 1974. He favours territorial expansion in N Africa, has supported rebels in

Chad, and has proposed mergers with a number of countries. During the ▷Gulf War, however, he advocated diplomacy rather than war.

Khartoum capital and trading centre of Sudan, at the junction of the Blue and White Nile; population (1983) 476,000, and of Khartoum North, across the Blue Nile, 341,000. Omdurman is also a suburb of Khartoum, giving the urban area a population of over 1.3 million.

Khmer or *Kmer* member of the largest ethnic group in Cambodia, numbering about 7 million. Khmer minorities also live in E Thailand and S Vietnam. The Khmer language belongs to the Mon-Khmer family of Austro-Asiatic languages.

Khmer Rouge communist movement in Cambodia (Kampuchea) formed in the 1960s. Controlling the country 1974–78, it was responsible for mass deportations and executions under the leadership of Pol Pot. Since then it has conducted guerrilla warfare, and in 1991 gained representation in the governing body. Its leader (from 1985) is Khieu Samphan.

Khomeini Ayatollah Ruhollah 1900–1989. Iranian Shi'ite Muslim leader, born in Khomein, central Iran. Exiled for opposition to the Shah from 1964, he returned when the Shah left the country 1979, and established a fundamentalist Islamic republic. His rule was marked by a protracted war with Iraq, and suppression of opposition within Iran, executing thousands of opponents.

Khrushchev Nikita Sergeyevich 1894–1971. Soviet politician, secretary general of the Communist Party 1953–64, premier 1958–64. His de-Stalinization programme gave rise to revolts in Poland and Hungary 1956. Because of problems with the economy and foreign affairs (a breach with China 1960; conflict with the USA in the Cuban missile crisis 1962), he was ousted by Leonid Brezhnev and Alexei Kosygin.

kidney in vertebrates, one of a pair of organs responsible for fluid regulation, excretion of waste products, and maintaining the ionic composition of the blood. The kidneys are situated on the rear wall of the abdomen. Each one consists of a number of long tubules; the outer parts filter the aqueous components of blood, and the inner parts selectively reabsorb vital salts, leaving waste products in the remaining fluid (urine), which is passed through the ureter to the bladder.

Kierkegaard Søren (Aabye) 1813–1855. Danish philosopher considered to be the founder of ▷existentialism. He argued that no system of thought could explain the unique experience of the individual. He defended Christianity, suggesting that God cannot be known through reason, but only through a 'leap of faith'. His chief works are *Enten-Eller/Either-Or* 1843, *Begrebet Angest/Concept of Dread* 1844, and *Efterskrift/Postscript* 1846.

Kiev capital of Ukraine, industrial centre on the confluence of the Desna and Dnieper rivers; population (1987) 2,554,000. It was the capital of Russia in the Middle Ages.

Kigali capital of Rwanda, central Africa, 80 km/50 mi E of Lake Kivu; population (1981) 157,000.

Kikuyu member of Kenya's dominant ethnic group, numbering about three million. The Kikuyu are primarily cultivators, although many are highly educated and have entered the professions. Their language belongs to the Bantu branch of the Niger-Congo family.

Kildare county of the Republic of Ireland, in the province of Leinster; county town Naas; area 1,690 sq km/652 sq mi; population (1991) 122,516. It is wet and boggy in the N and includes part of the Bog of Allen; the village of Maynooth, with a training college for Roman Catholic priests; and the Curragh, a plain that is the site of the national stud and headquarters of Irish horse racing at Tully.

Kilimanjaro volcano in ◊Tanzania, the highest mountain in Africa, 5,900 m/19,364 ft.

Kilkenny county of the Republic of Ireland, in the province of Leinster; county town Kilkenny; area 2,060 sq km/795 sq mi; population (1991) 73,600. It has the rivers Nore, Suir, and Barrow.

kilobyte (K or KB) in computing, a unit of memory equal to 1,024 ◊bytes. It is sometimes used, less precisely, to mean 1,000 bytes.

Kim Il Sung 1912–1994. North Korean communist politician and marshal. He became prime minister 1948 and president 1972, retaining the presidency of the Communist Workers' party. He liked to be known as the 'Great Leader' and campaigned constantly for the reunification of Korea. His son *Kim Jong Il* (1942–), known as the 'Dear Leader', succeeded him.

kinesis (plural *kineses*) in biology, a nondirectional movement in response to a stimulus; for example, woodlice move faster in drier surroundings. *Taxis* is a similar pattern of behaviour, but there the response is directional.

kinetic energy the energy of a body resulting from motion. It is contrasted with ◊potential energy.

kinetics branch of ◊dynamics dealing with the action of forces producing or changing the motion of a body; *kinematics* deals with motion without reference to force or mass.

kinetic theory theory describing the physical properties of matter in terms of the behaviour – principally movement – of its component atoms or molecules. The temperature of a substance is dependent on the velocity of movement of its constituent particles, increased temperature being accompanied by increased movement. A gas consists of rapidly moving atoms or molecules and, according to kinetic theory, it is their continual impact on the walls of the containing vessel that accounts for the pressure of the gas. The slowing of molecular motion as temperature falls, according to kinetic theory, accounts for the physical properties of liquids and solids, culminating in the concept of no molecular motion at absolute zero (0K/−273°C).

King Martin Luther Jr 1929–1968. US civil-rights campaigner, black leader, and Baptist minister. He first came to national attention as leader of the Montgomery, Alabama, bus boycott 1955, and was one of the organizers of the massive (200,000 people) march on Washington DC 1963 to demand racial equality. He was assassinated in Memphis, Tennessee, by James Earl Ray (1928–). Nobel Peace Prize 1964.

kingdom the primary division in biological ◊classification. At one time, only two kingdoms were recognized: animals and plants. Today most biologists prefer a five-kingdom system, even though it still involves grouping together organisms that are probably unrelated. One widely accepted scheme is as follows: *Kingdom Animalia* (all multicellular animals); *Kingdom Plantae* (all plants, including seaweeds and other algae, except blue- green); *Kingdom Fungi* (all fungi, including the unicellular yeasts, but not slime moulds); *Kingdom Protista* or *Protoctista* (protozoa, diatoms, dinoflagellates, slime moulds, and various other lower organisms with eukaryotic cells); and *Kingdom Monera* (all prokaryotes – the bacteria and cyanobacteria, or ◊blue-green algae). The first four of these kingdoms make up the eukaryotes.

Kingsley Charles 1819–1875. English author. A rector, he was known as the 'Chartist clergyman' because of such social novels as *Alton Locke* 1850. His historical novels include *Westward Ho!* 1855. He also wrote, for children, *The Water Babies* 1863.

Kingston capital and principal port of Jamaica, West Indies, the cultural and commercial centre of the island; population (1983) 101,000, metropolitan area 525,000. Founded 1693, Kingston became the capital of Jamaica 1872.

Kingstown capital and principal port of St Vincent and the Grenadines, West Indies, in the SW of the island of St Vincent; population (1989) 29,400.

Kinnock Neil 1942– . British Labour politician, party leader 1983–92. Born and educated in Wales, he adopted a moderate position as party leader, initiating a major policy review 1988–89. He resigned after Labour's defeat in the 1992 general election. In 1994 he left parliament to become a European commissioner.

Kinshasa formerly *Léopoldville* capital of Zaire on the river Zaire, 400 km/250 mi inland from the port of Matadi; population (1984) 2,654,000. It was founded by the explorer Henry Stanley 1887.

Kipling (Joseph) Rudyard 1865–1936. English writer, born in India. *Plain Tales from the Hills* 1888, about Anglo-Indian society, contains the earliest of his masterly short stories. His books for children, including *The Jungle Book* 1894–95, *Just So Stories* 1902, *Puck of Pook's Hill* 1906, and the novel *Kim* 1901, reveal his imaginative identification with the exotic. Nobel Prize for Literature 1907.

Kiribati Republic of; *area* 717 sq km/277 sq mi; *capital* (and port) Bairiki (on Tarawa Atoll); *environment* threatened by the possibility of a rise in sea level caused by global warming. A rise of approximately 30 cm/1 ft by the year 2040 will make existing fresh water undrinkable; *features* island groups crossed by equator and International Date Line; *political system* liberal democracy; *population* (1993 est) 77,000 (Micronesian); growth rate 1.7% p.a.; *languages* English (official), Gilbertese; *religions* Roman Catholic 48%, Protestant 45%.

Kissinger Henry 1923– . German-born US diplomat. After a brilliant academic career at Harvard University, he was appointed national security adviser 1969 by President Nixon, and was secretary of state 1973–77. His missions to the USSR and China improved US relations with both countries, and he took part in negotiating US withdrawal from Vietnam 1973 and in Arab-Israeli peace negotiations 1973–75. Nobel Peace Prize 1973.

Kitchener Horatio Herbert, Earl Kitchener of Khartoum 1850–1916. British soldier and administrator. He defeated the Sudanese dervishes at Omdurman 1898 and reoccupied Khartoum. In South Africa, he was Chief of Staff 1900–02 during the Boer War, and commanded the forces in India 1902–09. He was appointed war minister on the outbreak of World War I, and drowned when his ship was sunk on the way to Russia.

Klee Paul 1879–1940. Swiss artist. He was one of the most original artists of the 20th century. He settled in Munich 1906, joined the *Blaue Reiter* group of German Expressionist painters 1912, and worked at the Bauhaus school of design 1920–31, returning to Switzerland 1933. His works are an exploration of the potential of line, plane, and colour and based on the belief in a reality beyond appearances. *Twittering Machine* 1922 (Museum of Modern Art, New York) is typical.

Klimt Gustav 1862–1918. Austrian painter. He was influenced by Jugendstil (Art Nouveau) and Symbolism and was a founding member of the Vienna Sezession group 1897. His paintings have a jewelled effect similar to mosaics, for example *The Kiss* 1909 (Musée des Beaux-Arts, Strasbourg).

Knossos chief city of ◊Minoan Crete, near present-day Iráklion, 6 km/4 mi SE of Candia. The archaeological site, excavated by Arthur ◊Evans (1899–1935), dates from about 2000–1400 BC, and includes the palace throne room, the remains of frescoes, and construction on more than one level.

knot in navigation, unit by which a ship's speed is measured, equivalent to one nautical mile per hour (one knot equals about 1.15 miles per hour). It is also sometimes used in aviation.

knowledge-based system (KBS) computer program that uses an encoding of human knowledge to help solve problems. It was discovered during research into artificial intelligence that adding heuristics (rules of thumb) enabled programs to tackle problems that were otherwise difficult to solve by the usual techniques of computer science.

Knox John *c.* 1505–1572. Scottish Protestant reformer, founder of the Church of Scotland. He spent several years in exile for his beliefs, including a period in Geneva where he met John ◊Calvin. He returned to Scotland 1559 to promote Presbyterianism. His books include *First Blast of the Trumpet Against the Monstrous Regiment of Women* 1558.

koala marsupial *Phascolarctos cinereus* of the family Phalangeridae, found only in E Australia. It feeds almost entirely on eucalyptus shoots. It is about 60 cm/2 ft long, and resembles a bear. The popularity of its greyish fur led to its almost complete extermination by hunters. Under protection since 1936, it has rapidly increased in numbers.

Kobe deep-water port in S Honshu, Japan; population (1990) 1,477,400. *Port Island*, an artificial island of 5 sq km/2 sq mi in Kobe harbour, was created 1960–68 from the rock of nearby mountains. It was one of the world's largest construction projects, and is now a residential and recreation area with a luxury hotel, amusement park, and conference centres. It is linked to the city by a driverless, computerised monorail. In 1994 it was devastated by an earthquake of 7.2 magnitude, with over 4,000 casualties.

Koestler Arthur 1905–1983. Hungarian-born English author. Imprisoned by the Nazis in France 1940, he escaped to England. His novel *Darkness at Noon* 1940, regarded as his masterpiece, is a fictional account of the Stalinist purges, and draws on his experiences as a prisoner under sentence of death during the Spanish Civil War.

Kohl Helmut 1930– . German conservative politician, leader of the Christian Democratic Union (CDU) from 1976, West German chancellor (prime minister) 1982–90, and the first chancellor of reunited Germany from 1990. He oversaw the reunification of East and West Germany 1989–90 but his miscalculation of the immediate adverse effects on the economy led to his unpopularity. However, as the economy recovered, so did his public esteem, and he won a historic third electoral victory Oct 1994.

Koran (alternatively transliterated as *Quran*) sacred book of ◊Islam. Written in the purest Arabic, it contains 114 *suras* (chapters), and is stated to have been divinely revealed to the prophet Muhammad about 616.

Korean native to or inhabitant of Korea; also the language and culture. There are approximately 33 million Koreans in South Korea, 15 million in North Korea, and 3 million elsewhere, principally in Japan, China (Manchuria), Russia, Kazakhstan, Uzbekistan, and the USA.

Korea, North Democratic People's Republic of (*Chosun Minchu-chui Inmin Konghwa-guk*); *area* 120,538 sq km/ 46,528 sq mi; *capital* Pyongyang; *environment* the building of a hydroelectric dam at Kumgangsan on a tributary of the Han River has been opposed by South Korea as a potential flooding threat to central Korea; *features* separated from South Korea by a military demarcation line; the richer of the two Koreas in mineral resources; *political system* communism; *population* (1993 est) 22,600,000; growth rate 2.5% p.a.; *language* Korean; *religions* traditionally Buddhist, Confucian, but religious activity curtailed by the state.

Korean War war 1950–53 between North Korea, supported by China, and South Korea, aided by the United Nations (UN). North Korean forces invaded the South 25 June 1950, and the UN voted to oppose them. The North Koreans held most of the South when UN–US reinforcements arrived Sept 1950. Negotiations started 1951 finally ended the war 1953.

Korea, South Republic of Korea (*Daehan Minguk*); *area* 98,799 sq km/ 38,161 sq mi; *capital* Seoul; *features* Chomsongdae (world's earliest observatory); giant Popchusa Buddha; granite peaks of Soraksan National Park; *political system* emergent democracy; *population* (1993 est) 44,200,000; growth rate 1.4% p.a.; *language* Korean; *religions* traditionally Buddhist, Confucian, and Chondokyo; Christian 28%.

Krebs Hans 1900–1981. German-born British biochemist who discovered the citric acid cycle, also known as the *Krebs cycle*, the final pathway by which food molecules are converted into energy in living tissues. For this work he shared with Fritz Lipmann the 1953 Nobel Prize for Medicine.

krill any of several Antarctic crustaceans of the order Euphausiacea, the most common species being *Euphausia superba*. Shrimplike, it is about 6 cm/2.5 in long, with two antennae, five pairs of legs, seven pairs of light organs along the body, and is coloured orange above and green beneath.

Krishna incarnation of the Hindu god ◊Vishnu. The devotion of the bhakti movement is usually directed towards Krishna; an example of this is the International Society for Krishna Consciousness. Many stories are told of Krishna's mischievous youth, and he is the charioteer of Arjuna in the *Bhagavad-Gita*.

Kronos or *Cronus* in Greek mythology, the ruler of the world and one of the ◊Titans. He was the father of Zeus, who overthrew him.

krypton colourless, odourless, gaseous, nonmetallic element, symbol Kr, atomic number 36, relative atomic mass 83.80. It is grouped with the inert gases and was long believed not to enter into reactions, but it is now known to combine with fluorine under certain conditions; it remains inert to all other reagents. It is present in very small quantities in the air (about 114 parts per million). It is used chiefly in fluorescent lamps, lasers, and gas-filled electronic valves.

Kuala Lumpur capital of the Federation of Malaysia; area 240 sq km/93 sq mi; population (1990) 1,237,900. The city developed after 1873 with the expansion of tin and rubber trading. Formerly within the state of Selangor, of which it was also the capital, it was created a federal territory 1974.

Kublai Khan 1216–1294. Mongol emperor of China from 1259. He completed his grandfather ◊Genghis Khan's conquest of N China from 1240, and on his brother Mungo's death 1259 established himself as emperor of China. He moved the capital to Beijing and founded the Yuan dynasty, successfully expanding his empire into Indochina, but was defeated in an attempt to conquer Japan 1281.

Kubrick Stanley 1928– . US film director, producer, and screenwriter. His films include *Paths of Glory* 1957, *Dr Strangelove* 1964, *2001: A Space Odyssey* 1968, *A Clockwork Orange* 1971, and *The Shining* 1979.

Ku Klux Klan US secret society dedicated to white supremacy, founded 1866 in the southern states of the USA to oppose Reconstruction after the American ◊Civil War and to deny political rights to the black population. Members wore hooded white robes to hide their identity, and burned crosses at their night-time meetings. The Klan has evolved into a paramilitary extremist group.

kung fu Chinese art of unarmed combat (Mandarin *ch'üan fa*), one of the ◊martial arts. It is practised in many forms, the most popular being *wing chun*, 'beautiful springtime'. The basic principle is to use attack as a form of defence.

Kurd member of the Kurdish culture, living mostly in the Taurus and Sagros mountains of W Iran and N Iraq in the region called Kurdistan. There are also around 8 million Kurds in Turkey, and several million live elsewhere throughout the world. Around 25,000 Kurds were killed during chemical-weapon attacks by Iraq 1984–89, and after the Gulf War 1991 more than a million were forced to flee their homes in N Iraq. They are predominantly

Sunni Muslims, although there are some Shi'ites in Iran. The *Kurdish language* belongs to the Indo-Iranian branch of the Indo-European family, closely related to Farsi (Persian).

Kuwait State of (*Dowlat al Kuwait*); *area* 17,819 sq km/6,878 sq mi; *capital* Kuwait (also chief port); *environment* during the Gulf War 1990–91, oil wells were set alight and about 300,000 tonnes of oil were released into the waters of the Gulf leading to pollution haze, photochemical smog, acid rain, soil contamination, and water pollution; *features* there are no rivers and rain is light; the world's largest desalination plants, built in the 1950s; *political system* absolute monarchy; *population* (1993 est) 1,600,000 (Kuwaitis 40%, Palestinians 30%); growth rate 5.5% p.a.; *languages* Arabic 78%, Kurdish 10%, Farsi 4%; *religion* Sunni Muslim 45%, Shi'ite minority 30%.

Kuwait City (Arabic *Al Kuwayt*) formerly *Qurein* chief port and capital of the state of Kuwait, on the southern shore of Kuwait Bay; population (1985) 44,300, plus the suburbs of Hawalli, population (1985) 145,100, Jahra, population (1985) 111,200, and as-Salimiya, population (1985) 153,400. Kuwait is a banking and investment centre. It was heavily damaged during the Gulf War.

Kyoto former capital of Japan 794–1868 (when the capital was changed to Tokyo) on Honshu Island, linked by canal with Biwa Lake; population (1989) 1,407,300.

Kyrgyzstan Republic of; *area* 198,500 sq km/76,641 sq mi; *capital* Bishkek (formerly Frunze); *political system* emergent democracy; *population* (1993 est) 4,600,000 (Kyrgyz 52%, Russian 22%, Uzbek 13%, Ukrainian 3%, German 2%); *language* Kyrgyz, a Turkic language; *religion* Sunni Muslim.

L

Labour Party UK political party based on socialist principles, originally formed to represent workers. It was founded in 1900 and first held office in 1924. The first majority Labour government 1945–51 introduced nationalization and the National Health Service, and expanded social security. Labour was again in power 1964–70 and 1974–79. The party leader (from 1994) is Tony ⊳Blair.

Labrador area of NE Canada, part of the province of Newfoundland, lying between Ungava Bay on the NW, the Atlantic Ocean on the E, and the Strait of Belle Isle on the SE; area 266,060 sq km/102,699 sq mi; population (1986) 28,741. It consists primarily of a gently sloping plateau with an irregular coastline of numerous bays, fjords, inlets, and cliffs (60-120 m/200-400 ft high).

lacrosse Canadian ball game, adopted from the North American Indians, and named after a fancied resemblance of the lacrosse stick (crosse) to a bishop's crosier. Thongs across the curved end of the crosse form a pocket to carry the small rubber ball. The field is approximately 100 m/110 yd long and a minimum of 55 m/60 yd wide in the men's game, which is played with 10 players per side; the women's field is larger, and there are 12 players per side. The goals are just under 2 m/6 ft square, with loose nets. The world championship was first held in 1967 for men, and in 1969 for women.

lactation secretion of milk in mammals, from the mammary glands. In late pregnancy, the cells lining the lobules inside the mammary glands begin extracting substances from the blood to produce milk. The supply of milk starts shortly after birth with the production of colostrum, a clear fluid consisting largely of water, protein, antibodies, and vitamins. The production of milk continues practically as long as the baby continues to suckle.

lactic acid or *2-hydroxypropanoic acid* $CH_3CHOHCOOH$ organic acid, a colourless, almost odourless liquid, produced by certain bacteria during fermentation and by active muscle cells when they are exercised hard and are experiencing oxygen debt. An accumulation of lactic acid in the muscles may cause cramp. It occurs in yoghurt, buttermilk, sour cream, poor wine, and certain plant extracts, and is used in food preservation and in the preparation of pharmaceuticals.

lactose white sugar, found in solution in milk; it forms 5% of cow's milk. It is commercially prepared from the whey obtained in cheese-making. Like table sugar (sucrose), it is a disaccharide, consisting of two basic sugar units (monosaccharides), in this case, glucose and galactose. Unlike sucrose, it is tasteless.

ladybird or *ladybug* beetle of the family Coccinellidae, generally red or yellow in colour, with black spots. There are numerous species which, as larvae and adults, feed on aphids and scale-insect pests.

Lady Day British name for the Christian festival (25 March) of the Annunciation of the Virgin Mary; until 1752 it was the beginning of the legal year in England, and it is still a quarter day (date for the payment of quarterly rates or dues).

La Fontaine Jean de 1621–1695. French poet. He was born at Château-Thierry, and from 1656 lived largely in Paris, the friend of the playwrights Molière and Racine, and the poet Boileau. His works include *Fables* 1668–94 and *Contes* 1665–74, a series of witty and bawdy tales in verse.

Lagos chief port and former capital of Nigeria, located at the western end of an island in a lagoon and linked by bridges with the mainland via Iddo Island; population (1983) 1,097,000. One of the most important slaving ports, Lagos was bombarded and occupied by the British 1851, becoming the colony of Lagos 1862. Abuja was designated the new capital 1982 (officially recognized as such 1992).

Lahore capital of the province of Punjab and second city of Pakistan; population (1981) 2,920,000. It is associated with the Mogul rulers Akbar, Jahangir, and Aurangzeb, whose capital it was in the 16th and 17th centuries.

Laing R(onald) D(avid) 1927–1989. Scottish psychoanalyst, originator of the 'social theory' of mental illness, for example that schizophrenia is promoted by family pressure for its members to conform to standards alien to themselves. His books include *The Divided Self* 1960 and *The Politics of the Family* 1971.

lake body of still water lying in depressed ground without direct communication with the sea. Lakes are common in formerly glaciated regions, along the courses of slow rivers, and in low land near the sea. The main classifications are by origin: *glacial lakes*, formed by glacial scouring; *barrier lakes*, formed by landslides and glacial moraines; *crater lakes*, found in volcanoes; and *tectonic lakes*, occurring in natural fissures.

Lake District region in Cumbria, England; area 1,800 sq km/700 sq mi. It contains the principal English lakes, which are separated by wild uplands rising to many peaks, including Scafell Pike (978 m/3,210 ft), the highest peak in England.

Lalique René 1860–1945. French designer and manufacturer of ◊Art Nouveau glass, jewellery, and house interiors. The Lalique factory continues in production at Wingen-sur-Moder, Alsace, under his son Marc and granddaughter Marie-Claude.

Lamaism religion of Tibet and Mongolia, a form of Mahāyāna Buddhism. Buddhism was introduced into Tibet in AD 640, but the real founder of Lamaism was the Indian missionary Padma Sambhava who began his activity about 750. The head of the church is the ◊Dalai Lama, who is considered an incarnation of the Bodhisattva Avalokiteśvara. On the death of the Dalai Lama great care is taken in finding the infant in whom he has been reincarnated.

Lamarck Jean Baptiste de 1744–1829. French naturalist whose theory of evolution, known as *Lamarckism*, was based on the idea that acquired characteristics (changes acquired in an individual's lifetime) are inherited, and that organisms have an intrinsic urge to evolve into better-adapted forms.

Lamartine Alphonse de 1790–1869. French poet. He wrote romantic poems, including *Méditations poétiques* 1820, followed by *Nouvelles méditations/New Meditations* 1823, and *Harmonies* 1830. His *Histoire des Girondins/History of the Girondins* 1847 helped to inspire the revolution of 1848.

Lamb Charles 1775–1834. English essayist and critic. He collaborated with his sister *Mary Lamb* (1764–1847) on *Tales from Shakespeare* 1807, and his *Specimens of English Dramatic Poets* 1808 helped to revive interest in Elizabethan plays. As 'Elia' he contributed essays to the *London Magazine* from 1820 (collected 1823 and 1833).

Lancashire county of NW England; *area* 3,040 sq km/1,173 sq mi; *features* Pennines; Forest of Bowland (moors and farming valleys); Pendle Hill; *population* (1991) 1,384,000.

Land Registry, HM official body which registers legal rights to land in England and Wales. Since its foundation in 1925, a move towards compulsory registration of land in different areas of the country has required the purchaser of land to provide details of his or her title and all other rights (such as mortgages) relating to the land. Once registered, the title to the land is guaranteed by the Land Registry, subject to those interests that cannot be registered.

Landseer Edwin Henry 1802–1873. English painter, sculptor, and engraver of animal studies. Much of his work reflects the Victorian taste for sentimental and moralistic pictures, for example *Dignity and Impudence* 1839 (Tate Gallery, London). His sculptures include the lions at the base of Nelson's Column in Trafalgar Square, London, 1857–67.

Lang Fritz 1890–1976. Austrian film director. His films are characterized by a strong sense of fatalism and alienation. His German films include *Metropolis* 1927, the sensational *M* 1931 and the series of Dr Mabuse films, after which he fled from the Nazis to Hollywood 1935. His US films include *Fury* 1936, *You Only Live Once* 1937, *Scarlet Street* 1945, *Rancho Notorious* 1952, and *The Big Heat* 1953.

language human communication through speech, writing, or both. Different nationalities or ethnic groups typically have different languages or variations on particular languages; for example, Armenians speaking the Armenian language and the British and Americans speaking distinctive varieties of the English language. One language may have various dialects, which may be seen by those who use them as languages in their own right.

Languedoc-Roussillon region of S France, comprising the *départements* of Aude, Gard, Hérault, Lozère, and Pyrénées- Orientales; area 27,400 sq km/ 10,576 sq mi; population (1986) 2,012,000. Its capital is Montpellier.

lanthanide any of a series of 15 metallic elements (also known as rare earths) with atomic numbers 57 (lanthanum) to 71 (lutetium). One of its members, promethium, is radioactive. All occur in nature. Lanthanides are grouped because of their chemical similarities (they are all bivalent), their properties differing only slightly with atomic number.

Laois or *Laoighis* county of the Republic of Ireland, in the province of Leinster; county town Port Laoise; area 1,720 sq km/664 sq mi; population (1991) 52,300. It was formerly known as *Queen's County*. It is flat, except for the Slieve Bloom Mountains in the NW, and there are many bogs.

Laos Lao People's Democratic Republic (*Saathiaranagroat Prach-hathippatay Prachhachhon Lao*); *area* 236,790 sq km/91,400 sq mi; *capital* Vientiane; *features* Plain of Jars, where prehistoric people carved stone jars large enough to hold a person; *political system* communism, one-party state; *population* (1993) 4,400,000 (Lao 48%, Thai 14%, Khmer 25%, Chinese 13%); growth rate 2.2% p.a.; *languages* Lao (official), French; *religions* Theravāda Buddhist 85%, animist beliefs among mountain dwellers.

Lao Zi or Lao Tzu *c.* 604–531 BC. Chinese philosopher, commonly regarded as the founder of ◊Taoism, with its emphasis on the Tao, the inevitable and harmonious way of the universe. Nothing certain is known of his life. The *Tao Tê Ching*, the Taoist scripture, is attributed to him but apparently dates from the 3rd century BC.

La Paz capital city of Bolivia, in Murillo province, 3,800 m/12,400 ft above sea level; population (1988) 1,049,800. Founded by the Spanish 1548 as Pueblo Nuevo de Nuestra Senôra de la Paz, it

has been the seat of government since 1898.

lapis lazuli rock containing the blue mineral lazurite in a matrix of white calcite with small amounts of other minerals. It occurs in silica-poor igneous rocks and metamorphic limestones found in Afghanistan, Siberia, Iran, and Chile. Lapis lazuli was a valuable pigment of the Middle Ages, also used as a gemstone and in inlaying and ornamental work.

Lapland region of Europe within the Arctic Circle in Norway, Sweden, Finland, and the Kola Peninsula of NW Russia, without political definition. Its chief resources are chromium, copper, iron, timber, hydroelectric power, and tourism. The indigenous population are the Saami (formerly known as Lapps), a seminomadic herding people. Lapland has low temperatures, with three months' continuous daylight in summer and three months' continuous darkness in winter. There is summer agriculture.

laptop computer portable microcomputer, small enough to be used on the operator's lap. It consists of a single unit, incorporating a keyboard, ◊floppy disc or ◊hard disc drives, and a screen. It uses a liquid-crystal or gas- plasma display, rather than the bulkier and heavier cathode-ray tubes found in most display terminals.

La Rochefoucauld François, duc de La Rochefoucauld 1613–1680. French writer. His *Réflexions, ou sentences et maximes morales/Reflections, or Moral Maxims* 1665 is a collection of brief, epigrammatic, and cynical observations on life and society, with the epigraph 'Our virtues are mostly our vices in disguise'.

larva stage between hatching and adulthood in those species in which the young have a different appearance and way of life from the adults. Examples include tadpoles (frogs) and caterpillars (butterflies and moths). Larvae are typical of the invertebrates, some of which (for example, shrimps) have two or more distinct larval stages. Among vertebrates, it is only the amphibians and some fishes that have a larval stage.

laryngitis inflammation of the larynx, causing soreness of the throat, a dry cough, and hoarseness. The acute form is due to a virus or other infection, excessive use of the voice, or inhalation of irritating smoke, and may cause the voice to be completely lost. With rest, the inflammation usually subsides in a few days.

larynx in mammals, a cavity at the upper end of the trachea (windpipe) containing the vocal cords. It is stiffened with cartilage and lined with mucous membrane. Amphibians and reptiles have much simpler larynxes, with no vocal cords. Birds have a similar cavity, called the *syrinx*, found lower down the trachea, where it branches to form the bronchi. It is very complex, with well-developed vocal cords.

Lascaux cave system in SW France with prehistoric wall paintings. It is richly decorated with realistic and symbolic paintings of buffaloes, horses, and red deer of the Upper Palaeolithic period, about 18,000 BC. The caves, near Montignac in the Dordogne, were discovered 1940. Similar paintings are found in Altamira, Spain. The opening of the Lascaux caves to tourists led to deterioration of the paintings; the caves were closed 1963 and a facsimile opened 1983.

laser (acronym for *light amplification by stimulated emission of radiation*) a device for producing a narrow beam of light, capable of travelling over vast distances without dispersion, and of being focused to give enormous power densities (10^8 watts per cm^2 for high-energy lasers). The laser operates on a principle similar to that of the ▷maser (a high-frequency microwave amplifier or oscillator). The uses of lasers include communications (a laser beam can carry much more information than can radio waves), cutting, drilling, welding, satellite tracking, medical and biological research, and surgery.

Las Palmas or *Las Palmas de Gran Canaria* tourist resort on the northeast coast of Gran Canaria, Canary Islands; population (1991) 347,700.

Lassa fever acute disease caused by a virus, first detected in 1969, and spread by a species of rat found only in W Africa. It is classified as a haemorrhagic fever and characterized by high fever, headache, muscle pain, and internal bleeding. There is no known cure, the survival rate being less than 50%.

Las Vegas city in Nevada, USA, known for its nightclubs and gambling casinos; population (1990) 258,300. Las Vegas entertains millions of visitors each year and is an important convention centre. Founded 1855 in a ranching area, the modern community developed with the coming of the railroad 1905. The first casino-hotel opened 1947.

latent heat in physics, the heat absorbed or radiated by a substance as it changes state (for example, from solid to liquid) at constant temperature and pressure.

Latin Indo-European language of ancient Italy. Latin has passed through four influential phases: as the language of (1) republican Rome, (2) the Roman Empire, (3) the Roman Catholic Church, and (4) W European culture, science, philosophy, and law during the Middle Ages and the Renaissance. During the third and fourth phases, much Latin vocabulary entered the English language. It is the parent form of the ◊Romance languages, noted for its highly inflected grammar and conciseness of expression.

Latin America large territory in the Western hemisphere south of the USA, consisting of Mexico, Central America, South America, and the West Indies. The main languages spoken are Spanish, Portuguese, and French.

latitude and longitude imaginary lines used to locate position on the globe. Lines of latitude are drawn parallel to the equator, with 0° at the equator and 90° at the north and south poles. Lines of longitude are drawn at right angles to these, with 0° (the Prime Meridian) passing through Greenwich, England.

Latvia Republic of; *area* 63,700 sq km/ 24,595 sq mi; *capital* Riga; *environment* coast littered with wrecks of Soviet vessels; ground water around former Soviet bases contaminated; *features* Riga is largest port on the Baltic after St Petersburg; *political system* emergent democratic republic; *population* (1993) 2,610,000 (Latvian 52%, Russian 34%, Byelorussian 5%, Ukrainian 3%); *language* Latvian; *religions* mostly Lutheran Protestant, with a Roman Catholic minority.

Laud William 1573–1645. English priest; archbishop of Canterbury from 1633. His attempt to impose the use of the Prayer Book on the Scots precipitated the English ◊Civil War. Impeached by Parliament 1640, he was imprisoned in the Tower of London, summarily condemned to death, and beheaded.

Laurel and Hardy Stan Laurel (stage name of Arthur Stanley Jefferson) 1890–1965 and Oliver Hardy 1892–1957. US film comedians. They were one of the most successful comedy teams in film history (Stan was slim, Oliver rotund). Their partnership began 1927, survived the transition from silent films to sound, and resulted in more than 200 short and feature-length films. Among these are *Pack Up Your Troubles* 1932, *Our Relations* 1936, and *A Chump at Oxford* 1940.

lava molten rock (usually 800–1100°C/ 1500–2000°F) that erupts from a ◊volcano and cools to form extrusive ◊igneous rock. It differs from magma in that it is molten rock on the surface; magma is molten rock below the surface. Lava that is high in silica is viscous and sticky and does not flow far; it forms a steep-sided conical volcano. Low-silica lava can flow for long distances and forms a broad flat volcano.

Laval Pierre 1883–1945. French right-wing politician. He was prime minister and foreign secretary 1931–32, and again 1935–36. In World War II he joined Pétain's ◊Vichy government as vice-premier in June 1940; dismissed in Dec 1940, he was reinstated by Hitler's orders as head of the government and foreign minister in 1942. After the war he was executed.

lavender sweet-smelling herb, genus *Lavandula*, of the mint family Labiatae, native to W Mediterranean countries. The bushy low-growing *L. angustifolia* has long, narrow, erect leaves of a silver-green colour. The flowers, borne on a terminal spike, vary in colour from lilac to deep purple and are covered with small fragrant oil glands. The oil is extensively used in pharmacy and the manufacture of perfumes.

Lavoisier Antoine Laurent 1743–1794. French chemist. He proved that combustion needed only a part of the air, which he called oxygen, thereby destroying the theory of phlogiston (an imaginary 'fire element' released during combustion). With Pierre de Laplace, the astronomer and mathematician, he showed that water was a compound of oxygen and hydrogen. In this way he established the basic rules of chemical combination.

Lawrence D(avid) H(erbert) 1885–1930. English writer. His work expresses his belief in emotion and the sexual impulse as creative and true to human nature. His writing first received attention after the publication of the semi-autobiographical *Sons and Lovers* 1913, which includes a portrayal of his mother (died 1911). Other novels include *The Rainbow* 1915, *Women in Love* 1921, and *Lady Chatterley's Lover* 1928.

Lawrence T(homas) E(dward), known as *Lawrence of Arabia* 1888–1935. British soldier, scholar, and translator. Appointed to the military intelligence department in Cairo, Egypt, during World War I, he took part in negotiations for an Arab revolt against the Ottoman Turks, and in 1916 attached himself to the emir Faisal. He became a guerrilla leader of genius, combining raids on Turkish communications with the organization of a joint Arab revolt, described in *The Seven Pillars of Wisdom* 1926.

Lazio (Roman *Latium*) region of W central Italy; area 17,200 sq km/6,639 sq mi; capital Rome; population (1990) 5,191,500. Home of the Latins from the 10th century BC, it was dominated by the Romans from the 4th century BC.

lead heavy, soft, malleable, grey, metallic element, symbol Pb (from Latin *plumbum*), atomic number 82, relative atomic mass 207.19. Usually found as an ore (most often in galena), it occasionally occurs as a free metal (native metal), and is the final stable product of the decay of uranium. Lead is the softest and weakest of the commonly used metals, with a low melting point; it is a poor conductor of electricity and resists acid corrosion. The metal is an effective shield against radiation and is used in batteries, glass, ceramics, and alloys such as pewter and solder.

leaded petrol petrol that contains antiknock, a mixture of the chemicals tetraethyl lead and dibromoethane. The lead from the exhaust fumes enters the atmosphere, mostly as simple lead compounds, which are poisonous to the developing nervous systems of children.

leaf lateral outgrowth on the stem of a plant, and in most species the primary organ of ⟡photosynthesis. The chief leaf types are cotyledons (seed leaves), scale leaves (on underground stems), foliage leaves, and bracts (in the axil of which a flower is produced).

League of Nations international organization formed after World War I to solve international disputes by arbitration. Established in Geneva, Switzerland, 1920, the league included representatives from states throughout the world, but was severely weakened by the US decision not to become a member, and had no power to enforce its decisions. It was dissolved 1946.

Leakey Louis (Seymour Bazett) 1903–1972. British archaeologist, born in Kenya. In 1958, with his archaeologist wife *Mary Leakey* (1913–), he discovered gigantic extinct-animal fossils in the Olduvai Gorge in Tanzania, as well as many remains of an early human type.

Leakey Richard 1944– Kenyan archaeologist and conservationist. In 1972 he discovered at Lake Turkana, Kenya, an apelike skull, estimated to be about 2.9 million years old; it had some human characteristics and a brain capacity of 800 cu cm. In 1984 his team found an almost complete skeleton of *Homo erectus* some 1.6 million years old. He is the son of Louis and Mary Leakey. He was director of the Kenya Wildlife Service 1989–94.

Lean David 1908–1991. English film director. His films, noted for their painstaking craftsmanship, include early work codirected with playwright Noël Coward. *Brief Encounter* 1946 established Lean as a leading talent. Among his later films are such epics as *The Bridge on the River Kwai* 1957 (Academy Award), *Lawrence of Arabia* 1962 (Academy Award), *Dr Zhivago* 1965, *Ryan's Daughter* 1970, and *A Passage to India* 1984.

Lear Edward 1812–1888. English artist and humorist. His *Book of Nonsense* 1846 popularized the limerick (a five-line humorous verse). He first attracted attention by his paintings of birds, and later turned to landscapes. He travelled to Italy, Greece, Egypt, and India, publishing books on his travels with his own illustrations, and spent most of his later life in Italy.

leather material prepared from the hides and skins of animals, by tanning with vegetable tannins and chromium salts. Leather is a durable and water-resistant material, and is used for bags, shoes, clothing, and upholstery. There are three main stages in the process of converting animal skin into leather: cleaning, tanning, and dressing. Tanning is often a highly polluting process.

Lebanon Republic of (*al-Jumhouria al-Lubnaniya*); *area* 10,452 sq km/4,034 sq mi; *capital* and port Beirut; *environment* water table polluted; deforestation has left only 3% of the country forested; solid waste has been dumped at sea; fertilizers have caused soil salinity; *features* Mount Hermon; Chouf Mountains; archaeological sites at Baalbeck, Byblos, Tyre; until the civil war, the financial centre of the Middle East; *political system* emergent democratic republic; *population* (1993 est) 2,900,000 (Lebanese 82%, Palestinian 9%, Armenian 5%); growth rate –0.1% p.a.; *languages* Arabic, French (both official), Armenian, English; *religions* Muslim 57% (Shiite 33%, Sunni 24%), Christian (Maronite and Orthodox) 40%, Druse 3%.

lecithin lipid (fat), containing nitrogen and phosphorus, that forms a vital part of the cell membranes of plant and animal cells. The name is from the Greek *lekithos* 'egg yolk', eggs being a major source of lecithin.

Leconte de Lisle Charles Marie René 1818–1894. French poet. He headed the anti-Romantic group *Les Parnassiens* 1866–76. His work drew inspiration from the ancient world, as in *Poèmes antiques/Antique Poems* 1852, *Poèmes barbares/Barbaric Poems* 1862, and *Poèmes tragiques/Tragic Poems* 1884.

Le Corbusier assumed name of Charles-Edouard Jeanneret 1887–1965. Swiss-born French architect. He was an early and influential exponent of the Modern Movement. His distinct brand of Functionalism first appears in his town-planning proposals of the early 1920s, which advocate 'vertical garden cities' (multi-storey villas, zoning of living and working areas, and traffic separation) as solutions to urban growth and chaos.

Leda in Greek mythology, the wife of Tyndareus and mother of Clytemnestra. Zeus, who came to her as a swan, was the father of her other children: ◊Helen of Troy and the twins Castor and Pollux.

leech annelid worm forming the class Hirudinea. Leeches inhabit fresh water, and in tropical countries infest damp forests. As bloodsucking animals they are injurious to people and animals, to whom they attach themselves by means of a strong mouth adapted to sucking.

Leeds industrial city in West Yorkshire, England, on the river Aire; population (1991 est) 680,700. Notable buildings include the Town Hall designed by Cuthbert Brodrick, Leeds University (1904), the Art Gallery (1844), Temple Newsam museum (early 16th century, altered *c.* 1630), and the Cistercian Abbey of Kirkstall (1147). It is a centre of communications where road, rail, and canal (to Liverpool and Goole) meet.

Leeuwenhoek Anton van 1632–1723. Dutch pioneer of microscopic research. He ground his own lenses, some of which magnified up to 200 times. With these he was able to see individual red blood cells, sperm, and bacteria, achievements not repeated for more than a century.

Leeward Islands (1) group of islands, part of the ◊Society Islands, in ◊French Polynesia, S Pacific; (2) general term for the northern half of the Lesser ◊Antilles in the West Indies; (3) former British colony in the West Indies (1871–1956) comprising Antigua, Montserrat, St Christopher (St Kitts)–Nevis, Anguilla, and the Virgin Islands.

legal aid public assistance with legal costs. In Britain it is given only to those below certain thresholds of income and unable to meet the costs. There are separate provisions for civil and criminal cases. Since 1989 legal aid is administered by the Legal Aid Board.

legume plant of the family Leguminosae, which has a pod containing dry seeds. The family includes peas, beans, lentils, clover, and alfalfa (lucerne). Legumes are important in agriculture because of their specialized roots, which have nodules containing bacteria capable of fixing nitrogen from the air and increasing the fertility of the soil. The edible seeds of legumes are called *pulses*.

Le Havre industrial port Normandy, NW France, on the river Seine; population (1990) 197,200. It is the largest port in Europe, and has transatlantic passenger links.

Leicestershire county of central England; *area* 2,550 sq km/984 sq mi; *towns and cities* Leicester (administrative headquarters), Loughborough, Melton Mowbray, Market Harborough; *features* river Soar; Rutland Water, one of Europe's largest reservoirs; Charnwood Forest; *population* (1991) 867,500.

Leinster southeastern province of the Republic of Ireland, comprising the counties of Carlow, Dublin, Kildare, Kilkenny, Laois, Longford, Louth,

Meath, Offaly, Westmeath, Wexford, and Wicklow; area 19,630 sq km/7,577 sq mi; capital Dublin; population (1991) 1,860,000.

Leitrim county of the Republic of Ireland, in the province of Connacht, bounded NW by Donegal Bay; county town Carrick-on-Shannon; area 1,530 sq km/591 sq mi; population (1991) 25,300. The rivers Shannon, Bonet, Drowes, and Duff run through it.

Lely Peter. Adopted name of Pieter van der Faes 1618–1680. Dutch painter. He was active in England from 1641, painting fashionable portraits in the style of van Dyck. His subjects included Charles I, Cromwell, and Charles II. He painted a series of admirals, *Flagmen* (National Maritime Museum, London), and one of *The Windsor Beauties* (Hampton Court, Richmond), fashionable women of Charles II's court.

Le Mans industrial city in Sarthe *département*, W France; population (1990) 148,500, conurbation 191,000. It has a motor-racing circuit where the annual endurance 24-hour race (established 1923) for sports cars and their prototypes is held.

lemon balm perennial herb *Melissa officinalis* of the mint family Labiatae, with lemon-scented leaves. It is widely used in teas, liqueurs, and medicines.

lemur prosimian ◊primate of the family Lemuridae, inhabiting Madagascar and the Comoro Islands. There are about 16 species, ranging from mouse-sized to dog-sized animals. Lemurs are arboreal, and some species are nocturnal. They have long, bushy tails, and feed on fruit, insects, and small animals. Many are threatened with extinction owing to loss of their forest habitat and, in some cases, from hunting.

Lenin Vladimir Ilyich. Adopted name of Vladimir Ilyich Ulyanov 1870–1924. Russian revolutionary, first leader of the USSR, and communist theoretician. Forced to leave Russia after the failure of the 1905 Revolution, he settled in Switzerland 1914, returning to Russia after the February revolution of 1917. He led the Bolshevik revolution Nov 1917 and became leader of a Soviet government, concluded peace with Germany, and organized a successful resistance to White Russian (pro-tsarist) uprisings and foreign intervention 1918–20. His modification of traditional Marxist doctrine to fit conditions in Russia became known as *Marxism-Leninism*, the basis of communist ideology.

Leningrad former name (1924–91) of the Russian city ◊St Petersburg.

lens in optics, a piece of a transparent material, such as glass, with two polished surfaces – one concave or convex, and the other plane, concave, or convex – that modifies rays of light. A convex lens brings rays of light together; a concave lens makes the rays diverge. Lenses are essential to spectacles, microscopes, telescopes, cameras, and almost all optical instruments.

Lent in the Christian church, the 40-day period of fasting that precedes Easter, beginning on Ash Wednesday, but omitting Sundays.

lentil annual Old World plant *Lens culinaris* of the pea family Leguminosae. The plant, which resembles vetch, grows 15–45 cm/6–18 in high and has white, blue, or purplish flowers. The seeds, contained in pods about 1.6 cm/0.6 in long, are widely used as food.

Leonardo da Vinci 1452–1519. Italian painter, sculptor, architect, engineer, and scientist. One of the greatest figures of the Italian Renaissance, he was active in Florence, Milan, and, from 1516, France. As state engineer and court painter to the duke of Milan, he painted the *Last Supper* mural about 1495 (Sta Maria delle Grazie, Milan), and on his return to Florence painted the *Mona Lisa* (Louvre, Paris) about 1503–06. His notebooks and drawings show an immensely inventive and enquiring mind, studying aspects of the natural world from anatomy to aerodynamics. He influenced many of his contemporaries, including Michelangelo, Raphael, Giorgione, and Bramante.

leopard or *panther* cat *Panthera pardus*, found in Africa and Asia. The background colour of the coat is golden, and the black spots form rosettes that differ according to the variety; black panthers are simply a colour variation and retain the patterning as a 'watered-silk' effect. The length is 1.5–2.5 m/5–8 ft, including the tail, which may measure 1 m/3 ft.

lepidoptera order of insects, including ▷butterflies and ▷moths, which have overlapping scales on their wings; the order consists of some 165,000 species.

leprosy or *Hansen's disease* chronic, progressive disease caused by a bacterium *Mycobacterium leprae* closely related to that of tuberculosis. The infection attacks the skin and nerves. Once common in many countries, leprosy is now confined almost entirely to the tropics. It is controlled with drugs.

lepton any of a class of light ▷elementary particles that are not affected by the strong nuclear force; they do not interact strongly with other particles or nuclei. The leptons are comprised of the ▷electron, ▷muon, and ▷tau, and their ▷neutrinos (the electron neutrino, muon neutrino, and tau neutrino), plus their six ▷antiparticles.

Lesotho Kingdom of; *area* 30,355 sq km/11,717 sq mi; *capital* Maseru; *features* Lesotho is an enclave within South Africa; *political system* constitutional monarchy; *population* (1993 est) 1,900,000; growth rate 2.7% p.a.; *languages* Sesotho, English (official), Zulu, Xhosa; *religions* Protestant 42%, Roman Catholic 38%.

Lessing Doris (May) (née Taylor) 1919– . English novelist, brought up in Rhodesia. Concerned with social and political themes, particularly the place of women in society, her work includes *The Grass is Singing* 1950, the five-novel series *Children of Violence* 1952–69, *The Golden Notebook* 1962, *The Good Terrorist* 1985, and *The Fifth Child* 1988.

Lesvos Greek island in the Aegean Sea, near the coast of Turkey; *area* 2,154 sq km/831 sq mi; *capital* Mytilene; *population* (1981) 104,620.

leukaemia any one of a group of cancers of the blood cells, with widespread involvement of the bone marrow and other blood-forming tissue. The central feature of leukaemia is runaway production of white blood cells that are immature or in some way abnormal. These rogue cells, which lack the defensive capacity of healthy white cells, overwhelm the normal ones, leaving the victim vulnerable to infection. Treatment is with radiotherapy and cytotoxic drugs to suppress replication of abnormal cells, or by bone-marrow transplantation.

lever simple machine consisting of a rigid rod pivoted at a fixed point called the fulcrum, used for shifting or raising a heavy load or applying force in a similar way. Levers are classified into orders according to where the effort is applied, and the load-moving force developed, in relation to the position of the fulcrum.

Lévi-Strauss Claude 1908–1990 French anthropologist who sought to find a universal structure governing all societies, as reflected in the way their myths are constructed. His works include *Tristes Tropiques* 1955 and *Mythologiques/Mythologies* 1964–71.

Lewis (Percy) Wyndham 1886–1957. English writer and artist. He pioneered Vorticism, which with its feeling of movement sought to reflect the age of industry. He had a hard and aggressive style in both his writing and his painting. His literary works include the novels *Tarr* 1918 and *The Childermass* 1928, the essay *Time and Western Man* 1927, and autobiographies.

Lhasa ('the Forbidden City') capital of the autonomous region of ▷Tibet, China, at 5,000 m/16,400 ft; population (1982) 105,000. Closed to Westerners until 1904, it is the holy city of ▷Lamaism.

Liberal Party British political party, the successor to the ▷Whig Party, with an ideology of liberalism. In the 19th century, it represented the interests of commerce and industry. Its outstanding leaders were Palmerston, Gladstone, and Lloyd George. From 1914 it declined, and the rise of the Labour Party pushed the Liberals into the

middle ground. The Liberals joined forces with the Social Democratic Party (SDP) as the Alliance for the 1983 and 1987 elections. In 1988, a majority of the SDP voted to merge with the Liberals to form the ▷Social and Liberal Democrats.

Liberia Republic of; *area* 111,370 sq km/42,989 sq mi; *capital* and port Monrovia; *features* nominally the world's largest merchant navy as minimal registration controls make Liberia's a flag of convenience; the world's largest rubber plantations; *political system* emergent democratic republic; *population* (1993 est) 2,700,000; growth rate 3% p.a.; *languages* English (official), over 20 Niger-Congo languages; *religions* animist 65%, Muslim 20%, Christian 15%.

libido in Freudian psychology, the psychic energy, or life force, that is to be found even in a newborn child. The libido develops through a number of phases, identified by Freud as the *oral stage*, when a child tests everything by mouth, the *anal stage*, when the child gets satisfaction from control of its body, and the *genital stage*, when sexual instincts find pleasure in the outward show of love.

Libya Great Socialist People's Libyan Arab Jamahiriya (*al-Jamahiriya al-Arabiya al-Libya al-Shabiya al-Ishtirakiya al-Uzma*); *area* 1,759,540 sq km/679,182 sq mi; *capital* Tripoli; *environment* plan to pump water from below the Sahara to the coast risks rapid exhaustion of nonrenewable supply (Great Manmade River Project); *features* Gulf of Sirte; rock paintings of about 3000 BC in the Fezzan; Roman city sites include Leptis Magna, Sabratha; *political system* one-party socialist state; *population* (1993 est) 4,700,000 (including 500,000 foreign workers);

growth rate 3.1% p.a.; *language* Arabic; *religion* Sunni Muslim 97%.

lichen any organism of the group Lichenes, which consists of a specific fungus and a specific alga existing in a mutually beneficial relationship. Found as coloured patches or spongelike masses adhering to trees, rocks, and other substrates, lichens flourish under adverse conditions.

Liechtenstein Principality of (*Fürstentum Liechtenstein*); *area* 160 sq km/ 62 sq mi; *capital* Vaduz; *features* no airport or railway station; easy tax laws make it an international haven for foreign companies and banks (some 50,000 companies are registered); *political system* constitutional monarchy; *population* (1993 est) 30,000 (33% foreign); growth rate 1.4% p.a.; *language* German (official); an Alemannic dialect is also spoken; *religions* Roman Catholic 87%, Protestant 8%.

life cycle in biology, the sequence of developmental stages through which members of a given species pass. Most vertebrates have a simple life cycle consisting of ◊fertilization of sex cells or ◊gametes, a period of development as an ◊embryo, a period of juvenile growth after hatching or birth, an adulthood including ◊sexual reproduction, and finally death. Invertebrate life cycles are generally more complex and may involve major reconstitution of the individual's appearance (◊metamorphosis) and completely different styles of life. Plants have a special type of life cycle with two distinct phases, known as alternation of generations. Many insects such as cicadas, dragonflies, and mayflies have a long larvae or pupae phase and a short adult phase. Dragonflies live an aquatic life as larvae and an aerial life during the adult phase. In many invertebrates and protozoa there is a sequence of stages in the life cycle, and in parasites different stages often occur in different host organisms.

ligament strong flexible connective tissue, made of the protein ◊collagen, which joins bone to bone at moveable joints. Ligaments prevent bone dislocation (under normal circumstances) but permit joint flexion.

light electromagnetic waves in the visible range, having a wavelength from about 400 nanometres in the extreme violet to about 770 nanometres in the extreme red. Light is considered to exhibit particle and wave properties, and the fundamental particle, or quantum, of light is called the photon. The speed of light (and of all electromagnetic radiation) in a vacuum is approximately 300,000 km/186,000 mi per second, and is a universal constant denoted by c.

light-emitting diode (LED) means of displaying symbols in electronic instruments and devices. An LED is made of ◊semiconductor material, such as gallium arsenide phosphide, that glows when electricity is passed through it. The first digital watches and calculators had LED displays, but many later models use ◊liquid-crystal displays.

lightning high-voltage electrical discharge between two charged rainclouds or between a cloud and the Earth, caused by the build-up of electrical charges. Air in the path of lightning ionizes (becomes conducting), and expands; the accompanying noise is heard as thunder. Currents of 20,000 amperes and temperatures of 30,000°C/54,000°F are common.

light year in astronomy, the distance travelled by a beam of light in a vacuum in one year, approximately 9.46 trillion (million million) km/5.88 trillion miles.

Liguria coastal region of NW Italy, which includes the resorts of the Italian Riviera, lying between the western Alps and the Mediterranean Gulf of Genoa. The region comprises the provinces of Genova, La Spezia, Imperia, and Savona, with a population (1990) of 1,719,200 and an area of 5,418 sq km/2,093 sq mi. Genoa is the chief city and port.

Lilongwe capital of Malawi since 1975, on the Lilongwe River; population (1987) 234,000. Capital Hill, 5 km/3 mi from the old city, is the site of government buildings and offices.

Lima capital of Peru, an industrial city with its port at Callao; population (1988) 418,000, metropolitan area 4,605,000. Founded by the Spanish conquistador Francisco Pizarro 1535, it was rebuilt after destruction by an earthquake 1746.

lime or *quicklime* CaO (technical name *calcium oxide*) white powdery substance used in making mortar and cement. It is made commercially by heating calcium carbonate ($CaCO_3$), obtained from limestone or chalk, in a lime kiln. Quicklime readily absorbs water to become calcium hydroxide (CaOH), known as slaked lime, which is used to reduce soil acidity.

Limerick county of the Republic of Ireland, in the province of Munster; county town Limerick; area 2,690 sq km/1,038 sq mi; population (1991) 161,900. The land is fertile, with hills in the S.

limestone sedimentary rock composed chiefly of calcium carbonate $CaCO_3$, either derived from the shells of marine organisms or precipitated from solution, mostly in the ocean. Various types of limestone are used as building stone.

Lincoln Abraham 1809–1865. 16th president of the USA 1861–65, a Republican. In the American ◊Civil War, his chief concern was the preservation of the Union from which the Confederate (Southern) slave states had seceded on his election. In 1863 he announced the freedom of the slaves with the Emancipation Proclamation. He was re-elected in 1864 with victory for the North in sight, but was assassinated at the end of the war.

Lindbergh Charles A(ugustus) 1902–1974. US aviator who made the first solo nonstop flight in 33.5 hours across the Atlantic (Roosevelt Field, Long Island, New York, to Le Bourget airport, Paris) 1927 in the *Spirit of St Louis*, a Ryan monoplane designed by him.

Linnaeus Carolus 1707–1778. Swedish naturalist and physician. His botanical work *Systema naturae* 1735 contained his system for classifying plants into groups depending on shared characteristics (such as the number of stamens in flowers), providing a much-needed framework for identification. He also devised the concise and precise system for naming plants and animals, using one Latin (or Latinized) word to represent the genus and a second to distinguish the species.

lion cat *Panthera leo*, now found only in Africa and NW India. The coat is tawny, the young having darker spot markings that usually disappear in the adult. The male has a heavy mane and a tuft at the end of the tail. Head and body measure about 2 m/6 ft, plus 1 m/3 ft of tail, the lioness being slightly smaller. Lions produce litters of two to six cubs, and often live in prides of several adult males and females with several young.

Li Peng 1928– . Chinese communist politician, a member of the Politburo from 1985, and head of government from 1987. During the prodemocracy demonstrations of 1989 he supported the massacre of students by Chinese troops and the subsequent execution of others. He sought improved relations with the USSR before its demise, and has favoured maintaining firm central and party control over the economy.

lipid any of a large number of esters of fatty acids, commonly formed by the reaction of a fatty acid with glycerol (see ⟩glyceride). They are soluble in alcohol but not in water. Lipids are the chief constituents of plant and animal waxes, fats, and oils.

Lippi Fra Filippo *c.* 1406–1469. Italian painter. His works include frescoes depicting the lives of St Stephen and St John the Baptist in Prato Cathedral 1452–66. He also painted many altarpieces of Madonnas and groups of saints.

liquid state of matter between a ⟩solid and a ⟩gas. A liquid forms a level surface and assumes the shape of its container. Its atoms do not occupy fixed positions as in a crystalline solid, nor do they have freedom of movement as in a gas. Unlike a gas, a liquid is difficult to compress since pressure applied at one point is equally transmitted throughout (Pascal's principle). ⟩Hydraulics makes use of this property.

liquid-crystal display (LCD) display of numbers (for example, in a calculator) or pictures (such as on a pocket television screen) produced by molecules of a substance in a semiliquid state with some crystalline properties, so that clusters of molecules align in parallel formations. The display is a blank until the application of an electric field, which 'twists' the molecules so that they reflect or transmit light falling on them.

Lisbon (Portuguese *Lisboa*) city and capital of Portugal, in the SW of the country, on the tidal lake and estuary formed by the river Tagus; population (1984) 808,000. It has been the capital since 1260.

Liszt Franz 1811–1886. Hungarian pianist and composer. An outstanding virtuoso of the piano, he was an established concert artist by the age of 12. His expressive, romantic, and frequently chromatic works include piano music (*Transcendental Studies* 1851), masses and oratorios, songs, organ music, and a symphony. Much of his music is programmatic; he also originated the symphonic poem.

litchi or *lychee* evergreen tree *Litchi chinensis* of the soapberry family Sapindaceae. The delicately flavoured ovate fruit is encased in a brownish rough outer skin and has a hard seed. The litchi is native to S China, where it has been cultivated for 2,000 years.

lithium soft, ductile, silver-white, metallic element, symbol Li, atomic number 3, relative atomic mass 6.941. It is one of the ⟩alkali metals, has a very low density (far less than most woods), and floats on water (specific gravity 0.57); it is the lightest of all metals. Lithium is used to harden alloys, and in batteries;

its compounds are used in medicine to treat manic depression.

lithography printmaking technique invented in 1798 by Aloys Senefelder, based on the mutual repulsion of grease and water. A drawing is made with greasy crayon on an absorbent stone, which is then wetted. The wet stone repels ink (which is greasy) applied to the surface and the crayon absorbs it, so that the drawing can be printed. Lithographic printing is used in book production, posters, and prints, and this basic principle has developed into complex processes.

Lithuania Republic of; *area* 65,200 sq km/25,174 sq mi; *capital* Vilnius; *features* river Nemen; white sand dunes on Kursiu Marios lagoon; *political system* emergent democracy; *population* (1994) 3,740,000 (Lithuanian 80%, Russian 9%, Polish 7%, Byelorussian 2%); *language* Lithuanian; *religion* predominantly Roman Catholic.

litmus dye obtained from various lichens and used in chemistry as an indicator to test the acidic or alkaline nature of aqueous solutions; it turns red in the presence of acid, and blue in the presence of alkali.

liver large organ of vertebrates, which has many regulatory and storage functions. The human liver is situated in the upper abdomen, and weighs about 2 kg/4.5 lb. It is divided into four lobes. The liver receives the products of digestion, converts glucose to glycogen (a long-chain carbohydrate used for storage), and breaks down fats. It removes excess amino acids from the blood, converting them to urea, which is excreted by the kidneys. The liver also synthesizes vitamins, produces bile and blood-clotting factors, and removes damaged red cells and toxins such as alcohol from the blood.

Liverpool city, seaport, and administrative headquarters of Merseyside, NW England; population (1991 est) 448,300. Liverpool is the UK's chief Atlantic port. The Mersey Tunnel (1886), rail tunnel, and Queensway Tunnel (1934), link Liverpool and Birkenhead. Kingsway Tunnel (1971) links Liverpool and Wallasey; *features* St George's Hall (1838–54), a fine example of Classical architecture; Anglican cathedral, designed by George Gilbert Scott 1980; the Tate Gallery in the N in former Albert Dock 1987; one of the finest public libraries in the country; all the members of the ▷Beatles were born here.

Livingstone David 1813–1873. Scottish missionary explorer. In 1841 he went to Africa, reached Lake Ngami 1849, followed the Zambezi to its mouth, saw the Victoria Falls 1855, and went to East and Central Africa 1858–64, reaching Lakes Shirwa and Malawi. From 1866, he tried to find the source of the river Nile, and reached Ujiji in Tanganyika in Nov 1871.

Livy (Titus Livius) 59 BC–AD 17. Roman historian. He was the author of a *History of Rome* from the city's foundation to 9 BC, based partly on legend. It was composed of 142 books, of which 35 survive, covering the periods from the arrival of Aeneas in Italy to 293 BC and from 218 to 167 BC.

lizard reptile of the suborder Lacertilia, which together with snakes constitutes the order Squamata. Lizards are generally distinguishable from snakes by having four legs, moveable eyelids, eardrums, and a fleshy tongue, but some lizards are legless and snakelike in appearance. There are over 3,000 species of lizard worldwide.

Ljubljana (German *Laibach*) capital and industrial city of Slovenia, near the confluence of the rivers Ljubljanica and Sava; population (1991) 276,100. It has a nuclear research centre and is linked with S Austria by the Karawanken road tunnel under the Alps (1979–83).

Lloyd George David 1863–1945. Welsh Liberal politician, prime minister of Britain 1916–22. A pioneer of social reform, as chancellor of the Exchequer 1908–15 he introduced old-age pensions 1908 and health and unemployment insurance 1911. The creation of the Irish Free State in 1921 and his pro-Greek policy against the Turks caused the collapse of his coalition government.

Lloyd Webber Andrew 1948– . English composer. His early musicals, with lyrics by Tim Rice, include *Joseph and the Amazing Technicolor Dreamcoat* 1968, *Jesus Christ Superstar* 1970, and *Evita* 1978, based on the life of the Argentine leader Eva Perón. He also wrote *Cats* 1981, based on T S Eliot's *Old Possum's Book of Practical Cats*, *Starlight Express* 1984, *The Phantom of the Opera* 1986, and *Aspects of Love* 1989.

Locarno, Pact of series of diplomatic documents initialled in Locarno, Switzerland, 16 Oct 1925 and formally signed in London 1 Dec 1925. The pact settled the question of French security, and the signatories – Britain, France, Belgium, Italy, and Germany – guaranteed Germany's existing frontiers with France and Belgium. Following the signing of the pact, Germany was admitted to the League of Nations.

Loch Ness Scottish lake; see ▷Ness, Loch.

lock construction installed in waterways to allow boats or ships to travel from one level to another. The earliest form, the *flash lock*, was first seen in the East in 1st-century AD – China and in the West in 11th-century – Holland. By this method barriers temporarily dammed a river and when removed allowed the flash flood to propel the waiting boat through any obstacle. This was followed in 12th-century China and 14th-century Holland by the *pound lock*. In this system the lock has gates at each end. Boats enter through one gate when the levels are the same both outside and inside. Water is then allowed in (or out of) the lock until the level rises (or falls) to the new level outside the other gate.

Locke John 1632–1704. English philosopher. His Essay concerning Human Understanding 1690 maintained that experience was the only source of knowledge (empiricism), and that 'we can have knowlege no farther than we have ideas' prompted by such experience. *Two Treatises on Government* 1690 helped to form contemporary ideas of liberal democracy.

locomotive engine for hauling railway trains. In 1804 Richard Trevithick built the first steam engine to run on rails. Locomotive design did not radically improve until British engineer George Stephenson built the *Rocket* 1829, which featured a multitube boiler and blastpipe, standard in all following *steam locomotives*. Today most locomotives are diesel or electric: *diesel locomotives* have a powerful diesel engine, and *electric locomotives* draw their power from either an overhead cable or a third rail alongside the ordinary track.

lode geological deposit rich in certain minerals, generally consisting of a large vein or set of veins containing ore minerals. A system of veins that can be mined directly forms a lode, for example the mother lode of the California gold rush.

logarithm or *log* the exponent or index of a number to a specified base – usually 10. For example, the logarithm to the base 10 of 1,000 is 3 because $10^3 = 1,000$; the logarithm of 2 is 0.3010 because $2 = 10^{0.3010}$. Before the advent of cheap electronic calculators, multiplication and division could be simplified by being replaced with the addition and subtraction of logarithms.

logic branch of philosophy that studies valid reasoning and argument. It is also the way in which one thing may be said to follow from, or be a consequence of, another (deductive logic). Logic is generally divided into the traditional formal logic of Aristotle and the symbolic logic derived from Friedrich Frege and Bertrand Russell.

logical positivism doctrine that the only meaningful propositions are those that can be verified empirically. Metaphysics, religion, and aesthetics are therefore meaningless.

Loire longest river in France, rising in the Cévennes Mountains, at 1,350 m/4,430 ft and flowing for 1,050 km/650 mi first N then W until it reaches the Bay of Biscay at St Nazaire, passing Nevers, Orléans, Tours, and Nantes. It gives its name to the *départements* of Loire, Haute-Loire, Loire-Atlantique, Indre-et-Loire, Maine-et-Loire, and Saône-et-Loire. There are many châteaux and vineyards along its banks.

Lollard follower of the English religious reformer John ▷Wycliffe in the 14th century. The Lollards condemned the doctrine of the transubstantiation of the bread and wine of the Eucharist, advocated the diversion of ecclesiastical property to charitable uses, and denounced war and capital punishment. They were active from about 1377.

Lombardy (Italian *Lombardia*) region of N Italy, including Lake Como; capital Milan; area 23,900 sq km/9,225 sq mi; population (1990) 8,939,400. It is the country's chief industrial area.

Lomé capital and port of Togo; population (1983) 366,000. It is a centre for gold, silver, and marble crafts.

Lomond, Loch largest freshwater Scottish lake, 37 km/21 mi long, area 70 sq km/27 sq mi, divided between Strathclyde and Central regions. It is overlooked by the mountain *Ben Lomond* (973 m/3,192 ft) and is linked to the Clyde estuary.

London capital of England and the United Kingdom, on the river Thames; its metropolitan area, *Greater London*, has an area of 1,580 sq km/610 sq mi and population (1991) of 6,679,700 (larger metropolitan area about 9 million). The *City of London*, known as the 'square mile', area 274 hectares/677 acres, is the financial and commercial centre of the UK. Roman *Londinium* was established soon after the Roman invasion AD 43. *features* the Tower of London, built by William the Conqueror on a Roman site, housing the crown jewels and the royal armouries; St Paul's Cathedral; Buckingham Palace; and Westminster Abbey; *museums*: British, Victoria and Albert, Natural History, Science; *galleries*: National Gallery,

National Portrait, Hayward, Wallace Collection, Courtauld Institute.

Londonderry former name (to 1984) of the county and city of ◊Derry in Northern Ireland.

lone pair in chemistry, a pair of electrons in the outermost shell of an atom that are not used in bonding. In certain circumstances, they will allow the atom to bond with atoms, ions, or molecules (such as boron trifluoride, BF_3) that are deficient in electrons, forming coordinate covalent (dative) bonds in which they provide both of the bonding electrons.

Longfellow Henry Wadsworth 1807–1882. US poet. He is remembered for his ballads ('Excelsior', 'The Village Blacksmith', 'The Wreck of the Hesperus') and the mythic narrative epics *Evangeline* 1847, *The Song of Hiawatha* 1855, and *The Courtship of Miles Standish* 1858.

Long Island island E of Manhattan and SE of Connecticut, USA, separated from the mainland by Long Island Sound and the East River; 120 mi/193 km long by about 30 mi/48km wide; area 1,400 sq mi/3,627 sq km; population (1984) 6,818,480.

longitude see ◊latitude and longitude.

long jump field event in athletics in which competitors sprint up to and leap from a take-off board into a sandpit measuring 9 metres in length. The take-off board is 1 metre from the landing area. Each competitor usually has six attempts, and the winner is the one with the longest jump.

Long March in Chinese history, the 10,000 km/6,000 mi trek undertaken 1934–35 by Mao Zedong and his communist forces from SE to NW China, under harassment from the Guomindang (nationalist) army.

Long Parliament English Parliament 1640–53 and 1659–60, which continued through the Civil War. After the Royalists withdrew in 1642 and the Presbyterian right was excluded in 1648, the remaining ◊Rump ruled England until expelled by Oliver Cromwell in 1653. Reassembled 1659–60, the Long Parliament initiated the negotiations for the restoration of the monarchy.

loom any machine for weaving yarn or thread into cloth. The first looms were used to weave sheep's wool about 5000 BC. A loom is a frame on which a set of lengthwise threads (warp) is strung. A second set of threads (weft), carried in a shuttle, is inserted at right angles over and under the warp.

Lorca Federico García 1898–1936. Spanish poet and playwright. His plays include *Bodas de sangre/Blood Wedding* 1933 and *La casa de Bernarda Alba/The House of Bernarda Alba* 1936. His poems include 'Lament', written for the bullfighter Mejías. Lorca was shot by the Falangists during the Spanish Civil War.

Lorenz Konrad 1903–1989. Austrian ethologist. Director of the Max Planck Institute for the Physiology of Behaviour in Bavaria 1955–73, he wrote the studies of ethology (animal behaviour) *King Solomon's Ring* 1952 and *On Aggression* 1966. In 1973 he shared the Nobel Prize for Medicine with Nikolaas Tinbergen and Karl von Frisch.

Lorraine region of NE France in the upper reaches of the Meuse and Moselle rivers; bounded N by Belgium, Luxembourg, and Germany and E by Alsace; area 23,600 sq km/9,095 sq mi; population (1986) 2,313,000. It comprises the *départements* of Meurthe-et- Moselle, Meuse, Moselle, and Vosges, and its capital is Nancy.

Los Angeles city and port in SW California, USA; population (1990) 3,485,400, metropolitan area of Los Angeles – Long Beach 14,531,530.

Lothian region of Scotland; *area* 1,800 sq km/695 sq mi; *towns and cities* Edinburgh (administrative headquarters), Livingston; *features* fertile lowlands bordering on the Firth of Forth in N and rising gently in S; hills: Lammermuir, Moorfoot, Pentland; Bass Rock in the Firth of Forth, noted for seabirds; *population* (1991) 726,000.

loudspeaker electromechanical device that converts electrical signals into sound waves, which are radiated into the air. The most common type of loudspeaker is the *moving-coil speaker*. Electrical signals from, for example, a radio are fed to a coil of fine wire wound around the top of a cone. The coil is surrounded by a magnet. When signals pass through it, the coil becomes an electromagnet, which by moving causes the cone to vibrate, setting up sound waves.

Louis XIV (called *the Sun King*) 1638–1715. King of France from 1643, when he succeeded his father Louis XIII; his mother was Anne of Austria. Until 1661 France was ruled by the chief minister, Jules Mazarin, but later Louis took absolute power, summed up in his saying *L'Etat c'est moi* ('I am the state'). Throughout his reign he was engaged in unsuccessful expansionist wars – 1667–68, 1672–78, 1688–97, and 1701–13 (the War of the ◊Spanish Succession) – against various European alliances, always including Britain and the Netherlands. He was a patron of the arts.

Louis XVI 1754–1793. King of France from 1774, grandson of Louis XV, and son of Louis the Dauphin. He was dominated by his queen, ◊Marie Antoinette, and French finances fell into such confusion that in 1789 the ◊States General (parliament) had to be summoned, and the ◊French Revolution began. Louis lost his personal popularity in June 1791 when he attempted to flee the country, and in Aug 1792 the Parisians stormed the Tuileries palace and took the royal family prisoner. Deposed in Sept 1792, Louis was tried in Dec, sentenced for treason in Jan 1793, and guillotined.

Louisiana state in S USA; *area* 135,900 sq km/52,457 sq mi; *capital* Baton Rouge; *features* New Orleans French Quarter: jazz, restaurants, Mardi Gras; Mississippi River delta; *population* (1990) 4,220,000; including Cajuns, descendants of 18th-century religious exiles from Canada, who speak a French dialect.

Louisiana Purchase purchase by the USA from France 1803 of an area covering about 2,144,000 sq km/828,000 sq mi, including the present-day states of Louisiana, Missouri, Arkansas, Iowa, Nebraska, North Dakota, South Dakota, and Oklahoma.

Lourdes town in Midi-Pyrénées region, SW France, on the Gave de Pau River; population (1982) 18,000. Its Christian shrine to St Bernadette has a reputation for miraculous cures and Lourdes is an important Catholic pilgrimage centre. The young peasant girl Bernadette Soubirous was shown the healing springs of the Grotte de Massabielle by a vision of the Virgin Mary 1858.

louse parasitic insect of the order Anoplura, which lives on mammals. It has a flat, segmented body without wings, and a tube attached to the head, used for sucking blood from its host.

Low Countries region of Europe that consists of ▷Belgium and the ▷Netherlands, and usually includes ▷Luxembourg.

Lower Saxony (German *Niedersachsen*) administrative region (German *Land*) of N Germany; *area* 47,400 sq km/18,296 sq mi; *capital* Hanover; *features* Lüneburg Heath; *population* (1988) 7,190,000; *religion* 75% Protestant, 20% Roman Catholic.

LSD (abbreviation for *lysergic acid diethylamide*) psychedelic drug, an ▷hallucinogen. Colourless, odourless, and easily synthesized, it is nonaddictive and nontoxic, but its effects are unpredictable. Its use is illegal in most countries.

Luanda formerly *Loanda* capital and industrial port of Angola; population (1988) 1,200,000. Founded 1575, it became a Portuguese colonial administrative centre as well as an outlet for slaves transported to Brazil.

Lucifer in Christian theology, another name for the ▷devil, the leader of the angels who rebelled against God. Lucifer is also another name for the morning star (the planet ▷Venus).

Lucretius (Titus Lucretius Carus) *c.* 99–55 BC. Roman poet and ▷Epicurean philosopher whose *De Rerum natura/On the Nature of The Universe* envisaged the whole universe as a combination of atoms, and had some concept of evolutionary theory.

Luddite one of a group of people involved in machine-wrecking riots in N England 1811–16. The organizer of the Luddites was referred to as General Ludd, but may not have existed. Many Luddites were hanged or transported to penal colonies, such as Australia.

Luftwaffe German air force used both in World War I and (as reorganized by the Nazi leader Hermann Goering in 1933) in World War II. The Luftwaffe also covered anti-aircraft defence and the launching of the flying bombs V1 and V2.

Luke, St traditionally, the compiler of the third Gospel and of the Acts of the Apostles in the New Testament. He is the patron saint of painters; his emblem is a winged ox, and his feast day 18 Oct.

lumbar puncture or *spinal tap* insertion of a hollow needle between two lumbar (lower back) vertebrae to withdraw a sample of cerebrospinal fluid (CSF) for testing. Normally clear and colourless, the CSF acts as a fluid buffer around the brain and spinal cord. Changes in its quantity, colour, or composition may indicate neurological damage or disease.

Lumière Auguste Marie 1862–1954 and Louis Jean 1864–1948. French brothers who pioneered cinematography. In 1895 they patented their cinematograph, a combined camera and projector operating at 16 frames per second, and opened the world's first cinema in Paris to show their films.

lung large cavity of the body, used for ▷gas exchange. It is essentially a sheet of thin, moist membrane that is folded so as to occupy less space. Most tetrapod (four-limbed) vertebrates have a pair of lungs occupying the thorax. The lung tissue, consisting of multitudes of air sacs and blood vessels, is very light and spongy, and functions by bringing inhaled air into close contact with the blood so that oxygen can pass into the organism and waste carbon dioxide can be passed out. The efficiency of lungs is enhanced by ◊breathing movements, by the thinness and moistness of their surfaces, and by a constant supply of circulating blood.

lungfish three genera of fleshy-finned bony fishes of the subclass Dipnoi, found in Africa, South America, and Australia. They have elongated bodies, and grow to about 2 m/6 ft, and in addition to gills have 'lungs' with which they can breathe air during periods of drought conditions.

Luoyang or *Loyang* industrial city in Henan province, China, S of the river Huang He; population 1,114,000. It was formerly the capital of China and an important Buddhist centre in the 5th and 6th centuries.

lupus in medicine, any of various diseases characterized by lesions of the skin. One form (lupus vulgaris) is caused by the tubercle bacillus (see ◊tuberculosis). The organism produces ulcers that spread and eat away the underlying tissues. Treatment is primarily with standard antituberculous drugs, but ultraviolet light may also be used.

Lusaka capital of Zambia from 1964 (of Northern Rhodesia 1935–64), 370 km/230 mi NE of Livingstone; it is a commercial and agricultural centre; population (1988) 870,000.

lute member of a family of stringed musical instruments of the 14th–18th century, including the mandore, theorbo, and chitarrone. Lutes are pear-shaped with up to seven courses of strings (single or double), plucked with the fingers. Music for lutes is written in special notation called tablature and chords are played simultaneously, not arpeggiated as for guitar. Modern lutenists include Julian Bream (1933–) and Anthony Rooley (1944–).

luteinizing hormone ◊hormone produced by the pituitary gland. In males, it stimulates the testes to produce androgens (male sex hormones). In females, it works together with follicle-stimulating hormone to initiate production of egg cells by the ovary. If fertilization occurs, it plays a part in maintaining the pregnancy by controlling the levels of the hormones oestrogen and progesterone in the body.

Luther Martin 1483–1546. German Christian church reformer, regarded as the instigator of the Protestant revolution. While a priest at the University of Wittenberg, he wrote an attack on the sale of indulgences. The Holy Roman emperor Charles V summoned him to the Diet of Worms in Germany 1521, where he refused to retract his objections. Originally intending reform, his protest led to schism, with the emergence, following the Augsburg Confession 1530 (a statement of the Protestant faith), of a new Protestant church. After the Confession, he gradually retired from the Protestant leadership.

Lutheranism form of Protestant Christianity derived from the life and teaching of Martin Luther; it is sometimes called Evangelical to distinguish it from the other main branch of European Protestantism, the Reformed. The most generally accepted statement of Lutheranism is that of the *Confession of Augsburg* 1530 but Luther's Shorter Catechism also carries great weight. It is the largest Protestant body and is the major religion of many N European countries, including Germany, Sweden, and Denmark.

Lutyens Edwin Landseer 1869–1944. English architect. His designs ranged from the picturesque, such as Castle Drogo, Devon, 1910–30, to Renaissance-style country houses, and ultimately evolved into a Classical style as seen in the Cenotaph, London, 1919, and the Viceroy's House, New Delhi, India, 1912–31.

Luxembourg capital of the country of Luxembourg, on the Alzette and Petrusse rivers; population (1985) 76,000. The 16th-century Grand Ducal Palace, European Court of Justice, and European Parliament secretariat are situated here, but plenary sessions of the parliament are now held only in Strasbourg, France.

Luxembourg Grand Duchy of (*Grand-Duché de Luxembourg*); *area* 2,586 sq km/998 sq mi; *capital* Luxembourg; *features* seat of the European Court of Justice, Secretariat of the European Parliament, international banking centre; economically linked with Belgium; *head of state* Grand Duke Jean from 1964; *head of government* Jacques Santer from 1984; *political system* liberal democracy; *population* (1993) 395,200; growth rate 0% p.a.; *languages* French (official), local Letzeburgesch, German; *religion* Roman Catholic 97%.

Luxor (Arabic *al-Uqsur*) small town in Egypt on the E bank of the river Nile. The ancient city of Thebes is on the W bank, with the temple of Luxor built by Amenhotep III (*c.* 1411–1375 BC) and the tombs of the pharaohs in the Valley of the Kings.

LW abbreviation for *long wave*, a radio wave with a wavelength of over 1,000 m/3,300 ft; one of the main wavebands into which radio frequency transmissions are divided.

lymph fluid found in the lymphatic system of vertebrates.

lymph nodes small masses of lymphatic tissue in the body that occur at various points along the major lymphatic vessels. Tonsils and adenoids are large lymph nodes. As the lymph passes through them it is filtered, and bacteria and other microorganisms are engulfed by cells known as macrophages.

lymphocyte type of white blood cell with a large nucleus, produced in the bone marrow. Most occur in the ◊lymph and blood, and around sites of infection. *B lymphocytes* or B cells are responsible for producing ◊antibodies. *T lymphocytes* or T cells have several roles in the mechanism of ◊immunity.

Lyon (English *Lyons*) industrial city and capital of Rhône *département*, Rhône-Alpes region, at the confluence of the rivers Rhône and Saône, 275 km/170 mi NNW of Marseille; population (1990) 422,400, conurbation 1,221,000. It is the third-largest city of France.

lyre stringed instrument of great antiquity. It consists of a soundbox with two curved arms extended upwards to a crosspiece to which four to ten strings are attached. It is played with a plectrum or the fingers. It originated in Asia, and was widespread in ancient Greece and Egypt.

M

Maastricht Treaty treaty on European union, agreed 10 Dec 1991 by leaders of European Community nations at a summit meeting at Maastricht in the Netherlands. Initially rejected by the Danish in a June 1992 referendum, it was eventually ratified by all member states and took effect 1 Nov 1993, from which date the European Community became known as the ▷European Union (EU).

Mabuse Jan. Adopted name of Jan Gossaert *c.* 1478–*c.* 1533. Flemish painter. He was active chiefly in Antwerp. His visit to Italy 1508 started a new vogue in Flanders for Italianate ornament and Classical detail in painting, including sculptural nude figures, as in his *Neptune and Amphitrite* about 1516 (Staatliche Museen, Berlin).

Macbeth King of Scotland from 1040. The son of Findlaech, hereditary ruler of Moray, he was commander of the forces of Duncan I, King of Scotia, whom he killed in battle 1040. His reign was prosperous until Duncan's son Malcolm III led an invasion and killed him at Lumphanan.

MacDonald (James) Ramsay 1866–1937. British politician, first Labour prime minister Jan–Oct 1924 and 1929–31. Failing to deal with worsening economic conditions, he left the party to form a coalition government 1931, which was increasingly dominated by Conservatives, until he was replaced by Stanley Baldwin 1935.

Macedonia ancient region of Greece, forming parts of modern Greece, Bulgaria, and the Former Yugoslav Republic of Macedonia. Macedonia gained control of Greece after Philip II's victory at Chaeronea 338 BC. His son, ▷Alexander the Great, conquered a vast empire. Macedonia became a Roman province 146 BC.

Macedonia Former Yugoslav Republic of; *area* 25,700 sq km/9,920 sq mi; *capital* Skopje; *political system* emergent democracy; *population* (1992) 2,060,000 (Albanian 20%, Turkish 4.8%, Hungarian 2.7%, Serb 2.2%); *language* Macedonian, closely allied to Bulgarian and written in Cyrillic; *religion* Christian, mainly Orthodox; Muslim 2.5%.

Macedonia (Greek *Makedhonia*) mountainous region of N Greece, part of the ancient country of Macedonia which was divided between Serbia, Bulgaria, and Greece after the Balkan Wars of 1912–13. Greek Macedonia is bounded W and N by Albania and the Former Yugoslav Republic of Macedonia; area 34,177 sq km/13,200 sq mi; population (1991) 2,263,000. The chief city is Thessaloniki. Mount Olympus rises to 2,918 m/9,570 ft on the border with Thessaly.

Macedonian person of Macedonian culture from the Former Yugoslav Republic of Macedonia and the surrounding area, especially Greece, Albania, and Bulgaria. Macedonian, a Slavic language belonging to the Indo-European family, has 1–1.5 million speakers. The Macedonians are predominantly members of the Greek Orthodox Church and write with a Cyrillic script. They are known for their folk arts.

Machiavelli Niccolò 1469–1527. Italian politician and author. His name is synonymous with cunning and cynical statecraft. In his most celebrated political writings, *Il principe/The Prince* 1513 and *Discorsi/Discourses* 1531, he discussed ways in which rulers can advance the interests of their states (and themselves) through an often amoral and opportunistic manipulation of other people.

machine device that allows a small force (the effort) to overcome a larger one (the load). There are three basic machines: the inclined plane (ramp), the lever, and the wheel and axle. All other machines are combinations of these three basic types. Simple machines derived from the inclined plane include the wedge, the gear, and the screw; the spanner is derived from the lever; the pulley from the wheel.

Mach number ratio of the speed of a body to the speed of sound in the undisturbed medium through which the body travels. Mach 1 is reached when a body (such as an aircraft) has a velocity greater than that of sound ('passes the sound barrier'), namely 331 m/1,087 ft per second at sea level. It is named after Austrian physicist Ernst Mach (1838–1916).

McKellen Ian (Murray) 1939– . English actor. Acclaimed as the leading Shakespearean player of his generation, his stage roles include Richard II 1968, Macbeth 1977, Max in Martin Sherman's *Bent* 1979, Platonov in Chekhov's *Wild Honey* 1986, Iago in *Othello* 1989, and Richard III 1990. His films include *Priest of Love* 1982 and *Plenty* 1985.

McKinley, Mount or *Denali* peak in Alaska, USA, the highest in North America, 6,194 m/20,320 ft; named after US president William McKinley.

Macmillan (Maurice) Harold, 1st Earl of Stockton 1894–1986. British Conservative politician, prime minister 1957–63; foreign secretary 1955 and chancellor of the Exchequer 1955–57. In 1963 he attempted to negotiate British entry into the European Economic Community, but was blocked by French president de Gaulle. Much of his career as prime minister was spent defending the retention of a UK nuclear weapon, and he was responsible for the purchase of US Polaris missiles 1962.

Madagascar Democratic Republic of (*Repoblika Demokratika n'i Madagaskar*); *area* 587,041 sq km/226,598 sq mi; *capital* Antananarivo; *environment* according to 1990 UN figures, 93% of the forest area has been destroyed and about 100,000 species have been made extinct; *features* one of the last places to be inhabited, it evolved in isolation with unique animals (such as the lemur, now under threat from deforestation); *political system* emergent democratic republic; *population* (1993 est) 13,000,000, mostly of Malayo-Indonesian origin; growth rate 3.2% p.a.; *languages* Malagasy (official), French, English; *religions* animist 50%, Christian 40%, Muslim 10%.

Madeira group of islands forming an autonomous region of Portugal off the NW coast of Africa, about 420 km/260 mi N of the Canary Islands. Madeira, the largest, and Porto Santo are the only inhabited islands. The Desertas and Selvagens are uninhabited islets. Their mild climate makes them a year-round resort; *area* 796 sq km/308 sq mi; *capital* Funchal, on Madeira; *population* (1986) 269,500.

Madhya Pradesh state of central India; the largest of the Indian states; *area* 442,700 sq km/170,921 sq mi; *capital* Bhopal; *population* (1991) 66,135,400; *language* Hindi.

Madras industrial port and capital of Tamil Nadu, India, on the Bay of Bengal; population (1981) 4,277,000. Fort St George 1639 remains from the East India Company when Madras was the chief port on the E coast.

Madrid industrial city and capital of Spain and of Madrid province; population (1991) 2,984,600. Built on an elevated plateau in the centre of the country, at 655 m/2,183 ft it is the highest capital city in Europe and has excesses of heat and cold. Madrid province has an area of 8,000 sq km/3,088 sq mi and a population of 4,855,000; *features* The Real Academia de Bellas Artes (1752); the Prado museum (1785); the royal palace (1764), built for Philip V; the 15th century Retiro Park; the Plaza Mayor (1617–20); the Akalá Arch; and the basilica of San Francisco el Grande (1761–84).

Mafia secret society reputed to control organized crime such as gambling, loan-sharking, drug traffic, prostitution, and protection; connected with the Camorra of Naples, a secret society founded in the 1820's and suppressed in 1911, but which still operates in the Naples area. It originated in Sicily in the late Middle Ages and now operates chiefly there and in countries to which Italians have emigrated, such as the USA and Australia. During the early 1990s it became increasingly evident that prominent Italian politicians had had dealings with the Mafia, and by 1993 many centre and right-wing politicians had been discredited.

Magellan Ferdinand 1480–1521. Portuguese navigator. In 1519 he set sail in the *Victoria* from Seville with the intention of reaching the East Indies by a westerly route. He sailed through the *Strait of Magellan* at the tip of South America, crossed an ocean he named the Pacific, and in 1521 reached the Philippines, where he was killed in a battle with the islanders.

Magellanic Clouds in astronomy, the two galaxies nearest to our own galaxy. They are irregularly shaped, and appear as detached parts of the ◊Milky Way, in the southern constellations Dorado and Tucana.

magi (singular *magus*) priests of the Zoroastrian religion of ancient Persia, noted for their knowledge of astrology. The term is used in the New Testament of the Latin Vulgate Bible where the Authorized Version gives 'wise men'. The magi who came to visit the infant Jesus with gifts of gold, frankincense, and myrrh (the *Adoration of the Magi*) were in later tradition described as 'the three kings' – Caspar, Melchior, and Balthazar.

magistrates' court in England and Wales, a local law court that mainly deals with minor criminal cases. A magistrates' court consists of between two and seven lay justices of the peace (who are advised on the law by a clerk to the justices), or a single paid lawyer called a stipendiary magistrate.

maglev (acronym for *magnetic levitation*) high-speed surface transport using the repellent force of superconductive magnets (see ▷superconductivity) to propel and support, for example, a train above a track.

magma molten rock material beneath the Earth's surface from which ▷igneous rocks are formed. ▷Lava is magma that has reached the surface and solidified, losing some of its components on the way.

Magna Carta in English history, the charter granted by King John 1215, traditionally seen as guaranteeing human rights against the excessive use of royal power. As a reply to the king's demands for excessive feudal dues and attacks on the privileges of the church, Archbishop Langton proposed to the barons the drawing-up of a binding document 1213. John was forced to accept this at Runnymede (now in Surrey) 15 June 1215.

magnesium lightweight, very ductile and malleable, silver-white, metallic element, symbol Mg, atomic number 12, relative atomic mass 24.305. It is one of the ▷alkaline- earth metals, and the lightest of the commonly used metals. Magnesium silicate, carbonate, and chloride are widely distributed in nature. The metal is used in alloys and flash photography. It is a necessary trace element in the human diet, and green plants cannot grow without it since it is an essential constituent of the photosynthetic pigment ▷chlorophyll ($C_{55}H_{72}MgN_4O_5$).

magnet any object that forms a magnetic field (displays ▷magnetism), either permanently or temporarily through induction, causing it to attract materials such as iron, cobalt, nickel, and alloys of these. It always has two magnetic poles, called north and south.

magnetic field region around a permanent magnet, or around a conductor carrying an electric current, in which a force acts on a moving charge or on a magnet placed in the field. The field can be represented by lines of force, which by convention link north and south poles and are parallel to the directions of a small compass needle placed on them. A magnetic field's magnitude and direction are given by the magnetic flux density, expressed in teslas.

magnetic resonance imaging (MRI) diagnostic scanning system based on the principles of nuclear magnetic resonance. MRI yields finely detailed three-dimensional images of structures within the body without exposing the patient to harmful radiation. The technique is invaluable for imaging the soft tissues of the body, in particular the brain and the spinal cord.

magnetism phenomena associated with ▷magnetic fields. Magnetic fields are produced by moving charged particles: in electromagnets, electrons flow through a coil of wire connected to a battery; in permanent magnets, spinning electrons within the atoms generate the field. Substances differ in the extent to which they can be magnetized by an external field.

magnification measure of the enlargement or reduction of an object in an imaging optical system. *Linear magnification* is the ratio of the size (height) of the image to that of the object. *Angular* *magnification* is the ratio of the angle subtended at the observer's eye by the image to the angle subtended by the object when viewed directly.

magnitude in astronomy, measure of the brightness of a star or other celestial object. The larger the number denoting the magnitude, the fainter the object. Zero or first magnitude indicates some of the brightest stars. Still brighter are those of negative magnitude, such as Sirius, whose magnitude is -1.46. *Apparent magnitude* is the brightness of an object as seen from Earth; *absolute magnitude* is the brightness at a standard distance of 10 parsecs (32.6 light years).

Magritte René 1898–1967. Belgian Surrealist painter. His work focuses on visual paradoxes and everyday objects taken out of context. Recurring motifs include bowler hats, apples, and windows, for example *Golconda* 1953 (private collection), in which men in bowler hats are falling from the sky to a street below.

Magyar member of the largest ethnic group in Hungary, comprising 92% of the population. Magyars are of mixed Ugric and Turkic origin, and they arrived in Hungary towards the end of the 9th century. The Magyar language (see Hungarian language) belongs to the Uralic group.

Maharashtra state in W central India; *area* 307,800 sq km/118,811 sq mi; *capital* Bombay; *features* cave temples of Ajanta, containing 200 BC–7th century AD Buddhist murals and sculptures; Ellora cave temples 6th–9th century with Buddhist, Hindu, and Jain sculptures; *population* (1991) 78,706,700; *language* Marathi 50%; *religions* Hindu 80%, Parsee, Jain, and Sikh minorities.

Mahfouz Naguib 1911– . Egyptian novelist and playwright. His novels, which deal with the urban working class, include the semi-autobiographical *Khan al-Kasrain/The Cairo Trilogy* 1956–57. His *Children of Gebelawi* 1959 was banned in Egypt because of its treatment of religious themes. Nobel Prize for Literature 1988.

Mahler Gustav 1860–1911. Austrian composer and conductor. His epic symphonies express a world-weary Romanticism in visionary tableaux incorporating folk music and pastoral imagery. He composed 14 symphonies (three unnumbered), many with voices, including *Symphony No 2 'Resurrection'* 1884–86, revised 1893–96, also orchestral lieder (songs) including *Das Lied von der Erde/The Song of the Earth* 1909 and *Kindertotenlieder/Dead Children's Songs* 1901–04.

mahogany timber from any of several genera of trees found in the Americas and Africa. Mahogany is a tropical hardwood obtained chiefly by rainforest logging. It has a warm red colour and takes a high polish. The species is under threat.

Mailer Norman 1923– . US writer and journalist. One of the most prominent figures of postwar American literature, he gained wide attention with his first, bestselling book *The Naked and the Dead* 1948, a naturalistic war novel. His later works, which use sexual and scatological material, show his personal engagement with history, politics, and psychology.

Maine northeasternmost state of the USA, largest of the New England states; *area* 86,200 sq km/33,273 sq mi; *capital* Augusta; *features* Acadia National Park; Roosevelt's Campobello International

Park; canoeing along the Allagush Wilderness Waterway; *population* (1990) 1,228,000.

mainframe large computer used for commercial data processing and other large-scale operations. Because of the general increase in computing power, the differences between the mainframe, supercomputer, minicomputer, and microcomputer (personal computer) are becoming less marked.

maize (North American *corn*) plant *Zea mays* of the grass family. Grown extensively in all subtropical and warm temperate regions, its range has been extended to colder zones by hardy varieties developed in the 1960s. It is widely used as animal feed.

Major John 1943– . British Conservative politician, prime minister from Nov 1990. He was foreign secretary 1989 and chancellor of the Exchequer 1989–90. His initial positive approach to European union was hindered from 1991 by divisions within the party. Major was returned to power in the April 1992 general election in spite of dissatisfaction with the poll tax, the National Health Service, and the recession. He won some support with the launch of a peace initiative on Northern Ireland 1993 and weathered local and European election defeats 1994.

Majorca (Spanish *Mallorca*) largest of the ◊Balearic Islands, belonging to Spain, in the W Mediterranean; *area* 3,640 sq km/1,405 sq mi; *capital* Palma; *features* the highest mountain is Puig Mayor, 1,445 m/4,741 ft; *population* (1981) 561,215.

Malabo port and capital of Equatorial Guinea, on the island of Bioko; population (1983) 15,253. It was founded in the 1820s by the British as *Port Clarence*. Under Spanish rule it was known as *Santa Isabel* (until 1973).

malaria infectious parasitic disease of the tropics transmitted by mosquitoes, marked by periodic fever and an enlarged spleen. When a female mosquito of the *Anopheles* genus bites a human who has malaria, it takes in with the human blood one of four malaria protozoa of the genus *Plasmodium*. This matures within the insect and is then transferred when the mosquito bites a new victim. Malaria affects some 267 million people in 103 countries, claiming more than a million lives a year.

Malawi Republic of (*Malawi*); *area* 118,000 sq km/45,560 sq mi; *capital* Lilongwe; *features* one-third is water, including lakes Malawi, Chilara, and Malombe; Great Rift Valley; Nyika, Kasungu, and Lengare national parks; Mulanje Massif; Shire River; *political system* emergent democratic republic; *population* (1993 est) 9,700,000 (nearly 1 million refugees from Mozambique); growth rate 3.3% p.a.; *languages* English, Chichewa (both official); *religions* Christian 75%, Muslim 20%.

Malay member of a large group of peoples, comprising the majority population of the Malay Peninsula and Archipelago, and also found in S Thailand and coastal Sumatra and Borneo. The *Malay language* is a member of the Western or Indonesian branch of the Malayo-Polynesian language family, used in the Malay peninsula and many of the islands of Malaysia and Indonesia. It can be written in either Arabic or Roman scripts.

Malaysia, Federation of; country in SE Asia, comprising Peninsular Malaysia (the nine Malay states – Johore, Kedah,

Kelantan, Negri Sembilan, Pahang, Perak, Perlis, Selangor, Trengganu – plus Malacca and Penang); and E Malaysia (Sabah and Sarawak) *area* 329,759 sq km/127,287 sq mi; *capital* Kuala Lumpur; *features* Mount Kinabalu (highest peak in SE Asia); Niah caves (Sarawak); *political system* liberal democracy; *population* (1993) 19,030,000 (Malaysian 47%, Chinese 32%, Indian 8%, others 13%); growth rate 2% p.a.; *languages* Malay (official), English, Chinese, Indian, and local languages; *religions* Muslim (official), Buddhist, Hindu, local beliefs.

Maldives Republic of (*Divehi Jumhuriya*); *area* 298 sq km/115 sq mi; *capital* Malé; *environment* the threat of rising sea level has been heightened by the frequency of flooding in recent years; *features* tourism developed since 1972; *political system* authoritarian nationalism; *population* (1993) 238,400; growth rate 3.7% p.a.; *languages* Divehi (Sinhalese dialect), English; *religion* Sunni Muslim.

Malé capital and chief atoll of the Maldives in the Indian Ocean; population (1990) 55,100.

Mali Republic of (*République du Mali*); *area* 1,240,142 sq km/478,695 sq mi; *capital* Bamako; *environment* a rising population coupled with recent droughts has affected marginal agriculture. Once in surplus, grain has had to be imported every year since 1965; *features* ancient town of Timbuktu; railway to Dakar is the only outlet to the sea; *political system* emergent democratic republic; *population* (1993 est) 8,750,000; growth rate 2.9% p.a.; *languages* French (official), Bambara; *religion* Sunni Muslim 90%, animist 9%, Christian 1%.

Mallarmé Stéphane 1842–1898. French poet. He founded the Symbolist school with Paul Verlaine. His belief that poetry should be evocative and suggestive was reflected in *L'Après-midi d'un faune/Afternoon of a Faun* 1876, which inspired the composer Debussy.

Malle Louis 1932– . French film director. After a period as assistant to director Robert Bresson, he directed *Les Amants/The Lovers* 1958, audacious for its time in its explicitness. His subsequent films, made in France and the USA, include *Zazie dans le métro* 1961, *Viva Maria* 1965, *Pretty Baby* 1978, *Atlantic City* 1980, *Au Revoir les Enfants* 1988, *Milou en mai* 1989, and *Damage* 1993.

Malory Thomas 15th century. English author. He is known for the prose romance *Le Morte d'Arthur* about 1470, a translation from the French, modified by material from other sources. It deals with the exploits of King Arthur's knights of the Round Table and the quest for the ◊Holy Grail.

Malraux André 1901–1976. French writer. An active antifascist, he gained international renown for his novel *La Condition humaine/Man's Estate* 1933, set during the Nationalist/Communist Revolution in China in the 1920s. *L'Espoir/Days of Hope* 1937 is set in Civil War Spain, where he was a bomber pilot in the International Brigade. In World War II he supported the Gaullist resistance, and was minister of cultural affairs 1960–69.

Malta Republic of (*Repubblika Ta' Malta*); *area* 320 sq km/124 sq mi; *capital* and port Valletta; *features* occupies strategic location in central Mediterranean; large commercial dock facilities; *political system* liberal democracy; *population* (1993) 364,600; growth rate 0.7% p.a.; *languages* Maltese, English; *religion* Roman Catholic 98%.

Malthus Thomas Robert 1766–1834. English economist and cleric. His *Essay on the Principle of Population* 1798 (revised 1803) argued for population control, since populations increase in geometric ratio and food supply only in arithmetic ratio, and influenced Charles Darwin's thinking on natural selection as the driving force of evolution.

mammal animal characterized by having mammary glands in the female; these are used for suckling the young. Other features of mammals are ▷hair (very reduced in some species, such as whales); a middle ear formed of three small bones (ossicles); a lower jaw consisting of two bones only; seven vertebrae in the neck; and no nucleus in the red blood cells. Mammals are divided into three groups: *placental mammals*, where the young develop inside the ▷uterus, receiving nourishment from the blood of the mother via the ▷placenta; *marsupials*, where the young are born at an early stage of development and develop further in a pouch on the mother's body; *monotremes*, where the young hatch from an egg outside the mother's body and are then nourished with milk. Platypus and echidna are the only surviving monotremes.

mammary gland in female mammals, a milk-producing gland derived from epithelial cells underlying the skin, active only after the production of young. In all but monotremes (egg-laying mammals), the mammary glands terminate in teats which aid infant suckling. The number of glands and their position vary between species. In humans there are 2, in cows 4, and in pigs between 10 and 14.

Managua capital and chief industrial city of Nicaragua, on the lake of the same name; population (1985) 682,000. It has twice been destroyed by earthquake and rebuilt, 1931 and 1972; it was also badly damaged during the civil war in the late 1970s.

Manama (Arabic *Al Manamah*) capital and free trade port of Bahrain, on Bahrain Island; population (1988) 152,000.

Manchester city in NW England, on the river Irwell, 50 km/31 mi E of Liverpool. It is a manufacturing and financial centre; population (1991) 404,900. It is linked by the Manchester Ship Canal (1894) to the river Mersey and the sea.

Manchester, Greater metropolitan county of NW England, created 1974; in 1986, most of the functions of the former county council were transferred to metropolitan district councils; *area* 1,290 sq km/498 sq mi; *towns and cities* Manchester, Bolton, Oldham, Rochdale, Salford, Stockport, and Wigan; *features* Manchester Ship Canal links it with the river Mersey and the sea; Old Trafford cricket ground at Stretford; football ground of Manchester United. *population* (1991) 2,499,400.

Mandalay chief city of the Mandalay division of Myanmar (formerly Burma), on the river Irrawaddy, about 495 km/370 mi N of Yangon (Rangoon); population (1983) 533,000.

Mandarin standard form of the Chinese language. Historically it derives from the language spoken by *mandarins*, Chinese imperial officials, from the 7th century onwards. It is used by 70% of the population and taught in schools of the People's Republic of China.

Mandela Nelson (Rolihlahla) 1918– . South African politician and lawyer, president from 1994. Imprisoned from 1964, as organizer of the then banned ◊African National Congress (ANC), he became a symbol of unity for the worldwide anti-apartheid movement. In Feb 1990 he was released, the ban on the ANC having been lifted, and as president of the ANC from 1991, entered into negotiations with the government about a multiracial future for South Africa. In May 1994 he was sworn in as South Africa's first post-apartheid president after the ANC won the universal suffrage elections. Nobel Prize for Peace jointly with South African president F W de Klerk 1993.

mandolin plucked string instrument with four to six pairs of strings (courses), tuned like a violin, which flourished 1600–1800. It takes its name from its almond-shaped body (Italian *mandorla* 'almond'). Vivaldi composed two concertos for the mandolin about 1736.

Manet Edouard 1832–1883. French painter. Active in Paris, he was one of the foremost French artists of the 19th century. Rebelling against the academic tradition, he developed a clear and unaffected realist style. His subjects were mainly contemporary, such as *A Bar at the Folies-Bergère* 1882 (Courtauld Art Gallery, London).

manganese hard, brittle, grey-white metallic element, symbol Mn, atomic number 25, relative atomic mass 54.9380. It resembles iron (and rusts), but it is not magnetic and is softer. It is used chiefly in making steel alloys, also alloys with aluminium and copper. It is used in fertilizers, paints, and industrial chemicals. It is a necessary trace element in human nutrition.

mangrove any of several shrubs and trees, especially of the mangrove family Rhizophoraceae, found in the muddy swamps of tropical and subtropical coasts and estuaries. By sending down aerial roots from their branches, they rapidly form close- growing mangrove thickets. Their timber is impervious to water and resists marine worms. Mangrove swamps are rich breeding grounds for fish and shellfish. These habitats are being destroyed in many countries.

Manhattan island 20 km/12.5 mi long and 4 km/2.5 mi wide, lying between the Hudson and East rivers and forming a borough of the city of ◊New York, USA. It includes the Wall Street business centre, Broadway and its theatres, Carnegie Hall (1891), the World Trade Centre (1973), the Empire State Building (1931), the United Nations headquarters (1952), Madison Square Garden, and Central Park.

manic depression or *bipolar disorder* mental disorder characterized by recurring periods of ◊depression, which may or may not alternate with periods of inappropriate elation (mania) or overactivity. Sufferers may be genetically predisposed to the condition. Some cases have been improved by taking prescribed doses of ◊lithium.

Manila industrial port and capital of the Philippines, on the island of Luzon; population (1990) 1,598,900, metropolitan area (including Quezon City) 5,926,000.

Manipur state of NE India; *area* 22,400 sq km/8,646 sq mi; *capital* Imphal; *features* Loktak Lake; original Indian home of polo; *population* (1991) 1,826,700; *language* Hindi; *religion* Hindu 70%.

Man, Isle of island in the Irish Sea, a dependency of the British crown, but not part of the UK; *area* 570 sq km/220 sq mi; *capital* Douglas; *features* Snaefell 620 m/2,035 ft; annual TT (Tourist Trophy) motorcycle races, gambling casinos, Britain's first free port, tax haven; tailless Manx cat; *population* (1991) 69,800; *language* English (Manx, nearer to Scottish than Irish Gaelic, has been almost extinct since the 1970s).

Manitoba prairie province of Canada; *area* 650,000 sq km/250,900 sq mi; *capital* Winnipeg; *features* lakes Winnipeg, Winnipegosis, and Manitoba (area 4,700 sq km/1,814 sq mi); 50% forested; *population* (1991) 1,092,600.

Mann Thomas 1875–1955. German novelist and critic. He was concerned with the theme of the artist's relation to society. His first novel was *Buddenbrooks* 1901, which, followed by *Der Zauberberg/The Magic Mountain* 1924, led to a Nobel prize 1929. Notable among his works of short fiction is 'Der Tod in Venedig/Death in Venice' 1913.

Mannerism in art and architecture, a style characterized by a subtle but conscious breaking of the 'rules' of classical composition – for example, displaying the human body in an off-centre, distorted pose, and using harsh, non-blending colours. The term was coined by Italian artist Giorgio Vasari (1511–74) to describe the 16th-century reaction to Renaissance Classicism, referring to the later works of Michelangelo, for example.

manor basic economic unit in ◊feudalism in Europe, established in England under the Norman conquest. It consisted of the lord's house and cultivated land, land rented by free tenants, land held by villagers, common land, woodland, and waste land.

Mansfield Katherine. Pen name of Kathleen Beauchamp 1888–1923. New Zealand writer. She lived most of her life in England. Her delicate artistry emerges not only in her volumes of short stories – such as *In a German Pension* 1911, *Bliss* 1920, and *The Garden Party* 1923 – but also in her *Letters* and *Journal*.

Mantegna Andrea *c.* 1431–1506. Italian Renaissance painter and engraver, active chiefly in Padua and Mantua, where some of his frescoes remain. Paintings such as *The Agony in the Garden* about 1455 (National Gallery, London) reveal a dramatic, linear style, mastery of perspective, and strongly Classical architectural detail.

Maoism form of communism based on the ideas and teachings of the Chinese communist leader ◊Mao Zedong. It involves an adaptation of ◊Marxism to suit conditions in China and apportions a much greater role to agriculture and the peasantry in the building of socialism, thus effectively bypassing the capitalist (industrial) stage envisaged by Marx. In addition, Maoism stresses ideological, as well as economic, transformation, based on regular contact between party members and the general population.

Maori member of the Polynesian people of pre- European New Zealand, who numbered 294,200 in 1986, about 10% of the total population. Their language, Maori, belongs to the eastern branch of the Austronesian family.

Mao Zedong or *Mao Tse-tung* 1893–1976. Chinese political leader and Marxist theoretician; a founder and leader of the Chinese Communist Party

(CCP) from 1921. He organized the ▷Long March 1934–35 and the war of liberation 1937–49, following which he established a People's Republic and communist rule in China; he headed the CCP and government until his death. His influence diminished with the failure of his 1958–60 Great Leap Forward, but he emerged dominant again during the 1966–69 ▷Cultural Revolution.

Maputo formerly (until 1975) *Lourenço Marques* capital of Mozambique, and Africa's second-largest port, on Delagoa Bay; population (1987) 1,006,800. Linked by rail with Zimbabwe and South Africa, it is a major outlet for minerals, steel, textiles, processed foods, and furniture.

marathon athletics endurance race over 42.195 km/26 mi 385 yd. It was first included in the Olympic Games in Athens 1896. The distance varied until it was standardized 1924. More recently, races have been opened to wider participation, including social runners as well as those competing at senior level.

marble metamorphosed ▷limestone that takes and retains a good polish; it is used in building and sculpture. In its pure form it is white and consists almost entirely of calcite $CaCO_3$. Mineral impurities give it various colours and patterns. Carrara, Italy, is known for white marble.

Marches boundary areas of England with Wales, and England with Scotland. In the Middle Ages these troubled frontier regions were held by lords of the Marches, sometimes called *marchiones* and later earls of March.

Marconi Guglielmo 1874–1937. Italian electrical engineer and pioneer in the invention and development of radio. In 1895 he achieved radio communication over more than a mile, and in England 1896 he conducted successful experiments that led to the formation of the company that became Marconi's Wireless Telegraph Company Ltd. He shared the Nobel Prize for Physics 1909.

Marcos Ferdinand 1917–1989. Filipino right-wing politician, president 1965–1986, when he was forced into exile in Hawaii by a popular front led by Corazon ▷Aquino. Backed by the USA when in power, in 1988 US authorities indicted him and his wife *Imelda Marcos*(1930–) for racketeering and embezzlement. She returned to Manila 1191 and was an unsuccessful candidate in the 1992 presidential elections.

Margaret (Rose) 1930– . Princess of the UK, younger daughter of George VI and sister of Elizabeth II. In 1960 she married Anthony Armstrong-Jones, later created Lord Snowdon, but they were divorced 1978. Their children are *David, Viscount Linley* (1961–) and *Lady Sarah Armstrong-Jones* (1964–).

Margaret, St 1045–1093. Queen of Scotland, the granddaughter of King Edmund Ironside of England. She went to Scotland after the Norman Conquest, and soon after married Malcolm III. The marriage of her daughter Matilda to Henry I united the Norman and English royal houses.

margarine butter substitute made from animal fats and/or vegetable oils. The French chemist Hippolyte Mège-Mouries invented margarine 1889. Today, margarines are usually made with vegetable oils, such as soya, corn, or sunflower oil, giving a product low in saturated fats (polyunsaturated) and fortified with vitamins A and D.

Margrethe II 1940– . Queen of Denmark from 1972, when she succeeded her father Frederick IX. In 1967, she married the French diplomat Count Henri de Laborde de Monpezat, who took the title Prince Hendrik. Her heir is Crown Prince Frederick (1968–).

Mariana Islands or *Marianas* archipelago in the NW Pacific E of the Philippines, divided politically into ▷*Guam* (an unincorporated territory of the USA) and the *Northern Mariana Islands* (a commonwealth of the USA with its own internal government).

Mariana Trench lowest region on the Earth's surface; the deepest part of the sea floor. The trench is 2,400 km/1,500 mi long and is situated 300 km/200 mi E of the Mariana Islands, in the NW Pacific Ocean. Its deepest part is the gorge known as the Challenger Deep, which extends 11,034 m/36,210 ft below sea level.

Marie Antoinette 1755–1793. Queen of France from 1774. She was the daughter of Empress Maria Theresa of Austria, and married ▷Louis XVI of France 1770. Her reputation for extravagance helped provoke the ▷French Revolution of 1789. She was tried for treason Oct 1793 and guillotined.

Marie de' Medici 1573–1642. Queen of France, wife of Henry IV from 1600, and regent (after his murder) for their son Louis XIII. She left the government to her favourites, the Concinis, until Louis XIII seized power and executed them 1617. She was banished but, after she led a revolt 1619, ▷Richelieu effected her reconciliation with her son. When she attempted to oust him again 1630, she was exiled.

marijuana dried leaves and flowers of the hemp plant ▷cannabis, used as a drug; it is illegal in most countries. Mexico is the world's largest producer.

marjoram aromatic herb of the mint family Labiatae. Wild marjoram *Origanum vulgare* is found both in Europe and Asia and has become naturalized in the Americas; the culinary sweet marjoram *O. majorana* is widely cultivated.

Mark Antony (Marcus Antonius) 83–30 BC. Roman politician and soldier. He served under Julius ▷Caesar until Caesar's assassination, when he formed the Second Triumvirate with Octavian (later ▷Augustus) and Lepidus. In 42 he defeated Brutus and Cassius at Philippi, taking Egypt as his share of the empire. He formed a liaison with ▷Cleopatra, but in 40 he returned to Rome to marry Octavia, the sister of Octavian. In 32 the Senate declared war on Cleopatra, and Antony, who had combined forces with Cleopatra, was defeated by Octavian at the battle of Actium 31 BC. He returned to Egypt and committed suicide.

Mark, St in the New Testament, Christian apostle and evangelist whose name is given to the second Gospel. It was probably written AD 65–70, and used by the authors of the first and third Gospels. He is the patron saint of Venice, and his emblem is a winged lion. Feast day 25 April.

Marlowe Christopher 1564–1593. English poet and dramatist. His work includes the blank-verse plays *Tamburlaine the Great c.* 1587, *The Jew of Malta c.* 1589, *Edward II* and *Dr Faustus*, both *c.* 1592, the poem *Hero and Leander* 1598, and a translation of Ovid's *Amores*.

Mars in Roman mythology, the god of war, depicted as a fearless warrior. The month of March is named after him. He is equivalent to the Greek Ares.

Mars fourth planet from the Sun, average distance 227.9 million km/ 141.6 million mi. It revolves around the Sun in 687 Earth days, and has a rotation period of 24 hr 37 min. It is much smaller than Venus or Earth, with a diameter 6,780 km/4,210 mi, and mass 0.11 that of Earth. Mars is slightly pear-shaped, with a low, level northern hemisphere, which is comparatively uncratered and geologically 'young', and a heavily cratered 'ancient' southern hemisphere.

Marseille (English *Marseilles*) chief seaport of France, industrial centre, and capital of the *département* of Bouches-du-Rhône, on the Golfe du Lion, Mediterranean Sea; population (1990) 807,700.

marsh low-lying wetland. Freshwater marshes are common wherever groundwater, surface springs, streams, or run-off cause frequent flooding or more or less permanent shallow water. A marsh is alkaline whereas a ◊bog is acid. Marshes develop on inorganic silt or clay soils. Rushes are typical marsh plants. Large marshes dominated by papyrus, cattail, and reeds, with standing water throughout the year, are commonly called swamps. Near the sea, salt marshes may form.

Marshall Islands *area* 180 sq km/69 sq mi; *capital* Dalap-Uliga-Darrit (on Majuro atoll); *features* the atolls of Eniwetok and Bikini were used for US atom-bomb tests 1946–63, where radioactivity is expected to last for 100 years; *political system* liberal democracy; *population* (1990) 31,600; *language* English

(official); *religions* Christian, mainly Roman Catholic, and local faiths.

Marshall Plan programme of US economic aid to Europe, set up at the end of World War II. Officially known as the European Recovery Programme, it was announced by Secretary of State George C Marshall to undermine the perceived danger of communist takeover in postwar Europe, which was the main reason for the aid effort.

Marston Moor, Battle of battle fought in the English Civil War 2 July 1644 on Marston Moor, 11 km/7 mi W of York. The Royalists were conclusively defeated by the Parliamentarians and Scots.

marsupial mammal in which the female has a pouch where she carries her young (born tiny and immature) for a considerable time after birth. Marsupials include omnivorous, herbivorous, and carnivorous species, among them the kangaroo, wombat, opossum, phalanger, bandicoot, dasyure, and wallaby.

martial arts any of several styles of armed and unarmed combat developed in the East from ancient techniques and arts. Common martial arts include aikido, ◊judo, jujitsu, ◊karate, kendo, and ◊kung fu.

Martinique French island in the West Indies (Lesser Antilles); *area* 1,079 sq km/417 sq mi; *capital* Fort-de-France; *features* several active volcanoes; Napoleon's empress Josephine was born in Martinique, and her childhood home is now a museum; *population* (1990) 359,600.

Martinmas in the Christian calendar, the feast of St Martin, 11 Nov.

Marvell Andrew 1621–1678. English metaphysical poet and satirist. His poems include 'To His Coy Mistress' and 'Horatian Ode upon Cromwell's Return from Ireland'. He was committed to the parliamentary cause, and was member of Parliament for Hull from 1659. He devoted his last years mainly to verse satire and prose works attacking repressive aspects of government.

Marx Karl (Heinrich) 1818–1883. German philosopher, economist, and social theorist whose account of change through conflict is known as historical, or dialectical, materialism (see ◊Marxism). His *Das Kapital/Capital* 1867–95 is the fundamental text of Marxist economics and exercised an enormous influence on later thinkers and political activists.

Marx Brothers family team of US film comedians: Leonard *Chico* (from the 'chicks' – women – he chased) 1887–1961; Adolph, the silent *Harpo* (from the harp he played) 1888–1964; Julius *Groucho* (from his temper) 1890–1977; and Herbert *Zeppo* (born at the time of the first zeppelins) 1901–1979. Their thirteen zany films included *Animal Crackers* 1930, *Monkey Business* 1931, and *Go West* 1940.

Marxism philosophical system, developed by the 19th-century German social theorists ◊Marx and ◊Engels, also known as *dialectical materialism*, under which matter gives rise to mind (materialism) and all is subject to change (from dialectic; see ◊Hegel). As applied to history, it supposes that the succession of feudalism, capitalism, socialism, and finally the classless society is inevitable. The stubborn resistance of any existing system to change necessitates its complete overthrow in the *class struggle* – in the case of capitalism, by the proletariat – rather than gradual modification.

Mary Queen of Scots 1542–1587. Queen of Scotland 1542–67. Also known as *Mary Stuart*, she was the daughter of James V. A champion of the Catholic cause, Elizabeth I held her prisoner while the Roman Catholics, who regarded Mary as rightful queen of England, formed many conspiracies to place her on the throne. For complicity in one of these plots she was executed.

Mary in the New Testament, the mother of Jesus through divine intervention, wife of ◊Joseph. The Roman Catholic Church maintains belief in her ◊Immaculate Conception and bodily assumption into heaven, and venerates her as a mediator. Feast day of the Assumption is 15 Aug.

Mary I (called *Bloody Mary*) 1516–1558. Queen of England from 1553. She was the eldest daughter of Henry VIII by Catherine of Aragon. When Edward VI died, Mary secured the crown in spite of the conspiracy to substitute Lady Jane ◊Grey. In 1554 Mary married Philip II of Spain, obtained the restoration of papal supremacy, and sanctioned the persecution of Protestants. She was succeeded by her half-sister Elizabeth I.

Mary II 1662–1694. Queen of England, Scotland, and Ireland from 1688. She was the Protestant elder daughter of the Catholic ◊James II, and in 1677 was married to her cousin ◊William of Orange. After the 1688 revolution she accepted the crown jointly with William.

Maryland state of E USA; *area* 31,600 sq km/12,198 sq mi; *capital* Annapolis; *features* Chesapeake Bay; yacht racing and the US Naval Academy at Annapolis; Fort Meade, a government electronic-listening centre; Baltimore harbour; *population* (1990) 4,781,500.

Mary Magdalene, St in the New Testament, the woman whom Jesus cured of possession by evil spirits, was present at the Crucifixion and burial, and was the first to meet the risen Jesus. She is often identified with the woman of St Luke's gospel who anointed Jesus' feet, and her symbol is a jar of ointment; feast day 22 July.

Masaccio (Tommaso di Giovanni di Simone Guidi) 1401–1428. Florentine painter. He was a leader of the early Italian Renaissance. His frescoes in Sta Maria del Carmine, Florence, 1425–28, which he painted with Masolino da Panicale, show a decisive break with Gothic conventions. He was the first painter to apply the scientific laws of perspective, newly discovered by the architect Brunelleschi, and achieved a remarkable sense of space and volume.

Masai member of an E African people whose territory is divided between Tanzania and Kenya, and who number about 250,000. They were originally warriors and nomads, breeding humped zebu cattle, but some have adopted a more settled life. Their cooperation is being sought by the Kenyan authorities to help in wildlife conservation. They speak a Nilotic language belonging to the Nilo-Saharan family.

maser (acronym for *microwave amplification by stimulated emission of radiation*) in physics, a high-frequency microwave amplifier or oscillator in which the signal to be amplified is used to stimulate unstable atoms into emitting energy at the same frequency. Atoms or molecules are raised to a higher energy level and then allowed to lose this energy by radiation emitted at a precise frequency. The principle has been extended to other parts of the electromagnetic spectrum as, for example, in the ◊laser.

Maseru capital of Lesotho, S Africa, on the Caledon River; population (1986) 289,000. Founded 1869, it is a centre for trade and diamond processing.

Mason–Dixon Line in the USA, the boundary line between Maryland and Pennsylvania (latitude 39° 43' 26.3" N), named after Charles Mason (1730–1787) and Jeremiah Dixon (died 1777), English astronomers and surveyors who surveyed it 1763–67. It was popularly seen as dividing the North from the South.

mass in physics, the quantity of matter in a body as measured by its inertia. Mass determines the acceleration produced in a body by a given force acting on it, the acceleration being inversely proportional to the mass of the body. The mass also determines the force exerted on a body by ◊gravity on Earth, although this attraction varies slightly from place to place. In the SI system, the base unit of mass is the kilogram.

Mass in Christianity, the celebration of the ◊Eucharist.

Massachusetts state of NE USA; nickname Bay State/Old Colony State; *area* 21,500 sq km/8,299 sq mi; *capital* Boston; *population* (1990) 6,016,400; *features* Harvard University and the Massachusetts Institute of Technology, Cambridge; Cape Cod National Seashore; Plymouth Rock.

Massif Central mountainous plateau region of S central France; area 93,000 sq km/36,000 sq mi, highest peak Puy de Sancy, 1,886 m/6,188 ft. It is a source of hydroelectricity.

Mata Hari stage name of Gertrud Margarete Zelle 1876–1917. Dutch courtesan, dancer, and probable spy. In World War I she had affairs with highly placed military and government officials on both sides and told Allied secrets to the Germans. She may have been a double agent, in the pay of both France and Germany. She was shot by the French on espionage charges.

materialism philosophical theory that there is nothing in existence over and above matter and matter in motion. Such a theory excludes the possibility of deities. It also sees mind as an attribute of the physical, denying idealist theories that see mind as something independent of body; for example, Descartes' theory of 'thinking substance'.

mathematics science of spatial and numerical relationships. The main divisions of *pure mathematics* include geometry, arithmetic, algebra, calculus, and trigonometry. Mechanics, statistics, numerical analysis, computing, the mathematical theories of astronomy, electricity, optics, thermodynamics, and atomic studies come under the heading of *applied mathematics*.

Matisse Henri 1869–1954. French painter, sculptor, illustrator, and designer. One of the most original creative forces in early 20th-century art. Influenced by Impressionism, Post-Impressionism, and later Cubism, among his favoured subjects were odalisques (women of the harem), bathers, and dancers; for example, *The Dance* 1910 (The Hermitage, St Petersburg). Later works include pure abstracts, as in his collages of coloured paper shapes (*gouaches découpées*).

matter in physics, anything that has mass and can be detected and measured. All matter is made up of ▷atoms, which in turn are made up of ▷elementary particles; it exists ordinarily as a solid, liquid, or gas. The history of science and philosophy is largely taken up with accounts of theories of matter, ranging from the hard 'atoms' of Democritus to the 'waves' of modern quantum theory.

Matterhorn (French *le Cervin*, Italian *il Cervino*) mountain peak in the Alps on the Swiss-Italian border; 4,478 m/14,690 ft.

Matthew, St Christian apostle and evangelist, the traditional author of the first Gospel. He is usually identified with Levi, who was a tax collector in the service of Herod Antipas, and was called by Jesus to be a disciple as he sat by the Lake of Galilee receiving customs dues. His emblem is a man with wings; feast day 21 Sept.

Maugham (William) Somerset 1874–1965. English writer. His work includes the novels *Of Human Bondage* 1915, *The Moon and Sixpence* 1919, and *Cakes and Ale* 1930; the short-story collections *The Trembling of a Leaf* 1921 and *Ashenden* 1928; and the plays *Lady Frederick* 1907 and *Our Betters* 1923.

Maundy Thursday in the Christian church, the Thursday before Easter. The ceremony of washing the feet of pilgrims on that day was instituted in commemoration of Jesus' washing of the apostles' feet and observed from the 4th century to 1754.

Maupassant Guy de 1850–1893. French author. He established a reputation with the short story 'Boule de suif/Ball of Fat' 1880 and wrote some

300 short stories in all. His novels include *Une Vie/A Woman's Life* 1883 and *Bel-Ami* 1885. He was encouraged as a writer by Gustave ▷Flaubert.

Mauritania Islamic Republic of (*République Islamique de Mauritanie*); *area* 1,030,700 sq km/397,850 sq mi; *capital* Nouakchott; *features* part of the Sahara Desert; dusty sirocco wind blows in March; *political system* emergent democratic republic; *population* (1993 est) 2,200,000 (Arab-Berber 30%, black African 30%, Haratine – descendants of black slaves, who remained slaves until 1980 – 30%); growth rate 3% p.a.; *languages* French (official), Hasaniya Arabic, black African languages; *religion* Sunni Muslim 99%.

Mauritius Republic of; *area* 1,865 sq km/720 sq mi; the island of Rodrigues is part of Mauritius; there are several small island dependencies; *capital* Port Louis; *features* unusual wildlife includes flying fox and ostrich; it was the home of the dodo (extinct from about 1680); *political system* liberal democratic republic; *population* (1993 est) 1,100,000, 68% of Indian origin; growth rate 1.5% p.a.; *languages* English (official), French, creole, Indian languages; *religions* Hindu 51%, Christian 30%, Muslim 17%.

Maxwell James Clerk 1831–1879. Scottish physicist. His main achievement was in the understanding of ▷electromagnetic waves: *Maxwell's equations* bring together electricity, magnetism, and light in one set of relations. He contributed to every branch of physical science – studying gases, optics, and the sensation of colour. His theoretical work in magnetism prepared the way for wireless telegraphy and telephony.

Maya member of an American Indian civilization originating in the Yucatán Peninsula in Central America about 2600 BC, with later sites in Mexico, Guatemala, and Belize, and enjoying a classical period AD 325–925, after which it declined. Today they are Roman Catholic, and live in Yucatán, Guatemala, Belize, and W Honduras. Many still speak Maya, a member of the Totonac-Mayan (Penutian) language family, as well as Spanish.

Mayo county of the Republic of Ireland, in the province of Connacht; county town Castlebar; area 5,400 sq km/2,084 sq mi; population (1991) 110,700. It has wild Atlantic coast scenery. It features Croagh Patrick 765 m/2,510 ft, the mountain where St Patrick spent the 40 days of Lent in 441, climbed by pilgrims on the last Sunday of July each year; and the village of Knock, where two women claimed to have seen a vision of the Virgin with two saints 1879, now a site of pilgrimage.

ME abbreviation for *myalgic encephalomyelitis*, a debilitating condition still not universally accepted as a genuine disease. The condition occurs after a flulike attack and has a diffuse range of symptoms. These strike and recur for years and include extreme fatigue, muscular pain, weakness, poor balance and coordination, joint pains, gastric upset, and depression.

mean in mathematics, a measure of the average of a number of terms or quantities. The simple *arithmetic mean* is the average value of the quantities, that is, the sum of the quantities divided by their number. The *weighted mean* takes into account the frequency of the terms that are summed; it is calculated by multiplying each term by the number of times it occurs, summing the results and dividing this total by the total number of occurrences. The *geometric mean* of *n* quantities is the *n*th root of their product. In statistics, it is a measure of central tendency of a set of data.

measles acute virus disease (rubeola), spread by airborne infection. Symptoms are fever, severe catarrh, small spots inside the mouth, and a raised, blotchy red rash appearing for about a week after two weeks' incubation. Prevention is by vaccination.

Mecca (Arabic *Makkah*) city in Saudi Arabia and, as birthplace of Muhammad, the holiest city of the Islamic world; population (1974) 367,000. In the centre of Mecca is the Great Mosque, in the courtyard of which is the Kaaba, the sacred shrine containing the black stone believed to have been given to Abraham by the angel Gabriel.

mechanics branch of physics dealing with the motions of bodies and the forces causing these motions, and also with the forces acting on bodies in equilibrium. It is usually divided into ◊dynamics and statics.

Medea in Greek mythology, the sorceress daughter of the king of Colchis. When ◊Jason reached Colchis, she fell in love with him, helped him acquire the ◊Golden Fleece, and they fled together. When Jason later married Creusa, daughter of the king of Corinth, Medea killed his bride with the gift of a poisoned garment, and then killed her own two children by Jason.

Medellin industrial city in the Central Cordillera, Colombia, 1,538 m/5,048 ft above sea level; population (1985) 2,069,000. It is a centre for the country's drug trade.

median in mathematics and statistics, the middle number of an ordered group of numbers. If there is no middle number (because there is an even number of terms), the median is the ◊mean (average) of the two middle numbers. For example, the median of the group 2, 3, 7, 11, 12 is 7; that of 3, 4, 7, 9, 11, 13 is 8 (the average of 7 and 9).

Medici noble family of Florence, the city's rulers from 1434 until they died out 1737. Family members included ◊Catherine de' Medici, Pope Leo X, Pope Clement VII and ◊Marie de' Medici.

Medici Cosimo de' 1389–1464. Italian politician and banker. Regarded as the model for Machiavelli's *The Prince*, he dominated the government of Florence from 1434 and was a patron of the arts. He was succeeded by his inept son *Piero de' Medici* (1416–1469).

Medina (Arabic *Madinah*) Saudi Arabian city, about 355 km/220 mi N of Mecca; population (1986 est) 500,000. It is the second holiest city in the Islamic world, and is believed to contain the tomb of Muhammad.

Mediterranean Sea inland sea separating Europe from N Africa, with Asia to the E; extreme length 3,700 km/2,300 mi; area 2,966,000 sq km/1,145,000 sq mi. It is linked to the Atlantic Ocean (at the Strait of Gibraltar), Red Sea, and Indian Ocean (by the Suez Canal), Black Sea (at the Dardanelles and Sea of Marmara). The main subdivisions are the Adriatic, Aegean, Ionian, and Tyrrhenian seas. It is highly polluted.

Medusa in Greek mythology, a mortal woman who was transformed into a Gorgon. Medusa was slain by Perseus;

the winged horse ◊Pegasus was supposed to have sprung from her blood. Her head was so hideous – even in death – that any beholder was turned to stone.

mega- prefix denoting multiplication by a million. For example, a megawatt (MW) is equivalent to a million watts.

megabyte (Mb) in computing, a unit of memory equal to 1,024 ◊kilobytes. It is sometimes used, less precisely, to mean 1 million bytes.

megalith prehistoric stone monument of the late Neolithic or early Bronze Age. Most common in Europe, megaliths include single, large uprights (*menhirs*, for example, the Five Kings, Northumberland, England); *rows* (for example, Carnac, Brittany, France); *circles*, generally with a central 'altar stone'; and the remains of burial chambers with the covering earth removed, looking like a hut (*dolmens*, for example Kits Coty, Kent, England).

Melanesia islands in the SW Pacific between Micronesia to the N and Polynesia to the E, embracing all the islands from the New Britain archipelago to Fiji.

Melanesian indigenous inhabitant of Melanesia; a member of any of the Pacific peoples of Melanesia. The Melanesian languages belong to the Austronesian family.

melanoma highly malignant tumour of the melanin- forming cells (melanocytes) of the skin. It develops from an existing mole in up to two thirds of cases, but can also arise in the eye or mucous membranes. Malignant melanoma is the most dangerous of the skin cancers; it is associated with brief but excessive exposure to sunlight. It is easily treated if caught early but deadly once it has spread. There is a genetic factor in some cases.

Melbourne capital of Victoria, Australia, near the mouth of the river Yarra; population (1990) 3,080,000.

melting point temperature at which a substance melts, or changes from solid to liquid form. A pure substance under standard conditions of pressure (usually one atmosphere) has a definite melting point. If heat is supplied to a solid at its melting point, the temperature does not change until the melting process is complete. The melting point of ice is 0°C or 32°F.

Melville Herman 1819–1891. US writer. His novel *Moby-Dick* 1851 was inspired by his whaling experiences in the South Seas and is now considered to be one of the masterpieces of American literature. Earlier fiction includes *Typee* 1846 and *Omoo* 1847. *Billy Budd, Sailor* was completed just before his death and published 1924.

membrane in living things, a continuous layer, made up principally of fat molecules, that encloses a ◊cell or ◊organelles within a cell. Certain small molecules can pass through the cell membrane, but most must enter or leave the cell via channels in the membrane made up of special proteins. The Golgi apparatus within the cell is thought to produce certain membranes.

Memphis ruined city beside the Nile, 19 km/12 mi S of Cairo, Egypt. Once the centre of the worship of Ptah, it was the earliest capital of a united Egypt under King Menes about 3200 BC, but was superseded by Thebes under the new empire 1570 BC.

Memphis industrial port city on the Mississippi River, in Tennessee, USA;

population (1990) 610,300. The French built a fort here 1739, but Memphis was not founded until 1819. Its musical history includes Beale Street, home of the blues composer W C Handy, and Graceland, home of Elvis Presley; its recording studios and record companies (Sun 1953–68, Stax 1960–75) made it a focus of the music industry.

Mendel Gregor Johann 1822–1884 Austrian biologist, founder of ◊genetics. His experiments with successive generations of peas gave the basis for his theory of particulate inheritance rather than blending, involving dominant and recessive characters. His results, published 1865–69, remained unrecognized until the early 20th century.

Mendeleyev Dmitri Ivanovich 1834–1907. Russian chemist who framed the periodic law in chemistry 1869, which states that the chemical properties of the elements depend on their relative atomic masses. This law is the basis of the ◊periodic table of the elements, in which the elements are arranged by atomic number and organized by their related groups.

Mendelssohn (-Bartholdy) (Jakob Ludwig) Felix 1809–1847. German composer, also a pianist and conductor. His music has a lightness and charm of Classical music, applied to Romantic and descriptive subjects. Among his best-known works are *A Midsummer Night's Dream* 1827; the *Fingal's Cave* overture 1832; and five symphonies, which include the 'Reformation' 1830, the 'Italian' 1833, and the 'Scottish' 1842. He was instrumental in promoting the revival of interest in J S Bach's music.

meningitis inflammation of the meninges (membranes) surrounding the brain, caused by bacterial or viral infection. Bacterial meningitis, though treatable by antibiotics, is the more serious threat. Diagnosis is by ◊lumbar puncture.

menopause in women, the cessation of reproductive ability, characterized by menstruation (see ◊menstrual cycle) becoming irregular and eventually ceasing. The onset is at about the age of 50, but varies greatly. Menopause is usually uneventful, but some women suffer from complications such as flushing, excessive bleeding, and nervous disorders. Since the 1950s, ◊hormone-replacement therapy (HRT), using ◊oestrogen alone or with progestogen, a synthetic form of ◊progesterone, has been developed to counteract such effects.

Menshevik member of the minority of the Russian Social Democratic Party, who split from the ◊Bolsheviks 1903. The Mensheviks believed in a large, loosely organized party and that, before socialist revolution could occur in Russia, capitalist society had to develop further. During the Russian Revolution they had limited power and set up a government in Georgia, but were suppressed 1922.

menstrual cycle cycle that occurs in female mammals of reproductive age, in which the body is prepared for pregnancy. At the beginning of the cycle, a Graafian (egg) follicle develops in the ovary, and the inner wall of the uterus forms a soft spongy lining. The egg is released from the ovary, and the uterus lining (endometrium) becomes vascularized (filled with blood vessels). If fertilization does not occur, the corpus luteum (remains of the Graafian follicle) degenerates, and the uterine lining breaks down, and is shed. This is what causes the loss of blood that marks menstruation. The cycle then begins again. Human menstruation takes place from puberty to menopause, except during pregnancy, occurring about every 28 days.

Menuhin Yehudi 1916– . US-born violinist and conductor. His solo repertoire extends from Vivaldi to Enescu. He recorded the Elgar *Violin Concerto* 1932 with the composer conducting, and commissioned the *Sonata* for violin solo 1944 from an ailing Bartók. He has appeared in concert with sitar virtuoso Ravi Shankar, and with jazz violinist Stephane Grappelli.

merchant navy the passenger and cargo ships of a country. Most are owned by private companies. To avoid strict regulations on safety, union rules on crew wages, and so on, many ships are today registered under 'flags of convenience', that is, flags of countries that do not have such rules.

mercury or *quicksilver* heavy, silver-grey, metallic element, symbol Hg (from Latin *hydrargyrum*), atomic number 80, relative atomic mass 200.59. It is a dense, mobile liquid with a low melting point (−38.87°C/−37.96°F). Its chief source is the mineral cinnabar, HgS, but it sometimes occurs in nature as a free metal.

Mercury in astronomy, the closest planet to the Sun, at an average distance of 58 million km/36 million mi. Its diameter is 4,880 km/3,030 mi, its mass 0.056 that of Earth. Mercury orbits the Sun every 88 days, and spins on its axis every 59 days. On its sunward side the surface temperature reaches over 400°C/752°F, but on the 'night' side it falls to −170°C/−274°F. Mercury has an atmosphere with minute traces of argon and helium. In 1974 the US space probe *Mariner 10* discovered that its surface is cratered by meteorite impacts. Mercury has no moons.

Mercury in Roman mythology, a god, identified with the Greek ◊Hermes, and like him represented with winged sandals and a winged staff entwined with snakes. He was the messenger of the gods, and was associated particularly with commerce.

meridian half a great circle drawn on the Earth's surface passing through both poles and thus through all places with the same longitude. Terrestrial longitudes are usually measured from the Greenwich Meridian.

merino breed of sheep. Its close-set, silky wool is highly valued. The merino, originally from Spain, is now found all over the world, and is the breed on which the Australian wool industry is built.

Merlin legendary magician and counsellor to King ◊Arthur. Welsh bardic literature has a cycle of poems attributed to him, and he may have been a real person.

Merseyside metropolitan county of NW England, created 1974; in 1986, most of the functions of the former county council were transferred to metropolitan district councils; *area* 650 sq km/251 sq mi; *towns and cities* Liverpool (administrative headquarters), Bootle, Birkenhead, St Helens, Wallasey, Southport; *features* river Mersey (length 112km/70 mi); Prescot Museum of clock-and watch-making; Speke Hall (Tudor); *population* (1991) 1,403,600.

Mesolithic the Middle Stone Age developmental stage of human technology and of ◊prehistory.

meson in physics, an unstable subatomic particle made up of two indivisible elementary particles called ◊quarks. It has a mass intermediate between that of the electron and that of the proton, is found in cosmic radiation, and is emitted by nuclei under bombardment by very high-energy particles.

Mesopotamia the land between the Tigris and Euphrates rivers, now part of Iraq. The civilizations of Sumer and Babylon flourished here. Sumer (3500 BC) may have been the earliest urban civilization.

mesosphere layer in the Earth's ◊atmosphere above the stratosphere and below the thermosphere. It lies between about 50 km/31 mi and 80 km/50 mi above the ground.

Mesozoic era of geological time 245–65 million years ago, consisting of the Triassic, Jurassic, and Cretaceous periods. At the beginning of the era, the continents were joined together as Pangaea; dinosaurs and other giant reptiles dominated the sea and air; and ferns, horsetails, and cycads thrived in a warm climate worldwide. By the end of the Mesozoic era, the continents had begun to assume their present positions, flowering plants were dominant, and many of the large reptiles and marine fauna were becoming extinct.

Messiaen Olivier 1908–1992. French composer, organist, and teacher. His music is mystical in character, vividly coloured, and incorporates transcriptions of birdsong. Among his works are the *Quartet for the End of Time* 1941, the large-scale *Turangalîla Symphony* 1949, and solo organ and piano pieces. As a teacher at the Paris Conservatoire from 1942, he influenced three generations of composers.

Messiah in Judaism and Christianity, the saviour or deliverer. Jews from the time of the Old Testament exile in Babylon have looked forward to the coming of the Messiah. Christians believe that the Messiah came in the person of ◊Jesus, and hence called him the Christ.

metabolism the chemical processes of living organisms enabling them to grow and to function. It involves a constant alternation of building up (*anabolism*) and breaking down (*catabolism*). For example, green plants build up complex organic substances from water, carbon dioxide, and mineral salts (photosynthesis); by digestion animals partially break down complex organic substances, ingested as food, and subsequently resynthesize them for use in their own bodies.

metal any of a class of chemical elements with certain chemical characteristics and physical properties: they are good conductors of heat and electricity; opaque but reflect light well; malleable, which enables them to be cold-worked and rolled into sheets; and ductile, which permits them to be drawn into thin wires.

metallurgy the science and technology of producing metals, which includes extraction, alloying, and hardening. Extractive, or *process, metallurgy* is concerned with the extraction of metals from their ◊ores and refining and adapting them for use. *Physical metallurgy* is concerned with their properties and application. *Metallography* establishes the microscopic structures that contribute to hardness, ductility, and strength.

metamorphic rock rock altered in structure and composition by pressure, heat, or chemically active fluids after original formation. (If heat is sufficient to melt the original rock, technically it becomes an igneous rock upon cooling.) The term was coined in 1833 by Scottish geologist Charles Lyell (1797–1875).

metamorphosis period during the life cycle of many invertebrates, most amphibians, and some fish, during which the individual's body changes from one form to another through a major reconstitution of its tissues. For example, adult frogs are produced by metamorphosis from tadpoles, and butterflies are produced from caterpillars following metamorphosis within a pupa.

metaphysical poets group of early 17th-century English poets whose work is characterized by ingenious, highly intricate wordplay and unlikely or paradoxical imagery. Among the exponents of this genre are John Donne, George Herbert, Andrew Marvell, Richard Crashaw, and Henry Vaughan.

metaphysics branch of philosophy that deals with first principles, in particular 'being' (ontology) and 'knowing' (epistemology), and that is concerned with the ultimate nature of reality. It has been maintained that no certain knowledge of metaphysical questions is possible.

meteor flash of light in the sky, popularly known as a *shooting* or *falling star*, caused by a particle of dust, a *meteoroid*, entering the atmosphere at speeds up to 70 kps/45 mps and burning up by friction at a height of around 100 km/60 mi. On any clear night, several *sporadic meteors* can be seen each hour.

meteorite piece of rock or metal from space that reaches the surface of the Earth, Moon, or other body. Most meteorites are thought to be fragments from asteroids, although some may be pieces from the heads of comets. Most are stony, although some are made of iron and a few have a mixed rock-iron composition. Meteorites provide evidence for the nature of the solar system and may be similar to the Earth's core and mantle, neither of which can be observed directly.

meteorology scientific observation and study of the ⟩atmosphere, so that weather can be accurately forecast. Data from meteorological stations and weather satellites are collated by computer at central agencies, and forecast and weather maps based on current readings are issued at regular intervals. Modern analysis can give useful forecasts for up to six days ahead.

methane CH_4 the simplest hydrocarbon of the paraffin series. Colourless, odourless, and lighter than air, it burns with a bluish flame and explodes when mixed with air or oxygen. It is the chief constituent of natural gas and also occurs in the explosive firedamp of coal mines.

Methodism evangelical Protestant Christian movement that was founded by John ⟩Wesley 1739 within the Church of England, but became a separate body 1795. The Methodist Episcopal Church was founded in the USA 1784. There are over 50 million Methodists worldwide.

methylated spirit alcohol that has been rendered undrinkable, and is used for industrial purposes, as a fuel for spirit burners or a solvent.

metric system system of weights and measures developed in France in the

18th century and recognized by other countries in the 19th century. In 1960 an international conference on weights and measures recommended the universal adoption of a revised International System (Système International d'Unités, or SI), with seven prescribed 'base units': the metre (m) for length, kilogram (kg) for mass, second (s) for time, ampere (A) for electric current, kelvin (K) for thermodynamic temperature, candela (cd) for luminous intensity, and mole (mol) for quantity of matter.

Metternich Klemens (Wenzel Lothar), Prince von Metternich 1773–1859. Austrian politician, the leading figure in European diplomacy after the fall of Napoleon. As foreign minister 1809–48 (as well as chancellor from 1821), he tried to maintain the balance of power in Europe, supporting monarchy and repressing liberalism.

Mexico United States of (*Estados Unidos Mexicanos*); *area* 1,958,201 sq km/756,198 sq mi; *capital* Mexico City; *environment* air is polluted by 130,000 factories and 2.5 million vehicles; *features* Rio Grande; 3,218 km/2,000 mi frontier with USA; resorts Acapulco, Mexicali; volcanoes, including Popocatepetl; *political system* federal democratic republic; *population* (1993 est) 91,600,000 (mixed descent 60%, Indian 30%, Spanish descent 10%); 50% under 20 years of age; growth rate 2.6% p.a.; *languages* Spanish (official) 92%, Nahuatl, Maya, Zapoteco, Mixteco, Otomi; *religion* Roman Catholic 97%.

Mexico City (Spanish *Ciudad de México*) capital, industrial and cultural centre of Mexico, 2,255 m/7,400 ft above sea level on the S edge of the central plateau; population (1986) 18,748,000. It is thought to be one of the world's most polluted cities because of its position in a volcanic basin 2,000 m/7,400 ft above sea level.

Miami industrial city and port in Florida, USA; population (1990) 358,500. It is the hub of finance, trade, and air transport for the USA, Latin America, and the Caribbean. There has been an influx of immigrants from Cuba, Haiti, Mexico, and South America since 1959.

Michaelmas Day in Christian church tradition, the festival of St Michael and all angels, observed 29 Sept.

Michelangelo 1475–1564. properly Michelangelo Buonarroti. Italian sculptor, painter, architect, and poet. He was active in his native Florence and in Rome. His giant talent dominated the High Renaissance. The marble *David* 1501–04 (Academia, Florence) set a new standard in nude sculpture. His massive figure style was translated into fresco in the Sistine Chapel 1508–12 and 1536–41 (Vatican). Other works in Rome include the dome of St Peter's basilica. His influence, particularly on the development of ◊Mannerism, was profound.

Michigan state in N central USA; *area* 151,600 sq km/58,518 sq mi; *capital* Lansing; *features* Great Lakes; over 50% forested; Isle Royale National Park; Henry Ford Museum; *population* (1990) 9,295,300.

microbiology the study of microorganisms, mostly viruses and single-celled organisms such as bacteria, protozoa, and yeasts. The practical applications of microbiology are in medicine (since many microorganisms cause disease); in brewing, baking, and other food and beverage processes, where the microorganisms carry out fermentation; and in genetic engineering, which is creating increasing interest in the field of microbiology.

Micronesia group of islands in the Pacific Ocean lying N of ▷Melanesia, including the Federated States of Micronesia, Belau, Kiribati, the Mariana and Marshall Islands, Nauru, and Tuvalu.

Micronesia Federated States of (FSM); *area* 700 sq km/270 sq mi; *capital* Kolonia, in Pohnpei state; *physical* an archipelago in the W Pacific; *features* equatorial, volcanic island chain, with extensive coral, limestone, and lava shores; *political system* democratic federal state; *population* (1990) 107,900; *languages* English (official) and local languages; *religion* Christianity.

microorganism or *microbe* living organism invisible to the naked eye but visible under a microscope. Microorganisms include viruses and single-celled organisms such as bacteria, protozoa, yeasts, and some algae. The term has no taxonomic significance in biology. The study of microorganisms is known as microbiology.

microphone primary component in a sound-reproducing system, whereby the mechanical energy of sound waves is converted into electrical signals by means of a transducer. One of the simplest is the telephone receiver mouthpiece, invented by Scottish–US inventor Alexander Graham Bell in 1876; other types of microphone are used with broadcasting and sound-film apparatus.

microprocessor complete computer ▷central processing unit contained on a single ▷integrated circuit, or chip. The microprocessor has led to a dramatic fall in the size and cost of computers.

Examples of microprocessors are the Intel 8086 family and the Motorola 68000 family.

microscope instrument for magnification with high resolution for detail. Optical and electron microscopes are the ones chiefly in use; other types include acoustic, scanning tunnelling, and atomic force microscopes. In 1988 a scanning tunnelling microscope was used to photograph a single protein molecule for the first time.

microwave ▷electromagnetic wave with a wavelength in the range 0. 3 to 30 cm/0.1 in to 12 in, or 300–300,000 megahertz (between radio waves and ▷infrared radiation). Microwaves are used in radar, in radio broadcasting, and in microwave heating and cooking.

Midas in Greek mythology, a king of Phrygia who was granted the gift of converting all he touched to gold. He soon regretted his gift, as his food and drink were also turned to gold. For preferring the music of Pan to that of Apollo, he was given ass's ears by the latter.

Middle Ages period of European history between the fall of the Roman Empire in the 5th century and the Renaissance in the 15th. Among the period's distinctive features were the unity of W Europe within the Roman Catholic Church, the feudal organization of political, social, and economic relations, and the use of art for largely religious purposes.

Mid Glamorgan (Welsh *Morgannwg Ganol*) county of S Wales, created 1974; *area* 1,020 sq km/394 sq mi; *towns and cities* Cardiff (administrative centre), Porthcawl, Aberdare, Merthyr Tydfil,

Bridgend, Pontypridd; *features* Caerphilly Castle, with its water defences; *population* (1991) 534,100; *languages* English, 8.5% Welsh-speaking.

Midi-Pyrénées region of SW France, comprising the *départements* of Ariège, Aveyron, Haute-Garonne, Gers, Lot, Hautes-Pyrénées, Tarn, and Tarn-et-Garonne; *area* 45,300 sq km/ 17,486 sq mi; *capital* Toulouse; *features* Lourdes; several spa towns, winter resorts, and prehistoric caves; *population* (1986) 2,355,000.

Milan (Italian *Milano*) industrial city, financial and cultural centre, capital of Lombardy, Italy; population (1988) 1,479,000.

milk secretion of the ▷mammary glands of female mammals, with which they suckle their young (during ▷lactation). Over 85% is water, the remainder comprising protein, fat, lactose (a sugar), calcium, phosphorus, iron, and vitamins. The milk of cows, goats, and sheep is often consumed by humans, but regular drinking of milk after infancy is principally a Western practice.

Milky Way faint band of light crossing the night sky, consisting of stars in the plane of our Galaxy. The name Milky Way is often used for the Galaxy itself. It is a spiral ▷galaxy, about 100,000 light years in diameter, containing at least 100 billion stars. The Sun is in one of its spiral arms, about 25,000 light years from the centre.

Mill John Stuart 1806–1873. English philosopher and economist who wrote *On Liberty* 1859, the classic philosophical defence of liberalism, and *Utilitarianism* 1863, a version of the 'greatest happiness for the greatest number' principle in ethics. His progressive views

inspired *On the Subjection of Women* 1869.

Millais John Everett 1829–1896. English painter. He was a founder member of the ▷*Pre- Raphaelite Brotherhood (PRB)* 1848. By the late 1850s he had left the PRB, and his style became more fluent and less detailed.

Miller Arthur 1915– . US dramatist. His plays deal with family relationships and contemporary American values, and include *Death of a Salesman* 1949 and *The Crucible* 1953. He was married 1956–61 to the film star Marilyn Monroe, for whom he wrote the film *The Misfits* 1960.

millet any of several grasses, family Gramineae, of which the grains are used as a cereal food and the stems as fodder.

Milošević Slobodan 1941– . Serbian communist politician, party chief and president of Serbia from 1986; re-elected Dec 1990 in multiparty elections and again Dec 1992. He wielded considerable influence over the Serb- dominated Yugoslav federal army during the 1991–92 civil war and appeared to back Serbian militia in Bosnia-Herzegovina 1992–94. He changed tactics during 1993, putting pressure on the Bosnian Serbs, to accept UN–EC negotiated peace terms.

Milton John 1608–1674. English poet. His epic *Paradise Lost* 1667 is one of the landmarks of English literature. Early poems including *Comus* (a masque performed 1634) and *Lycidas* (an elegy 1638) showed Milton's superlative lyric gift. Latin secretary to Oliver Cromwell during the Commonwealth period, he also wrote many pamphlets and prose works, including *Areopagitica* 1644, which opposed press censorship.

mineral naturally formed inorganic substance with a particular chemical composition and a regularly repeating internal structure. Either in their perfect crystalline form or otherwise, minerals are the constituents of ▷rocks. In more general usage, a mineral is any substance economically valuable for mining (including coal and oil, despite their organic origins). *Mineralogy* is the study of minerals; their classification is based chiefly on their chemical composition and the kind of chemical bonding that holds these atoms together.

Minerva in Roman mythology, the goddess of intelligence, and of handicrafts and the arts, equivalent to the Greek Athena. From the earliest days of ancient Rome, there was a temple to her on the Capitoline Hill, near the Temple of Jupiter.

Minimalism movement in art (mostly sculpture) and music towards severely simplified composition. Minimal art developed in the USA in the 1950s in reaction to Abstract Expressionism, shunning its emotive approach in favour of impersonality and elemental, usually geometric, shapes. It has found its fullest expression in sculpture, notably in the work of sculptor Carl André (1935–), who employs industrial materials in modular compositions. In music, from the 1960s, it manifested itself in large-scale statements, usually tonal or even diatonic, and often highly repetitive, based on a few 'minimal' musical ideas.

mining extraction of minerals from under the land or sea for industrial or domestic uses. Exhaustion of traditionally accessible resources has led to development of new mining techniques; for example, extraction of oil from offshore deposits and from land shale reserves. Technology is also under development for the exploitation of minerals from entirely new sources such as mud deposits and mineral nodules from the sea bed.

Minnesota state in N midwest USA; nickname Gopher State/North Star State; *area* 218,700 sq km/84,418 sq mi; *capital* St Paul; *features* Voyageurs National Park near the Canadian border; Minnehaha Falls at Minneapolis; more than 15,000 lakes; *population* (1990) 4,375,100.

Minoan civilization Bronze Age civilization on the Aegean island of Crete, divided into three main periods: early Minoan, about 3000–2200 BC; middle Minoan, about 2200–1580 BC; and late Minoan, about 1580–1100 BC. Each period was marked by cultural advances in copper and bronze weapons, pottery of increasingly intricate design, frescoes, and the construction of palaces and fine houses at Phaistos and Mallia, in addition to Knossos. About 1400 BC, in the late Minoan period, the civilization was suddenly destroyed by earthquake or war, and it became soon eclipsed by the ▷Mycenaean civilization of mainland Greece. In religion the Minoans seem to have worshipped principally a great mother goddess with whom was associated a young male god.

Minorca (Spanish *Menorca*) second largest of the ▷Balearic Islands in the Mediterranean; *area* 689 sq km/266 sq mi; *towns and cities* Mahon, Ciudadela; *population* (1985) 55,500.

Minotaur in Greek mythology, a monster, half man and half bull, offspring of Pasiphaë, wife of King Minos of Crete, and a bull. It lived in the Labyrinth at Knossos, and its victims were seven girls and seven youths, sent in annual tribute by Athens, until ▷Theseus killed it, with the aid of Ariadne, the daughter of Minos.

Miocene fourth epoch of the Tertiary period of geological time, 23.5–5.2 million years ago. At this time grasslands spread over the interior of continents, and hoofed mammals rapidly evolved.

Miró Joan 1893–1983. Spanish Surrealist painter. In the mid-1920s he developed an abstract style, lyrical and often witty, with amoeba shapes, some linear, some highly coloured, generally floating on a plain background.

miscarriage spontaneous expulsion of a fetus from the womb before it is capable of independent survival. Often, miscarriages are due to an abnormality in the developing fetus.

missile rocket-propelled weapon, which may be nuclear- armed. Modern missiles are often classified as surface-to-surface missiles (SSM), air-to-air missiles (AAM), surface-to-air missiles (SAM), or air-to-surface missiles (ASM). A *cruise missile* is in effect a pilotless, computer-guided aircraft; it can be sea-launched from submarines or surface ships, or launched from the air or the ground.

Mississippi river in the USA, the main arm of the great river system draining the USA between the Appalachian and the Rocky mountains. The length of the Mississippi is 3,780 km/2,350 mi; with its tributary the Missouri 6,020 km/3,740 mi.

Mississippi state in SE USA; *area* 123,600 sq km/47,710 sq mi; *capital* Jackson; *features* Vicksburg National Military Park (Civil War site); Seashore; mansions and plantations; *population* (1990) 2,573,200.

Missouri major river in the central USA, a tributary of the Mississippi, which it joins N of St Louis; length 4,320 km/2,683 mi.

Missouri state in central USA; *area* 180,600 sq km/69,712 sq mi; *capital* Jefferson City; *features* Pony Express Museum at St Joseph; Mark Twain and Ozark state parks; Harry S Truman Library at Independence; *population* (1990) 5,117,100.

Mitterrand François 1916– . French socialist politician, president 1981–95. He held ministerial posts in 11 governments 1947–58, and founded the French Socialist Party (PS) 1971. In 1985 he introduced proportional representation, allegedly to weaken the growing opposition from left and right. From 1982 his administrations combined economic orthodoxy with social reform.

Mizoram state of NE India; *area* 21,100 sq km/8,145 sq mi; *capital* Aizawl; *population* (1991) 686,200; *religion* 84% Christian.

Modernism in the arts, a general term used to describe the 20th century's conscious attempt to break with the artistic traditions of the 19th century; it is based on a concern with form and the exploration of technique as opposed to content and narrative. In the visual arts, for example, direct representationalism gave way to abstraction (see ▷abstract art).

Modigliani Amedeo 1884–1920. Italian artist. He was active in Paris from 1906. He painted and sculpted graceful nudes and portrait studies. His paintings – for example, the portrait of his mistress Jeanne Hébuterne, painted 1919 (Guggenheim Museum, New York) –

have a distinctive style, the forms elongated and sensual.

modulation in radio transmission, the intermittent change of frequency, or amplitude, of a radio carrier wave, in accordance with the audio characteristics of the speaking voice, music, or other signal being transmitted.

Mogadishu or *Mugdisho* capital and chief port of Somalia; population (1988) 1,000,000. During the struggle to overthrow President Barre and the ensuing civil war 1991–92, much of the city was devastated.

Mogul N Indian dynasty 1526–1858, established by Babur, Muslim descendant of Tamerlane, the 14th-century Mongol leader. The Mogul emperors ruled until the last one, Bahadur Shah II (1775–1862), was dethroned and exiled by the British; they included Akbar, Aurangzeb, and Shah Jahan. The Moguls established a more extensive and centralized empire than their Delhi sultanate forebears, and the Mogul era was one of great artistic achievement as well as urban and commercial development.

Mohammed alternative form of ▷Muhammad, founder of Islam.

Mohawk member of a North American Indian people, part of the Iroquois confederation, who lived in the Mohawk Valley, New York, and now live on reservations in Ontario, Québec (Canada), and New York State, as well as among the general population. Their language belongs to the Macro-Siouan group.

Mohican and Mohegan or *Mahican* two closely related North American Indian peoples, speaking an Algonquian language, who formerly occupied the Hudson Valley and parts

of Connecticut, respectively. The novelist James Fenimore ▷Cooper confused the two peoples in his fictional account *The Last of the Mohicans* 1826.

Mohs' scale scale of hardness for minerals (in ascending order): 1 talc; 2 gypsum; 3 calcite; 4 fluorite; 5 apatite; 6 orthoclase; 7 quartz; 8 topaz; 9 corundum; 10 diamond.

molar one of the large teeth found towards the back of the mammalian mouth. The structure of the jaw, and the relation of the muscles, allows a massive force to be applied to molars. In herbivores the molars are flat with sharp ridges of enamel and are used for grinding, an adaptation to a diet of tough plant material. Carnivores have sharp powerful molars called carnassials, which are adapted for cutting meat.

Moldova Republic of; *area* 33,700 sq km/13,012 sq mi; *capital* Chişinău (Kishinev); *features* Black Earth region; *political system* emergent democracy; *population* (1993 est) 4,500,000 (Moldavian 64%, Ukrainian 14%, Russian 13%, Gagauzi 4%, Bulgarian 2%); *language* Moldavian, allied to Romanian; *religion* Russian Orthodox.

molecule group of two or more ▷atoms bonded together. A molecule of an element consists of one or more like ▷atoms; a molecule of a compound consists of two or more different atoms bonded together. Molecules vary in size and complexity from the hydrogen molecule (H_2) to the large macromolecules of proteins. They are held together by ionic bonds, in which the atoms gain or lose electrons to form ▷ions, or by covalent bonds, where electrons from each atom are shared in a new molecular orbital.

Molière pen name of Jean-Baptiste Poquelin 1622–1673. French satirical dramatist and actor. Modern French comedy developed from his work. In 1655 he wrote his first play, *L'Etourdi/The Blunderer*. His satires include *L'Ecole des femmes/The School for Wives* 1662, *Tartuffe* 1664, (banned until 1697 for attacking the clergy), *Le Misanthrope* 1666, *Le Bourgeois Gentilhomme/The Would-Be Gentleman* 1670, and *Le Malade imaginaire/The Imaginary Invalid* 1673.

mollusc any invertebrate of the phylum Mollusca with a body divided into three parts, a head, a foot, and a visceral mass. The majority of molluscs are marine animals, but some inhabit fresh water, and a few are terrestrial. They include bivalves, mussels, octopuses, oysters, snails, slugs, and squids. The body is soft, limbless, and cold-blooded. There is no internal skeleton, but many species have a hard shell covering the body.

Mombasa industrial port in Kenya (serving also Uganda and Tanzania), built on Mombasa Island and adjacent mainland; population (1984) 481,000. It was founded by Arab traders in the 11th century and was an important centre for ivory and slave trading until the 16th century.

Monaco Principality of; *area* 1.95 sq km/0.75 sq mi; *capital* Monaco-Ville; *features* aquarium and oceanographic centre; Monte Carlo film festival, motor races, and casinos; world's second- smallest state; *political system* constitutional monarchy under French protectorate; *population* (1990) 30,000; growth rate –0.5% p.a.; *languages* French (official), English, Italian; *religion* Roman Catholic 95%.

Monaghan (Irish *Mhuineachain*) county of the Republic of Ireland, in the province of Ulster; county town Monaghan; area 1,290 sq km/498 sq mi; population (1991) 51,300. The county is low and rolling, and includes the rivers Finn and Blackwater.

Mondrian Piet (Pieter Mondriaan) 1872–1944. Dutch painter. A pioneer of abstract art, he lived in Paris 1919–38, then in London, and from 1940 in New York. He was a founder member of the De Stijl movement and chief exponent of Neo-Plasticism, a rigorous abstract style based on the use of simple geometric forms and pure colours. His *Composition in Red, Yellow and Blue* 1920 (Stedelijk, Amsterdam) is typical.

Monet Claude 1840–1926. French painter. He was a pioneer of Impressionism and a lifelong exponent of its ideals; his painting *Impression, Sunrise* 1872 gave the movement its name. In the 1870s he began painting the same subjects at different times of day to explore the ever-changing effects of light on colour and form; the *Haystacks* and *Rouen Cathedral* series followed in the 1890s, and from 1899 he painted a series of *Water Lilies* in the garden of his house at Giverny, Normandy (now a museum).

monetarism economic policy, advocated by the economist Milton Friedman and the Chicago school of economists, that proposes control of a country's money supply to keep it in step with the country's ability to produce goods, with the aim of curbing inflation. Cutting government spending is advocated, and the long-term aim is to return as much of the economy as possible to the private sector, allegedly in the interests of efficiency.

money any common medium of exchange acceptable in payment for goods or services or for the settlement of debts; legal tender. Money is usually coinage (invented by the Chinese in the second millennium BC) and paper notes (used by the Chinese from about AD 800). Developments such as the cheque and credit card fulfill many of the traditional functions of money. In 1994 Mondex electronic money was introduced experimentally in Swindon, Wiltshire, England.

Mongol member of any of the various Mongol (or Mongolian) ethnic groups of Central Asia. Mongols live in Mongolia, Russia, Inner Mongolia (China), Tibet, and Nepal. The Mongol language belongs to the Altaic family; some groups of Mongol descent speak languages in the Sino-Tibetan family, however.

Mongol Empire empire established by ◊Genghis Khan, who extended his domains from Russia to N China and became khan of the Mongol tribes 1206. His grandson ◊Kublai Khan conquered China and used foreigners (such as the Venetian traveller Marco Polo) as well as subjects to administer his empire. The Mongols lost China 1367 and suffered defeats in the west 1380; the empire broke up soon afterwards.

Mongolia State of (*Outer Mongolia* until 1924; *People's Republic of Mongolia* until 1991); *area* 1,565,000 sq km/ 604,480 sq mi; *capital* Ulaanbaatar; *features* Altai Mountains in SW; salt lakes; part of Gobi Desert in SE; contains both the world's southernmost permafrost and northernmost desert; *political system* emergent democracy; *population* (1993 est) 2,360,000; growth rate 2.8% p.a.; *languages* Khalkha Mongolian (official), Chinese, Russian, and Turkic

languages; *religion* officially none (Tibetan Buddhist Lamaism suppressed 1930s).

monkey any of the various smaller, mainly tree-dwelling anthropoid primates, excluding humans and the ◊apes. The 125 species live in Africa, Asia, and tropical Central and South America. Monkeys eat mainly leaves and fruit, and also small animals. Several species are endangered due to loss of forest habitat, for example the woolly spider monkey and black saki of the Amazonian forest.

monomer chemical compound composed of simple molecules from which ◊polymers can be made. Under certain conditions the simple molecules (of the monomer) join together (polymerize) to form a very long chain molecule (macromolecule) called a polymer. For example, the polymerization of ethene (ethylene) monomers produces the polymer polyethene (polyethylene).

monotreme any member of the order Monotremata, the only living egg-laying mammals, found in Australasia. They include the echidnas and the platypus.

Monroe Marilyn. Stage name of Norma Jean Mortenson or Baker 1926–1962. US film actress. The voluptuous blonde sex symbol of the 1950s, she made adroit comedies such as *Gentlemen Prefer Blondes* 1953, *How to Marry a Millionaire* 1953, *The Seven Year Itch* 1955, *Bus Stop* 1956, and *Some Like It Hot* 1959. Her third husband was playwright Arthur ◊Miller. She committed suicide.

Monrovia capital and port of Liberia; population (1985) 500,000.

monsoon wind pattern that brings seasonally heavy rain to S Asia; it blows towards the sea in winter and towards the land in summer. The monsoon may cause destructive flooding all over India and SE Asia from April to Sept, leaving thousands of people homeless each year.

Montaigne Michel Eyquem de 1533–1592. French writer. He is regarded as the creator of the essay form. In 1580 he published the first two volumes of his *Essais*; the third volume appeared 1588. Montaigne deals with all aspects of life from an urbanely sceptical viewpoint. Through the translation by John Florio 1603, he influenced Shakespeare and other English writers.

Montana state in western USA, on the Canadian border; *area* 318,100 sq km/ 147,143 sq mi; *capital* Helena; *features* Glacier National Park on the Continental Divide and Yellowstone National Park; Museum of the Plains Indian; Custer Battlefield National Monument; *population* (1990) 799,100.

Mont Blanc (Italian *Monte Bianco*) highest mountain in the ▷Alps, between France and Italy; height 4,807 m/15,772 ft. It was first climbed 1786 by Jacques Balmat and Michel Paccard of Chamonix.

Monte Carlo town and luxury resort in the principality of ▷Monaco, situated on a rocky promontory NE of Monaco town; population (1982) 12,000. It is known for its Casino (1878) designed by architect Charles Garnier, and the Monte Carlo car rally and Monaco Grand Prix.

Montenegro (Serbo-Croatian *Crna Gora*) constituent republic of Yugoslavia; *area* 13,800 sq km/5,327 sq mi; *capital* Podgorica; *features* Skadarsko Jezero (Lake Scutari) shared with Albania; Mount Lovćen (1,749 m/5,738 ft); *population* (1991) 615,300, including

c. 397,000 Montenegrins, 79,500 Muslims, and 39,500 Albanians; *language* Serbian variant of Serbo-Croat; *religion* Serbian Orthodox.

Monteverdi Claudio (Giovanni Antonio) 1567–1643. Italian composer. He contributed to the development of the opera with *La favola d'Orfeo/The Legend of Orpheus* 1607 and *L'incoronazione di Poppea/The Coronation of Poppea* 1642. He also wrote madrigals, motets, and sacred music, notably the *Vespers* 1610.

Montevideo capital and chief port of Uruguay, on the Rio de la Plata; population (1985) 1,250,000.

Montgomery Bernard Law, 1st Viscount Montgomery of Alamein 1887–1976. British field marshal. In World War II he commanded the 8th Army in N Africa in the Second Battle of El Alamein 1942. As commander of British troops in N Europe from 1944, he received the German surrender 1945.

Montréal inland port, industrial city of Québec, Canada, on Montréal Island at the junction of the Ottawa and St Lawrence rivers; population (1986) 2,921,000.

moon in astronomy, any natural ▷satellite that orbits a planet. Mercury and Venus are the only planets in the Solar System that do not have moons.

Moon natural satellite of Earth, 3,476 km/2,160 mi in diameter, with a mass 0.012 (approximately one-eightieth) that of Earth. Its surface gravity is only 0.16 (one-sixth) that of Earth. Its average distance from Earth is 384,400 km/238,855 mi, and it orbits in a west-to-east direction every 27.32 days (the *sidereal month*). It spins on its axis with one side permanently turned towards

Earth. The Moon has no atmosphere or water.

Moor any of the NW African Muslims, of mixed Arab and Berber origin, who conquered Spain and ruled its southern part from 711 to 1492, when they were forced to renounce their faith and became Christian (they were then known as *Moriscos*). The name (English form of Latin *Maurus*) was originally applied to an inhabitant of the Roman province of Mauritania, in NW Africa.

Moore Henry 1898–1986. English sculptor. His subjects include the reclining nude, mother and child groups, the warrior, and interlocking abstract forms. Many of his post-1945 works are in bronze or marble, including monumental semi-abstracts such as *Reclining Figure* 1957–58 (outside the UNESCO building, Paris), and often designed to be placed in landscape settings.

More (St) Thomas 1478–1535. English politician and author. From 1509 he was favoured by ◊Henry VIII and employed on foreign embassies. He was a member of the privy council from 1518 and Lord Chancellor from 1529 but resigned over Henry's break with the pope. For refusing to accept the king as head of the church, he was executed. The title of his political book *Utopia* 1516 has come to mean any supposedly perfect society.

Mormon or *Latter-day Saint* member of a Christian sect, the *Church of Jesus Christ of Latter-day Saints*, founded at Fayette, New York, in 1830 by Joseph ◊Smith. According to Smith, Mormon was an ancient prophet in North America whose *Book of Mormon*, of which Smith claimed divine revelation, is accepted by Mormons as part of the Christian scriptures. In the 19th century

the faction led by Brigham Young was polygamous. It is a missionary church with headquarters in Utah and a worldwide membership of about 6 million.

Morocco Kingdom of (*al-Mamlaka al-Maghrebia*); *area* 458,730 sq km/ 177,070 sq mi (excluding Western Sahara); *capital* Rabat; *features* Atlas Mountains; the towns Ceuta (from 1580) and Melilla (from 1492) are held by Spain; tunnel crossing the Strait of Gibraltar to Spain proposed 1985; *political system* constitutional monarchy; *population* (1993 est) 27,000,000; growth rate 2.5% p.a.; *languages* Arabic (official) 75%, Berber 25%, French, Spanish; *religion* Sunni Muslim 99%.

Moroni capital of the Comoros Republic, on Njazidja (Grand Comore); population (1980) 20,000. It has a small natural harbour.

morphine narcotic alkaloid $C_{17}H_{19}NO_3$ derived from ◊opium and prescribed only to alleviate severe pain. Its use produces serious side effects, including nausea, constipation, tolerance, and addiction, but it is highly valued for the relief of the terminally ill.

Morris William 1834–1896. English designer. A founder of the Arts and Crafts movement, also a socialist and writer, he shared the Pre-Raphaelite painters' fascination with medieval settings. In 1861 he cofounded a firm that designed and produced furniture, carpets, and a wide range of decorative wallpapers, many of which are still produced today. His Kelmscott Press, set up 1890, greatly influenced printing and book design.

morris dance English folk dance. In early times it was usually performed by six men, one of whom wore girl's clothing while another portrayed a horse. The others wore costumes decorated with bells. Morris dancing probably originated in pre-Christian ritual dances and is still popular in the UK and USA.

Morse code international code for transmitting messages by wire or radio using signals of short (dots) and long (dashes) duration, originated by US inventor Samuel Morse for use on his invention, the telegraph.

mosaic design or picture, usually for a floor, wall or vault, produced by setting small pieces of marble, glass, or other materials in a cement ground. The ancient Greeks were the first to use a form of mosaic (for example, the Macedonian royal palace at Pella). Mosaic was commonly used by the Romans for their baths and villas (for example Hadrian's Villa at Tivoli) and reached its highest development in the early Byzantine period (for example, San Vitale, Ravenna).

Moscow (Russian *Moskva*) industrial city, capital of Russia and of the Moskva region, and formerly (1922–91) of the USSR, on the Moskva River 640 km/400 mi SE of St Petersburg; population (1987) 8,815,000.

Moses Hebrew lawgiver and judge who led the Israelites out of Egypt to the promised land of Canaan. On Mount Sinai he claimed to have received from Jehovah the oral and written Law, including the *Ten Commandments* engraved on tablets of stone. The first five books of the Old Testament – in Judaism, the *Torah* – are ascribed to him.

mosque in Islam, a place of worship. Chief features are: the dome; the minaret, a balconied turret from which the faithful are called to prayer; the *mihrab*, or prayer niche, in one of the interior walls, showing the direction of the holy city of Mecca; and an open court surrounded by porticoes.

mosquito any fly of the family Culicidae. The female mosquito has needle-like mouthparts and sucks blood before laying eggs. Males feed on plant juices. Some mosquitoes carry diseases such as ▷malaria.

moss small nonflowering plant of the class Musci (10,000 species), forming with the liverworts and the hornworts the order Bryophyta. The stem of each plant bears rhizoids that anchor it; there are no true roots. Leaves spirally arranged on its lower portion have sexual organs at their tips. Most mosses flourish best in damp conditions where other vegetation is thin.

moth any of the various families of mainly night-flying insects of the order Lepidoptera, which also includes the butterflies. Their wings are covered with microscopic scales. The mouthparts are formed into a sucking proboscis, but certain moths have no functional mouthparts, and rely upon stores of fat and other reserves built up during the caterpillar stage. At least 100,000 different species of moth are known.

mot juste (French) the right word, just the word to suit the occasion.

motor anything that produces or imparts motion; a machine that provides mechanical power – for example, an electric motor. Machines that burn fuel (petrol, diesel) are usually called engines, but the internal-combustion engine that propels vehicles has long been called a motor, hence 'motoring' and 'motorcar'. Actually the motor is a part of the car engine.

motorcycle or *motorbike* two-wheeled vehicle propelled by a ◊petrol engine. The first successful motorized bicycle was built in France 1901, and British and US manufacturers first produced motorbikes 1903.

motorcycle racing speed contests on motorcycles. It has many different forms: *road racing* over open roads; *circuit racing* over purpose-built tracks; *speedway* over oval-shaped dirt tracks; *motocross* over natural terrain, incorporating hill climbs; and *trials*, also over natural terrain, but with the addition of artificial hazards.

motor neurone disease or *amyotrophic lateral sclerosis* chronic disease in which there is progressive degeneration of the nerve cells. It leads to weakness, wasting, and loss of muscle function and usually proves fatal within two to three years of onset. It occurs in hereditary and sporadic forms but its causes remain unclear. A gene believed to be implicated in familial cases was discovered 1993.

motor racing competitive racing of motor vehicles. It has forms as diverse as hill-climbing, stock-car racing, rallying, sports-car racing, and Formula One Grand Prix racing. The first organized race was from Paris to Rouen 1894.

mould mainly saprophytic fungi (see ◊fungus) living on foodstuffs and other organic matter, a few being parasitic on plants, animals, or each other. Many moulds are of medical or industrial importance; for example, penicillin.

mountain natural upward projection of the Earth's surface, higher and steeper than a hill. The process of mountain building (orogeny) consists of volcanism, folding, faulting, and thrusting, resulting from the collision and welding together of two tectonic plates (see ◊plate tectonics). This process deforms the rock and compresses the sediment between the two plates into mountain chains.

Mountbatten Louis, 1st Earl Mountbatten of Burma 1900–1979. British admiral and administrator. In World War II he became chief of combined operations 1942 and commander in chief in SE Asia 1943. As last viceroy of India 1947 and first governor general of India until 1948, he oversaw that country's transition to independence. He was killed by an Irish Republican Army bomb aboard his yacht in the Republic of Ireland.

mouse in zoology, one of a number of small rodents with small ears and a long, thin tail, belonging largely to the Old World family Muridae. The house mouse *Mus musculus* is distributed worldwide. It is 75 mm/3 in long, with a naked tail of equal length, and has a grey-brown body.

Mozambique People's Republic of (*República Popular de Moçambique*); *area* 799,380 sq km/308,561 sq mi; *capital* and chief port Maputo; *features* rivers Zambezi, Limpopo; 'Beira Corridor' rail, road, and pipeline link with Zimbabwe; *political system* emergent democratic republic; *population* (1993 est) 16,600,000 (mainly indigenous Bantu peoples; Portuguese 50,000); growth rate 2.8% p.a.; *languages* Portuguese (official), 16 African languages; *religion* animist 60%, Roman Catholic 18%, Muslim 16%.

Mozart Wolfgang Amadeus 1756–1791. Austrian composer and performer. His prolific works include 27 piano concertos, 23 string quartets, 35 violin sonatas, and over 50 symphonies including the E flat K543, G minor K550, and C major K551 ('Jupiter') symphonies, all composed 1788. His operas include *Idomeneo* 1780, *Entführung aus dem Serail/The Abduction from the Seraglio* 1782, *Le Nozze di Figaro/The Marriage of Figaro* 1786, *Don Giovanni* 1787, *Così fan tutte/Thus Do All Women* 1790, and *Die Zauberflöte/The Magic Flute* 1791.

MS-DOS (abbreviation for *Microsoft Disc Operating System*) computer *operating system* produced by Microsoft Corporation, widely used on microcomputers with Intel × 86 family microprocessors. A version called PC-DOS is sold by IBM specifically for its personal computers. MS-DOS and PC-DOS are usually referred to as DOS. MS-DOS first appeared 1981.

mucous membrane thin skin lining all animal body cavities and canals that come into contact with the air (for example, eyelids, breathing and digestive passages, genital tract). It secretes mucus, a moistening, lubricating, and protective fluid.

Mubarak Hosni 1928– . Egyptian politician, president from 1981. Vice president to Anwar Sadat from 1975, Mubarak succeeded him on his assassination. He has continued to pursue Sadat's moderate policies, and has significantly increased the freedom of the press and of political association, while trying to repress the growing Islamic fundamentalist movement. He was re-elected (uncontested) 1987 and 1993.

Mugabe Robert (Gabriel) 1925– . Zimbabwean politician, prime minister from 1980 and president from 1987. He was in detention in Rhodesia for nationalist activities 1964–74, then carried on guerrilla warfare from Mozambique. As leader of ZANU he was in an uneasy alliance with Joshua Nkomo (1917–) of ZAPU (Zimbabwe African People's Union) from 1976.

Muhammad or *Mohammed*, *Mahomet* c. 570–632. Founder of Islam, born in Mecca on the Arabian peninsula. In about 616 he claimed to be a prophet and that the *Koran* was revealed to him by God (it was later written down by his followers), through the angel Jibra'el (Gabriel). He fled from persecution to the town now known as Medina in 622: the flight, *Hegira*, marks the beginning of the Islamic era.

multiple sclerosis (MS) or *disseminated sclerosis* incurable chronic disease of the central nervous system, occurring in young or middle adulthood. Most prevalent in temperate zones, it affects more women than men. It is characterized by degeneration of the myelin sheath that surrounds nerves in the brain and spinal cord.

mumps or *infectious parotitis* virus infection marked by fever, pain, and swelling of one or both parotid salivary glands (situated in front of the ears). It is usually shortlived in children, although meningitis is a possible complication. In adults the symptoms are more serious and it may cause sterility in men.

Munch Edvard 1863–1944. Norwegian painter and printmaker. He studied in Paris and Berlin, and his major works date from the period 1892–1908, when he lived mainly in Germany. His paintings often focus on neurotic emotional states. The *Frieze of Life* 1890s, a sequence of highly charged, symbolic paintings, includes some of his most characteristic images, such as *Skriket/The Scream* 1893. He later reused these in etchings, lithographs, and woodcuts.

Munich (German *München*) industrial city, capital of Bavaria, Germany, on the river Isar; population (1986) 1,269,400.

Munich Agreement pact signed on 29 Sept 1938 by the leaders of the UK (Neville ▷Chamberlain), France (Edouard Daladier), Germany (Hitler), and Italy (Mussolini), under which Czechoslovakia was compelled to surrender its Sudeten-German districts (the *Sudetenland*) to Germany. Chamberlain claimed it would guarantee 'peace in our time', but it did not prevent Hitler from seizing the rest of Czechoslovakia in March 1939.

Munster southern province of the Republic of Ireland, comprising the counties of Clare, Cork, Kerry, Limerick, North and South Tipperary, and Waterford; area 24,140 sq km/9,318 sq mi; population (1991) 1,008,400.

muon an ▷elementary particle similar to the electron except for its mass which is 207 times greater than that of the electron. It has a half-life of 2 millionths of a second, decaying into electrons and ▷neutrinos. The muon was originally thought to be a ▷meson and is thus sometimes called a mu meson, although current opinion is that it is a ▷lepton.

Murray principal river of Australia, 2,575 km/1,600 mi long. It rises in the Australian Alps near Mount Kosciusko and flows W, forming the boundary between New South Wales and Victoria, and reaches the sea at Encounter Bay, South Australia. With its main tributary, the Darling, it is 3,750 km/2,330 mi long.

Muscat or *Masqat* capital of Oman, E Arabia, adjoining the port of Matrah, which has a deep-water harbour; combined population (1982) 80,000.

muscle contractile animal tissue that produces locomotion and power, and maintains the movement of body substances. Muscle is made of long cells that can contract to between one-half and one-third of their relaxed length.

muscular dystrophy any of a group of inherited chronic muscle disorders marked by weakening and wasting of muscle. Muscle fibres degenerate, to be replaced by fatty tissue, although the nerve supply remains unimpaired. Death occurs in early adult life.

Muse in Greek mythology, one of the nine daughters of Zeus and Mnemosyne (goddess of memory) and inspirers of creative arts: Calliope, epic poetry; Clio, history; Erato, love poetry; Euterpe, lyric poetry; Melpomene, tragedy; Polyhymnia, sacred song; Terpsichore, dance; Thalia, comedy; and Urania, astronomy.

mushroom fruiting body of certain fungi, consisting of an upright stem and a spore-producing cap with radiating gills on the undersurface. There are many edible species belonging to the genus *Agaricus*. See also ▷fungus and ▷toadstool.

Muslim or *Moslem*, a follower of ▷Islam.

Mussolini Benito 1883–1945. Italian dictator 1925–43. Founder of the Fascist Movement 1919 and prime minister from 1922, he became known as *Il Duce* ('the leader'). He invaded Ethiopia 1935–36, intervened in the Spanish Civil War 1936–39 in support of Franco, and conquered Albania 1939. In June 1940 Italy entered World War II supporting Hitler. Forced by military and domestic setbacks to resign 1943, Mussolini established a breakaway government in N Italy 1944–45, but was killed trying to flee the country.

Mussorgsky Modest Petrovich 1839–1881. Russian nationalist composer. He was a member of the group of five composers 'The Five'. His opera masterpiece was *Boris Godunov* 1869, revised 1871–72 and his other works include *Pictures at an Exhibition* 1874 for piano.

mustard any of several annual plants of the family Cruciferae, with sweet-smelling yellow flowers. Brown and white mustard are cultivated as a condiment in Europe and North America. The seeds of brown mustard *Brassica juncea* and white mustard *Sinapis alba* are used in the preparation of table mustard.

mutation in biology, a change in the genes produced by a change in the ◊DNA that makes up the hereditary material of all living organisms. Mutations, the raw material of evolution, result from mistakes during replication (copying) of DNA molecules. Only a few such mutations improve the organism's performance and are therefore favoured by ◊natural selection. Mutation rates are increased by certain chemicals and by radiation.

Myanmar Union of (*Thammada Myanmar Naingngandaw*) (formerly *Burma*, until 1989); *area* 676,577 sq km/ 261,228 sq mi; *capital* (and chief port) Yangon (formerly Rangoon); *environment* landslides and flooding during the rainy season (June–Sept) are becoming more frequent as a result of deforestation; *features* ruined cities of Pagan and Mingun; *political system* military republic; *population* (1993) 42,330,000; growth rate 1.9% p.a. (includes Shan, Karen, Raljome, Chinese, and Indian minorities); *language* Burmese; *religions* Hinayana Buddhist 85%, animist, Christian.

Mycenaean civilization Bronze Age civilization that flourished in Crete, Cyprus, mainland Greece, the Aegean Islands, and W Anatolia about 3000–1000 BC. Strongly influenced by the ◊Minoan civilization from Crete from about 1600 BC, it continued to thrive, with its centre at Mycenae, after the decline of Crete in about 1400. The Mycenaeans used a form of Greek called Linear B, discovered on large numbers of clay tablets containing administrative records. Their palaces were large and luxurious, and their tombs were massive and impressive monuments. Pottery, frescoes, and metalwork reached a high artistic level. Evidence of the civilization was brought to light by the excavations of Heinrich ◊Schliemann at Troy, Mycenae, and Tiryns from 1870 onwards, and of Arthur ◊Evans in Crete from 1899.

myopia or *short-sightedness* defect of the eye in which a person can see clearly only those objects that are close up. It is caused either by the eyeball being too long or by the cornea and lens system of the eye being too powerful, both of which cause the images of distant objects to be formed in front of the retina instead of on it. Myopia can be corrected by suitable glasses or contact lenses.

myrrh gum resin produced by small trees of the genus *Commiphora* of the bursera family, especially *C. myrrha*, found in Ethiopia and Arabia. In ancient times it was used for incense and perfume and in embalming.

myrtle evergreen shrub of the Old World genus *Myrtus*, family Myrtaceae. The commonly cultivated Mediterranean myrtle *M. communis* has oval opposite leaves and white flowers followed by purple berries, all of which are fragrant.

mysticism religious belief or spiritual experience based on direct, intuitive communion with the divine. It does not always involve an orthodox deity, though it is found in all the major religions – for example, kabbalism in Judaism, Sufism in Islam, and the bhakti movement in Hinduism. The mystical experience is often rooted in ascetism and can involve visions, trances, and ecstasies. Official churches fluctuate between acceptance of mysticism as a form of special grace, and suspicion of it as a dangerous deviation, verging on the heretical.

mythology body of traditional stories concerning the gods, supernatural beings, creation stories, and heroes of a given culture, with whom humans may have relationships. Often a mythology may be intended to explain the workings of the universe, nature, or human history.

N

Nabokov Vladimir 1899–1977. US writer. He left his native Russia 1917 and began writing in English in the 1940s. His most widely known book is *Lolita* 1955; his other books, remarkable for their word play and ingenious plots, include *Laughter in the Dark* 1938, *The Real Life of Sebastian Knight* 1945, *Pnin* 1957, and his memoirs *Speak, Memory* 1947.

Nagasaki industrial port on Kyushu Island, Japan; population (1990) 444,600. Nagasaki was the only Japanese port open to European trade from the 16th century until 1859. An atom bomb was dropped on it by the USA 9 Aug 1945.

Nairobi capital of Kenya, in the central highlands at 1,660 m/5,450 ft; population (1985) 1,100,000. It is the headquarters of the United Nations Environment Programme.

Namibia Republic of (formerly *South West Africa*); *area* 824,300 sq km/ 318,262 sq mi; *capital* Windhoek; *environment* 83% of rainfall evaporates as it hits the ground, making it the driest country in sub-Saharan Africa; *features* Namib and Kalahari deserts; Orange River; Caprivi Strip links Namibia to Zambezi River; includes the enclave of Walvis Bay (area 1,120 sq km/432 sq mi); *political system* democratic republic; *population* (1993 est) 1,550,000 (black African 85%, European 6%); *languages* Afrikaans (spoken by 60% of white population), German, English (all official), several indigenous languages; *religion* 51% Lutheran, 19% Roman Catholic, 6% Dutch Reformed Church, 6% Anglican.

Nanak 1469–*c.* 1539. Indian guru and founder of Sikhism, a religion based on the unity of God and the equality of all human beings. He was strongly opposed to caste divisions.

napalm fuel used in flamethrowers and incendiary bombs. Produced from jellied petrol, it is a mixture of *na*phthenic and *palm*itic acids. Napalm causes extensive burns because it sticks to the skin even when aflame. It was widely used by the US Army during the Vietnam War.

Napier John 1550–1617. Scottish mathematician who invented ♭logarithms 1614 and 'Napier's bones', an early mechanical calculating device for multiplication and division.

Naples (Italian *Napoli*) industrial port and capital of Campania, Italy, on the Tyrrhenian Sea; population (1988) 1,201,000. To the south is the Isle of Capri, and behind the city is Mount Vesuvius, with the ruins of Pompeii at its foot.

Napoleon I (Napoleon Bonaparte) 1769–1821. Emperor of the French 1804–14 and 1814–15. A general from

1796 in the Revolutionary War, in 1799 he overthrew the ruling Directory (see ◊French Revolution) and made himself dictator. From 1803 he conquered most of Europe (the *Napoleonic Wars*) and installed his brothers as puppet kings (see ◊Bonaparte). After the Peninsular War and retreat from Moscow 1812, he was forced to abdicate 1814 and was banished to the island of Elba. In March 1815 he reassumed power but was defeated by British and Prussian forces at the Battle of ◊Waterloo and exiled to the island of St Helena. His internal administrative reforms and laws are still evident in France.

Napoleon III 1808–1873. Emperor of the French 1852–70, known as *Louis-Napoleon*. After two attempted coups (1836 and 1840) he was jailed, then went into exile, returning for the revolution of 1848, when he became president of the Second Republic but proclaimed himself emperor 1852. In 1870 he was manoeuvred by the German chancellor Bismarck into war with Prussia (see ◊Franco-Prussian war); he was forced to surrender at Sedan, NE France, and the empire collapsed.

Narcissus in Greek mythology, a beautiful youth who rejected the love of the nymph Echo and was condemned to fall in love with his own reflection in a pool. He pined away and in the place where he died a flower sprang up that was named after him.

narcotic pain-relieving and sleep-inducing drug. The term is usually applied to ◊heroin, ◊morphine, and other opium derivatives, but may also be used for other drugs which depress brain activity, including anaesthetic agents and hypnotics.

NASA (acronym for *National Aeronautics and Space Administration*) US government agency, founded 1958, for spaceflight and aeronautical research. Its headquarters are in Washington DC and its main installation is at the Kennedy Space Center in Florida.

Nash John 1752–1835. English architect. He laid out Regent's Park, London, and its approaches, a vast grandiose scheme of terraces and crescents and palatial-style houses with ornate stucco façades. Between 1811 and 1821 he planned Regent Street (later rebuilt) and repaired and enlarged Buckingham Palace (for which he designed Marble Arch).

Nashville port on the Cumberland River and capital of Tennessee, USA; population (1990) 488,300. It is a banking and commercial centre, and has large printing, music-publishing, and recording industries; it is the hub of the country-music business in the USA.

Nasser Gamal Abdel 1918–1970. Egyptian politician, prime minister 1954–56 and from 1956 president of Egypt (the United Arab Republic 1958–71). In 1952 he was the driving power behind the Neguib coup, which ended the monarchy. His nationalization of the Suez Canal 1956 led to an Anglo-French invasion and the ◊Suez Crisis, and his ambitions for an Egyptian-led union of Arab states led to disquiet in the Middle East (and in the West). Nasser was also an early and influential leader of the nonaligned movement.

Natal province of South Africa, NE of Cape Province, bounded on the east by the Indian Ocean; *area* 91,785 sq km/ 35,429 sq mi; *capital* Pietermaritzburg; *features* St Lucia National Park, an area extending 324 sq km/125 sq mi from the coral reefs of the Indian Ocean to the swamps of Lake St Lucia, 324 sq km/ 125 sq mi; *population* (1985) 2,145,000.

NATO acronym for ▷*North Atlantic Treaty Organization.*

natural gas mixture of flammable gases found in the Earth's crust (often in association with petroleum). It is one of the world's three main fossil fuels (with coal and oil). Natural gas is a mixture of ▷hydrocarbons, chiefly methane, with ethane, butane, and propane.

natural selection the process whereby gene frequencies in a population change through certain individuals producing more descendants than others because they are better able to survive and reproduce in their environment. The accumulated effect of natural selection is to produce ▷adaptations such as the insulating coat of a polar bear or the spadelike forelimbs of a mole. The process is slow, relying firstly on random variation in the genes of an organism being produced by ▷mutation and secondly on the genetic ▷recombination of sexual reproduction. It was recognized by Charles Darwin and English naturalist Alfred Russel Wallace as the main process driving ▷evolution.

nature–nurture controversy or *environment–heredity controversy* long-standing dispute among philosophers and psychologists over the relative importance of environment, that is upbringing, experience and learning ('nurture'), and heredity, that is genetic inheritance ('nature'), in determining the make-up of an organism, as related to human personality and intelligence.

Nauru Republic of (*Naoero*); *area* 21 sq km/8 sq mi; *capital* (seat of government) Yaren District; *features* lies just S of equator; one of three phosphate rock islands in the Pacific; *political system* liberal democracy; *population* (1993 est) 10,000 (mainly Polynesian; Chinese 8%, European 8%); growth rate 1.7% p.a.; *languages* Nauruan (official), English; *religion* Protestant 66%, Roman Catholic 33%.

Navarre (Spanish *Navarra*) autonomous mountain region of N Spain; *area* 10,400 sq km/4,014 sq mi; *capital* Pamplona; *features* Monte Adi 1,503 m/4,933 ft; rivers: Ebro, Arga; *population* (1986) 513,000.

Navarre, Kingdom of former kingdom comprising the Spanish province of Navarre and part of what is now the French *département* of Basses-Pyrénées. It resisted the conquest of the ▷Moors and was independent until it became French 1284 on the marriage of Philip IV to the heiress of Navarre. In 1479 Ferdinand of Aragon annexed Spanish Navarre, with French Navarre going to Catherine of Foix (1483–1512), who kept the royal title. Her grandson became Henry IV of France, and Navarre was absorbed in the French crown lands 1620.

navigation the science and technology of finding the position, course, and distance travelled by a ship, plane, or other craft. Traditional methods include the magnetic ▷compass and sextant. Today the gyrocompass is usually used, together with highly sophisticated electronic methods, employing beacons of radio signals, such as Decca, Loran, and Omega. Satellite navigation uses satellites that broadcast time and position signals.

Navratilova Martina 1956– . Czech tennis player who became a naturalized US citizen 1981. The most outstanding woman player of the 1980s, she had 55 Grand Slam victories by 1991, including 18 singles titles. She won the Wimbledon singles title a record nine times, including six in succession 1982–87. She was defeated by Conchita Martinez in the final of her last Wimbledon 1994; she retired from professional tennis later in the same year.

Nazareth town in Galilee, N Israel, SE of Haifa; population (1981) 64,000. According to the New Testament, it was the boyhood home of Jesus.

Nazism ideology based on racism, nationalism, and the supremacy of the state over the individual. The German Nazi party, the *Nationalsozialistiche Deutsche Arbeiterpartei* (National Socialist German Workers' Party), was formed from the German Workers' Party (founded 1919) and led by Adolf ◊Hitler 1921–45.

Neagh, Lough lake in Northern Ireland, 25 km/15 mi W of Belfast; area 396 sq km/153 sq mi. It is the largest lake in the British Isles.

Neanderthal hominid of the Mid-Late Palaeolithic, named after the Neander Thal (valley) near Düsseldorf, Germany, where a skeleton was found 1856. *Homo sapiens neanderthalensis* lived from about 150,000 to 35,000 years ago and was similar in build to present-day people, but slightly smaller, stockier, and heavier-featured with a strong jaw and prominent brow ridges on a sloping forehead. The condition of the Neanderthal teeth that have been found suggests that they were used as clamps for holding objects with the hands.

Nebraska state in central USA; *area* 200,400 sq km/77,354 sq mi; *capital* Lincoln; *population* (1990) 1,578,400; *features* Rocky Mountain foothills; the ranch of Buffalo Bill.

Nebuchadnezzar or *Nebuchadrezzar II* king of Babylonia from 604 BC. Shortly before his accession he defeated the Egyptians at Carchemish and brought Palestine and Syria into his empire. Judah revolted, with Egyptian assistance, 596 and 587–586 BC; on both occasions he captured Jerusalem and took many Hebrews into captivity. He largely rebuilt Babylon and constructed the hanging gardens.

nebula cloud of gas and dust in space. Nebulae are the birthplaces of stars, but some nebulae are produced by gas thrown off from dying stars (see ◊supernova). Nebulae are classified depending on whether they emit, reflect, or absorb light.

Nehru Jawaharlal 1889–1964. Indian nationalist politician, prime minister from 1947. Before the partition (the division of British India into India and Pakistan), he led the socialist wing of the nationalist Congress Party, and was second in influence only to Mahatma Gandhi. He was imprisoned nine times by the British 1921–45 for political activities. His daughter was Prime Minister Indira Gandhi.

Nelson Horatio, Viscount Nelson 1758–1805. English admiral. He joined the navy in 1770. In the Revolutionary Wars against France he lost the sight in his right eye 1794 and lost his right arm 1797. He became a national hero, and rear admiral, after the victory off Cape St Vincent, Portugal. In 1798 he tracked the French fleet to Aboukir Bay where he almost entirely destroyed it. In 1801 he won a decisive victory over Denmark at the Battle of Copenhagen, and in 1805, after two years of blockading Toulon, another over the Franco-Spanish fleet at the Battle of ◊Trafalgar, near Gibraltar.

nematode unsegmented worm of the phylum Nematoda. Nematodes are pointed at both ends, with a tough, smooth outer skin. They include many free-living species found in soil and water, including the sea, but a large number are parasites, such as the round-worms and pinworms that live in humans, or the eelworms that attack plant roots.

Neo-Classicism movement in art, architecture, and design in Europe and North America about 1750–1850, characterized by a revival of classical Greek and Roman styles. It was inspired both by the excavation of Pompeii and Herculaneum (which revived Roman styles) and by the theories of the German art historian J J Winckelmann (1717–68) (which did much to revive Greek styles). Leading figures of the movement included the architect Robert Adam (1728–92), the painter Ingres (1780–1867), and the sculptor Antonio Canova (1757– 1822).

Neo-Impressionism movement in French painting in the 1880s, an extension of Impressionist technique. It drew on contemporary theories on colour and perception, building up form and colour by painting dots side by side. ◊Seurat was the chief exponent; his minute technique became known as *Pointillism*. Signac and Pissarro practised the style for a few years.

Neolithic last period of the ◊Stone Age, characterized by settled communities based on agriculture and domesticated animals, and identified by sophisticated, finely honed stone tools, and ceramic wares. The earliest Neolithic communities appeared about 9000 BC in the Middle East, followed by Egypt, India, and China. In Europe farming began in about 6500 BC in the Balkans and Aegean, spreading north and east by 1000 BC.

neon colourless, odourless, nonmetallic, gaseous element, symbol Ne, atomic number 10, relative atomic mass 20.183. It is grouped with the ◊inert gases, is non-reactive, and forms no compounds. It occurs in small quantities in the Earth's atmosphere.

neo-Nazism the upsurge in racial and political intolerance in Western Europe of the early 1990s. In Austria, Belgium, France, Germany, and Italy, the growth of extreme right-wing political groupings, coupled with racial violence, particularly in Germany, has revived memories of the Nazi period in Hitler's Germany. Ironically, the liberalization of politics in the post-Cold War world unleashed anti-liberal and neo-fascist forces hitherto checked by authoritarian regimes.

Nepal Kingdom of (*Nepal Adhirajya*); *area* 147,181 sq km/56,850 sq mi; *capital* Katmandu; *environment* described as the world's highest rubbish dump; an estimated 500 kg/1,100 lb of rubbish is left by each expedition trekking or climbing in the Himalayas; *features* Mount Everest, Mount Kangchenjunga; the only Hindu kingdom in the world; Lumbini, birthplace of the Buddha; *political system* constitutional monarchy; *population* (1993 est) 20,400,000 (mainly known by name of predominant clan, the Gurkhas; the Sherpas are a Buddhist minority of NE Nepal); growth rate 2.3%

p.a.; *language* Nepali (official); 20 dialects spoken; *religion* Hindu 90%; Buddhist, Muslim, Christian.

Neptune in Roman mythology, the god of the sea, equivalent of the Greek ▷Poseidon.

Neptune in astronomy, the eighth planet in average distance from the Sun. Neptune orbits the Sun every 164.8 years at an average distance of 4.497 billion km/2.794 billion mi. It is a giant gas (hydrogen, helium, methane) planet, with a diameter of 48,600 km/30,200 mi and a mass 17.2 times that of Earth. Its rotation period is 16 hours 7 minutes, and it has the highest winds in the Solar System. It has eight known moons.

Nero adopted name of Lucius Domitius Ahenobarbus AD 37–68. Roman emperor from 54. In 59 he had his mother Agrippina and his wife Octavia put to death. The great fire at Rome 64 was blamed on the Christians, whom he subsequently persecuted. In 65 a plot against Nero was discovered. Further revolts followed 68, and he committed suicide.

Neruda Pablo. Pen name of Neftali Ricardo Reyes y Basualto 1904–1973. Chilean poet and diplomat. His work includes lyrics and the epic poem of the American continent *Canto General* 1950. Nobel Prize for Literature 1971.

nerve bundle of nerve cells enclosed in a sheath of connective tissue and transmitting nerve impulses to and from the brain and spinal cord. A single nerve may contain both ▷motor and sensory nerve cells, but they function independently.

nerve cell or *neuron* elongated cell, the basic functional unit of the ▷nervous system that transmits information rapidly between different parts of the body. Each nerve cell has a cell body, containing the nucleus, from which trail processes called dendrites, responsible for receiving incoming signals. The unit of information is the *nerve impulse*, a travelling wave of chemical and electrical changes involving the membrane of the nerve cell. The cell's longest process, the axon, carries impulses away from the cell body.

nervous system the system of interconnected ▷nerve cells of most invertebrates and all vertebrates. It is composed of the ▷central and ▷autonomic nervous systems. It may be as simple as the nerve net of coelenterates (for example, jellyfishes) or as complex as the mammalian nervous system, with a central nervous system comprising brain and spinal cord, and a peripheral nervous system connecting up with sensory organs, muscles, and glands.

Ness, Loch lake in Highland Region, Scotland, forming part of the Caledonian Canal; 36 km/22.5 mi long, 229 m/754 ft deep. There have been unconfirmed reports of a *Loch Ness monster* since the 15th century.

Netherlands Kingdom of the (*Koninkrijk der Nederlanden*), popularly referred to as *Holland*; *area* 41,863 sq km/16,169 sq mi; *capital* Amsterdam; *environment* lies at the mouths of three of Europe's most polluted rivers, the Maas, Rhine, and Scheldt; *features* polders (reclaimed land) make up over 40% of the land area; *head of state* Queen Beatrix Wilhelmina Armgard from 1980; *head of government* Wim Kok from 1994; *political system* constitutional monarchy; *population* (1993) 15,240,000; growth rate 0.4% p.a.; *language* Dutch; *religions* Roman Catholic 40%, Protestant 31%.

nettle any plant of the genus *Urtica*, family Urticaceae. Stinging hairs on the generally ovate leaves can penetrate the skin, causing inflammation. The common nettle *U. dioica* grows on waste ground in Europe and North America, where it was introduced.

network in computing, a method of connecting computers so that they can share data and peripheral devices, such as printers. The main types are classified by the pattern of the connections – star or ring network, for example – or by the degree of geographical spread allowed; for example, *local area networks* (LANs) for communication within a room or building, and *wide area networks* (WANs) for more remote systems. The ◊Internet is the largest global network, with over 40 million users by the end of 1994.

neurology medical speciality concerned with the study and treatment of disorders of the brain, spinal cord, and peripheral nerves.

neuron another name for a ◊nerve cell.

neurosis in psychology, a general term referring to emotional disorders, such as anxiety, depression, and phobias. The main disturbance tends to be one of mood; contact with reality is relatively unaffected, in contrast to ◊psychosis.

neurotransmitter chemical that diffuses across a ◊synapse, and thus transmits impulses between ◊nerve cells, or between nerve cells and effector organs (for example, muscles). Common neurotransmitters are noradrenaline (which also acts as a hormone) and acetylcholine, the latter being most frequent at junctions between nerve and muscle. Nearly 50 different neurotransmitters have been identified.

neutralization in chemistry, a process occurring when the excess acid (or excess base) in a substance is reacted with added base (or added acid) so that the resulting substance is neither acidic nor basic.

neutrino in physics, any of three uncharged ◊elementary particles (and their antiparticles) of the ◊lepton class, having a mass too close to zero to be measured. The most familiar type, the antiparticle of the electron neutrino, is emitted in the beta decay of a nucleus. The other two are the muon and tau neutrinos.

neutron one of the three main subatomic particles, the others being the proton and the electron. The neutron is a composite particle, being made up of three ◊quarks, and therefore belongs to the ◊baryon group of the ◊hadrons. Neutrons have about the same mass as protons but no electric charge, and occur in the nuclei of all atoms except hydrogen. They contribute to the mass of atoms but do not affect their chemistry.

Nevada state in western USA; *area* 286,400 sq km/110,550 sq mi; *capital* Carson City; *population* (1990) 1,201,800; *environment* decontamination project underway after discovery of plutonium and other radioactive materials around an underground nuclear weapons testing site, ground water and wild animals near the site have been found to be contaminated; *features* legal gambling and prostitution (in some counties); entertainment at Las Vegas and Reno casinos; Lehman Caves National Monument.

New Brunswick maritime province of E Canada; *area* 73,400 sq km/28,332 sq mi; *capital* Fredericton; *features* Grand

Lake, St John River; Bay of Fundy; *population* (1991) 725,600; 37% French- speaking.

New Caledonia island group in the S Pacific, a French overseas territory between Australia and the Fiji Islands; *area* 18,576 sq km/7,170 sq mi; *capital* Nouméa; *population* (1983) 145,300 (43% Kanak (Melanesian), 37% European, 8% Wallisian, 5% Vietnamese and Indonesian, 4% Polynesian); *language* French (official); *religions* Roman Catholic 60%, Protestant 30%.

Newcastle-upon-Tyne industrial port and commercial and cultural centre, in Tyne and Wear, NE England, on the river Tyne opposite Gateshead; administrative headquarters of Tyne and Wear and Northumberland; population (1991) 259,500.

New Deal in US history, programme introduced by President F D Roosevelt 1933 to counter the Great ◊Depression. The programme included employment on public works, farm loans at low rates, and social reforms such as old-age and unemployment insurance, prevention of child labour, protection of employees against unfair practices by employers, and loans to local authorities for slum clearance.

New Delhi city adjacent to Old Delhi on the Yamuna River in the Union Territory of Delhi, N India; population (1991) 294,000. It is the administrative centre of Delhi, and was designated capital of India by the British 1911. Largely designed by British architect Edwin Lutyens, New Delhi was officially inaugurated after its completion 1931.

New England region of NE USA, comprising the states of Maine, New Hampshire, Vermont, Massachusetts, Rhode Island, and Connecticut. It is a geographic region rather than a political entity, with an area of 172,681 sq km/ 66,672 sq mi. Boston is the principal urban centre of the region, and Harvard and Yale are its major universities.

Newfoundland Canadian province on the Atlantic Ocean; *area* 405,700 sq km/ 156,600 sq mi; *capital* St John's; *features* Grand Banks section of the continental shelf rich in cod; home of the Newfoundland and Labrador dogs; *population* (1991) 571,600.

New Guinea island in the SW Pacific, N of Australia, comprising Papua New Guinea and the Indonesian province of Irian Jaya; total area about 885,780 sq km/342,000 sq mi. Part of the Dutch East Indies from 1828, West Irian was ceded by the United Nations to Indonesia 1963.

New Hampshire state in NE USA; *area* 24,000 sq km/9,264 sq mi; *capital* Concord; *population* (1990) 1,109,300; *features* White Mountains; no state income tax or sales tax.

New Jersey state in NE USA; *area* 20,200 sq km/7,797 sq mi; *capital* Trenton; *population* (1990) 7,730,200; *features* about 200 km/125 mi of seashore; legalized gambling in Atlantic City and Cape May; Statue of Liberty National Monument (shared with New York).

Newman John Henry 1801–1890. English Roman Catholic theologian. While still an Anglican, he wrote a series of *Tracts for the Times*, which gave their name to the Tractarian Movement (subsequently called the Oxford Movement) for the revival of Catholicism. He became a Catholic 1845 and was made a cardinal 1879. In 1864 his autobiography, *Apologia pro vita sua*, was published.

New Mexico state in southwestern USA; *area* 315,000 sq km/121,590 sq mi; *capital* Santa Fe; *population* (1990) 1,515,100; *features* Great Plains; Rocky Mountains; Rio Grande; White Sands Missile Range (also used by space shuttle); Navaho and Hopi Indian reservations.

New Orleans commercial and industrial city (banking, oil refining, rockets) and Mississippi river port in Louisiana, USA; population (1990) 496,900. It is the traditional birthplace of jazz.

New South Wales state of SE Australia; *area* 801,600 sq km/309,418 sq mi; *capital* Sydney; *features* Siding Spring Mountain 859 m/2,817 ft, NW of Sydney, with telescopes that can observe the central sector of the Galaxy; *population* (1987) 5,570,000 (60% in Sydney).

New Testament the second part of the ▷Bible, recognized by the Christian church from the 4th century as sacred doctrine. The New Testament includes the Gospels, which tell of the life and teachings of Jesus, the history of the early church, the teachings of St Paul, and mystical writings. It was written in Greek during the 1st and 2nd centuries AD, and the individual sections have been ascribed to various authors by Biblical scholars.

newton SI unit (symbol N) of ▷force. One newton is the force needed to accelerate an object with mass of one kilogram by one metre per second per second. The weight of a medium size (100 g/3 oz) apple is one newton.

Newton Isaac 1642–1727. English physicist and mathematician who laid the foundations of physics as a modern discipline. He discovered the law of gravity, created calculus, discovered that white light is composed of many colours, and developed the three standard laws of motion still in use today. During 1665–66, he discovered the binomial theorem, and differential and integral calculus, and also began to investigate the phenomenon of gravitation. In 1685, he expounded his universal law of gravitation.

Newton's laws of motion in physics, three laws that form the basis of Newtonian mechanics. (1) Unless acted upon by a net force, a body at rest stays at rest, and a moving body continues moving at the same speed in the same straight line. (2) A net force applied to a body gives it a rate of change of momentum proportional to the force and in the direction of the force. (3) When a body A exerts a force on a body B, B exerts an equal and opposite force on A; that is, to every action there is an equal and opposite reaction.

New World the Americas, so called by the first Europeans who reached them. The term also describes animals and plants of the western hemisphere.

New York largest city in the USA, industrial port, and cultural, financial, and commercial centre, in S New York State, at the junction of the Hudson and East rivers and including New York Bay. It comprises the boroughs of the Bronx, Brooklyn, Manhattan, Queens, and Staten Island; population (1990) 7,322,600, white 43.2%, black 25.2%, Hispanic 24.4%. New York is also known as the Big Apple.

New York state in NE USA; *area* 127,200 sq km/49,099 sq mi; *capital* Albany; *population* (1990) 17,990,500; *features* mountains: Adirondacks, Catskills; lakes: Champlain, Placid, Erie, Ontario; rivers: Mohawk, Hudson, St Lawrence (with Thousand Islands); Niagara Falls; Long Island; New York Bay.

New Zealand Dominion of; *area* 268,680 sq km/103,777 sq mi; *capital* and port Wellington; *features* Ruapehu volcano in the North Island, 2,797 m/9,180 ft; geysers and hot springs of the Rotorua district; Southern Alps; Canterbury Plains; *head of state* Elizabeth II from 1952 represented by governor general Catherine Tizard from 1990; *head of government* Jim Bolger from 1990; *political system* constitutional monarchy; *population* (1993) 3,490,000 (European, mostly British, 87%; Polynesian, mostly Maori, 12%); growth rate 0.9% p.a.; *languages* English (official), Maori; *religions* Protestant 50%, Roman Catholic 15%.

Niagara Falls two waterfalls on the Niagara River, on the Canada–USA border, between lakes Erie and Ontario and separated by Goat Island. The *American Falls* are 51 m/167 ft high, 330 m/1,080 ft wide; *Horseshoe Falls*, in Canada, are 49 m/160 ft high, 790 m/2,600 ft across.

Niamey river port and capital of ◊Niger; population (1983) 399,000.

Nicaragua Republic of (*República de Nicaragua*); *area* 127,849 sq km/49,363 sq mi; *capital* Managua; *features* largest state of Central America and most thinly populated; Mosquito Coast, Fonseca Bay, Corn Islands; *political system* emergent democracy; *population* (1993 est) 4,200,000 (mestizo 70%, Spanish descent 15%, Indian or black 10%); growth rate 3.3% p.a.; *languages* Spanish (official), Indian, English; *religion* Roman Catholic 95%.

Nice city on the French Riviera; population (1990) 345,700. Founded in the 3rd century BC, it repeatedly changed hands between France and the Duchy of Savoy from the 14th to the 19th century. In 1860 it was finally transferred to France.

Nicene Creed one of the fundamental ◊creeds of Christianity, promulgated by the Council of ◊Nicaea 325.

Nicholas II 1868–1918. Tsar of Russia 1894–1917. He was dominated by his wife, Tsarina Alexandra, who was under the influence of the religious charlatan ◊Rasputin. The tsar's mismanagement of the Russo-Japanese War and of internal affairs led to the revolution of 1905, which he suppressed, although he was forced to grant limited constitutional reforms. He took Russia into World War I in 1914, was forced to abdicate in 1917 after the ◊Russian Revolution, and was executed with his family.

Nicholas, St also known as *Santa Claus* In the Christian church, patron saint of Russia, children, merchants, sailors, and pawnbrokers; bishop of Myra (now in Turkey). His legendary gifts of dowries to poor girls led to the custom of giving gifts to children on the eve of his feast day, 6 Dec, still retained in some countries, such as the Netherlands; elsewhere the custom has been transferred to Christmas Day. His emblem is three balls.

nickel hard, malleable and ductile, silver-white metallic element, symbol Ni, atomic number 28, relative atomic mass 58.71. It occurs in igneous rocks and as a free metal (native metal), occasionally occurring in fragments of iron-nickel meteorites. It is a component of the Earth's core, which is held to consist principally of iron with some nickel. It has a high melting point, low electrical and thermal conductivity, and can be magnetized. It does not tarnish and therefore is much used for alloys, electroplating, and for coinage.

Nicosia capital of Cyprus; population (1987) 165,000. The Venetians, who took Cyprus 1489, surrounded Nicosia with a high wall, which still exists.

nicotine $C_{10}H_{14}N_2$ alkaloid (nitrogenous compound) obtained from the dried leaves of the tobacco plant *Nicotiana tabacum* and used as an insecticide. A colourless oil, soluble in water, it turns brown on exposure to the air.

Nietzsche Friedrich Wilhelm 1844–1900. German philosopher who rejected the accepted absolute moral values and the 'slave morality' of Christianity. He argued that 'God is dead' and therefore people were free to create their own values. His ideal was the *Übermensch*, or 'Superman', who would impose his will on the weak and worthless. Nietzsche claimed that knowledge is never objective but always serves some interest or unconscious purpose.

Niger third-longest river in Africa, 4,185 km/2,600 mi. It rises in the highlands bordering Sierra Leone and Guinea, flows NE through Mali, then SE through Niger and Nigeria to an inland delta on the Gulf of Guinea. Its flow has been badly affected by the expansion of the Sahara Desert.

Niger Republic of (*République du Niger*); *area* 1,186,408 sq km/457,953 sq mi; *capital* Niamey; *features* part of the Sahara Desert and subject to Sahel droughts; *political system* emergent democratic republic; *population* (1993 est) 8,500,000; growth rate 2.8% p.a.; *languages* French (official), Hausa, Djerma, and other minority languages; *religions* Sunni Muslim 85%, animist 15%.

Niger-Congo languages the largest group of languages (about 1,000) in Africa. It is divided into groups and subgroups; the most widely spoken Niger-Congo languages are Swahili (spoken on the E coast), the members of the Bantu group (southern Africa), and Yoruba (Nigeria).

Nigeria Federal Republic of; *area* 923,773 sq km/356,576 sq mi; *capital* Abuja; *environment* toxic waste from northern industrialized countries has been dumped in Nigeria; *features* harmattan (dry wind from the Sahara); rich artistic heritage, for example, Benin bronzes; *political system* military republic; *population* (1993 est) 92,800,000 (Yoruba in W, Ibo in E, and Hausa-Fulani in N); growth rate 3.3% p.a.; *religions* Sunni Muslim 50% (in N), Christian 40% (in S), local religions 10%.

Nightingale Florence 1820–1910. English nurse, the founder of nursing as a profession. She took a team of nurses to Scutari (now Üsküdar, Turkey) in 1854 and reduced the ◊Crimean War hospital death rate from 42% to 2%. In 1856 she founded the Nightingale School and Home for Nurses in London.

Nihilist member of a group of Russian revolutionaries in the reign of Alexander II 1855–81. Despairing of reform, they saw change as possible only through the destruction of morality, justice, marriage, property, and the idea of God. In 1878 the Nihilists launched a guerrilla campaign leading to the murder of the tsar 1881.

Nijinsky Vaslav 1890–1950. Russian dancer and choreographer. Noted for his powerful but graceful technique, he was a legendary member of ▷Diaghilev's Ballets Russes, for whom he choreographed Debussy's *Prélude à l'après-midi d'un faune* 1912 and *Jeux* 1913, and Stravinsky's *Le Sacre du printemps/The Rite of Spring* 1913.

Nile river in Africa, the world's longest, 6,695 km/4,160 mi. The *Blue Nile* rises in Lake Tana, Ethiopia, the *White Nile* at Lake Victoria, and they join at Khartoum, Sudan. The river enters the Mediterranean Sea at a vast delta in N Egypt.

Nineveh capital of the Assyrian Empire from the 8th century BC until its destruction by the Medes under King Cyaxares in 612 BC. It was situated on the river Tigris (opposite the present city of Mosul, Iraq) and was adorned with palaces.

nirvana (Sanskrit 'a blowing out') in Buddhism, the attainment of perfect serenity by the eradication of all desires. To some Buddhists it means complete annihilation, to others it means the absorption of the self in the infinite.

nitrate salt or ester of nitric acid, containing the NO^{3-} ion. Nitrates are used in explosives, in the chemical and pharmaceutical industries, in curing meat (see ▷nitre), and as fertilizers. They are the most water-soluble salts known and play a major part in the nitrogen cycle. Nitrates in the soil, whether naturally occurring or from inorganic or organic fertilizers, can be used by plants to make proteins and nucleic acids. However, runoff from fields can result in ▷nitrate pollution.

nitre or *saltpetre* potassium nitrate, KNO_3, a mineral found on and just under the ground in desert regions; used in explosives. Nitre occurs in Bihar, India, Iran, and Cape Province, South Africa. The salt was formerly used for the manufacture of gunpowder, but the supply of nitre for explosives is today largely met by making the salt from nitratine (also called Chile saltpetre, $NaNO_3$). Saltpetre is a preservative and is widely used for curing meats.

nitric acid or *aqua fortis* HNO_3 fuming acid obtained by the oxidation of ammonia or the action of sulphuric acid on potassium nitrate. It is a highly corrosive acid, dissolving most metals, and a strong oxidizing agent. It is used in the nitration and esterification of organic substances, and in the making of sulphuric acid, nitrates, explosives, plastics, and dyes.

nitrite salt or ester of nitrous acid, containing the nitrite ion (NO^{2-}). Nitrites are used as preservatives (for example, to prevent the growth of botulism spores) and as colouring agents in cured meats such as bacon and sausages.

nitrogen colourless, odourless, tasteless, gaseous, nonmetallic element, symbol N, atomic number 7, relative atomic mass 14.0067. It forms almost 80% of the Earth's atmosphere by volume and is a constituent of all plant and animal tissues (in proteins and nucleic acids). Nitrogen is obtained for industrial use by the liquefaction and fractional distillation of air. Its compounds are used in the manufacture of foods, drugs, fertilizers, dyes, and explosives.

nitrogen cycle the process of nitrogen passing through the ecosystem. Nitrogen, in the form of inorganic compounds (such as nitrates) in the soil, is absorbed by plants and turned into organic compounds (such as proteins) in plant tissue. A proportion of this nitrogen is eaten by ▷herbivores, with some of this in turn being passed on to the carnivores, which feed on the herbivores. The nitrogen is ultimately returned to the soil as excrement and when organisms die and are converted back to inorganic form by decomposers.

nitrogen fixation process by which nitrogen in the atmosphere is converted into nitrogenous compounds by the action of microorganisms, such as cyanobacteria (see ▷blue-green algae) and bacteria, in conjunction with certain ▷legumes. Several chemical processes duplicate nitrogen fixation to produce fertilizers; see ▷nitrogen cycle.

nitroglycerine $C_3H_5(ONO_2)_3$ flammable, explosive oil produced by the action of nitric and sulphuric acids on glycerol. Although poisonous, it is used in cardiac medicine. It explodes with great violence if heated in a confined space and is used in the preparation of dynamite, cordite, and other high explosives.

Nixon Richard (Milhous) 1913–1994. 37th president of the USA 1969–74, a Republican. He attracted attention as a member of the Un-American Activities Committee 1948, and was vice president to Eisenhower 1953–61. As president he was responsible for US withdrawal from Vietnam, and forged new links with China, but at home his culpability in the cover-up of the Watergate scandal led to his resignation 1974.

Noah in the Old Testament, the son of Lamech and father of Shem, Ham, and Japheth, who, according to God's instructions, built a ship, the ark, so that he and his family and specimens of all existing animals might survive the ▷Flood. There is also a Babylonian version of the tale, *The Epic of Gilgamesh*.

Nobel prize annual international prize, first awarded 1901 under the will of Alfred Nobel, Swedish chemist, who invented dynamite. The interest on the Nobel endowment fund is divided annually among the persons who have made the greatest contributions in the fields of physics, chemistry, medicine, literature, and world peace. *(See table on page 557.)*

noble gas alternative name for ▷inert gas.

Nonconformist in religion, originally a member of the Puritan section of the Church of England clergy who, in the Elizabethan age, refused to conform to certain practices, for example the wearing of the surplice and kneeling to receive Holy Communion.

nonmetal one of a set of elements (around 20 in total) with certain physical and chemical properties opposite to those of metals. Nonmetals accept electrons and are sometimes called electronegative elements.

nonrenewable resource natural resource, such as coal or oil, that takes thousands or millions of years to form naturally and can therefore not be replaced once it is consumed. The main energy sources used by humans are nonrenewable ones; renewable resources, such as solar, tidal, and geothermal power, have so far been less exploited.

Norfolk county of E England; *area* 5,360 sq km/2,069 sq mi; *towns and cities* Norwich (administrative headquarters), King's Lynn; resorts: Great Yarmouth, Cromer; *features* the Fens; Norfolk Broads; residence of Elizabeth II at Sandringham (built 1869–71); *population* (1991) 745,600.

Noriega Manuel (Antonio Morena) 1940– . Panamanian soldier and politician, effective ruler of Panama from 1982, as head of the National Guard, until deposed by the USA 1989. An informer for the US Central Intelligence Agency, he was known to be involved in drug trafficking as early as 1972. He enjoyed US support until 1987. In the 1989 US invasion of Panama, he was forcibly taken to the USA. He was tried and convicted of trafficking 1992.

Norman any of the descendants of the Norsemen (to whose chief, Rollo, Normandy was granted by Charles III of France 911) who adopted French language and culture. During the 11th and 12th centuries they conquered England 1066 (under William the Conqueror), Scotland 1072, parts of Wales and Ireland, S Italy, Sicily, and Malta, and took a prominent part in the Crusades.

Normandy former duchy of NW France now divided into two regions: ▷Haute-Normandie and Basse-Normandie.

Norseman early inhabitant of Norway. The term Norsemen is also applied to Scandinavian ▷Vikings who during the 8th–11th centuries raided and settled in Britain, Ireland, France, Russia, Iceland, and Greenland.

North America third-largest of the continents (including Greenland and Central America), and over twice the size of Europe; *area* 24,000,000 sq km/9,400,000 sq mi; *largest cities* (population over 1 million) Mexico City, New York, Chicago, Toronto, Los Angeles, Montréal, Guadalajara, Monterrey, Philadelphia, Houston, Guatemala City, Vancouver, Detroit, San Diego, Dallas; *features* Lake Superior (the largest body of fresh water in the world); Grand Canyon on the Colorado River; San Andreas Fault, California; deserts: Death Valley, Mojave, Sonoran; rivers (over 1,600 km/1,000 mi) include Mississippi, Missouri, Mackenzie, Rio Grande, Yukon, Arkansas, Colorado, Saskatchewan-Bow, Columbia, Red, Peace, Snake; *population* (1988) 395 million, rising to an estimated 450 million by 2000.

Northamptonshire county of central England; *area* 2,370 sq km/915 sq mi; *towns and cities* Northampton (administrative headquarters), Kettering; *features* Canons Ashby, Tudor house, home of the Drydens for 400 years; churches with broached spires; *population* (1991) 578,800.

North Atlantic Treaty Organization (NATO) association set up 1949 to provide for the collective defence of the major W European and North American states against the perceived threat from the USSR. The collapse of communism in eastern Europe from 1990 prompted a radical review of its policy and defence strategy. In 1994 a 'partnership for peace' programme was launched, inviting former members of the Warsaw Pact and ex-Soviet republics to take part in a wide range of military cooperation agreements. By mid-1994 most had joined.

North Carolina state in E USA; *area* 136,400 sq km/52,650 sq mi; *capital*

Raleigh; *features* Appalachian Mountains, including Blue Ridge and Great Smoky mountains; *population* (1990) 6,628,600.

North Dakota state in N USA; *area* 183,100 sq km/70,677 sq mi; *capital* Bismarck; *features* fertile Red River valley, Missouri Plateau; Garrison Dam on the Missouri River; International Peace Garden, on Canadian border; *population* (1990) 638,800.

Northern Ireland see ▷Ireland, Northern.

North Pole the northern point where an imaginary line penetrates the Earth's surface by the axis about which it revolves; see also ▷Poles and ▷Arctic.

North Rhine–Westphalia (German *Nordrhein-Westfalen*) administrative *Land* of Germany; *area* 34,100 sq km/ 13,163 sq mi; *capital* Düsseldorf; *features* valley of the Rhine; Ruhr industrial district; *population* (1988) 16,700,000; *religion* 53% Roman Catholic, 42% Protestant.

North Sea sea to the E of Britain and bounded by the coasts of Belgium, the Netherlands, Germany, Denmark, and Norway; part of the Atlantic Ocean; area 523,000 sq km/202,000 sq mi; average depth 55 m/180 ft, greatest depth 660 m/2,165 ft. In the NE it joins the Norwegian Sea, and in the S it meets the Strait of Dover.

Northumberland county of N England; *area* 5,030 sq km/1,942 sq mi; *towns and cities* Morpeth (administrative headquarters), Berwick-upon-Tweed, Hexham, Newcastle-upon-Tyne; *features* Cheviot Hills; Northumberland National Park; Holy Island; a segment of Hadrian's Wall; Alnwick and Bamburgh castles; *population* (1991) 304,700.

Northumbria Anglo-Saxon kingdom that covered NE England and SE Scotland, comprising the 6th-century kingdoms of Bernicia (Forth–Tees) and Deira (Tees–Humber), united in the 7th century. It accepted the supremacy of Wessex 827 and was conquered by the Danes in the late 9th century.

Northwest Territories territory of Canada; *area* 3,426,300 sq km/ 1,322,552 sq mi; *capital* Yellowknife; *features* Mackenzie River; lakes: Great Slave, Great Bear; Miles Canyon; *population* (1991) 54,000; over 50% native peoples (Indian, Inuit).

North Yorkshire county of NE England, created 1974 from most of the North Riding and parts of East and West Ridings of Yorkshire; *area* 8,320 sq km/ 3,212 sq mi; *towns and cities* Northallerton (administrative headquarters), York; resorts: Harrogate, Scarborough, Whitby; *features* England's largest county; part of the Pennines, the Vale of York, North Yorkshire Moors, Rievaulx Abbey; Bolton Abbey; York Minster; Castle Howard, designed by Vanbrugh; *population* (1991) 702,200.

Norway Kingdom of (*Kongeriket Norge*); *area* 387,000 sq km/149,421 sq mi (includes Svalbard and Jan Mayen); *capital* Oslo; *environment* an estimated 80% of the lakes and streams in the southern half of the country have been severely acidified by acid rain; *features* fjords, including Hardanger and Sogne, longest 185 km/115 mi, deepest 1,245 m/4,086 ft; glaciers in north; midnight sun and northern lights; *head of state* Harald V from 1991; *head of government* Gro Harlem Brundtland from 1990; *political system* constitutional monarchy; *population* (1993 est) 4,300,000; growth rate 0.3% p.a.; *languages* Norwegian (official); there are Saami-(Lapp) and

Finnish- speaking minorities; *religion* Evangelical Lutheran (endowed by state) 94%.

Norwich cathedral city in Norfolk, E England, on the river Wensum; administrative headquarters of Norfolk; population (1991) 120,900. It has a Norman castle, a 15th-century Guildhall, medieval churches, Tudor houses, and a Georgian Assembly House.

nose in humans, the upper entrance of the respiratory tract; the organ of the sense of smell. The external part is divided down the middle by a septum of ◊cartilage. The nostrils contain plates of cartilage that can be moved by muscles and have a growth of stiff hairs at the margin to prevent foreign objects from entering. The whole nasal cavity is lined with a ◊mucous membrane that warms and moistens the air as it enters and ejects dirt. In the upper parts of the cavity the membrane contains 50 million olfactory receptor cells (cells sensitive to smell).

Nottinghamshire county of central England; *area* 2,160 sq km/834 sq mi; *towns and cities* Nottingham (administrative headquarters), Mansfield, Worksop, Newark; *features* the remains of Sherwood Forest (home of Robin Hood); *population* (1991) 980,600.

Nouakchott capital of Mauritania; population (1985) 500,000.

nova (plural *novae*) faint star that suddenly erupts in brightness by 10,000 times or more. Novae are believed to occur in close ◊binary star systems, where gas from one star flows to a companion ◊white dwarf. The gas ignites and is thrown off in an explosion at speeds of 1,500 kps/930 mps or more. Unlike a ◊supernova, the star is not completely disrupted by the outburst. After a few weeks or months it subsides to its previous state; it may erupt many more times.

Nova Scotia maritime province of E Canada; *area* 55,500 sq km/21,423 sq mi; *capital* Halifax (chief port); *features* Strait of Canso Superport, the largest deepwater harbour on the Atlantic coast of North America; *population* (1991) 897,500.

nuclear energy or *atomic energy* energy released from the inner core, or ◊nucleus, of the atom. Energy produced by ◊*nuclear fission* (the splitting of uranium or plutonium nuclei) has been harnessed since the 1950s to generate electricity, and research continues into the possible controlled use of nuclear fusion (the fusing, or combining, of atomic nuclei).

nuclear physics study of the properties of the nucleus of the ◊atom, including the structure of nuclei; nuclear forces; the interactions between particles and nuclei; and the study of radioactive decay. The study of elementary particles is ◊particle physics.

nuclear reactor device for producing ◊nuclear energy in a controlled manner. There are various types of reactor in use, all using nuclear fission. In a *gas-cooled reactor*, a circulating gas under pressure (such as carbon dioxide) removes heat from the core of the reactor, which usually contains natural uranium. The efficiency of the fission process is increased by slowing neutrons in the core by using a moderator such as carbon. The reaction is controlled with neutron-absorbing rods made of boron. An *advanced gas-cooled reactor* (AGR) generally has enriched uranium as its fuel. A *water-cooled reactor*, such as the steam-generating heavy water (deuterium oxide) reactor, has water circulating through the hot core. The water is converted to steam, which drives turbo-alternators for generating electricity. The most widely used reactor is the *pressurized-water reactor* (PWR), which contains a sealed system of pressurized water that is heated to form steam in heat exchangers in an external circuit. The *fast reactor* has no moderator and uses fast neutrons to bring about fission. It uses a mixture of plutonium and uranium oxide as fuel. When operating, uranium is converted to plutonium, which can be extracted and used later as fuel. It is also called the fast breeder because it produces more plutonium than it consumes. Heat is removed from the reactor by a coolant of liquid sodium.

nuclear waste the radioactive and toxic by-products of the nuclear-energy and nuclear-weapons industries. Nuclear waste may have an active life of several thousand years.

nucleon in particle physics, either a ⊳proton or a ⊳neutron, both particles present in the atomic nucleus. *Nucleon number* is an alternative name for the mass number of an atom.

nucleus in physics, the positively charged central part of an ⊳atom, which constitutes almost all its mass. Except for hydrogen nuclei, which have only protons, nuclei are composed of both protons and neutrons. Surrounding the nuclei are electrons, of equal and opposite charge to that of the protons, thus giving the atom a neutral charge.

nucleus in biology, the central, membrane-enclosed part of a eukaryotic cell, containing the chromosomes.

Nukua'lofa capital and port of Tonga on Tongatapu Island; population (1986) 29,000.

number symbol used in counting or measuring. In mathematics, there are various kinds of numbers. The everyday number system is the decimal ('proceeding by tens') system, using the base ten. *Real numbers* include all rational numbers (integers, or whole numbers, and fractions) and irrational numbers (those not expressible as fractions). *Complex numbers* include the real and unreal numbers (real-number multiples of the square root of -1). The ⊳binary number system, used in computers, has two as its base. The ordinary numerals, 0, 1, 2, 3, 4, 5, 6, 7, 8, and 9, give a counting system that, in the decimal system, continues 10, 11, 12, 13, and so on. These are whole numbers (integers), with fractions represented as, for example, $\frac{1}{4}$, $\frac{1}{2}$, $\frac{3}{4}$, or as decimal fractions (0.25, 0.5, 0.75). They are also *rational numbers*. *Irrational numbers* cannot be represented in this way and require symbols, such as $\sqrt{2}$, π, and e. They can be expressed numerically only as the (inexact) approximations 1.414, 3.142 and 2.718 (to three places of decimals) respectively. The symbols π and e are also examples of *transcendental numbers*, because they (unlike $\sqrt{2}$) cannot be derived by solving a polynomial equation (an equation with one ⊳variable quantity) with rational coefficients (multiplying factors). Complex numbers, which include the real numbers as well as unreal numbers, take the general form $a + bi$, where i $= \sqrt{-1}$ (that is, $i^2 = -1$), and a is the real part and bi the unreal part.

Nuremberg (German *Nürnberg*) industrial city in Bavaria, Germany; population (1988) 467,000. From 1933 the Nuremberg rallies were held here, and in 1945 the Nuremberg trials of war criminals.

Nuremberg trials after World War II, the trials of the 24 chief ⊳Nazi war criminals Nov 1945–Oct 1946 by an international military tribunal consisting of four judges and four prosecutors: one of each from the USA, UK, USSR, and France. An appendix accused the German cabinet, general staff, high command, Nazi leadership corps, ⊳SS, Sturmabteilung, and ⊳Gestapo of criminal behaviour.

Nureyev Rudolf 1938–1993. Russian dancer and choreographer. A soloist with the Kirov Ballet, he defected to the West during a visit to Paris 1961. Mainly associated with the Royal Ballet (London) and as Margot ⊳Fonteyn's principal partner, he was one of the most brilliant dancers of the 1960s and 1970s. Nureyev danced in such roles as Prince Siegfried in *Swan Lake* and Armand in *Marguerite and Armand*, which was created especially for Fonteyn and Nureyev.

nut any dry, single-seeded fruit that does not split open to release the seed, such as the chestnut. A nut is formed from more than one carpel, but only one seed becomes fully formed, the remainder aborting. The wall of the fruit, the pericarp, becomes hard and woody, forming the outer shell.

nylon synthetic long-chain polymer similar in chemical structure to protein. Nylon was the first all-synthesized fibre, made from petroleum, natural gas, air, and water by the Du Pont firm in 1938. It is used in the manufacture of moulded articles, textiles, and medical sutures. Nylon fibres are stronger and more elastic than silk and are relatively insensitive to moisture and mildew. Nylon is used for hosiery and woven goods, simulating other materials such as silks and furs; it is also used for carpets.

nymph in Greek mythology, a guardian spirit of nature. *Hamadryads* or *dryads* guarded trees; *naiads*, springs and pools; *oreads*, hills and rocks; and *Nereids*,the sea.

O

oak any tree or shrub of the genus *Quercus* of the beech family Fagaceae, with over 300 known species widely distributed in temperate zones. Oaks are valuable for timber, the wood being durable and straight-grained. Their fruits are called acorns.

oasis area of land made fertile by the presence of water near the surface in an otherwise arid region. The occurrence of oases affects the distribution of plants, animals, and people in the desert regions of the world.

oat type of grass, genus *Avena*, a cereal food. The plant has long, narrow leaves and a stiff straw stem; the panicles of flowers, and later of grain, hang downwards. The cultivated oat *Avena sativa* is produced for human and animal food.

Oates Titus 1649–1705. English conspirator. A priest, he entered the Jesuit colleges at Valladolid, Spain, and St Omer, France, as a spy 1677–78, and on his return to England announced he had discovered a 'Popish Plot' to murder Charles II and re-establish Catholicism. Although this story was almost entirely false, many innocent Roman Catholics were executed during 1678–80 on Oates's evidence.

oboe musical instrument of the woodwind family, a refined treble shawm of narrow tapering bore and exposed double reed. The oboe was developed by the Hotteterre family of makers about 1700 and was incorporated in the court ensemble of Louis XIV. In B flat, it has a rich tone of elegant finish.

obsidian black or dark-coloured glassy volcanic rock, chemically similar to ◊granite, but formed by cooling rapidly on the Earth's surface at low pressure.

ocean great mass of salt water. Strictly speaking three oceans exist – the Atlantic, Indian, and Pacific – to which the Arctic is often added. They cover approximately 70% or 363,000,000 sq km/140,000,000 sq mi of the total surface area of the Earth. Water levels recorded in the world's oceans have shown an increase of 10–15 cm/4–6 in over the past 100 years. (*See table on page 565.*)

Oceania general term for the islands of the central and S Pacific, including Australia, New Zealand, and the eastern half of New Guinea; although not strictly a continent, Oceania is often referred to as such to facilitate handling of global statistics; *area* 8,500,000 sq km/3,300,000 sq mi (land area); *largest cities* (population over 500,000) Sydney, Melbourne, Brisbane, Perth, Adelaide, Auckland; *features* the Challenger Deep in the Mariana Trench –11,034 m/–36,201 ft is the greatest known depth of sea in the world; Ayers Rock in Northern Territory, Australia, is the world's largest monolith; the Great Barrier Reef is the longest coral reef in the world; Mount Kosciusko 2,229 m/ 7,316 ft in New South Wales is the highest peak in Australia; Mount Cook 3,764 m/12,349 ft is the highest peak in New Zealand.

Odin chief god of Scandinavian mythology, the *Woden* or *Wotan* of the Germanic peoples. A sky god, he lives in Asgard, at the top of the world-tree, and from the Valkyries (the divine maidens) receives the souls of half of the heroic slain warriors, feasting with them in his great hall, Valhalla. The son of Odin and his wife Freya is Thor. Wednesday is named after Odin.

Odysseus chief character of Homer's *Odyssey*, king of the island of Ithaca and also mentioned in Homer's *Iliad* (both 8th century BC) as one of the leaders of the Greek forces at the siege of Troy. Odysseus was distinguished among Greek leaders for his cleverness and cunning. He appears in other later tragedies.

Oedipus in Greek mythology, king of Thebes who unwittingly killed his father, Laius, and married his mother, Jocasta, in fulfilment of a prophecy. When he learned what he had done, he put out his eyes; Jocasta hanged herself. His story was dramatized by the Greek tragedian ◊Sophocles.

Oedipus complex in psychology, term coined by Sigmund ◊Freud for the unconscious antagonism of a son to his father, whom he sees as a rival for his mother's affection. For a girl antagonistic to her mother, as a rival for her father's affection, the term is *Electra complex*.

oestrogen any of a group of hormones produced by the ◊ovaries of vertebrates; the term is also used for various synthetic hormones that mimic their effects. The principal oestrogen in mammals is oestradiol. Oestrogens control female sexual development, promote the growth of female secondary sexual characteristics, stimulate egg production, and, in mammals, prepare the lining of the uterus for pregnancy.

oestrus in mammals, the period during a female's reproductive cycle (also known as the oestrus cycle or ◊menstrual cycle) when mating is most likely to occur. It usually coincides with ovulation.

Offa's Dyke defensive earthwork along the Welsh border, of which there are remains from the mouth of the river Dee to that of the river Severn. It represents the boundary secured by Offa, King of Mercia, England, in the 8th century, during his wars with Wales.

Ohio state in N central USA; nickname Buckeye State; *area* 107,100 sq km/ 41,341 sq mi; *capital* Columbus; *population* (1990) 10,847,100; *features* Ohio River; Lake Erie.

oil flammable substance, usually insoluble in water, and composed chiefly of carbon and hydrogen. Oils may be solids (fats and waxes) or liquids. The three main types are: *essential oils*, obtained from plants; *fixed oils*, obtained from animals and plants; and *mineral oils*, obtained chiefly from the refining of ◊petroleum.

O'Keeffe Georgia 1887–1986. US painter. She is known chiefly for her large, semi-abstract studies of flowers and bones, such as *Black Iris* 1926 (Metropolitan Museum of Art, New York) and the *Pelvis Series* of the 1940s.

Oklahoma state in S central USA; *area* 181,100 sq km/69,905 sq mi; *capital* Oklahoma City; *features* Arkansas, Red, and Canadian rivers; Wichita and Ozark mountain ranges; Indian reservations on the high plains; *population* (1990) 3,145,600.

Old English general name for the range of dialects spoken by Germanic settlers in England between the 5th and 11th centuries AD, also known as ◊Anglo-Saxon. The literature of the period includes *Beowulf*, an epic in West Saxon dialect.

Old Testament Christian term for the Hebrew ◊Bible, which is the first part of the Christian Bible. It contains 39 (according to Christianity) or 24 (according to Judaism) books, which include the origins of the world, the history of the ancient Hebrews and their covenant with God, prophetical writings, and religious poetry. The first five books (*The five books of Moses*) are traditionally ascribed to Moses and known as the Pentateuch (by Christians) or the Torah (by Jews).

Olduvai Gorge deep cleft in the Serengeti steppe, Tanzania, where Louis and Mary ◊Leakey found prehistoric stone tools in the 1930s. They discovered Pleistocene remains of prehumans and gigantic animals 1958–59. The gorge has given its name to the *Olduvai culture*, a simple stone-tool culture of prehistoric hominids, dating from 2–0.5 million years ago.

Old World the continents of the eastern hemisphere, so called because they were familiar to Europeans before the Americas. The term is used as an adjective to describe animals and plants that live in the eastern hemisphere.

Oligocene third epoch of the Tertiary period of geological time, 35.5–3.25 million years ago. The name, from Greek, means 'a little recent', referring to the presence of the remains of some modern types of animals existing at that time.

olive evergreen tree *Olea europaea* of the family Oleaceae. Native to Asia but widely cultivated in Mediterranean and subtropical areas, it grows up to 15 m/50 ft high, with twisted branches and opposite, lance-shaped silvery leaves. The white flowers are followed by green oval fruits that ripen a bluish black. They are preserved in brine or oil, dried, or pressed to make olive oil.

Olivier Laurence (Kerr), Baron Olivier 1907–1989. English actor and director. For many years associated with the Old Vic theatre, he was director of the National Theatre company 1962–73. His stage roles include Henry V, Hamlet, Richard III, and Archie Rice in John Osborne's *The Entertainer* 1957 (filmed 1960). His acting and direction of filmed versions of Shakespeare's plays received critical acclaim for example, *Henry V* 1944 and *Hamlet* 1948 (Academy Award).

Olympic Games sporting contests originally held in Olympia, ancient Greece, every four years during a sacred truce; records were kept from 776 BC. Women were forbidden to be present, and the male contestants were naked. The ancient Games were abolished AD 394. From 1896–1994, the present-day games were held every four years with (since 1924) a separate winter Games programme; the winter and summer Games are now held two years apart.

Olympus (Greek *Olimbos*) any of several mountains in Greece and elsewhere, one of which is *Mount Olympus* in N Thessaly, Greece, 2,918 m/9,577 ft high. In ancient Greece it was considered the home of the gods.

Oman Sultanate of (*Saltanat 'Uman*); *area* 272,000 sq km/105,000 sq mi; *capital* Muscat; *features* Jebel Akhdar highlands; Kuria Muria islands; Masirah Island is used in aerial reconnaissance of the Arabian Sea and Indian Ocean; exclave on Musandam Peninsula controlling Strait of Hormuz; *political system* absolute monarchy; *population* (1993 est) 1,650,000; growth rate 3.0% p.a.; *languages* Arabic (official), English, Urdu, other Indian languages; *religions* Ibadhi Muslim 75%, Sunni Muslim, Shi'ite Muslim, Hindu.

Omar Khayyám *c.* 1050–1123. Persian astronomer, mathematician, and poet. In the West, he is chiefly known as a poet through Edward ◊Fitzgerald's version of *The Rubaiyat of Omar Khayyám* 1859.

ombudsman official who acts on behalf of the private citizen in investigating complaints against the government. The post is of Scandinavian origin; it was introduced in Sweden 1809, Denmark 1954, and Norway 1962, and spread to other countries from the 1960s.

omnivore animal that feeds on both plant and animal material. Omnivores have digestive adaptations intermediate between those of ◊herbivores and ◊carnivores, with relatively unspecialized digestive systems and gut microorganisms that can digest a variety of foodstuffs.

O'Neill Eugene (Gladstone) 1888–1953. US playwright. Widely regarded as the greatest US dramatist, the 'down-to-earth' element in his plays was a radical departure from the romantic and melodramatic American theatre of the day. His works include *Beyond the Horizon* and *Emperor Jones* 1920, *Anna Christie* 1921, *The Iceman Cometh* 1946, and the posthumously produced *A Long Day's Journey into Night* 1956. Nobel Prize for Literature 1936.

Ontario province of central Canada; *area* 1,068,600 sq km/412,480 sq mi; *capital* Toronto; *features* Black Creek Pioneer Village; ◊Niagara Falls; *population* (1986) 9,114,000.

Op art (abbreviation for *Optical art*) movement in abstract art during the late 1950s and 1960s, in which colour and pattern were used to create optical effects, particularly the illusion of movement. Exponents include Victor Vasarély (1908–) and Bridget Riley (1931–).

OPEC acronym for ◊*Organization of Petroleum-Exporting Countries.*

opera dramatic musical work in which singing takes the place of speech; the music accompanying the action has paramount importance, although dancing and spectacular staging may also play their parts. Opera originated in late 16th-century Florence and developed from Classical Greek drama. *Operetta*, a light form of opera, contains music, dance, and spoken dialogue, and has a story line that is romantic and sentimental, often employing farce and parody.

operating system (OS) in computing, a program that controls the basic operation of a computer. A typical OS controls the peripheral devices, organizes the filing system, provides a means of communicating with the operator, and runs other programs.

opium drug extracted from the unripe seeds of the opium poppy *Papaver somniferum* of SW Asia. An addictive ◊narcotic, it contains several alkaloids, including *morphine*, one of the most powerful natural painkillers and addictive narcotics known, and *codeine*, a milder painkiller.

Opium Wars two wars, the First Opium War 1839–42 and the Second Opium War 1856–60, waged by Britain against China to enforce the opening of Chinese ports to trade in opium. Opium from British India paid for Britain's imports from China, such as porcelain, silk, and, above all, tea.

optical fibre very fine, optically pure glass fibre through which light can be reflected to transmit images or data from one end to the other. Although expensive to produce and install, optical fibres can carry more data than traditional cables, and are less susceptible to interference.

optics branch of physics that deals with the study of ◊light and vision – for example, shadows and mirror images, lenses, microscopes, telescopes, and cameras. For all practical purposes light rays travel in straight lines, although Albert ◊Einstein demonstrated that they may be 'bent' by a gravitational field. On striking a surface they are reflected or refracted with some absorption of energy, and the study of this is known as geometrical optics.

oracle Greek sacred site where answers (also called oracles) were given by priests of a deity to enquirers about personal affairs or state policy. These were often ambivalent. The most celebrated was that of Apollo at ◊Delphi.

Orange Free State province of the Republic of South Africa; *area* 127,993 sq km/49,405 sq mi; *capital* Bloemfontein; *features* plain of the High Veld; Lesotho forms an enclave on the Natal–Cape Province border; *population* (1987) 1,863,000; 82% ethnic Africans.

orang-utan ape *Pongo pygmaeus*, found solely in Borneo and Sumatra. Up to 1.65 m/5.5 ft in height, it is covered with long, red-brown hair and mainly lives a solitary, arboreal life, feeding chiefly on fruit. Now an endangered species, it is officially protected because its habitat is being systematically destroyed by ◊deforestation.

oratorio dramatic, non-scenic musical setting of religious texts, scored for orchestra, chorus, and solo voices. Its origins lie in the *Laude spirituali* performed by St Philip Neri's Oratory in Rome in the 16th century, followed by the first definitive oratorio in the 17th century by Cavalieri. The form reached perfection in such works as J S Bach's *Christmas Oratorio*, and Handel's *Messiah*.

orbit path of one body in space around another, such as the orbit of Earth around the Sun, or the Moon around Earth. When the two bodies are similar in mass, as in a ◊binary star, both bodies move around their common centre of mass. The movement of objects in orbit follows Johann ◊Kepler's laws, which apply to artificial satellites as well as to natural bodies.

orchestra group of musicians playing together on different instruments. In Western music, an orchestra typically contains various bowed string instruments and sections of wind, brass, and percussion. The size and format may vary according to the needs of composers.

order in biological classification, a group of related families. For example, the horse, rhinoceros, and tapir families are grouped in the order Perissodactyla, the odd-toed ungulates, because they all have either one or three toes on each foot. The names of orders are not shown in italic (unlike genus and species names) and by convention they have the ending '-formes' in birds and fish; '-a' in mammals, amphibians, reptiles, and other animals; and '-ales' in fungi and plants. Related orders are grouped together in a ◊class.

ordinal number in mathematics, one of the series first, second, third, fourth, ... Ordinal numbers relate to order, whereas ◊cardinal numbers (1, 2, 3, 4, ...) relate to quantity, or count.

Ordovician period of geological time 510–439 million years ago; the second period of the ◊Palaeozoic era. Animal life was confined to the sea: reef-building algae and the first jawless fish are characteristic.

ore body of rock, a vein within it, or a deposit of sediment, worth mining for the economically valuable mineral it contains. The term is usually applied to sources of metals. Occasionally metals are found uncombined (native metals), but more often they occur as compounds such as carbonates, sulphides, or oxides. The ores often contain unwanted impurities that must be removed when the metal is extracted.

oregano any of several perennial herbs of the Labiatae family, especially the aromatic *Origanum vulgare*, also known as wild marjoram. It is native to the Mediterranean countries and W Asia and naturalized in the Americas. Oregano is extensively used to season Mediterranean cooking.

Oregon state in NW USA, on the Pacific coast; nickname Beaver State;

area 251,500 sq km/97,079 sq mi; *capital* Salem; *population* (1990) 2,842,300; *features* Crater Lake, deepest in the USA (589 m/1,933 ft); mountains.

organ musical wind instrument of ancient origin. It produces sound from pipes of various sizes under applied pressure and has keyboard controls. Apart from its continued use in serious compositions and for church music, the organ has been adapted for light entertainment.

organ in biology, part of a living body, such as the liver or brain, that has a distinctive function or set of functions.

organelle discrete and specialized structure in a living cell; organelles include mitochondria, chloroplasts, lysosomes, ribosomes, and the nucleus.

organic chemistry branch of chemistry that deals with carbon compounds. Organic compounds form the chemical basis of life and are more abundant than inorganic compounds. In a typical organic compound, each carbon atom forms bonds covalently with each of its neighbouring carbon atoms in a chain or ring, and additionally with other atoms, commonly hydrogen, oxygen, nitrogen, or sulphur.

organic farming farming without the use of synthetic fertilizers (such as ◊nitrates and phosphates) or ◊pesticides (herbicides, insecticides, and fungicides) or other agrochemicals (such as hormones, growth stimulants, or fruit regulators).

Organization of Petroleum-Exporting Countries (OPEC) body established 1960 to coordinate price and supply policies of oil-producing states. Its concerted action in raising prices in the 1970s triggered worldwide recession but also lessened demand so that its influence was reduced by the mid-1980s. OPEC members in 1994 were: Algeria, Gabon, Indonesia, Iran, Iraq, Kuwait, Libya, Nigeria, Qatar, Saudi Arabia, the United Arab Emirates, and Venezuela.

Orinoco river in N South America, flowing for about 2,400 km/1,500 mi through Venezuela and forming for about 320 km/200 mi the boundary with Colombia; tributaries include the Guaviare, Meta, Apure, Ventuari, Caura, and Caroni. It is navigable by large steamers for 1,125 km/700 mi from its Atlantic delta; rapids obstruct the upper river.

Orion in astronomy, a very prominent constellation in the equatorial region of the sky, identified with the hunter of Greek mythology. It contains the bright stars Betelgeuse and Rigel, as well as a distinctive row of three stars that make up Orion's belt. Beneath the belt, marking the sword of Orion, is the Orion nebula; nearby is one of the most distinctive dark nebulae, the Horsehead.

Orkney Islands island group off the northeast coast of Scotland; *area* 970 sq km/375 sq mi; *features* comprises about 90 islands and islets, low-lying and treeless; mild climate owing to the Gulf Stream; Skara Brae, a well-preserved Neolithic village on Mainland; Scapa Flow, between Mainland and Hoy, was a naval base in both world wars; *population* (1989) 19,600.

ornithology study of birds. It covers scientific aspects relating to their structure and classification, and their habits, song, flight, and value to agriculture as destroyers of insect pests. Worldwide scientific banding (or the fitting of coded rings to captured specimens) has resulted in accurate information on bird movements and distribution. There is an International Council for Bird Preservation with its headquarters at the Natural History Museum, London.

Orpheus mythical Greek poet and musician. The son of Apollo and a muse, he married Eurydice, who died from the bite of a snake. Orpheus went down to Hades to bring her back and her return to life was granted on condition that he walk ahead of her without looking back. He did look back and Eurydice was irretrievably lost. In his grief, he offended the Maenad women of Thrace, and was torn to pieces by them.

Orthodox Church or *Eastern Orthodox Church* or *Greek Orthodox Church* federation of self-governing Christian churches mainly found in E and SE Europe and parts of Asia. The centre of worship is the Eucharist. There is a married clergy, except for bishops; the Immaculate Conception is not accepted. The highest rank in the church is that of ecumenical patriarch, or bishop of Istanbul.

Orwell George. Pen name of Eric Arthur Blair 1903–1950. English author. His books include the satirical fable *Animal Farm* 1945 and the prophetic *Nineteen Eighty-Four* 1949, portraying the catastrophic excesses of state control over the individual. A deep sense of social conscience and antipathy towards political dictatorship characterize his work.

Osaka industrial port on Honshu Island, Japan; population (1990) 2,623,800, metropolitan area 8,000,000. It is the oldest city of Japan and was at times the seat of government in the 4th–8th centuries.

Osborne John (James) 1929–1994. English dramatist. He became one of the

ovary

first Angry Young Men (anti- establishment writers of the 1950s) of British
theatre with his debut play, *Look Back
in Anger* 1956. Other plays include *The
Entertainer* 1957, *Luther* 1960, *Inadmissible Evidence* 1964, and *A Patriot
for Me* 1965.

Osiris ancient Egyptian god, the
embodiment of goodness, who ruled the
underworld after being killed by Set.
The sister-wife of Osiris was ◊Isis or
Hathor, and their son Horus captured
his father's murderer. The pharaohs
were thought to be his incarnation.

Oslo capital and industrial port of
Norway; population (1991) 461,600.
The first recorded settlement was made
in the 11th century by Harald III Hardrada, but after a fire 1624, it was entirely
replanned by Christian IV and renamed
Christiania 1624–1924.

osmosis movement of solvent (liquid)
through a semipermeable membrane
separating solutions of different concentrations. The solvent passes from a less
concentrated solution to a more concentrated solution until the two concentrations are equal. Applying external
pressure to the solution on the more
concentrated side arrests osmosis, and
is a measure of the osmotic pressure of
the solution.

osteopathy system of alternative
medical practice that relies on physical
manipulation to treat mechanical stress.
It was developed over a century ago by
US physician Andrew Taylor Still, who
maintained that most ailments can be
prevented or cured by techniques of
spinal manipulation.

osteoporosis disease in which the
bone substance becomes porous and
brittle. It is common in older people,

affecting more women than men. It may
be treated with calcium supplements
and etidronate.

ostrich large flightless bird *Struthio
camelus*, found in Africa. The male may
be about 2.5 m/8 ft tall and weigh 135
kg/300 lb, and is the largest living bird.
It has exceptionally strong legs and feet
(two-toed) that enable it to run at high
speed, and are also used in defence. It
lives in family groups of one cock with
several hens, each of which incubates
about 14 eggs.

Ottawa capital of Canada, in E
Ontario, on the hills overlooking the
Ottawa River and divided by the Rideau
Canal into the Upper (western) and
Lower (eastern) towns; population
(1986) 301,000, metropolitan area (with
adjoining Hull, Québec) 819,000.

Ottoman Empire Muslim empire of
the Turks 1300–1920, the successor of
the Seljuk Empire. It was founded 1299
by Osman I (1259–1326) and reached
its height with ◊Suleiman in the 16th
century. Its capital was Istanbul (formerly Constantinople).

Ouagadougou capital and industrial
centre of Burkina Faso; population
(1985) 442,000. The city has the palace
of Moro Naba, emperor of the Mossi
people, a neo-Romanesque cathedral,
and a central avenue called the Champs
Elysées. It was the capital of the Mossi
empire from the 15th century.

ovary in female animals, the organ that
generates the ◊ovum. In humans, the
ovaries are two whitish rounded bodies
about 25 mm/1 in by 35 mm/1.5 in,
located in the lower abdomen to either
side of the uterus. Every month, from
puberty to the onset of the menopause,
an ovum is released from the ovary.

This is called ovulation, and forms part of the ⬦menstrual cycle. In botany, an ovary is the expanded basal portion of the ⬦carpel of flowering plants, containing one or more ovules. It is hollow with a thick wall to protect the ovules. Following fertilization of the ovum, it develops into the fruit wall or pericarp.

Ovid (Publius Ovidius Naso) 43 BC–AD 17. Latin poet. His poetry deals mainly with the themes of love (*Amores* 20 BC, *Ars amatoria/The Art of Love* 1 BC), mythology (*Metamorphoses* AD 2), and exile (*Tristia* AD 9–12).

ovovivipary method of animal reproduction in which fertilized eggs develop within the female (unlike ovipary), and the embryo gains no nutritional substances from the female (unlike vivipary). It occurs in some invertebrates, fishes, and reptiles.

ovulation in female animals, the process of releasing egg cells (ova) from the ⬦ovary. In mammals it occurs as part of the ⬦menstrual cycle.

ovum (plural *ova*) female gamete (sex cell) before fertilization. In animals it is called an egg, and is produced in the ovaries. In plants, where it is also known as an egg cell or oosphere, the ovum is produced in an ovule. The ovum is nonmotile. It must be fertilized by a male gamete before it can develop further, except in cases of ⬦parthenogenesis.

Owen Wilfred 1893–1918. English poet. His verse, owing much to the encouragement of Siegfried Sassoon (1886–1918), expresses his hatred of war, for example *Anthem for Doomed Youth*, published 1921.

owl any bird of the order Strigiformes, found worldwide. They are mainly nocturnal birds of prey, with mobile heads, soundless flight, acute hearing, and forward-facing immobile eyes, surrounded by 'facial discs' of rayed feathers. All species lay white eggs, and begin incubation as soon as the first is laid. They regurgitate indigestible remains of their prey in pellets (castings).

Oxford university city and administrative centre of Oxfordshire in S central England, at the confluence of the rivers Thames (called the Isis around Oxford) and Cherwell; population (1991) 110,000. Oxford University has 36 colleges, the oldest being University College (1249). Among its historical buildings are Christ Church cathedral (12th century) and the Sheldonian Theatre designed by Christopher Wren. Its museums include the Ashmolean and the Pitt-Rivers.

Oxfordshire county of S central England; *area* 2,610 sq km/1,007 sq mi; *towns and cities* Oxford (administrative headquarters), Abingdon, Banbury, Henley-on-Thames, Witney, Woodstock; *features* Cotswolds and Chiltern Hills; Vale of the White Horse (chalk hill figure at Uffington, 114 m/374 ft long); Oxford University; Blenheim Palace, Woodstock (built 1705–22 by Vanbrugh) *population* (1991) 553,800.

oxidation in chemistry, the loss of ⬦electrons, gain of oxygen, or loss of hydrogen by an atom, ion, or molecule during a chemical reaction.

oxide compound of oxygen and another element, frequently produced by burning the element or a compound of it in air or oxygen.

oxygen colourless, odourless, tasteless, nonmetallic, gaseous element, symbol O, atomic number 8, relative atomic mass 15.9994. It is the most abundant element in the Earth's crust (almost 50% by mass), forms about 21% by volume of the atmosphere, and is present in combined form in water and many other substances. Life on Earth evolved using oxygen, which is a by-product of ◊photosynthesis and the basis for ◊respiration in plants and animals.

ozone O_3 highly reactive pale-blue gas with a penetrating odour. Ozone is an allotrope of oxygen (see ◊allotropy), made up of three atoms of oxygen. Ozone is an allotrope of oxygen (see ◊allotropy), made up of three atoms of oxygen. It is formed when the molecule of the stable form of oxygen (O_2) is split by ultraviolet radiation or electrical discharge. It forms a thin layer in the upper atmosphere, which protects life on Earth from ultraviolet rays, a cause of skin cancer.

ozone depleter any chemical that destroys the ozone in the stratosphere. Most ozone depleters are chemically stable compounds containing chlorine or bromine, which remain unchanged for long enough to drift up to the upper atmosphere. The best known are ◊chlorofluorocarbons (CFCs), but many other ozone depleters are known, including halons, used in some fire extinguishers; methyl chloroform and carbon tetrachloride, both solvents; some CFC substitutes; and the pesticide methyl bromide.

P

pacemaker or *sinoatrial node* (SA node) in vertebrates, a group of muscle cells in the wall of the heart that contracts spontaneously and rhythmically, setting the pace for the contractions of the rest of the heart. The pacemaker's intrinsic rate of contraction is increased or decreased, according to the needs of the body, by stimulation from the ▷autonomic nervous system. The term also refers to a medical device implanted under the skin of a patient whose heart beats inefficiently. It delivers minute electric shocks to stimulate the heart muscles at regular intervals and restores normal heartbeat.

Pacific Ocean world's largest ocean, extending from Antarctica to the Bering Strait; area 166,242,500 sq km/64,170,000 sq mi; average depth 4,188 m/13,749 ft; greatest depth of any ocean 11,034 m/36,210 ft in the Mariana Trench.

Paisley Ian (Richard Kyle) 1926– . Northern Ireland politician and cleric, leader of the Democratic Unionist Party from 1972. He has represented North Antrim in the House of Commons since 1974. An almost fanatical loyalist, his blunt and forthright manner, stentorian voice, and pugnaciousness are hallmarks of his political career.

Pakistan Islamic Republic of; *area* 796,100 sq km/307,295 sq mi; one-third of Kashmir under Pakistani control; *capital* Islamabad; *environment* about 68% of irrigated land is waterlogged or suffering from salinization; *features* the 'five rivers' (Indus, Jhelum, Chenab, Ravi, and Sutlej) feed the world's largest irrigation system; sites of the Indus Valley civilization; *political system* emergent democracy; *population* (1993 est) 122,400,000 (Punjabi 66%, Sindhi 13%); growth rate 3.1% p.a.; *languages* Urdu and English (official); Punjabi, Sindhi, Pashto, Baluchi, other local dialects; *religion* Sunni Muslim 75%, Shi'ite Muslim 20%, Hindu 4%.

Palaeocene first epoch of the Tertiary period of geological time, 65–56.5 million years ago. Many types of mammals spread rapidly after the disappearance of the great reptiles of the Mesozoic. Flying mammals replaced the flying reptiles, swimming mammals replaced the swimming reptiles, and all the ecological niches vacated by the reptiles were adopted by mammals.

Palaeolithic the Old Stone Age period, the earliest stage of human technology.

palaeontology in geology, the study of ancient life that encompasses the structure of ancient organisms and their environment, evolution, and ecology, as revealed by their ▷fossils. The practical aspects of palaeontology are based on using the presence of different fossils to date particular rock strata and to identify rocks that were laid down under particular conditions, for instance giving rise to the formation of oil.

Palaeozoic era of geological time 570–245 million years ago. It comprises the Cambrian, Ordovician, Silurian, Devonian, Carboniferous, and Permian periods. The Cambrian, Ordovician, and Silurian constitute the Lower or Early Palaeozoic; the Devonian, Carboniferous, and Permian make up the Upper or Late Palaeozoic. The era includes the evolution of hard-shelled multicellular life forms in the sea; the invasion of land by plants and animals; and the evolution of fish, amphibians, and early reptiles. The earliest identifiable fossils date from this era.

Palermo capital and seaport of Sicily; population (1988) 729,000. It was founded by the Phoenicians in the 8th century BC.

Palestine historic geographical area at the E end of the Mediterranean sea, also known as the Holy Land because of its historic and symbolic importance for Jews, Christians, and Muslims. Early settlers included the Canaanites, Hebrews, and Philistines. Over the centuries it became part of the Egyptian, Assyrian, Babylonian, Macedonian, Ptolemaic, Seleucid, Roman, Byzantine, Arab, and Ottoman empires. Today, it comprises parts of modern Israel, and Jordan.

Palestine Liberation Organization (PLO) Arab organization founded 1964 whose main aim emerged as the establishment of a Palestinian state alongside that of Israel. Its president (from 1969) is Yassir ▷Arafat. In 1993 a peace agreement based on mutual recognition was reached with Israel. In 1994 Arafat returned to the newly liberated territories of Gaza and Jericho to head an interim civilian administration, the Palestinian National Authority.

Palladio Andrea 1518–1580. Italian Renaissance architect. He was noted for his harmonious and balanced classical structures. He designed numerous palaces and country houses in and around Vicenza, Italy, making use of Roman classical forms, symmetry, and proportion. He also designed churches in Venice and published his studies of classical form in several illustrated books.

palm plant of the family Palmae, characterized by a single tall stem bearing a thick cluster of large palmate or pinnate leaves at the top. The majority of the numerous species are tropical or subtropical. Some, such as the coconut, date, sago, and oil palms, are important economically.

Palma (Spanish *Palma de Mallorca*) industrial port, resort, and capital of the Balearic Islands, Spain, on Majorca; population (1991) 308,600. Palma was founded 276 BC as a Roman colony. It has a Gothic cathedral, begun 1229.

Palmerston Henry John Temple, 3rd Viscount Palmerston 1784–1865. British politician. He was prime minister 1855–58 and 1859–65. Initially a Tory, in Parliament from 1807, he was secretary-at-war 1809–28. He broke with the Tories 1830 and sat in the Whig cabinets of 1830–34, 1835–41, and 1846–51 as foreign secretary.

Palm Sunday in the Christian calendar, the Sunday before Easter and first day of Holy Week, commemorating Jesus' entry into Jerusalem, when the crowd strewed palm leaves in his path.

Pan in Greek mythology, the god of flocks and herds (Roman Sylvanus), shown as a man with the horns, ears, and hoofed legs of a goat, and playing a shepherd's panpipe (or syrinx).

Panama Republic of (*República de Panamá*); *area* 77,100 sq km/29,768 sq mi; *capital* Panamá (Panama City); *features* Panama Canal; Smithsonian Tropical Research Institute; *political system* emergent democratic republic; *population* (1993 est) 2,510,000 (mestizo, or mixed race, 70%; West Indian 14%; European descent 10%; Indian (Cuna, Choco, Guayami) 6%); growth rate 2.2% p.a.; *languages* Spanish (official), English; *religions* Roman Catholic 93%, Protestant 6%.

Panama Canal canal across the Panama isthmus in Central America, connecting the Pacific and Atlantic oceans; length 80 km/50 mi, with 12 locks. Built by the USA 1904–14 after an unsuccessful attempt by the French, it was formally opened 1920. The *Panama Canal Zone* was acquired 'in perpetuity' by the USA 1903, comprising land extending about 5 km/3 mi on either side of the canal. The zone passed to Panama 1979, and control of the canal itself was ceded to Panama by the USA Jan 1990 under the terms of the Panama Canal Treaty 1977. The Canal Zone has several US military bases.

pancreas in vertebrates, an accessory gland of the digestive system located close to the duodenum. When stimulated by the hormone secretin, it releases enzymes into the duodenum that digest starches, proteins, and fats. In humans, it is about 18 cm/7 in long, and lies behind and below the stomach. It contains groups of cells called the *islets of Langerhans*, which secrete the hormones insulin and glucagon that regulate the blood sugar level.

panda one of two carnivores of different families, native to NW China and Tibet. The *giant panda* Ailuropoda melanoleuca has black-and-white fur with black eye patches and feeds mainly on bamboo shoots, consuming about 8 kg/17.5 lb of bamboo per day. It can grow up to 1.5 m/4.5 ft long, and weigh up to 140 kg/300 lb. It is an endangered species. The *lesser*, or *red*, *panda* Ailurus fulgens, of the raccoon family, is about 50 cm/1.5 ft long, and is black and chestnut, with a long tail.

Pandora in Greek mythology, the first mortal woman. Zeus sent her to Earth with a box of evils (to counteract the blessings brought to mortals by ▷Prometheus' gift of fire); she opened the box, and the evils all flew out. Only hope was left inside as a consolation.

pantheism doctrine that regards all of reality as divine, and God as present in all of nature and the universe. It is expressed in Egyptian religion and Brahmanism; stoicism, Neo-Platonism, Judaism, Christianity, and Islam can be interpreted in pantheistic terms. Pantheistic philosophers include Bruno, Spinoza, Fichte, Schelling, and Hegel.

Papandreou Andreas 1919– . Greek socialist politician, founder of the Pan-Hellenic Socialist Movement (PASOK); prime minister 1981–89 and again from 1993. He lost the election 1989 after being implicated in an alleged embezzlement scandal, but was cleared of all charges 1992 and re-elected prime minister Oct 1993.

paper thin, flexible material made in sheets from vegetable fibres (such as wood pulp) or rags and used for writing, drawing, printing, packaging, and various household needs. The name comes from papyrus, a form of writing material made from water reed, used in ancient Egypt. The invention of true paper, originally made of pulped fishing nets and rags, is credited to Tsai Lun, Chinese minister of agriculture, AD 105.

Papua New Guinea *area* 462,840 sq km/178,656 sq mi; *capital* Port Moresby (on E New Guinea); *features* one of world's largest swamps on SW coast; world's largest butterfly, orchids; Sepik River; *political system* liberal democracy; *population* (1993 est) 3,900,000 (Papuans, Melanesians, Negritos, various minorities); growth rate 2.6% p.a.; *languages* English (official); pidgin English, 715 local languages; *religions* Protestant 63%, Roman Catholic 31%, local faiths.

paraffin common name for ▷alkane, any member of the series of hydrocarbons with the general formula C_nH_{2n+2}. The lower members are gases, such as methane (marsh or natural gas). The middle ones (mainly liquid) form the basis of petrol, kerosene, and lubricating oils, while the higher ones (paraffin waxes) are used in ointment and cosmetic bases.

Paraguay Republic of (*República del Paraguay*); *area* 406,752 sq km/157,006 sq mi; *capital* Asunción; *features* Itaipú dam on border with Brazil; Gran Chaco plain with huge swamps; *political system* emergent democratic republic; *population* (1993) 4,500,000 (95% mixed Guarani Indian–Spanish descent); growth rate 3.0% p.a.; *religion* Roman Catholic 97%.

parallelogram in mathematics, a quadrilateral (four-sided plane figure) with opposite pairs of sides equal in length and parallel, and opposite angles equal. The diagonals of a parallelogram

bisect each other. Its area is the product of the length of one side and the perpendicular distance between this and the opposite side. In the special case when all four sides are equal in length, the parallelogram is known as a rhombus, and when the internal angles are right angles, it is a rectangle or square.

parallel processing emerging computer technology that allows more than one computation at the same time. Although in the 1980s this technology enabled only a small number of computer processor units to work in parallel, in theory thousands or millions of processors could be used at the same time.

paralysis loss of voluntary movement due to failure of nerve impulses to reach the muscles involved. It may result from almost any disorder of the nervous system, including brain or spinal cord injury, poliomyelitis, stroke, tumour or multiple sclerosis. Paralysis may also involve loss of sensation due to sensory nerve disturbance. Paralysis of the legs, involving loss of both movement and sensation, and usually caused by spinal injury, is termed *paraplegia*.

parasite organism that lives on or in another organism (called the host) and depends on it for nutrition, often at the expense of the host's welfare. Parasites that live inside the host, such as liver flukes and tapeworms, are called *endoparasites*; those that live on the exterior, such as fleas and lice, are called *ectoparasites*.

Paris port and capital of France, on the river Seine; *département* in the Île de France region; area 105 sq km/40.5 sq mi; population (1990) 2,175,200.

Park Mungo 1771–1806. Scottish explorer who traced the course of the

Niger River 1795–97. He disappeared and probably drowned during a second African expedition 1805–06. He published *Travels in the Interior of Africa* 1799.

Parker Charlie (Charles Christopher 'Bird', 'Yardbird') 1920–1955. US alto saxophonist and jazz composer. He was associated with the trumpeter Dizzy Gillespie in developing the bebop style.

Parkinson's disease or *parkinsonism* or *paralysis agitans* degenerative disease of the brain characterized by a progressive loss of mobility, muscular rigidity, tremor, and speech difficulties. The condition is mainly seen in people over the age of 50.

parliament legislative body of a country. The world's oldest parliament is the Icelandic Althing which dates from about 930. The UK Parliament is usually dated from 1265. The legislature of the USA is called Congress and comprises the House of Representatives and the Senate. The European Parliament is the governing body of the European Union.

Parnassus mountain in central Greece, height 2,457 m/8,064 ft, revered by the ancient Greeks as the abode of Apollo and the Muses. The sacred site of Delphi lies on its southern flank.

Parnell Charles Stewart 1846–1891. Irish nationalist politician. He supported a policy of obstruction and violence to attain ◊Home Rule, and became the president of the Nationalist Party 1877. In 1879 he approved the Land League, and his attitude led to his imprisonment 1881.

parrot any bird of the order Psittaciformes, abundant in the tropics, especially in Australia and South America. They are mainly vegetarian, and range in size from the 8.5 cm/3.5 in pygmy parrot to the 100 cm/40 in Amazon parrot. The smaller species are commonly referred to as parakeets. The plumage is often very colourful, and the call is usually a harsh screech. Several species are endangered.

parsec in astronomy, a unit (symbol pc) used for distances to stars and galaxies. One parsec is equal to 3.2616 ◊light years, 2.063×10^5 ◊astronomical units, and 3.086×10^{13} km.

parthenogenesis development of an ovum (egg) without any genetic contribution from a male. Parthenogenesis is the normal means of reproduction in a few plants (for example, dandelions) and animals (for example, certain fish). Some sexually reproducing species, such as aphids, show parthenogenesis at some stage in their life cycle.

particle physics study of the particles that make up all atoms, and of their interactions. More than 300 subatomic particles have now been identified by physicists, categorized into several classes according to their mass, electric charge, spin, magnetic moment, and interaction. Subatomic particles include the ◊elementary particles (◊quarks, ◊leptons, and ◊gauge bosons), which are believed to be indivisible and so may be considered the fundamental units of matter; and the ◊hadrons (baryons, such as the proton and neutron, and mesons), which are composite particles, made up of two or three quarks. The proton, electron, and neutrino are the only stable particles (the neutron being stable only when in the atomic nucleus). The unstable particles decay rapidly into other particles, and are known from experiments with particle accelerators and cosmic radiation. See ◊atomic structure.

Pascal Blaise 1623–1662. French philosopher and mathematician. He contributed to the development of hydraulics, the ◊calculus, and the mathematical theory of probability.

Passover also called *Pesach* in Judaism, an eight-day spring festival which commemorates the exodus of the Israelites from Egypt and the passing over by the Angel of Death of the Jewish houses, so that only the Egyptian firstborn sons were killed, in retribution for Pharaoh's murdering of all Jewish male infants.

Pasternak Boris Leonidovich 1890–1960. Russian poet and novelist. His novel *Dr Zhivago* 1957 was originally banned in the USSR, but was awarded a Nobel prize 1958 (which Pasternak declined). The ban on *Dr Zhivago* has since been lifted and Pasternak has been posthumously rehabilitated.

Pasteur Louis 1822–1895. French chemist and microbiologist who discovered that fermentation is caused by microorganisms. He developed a rabies vaccine, which led to the foundation of the Institut Pasteur in Paris 1888.

pasteurization treatment of food to reduce the number of microorganisms it contains and so protect consumers from disease. For milk, the method involves heating it to 72°C/161°F for 15 seconds followed by rapid cooling to 10°C/50°F or lower.

pathogen in medicine, any microorganism that causes disease. Most pathogens are ◊parasites, and the diseases they cause are incidental to their search for food or shelter inside the host. Non-parasitic organisms, such as soil bacteria

or those living in the human gut and feeding on waste foodstuffs, can also become pathogenic to a person whose immune system or liver is damaged. The larger parasites that can cause disease, such as nematode worms, are not usually described as pathogens.

Patrick, St 389–*c.* 461. Patron saint of Ireland. Born in Britain, probably in S Wales, he was carried off by pirates to six years' slavery in Antrim, Ireland, before escaping either to Britain or Gaul to train as a missionary. Said to have landed again in Ireland 432 or 456, his work was a vital factor in the spread of Christian influence there. His symbols are snakes and shamrocks; feast day 17 March.

Paul, St *c.* AD 3–*c.* AD 68. Christian missionary and martyr; in the New Testament, one of the apostles and author of 13 epistles. Originally opposed to Christianity, he took part in the stoning of St Stephen. He is said to have been converted by a vision on the road to Damascus, after which he made great missionary journeys, for example to Philippi and Ephesus. His emblems are a sword and a book; feast day 29 June.

Pavlov Ivan Petrovich 1849–1936. Russian physiologist who studied conditioned reflexes in animals. His work had a great impact on behavioural theory and learning theory. See also ◊conditioning. Nobel Prize for Medicine 1904.

Pavlova Anna 1881–1931. Russian dancer. Prima ballerina of the Imperial Ballet from 1906, she left Russia 1913, and went on to become one of the world's most celebrated exponents of classical ballet. She influenced dancers worldwide with roles such as Mikhail Fokine's *The Dying Swan* solo 1907.

Pays de la Loire agricultural region of W France, comprising the *départements* of Loire-Atlantique, Maine-et-Loire, Mayenne, Sarthe, and Vendée; capital Nantes; area 32,100 sq km/ 12,391 sq mi; population (1986) 3,018,000.

Paz Octavio 1914– . Mexican poet and essayist. His works reflect many influences, including Marxism, Surrealism, and Aztec mythology. His long poem *Piedra del sol/Sun Stone* 1957 uses contrasting images, centring upon the Aztec Calendar Stone (representing the Aztec universe), to symbolize the loneliness of individuals and their search for union with others. Nobel Prize for Literature 1990.

peacock technically, the male of any of various large pheasants. The name is most often used for the common peacock *Pavo cristatus*, a bird of the pheasant family, native to S Asia. It is rather larger than a pheasant. The male has a large fan-shaped tail, brightly coloured with blue, green, and purple 'eyes' on a chestnut background. The female (peahen) is brown with a small tail.

peanut or *groundnut* or *monkey nut* South American vinelike annual plant *Arachis hypogaea*, family Leguminosae. After flowering, the flower stalks bend and force the pods into the earth to ripen underground. The nuts are a staple food in many tropical countries and are widely grown in the S USA. They yield a valuable edible oil and are the basis for numerous processed foods.

pearl shiny, hard, rounded abnormal growth composed of nacre (or mother-of-pearl), a chalky substance. Nacre is secreted by many molluscs, and deposited in thin layers on the inside of the shell around a parasite, a grain of

sand, or some other irritant body. After several years of the mantle (the layer of tissue between the shell and the body mass) secreting this nacre, a pearl is formed.

Pearl Harbor US Pacific naval base in Oahu, Hawaii, USA, the scene of a Japanese aerial attack 7 Dec 1941, which brought the USA into World War II. The attack took place while Japanese envoys were holding so-called peace talks in Washington. More than 2,000 members of US armed forces were killed, and a large part of the US Pacific fleet was destroyed or damaged.

Pearson Lester Bowles 1897–1972. Canadian politician, leader of the Liberal Party from 1958, prime minister 1963–68. As foreign minister 1948–57, he represented Canada at the United Nations, playing a key role in settling the ♢Suez Crisis 1956. Nobel Peace Prize 1957.

Peasants' Revolt the rising of the English peasantry in June 1381, the result of economic, social, and political disillusionment. It was sparked off by the imposition of a new poll tax, three times the rates of those imposed in 1377 and 1379. Led by Wat ♢Tyler and John Ball (d. 1381), rebels from SE England marched on London and demanded reforms. The authorities put down the revolt by deceit and force.

peat fibrous organic substance found in bogs and formed by the incomplete decomposition of plants such as sphagnum moss. N Asia, Canada, Finland, Ireland, and other places have large deposits, which have been dried and used as fuel from ancient times. Peat can also be used as a soil additive.

Peel Robert 1788–1850. British Conservative politician. As home secretary 1822–27 and 1828–30, he founded the modern police force and in 1829 introduced Roman Catholic emancipation. He was prime minister 1834–35 and 1841–46, when his repeal of the ⊳Corn Laws caused him and his followers to break with the party.

Pegasus in Greek mythology, the winged horse that sprang from the blood of the Gorgon Medusa. He was transformed into a constellation.

Peking alternative transcription of ⊳Beijing, the capital of China.

Pelé adopted name of Edson Arantes do Nascimento 1940– . Brazilian soccer player. A prolific goal scorer, he appeared in four World Cup competitions 1958–70 and led Brazil to three championships (1958, 1962, 1970).

Peloponnese (Greek *Peloponnesos*) peninsula forming the S part of Greece; area 21,549 sq km/8,318 sq mi; population (1991) 1,077,000. It is joined to the mainland by the narrow isthmus of Corinth and is divided into the nomes (administrative areas) of Argolis, Arcadia, Achaea, Elis, Corinth, Lakonia, and Messenia, representing its seven ancient states.

Peloponnesian conflict between Athens and Sparta, backed by their respective allies, 431–404 BC, originating in suspicions about the ambitions of the Athenian leader Pericles. It was ended by the Spartan general Lysander's capture of the Athenian fleet in 405, and his starving the Athenians into surrender in 404. Sparta's victory meant the destruction of the political power of Athens.

Penang (Malay Pulau Pinang) state in W Peninsular Malaysia, formed of *Penang Island*, Province Wellesley, and the Dindings on the mainland; area 1,030 sq km/398 sq mi; capital Penang (George Town); population (1990) 1,142,200. Penang Island was bought by Britain from the ruler of Kedah 1785; Province Wellesley was acquired 1800.

penguin any of an order (Sphenisciformes) of marine flightless birds, mostly black and white, found in the southern hemisphere. They range in size from 40 cm/1.6 ft to 1.2 m/4 ft tall, and have thick feathers to protect them from the intense cold. They are awkward on land, but their wings have evolved into flippers, making them excellent swimmers. Penguins congregate to breed in 'rookeries', and often spend many months incubating their eggs while their mates are out at sea feeding.

penicillin any of a group of ⊳antibiotic (bacteria killing) compounds obtained from filtrates of moulds of the genus *Penicillium* (especially *P. notatum*) or produced synthetically. Penicillin was the first antibiotic to be discovered (by Alexander ⊳Fleming); it kills a broad spectrum of bacteria, many of which cause disease in humans.

penis male reproductive organ containing the urethra, the channel through which urine and ⊳semen are voided. It transfers sperm to the female reproductive tract to fertilize the ovum. In mammals, the penis is made erect by vessels that fill with blood, and in most mammals (but not humans) is stiffened by a bone.

Pennines mountain system, 'the backbone of England', broken by a gap through which the river Aire flows to the E and the Ribble to the W; length

(Scottish border to the Peaks in Derbyshire) 400 km/250 mi. It is the watershed for the main rivers of NE England. The rocks are carboniferous limestone and millstone grit, the land high moorland and fell.

Pennsylvania state in NE USA; *area* 117,400 sq km/45,316 sq mi; *capital* Harrisburg; *features* Allegheny Mountains; Gettysburg Civil War battlefield; *population* (1990) 11,881,600.

Pentagon the headquarters of the US Department of Defense, Arlington, Virginia. One of the world's largest office buildings (five-sided with a pentagonal central court), it houses the administrative and command headquarters for the US armed forces and has become synonymous with the military establishment bureaucracy.

Pentecost in Judaism, the festival of *Shavuot*, celebrated on the 50th day after ▷Passover in commemoration of the giving of the Ten Commandments to Moses on Mount Sinai, and the end of the grain harvest; in the Christian church, Pentecost is the day on which the apostles experienced inspiration of the Holy Spirit, commemorated on Whit Sunday.

Pentecostal movement Christian revivalist movement inspired by the baptism in the Holy Spirit with 'speaking in tongues' experienced by the apostles at the time of Pentecost. It represents a reaction against the rigid theology and formal worship of the traditional churches, but believes in the literal word of the Bible and disapproves of alcohol, tobacco, dancing, theatre, and so on.

Pepin the Short *c.* 714–*c.* 768. King of the Franks from 751. The son of Charles Martel, he acted as Mayor of the Palace to the last Merovingian king, Childeric III, deposed him and assumed the royal title himself, founding the ▷Carolingian dynasty. He was ▷Charlemagne's father.

pepper climbing plant *Piper nigrum* native to the E Indies, of the Old World pepper family Piperaceae. When gathered green, the berries are crushed to release the seeds for the spice called black pepper. When the berries are ripe, the seeds are removed and their outer skin is discarded, to produce white pepper. Chilli pepper, cayenne or red pepper, and the sweet peppers used as a vegetable come from ▷capsicums native to the New World.

peptide molecule comprising two or more ▷amino acid molecules (not necessarily different) joined by *peptide bonds*, whereby the acid group of one acid is linked to the amino group of the other (–CO.NH). The number of amino acid molecules in the peptide is indicated by referring to it as a di-, tri-, or polypeptide (two, three, or many amino acids).

Pepys Samuel 1633–1703. English diarist. His diary 1659–69 was a unique record of both the daily life of the period and his own intimate feelings. Written in shorthand, it was not deciphered until 1825. Pepys was imprisoned 1679 in the Tower of London on suspicion of being connected with the Popish Plot (see Titus ▷Oates).

perch any of the largest order of spiny-finned bony fishes, the Perciformes, with some 8,000 species. This order includes the sea basses, cichlids, damselfishes, mullets, barracudas, wrasses, and gobies. Perches of the freshwater genus *Perca* are found in Europe, Asia, and

North America. They have varied shapes and are usually a greenish colour. They are very prolific, spawning when about three years old, and have voracious appetites.

percussion instrument musical instrument played by being struck with the hand or a beater. Percussion instruments can be divided into those that can be tuned to produce a sound of definite pitch, such as the timpani, tubular bells, glockenspiel, and xylophone, and those of indefinite pitch, including bass drum, tambourine, triangle, cymbals, and castanets.

Peres Shimon 1923–   . Israeli socialist politician, prime minister 1984–86. As foreign minister in Yitzhak Rabin's Labour government from 1992, he negotiated the 1993 peace agreement with the Palestine Liberation Organization (PLO). Nobel Prize for Peace jointly with Israeli president, Rabin, and PLO leader, Yassir Arafat 1994.

pericarp wall of a ⟩fruit. It encloses the seeds and is derived from the ⟩ovary wall. In fruits such as the acorn, the pericarp becomes dry and hard, forming a shell around the seed. In fleshy fruits the pericarp is typically made up of three distinct layers. The *epicarp*, or *exocarp*, forms the tough outer skin of the fruit, while the *mesocarp* is often fleshy and forms the middle layers. The innermost layer or *endocarp*, which surrounds the seeds, may be membranous or thick and hard, as in the stone of cherries, plums, and apricots.

periodic table of the elements in chemistry, a table in which the elements are arranged in order of their atomic number. The table summarizes the major properties of the elements and enables predictions to be made about their behaviour.

Permian period of geological time 290–245 million years ago, the last period of the Palaeozoic era. Its end was marked by a significant change in marine life, including the extinction of many corals and trilobites. Deserts were widespread, and terrestrial amphibians and mammal-like reptiles flourished. Cone-bearing plants (gymnosperms) came to prominence.

Perón Juan (Domingo) 1895–1974. Argentine politician, dictator 1946–55 and from 1973 until his death. His populist appeal to the poor was enhanced by the charisma and political work of his second wife Eva (Evita) Perón (1919–52). After her death his popularity waned, and he was deposed in a military coup 1955. He returned from exile to the presidency 1973, but died in office 1974, and was succeeded as president by his third wife Isabel Perón (1931–   ) until 1976.

perpendicular in mathematics, at a right angle; also, a line at right angles to another or to a plane. For a pair of skew lines (lines in three dimensions that do not meet), there is just one common perpendicular, which is at right angles to both lines; the nearest points on the two lines are the feet of this perpendicular.

Persian Gulf or *Arabian Gulf* large shallow inlet of the Arabian Sea; area 233,000 sq km/90,000 sq mi. It divides the Arabian peninsula from Iran and is linked by the Strait of Hormuz and the Gulf of Oman to the Arabian Sea. Oilfields surround it in the Gulf States of Bahrain, Iran, Iraq, Kuwait, Oman, Qatar, Saudi Arabia, and the United Arab Emirates.

Persian Wars series of conflicts between Greece and Persia 499–449 BC. The eventual victory of Greece marked the end of Persian domination of the ancient world and the beginning of Greek supremacy.

Perth capital of Western Australia, with its port at nearby Fremantle on the Swan River; population (1990) 1,190,100. It was founded 1829 and is the commercial and cultural centre of the state.

Peru Republic of (*República del Perú*); *area* 1,285,200 sq km/496,216 sq mi; *capital* Lima, including port of Callao; *environment* an estimated 38% of the 8,000 sq km/3,100 sq mi of coastal lands under irrigation are either waterlogged or suffering from saline water. Only half the population has access to clean drinking water; *features* Lake Titicaca; Atacama Desert; Nazca lines, monuments of Machu Picchu, Chan Chan, Charin de Huantar; *political system* democratic republic; *population* (1993) 22,130,000 (Indian, mainly Quechua and Aymara, 46%; mixed Spanish–Indian descent 43%); growth rate 2.6% p.a.; *languages* Spanish 68%, Quechua 27% (both official), Aymara 3%; *religion* Roman Catholic 90%.

pesticide any chemical used in farming, gardening, or indoors to combat pests. Pesticides are of three main types: *insecticides* (to kill insects), *fungicides* (to kill fungal diseases), and *herbicides* (to kill plants, mainly those considered weeds). Pesticides cause a number of pollution problems through spray drift onto surrounding areas, direct contamination of users or the public, and as residues on food.

Peter (I) the Great 1672–1725. Tsar of Russia from 1682. He assumed control of the government 1689. He attempted to reorganize the country on Western lines; the army was modernized, a fleet was built, the administrative and legal systems were remodelled, education was encouraged, and the church was brought under state control. On the Baltic coast he built St Petersburg as his new capital.

Peter, St Christian martyr, the author of two epistles in the New Testament and leader of the apostles. He is regarded as the first bishop of Rome, whose mantle the pope inherits. His real name was Simon, but he was nicknamed Kephas ('Peter', from the Greek for 'rock') by Jesus, as being the rock upon which he would build his church. His emblem is two keys; feast day 29 June.

Petipa Marius 1818–1910. French choreographer. He created some of the most important ballets in the classical repertory. For the Imperial Ballet in Russia he created masterpieces such as *Don Quixote* 1869, *La Bayadère* 1877, *The Sleeping Beauty* 1890, *Swan Lake* 1895, and *Raymonda* 1898.

Petrarch (Italian *Petrarca*) Francesco 1304–1374. Italian poet. He was a devotee of the Classical tradition. His *Il Canzoniere* is composed of sonnets in praise of his idealized love, 'Laura', whom he first saw 1327 (she was a married woman and refused to become his mistress). The dialogue *Secretum meum/My Secret* is a spiritual biography.

petrol mixture of hydrocarbons derived from petroleum, mainly used as a fuel for internal combustion engines. It is colourless and highly volatile. *Leaded petrol* contains antiknock (a mixture of tetraethyl lead and dibromoethane), which improves the combustion of petrol and the performance of a car engine. The lead from the exhaust fumes enters the atmosphere, mostly as simple lead compounds.

petrol engine the most commonly used source of power for motor vehicles, introduced by the German engineers Gottlieb Daimler and Karl Benz 1885. The petrol engine is a complex piece of machinery made up of about 150 moving parts. It is a reciprocating piston engine, in which a number of pistons move up and down in cylinders. The motion of the pistons rotate a crankshaft, at the end of which is a heavy flywheel. From the flywheel the power is transferred to the car's driving wheels via the transmission system of clutch, gearbox, and final drive.

petroleum or *crude oil* natural mineral oil, a thick greenish-brown flammable liquid found underground in permeable rocks. Petroleum consists of hydrocarbons mixed with oxygen, sulphur, nitrogen, and other elements in varying proportions. It is thought to be derived from ancient organic material that has been converted by, first, bacterial action, then heat and pressure (but its origin may be chemical also). From crude petroleum, various products are made by distillation and other processes; for example, fuel oil, petrol, kerosene, diesel, lubricating oil, paraffin wax, and petroleum jelly.

pewter any of various alloys of mostly tin with varying amounts of lead, copper, or antimony. Pewter has been known for centuries and was once widely used for domestic utensils but is now used mainly for ornamental ware.

pH scale from 0 to 14 for measuring acidity or alkalinity. A pH of 7.0 indicates neutrality, below 7 is acid, while above 7 is alkaline. Strong acids, such as those used in car batteries, have a pH of about 2; strong alkalis such as sodium hydroxide are pH 13.

Phanerozoic eon in Earth history, consisting of the most recent 570 million years. It comprises the Palaeozoic, Mesozoic, and Cenozoic eras. The vast majority of fossils come from this eon, owing to the evolution of hard shells and internal skeletons. The name means 'interval of well- displayed life'.

Pharisee member of a conservative Jewish sect that arose in the 2nd century BC in protest against all movements favouring compromise with Hellenistic culture. The Pharisees were devout adherents of the law, both as found in the Torah and in the oral tradition known as the Mishnah.

phenol member of a group of aromatic chemical compounds with weakly acidic properties, which are characterized by a hydroxyl (OH) group attached directly to an aromatic ring. The simplest of the phenols, derived from benzene, is also known as phenol and has the formula C_6H_5OH. It is sometimes called *carbolic acid* and can be extracted from coal tar.

phenotype in genetics, visible traits, those actually displayed by an organism. The phenotype is not a direct reflection of the ◊genotype because some alleles are masked by the presence of other, dominant alleles. The phenotype is further modified by the effects of the environment (for example, poor nutrition stunts growth).

pheromone chemical signal (such as an odour) that is emitted by one animal and affects the behaviour of others. Pheromones are used by many animal species to attract mates.

Phidias or *Pheidias* Greek sculptor. He supervised the sculptural programme for the Parthenon (most of it is preserved in the British Museum, London, and known as the Elgin marbles). He also executed the colossal statue of Zeus at Olympia, one of the Seven Wonders of the World.

Philadelphia industrial city and port on the Delaware River in Pennsylvania, USA; population (1990) 1,585,600, metropolitan area 5,899,300. Founded 1682, it was the first capital of the USA 1790–1800.

Philip Duke of Edinburgh 1921– . Prince of the UK, husband of Elizabeth II, a grandson of George I of Greece and a great-great-grandson of Queen Victoria. He was born in Corfu, Greece, but brought up in England.

Philip II 1527–1598. King of Spain from 1556. Son of the Habsburg emperor Charles V, he married Queen Mary of England 1554. On his father's abdication 1556 he inherited Spain, the Netherlands, and the Spanish possessions in Italy and the Americas, and in 1580 annexed Portugal. His intolerance of the Netherlanders drove them into revolt. The defeat of the Spanish Armada by the English 1588 marked the beginning of the decline of Spanish power. He was at war with France from 1589.

Philippines Republic of the (*Republika ng Pilipinas*); *area* 300,000 sq km/ 115,800 sq mi; *capital* Manila (on Luzon); *environment* cleared for timber, tannin, and the creation of fish ponds, the mangrove forest was reduced from 5,000 sq km/1,930 sq mi to 380 sq km/ 146 sq mi between 1920 and 1988; *features* Luzon, site of Clark Field, US air base used as a logistical base in Vietnam War; Pinatubo volcano (1,759 m/5,770 ft); Mindanao has active volcano Apo (2,954 m/9,690 ft) and mountainous rainforest; *political system* emergent democracy; *population* (1993) 65,650,000 (93% Malaysian); growth rate 2.4% p.a.; *languages* Tagalog (Filipino, official); English and Spanish; *religions* Roman Catholic 84%, Protestant 9%, Muslim 5%.

Philistine member of a seafaring people of non-Semitic origin who founded city-states on the Palestinian coastal plain in the 12th century BC, adopting a Semitic language and religion.

philosophy branch of learning concerned with fundamental problems – including the nature of mind and matter, perception, self, free will, causation, time and space, and the existence of moral judgements – which cannot be resolved by a specific method. ◊Socrates, ◊Plato, and ◊Aristotle were the major philosophers of ancient time, influencing the work of medieval scholars and leading to the rationalism of French philosopher ◊Descartes (1596–1650), whose rationalism contrasted with the philosophy of ◊Locke and, later, ◊Hume in Britain. In Germany in the 18th century ◊Kant was the precursor of the 19th-century idealism propounded by ◊Hegel and ◊Nietzsche amongst others. Philosophy in the 20th century has ranged from the existentialism of ◊Satre to the logical analysis and study of language of Bertrand Russell (1872–1970) in England and Austrian philospher Ludwig Wittgenstein (1889–1951).

phloem tissue found in vascular plants whose main function is to conduct sugars and other food materials from the leaves, where they are produced, to all other parts of the plant.

Phnom Penh capital of Cambodia, on the Mekong River, 210 km/130 mi NW of Saigon; population (1989) 800,000. It has been Cambodia's capital since the 15th century, and has royal palaces, museums, and pagodas.

Phoenicia ancient Greek name for N ◊Canaan on the E coast of the Mediterranean. The Phoenician civilization flourished from about 1200 until the capture of Tyre by Alexander the Great in 332 BC. Seafaring traders and artisans, they are said to have circumnavigated Africa and established colonies in Cyprus, N Africa (for example, Carthage), Malta, Sicily, and Spain.

phoenix mythical Egyptian bird that burned itself to death on a pyre every 500 years and rose rejuvenated from the ashes.

Phoenix capital of Arizona, USA; industrial city and tourist centre on the Salt River; population (1990) 983,400.

phosphate salt or ester of phosphoric acid. Incomplete neutralization of phosphoric acid gives rise to acid phosphates (see ◊acid salts and buffer). Phosphates are used as fertilizers, and are required for the development of healthy root systems. They are involved in many biochemical processes, often as part of complex molecules, such as ◊ATP.

phosphorescence in physics, the emission of light by certain substances after they have absorbed energy, whether from visible light, other electromagnetic radiation such as ultraviolet rays or X-rays, or cathode rays (a beam of electrons). When the stimulating energy is removed phosphorescence ceases, although it may persist for a short time after (unlike fluorescence, which stops immediately).

phosphorus highly reactive, nonmetallic element, symbol P, atomic number 15, relative atomic mass 30.9738. It occurs in nature as phosphates (commonly in the form of the mineral apatite), and is essential to plant and animal life. Compounds of phosphorus are used in fertilizers, various organic chemicals, for matches and fireworks, and in glass and steel.

photochemical reaction any chemical reaction in which light is produced or light initiates the reaction. Light can initiate reactions by exciting atoms or molecules and making them more reactive: the light energy becomes converted to chemical energy. Many photochemical reactions set up a ◊chain reaction and produce ◊free radicals.

photography process for reproducing images on sensitized materials by various forms of radiant energy, including visible light, ultraviolet, infrared, X-rays, atomic radiations, and electron beams. Photography was developed in the 19th century; among the pioneers were L J M ◊Daguerre in France and Fox Talbot in the UK. Colour photography dates from the early 20th century.

photon in physics, the ◊elementary particle or 'package' (quantum) of energy in which light and other forms of electromagnetic radiation are emitted. The photon has both particle and wave properties; it has no charge, is considered massless but possesses momentum and energy. It is one of the ◊gauge bosons, a particle that cannot be subdivided, and is the carrier of the ◊electromagnetic force, one of the fundamental forces of nature.

photosynthesis process by which green plants trap light energy and use it to drive a series of chemical reactions, leading to the formation of carbohydrates. All animals ultimately depend on photosynthesis because it is the method by which the basic food (sugar) is created. For photosynthesis to occur, the plant must possess ▷chlorophyll and must have a supply of carbon dioxide and water. Actively photosynthesizing green plants store excess sugar as starch (this can be tested for using iodine).

phylum (plural *phyla*) major grouping in biological classification. Mammals, birds, reptiles, amphibians, fishes, and tunicates belong to the phylum Chordata; the phylum Mollusca consists of snails, slugs, mussels, clams, squid, and octopuses; the phylum Porifera contains sponges; and the phylum Echinodermata includes starfish, sea urchins, and sea cucumbers. In classifying plants (where the term 'division' often takes the place of 'phylum'), there are between four and nine phyla depending on the criteria used; all flowering plants belong to a single phylum, Angiospermata, and all conifers to another, Gymnospermata. Related phyla are grouped together in a ▷kingdom; phyla are subdivided into ▷classes.

physical chemistry branch of chemistry concerned with examining the relationships between the chemical compositions of substances and the physical properties that they display. Most chemical reactions exhibit some physical phenomenon (change of state, temperature, pressure, or volume, the use or production of electricity), and the measurement and study of such phenomena has led to many chemical theories and laws.

physics branch of science concerned with the laws that govern the structure of the universe, and the forms of matter and energy and their interactions. For convenience, physics is often divided into branches such as nuclear physics, particle physics, solid- and liquid-state physics, electricity, electronics, magnetism, optics, acoustics, heat, and thermodynamics. Before the 20th century, physics was known as *natural philosophy*.

physiology branch of biology that deals with the functioning of living organisms, as opposed to anatomy, which studies their structures.

pi symbol π, the ratio of the circumference of a circle to its diameter. The value of pi is 3.1415926, correct to seven decimal places. Common approximations to pi are $^{22}/_7$ and 3.14, although the value 3 can be used as a rough estimation.

piano or *pianoforte* (originally *fortepiano*) stringed musical instrument played by felt-covered hammers activated from a keyboard. It is capable of dynamic gradation between soft (piano) and loud (forte) tones, hence its name. The first piano was constructed 1704 and introduced 1709 by Bartolommeo Cristofori, a harpsichord maker in Padua. It uses a clever mechanism to make the keyboard touch-sensitive.

Picardy (French *Picardie*) region of N France, including Aisne, Oise, and Somme *départements*; *area* 19,400 sq km/7,488 sq mi; *population* (1986) 1,774,000.

Picasso Pablo Ruiz y 1881–1973. Spanish artist. Active chiefly in France, he was one of the most inventive and prolific talents in 20th-century art. His

Blue Period 1901–1904 and Rose Period 1905–1906 preceded the revolutionary *Les Demoiselles d'Avignon* 1907 (Museum of Modern Art, New York), which paved the way for Cubism. In the early 1920s he was considered a leader of the Surrealist movement. In the 1930s his work included metal sculpture, book illustration.

Pict Roman term for a member of the peoples of N Scotland, possibly meaning 'painted' (tattooed). Of pre- Celtic origin, and speaking a Celtic language which died out in about the 10th century, the Picts are thought to have inhabited much of England before the arrival of the Celtic Britons. They were united with the Celtic Scots under the rule of Kenneth MacAlpin 844. Their greatest monument is a series of carved stones, whose symbols remain undeciphered.

Piedmont (Italian *Piemonte*) region of N Italy, bordering Switzerland to the N and France to the W, and surrounded, except to the E, by the Alps and the Apennines; area 25,400 sq km/9,804 sq mi; population (1990) 4,356,200. Its capital is Turin. It includes the fertile Po river valley.

Piero della Francesca *c.* 1420–1492. Italian painter. Active in Arezzo and Urbino, he was one of the major artists of the 15th century. His work has a solemn stillness and unusually solid figures, luminous colour, and carefully calculated compositional harmonies. It includes a fresco series, *The Legend of the True Cross* (San Francesco, Arezzo), begun about 1452, and the *Flagellation of Christ* (Galleria della Marche, Palazzo Ducale, Urbino) 1450s.

Pilate Pontius early 1st century AD. Roman procurator of Judea AD 26–36. The New Testament Gospels describe his reluctant ordering of Jesus' crucifixion, but there has been considerable debate about his actual role in it.

Pilgrims the emigrants who sailed from Plymouth, Devon, England, in the *Mayflower* on 16 Sept 1620 to found the first colony in New England at New Plymouth, Massachusetts. Of the 102 passengers fewer than a quarter were Puritan refugees.

Pill, the commonly used term for the contraceptive pill, based on female hormones. The combined pill, which contains synthetic hormones similar to oestrogen and progesterone, stops the production of eggs, and makes the mucus produced by the cervix hostile to sperm. It is the most effective form of contraception apart from sterilization, being more than 99% effective.

Pinatubo, Mount active volcano on Luzon Island, the Philippines, 88 km/55 mi N of Manila. Dormant for 600 years, it erupted June 1991, killing 343 people and leaving as many as 200,000 homeless. Surrounding rice fields were covered with 3 m/10 ft of volcanic ash.

pineal body or *pineal gland* a cone-shaped outgrowth of the vertebrate brain. In some lower vertebrates, it develops a rudimentary lens and retina, which show it to be derived from an eye, or pair of eyes, situated on the top of the head in ancestral vertebrates. In fishes that can change colour to match their background, the pineal perceives the light level and controls the colour change. In birds, the pineal detects changes in daylight and stimulates breeding behaviour as spring approaches. Mammals also have a pineal gland, but it is located deeper within the brain. It secretes a hormone, melatonin, thought to influence rhythms of activity. In humans, it is a small piece of tissue attached by a stalk to the rear wall of the third ventricle of the brain.

Pinochet (Ugarte) Augusto 1915– . Military ruler of Chile from 1973, when a coup backed by the US Central Intelligence Agency ousted and killed President Salvador Allende. Pinochet took over the presidency and governed ruthlessly, crushing all opposition. He was voted out of power when general elections were held Dec 1989 but remained head of the armed forces.

Pinter Harold 1930– . English dramatist, originally an actor. He specializes in the tragicomedy of the breakdown of communication, broadly in the tradition of the Theatre of the Absurd – for example, *The Birthday Party* 1958 and *The Caretaker* 1960. Later plays include *The Homecoming* 1965, *Old Times* 1971, *Betrayal* 1978, and *Moonlight* 1993.

Pirandello Luigi 1867–1936. Italian playwright, novelist, and short-story writer. His plays, which often deal with the themes of illusion and reality, and the tragicomic absurdity of life, include *Sei personaggi in cerca d'autore/Six Characters in Search of an Author* 1921, and *Enrico IV/Henry IV* 1922. The themes and innovative techniques of his plays anticipated the work of Brecht, O'Neill, Anouilh, and Genet. Nobel Prize 1934.

piranha any South American freshwater fish of the genus *Serrusalmus*, in the same order as cichlids. They can grow to 60 cm/2 ft long, and have razor-sharp teeth; some species may rapidly devour animals, especially if attracted by blood.

Pisa city in Tuscany, Italy; population (1988) 104,000. It has an 11th–12th-century cathedral. Its famous campanile, the Leaning Tower of Pisa (repaired 1990), is 55 m/180 ft high and about 5 m/16.5 ft out of perpendicular. It has foundations only about 3 m/10 ft deep.

pistil general term for the female part of a flower, either referring to one single ▷carpel or a group of several fused carpels.

piston barrel-shaped device used in reciprocating engines (steam, petrol, diesel oil) to harness power. Pistons are driven up and down in cylinders by expanding steam or hot gases. They pass on their motion via a connecting rod and crank to a crankshaft, which turns the driving wheels. In a pump or compressor, the role of the piston is reversed, being used to move gases and liquids. See also ▷internal-combustion engine.

Pitcairn Islands British colony in Polynesia, 5,300 km/3,300 mi NE of New Zealand; *area* 27 sq km/10 sq mi; *capital* Adamstown; *features* the uninhabited Henderson Islands, an unspoiled coral atoll with a rare ecology, and tiny Ducie and Oeno islands, annexed by Britain 1902; *population* (1990) 52; *language* English.

pitchblende or *uraninite* brownish-black mineral, the major constituent of uranium ore, consisting mainly of uranium oxide (UO_2). It also contains some lead (the final, stable product of uranium decay) and variable amounts of most of the naturally occurring radioactive elements, which are products of either the decay or the fissioning of uranium isotopes. The uranium yield is 50–80%; it is also a source of radium, polonium, and actinium.

Pitchblende was first studied by Pierre and Marie ◊Curie, who found radium and polonium in its residues in 1898.

Pitt William, *the Elder* 1st Earl of Chatham 1708–1778. British Whig politician, 'the Great Commoner'. He served effectively as prime minister in coalition governments 1756–61 and 1766–68.

Pitt William, *the Younger* 1759–1806. British Tory prime minister 1783–1801 and 1804–06. He raised the importance of the House of Commons, carried out fiscal reforms, and effected the union with Ireland. He underestimated the importance of the French Revolution and became embroiled in wars with France from 1793. He died on hearing of Napoleon's victory at Austerlitz.

Pittsburgh industrial city in the NE USA and the nation's largest inland port, where the Allegheny and Monongahela rivers join to form the Ohio River in Pennsylvania; population (1990) 369,900, metropolitan area 2,242,800.

pituitary gland major ◊endocrine gland of vertebrates, situated in the centre of the brain. It is attached to the hypothalamus by a stalk. The pituitary consists of two lobes. The posterior lobe is an extension of the hypothalamus, and is in effect nervous tissue. It stores two hormones synthesized in the hypothalamus: ADH (antidiuretic hormone) and oxytocin. The anterior lobe secretes six hormones, some of which control the activities of other glands (thyroid, gonads, and adrenal cortex); others are direct-acting hormones affecting milk secretion and controlling growth.

pixel (acronym for *picture element*) single dot on a computer screen. All screen images are made up of a collection of pixels, with each pixel being either off (dark) or on (illuminated, possibly in colour). The number of pixels available determines the screen's resolution. Typical resolutions of microcomputer screens vary from 320 × 200 pixels to 640 × 480 pixels, but screens with 1,024 x 768 pixels are now quite common for high-quality graphic (pictorial) displays.

placenta organ that attaches the developing ◊embryo or ◊fetus to the ◊uterus in placental mammals (mammals other than marsupials, platypuses, and echidnas). Composed of maternal and embryonic tissue, it links the blood supply of the embryo to the blood supply of the mother, allowing the exchange of oxygen, nutrients, and waste products. The two blood systems are not in direct contact, but are separated by thin membranes, with materials diffusing across from one system to the other. The placenta also produces hormones that maintain and regulate pregnancy. It is shed as part of the afterbirth.

plague term applied to any epidemic disease with a high mortality rate, but it usually refers to the bubonic plague. This is a disease transmitted by fleas (carried by the black rat) which infect the sufferer with the bacillus *Yersinia pestis*. An early symptom is swelling of lymph nodes, usually in the armpit and groin; such swellings are called 'buboes'. It causes virulent blood poisoning and the death rate is high.

Planck Max 1858–1947. German physicist who framed the quantum theory 1900. His research into the manner in which heated bodies radiate energy led him to report that energy is emitted only in indivisible amounts, called quanta, the magnitudes of which are proportional to the frequency of the radiation. His discovery ran counter to classical physics and is held to have marked the commencement of the modern science. Nobel Prize for Physics 1918.

planet large celestial body in orbit around a star, composed of rock, metal, or gas. There are nine planets in the Solar System: Mercury, Venus, Earth, Mars, Jupiter, Saturn, Neptune, Uranus, and Pluto. The inner four, called the *terrestrial planets*, are small and rocky, and include the planet Earth. The outer planets, with the exception of Pluto, are called the giant planets, large balls of rock, liquid, and gas; the largest is Jupiter, which contains more than twice as much mass as all the other planets combined. Planets do not produce light, but reflect the light of their parent star.

plankton small, often microscopic, forms of plant and animal life that live in the upper layers of fresh and salt water, and are an important source of food for larger animals. Marine plankton is concentrated in areas where rising currents bring mineral salts to the surface.

plant organism that carries out ⊳photosynthesis, has cellulose cell walls and complex cells, and is immobile. A few parasitic plants have lost the ability to photosynthesize but are still considered to be plants. Plants are autotrophs, that is, they make carbohydrates from water and carbon dioxide, and are the primary producers in all food chains, so that all animal life is dependent on them. They play a vital part in the carbon cycle, removing carbon dioxide from the atmosphere and generating oxygen. The study of plants is known as botany.

Plantagenet English royal house, reigning 1154–1399, whose name comes from the nickname of Geoffrey, Count of Anjou (1113–1151), father of Henry II, who often wore in his hat a sprig of broom, *planta genista*. In the 1450s, Richard, Duke of York, took 'Plantagenet' as a surname to emphasize his superior claim to the throne over Henry VI's.

plant classification taxonomy or classification of plants. Originally the plant kingdom included bacteria, diatoms, dinoflagellates, fungi, and slime moulds, but these are not now thought of as plants. The groups that are always classified as plants are the bryophytes (mosses and liverworts), pteridophytes (ferns, horsetails, and club mosses), gymnosperms (conifers, yews, cycads, and ginkgos), and angiosperms (flowering plants). The angiosperms are split into monocotyledons (for example, orchids, grasses, lilies) and dicotyledons (for example, oak, buttercup, geranium, and daisy).

plasma in biology, the liquid component of the ⊳blood.

plasma in physics, an ionized gas produced at extremely high temperatures, as in the Sun and other stars, which contains positive and negative charges in approximately equal numbers. It is a good electrical conductor. In thermonuclear reactions the plasma produced is confined through the use of magnetic fields.

plastic any of the stable synthetic materials that are fluid at some stage in their manufacture, when they can be shaped, and that later set to rigid or semi-rigid solids. Plastics today are chiefly derived from petroleum. Most are polymers, made up of long chains of identical molecules.

plate tectonics theory formulated in the 1960s to explain the phenomena of ◊continental drift and seafloor spreading, and the formation of the major physical features of the Earth's surface. The Earth's outermost layer is regarded as a jigsaw of rigid major and minor plates up to 100 km/62 mi thick, which move relative to each other, probably under the influence of convection currents in the mantle beneath. Major landforms occur at the margins of the plates, where plates are colliding or moving apart – for example, volcanoes, fold mountains, ocean trenches, and ocean ridges.

Plath Sylvia 1932–1963. US poet and novelist. Her powerful, highly personal poems, often expressing a sense of desolation, are distinguished by their intensity and sharp imagery. Her works include her autobiographical novel *The Bell Jar* 1961 and *Collected Poems* 1981.

platinum heavy, soft, silver-white, malleable and ductile, metallic element, symbol Pt, atomic number 78, relative atomic mass 195.09. It is the first of a group of six metallic elements (platinum, osmium, iridium, rhodium, ruthenium, and palladium) that possess similar traits, such as resistance to tarnish, corrosion, and attack by acid, and that often occur as free metals (native metals). They often occur in natural alloys with each other, the commonest of which is osmiridium. Both pure and as an alloy, platinum is used in dentistry, jewellery, and as a catalyst.

Plato *c.* 428–347 BC. Greek philosopher. He was a pupil of Socrates, teacher of Aristotle, and founder of the Academy school of philosophy. He was the author of philosophical dialogues on such topics as metaphysics, ethics, and politics. Central to his teachings is the notion of Forms, which are located outside the everyday world – timeless, motionless, and absolutely real.

platypus monotreme, or egg-laying, mammal *Ornithorhynchus anatinus*, found in Tasmania and E Australia. Semiaquatic, it has small eyes and no external ears, and jaws resembling a duck's beak. It lives in long burrows along river banks, where it lays two eggs in a rough nest. It feeds on water worms and insects, and when full-grown is 60 cm/2 ft long.

plebiscite referendum or direct vote by all the electors of a country or district on a specific question.

Pleistocene first epoch of the Quaternary period of geological time, beginning 1.64 million years ago and ending 10,000 years ago. The polar ice caps were extensive and glaciers were abundant during the ice age of this period, and humans evolved into modern *Homo sapiens sapiens* about 100,000 years ago.

Pliocene fifth and last epoch of the Tertiary period of geological time, 5.2–1.64 million years ago. The earliest hominid, the humanlike ape *Australopithecines*, evolved in Africa.

PLO abbreviation for ◊*Palestine Liberation Organization.*

Plutarch *c.* AD 46–120. Greek biographer and essayist. His *Parallel Lives* comprise paired biographies of famous Greek and Roman soldiers and politicians, followed by comparisons between the two. Thomas North's 1579 translation inspired Shakespeare's Roman plays.

Pluto in astronomy, the smallest and, usually, outermost planet of the Solar System. The existence of Pluto was predicted by calculation by Percival Lowell and the planet was located by Clyde ◊Tombaugh in 1930. It orbits the Sun every 248.5 years at an average distance of 5.8 billion km/3.6 billion mi. Its highly elliptical orbit occasionally takes it within the orbit of Neptune, as in 1979–99. Pluto has a diameter of about 2,300 km/1,400 mi, and a mass about 0.002 of that of Earth. It is of low density, composed of rock and ice, with frozen methane on its surface and a thin atmosphere.

Pluto in Greek mythology, the lord of the underworld (Roman Dis), sometimes known as Hades. He was the brother of Zeus and Poseidon.

plutonium silvery-white, radioactive, metallic element of the ◊actinide series, symbol Pu, atomic number 94, relative atomic mass 239.13. It occurs in nature in minute quantities in ◊pitchblende and other ores, but is produced in quantity only synthetically. It has six allotropic forms (see ◊allotropy) and is one of three fissile elements (elements capable of splitting into other elements – the others are thorium and uranium). The element has awkward physical properties and is the most toxic substance known.

Plymouth city and seaport in Devon, England, at the mouth of the river Plym, with dockyard, barracks, and a naval base at Devonport; population (1981) 243,400. The *Mayflower* ◊Pilgrims sailed from here 1620.

pneumonia inflammation of the lungs, generally due to bacterial or viral infection but also to particulate matter or gases. It is characterized by a build-up of fluid in the alveoli, the clustered air sacs (at the ends of the air passages) where oxygen exchange takes place.

Poe Edgar Allan 1809–1849. US writer and poet. His short stories are renowned for their horrific atmosphere, as in 'The Fall of the House of Usher' 1839 and 'The Masque of the Red Death' 1842, and for their acute reasoning (ratiocination), as in 'The Gold Bug' 1843 and 'The Murders in the Rue Morgue' 1841. His poems include 'The Raven' 1845.

poet laureate poet of the British royal household, so called because of the laurel wreath awarded to eminent poets in the Graeco-Roman world. Early poets with unofficial status were Geoffrey Chaucer, John Skelton, Edmund Spenser, Samuel Daniel, and Ben Jonson. Ted ◊Hughes was appointed poet laureate 1984.

pogrom unprovoked violent attack on an ethnic group, particularly Jews, carried out with official sanction. The Russian pogroms against Jews began 1881, after the assassination of Tsar Alexander II, and again in 1903–06; persecution of the Jews remained constant until the Russian Revolution. Later there were pogroms in E Europe, especially in Poland after 1918, and in Germany under Hitler (see ◊Holocaust).

poikilothermy the condition in which an animal's body temperature is largely dependent on the temperature of the air or water in which it lives. It is characteristic of all animals except birds and mammals, which maintain their body temperatures by homeothermy (they are 'warm-blooded').

poinsettia or *Christmas flower* winterflowering shrub *Euphorbia pulcherrima*, with large red leaves encircling small greenish-yellow flowers. It is native to Mexico and tropical America and is a popular houseplant in North America and Europe.

poison or *toxin* any chemical substance that, when introduced into or applied to the body, is capable of injuring health or destroying life. The liver removes some poisons from the blood. The majority of poisons may be divided into *corrosives*, such as sulphuric, nitric, and hydrochloric acids; *irritants*, including arsenic and copper sulphate; *narcotics* such as opium, and carbon monoxide; and *narcotico-irritants* from any substances of plant origin including carbolic acid and tobacco.

Poitou-Charentes region of W central France, comprising the *départements* of Charente, Charente- Maritime, Deux-Sèvres, and Vienne; *capital* Poitiers; *area* 25,800 sq km/9,959 sq mi; *population* (1986) 1,584,000.

Poland Republic of (*Polska Rzeczpospolita*); *area* 127,886 sq km/49,325 sq mi; *capital* Warsaw; *environment* severe atmospheric pollution and toxic waste from industry have resulted in the designation of 27 ecologically endangered areas. 75% of the country's drinking water does not meet official health standards; *features* last wild European bison (only in protected herds); *head of state* Lech Wałesa from 1990; *political system* emergent democratic republic; *population* (1993) 38,310,000; growth rate 0.6% p.a.; *languages* Polish (official), German; *religion* Roman Catholic 95%.

Polanski Roman 1933– . Polish film director. His films include *Repulsion* 1965, *Cul de Sac* 1966, *Rosemary's Baby* 1968, *Tess* 1979, *Frantic* 1988, and *Bitter Moon* 1992.

Polaris or *Pole Star* or *North Star* the bright star closest to the north celestial pole, and the brightest star in the constellation Ursa Minor. Its position is indicated by the 'pointers' in Ursa Major. Polaris is a yellow ⊳supergiant about 500 light years away.

Polaroid camera instant-picture camera, invented by Edwin Land in the USA 1947. The original camera produced black-and-white prints in about one minute. Modern cameras can produce black-and-white prints in a few seconds, and colour prints in less than a minute. An advanced model has automatic focusing and exposure. It ejects a piece of film on paper immediately after the picture has been taken.

polar reversal changeover in polarity of the Earth's magnetic poles. Studies of the magnetism retained in rocks at the time of their formation have shown that in the past the Earth's north magnetic pole repeatedly became the south magnetic pole, and vice versa.

pole either of the geographic north and south points of the axis about which the Earth rotates. The geographic poles differ from the magnetic poles, which are the points towards which a freely suspended magnetic needle will point.

Pole person of Polish culture from Poland and the surrounding area. The Poles are predominantly Roman Catholic, though there is an Orthodox Church minority. They are known for their distinctive cooking, folk festivals, and folk arts. There are 37–40 million speakers of Polish (including some in the USA), a Slavic language belonging to the Indo-European family.

Pole Star another name for ◊Polaris, the northern pole star. There is no bright star near the southern celestial pole.

polio (*poliomyelitis*) viral infection of the central nervous system affecting nerves that activate muscles. The disease used to be known as infantile paralysis. Two kinds of vaccine are available, one injected (see ◊Salk) and one given by mouth. The World Health Organization expects that polio will be eradicated by 2000.

pollen the grains of ◊seed plants that contain the male gametes. In ◊angiosperms (flowering plants) pollen is produced within anthers; in most ◊gymnosperms (cone-bearing plants) it is produced in male cones. A pollen grain is typically yellow and, when mature, has a hard outer wall. Pollen of insect-pollinated plants (see ◊pollination) is often sticky and spiny and larger than the smooth, light grains produced by wind-pollinated species.

pollination the process by which pollen is transferred from one plant to another. The male ◊gametes are contained in pollen grains, which must be transferred from the anther to the stigma in ◊angiosperms (flowering plants), and from the male cone to the female cone in ◊gymnosperms (cone-bearing plants). Fertilization (not the same as pollination) occurs after the growth of the pollen tube to the ovary. Self-pollination occurs when pollen is transferred to a stigma of the same flower, or to another flower on the same plant; cross-pollination occurs when pollen is transferred to another plant. This involves external pollen-carrying agents, such as wind (anemophily), water (hydrophily), insects, birds (ornithophily), bats, and other small mammals.

Pollock Jackson 1912–1956. US painter. He was a pioneer of Abstract Expressionism and one of the foremost exponents of action painting. His style is characterized by complex networks of swirling, interwoven lines of great delicacy and rhythmic subtlety.

pollution the harmful effect on the environment of by-products of human activity, principally industrial and agricultural processes – for example, noise, smoke, car emissions, chemical and radioactive effluents in air, seas, and rivers, pesticides, radiation, sewage, and household waste. Pollution contributes to the ◊greenhouse effect.

polo stick-and-ball game played between two teams of four on horseback. It is played on the largest field of any game, measuring up to 274 m/300 yd by 182 m/200 yd. A small solid ball is struck with the side of a long-handled mallet through goals at each end of the field. A typical match lasts about an hour, and is divided into 'chukkas' of 7½ minutes each.

Polo Marco 1254–1324. Venetian traveller and writer. He travelled overland to China 1271–75, and served the emperor Kublai Khan until he returned to Europe by sea 1292–95. He was captured while fighting for Venice against Genoa, and, while in prison 1296–98, dictated an account of his travels.

Pol Pot (also known as *Saloth Sar*, *Tol Saut*, and *Pol Porth*) 1925– . Cambodian politician and leader of the Khmer Rouge communist movement that overthrew the government 1975. After widespread atrocities against the civilian population, his regime was deposed by a Vietnamese invasion 1979. Pol Pot continued to help lead the

Khmer Rouge despite officially resigning from all positions in 1989.

polyester synthetic resin formed by the ▷condensation of polyhydric alcohols (alcohols containing more than one hydroxyl group) with dibasic acids (acids containing two replaceable hydrogen atoms). Polyesters are thermosetting ▷plastics, used in making synthetic fibres, such as Dacron and Terylene, and constructional plastics. With glass fibre added as reinforcement, polyesters are used in car bodies and boat hulls.

polyethylene or *polyethene* polymer of the gas ethylene (technically called ethene, C_2H_4). It is a tough, white, translucent, waxy thermoplastic (which means it can be repeatedly softened by heating). It is used for packaging, bottles, toys, wood preservation, electric cable, pipes and tubing.

polymer compound made up of a large long-chain or branching matrix composed of many repeated simple units (*monomers*). There are many polymers, both natural (cellulose, chitin, lignin) and synthetic (polyethylene and nylon, types of plastic). Synthetic polymers belong to two groups: thermosoftening and thermosetting (see ▷plastic).

Polynesia islands of Oceania E of 170° E latitude, including Hawaii, Kiribati, Tuvalu, Fiji, Tonga, Tokelau, Samoa, Cook Islands, and French Polynesia.

polysaccharide long-chain ▷carbohydrate made up of hundreds or thousands of linked simple sugars (monosaccharides) such as glucose and closely related molecules.

polyunsaturate type of ▷fat or oil containing a high proportion of triglyceride molecules whose ▷fatty acid chains contain several double bonds. By contrast, the fatty-acid chains of the triglycerides in saturated fats (such as lard) contain only single bonds. Medical evidence suggests that polyunsaturated fats, used widely in margarines and cooking fats, are less likely to contribute to cardiovascular disease than saturated fats, but there is also some evidence that they may have adverse effects on health.

Pompeii ancient city in Italy, near the volcano ▷Vesuvius, 21 km/13 mi SE of Naples. In AD 63 an earthquake destroyed much of the city, which had been a Roman port and pleasure resort; it was completely buried beneath volcanic ash when Vesuvius erupted AD 79. Over 2,000 people were killed. Pompeii was rediscovered 1748 and the systematic excavation begun 1763 still continues.

Pompidou Georges 1911–1974. French conservative politician, president 1969–74. He negotiated a settlement with the Algerians 1961 and, as prime minister 1962–68, with the students in the revolt of May 1968.

Pondicherry union territory of SE India; area 480 sq km/185 sq mi; population (1991) 789,400. Founded by the French 1674, Pondicherry was transferred to the government of India 1954, together with Karaikal, Yanam, and Mahé, becoming the Union Territory of Pondicherry 1962. Its capital is Pondicherry. Languages spoken include French, English, Tamil, Telegu, and Malayalam.

Pop art movement of British and American artists in the mid-1950s and 1960s, reacting against the elitism of abstract art. Pop art imagery was drawn from advertising, comic strips, film, and television. Early exponents included Richard Hamilton in the UK, and Jasper Johns, Andy Warhol, and Roy Lichtenstein in the USA. In its eclecticism and its sense of irony and playfulness, Pop art helped to prepare the way for the Post-Modernism of the 1970s and 1980s.

Pope Alexander 1688–1744. English poet and satirist. He established his reputation with the precocious *Pastorals* 1709 and *Essay on Criticism* 1711, which were followed by a parody of the heroic epic *The Rape of the Lock* 1712–14 and 'Eloisa to Abelard' 1717. Other works include a highly Neo-Classical translation of Homer's *Iliad* and *Odyssey* 1715–26.

porcelain (hardpaste) translucent ceramic material with a shining finish, see ◊pottery and porcelain.

Port-au-Prince capital and industrial port of Haiti; population (1982) 763,000.

Porter Cole (Albert) 1892–1964. US composer and lyricist. He wrote mainly musical comedies. His witty, sophisticated songs like 'Let's Do It' 1928, 'I Get a Kick Out of You' 1934, and 'Don't Fence Me In' 1944 have been widely recorded and admired. His shows, many of which were made into films, include *The Gay Divorce* 1932 (filmed 1934 as *The Gay Divorcee*), and *Kiss Me Kate* 1948.

Port Moresby capital and port of Papua New Guinea on the S coast of New Guinea; population (1987) 152,000.

Pôrto Alegre port and capital of Rio Grande dɔ Sul state, S Brazil; population (1991) 1,254,600. It is a freshwater port for ocean-going vessels and is Brazil's major commercial centre.

Port-of-Spain port and capital of Trinidad and Tobago, on the island of Trinidad; population (1988) 58,000. It has a cathedral (1813–28) and the San Andres Fort (1785).

Porto Novo capital of Benin, W Africa; population (1982) 208,258. It was a former Portuguese centre for the slave and tobacco trade with Brazil and became a French protectorate 1863.

Portugal Republic of (*República Portuguesa*); *area* 92,000 sq km/35,521 sq mi (including the Azores and Madeira); *capital* Lisbon; *features* rivers Minho, Douro, Tagus (Tejo), Guadiana; Serra da Estrêla mountains; *political system* democratic republic; *population* (1993 est) 10,450,000; growth rate 0.5% p.a.; *language* Portuguese; *religion* Roman Catholic 97%.

Portuguese inhabitant of Portugal. The Portuguese have a mixed cultural heritage that can be traced back to the Lusitanian Celts who were defeated by the Romans about 140 BC. They are predominantly Roman Catholic. The *Portuguese language* is a member of the Romance branch of the Indo-European language family; spoken by 120–135 million people worldwide, it is the national language of Portugal, closely related to Spanish and strongly influenced by Arabic.

Poseidon in Greek mythology, the chief god of the sea (Roman Neptune), brother of Zeus and Pluto. The brothers dethroned their father, Kronos, and divided his realm, Poseidon taking the sea;

he was also worshipped as god of earth-quakes. His sons were the merman sea god Triton and the Cyclops Poly-phemus.

positron in physics, the antiparticle of the electron; an ▷elementary particle having the same magnitude of mass and charge as an electron but exhibiting a positive charge. The positron was disco-vered in 1932 by US physicist Carl Anderson at Caltech, USA, its existence having been predicted by the British physicist Paul Dirac 1928.

Post-Impressionism movement in painting that followed ▷Impressionism in the 1880s and 1890s, incorporating various styles. The term was first used by the English critic Roger Fry 1910 to describe the works of Cézanne, van Gogh, and Gauguin. Though differing greatly in style and aims, these painters sought to go beyond Impressionism's concern with the ever-changing effects of light.

potassium soft, waxlike, silver-white, metallic element, symbol K (Latin *kalium*), atomic number 19, relative atomic mass 39.0983. It is one of the ▷alkali metals and has a very low density – it floats on water, and is the second lightest metal (after lithium). It oxidizes rapidly when exposed to air and reacts violently with water. Of great abundance in the Earth's crust, it is widely distrib-uted with other elements and found in salt and mineral deposits in the form of potassium aluminium silicates.

potato perennial plant *Solanum tub-erosum*, family Solanaceae, with edible tuberous roots that are rich in starch. Used by the Andean Indians for at least 2,000 years before the Spanish Con-quest, the potato was introduced to Europe by the mid-16th century, and reputedly to England by the explorer Walter Raleigh.

potential difference (pd) measure of the electrical potential energy converted to another form for every unit charge moving between two points in an elec-tric circuit (see ▷potential, electric). The unit of potential difference is the volt.

potential, electric in physics, the rela-tive electrical state of an object. A charged conductor, for example, has a higher potential than the Earth, whose potential is taken by convention to be zero. An electric ▷cell (battery) has a potential in relation to emf (▷electromo-tive force), which can make current flow in an external circuit. The difference in potential between two points – the ▷potential difference – is expressed in ▷volts; that is, a 12 V battery has a potential difference of 12 volts between its negative and positive terminals.

potential energy ▷energy possessed by an object by virtue of its relative position or state (for example, as in a compressed spring). It is contrasted with kinetic energy, the form of energy pos-sessed by moving bodies.

potentiometer in physics, an electrical resistor that can be divided so as to compare, measure, or control voltages. In radio circuits, any rotary variable resistance (such as volume control) is referred to as a potentiometer.

pottery and porcelain ▷ceramics in domestic and ornamental use including: *earthenware*, unglazed (porous) or glazed; *stoneware* made of non-porous clay with a high silica content, fired at high temperature, which is very hard; *bone china* (softpaste) semi-porcelain made of 5% bone ash and china clay; *porcelain* (hardpaste) characterized by its hardness, ringing sound when struck, translucence, and shining finish. Made of kaolin and petuntse (fusible ⊳feldspar consisting chiefly of silicates reduced to a fine, white powder, porcelain is high-fired at 1,400°C/2,552°F.

poultry domestic birds such as chickens, turkeys, ducks, and geese. They were domesticated for meat and eggs by early farmers in China, Europe, Egypt, and the Americas. Chickens were domesticated from the SE Asian jungle fowl *Gallus gallus* and then raised in the East as well as the West. Turkeys are New World birds, domesticated in ancient Mexico. Geese and ducks were domesticated in Egypt, China, and Europe.

Pound Ezra 1885–1972. US poet and cultural critic. He is regarded as one of the most important figures of 20th-century literature, and his work revolutionized modern poetry. His *Personae* and *Exultations* 1909 established and promoted the principles of Imagism, and influenced numerous poets, including T S ⊳Eliot.

Poussin Nicolas 1594–1665. French painter. Active chiefly in Rome, he was also court painter to Louis XIII 1640–43. He was the foremost exponent of 17th-century Baroque Classicism. He painted mythological and literary scenes in a strongly Classical style; for example, *Et in Arcadia Ego* 1638–39 (Louvre, Paris).

power in mathematics, that which is represented by an exponent or index, denoted by a superior small numeral. A number or symbol raised to the power of 2 – that is, multiplied by itself – is said to be squared (for example, 3^2, x^2), and when raised to the power of 3,

it is said to be cubed (for example, 2^3, y^3).

power in physics, the rate of doing work or consuming energy. It is measured in watts (joules per second) or other units of work per unit time.

Powys county of central Wales, created 1974; *area* 5,080 sq km/1,961 sq mi; *towns* Llandrindod Wells (administrative headquarters); *features* Brecon Beacons National Park; Black Mountains; rivers: Wye and Severn; Lake Vyrnwy, artificial reservoir supplying Liverpool and Birmingham; *population* (1991) 117,500; *languages* English, 20% Welsh-speaking.

Prague (Czech *Praha*) city and capital of the Czech Republic on the river Vltava; population (1991) 1,212,000. It was the capital of Czechoslovakia 1918–93.

Praia port and capital of the Republic of Cape Verde, on the island of São Tiago (Santiago); population (1980) 37,500. Industries include fishing and shipping.

Precambrian in geology, the time from the formation of Earth (4.6 billion years ago) up to 570 million years ago. Its boundary with the succeeding Cambrian period marks the time when animals first developed hard outer parts (exoskeletons) and so left abundant fossil remains. It comprises about 85% of geological time and is divided into two periods: the Archaean, in which no life existed, and the Proterozoic, in which there was life in some form.

precession slow wobble of the Earth on its axis, like that of a spinning top. The gravitational pulls of the Sun and Moon on the Earth's equatorial bulge cause the Earth's axis to trace out a circle on the sky every 25,800 years. The position of the celestial poles is constantly changing owing to precession, as are the positions of the equinoxes (the points at which the celestial equator intersects the Sun's path around the sky). The *precession of the equinoxes* means that there is a gradual westward drift in the ecliptic – the path that the Sun appears to follow – and in the coordinates of objects on the celestial sphere.

precipitation in chemistry, the formation of an insoluble solid in a liquid as a result of a reaction within the liquid between two or more soluble substances. If the solid settles, it forms a *precipitate*; if the particles of solid are very small, they will remain in suspension, forming a *colloidal precipitate* (see ▷colloid).

predestination in Christian theology, the doctrine asserting that God has determined all events beforehand, including the ultimate salvation or damnation of the individual human soul. Today Christianity in general accepts that humanity has free will, though some forms, such as Calvinism, believe that salvation can only be attained by the gift of God. The concept of predestination is also found in Islam.

pregnancy in humans, the period during which an embryo grows within the womb. It begins at conception and ends at birth, and the normal length is 40 weeks. Menstruation usually stops on conception. About one in five pregnancies fails, but most of these failures occur very early on, so the woman may notice only that her period is late. After the second month, the breasts become tense and tender, and the areas round the nipples become darker. Enlargement of the uterus can be felt at about the end of the third month, and thereafter the abdomen enlarges progressively. Pregnancy in animals is called ▷gestation.

prehistory human cultures before the use of writing. A classification system, the Three Age system, was devised 1816 by Danish archaeologist Christian Thomsen, based on the predominant materials used by early humans for tools and weapons: ▷Stone Age, ▷Bronze Age, ▷Iron Age.

premenstrual tension (PMT) or *premenstrual syndrome* medical condition caused by hormone changes and comprising a number of physical and emotional features that occur cyclically before menstruation and disappear with its onset. Symptoms include mood changes, breast tenderness, a feeling of bloatedness, and headache.

Pre-Raphaelite Brotherhood (PRB) group of British painters 1848–53; Dante Gabriel Rossetti, John Everett Millais, and Holman Hunt were founding members. They aimed to paint serious subjects, to study nature closely, and to shun the influence of the styles of painters after Raphael. Their subjects were mainly biblical and literary, painted with obsessive naturalism and attention to detail.

Presbyterianism system of Christian Protestant church government, expounded during the Reformation by John Calvin, which gives its name to the established Church of Scotland, and is also practised in England, Wales, Ireland, Switzerland, North America, and elsewhere. There is no compulsory form of worship and each congregation is governed by presbyters or elders (clerical or lay), who are of equal rank.

Presley Elvis (Aron) 1935–1977. US singer and guitarist. He was the most influential performer of the rock- and-roll era. With his recordings for Sun Records in Memphis, Tennessee, 1954–55 and early hits such as 'Heartbreak Hotel', 'Hound Dog', and 'Love Me Tender', all 1956, he created an individual vocal style, influenced by Southern blues, gospel music, country music, and rhythm and blues.

pressure in physics, the force acting normally (at right angles) to a body per unit surface area. The SI unit of pressure is the pascal (newton per square metre), equal to 0.01 millibars. In a fluid (liquid or gas), pressure increases with depth. At the edge of Earth's atmosphere, pressure is zero, whereas at sea level atmospheric pressure due to the weight of the air above is about 100 kilopascals (1,013 millibars or 1 atmosphere). Pressure is commonly measured by means of a ⊳barometer, manometer, or Bourdon gauge.

Pretoria administrative capital of the Union of South Africa from 1910 and capital of Transvaal province from 1860; population (1985) 741,300. Founded 1855, it was named after Boer leader Andries Pretorius (1799–1853).

Previn André (George) 1929– . German-born US conductor and composer. He was principal conductor of the London Symphony Orchestra 1968–79, music director of Britain's Royal Philharmonic Orchestra 1985, and its principal director 1985–91. He was also principal conductor of the Los Angeles Philharmonic 1986–89 and is now a guest conductor of many orchestras in Europe and the USA. His compositions concertos for piano 1971 and guitar 1984.

Priestley J(ohn) B(oynton) 1894–1984. English novelist and playwright.

His first success was a novel about travelling theatre, *The Good Companions* 1929. He followed it with a realist novel about London life, *Angel Pavement* 1930. As a playwright he was often preoccupied with theories of time, as in *An Inspector Calls* 1945.

primate in zoology, any member of the order of mammals that includes monkeys, apes, and humans (together called *anthropoids*), as well as lemurs, bushbabies, lorises, and tarsiers (together called *prosimians*). Generally, they have forward-directed eyes, gripping hands and feet, opposable thumbs, and big toes. They tend to have nails rather than claws, with gripping pads on the ends of the digits, all adaptations to the arboreal, climbing mode of life.

prime number number that can be divided only by 1 or itself, that is, having no other factors. There is an infinite number of primes, the first ten of which are 2, 3, 5, 7, 11, 13, 17, 19, 23, and 29 (by definition, the number 1 is excluded from the set of prime numbers). The number 2 is the only even prime because all other even numbers have 2 as a factor.

Prince Edward Island province of E Canada; *area* 5,700 sq km/2,200 sq mi; *capital* Charlottetown; *features* Prince Edward Island National Park; Summerside Lobster Carnival; *population* (1991) 129,900.

printer in computing, an output device for producing printed copies of text or graphics. Types include the *daisywheel printer*, which produces good-quality text but no graphics; the *dot matrix printer*, which produces text and graphics by printing a pattern of small dots; the *ink- jet printer*, which creates text and graphics by spraying a fine jet of quick-drying ink onto the paper; and the *laser printer*, which uses electrostatic technology very similar to that used by a photocopier to produce high-quality text and graphics.

printing reproduction of text or illustrative material on paper, as in books or newspapers, or on an increasing variety of materials; for example, on plastic containers. The first printing used woodblocks, followed by carved wood type or moulded metal type and hand-operated presses. Modern printing is effected by electronically controlled machinery. Current printing processes include electronic phototypesetting with offset printing, and gravure print.

prism in optics, a triangular block of transparent material (plastic, glass, silica) commonly used to 'bend' a ray of light or split a beam into its spectral colours. Prisms are used as mirrors to define the optical path in binoculars, camera viewfinders, and periscopes. The dispersive property of prisms is used in the spectroscope.

Privy Council council composed originally of the chief royal officials of the Norman kings in Britain; under the Tudors and early Stuarts it became the chief governing body. It was replaced from 1688 by the ◊cabinet, originally a committee of the council, and the council itself now retains only formal powers in issuing royal proclamations and orders in council. Cabinet ministers are automatically members, and it is presided over by the Lord President of the Council.

processor in computing, another name for the ◊central processing unit or ◊microprocessor of a computer.

procurator fiscal officer of a Scottish sheriff's court who (combining the role of public prosecutor and coroner) inquires into suspicious deaths and carries out the preliminary questioning of witnesses to crime.

productivity in economics, the output produced by a given quantity of labour, usually measured as output per person employed in the firm, industry, sector, or economy concerned. Productivity is determined by the quality and quantity of the fixed capital used by labour, and the effort of the workers concerned.

progesterone ◊steroid hormone that occurs in vertebrates. In mammals, it regulates the menstrual cycle and pregnancy. Progesterone is secreted by the corpus luteum (the ruptured Graafian follicle of a discharged ovum).

program in computing, a set of instructions that controls the operation of a computer. There are two main kinds: applications programs, which carry out tasks for the benefit of the user – for example, word processing; and systems programs, which control the internal workings of the computer. A utility program is a systems program that carries out specific tasks for the user. Programs can be written in any of a number of ◊programming languages but are always translated into machine code before they can be executed by the computer.

programming language in computing, a special notation in which instructions for controlling a computer are written. Programming languages are designed to be easy for people to write and read, but must be capable of being mechanically translated (by a compiler or an interpreter) into the machine code that the computer can execute. Programming languages may be classified as high-level languages or low-level languages.

Prohibition in US history, the period 1920–33 when alcohol was illegal, representing the culmination of a long campaign by church and women's organizations, temperance societies, and the Anti-Saloon League. This led to bootlegging (the illegal distribution of liquor, often illicitly distilled), to the financial advantage of organized crime, and public opinion insisted on repeal 1933.

prokaryote in biology, an organism whose cells lack organelles (specialized segregated structures such as nuclei, mitochondria, and chloroplasts). Prokaryote DNA is not arranged in chromosomes but forms a coiled structure called a *nucleoid*. The prokaryotes comprise only the *bacteria* and *cyanobacteria* (see ◊blue- green algae); all other organisms are eukaryotes.

Prokofiev Sergey (Sergeyevich) 1891–1953. Soviet composer. His music includes operas such as *The Love for Three Oranges* 1921; ballets for Sergei Diaghilev, including *Romeo and Juliet* 1935; seven symphonies including the *Classical Symphony* 1916–17; music for film, including Eisenstein's *Alexander Nevsky* 1938; piano and violin concertos; songs and cantatas and *Peter and the Wolf* 1936 for children, to his own libretto after a Russian folk tale.

PROM (acronym for *programmable read-only memory*) in computing, a memory device in the form of an integrated circuit (chip) that can be programmed after manufacture to hold information permanently. PROM chips are empty of information when manufactured, unlike ROM (read-only memory) chips, which have information built into them. Other memory devices are EPROM (erasable programmable read-only memory) and ◊RAM (random-access memory).

Prometheus in Greek mythology, a ◊Titan who stole fire from heaven for the human race. In revenge, Zeus had him chained to a rock where an eagle came each day to feast on his liver, which grew back each night, until he was rescued by the hero ◊Heracles.

propane C_3H_8 gaseous hydrocarbon of the ◊alkane series, found in petroleum and used as fuel.

Prost Alain 1955– . French motor-racing driver who was world champion 1985, 1986, 1989, and 1993, and the first French world drivers' champion. To the end of the 1993 season he had won 51 Grand Prix from 199 starts. He retired 1993.

prostaglandin any of a group of complex fatty acids present in the body that act as messenger substances between cells. Effects include stimulating the contraction of smooth muscle (for example, of the womb during birth), regulating the production of stomach acid, and modifying hormonal activity. In excess, prostaglandins may produce inflammatory disorders such as arthritis. Synthetic prostaglandins are used to induce labour in humans and domestic animals.

prostate gland gland surrounding and opening into the urethra at the base of the ◊bladder in male mammals.

prosthesis artificial device used to substitute for a body part which is defective or missing. Prostheses include artificial limbs, hearing aids, false teeth and eyes, heart ◊pacemakers and plastic heart valves and blood vessels.

protein complex, biologically important substance composed of amino acids joined by ▷peptide bonds. Proteins are essential to all living organisms. As *enzymes* they regulate all aspects of metabolism. Structural proteins such as *keratin* and *collagen* make up the skin, claws, bones, tendons, and ligaments; *muscle* proteins produce movement; *haemoglobin* transports oxygen; and *membrane* proteins regulate the movement of substances into and out of cells. For humans, protein is an essential part of the diet, and is found in greatest quantity in soya beans and other grain legumes, meat, eggs, and cheese.

Proterozoic eon of geological time, possible 3.5 billion to 570 million years ago, the second division of the Precambrian. It is defined as the time of simple life, since many rocks dating from this eon show traces of biological activity, and some contain the fossils of bacteria and algae.

Protestantism one of the main divisions of Christianity, which emerged from Roman Catholicism at the ▷Reformation. The chief denominations are the Anglican Communion (Episcopalian in the USA), Baptists, Lutherans, Methodists, Pentecostals, and Presbyterians, with a total membership of about 300 million.

protist in biology, a single-celled organism which has a eukaryotic cell, but which is not member of the plant, fungal, or animal kingdoms. The main protists are ▷protozoa.

proton in physics, a positively charged subatomic particle, a constituent of the nucleus of all atoms. It belongs to the ▷baryon subclass of the ▷hadrons. A proton is extremely long-lived, with a lifespan of at least 10^{32} years. It carries a unit positive charge equal to the negative charge of an ▷electron. Its mass is almost 1,836 times that of an electron, or 1.67×10^{-24} g. Protons are composed of two up ▷quarks and one down quark held together by ▷gluons. The number of protons in the atom of an element is equal to the atomic number of that element.

protoplasm contents of a living cell. Strictly speaking it includes all the discrete structures (organelles) in a cell, but it is often used simply to mean the jellylike material in which these float. The contents of a cell outside the nucleus are called ▷cytoplasm.

protozoa group of single-celled organisms without rigid cell walls. Some, such as amoeba, ingest other cells, but most are saprotrophs or parasites. The group is polyphyletic (containing organisms which have different evolutionary origins).

Proust Marcel 1871–1922. French novelist and critic. His immense autobiographical work *A la Recherche du temps perdu/Remembrance of Things Past* 1913–27, consisting of a series of novels, is the expression of his childhood memories coaxed from his subconscious; it is also a precise reflection of life in France at the end of the 19th century.

Prussia N German state 1618–1945 on the Baltic coast. It was an independent kingdom until 1867, when it became, under Otto von ▷Bismarck, the military power of the North German Confederation and part of the German Empire 1871 under the Prussian king Wilhelm I. West Prussia became part of Poland under the Treaty of ▷Versailles, and East

Prussia was largely incorporated into the USSR after 1945.

psoriasis chronic, recurring skin disease characterized by raised, red, scaly patches, on the scalp, elbows, knees, and elsewhere. Tar preparations, steroid creams, and ultraviolet light are used to treat it, and sometimes it disappears spontaneously. Psoriasis may be accompanied by a form of arthritis (inflammation of the joints).

psychiatry branch of medicine dealing with the diagnosis and treatment of mental disorder, normally divided into the areas of *neurotic conditions*, including anxiety, depression, and hysteria and *psychotic disorders* such as schizophrenia. Psychiatric treatment consists of drugs, analysis, or electroconvulsive therapy.

psychoanalysis theory and treatment method for neuroses, developed by Sigmund ▷Freud. The main treatment method involves the free association of ideas, and their interpretation by patient and analyst. It is typically prolonged.

psychology systematic study of human and animal behaviour. The subject includes diverse areas of study and application, among them the roles of instinct, heredity, environment, and culture; the processes of sensation, perception, learning, and memory; the bases of motivation and emotion; and the functioning of thought, intelligence, and language. Significant psychologists have included Gustav Fechner, founder of psychophysics; Wolfgang Köhler, one of the ▷gestalt or 'whole' psychologists; Sigmund Freud and his associates Carl Jung, Alfred Adler, and Hermann Rorschach; William James, Jean Piaget; Carl Rogers; Hans Eysenck; J B Watson; and B F Skinner.

psychosis or *psychotic disorder* general term for a serious mental disorder where the individual commonly loses contact with reality and may experience hallucinations (seeing or hearing things that do not exist) or delusions (fixed false beliefs). For example, in a paranoid psychosis, an individual may believe that others are plotting against him or her. A major type of psychosis is ▷schizophrenia.

psychotherapy psychological treatment for mental disorder, rather than physical treatments, such as electroconvulsive therapy (ECT) or drugs. Examples include cognitive therapy and psychoanalysis.

pteridophyte simple type of vascular plant. The pteridophytes comprise four classes: the Psilosida, including the most primitive vascular plants, found mainly in the tropics; the Lycopsida, including the club mosses; the Sphenopsida, including the horsetails; and the Pteropsida, including the ferns. They do not produce seeds.

Ptolemy (Claudius Ptolemaeus) *c.* 100–AD 170. Egyptian astronomer and geographer who worked in Alexandria. His *Almagest* developed the theory that Earth is the centre of the universe, with the Sun, Moon, and stars revolving around it. In 1543 the Polish astronomer ▷Copernicus proposed an alternative to the *Ptolemaic system*. Ptolemy's *Geography* was a standard source of information until the 16th century.

puberty stage in human development when the individual becomes sexually mature. It may occur from the age of ten upwards. The sexual organs take on their adult form and pubic hair grows. In girls, menstruation begins, and the breasts develop; in boys, the voice breaks and becomes deeper, and facial hair develops.

public sector part of the economy that is owned and controlled by the state, namely central government, local government, and government enterprises. In a command economy, the public sector allocates most of the resources in the economy. The opposite of the public sector is the private sector, where resources are allocated by private individuals and business organizations.

Puccini Giacomo (Antonio Domenico Michele Secondo Maria) 1858–1924. Italian opera composer. His music shows a strong gift for melody and dramatic effect and his operas combine exotic plots with elements of *verismo* (realism). They include *Manon Lescaut* 1893, *La Bohème* 1896, *Tosca* 1900, *Madame Butterfly* 1904, and the unfinished *Turandot* 1926.

Puerto Rico the Commonwealth of; easternmost island of the Greater Antilles, situated between the US Virgin Islands and the Dominican Republic; *area* 9,000 sq km/3,475 sq mi; *capital* San Juan; *features* volcanic mountains run E–W; the islands of Vieques and Culebra belong to Puerto Rico; *population* (1990) 3,522,000; *languages* Spanish and English (official); *religion* Roman Catholic.

Pugin Augustus Welby Northmore 1812–1852. English architect. He collaborated with Charles ◊Barry in the detailed design of the Houses of Parliament. He did much to instigate the Gothic Revival in England, largely through his book *Contrasts* 1836.

P'u-i (or *Pu-Yi*) Henry 1906–1967. Last emperor of China (as Hsuan Tung) from 1908 until his deposition 1912; he was restored for a week 1917. After his deposition he chose to be called Henry. He was president 1932– 34 and emperor 1934–45 of the Japanese puppet state of Manchukuo.

pulley simple machine consisting of a fixed, grooved wheel, sometimes in a block, around which a rope or chain can be run. A simple pulley serves only to change the direction of the applied effort (as in a simple hoist for raising loads). The use of more than one pulley results in a mechanical advantage, so that a given effort can raise a heavier load.

pulsar celestial source that emits pulses of energy at regular intervals, ranging from a few seconds to a few thousandths of a second. Pulsars are thought to be rapidly rotating neutron stars, which flash at radio and other wavelengths as they spin. They were discovered in 1967 by Jocelyn ◊Bell (now Burnell) and Antony Hewish at the Mullard Radio Astronomy Observatory, Cambridge, England. Over 500 radio pulsars are now known in our Galaxy, although a million or so may exist.

pulse crop such as peas and beans. Pulses are grown primarily for their seeds, which provide a concentrated source of vegetable protein, and make a vital contribution to human diets in poor countries where meat is scarce, and among vegetarians. Soya beans are the major temperate protein crop in the West; most are used for oil production or for animal feed. In Asia, most are processed into soya milk and beancurd. Peanuts dominate pulse production in the tropical world and are generally consumed as human food.

pulse impulse transmitted by the heartbeat throughout the arterial systems of vertebrates. When the heart muscle contracts, it forces blood into the aorta (the chief artery). Because the arteries are elastic, the sudden rise of pressure causes a throb or sudden swelling through them. The actual flow of the blood is about 60 cm/2 ft a second in humans. The average adult pulse rate is generally about 70 per minute. The pulse can be felt where an artery is near the surface, for example in the wrist or the neck.

Punic Wars three wars between ⟩Rome and ⟩Carthage: *First Punic War* 264–241 BC, resulted in the defeat of the Carthaginians; *Second Punic War* 218–201 BC, Hannibal invaded Italy and defeated the Romans but was finally defeated himself by Scipio Africanus Major; *Third Punic War* 149–146 BC, ended in the destruction of Carthage, and its possessions becoming the Roman province of Africa.

Punjab state of NW India; *area* 50,400 sq km/19,454 sq mi; *capital* Chandigarh; *features* Harappa has ruins from the ⟩Indus Valley civilization 2500 to 1600 BC; *population* (1991) 20,190,800; *language* Punjabi; *religion* 60% Sikh, 30% Hindu; there is friction between the two groups.

Punjab state of NE Pakistan; *area* 205,344 sq km/79,263 sq mi; *capital* Lahore; *features* wheat cultivation (by irrigation); *population* (1981) 47,292,000; *languages* Punjabi, Urdu; *religion* Muslim..

Punjabi majority ethnic group living in the Punjab, divided between India and Pakistan. Approximately 37 million live in the Pakistan half of Punjab with another 14 million on the Indian side of the border. In addition to Sikhs, there are Rajputs in Punjab, some of whom have adopted Islam. The *Punjabi language* belongs to the Indo-Iranian branch of the Indo-European family.

pupa nonfeeding, largely immobile stage of some insect life cycles, in which larval tissues are broken down, and adult tissues and structures are formed.

Purcell Henry 1659–1695. English Baroque composer. His music balances high formality with melodic expression of controlled intensity, for example, the opera *Dido and Aeneas* 1689 and music for Dryden's *King Arthur* 1691 and for *The Fairy Queen* 1692. He wrote more than 500 works, ranging from secular operas and incidental music for plays to cantatas and church music.

Purim Jewish festival celebrated in Feb or March (the 14th of Adar in the Jewish calendar), commemorating Esther, who saved the Jews from destruction in 473 BC during the Persian occupation.

Puritan from 1564, a member of the Church of England who wished to eliminate Roman Catholic survivals in church ritual, or substitute a presbyterian for an episcopal form of church government. The term also covers the separatists who withdrew from the church altogether. The Puritans were identified with the parliamentary opposition under James I and Charles I, and after the Restoration were driven from the church, and more usually known as Dissenters or ⟩Nonconformists.

Pushkin Aleksandr 1799–1837. Russian poet and writer. His works include the novel in verse *Eugene Onegin* 1823–31 and the tragic drama *Boris Godunov* 1825. Pushkin's range was wide, and his willingness to experiment freed later Russian writers from many of the archaic conventions of the literature of his time.

Pygmy (sometimes *Negrillo*) member of any of several groups of small-statured, dark- skinned peoples of the rain forests of equatorial Africa. They were probably the aboriginal inhabitants of the region, before the arrival of farming peoples from elsewhere. They live nomadically in small groups, as hunter-gatherers; they also trade with other, settled people in the area.

pyramid four-sided building with triangular sides. Pyramids were used in ancient Egypt to enclose a royal tomb; for example, the Great Pyramid of Khufu/Cheops at El Gîza, near Cairo, 230 m/755 ft square and 147 m/481 ft high. The three pyramids at Gîza were considered one of the ▷Seven Wonders of the World. In Babylon and Assyria, broadly stepped pyramids (▷ziggurats) were used as the base for a shrine to a god: the Tower of Babel was probably one of these.

Pyrenees (French *Pyrénées*; Spanish *Pirineos*) mountain range in SW Europe between France and Spain; length about 435 km/270 mi; highest peak Aneto (French Néthon) 3,404 m/11,172 ft. ▷Andorra is entirely within the range.

Hydroelectric power has encouraged industrial development in the foothills.

pyrethrum popular name for some flowers of the genus *Chrysanthemum*, family Compositae. The ornamental species *C. coccineum*, and hybrids derived from it, are commonly grown in gardens. Pyrethrum powder, made from the dried flower heads of some species, is a powerful contact pesticide for aphids and mosquitoes.

Pythagoras' theorem in geometry, a theorem stating that in a right-angled triangle, the area of the square on the hypotenuse (the longest side) is equal to the sum of the areas of the squares drawn on the other two sides. If the hypotenuse is h units long and the lengths of the other sides are a and b, then $h^2 = a^2 + b^2$. The theorem was formulated by Greek mathematician and philosopher *Pythagoras* (*c.* 580–500 BC).

python any constricting snake of the Old World subfamily Pythoninae of the family Boidae, which also includes boas and the anaconda. Pythons are found in the tropics of Africa, Asia, and Australia. Unlike boas, they lay eggs rather than produce living young. Some species are small, but the reticulated python *Python reticulatus* of SE Asia can grow to 10 m/33 ft.

Q

qat shrub *Catha edulis* of the staff-tree family Celastraceae. The leaves are chewed as a mild narcotic in some Arab countries. Its use was banned in Somalia 1983.

Qatar State of (*Dawlat Qatar*); *area* 11,400 sq km/4,402 sq mi; *capital* and chief port Doha; *features* negligible rain and surface water; only 3% is fertile, but irrigation allows self-sufficiency in fruit and vegetables; extensive oil discoveries since World War II; *political system* absolute monarchy; *population* (1993 est) 510,000 (half in Doha; Arab 40%, Indian 18%, Pakistani 18%); growth rate 3.7% p.a.; *languages* Arabic (official), English; *religion* Sunni Muslim 95%.

quail any of several genera of small ground-dwelling birds of the family Phasianidae, which also includes grouse, pheasants, bobwhites, and prairie chickens.

Quaker popular name, originally derogatory, for a member of the Society of ▷Friends.

quantum theory or *quantum mechanics* in physics, the theory that ▷energy does not have a continuous range of values, but is, instead, absorbed or radiated discontinuously, in multiples of definite, indivisible units called quanta. Just as earlier theory showed how light, generally seen as a wave motion, could also in some ways be seen as composed of discrete particles (▷photons), quantum theory shows how atomic particles such as electrons may also be seen as having wavelike properties. Quantum theory is the basis of particle physics, modern theoretical chemistry, and the solid-state physics that describes the behaviour of the silicon chips used in computers.

quark in physics, the ▷elementary particle that is the fundamental constituent of all ▷hadrons (baryons, such as neutrons and protons, and mesons). There are six types, or 'flavours': up, down, top, bottom, strange, and charmed, each of which has three varieties, or 'colours': red, yellow, and blue (visual colour is not meant, although the analogy is useful in many ways). To each quark there is an antiparticle, called an antiquark.

quartz crystalline form of ▷silica SiO_2, one of the most abundant minerals of the Earth's crust (12% by volume). Quartz occurs in many different kinds of rock, including sandstone and granite. It ranks 7 on the Mohs' scale of hardness and is resistant to chemical or mechanical breakdown. Quartzes vary according to the size and purity of their crystals. Crystals of pure quartz are coarse, colourless, and transparent, and this form is usually called rock crystal. Impure coloured varieties, often used as gemstones, include agate, citrine quartz, and ◊amethyst. Quartz is used in ornamental work and industry, where its reaction to electricity makes it valuable in electronic instruments. Quartz can also be made synthetically.

quasar (from *quasi*-stel*lar* object or QSO) one of the most distant extragalactic objects known, discovered 1963. Quasars appear starlike, but each emits more energy than 100 giant galaxies. They are thought to be at the centre of galaxies, their brilliance emanating from the stars and gas falling towards an immense ◊black hole at their nucleus.

Quaternary period of geological time that began 1.64 million years ago and is still in process. It is divided into the ◊Pleistocene and ◊Holocene epochs.

Québec capital and industrial port of Québec province, on the St Lawrence River, Canada; population (1986) 165,000, metropolitan area 603,000.

Québec province of E Canada; *area* 1,540,700 sq km/594,710 sq mi; *capital* Quebec; *features* immense water-power resources (for example, the James Bay project); *population* (1991) 6,811,800; *language* French (the only official language since 1974, although 17% speak English). Language laws 1989 prohibit the use of English on street signs.

Quechua or *Quichua* or *Kechua* member of the largest group of South American Indians. The Quechua live in the Andean region. Their ancestors included the Inca, who established the Quechua language in the region. Quechua is the second official language of Peru.

Queensland state in NE Australia; *area* 1,727,200 sq km/666,699 sq mi; *capital* Brisbane; *features* Great Dividing Range; Great Barrier Reef; Sunshine Coast, a 100-km/60-mi stretch of coast N of Brisbane; *population* (1987) 2,650,000.

quetzal long-tailed Central American bird *Pharomachus mocinno* of the trogon family. The male is brightly coloured, with green, red, blue, and white feathers, and is about 1.3 m/4.3 ft long including tail. The female is smaller and lacks the tail and plumage.

quinine antimalarial drug extracted from the bark of the cinchona tree. Peruvian Indians taught French missionaries how to use the bark in 1630, but quinine was not isolated until 1820. It is a bitter alkaloid $C_{20}H_{24}N_2O_2$.

Quito capital and industrial city of Ecuador, about 3,000 m/9,850 ft above sea level; population (1986) 1,093,300. It was an ancient settlement, taken by the Incas about 1470 and by the Spanish 1534. It has a temperate climate all year.

R

Rabat capital of Morocco, industrial port on the Atlantic coast, 177 km/110 mi W of Fez; population (1982) 519,000, Rabat-Salé 842,000. It is named after its original *ribat* or fortified monastery.

rabbit any of several genera of hopping mammals of the order Lagomorpha, which together with ◊hares constitute the family Leporidae. Rabbits differ from hares in bearing naked, helpless young and in occupying burrows.

Rabelais François 1495–1553. French satirist, monk, and physician. The author of works including *La Vie inestimable de Gargantua/The Inestimable Life of Gargantua* 1535 and *Faits et dits héroïques du grand Pantagruel/Heroic Deeds and Sayings of the Great Pantagruel* 1533, about two giants (father and son), his name has become synonymous with bawdy humour.

rabies or *hydrophobia* viral disease of the central nervous system that can afflict all warm-blooded creatures. It is almost invariably fatal once symptoms have developed. Its transmission to humans is generally by a bite from an infected animal.

Rabin Yitzhak 1922– . Israeli Labour politician, prime minister 1974– 77 and again from 1992. In Sept 1993 he signed a historic peace agreement with the ◊Palestinian Liberation Organization (PLO), leading to a withdrawal of Israeli forces from Gaza and Jericho. Nobel Prize for Peace jointly with Israeli foreign minister, Shimon Peres, and PLO leader, Yassir Arafat 1994.

Rachmaninov Sergei (Vasilevich) 1873–1943. Russian composer, conductor, and pianist. After the 1917 Revolution he emigrated to the USA. His music is melodious and emotional and includes operas, such as *Francesca da Rimini* 1906, three symphonies, four piano concertos, piano pieces, and songs. Among his other works are the *Prelude in C-Sharp Minor* 1882 and *Rhapsody on a Theme of Paganini* 1934 for piano and orchestra.

Racine Jean 1639–1699. French dramatist. He was an exponent of the classical tragedy in French drama, taking his subjects from Greek mythology and observing the rules of classical Greek drama. Most of his tragedies have women in the title role, for example *Andromaque* 1667, *Iphigénie* 1674, and *Phèdre* 1677.

racism belief in, or set of implicit assumptions about, the superiority of one's own race or ethnic group, often accompanied by prejudice against members of an ethnic group different from one's own. Racism may be used to justify ◊discrimination, verbal or physical abuse, or even genocide, as in Nazi Germany, or as practised by European settlers against American Indians in both North and South America.

rad unit of absorbed radiation dose, now replaced in the SI system by the ▷gray (one rad equals 0.01 gray), but still commonly used. It is defined as the dose when one kilogram of matter absorbs 0.01 joule of radiation energy (formerly, as the dose when one gram absorbs 100 ergs).

radar (acronym for *radio direction and ranging*) device for locating objects in space, direction finding, and navigation by means of transmitted and reflected high-frequency radio waves.

radian SI unit (symbol rad) of plane angles, an alternative unit to the ▷degree. It is the angle at the centre of a circle when the centre is joined to the two ends of an arc (part of the circumference) equal in length to the radius of the circle. There are 2π (approximately 6.284) radians in a full circle (360°).

radiation in physics, emission of radiant ▷energy as particles or waves – for example, heat, light, alpha particles, and beta particles (see ▷electromagnetic waves and ▷radioactivity).

radical in chemistry, a group of atoms forming part of a molecule, which acts as a unit and takes part in chemical reactions without disintegration, yet often cannot exist alone; for example, the methyl radical $-CH_3$, or the carboxyl radical $-COOH$.

radio transmission and reception of radio waves. In radio transmission a microphone converts ▷sound waves (pressure variations in the air) into ▷electromagnetic waves that are then picked up by a receiving aerial and fed

to a loudspeaker, which converts them back into sound waves.

radioactive decay process of continuous disintegration undergone by the nuclei of radioactive elements, such as radium and various isotopes of uranium and the transuranic elements. This changes the element's atomic number, thus transmuting one element into another, and is accompanied by the emission of radiation. Alpha and beta decay are the most common forms.

radioactivity spontaneous alteration of the nuclei of radioactive atoms, accompanied by the emission of radiation. It is the property exhibited by the radioactive ▷isotopes of stable elements and all isotopes of radioactive elements, and can be either natural or induced. See ▷radioactive decay.

radio astronomy study of radio waves emitted naturally by objects in space, by means of a ▷radio telescope. Radio emission comes from hot gases (*thermal radiation*); electrons spiralling in magnetic fields (*synchrotron radiation*); and specific wavelengths (*lines*) emitted by atoms and molecules in space, such as the 21 cm/8 in line emitted by hydrogen gas.

radiocarbon dating or *carbon dating* method of dating organic materials (for example, bone or wood), used in archaeology. Plants take up carbon dioxide gas from the atmosphere and incorporate it into their tissues, and some of that carbon dioxide contains the radioactive isotope of carbon, carbon-14. This decays at a known rate (half of it decays every 5,730 years); the time elapsed since the plant died can therefore be measured in a laboratory. Animals take carbon-14 into their bodies from eating plant tissues and their remains can be similarly dated. After 120,000 years so little carbon-14 is left that no measure is possible (see ▷half-life).

radio galaxy galaxy that is a strong source of electromagnetic waves of radio wavelengths. All galaxies, including our own, emit some radio waves, but radio galaxies are up to a million times more powerful.

radiography branch of science concerned with the use of radiation (particularly ▷X-rays) to produce images on photographic film or fluorescent screens. X-rays penetrate matter according to its nature, density, and thickness. In doing so they can cast shadows on photographic film, producing a radiograph. Radiography is widely used in medicine for examining bones and tissues and in industry for examining solid materials; for example, to check welded seams in pipelines.

radioisotope (contraction of *radioactive ▷isotope*) in physics, a naturally occurring or synthetic radioactive form of an element. Most radioisotopes are made by bombarding a stable element with neutrons in the core of a nuclear reactor. The radiations given off by radioisotopes are easy to detect (hence their use as tracers), can in some instances penetrate substantial thicknesses of materials, and have profound effects (such as genetic ▷mutation) on living matter. Although dangerous, radioisotopes are used in the fields of medicine, industry, agriculture, and research.

radio telescope instrument for detecting radio waves from the universe in ▷radio astronomy. Radio telescopes usually consist of a metal bowl that collects and focuses radio waves the way a concave mirror collects and focuses light waves. Radio telescopes are much larger than optical telescopes, because the wavelengths they are detecting are much longer than the wavelength of light. The largest single dish is 305 m/1,000 ft across, at Arecibo, Puerto Rico.

radiotherapy treatment of disease by ▷radiation from X-ray machines or radioactive sources. Radiation, which reduces the activity of dividing cells, is of special value for its effect on malignant tissues, certain nonmalignant tumours, and some diseases of the skin.

radio wave electromagnetic wave possessing a long wavelength (ranging from about 10^{-3} to 10^4 m) and a low frequency (from about 10^5 to 10^{11} Hz). Included in the radio-wave part of the spectrum are ▷microwaves, used for both communications and for cooking; ultra high- and very high-frequency waves, used for television and FM (frequency modulation) radio communications; and short, medium, and long waves, used for AM (amplitude modulation) radio communications. Radio waves that are used for communications have all been modulated to carry information. Stars emit radio waves, which may be detected and studied using ▷radio telescopes.

radium white, radioactive, metallic element, symbol Ra, atomic number 88, relative atomic mass 226.02. It is one of the ▷alkaline-earth metals, found in nature in ▷pitchblende and other uranium ores. Of the 16 isotopes, the commonest, Ra-226, has a half-life of 1.622 years. The element was discovered and named in 1898 by Pierre and Marie ▷Curie, who were investigating the residues of pitchblende.

radon colourless, odourless, gaseous, radioactive, nonmetallic element, symbol Rn, atomic number 86, relative atomic mass 222. It is grouped with the ◊inert gases and was formerly considered non-reactive, but is now known to form some compounds with fluorine. Of the 20 known isotopes, only three occur in nature; the longest half-life is 3.82 days.

Rafsanjani Hojatoleslam Ali Akbar Hashemi 1934– . Iranian politician and cleric, president from 1989. When his former teacher Ayatollah ◊Khomeini returned after the revolution of 1979–80, Rafsanjani became the speaker of the Iranian parliament and, after Khomeini's death, state president and effective political leader.

railway method of transport in which trains convey passengers and goods along a twin rail track. Following the work of English steam pioneers such as Scottish engineer James Watt, English engineer George ◊Stephenson built the first public steam railway, from Stockton to Darlington, England, in 1825. This heralded extensive railway building in Britain, continental Europe, and North America, providing a fast and economical means of transport and communication. After World War II, steam engines were replaced by electric and diesel engines. At the same time, the growth of road building, air services, and car ownership destroyed the supremacy of the railways.

rainforest dense forest usually found on or near the ◊equator where the climate is hot and wet. Heavy rainfall results as the moist air brought by the converging tradewinds rises because of the heat. Over half the tropical rainforests are in Central and South America, the rest in SE Asia and Africa.

They provide the bulk of the oxygen needed for plant and animal respiration. Tropical rainforest once covered 14% of the Earth's land surface, but are now being destroyed at an increasing rate as their valuable timber is harvested and the land cleared for agriculture, causing problems of ◊deforestation. Although by 1991 over 50% of the world's rainforest had been removed, they still comprise about 50% of all growing wood on the planet, and harbour at least 40% of the Earth's species (plants and animals).

Raleigh or *Ralegh* Walter *c.* 1552–1618. English adventurer, writer, and courtier to Queen Elizabeth I. His attempts to colonize North America 1584–87 were unsuccessful. He went on to make exploratory voyages to South America 1595 and 1616. Imprisoned for treason 1603–16, he was executed on his return from an unsuccessful expedition to South America. He is traditionally credited with introducing the potato to Europe and popularizing the use of tobacco.

RAM (acronym for *random-access memory*) in computing, a memory device in the form of a collection of integrated circuits (chips), frequently used in microcomputers. Unlike ◊ROM (read-only memory) chips, RAM chips can be both read from and written to by the computer, but their contents are lost when the power is switched off. Microcomputers of the 1990s may have 16–32 megabytes of RAM.

Ramadan in the Muslim calendar, the ninth month of the year. Throughout Ramadan a strict fast is observed during the hours of daylight; Muslims are encouraged to read the whole Koran in commemoration of the Night of Power (which falls during the month) when, it is believed, Muhammad first received his revelations from the angel Gabriel.

Rambert Marie. Adopted name of Cyvia Rambam 1888–1982. Polish-born British ballet dancer and teacher. One of the major innovative and influential figures in modern ballet, she worked with the Diaghilev ballet 1912–13, opened the Rambert School 1920, and in 1926 founded the Ballet Rambert which she directed. It became a modern-dance company from 1966 and renamed the Rambert Dance Company 1987.

Rao P(amulaparti) V(enkata) Narasimha 1921– . Indian politician, prime minister of India from 1991 and Congress (I) leader. He took over the party leadership after the assassination of Rajiv Gandhi. Elected prime minister the following month, he instituted a reform of the economy. He survived a vote of confidence 1993.

rape in botany, two plant species of the mustard family Cruciferae, *Brassica rapa* and *B. napus*, grown for their seeds, which yield a pungent edible oil. The common turnip is a variety of the former, and the swede turnip of the latter.

Raphael Sanzio (Raffaello Sanzio) 1483–1520. Italian painter. He was one of the greatest artists of the High Renaissance, active in Perugia, Florence, and Rome (from 1508), where he painted frescoes in the Vatican and for secular patrons. Many of his designs were engraved, and much of his later work was the product of his studio.

Rasputin (Russian 'dissolute') Grigory Efimovich 1871–1916. Siberian Eastern Orthodox mystic who acquired influence over the tsarina Alexandra, wife of ▷Nicholas II, and was able to make political and ecclesiastical appointments. His abuse of power and notorious debauchery (reputedly including the tsarina) led to his murder by a group of nobles.

Rastafarianism religion originating in the West Indies, based on the ideas of Marcus Garvey, who called on black people to return to Africa and set up a black-governed country there. When Haile Selassie (*Ras Tafari*, 'Lion of Judah') was crowned emperor of Ethiopia 1930, this was seen as a fulfilment of prophecy and some Rastafarians acknowledged him as an incarnation of God (*Jah*), others as a prophet. The use of ganja (marijuana) is a sacrament. There are no churches. There were about one million Rastafarians by 1990.

rationalism in theology, the belief that human reason rather than divine revelation is the correct means of ascertaining truth and regulating behaviour. In philosophy, rationalism takes the view that self-evident propositions deduced by reason are the sole basis of all knowledge (disregarding experience of the senses). It is usually contrasted with ▷empiricism, which argues that all knowledge must ultimately be derived from the senses.

Ravel (Joseph) Maurice 1875–1937. French composer and pianist. His work is characterized by its sensuousness, exotic harmonics, and dazzling orchestral effects. Examples are the piano pieces *Pavane pour une infante défunte/Pavane for a Dead Infanta* 1899 and *Jeux d'eau/Waterfall* 1901, and the ballets *Daphnis et Chloë* 1912 and *Boléro* 1928.

ray any of several orders (especially Ragiformes) of cartilaginous fishes with a flattened body, winglike pectoral fins, and a whiplike tail.

rayon any of various shiny textile fibres and fabrics made from ◊cellulose. It is produced by pressing whatever cellulose solution is used through very small holes and solidifying the resulting filaments. A common type is ◊viscose, which consists of regenerated filaments of pure cellulose. Acetate and triacetate are kinds of rayon consisting of filaments of cellulose acetate and triacetate.

reaction in chemistry, the coming together of two or more atoms, ions, or molecules with the result that a chemical change takes place. The nature of the reaction is portrayed by a chemical equation.

Reagan Ronald (Wilson) 1911– . 40th president of the USA 1981–89, a Republican. Governor of California 1966–74, he was a former Hollywood actor. In 1987 during the Irangate investigation Reagan admitted that US–Iran negotiations had become an 'arms for hostages deal', but denied knowledge of resultant funds being illegally sent to the Contras in Nicaragua. He increased military spending, cut social programmes, introduced deregulation of domestic markets, and cut taxes.

realism in the arts generally, an unadorned, naturalistic approach to subject matter. More specifically, *Realism* refers to a movement in mid-19th-century European art and literature, a reaction against Romantic and Classical idealization in favour of everyday life in carefully observed social settings.

real number in mathematics, any of the rational numbers (which include the integers) or irrational numbers. Real numbers exclude imaginary numbers, found in complex numbers of the general form $a + bi$ where $i = \sqrt{-1}$, although these do include a real component a.

recessive gene in genetics, an ◊allele (alternative form of a gene) that will show in the ◊phenotype (observed characteristics of an organism) only if its partner allele on the paired chromosome is similarly recessive. Such an allele will not show if its partner is dominant, that is if the organism is heterozygous for a particular characteristic. Alleles for blue eyes in humans, and for shortness in pea plants are recessive. Most mutant alleles are recessive and therefore are only rarely expressed (see ◊haemophilia and ◊sickle-cell disease).

recombination in genetics, any process that recombines, or 'shuffles', the genetic material, thus increasing genetic variation in the offspring. The two main processes of recombination both occur during meiosis (reduction division of cells). One is *crossing over*, in which chromosome pairs exchange segments; the other is the random reassortment of chromosomes that occurs when each gamete (sperm or egg) receives only one of each chromosome pair.

Reconstruction in US history, the period 1865–77 after the Civil War during which the nation was reunited under the federal government after the defeat of the Southern Confederacy.

recorder any of a widespread range of woodwind instruments of the whistle type which flourished in consort ensembles in the Renaissance and Baroque eras, along with viol consorts, as an instrumental medium for polyphonic music. A modern consort may include a sopranino in F5, soprano (descant) in

C4, alto (treble) in F3, tenor in C3, bass in F2, and great bass in C2.

rectifier in electrical engineering, a device used for obtaining one-directional current (DC) from an alternating source of supply (AC). (The process is necessary because almost all electrical power is generated, transmitted, and supplied as alternating current, but many devices, from television sets to electric motors, require direct current.) Types include plate rectifiers, thermionic ◊diodes, and ◊semiconductor diodes.

recycling processing of industrial and household waste (such as paper, glass, and some metals and plastics) so that it can be reused. This saves expenditure on scarce raw materials, slows down the depletion of ◊nonrenewable resources, and helps to reduce pollution.

red blood cell or *erythrocyte* the most common type of blood cell, responsible for transporting oxygen around the body. It contains haemoglobin, which combines with oxygen from the lungs to form oxyhaemoglobin. When transported to the tissues, these cells are able to release the oxygen because the oxyhaemoglobin splits into its original constituents.

Red Cross international relief agency founded by the Geneva Convention 1864 to assist the wounded and prisoners in war. Its symbol is a symmetrical red cross on a white ground. In addition to dealing with associated problems of war, such as refugees and the care of the disabled, the Red Cross is increasingly concerned with victims of natural disasters – floods, earthquakes, epidemics, and accidents.

red dwarf any star that is cool, faint, and small (about one-tenth the mass and diameter of the Sun). Red dwarfs burn slowly, and have estimated lifetimes of 100 billion years. They may be the most abundant type of star, but are difficult to see because they are so faint. Two of the closest stars to the Sun, Proxima Centauri and Barnard's Star, are red dwarfs.

Redford (Charles) Robert 1937– . US actor and film director. His blond good looks and versatility earned him his first starring role in *Barefoot in the Park* 1967, followed by *Butch Cassidy and the Sundance Kid* 1969 and *The Sting* 1973 (both with Paul Newman).

red giant any large bright star with a cool surface. It is thought to represent a late stage in the evolution of a star like the Sun, as it runs out of hydrogen fuel at its centre. Red giants have diameters between 10 and 100 times that of the Sun. They are very bright because they are so large, although their surface temperature is lower than that of the Sun, about 2,000–3,000K (1,700–2,700°C/3,000°–5,000°F). See also red ◊supergiants.

Redgrave Michael 1908–1985. English actor. His stage roles included Hamlet and Lear (Shakespeare), Uncle Vanya (Chekhov), and the schoolmaster in Rattigan's *The Browning Version* (filmed 1951). On screen he appeared in *The Lady Vanishes* 1938, *The Importance of Being Earnest* 1952, and *Goodbye Mr Chips* 1959. He was the father of actresses Vanessa (1937–) and Lynn Redgrave (1944–).

Red Sea submerged section of the Great ◊Rift Valley (2,000 km/1,200 mi long and up to 320 km/200 mi wide). Egypt, Sudan, Ethiopia, and Eritrea (in

Africa) and Saudi Arabia (Asia) are on its shores.

red shift in astronomy, the lengthening of the wavelengths of light from an object as a result of the object's motion away from us. It is an example of the ▷Doppler effect. The red shift in light from galaxies is evidence that the universe is expanding.

reduction in chemistry, the gain of electrons, loss of oxygen, or gain of hydrogen by an atom, ion, or molecule during a chemical reaction.

reed any of various perennial tall, slender grasses of wet or marshy environments; in particular, species of the genera *Phragmites* and *Arundo*; also the stalk of any of these plants. The common reed *P. australis* attains a height of 3 m/10 ft, having stiff, erect leaves and straight stems bearing a plume of purplish flowers.

referendum procedure whereby a decision on proposed legislation is referred to the electorate for settlement by direct vote of all the people. It is most frequently employed in Switzerland, the first country to use it, but has become increasingly widespread. In 1992 several European countries (Ireland, Denmark, France) held referendums on whether to ratify the ▷Maastricht Treaty on closer European union.

reflection the throwing back or deflection of waves, such as ▷light or ▷sound waves, when they hit a surface. The *law of reflection* states that the angle of incidence (the angle between the ray and a perpendicular line drawn to the surface) is equal to the angle of reflection (the angle between the reflected ray and a perpendicular to the surface).

reflex in animals, a very rapid involuntary response to a particular stimulus. It is controlled by the ▷nervous system. A reflex involves only a few nerve cells, unlike the slower but more complex responses produced by the many processing nerve cells of the brain.

Reform Acts UK acts of Parliament 1832, 1867, and 1884 that extended voting rights and redistributed parliamentary seats; also known as Representation of the People Acts.

Reformation religious and political movement in 16th-century Europe to reform the Roman Catholic church, which led to the establishment of Protestant churches. Anticipated from the 12th century by the Waldenses, Lollards, and Hussites, it was set off by German priest Martin ▷Luther 1517, and became effective when the absolute monarchies gave it support by challenging the political power of the papacy and confiscating church wealth.

refraction the bending of a wave of light, heat, or sound when it passes from one medium to another. Refraction occurs because waves travel at different velocities in different media.

refrigeration use of technology to transfer heat from cold to warm, against the normal temperature gradient, so that a body can remain substantially colder than its surroundings. Refrigeration equipment is used for the chilling and deep-freezing of food in food technology, and in air conditioners and industrial processes.

refugee person fleeing from oppressive or dangerous conditions (such as political, religious, or military persecution) and seeking refuge in a foreign country.

In 1993 there were an estimated 18 million refugees worldwide, whose resettlement and welfare were the responsibility of the United Nations High Commission for Refugees (UNHCR). An estimated average of 10,000 people a day become refugees.

Regency style style of architecture and interior furnishings popular in England during the late 18th and early 19th centuries. It is characterized by restrained simplicity and the imitation of ancient classical elements, often Greek.

regeneration in biology, regrowth of a new organ or tissue after the loss or removal of the original. It is common in plants, where a new individual can often be produced from a 'cutting' of the original. In animals, regeneration of major structures is limited to lower organisms; certain lizards can regrow their tails if these are lost, and new flatworms can grow from a tiny fragment of an old one. In mammals, regeneration is limited to the repair of tissue in wound healing and the regrowth of peripheral nerves following damage.

Reims (English *Reims*) capital of Champagne-Ardenne region, France; population (1990) 185,200. It is the centre of the champagne industry. In World War II, the German High Command formally surrendered here to US general Eisenhower 7 May 1945.

reincarnation belief that after death the human soul or the spirit of a plant or animal may live again in another human or animal. It is part of the teachings of many religions and philosophies, for example ancient Egyptian and Greek (the philosophies of Pythagoras and Plato), Buddhism, Hinduism, Jainism, certain Christian heresies (such as the Cathars), and theosophy. It is also referred to as *transmigration* or metempsychosis.

reindeer or *caribou* deer *Rangifer tarandus* of Arctic and subarctic regions, common to North America and Eurasia. About 120 cm/4 ft at the shoulder, it has a thick, brownish coat and broad hooves well adapted to travel over snow. It is the only deer in which both sexes have antlers; these can grow to 150 cm/5 ft long, and are shed in winter.

relative atomic mass the mass of an atom relative to one-twelfth the mass of an atom of carbon-12. It depends on the number of protons and neutrons in the atom, the electrons having negligible mass. If more than one ◊isotope of the element is present, the relative atomic mass is calculated by taking an average that takes account of the relative proportions of each isotope, resulting in values that are not whole numbers. The term *atomic weight*, although commonly used, is strictly speaking incorrect.

relativity in physics, the theory of the relative rather than absolute character of motion and mass, and the interdependence of matter, time, and space, as developed by German physicist Albert ◊Einstein in two phases:
special theory (1905) Starting with the premises that (1) the laws of nature are the same for all observers in unaccelerated motion, and (2) the speed of light is independent of the motion of its source, Einstein postulated that the time interval between two events was longer for an observer in whose frame of reference the events occur in different places than for the observer for whom they occur at the same place.
general theory of relativity (1915) The geometrical properties of space-time were to be conceived as modified locally

by the presence of a body with mass. A planet's orbit around the Sun (as observed in three-dimensional space) arises from its natural trajectory in modified space-time; there is no need to invoke, as Isaac Newton did, a force of ◊gravity coming from the Sun and acting on the planet.

Einstein's theory predicted slight differences in the orbits of the planets from Newton's theory, which were observable in the case of Mercury. The new theory also said light rays should bend when they pass by a massive object, owing to the object's effect on local space-time. The predicted bending of starlight was observed during the eclipse of the Sun 1919, when light from distant stars passing close to the Sun was not masked by sunlight.

Rembrandt Harmensz van Rijn 1606–1669. Dutch painter and etcher. He was one of the most prolific and significant artists in Europe of the 17th century. Between 1629 and 1669 he painted some 60 penetrating self-portraits. He also painted religious subjects, and produced about 300 etchings and over 1,000 drawings. His major group portraits include *The Anatomy Lesson of Dr Tulp* 1632 (Mauritshuis, The Hague) and *The Night Watch* 1642 (Rijksmuseum, Amsterdam).

remote sensing gathering and recording information from a distance. Space probes have sent back photographs and data about planets as distant as Neptune. In archaeology, surface survey techniques provide information without disturbing subsurface deposits.

REM sleep (acronym for *rapid-eye-movement* sleep) phase of sleep that recurs several times nightly in humans and is associated with dreaming. The eyes flicker quickly beneath closed lids.

Renaissance period and intellectual movement in European cultural history that is traditionally seen as ending the Middle Ages and beginning modern times. The Renaissance started in Italy in the 14th century and flourished in W Europe until about the 17th century. The aim of Renaissance education was to produce the 'complete human being' (*Renaissance man*), conversant in the humanities, mathematics and science, the arts and crafts, and athletics and sport; to enlarge the bounds of learning and geographical knowledge; and the study and imitation of Greek and Latin literature and art.

Renaissance art movement in European art of the 15th and 16th centuries. It began in Florence, Italy, with the rise of a spirit of humanism and a new appreciation of the Classical Greek and Roman past. The 15th century is known as the *Classical Renaissance*; the *High Renaissance* (early 16th century) covers the careers of Leonardo da Vinci, Raphael, Michelangelo, and Titian in Italy and Dürer in Germany.

renewable energy power from any source that replenishes itself. Most renewable systems rely on ◊solar energy directly or through the weather cycle as ◊wave power, ◊hydroelectric power, or wind power via ◊wind turbines, or solar energy collected by plants (alcohol fuels, for example). In addition, the gravitational force of the Moon can be harnessed through tidal power stations, and the heat trapped in the centre of the Earth is used via ◊geothermal energy systems.

Renoir Pierre-Auguste 1841–1919. French Impressionist painter. He met Monet and Sisley in the early 1860s, and together they formed the nucleus of the Impressionist movement. He developed a lively, colourful painting style with feathery brushwork (known as his 'rainbow style') and painted many voluptuous female nudes, such as *The Bathers* about 1884–87 (Philadelphia Museum of Art, USA).

repetitive strain injury (RSI) inflammation of tendon sheaths, mainly in the hands and wrists, which may be disabling. It is found predominantly in factory workers involved in constant repetitive movements, and in high-speed typists. Some victims have successfully sued their employers for damages.

reproduction in biology, process by which a living organism produces other organisms similar to itself. There are two kinds: ⊳asexual reproduction and ⊳sexual reproduction.

reptile any member of a class (Reptilia) of vertebrates. Unlike amphibians, reptiles have hard-shelled, yolk- filled eggs that are laid on land and from which fully formed young are born. Some snakes and lizards retain their eggs and give birth to live young. Reptiles are cold-blooded and produced from eggs, and the skin is usually covered with scales. The metabolism is slow, and in some cases (certain large snakes) intervals between meals may be months. Reptiles date back over 300 million years.

Republican Party one of the USA's two main political parties, formed 1854. It is considered more conservative than the Democratic Party, favouring capital and big business and opposing state subvention and federal controls. In the late 20th century most presidents have come from the Republican Party, but in Congress Republicans have generally been outnumbered. In the 1994 midterm elections Republicans gained control of both houses of Congress.

resistance in physics, that property of a substance that restricts the flow of electricity through it, associated with the conversion of electrical energy to heat; also the magnitude of this property. Resistance depends on many factors, such as the nature of the material, its temperature, dimensions, and thermal properties; degree of impurity; the nature and state of illumination of the surface; and the frequency and magnitude of the current. The SI unit of resistance is the ohm.

respiration biochemical process whereby food molecules are progressively broken down (oxidized) to release energy in the form of ⊳ATP. In most organisms this requires oxygen, but in some bacteria the oxidant is the nitrate or sulphate ion instead. In all higher organisms, respiration occurs in the mitochondria. Respiration is also used to mean breathing, in which oxygen is exchanged for carbon dioxide in the lung alveoli, though this is more accurately described as a form of ⊳gas exchange.

Restoration in English history, the period when the monarchy, in the person of Charles II, was re-established after the English Civil War and the fall of the Protectorate 1660.

resurrection in Christian, Jewish, and Muslim belief, the rising from the dead that all souls will experience at the Last Judgement. The Resurrection also refers to Jesus rising from the dead on the third day after his crucifixion, a belief central to Christianity and celebrated at Easter.

retrovirus any of a family of ▷viruses (Retroviridae) containing the genetic material ▷RNA rather than the more usual ▷DNA.

Réunion French island of the Mascarenes group, in the Indian Ocean, 650 km/400 mi E of Madagascar and 180 km/110 mi SW of Mauritius; *area* 2,512 sq km/970 sq mi; *capital* St Denis; *features* administers five uninhabited islands, also claimed by Madagascar; *population* (1990) 597,800.

revolutions of 1848 series of revolts in various parts of Europe against monarchical rule. While some of the revolutionaries had republican ideas, many more were motivated by economic grievances. The revolution began in France with the overthrow of Louis Philippe and then spread to Italy, the Austrian Empire, and Germany. Most of the Revolutions were violently suppressed within a few months.

Reykjavik capital (from 1918) and chief port of Iceland, on the SW coast; population (1988) 93,000. It is heated by underground mains fed by volcanic springs.

Reynolds Albert 1933– . Irish politician, prime minister 1992–94. He joined Fianna Fail 1977, becoming prime minister over a Fianna Fáil–Labour coalition on the forced resignation of Charles Haughey Jan 1992. In Dec 1993, he and UK prime minister John Major issued a joint peace initiative for Northern Ireland, the 'Downing Street Declaration', which led to a general cease-fire. He resigned as premier and Fianna Fáil leader Nov 1994.

Reynolds Joshua 1723–1792. English portrait painter. He was active in London from 1752 and became the first president of the Royal Academy 1768. His portraits display a facility for striking and characterful compositions in a consciously grand manner. He often borrowed classical poses, for example *Mrs Siddons as the Tragic Muse* 1784 (San Marino, California).

rhesus factor group of ▷antigens on the surface of red blood cells of humans which characterize the rhesus blood group system. Most individuals possess the main rhesus factor (Rh+), but those without this factor (Rh–) produce ▷antibodies if they come into contact with it. The name comes from rhesus monkeys, in whose blood rhesus factors were first found.

rheumatic fever or *acute rheumatism* acute or chronic illness characterized by fever and painful swelling of joints. Some victims also experience involuntary movements of the limbs and head, a form of chorea. It is now rare in the developed world.

Rhine (German *Rhein*, French *Rhin*) European river rising in Switzerland and reaching the North Sea via Germany and the Netherlands; length 1,320 km/820 mi. Tributaries include the Moselle and the Ruhr. It is linked with the Mediterranean by the Rhine– Rhône Waterway, and with the Black Sea by the Rhine–Main–Danube Waterway. It is the longest, and the dirtiest, river in Europe.

rhinoceros odd-toed hoofed mammal of the family Rhinocerotidae. The one-horned Indian rhinoceros *Rhinoceros unicornis* is up to 2 m/6 ft high at the shoulder, with a tubercled skin, folded into shieldlike pieces; the African rhinoceroses are smooth-skinned and two-horned. All are in danger of becoming extinct.

Rhode Island smallest state of the USA, in New England; *area* 3,100 sq km/ 1,197 sq mi; *capital* Providence; *features* Narragansett Bay runs inland 28 mi/45 km; *population* (1990) 1,003,500.

Rhodes (Greek *Ródhos*) Greek island, largest of the Dodecanese, in the E Aegean Sea; *area* 1,412 sq km/545 sq mi; *capital* Rhodes; *population* (1981) 88,000.

Rhodes Cecil (John) 1853–1902. South African politician, born in the UK, prime minister of Cape Colony 1890–96. He formed the British South Africa Company in 1889, which occupied Mashonaland and Matabeleland, thus forming *Rhodesia* (now Zambia and Zimbabwe).

Rhône river of S Europe; length 810 km/500 mi. It rises in Switzerland and flows through Lake Geneva to Lyon in France, where at its confluence with the Saône the upper limit of navigation is reached. The river turns due south, passes Vienne and Avignon, and takes in the Isère and other tributaries. Near Arles it divides into the *Grand* and *Petit Rhône*, flowing respectively SE and SW into the Mediterranean W of Marseille.

riboflavin or *vitamin B2* ◊vitamin of the B complex important in cell respiration. It is obtained from eggs, liver, and milk. A deficiency in the diet causes stunted growth.

ribonucleic acid full name of ◊RNA.

ribosome in biology, the protein-making machinery of the cell. Ribosomes are located on the endoplasmic reticulum (ER) of eukaryotic cells, and are made of proteins and a special type of ◊RNA, ribosomal RNA. They receive messenger RNA (copied from the ◊DNA) and ◊amino acids, and 'translate' the messenger RNA by using its chemically coded instructions to link amino acids in a specific order, to make a strand of a particular protein.

rice principal cereal of the wet regions of the tropics; derived from grass of the species *Oryza sativa*, probably native to India and SE Asia. It is unique among cereal crops in that it is grown standing in water. The yield is very large, and rice is said to be the staple food of one-third of the world population.

Richard (I) the Lion-Heart (French *Coeur-de- Lion*) 1157–1199. King of England from 1189, who spent all but six months of his reign abroad. He was the third son of Henry II, against whom he twice rebelled. Returning from the third ◊Crusade 1191–92, he was captured by the Duke of Austria, and handed over to Emperor Henry VI, but freed for a large ransom. He returned briefly to England, but his later years were spent in warfare in France, where he was killed.

Richard III 1452–1485. King of England from 1483. He was created Duke of Gloucester by his brother Edward IV, upon whose death 1483 he became protector to his nephew Edward V. He soon secured the crown for himself on the plea that Edward IV's sons were illegitimate. He proved a capable ruler, but the suspicion that he had murdered Edward V and his brother undermined his popularity. Richard III was defeated and killed by Henry VII at ◊Bosworth.

Richardson Ralph (David) 1902–1983. English actor. He played many stage parts, including Falstaff (Shakespeare), Peer Gynt (Ibsen), and Cyrano de Bergerac (Rostand). He shared the management of the Old Vic theatre with Laurence Olivier 1944–50. In later years he revealed himself as an accomplished deadpan comic.

Richardson Samuel 1689–1761. English novelist. He was one of the founders of the modern novel. *Pamela* 1740–41, written in the form of a series of letters and containing much dramatic conversation, was sensationally popular all across Europe, and was followed by *Clarissa* 1747–48 and *Sir Charles Grandison* 1753–54.

Richelieu Armand Jean du Plessis de 1585–1642. French cardinal and politician, chief minister from 1624. He ruthlessly crushed opposition to the monarchy and destroyed the political power of the ⬦Huguenots. Abroad, he sought to establish French supremacy by breaking the power of the Habsburgs, involving France in the Thirty Years' War from 1635.

Richter scale scale based on measurement of seismic waves, used to determine the magnitude of an ⬦earthquake at its epicentre. The magnitude of an earthquake differs from its intensity, measured by the Mercalli scale, which is subjective and varies from place to place for the same earthquake. The scale is named after US seismologist Charles Richter.

rickets defective growth of bone in children due to an insufficiency of calcium deposits. The bones, which do not harden adequately, are bent out of shape. It is usually caused by a lack of vitamin D and insufficient exposure to sunlight. Renal rickets, also a condition

of malformed bone, is associated with kidney disease.

Rift Valley, Great volcanic valley formed 10–20 million years ago by a crack in the Earth's crust and running about 8,000 km/5,000 mi from the Jordan Valley through the Red Sea to central Mozambique in SE Africa. It is marked by a series of lakes, including Lake Turkana (formerly Lake Rudolf), and volcanoes, such as Mount Kilimanjaro.

Riga capital and port of Latvia; population (1987) 900,000.

Rights of Man and the Citizen, Declaration of the historic French document. According to the statement of the French National Assembly 1789, these rights include representation in the legislature; equality before the law; equality of opportunity; freedom from arbitrary imprisonment; freedom of speech and religion; taxation in proportion to ability to pay; and security of property.

Rimbaud (Jean Nicolas) Arthur 1854–1891. French Symbolist poet. His verse was chiefly written before the age of 20, notably *Les Illuminations* published 1886. From 1871 he lived with the poet Paul ⬦Verlaine.

Rimsky-Korsakov Nikolay Andreyevich 1844–1908. Russian nationalist composer. His operas include *The Maid of Pskov* 1873, *The Snow Maiden* 1882, *Mozart and Salieri* 1898, and *The Golden Cockerel* 1907, a satirical attack on despotism that was banned until 1909. He also wrote an influential text on orchestration.

ringworm any of various contagious skin infections due to related kinds of fungus, usually resulting in circular, itchy, discoloured patches covered with scales or blisters. The scalp and feet (athlete's foot) are generally involved. Treatment is with antifungal preparations.

Rio de Janeiro port and resort in E Brazil; population (1991) 5,487,300. Sugar Loaf Mountain stands at the entrance to the harbour. Rio was the capital of Brazil 1763–1960. The city is the capital of the state of Rio de Janeiro, which has a population of 13,267,100 (1987 est).

Rio Grande river rising in the Rocky Mountains in S Colorado, USA, and flowing S to the Gulf of Mexico, where it is reduced to a trickle by irrigation demands on its upper reaches; length 3,050 km/1,900 mi. Its last 2,400 km/1,500 mi form the US–Mexican border (Mexican name *Rio Bravo del Norte*).

Risorgimento 19th-century movement for Italian national unity and independence, begun 1815. Uprisings 1848–49 failed, but with help from France in a war against Austria – to oust it from Italian provinces in the north – an Italian kingdom was founded 1861. Unification was finally completed with the addition of Venetia 1866 and the Papal States 1870.

river long water course that flows down a slope along a channel. It originates at a point called its *source*, and enters a sea or lake at its *mouth*. Along its length it may be joined by smaller rivers called *tributaries*. A river and its tributaries are contained within a drainage basin.

Riviera the Mediterranean coast of France and Italy from Marseille to La Spezia. The most exclusive stretch of the Riviera, with the finest climate, is the Côte d'Azur, from Menton to St Tropez, which includes Monaco.

Riyadh (Arabic *Ar Riyād*) capital of Saudi Arabia and of the Central Province, formerly the sultanate of Nejd, in an oasis, connected by rail with Dammam on the Arabian Gulf; population (1986) 1,500,000.

RNA *ribonucleic acid* nucleic acid involved in the process of translating the genetic material ◊DNA into proteins. It is usually single- stranded, unlike the double-stranded DNA, and consists of a large number of nucleotides strung together, each of which comprises the sugar ribose, a phosphate group, and one of four bases (uracil, cytosine, adenine, or guanine). RNA is copied from DNA by the formation of ◊base pairs, with uracil taking the place of thymine.

Robbia, della Italian family of sculptors and architects. *Luca della Robbia* (1400–1482) created a number of major works in Florence, notably the marble *cantoria* (singing gallery) in the cathedral 1431–38 (Museo del Duomo), with lively groups of choristers.

Robert (I) the Bruce 1274–1329. King of Scotland from 1306. He shared in the national uprising led by William Wallace, and, after Wallace's execution 1305, rose once more against Edward I of England, and was crowned at Scone 1306. He defeated Edward II at ◊Bannockburn 1314. In 1328 the treaty of Northampton recognized Scotland's independence and Robert as king.

Robespierre Maximilien François Marie Isidore de 1758–1794. French politician in the ◊French Revolution. As leader of the ◊Jacobins in the National Convention, he supported the execution of Louis XVI and the overthrow of the right-wing republican Girondins, and in July 1793 was elected to the Committee of Public Safety. A year later he was guillotined.

Robin Hood in English legend, an outlaw and champion of the poor against the rich, said to have lived in Sherwood Forest, Nottinghamshire, during the reign of Richard I (1189–99). He feuded with the sheriff of Nottingham, accompanied by Maid Marian and a band of followers known as his 'merry men'.

Robinson Mary 1944– . Irish Labour politician, president from 1990. She became a professor of law at 25. A strong supporter of women's rights, she has campaigned for the liberalization of Ireland's laws prohibiting divorce and abortion.

Robinson W(illiam) Heath 1872–1944. English cartoonist and illustrator. He made humorous drawings of bizarre machinery for performing simple tasks, such as raising one's hat. A clumsily designed apparatus is often described as a 'Heath Robinson' contraption.

robot any computer-controlled machine that can be programmed to move or carry out work. Robots are often used in industry to transport materials or to perform repetitive tasks. For instance, robotic arms, fixed to a floor or workbench, may be used to paint machine parts or assemble electronic circuits. Other robots are designed to work in situations that would be dangerous to humans – for example, in defusing bombs or in space and deep-sea exploration.

rock constituent of the Earth's crust, composed of mineral particles and/or materials of organic origin consolidated into a hard mass as ◊igneous, ◊sedimentary, or ◊metamorphic rocks.

Rockefeller John D(avison) 1839–1937. US millionaire, founder of Standard Oil 1870 (which achieved control of 90% of US refineries by 1882). He founded the philanthropic *Rockefeller Foundation* 1913, to which his son *John D(avison) Rockefeller Jr* (1874–1960) devoted his life.

rocket projectile driven by the reaction of gases produced by a fast-burning fuel. Unlike jet engines, which are also reaction engines, modern rockets carry their own oxygen supply to burn their fuel and do not require any surrounding atmosphere. For warfare, rocket heads carry an explosive device.

Rocky Mountains or *Rockies* largest North American mountain system. It extends from the junction with the Mexican plateau, N through the W central states of the US, through Canada to the Alaskan border, and then forms part of the Continental Divide, which separates rivers draining into the Atlantic or Arctic oceans from those flowing toward the Pacific Ocean. Mount Elbert is the highest peak, 14,433 ft/4,400 m. Some geographers consider the Yukon and Alaska ranges as part of the system, making the highest point Mount Mckinley (Denali) 20,320 ft/6,194 m.)

Rococo movement in the arts and architecture in 18th-century Europe, tending towards lightness, elegance, delicacy, and decorative charm. The term 'Rococo' is derived from the French *rocaille* (rock- or shell-work), a style of interior decoration based on S-curves and scroll-like forms. In the 1730s the movement became widespread in

Europe, notably in the churches and palaces of S Germany and Austria.

rodent any mammal of the worldwide order Rodentia, making up nearly half of all mammal species. Besides ordinary 'cheek teeth', they have a single front pair of incisor teeth in both upper and lower jaw, which continue to grow as they are worn down.

Rodgers Richard (Charles) 1902–1979. US composer. He collaborated with librettist Lorenz Hart (1895–1943) on songs like 'Blue Moon' 1934 and musicals like *On Your Toes* 1936. With Oscar Hammerstein II, he wrote many musicals, including *Oklahoma!* 1943, *South Pacific* 1949, *The King and I* 1951, and *The Sound of Music* 1959.

Rodin Auguste 1840–1917. French sculptor. He is considered the greatest of his day. He freed sculpture from the idealizing conventions of the time by his realistic treatment of the human figure, introducing a new boldness of style and expression. Examples are *Le Penseur/The Thinker* 1880 (Musée Rodin, Paris), *Le Baiser/The Kiss* 1886 (marble version in the Louvre, Paris), and *The Burghers of Calais* 1884–86 (copy in Embankment Gardens, Westminster, London).

roentgen or *röntgen* unit (symbol R) of radiation exposure, used for X-rays and gamma rays. It is defined in terms of the number of ions produced in one cubic centimetre of air by the radiation. Exposure to 1,000 roentgens gives rise to an absorbed dose of about 870 rads (8.7 grays), which is a dose equivalent of 870 rems (8.7 sieverts).

Rolling Stones, the British band formed 1962, once notorious as the 'bad

boys' of rock. Original members were Mick Jagger (1943–), Keith Richards (1943–), Brian Jones (1942–1969), Bill Wyman (1936–), Charlie Watts (1941–), and the pianist Ian Stewart (1938–1985).

Rolls-Royce industrial company manufacturing cars and aeroplane engines, founded 1906 by Henry ◊Royce and Charles Rolls. The Silver Ghost car model was designed 1906, and produced until 1925, when the Phantom was introduced. In 1914, Royce designed the Eagle aircraft engine, used extensively in World War I. Royce also designed the Merlin engine, used in Spitfires and Hurricanes in World War II. Jet engines followed, and became an important part of the company.

ROM (acronym for *read-only memory*) in computing, a memory device in the form of a collection of integrated circuits (chips), frequently used in microcomputers. ROM chips are loaded with data and programs during manufacture and, unlike ◊RAM (random- access memory) chips, can subsequently only be read, not written to, by computer. However, the contents of the chips are not lost when the power is switched off, as happens in RAM.

Roman Catholicism one of the main divisions of the Christian religion, separate from the Eastern Orthodox Church from 1054, and headed by the pope. For history and beliefs, see ◊Christianity. Membership is about 585 million worldwide, concentrated in S Europe, Latin America, and the Philippines.

Romance languages branch of Indo-European languages descended from the Latin of the Roman Empire ('popular' or 'vulgar' as opposed to 'classical' Latin). The present-day Romance languages with national status are French, Italian, Portuguese, Romanian, and Spanish.

Roman Empire from 27 BC to the 5th century AD ; see ▷Rome, ancient.

Romania Republic of; *area* 237,500 sq km/91,699 sq mi; *capital* Bucharest; *environment* although sulphur-dioxide levels are low, only 20% of the country's rivers provide drinkable water; *features* Carpathian Mountains, Transylvanian Alps; river Danube; Black Sea coast; mineral springs; *political system* emergent democratic republic; *population* (1993 est) 23,200,000 (Romanians 89%, Hungarians 7.9%, Germans 1.6%); growth rate 0.5% p.a.; *languages* Romanian (official), Hungarian, German; *religions* Romanian Orthodox 80%, Roman Catholic 6%.

Romanian member of the Romance branch of the Indo- European language family, spoken in Romania, Macedonia, Albania, and parts of N Greece. It has been strongly influenced by the Slavonic languages and by Greek. The Cyrillic alphabet was used until the 19th century, when a variant of the Roman alphabet was adopted.

Roman law legal system of ancient Rome that is now the basis of ▷civil law, one of the main European legal systems.

Roman numerals ancient European number system using symbols different from Arabic numerals (the ordinary numbers 1, 2, 3, 4, 5, and so on). The seven key symbols in Roman numerals, as represented today, are I (1), V (5), X (10), L (50), C (100), D (500), and M (1,000). There is no zero, and therefore no place-value as is fundamental to the Arabic system. The first ten Roman numerals are I, II, III, IV (or IIII), V, VI, VII, VIII, IX, and X. When a Roman symbol is preceded by a symbol of equal or greater value, the values of the symbols are added (XVI = 16).

Romanticism in literature, the visual arts, and music, a style that emphasizes the imagination, emotions, and creativity of the individual artist. Romanticism also refers specifically to late-18th- and early-19th-century European culture, as contrasted with 18th-century ▷Classicism.

Romany member of a nomadic people, also called *Gypsy* (a corruption of 'Egyptian', since they were erroneously thought to come from Egypt). They are now believed to have originated in NW India, and live throughout the world. The Romany language, spoken in several different dialects, belongs to the Indic branch of the Indo-European family.

Rome (Italian *Roma*) capital of Italy and of Lazio region, on the river Tiber, 27 km/17 mi from the Tyrrhenian Sea; population (1987) 2,817,000. It is an important cultural centre. Remains of the ancient city include the Forum, Colosseum, and Pantheon.

Rome, ancient civilization based in Rome, which lasted for about 800 years. Traditionally founded 753 BC, Rome became a republic 510 BC. From then, its history is one of almost continual expansion until the murder of Julius ▷Caesar and foundation of the empire under ▷Augustus and his successors. At its peak under Trajan, the Roman Empire stretched from Britain to Mesopotamia and the Caspian Sea. A long train of emperors ruling by virtue of military, rather than civil, power marked the beginning of Rome's long decline; under ▷Diocletian, the empire was divided into two parts – East and

West – although temporarily reunited under ◊Constantine, the first emperor formally to adopt Christianity. The end of the Roman Empire is generally dated by the deposition of the last emperor in the west AD 476. The Eastern Empire continued until 1453 at ◊Constantinople.

Rommel Erwin 1891–1944. German field marshal. He served in World War I, and in World War II he played an important part in the invasions of central Europe and France. He was commander of the N African offensive from 1941 (when he was nicknamed 'Desert Fox') until defeated in the Battles of El Alamein and he was expelled from Africa March 1943.

Röntgen (or *Roentgen*) Wilhelm Konrad 1845–1923. German physicist who discovered X-rays 1895. While investigating the passage of electricity through gases, he noticed the ◊fluorescence of a barium platinocyanide screen. This radiation passed through some substances opaque to light, and affected photographic plates. Developments from this discovery have revolutionized medical diagnosis.

root the part of a plant that is usually underground, and whose primary functions are anchorage and the absorption of water and dissolved mineral salts. Roots usually grow downwards and towards water (see ◊tropism). Plants such as epiphytic orchids, which grow above ground, produce aerial roots that absorb moisture from the atmosphere. Others, such as ivy, have climbing roots arising from the stems, which serve to attach the plant to trees and walls. *Root crops* are cultivated for their swollen edible root. Potatoes are the major temperate root crop; the major tropical root crops are cassava, yams, and sweet potatoes. Root crops are second in importance only to cereals as human food.

root of an equation, a value that satisfies the equality. For example, $x = 0$ and $x = 5$ are roots of the equation $x^2 - 5x = 0$.

Roscommon (originally Ros-Comain, 'wood around a monastery') county of the Republic of Ireland, in the province of Connacht; county town Roscommon; area 2,460 sq km/950 sq mi; population (1991) 51,900. It has rich pastures and is bounded on the E by the river Shannon, with lakes (Gara, Key, Allen) and bogs. It has the remains of a 13th-century castle.

Roseau formerly *Charlotte Town* capital of ◊Dominica, West Indies, on the SW coast of the island; population (1981) 20,000.

Roses, Wars of the civil wars in England 1455–85 between the houses of Lancaster (badge, red rose) and ◊York (badge, white rose), both of whom claimed the throne through descent from the sons of Edward III. As a result of Henry VI's lapse into insanity 1453, Richard, Duke of York, was installed as protector of the realm. Upon his recovery, Henry forced York to take up arms in self-defence.

Rosh Hashanah two-day holiday that marks the start of the Jewish New Year (first new moon after the autumn equinox), traditionally announced by blowing a ram's horn (a shofar).

Rossetti Christina (Georgina) 1830–1894. English poet. She was the sister of Dante Gabriel Rossetti and a devout High Anglican. Her verse includes *Goblin Market and Other Poems* 1862 and expresses unfulfilled spiritual yearning and frustrated love. She was a skilful technician and made use of irregular rhyme and line length.

Rossetti Dante Gabriel 1828–1882. English painter and poet. He was a founding member of the ◊*Pre- Raphaelite Brotherhood (PRB)* 1848. As well as romantic medieval scenes, he produced many idealized portraits of women, including the spiritual *Beata Beatrix* 1864. His verse includes 'The Blessed Damozel' 1850.

Rossini Gioacchino (Antonio) 1792–1868. Italian composer. His first success was the opera *Tancredi* 1813. In 1816 his 'opera buffa' *Il barbiere di Siviglia/The Barber of Seville* was produced in Rome. During 1815–23 he produced 20 operas, and created (with Donizetti and Bellini) the 19th-century Italian operatic style.

Rotterdam industrial port in the Netherlands and one of the foremost ocean cargo ports in the world, in the Rhine-Maas delta, linked by canal 1866–90 with the North Sea; population (1991) 582,266.

Rouault Georges 1871–1958. French painter, etcher, illustrator, and designer. He was one of the major religious artists of the 20th century. Early in his career he was associated with the ◊Fauves but created his own style using rich, dark colours and heavy outlines. His subjects include sad clowns, prostitutes, and evil lawyers. From about 1940 he painted mainly religious works.

Roundhead member of the Parliamentary party during the English Civil War 1640–60, opposing the royalist Cavaliers. The term referred to the short hair then worn only by men of the lower classes.

Rousseau Henri 'Le Douanier' 1844–1910. French painter. A self-taught naive artist, his subjects include scenes of the Parisian suburbs and exotic junglescapes, painted with painstaking detail; for example, *Tropical Storm with a Tiger* 1891 (National Gallery, London).

Rousseau Jean-Jacques 1712–1778. French social philosopher and writer whose *Du Contrat social/Social Contract* 1762, emphasizing the rights of the people over those of the government, was a significant influence on the French Revolution. In the novel *Emile* 1762 he outlined a new theory of education.

rowing propulsion of a boat by oars, either by one rower with two oars (sculling) or by crews (two, four, or eight persons) with one oar each, often with a coxswain. Major events include the world championship, first held 1962 for men and 1974 for women, and the Boat Race (between England's Oxford and Cambridge universities), first held 1829.

Royal Greenwich Observatory the national astronomical observatory of the UK, founded 1675 at Greenwich, E London, England, to provide navigational information for sailors. After World War II it was moved to Herstmonceux Castle, Sussex; in 1990 it was transferred to Cambridge. It also operates telescopes on La Palma in the Canary Islands, including the 4.2-m/165-in William Herschel Telescope, commissioned 1987.

rubber coagulated latex of a variety of plants, mainly from the New World. Most important is Para rubber, which derives from the tree *Hevea brasiliensis* of the spurge family. It was introduced from Brazil to SE Asia, where most of the world supply is now produced, the chief exporters being Peninsular Malaysia, Indonesia, Sri Lanka, Cambodia, Thailand, Sarawak, and Brunei. At about seven years the tree, which may grow to 20 m/60 ft, is ready for 'tapping'. Small incisions are made in the trunk and the latex drips into collecting cups. In pure form, rubber is white and has the formula $(C_5H_8)n$.

rubella technical term for ▷German measles.

Rubens Peter Paul 1577–1640. Flemish painter. He brought the exuberance of Italian Baroque to N Europe, creating, with an army of assistants, innumerable religious and allegorical paintings for churches and palaces. These show mastery of drama in large compositions, and love of rich colour. He also painted portraits and, in his last years, landscapes.

Rubicon ancient name of the small river flowing into the Adriatic that, under the Roman Republic, marked the boundary between Italy proper and Cisalpine Gaul. When ▷Caesar led his army across it 49 BC, he therefore declared war on the republic; hence to 'cross the Rubicon' means to take an irrevocable step.

Rugby League professional form of rugby football founded in England 1895 as the Northern Union when a dispute about pay caused northern clubs to break away from the Rugby Football Union. The game is similar to Rugby Union, but the number of players was reduced from 15 to 13 in 1906, and other rule changes have made the game more open and fast- moving.

Rugby Union amateur form of rugby football in which there are 15 players on each side. 'Tries' are scored by 'touching

down' the ball beyond the goal line or by kicking goals from penalties. The Rugby Football Union was formed 1871 and has its headquarters in England (Twickenham, Middlesex).

Ruisdael or **Ruysdael** Jacob van c. 1628–1682. Dutch landscape painter. He painted rural scenes near his native town of Haarlem and in Germany, and excelled in depicting gnarled and weatherbeaten trees. A notable example of his work is *The Jewish Cemetery* about 1660 (Gemäldegalerie, Dresden). The few figures in his pictures were painted by other artists.

ruminant any even-toed hoofed mammal with a rumen, the 'first stomach' of its complex digestive system. Plant food is stored and fermented before being brought back to the mouth for chewing (chewing the cud) and then is swallowed to the next stomach. Ruminants include cattle, antelopes, goats, deer, and giraffes, all with a four-chambered stomach. Camels are also ruminants, but they have a three-chambered stomach.

Rump, the English parliament formed between Dec 1648 and Nov 1653 after Pride's purge of the ▷Long Parliament to ensure a majority in favour of trying Charles I. It was dismissed 1653 by Cromwell, who replaced it with the ▷Barebones Parliament.

rune character in the oldest Germanic script, chiefly adapted from the Latin alphabet, the earliest examples being from the 3rd century, and found in Denmark. Runes were scratched on wood, metal, stone, or bone.

rush any grasslike plant of the genus *Juncus*, family Juncaceae, found in wet places in cold and temperate regions.

The round stems and flexible leaves of some species have been used for making mats and baskets since ancient times.

Rushdie (Ahmed) Salman 1947– . British writer. He was born in India of a Muslim family. His novel *The Satanic Verses* 1988 (the title refers to verses deleted from the Koran) offended many Muslims with alleged blasphemy. In 1989 the Ayatollah Khomeini of Iran called for Rushdie and his publishers to be killed.

Ruskin John 1819–1900. English art critic and social critic. He published five volumes of *Modern Painters* 1843–60 and *The Seven Lamps of Architecture* 1849, in which he stated his philosophy of art. His writings hastened the appreciation of painters considered unorthodox at the time, such as J M W ◊Turner and the ◊Pre-Raphaelite Brotherhood. His later writings were concerned with social and economic problems.

Russell Bertrand (Arthur William), 3rd Earl Russell 1872–1970. English philosopher and mathematician who contributed to the development of modern mathematical logic and wrote about social issues. His works include *Principia Mathematica* 1910–13 (with A N Whitehead (1861–1947)), in which he attempted to show that mathematics could be reduced to a branch of logic; *The Problems of Philosophy 1912*; and *A History of Western Philosophy 1946*. He was an outspoken liberal pacifist.

Russia originally the prerevolutionary Russian Empire (until 1917), now accurately restricted to the ◊Russian Federation.

Russian member of the majority ethnic group living in Russia. Russians are also often the largest minority in neighbouring republics. The ancestors of the Russians migrated from central Europe between the 6th and 8th centuries AD .The *Russian language* is a member of the East Slavonic branch of the Indo-European language family, written in the Cyrillic alphabet.

Russian Federation formerly (until 1991); *Russian; Soviet Federal Socialist Republic (RSFSR) area* 17,075,500 sq km/6,591,100 sq mi; *capital* Moscow; *features* sixteen autonomous republics: Bashkir; Buryat; Checheno-Ingush; Chuvash; Dagestan; Kabardino-Balkar; Kalmyk; Karelia; Komi; Mari; Mordovia; Vladikavkaz; Tatarstan; Tuva; Udmurt; Yakut; *head of state* Boris Yeltsin from 1990/91; *head of government* Viktor Chernomyrdin from 1992; *political system* emergent democracy; *population* (1993 est) 150,000,000 (82% Russian, Tatar 4%, Ukrainian 3%, Chuvash 1%); *language* Great Russian; *religion* traditionally Russian Orthodox.

Russian Revolution two revolutions of Feb and Oct 1917 (Julian calendar) that began with the overthrow of the Romanov dynasty and ended with the establishment of a communist soviet (council) state, the Union of Soviet Socialist Republics (USSR). In Oct Bolshevik workers and sailors under ◊Lenin seized government buildings and took over power.

Russo-Japanese War war between Russia and Japan 1904–05, which arose from conflicting ambitions in Korea and Manchuria, specifically, the Russian occupation of Port Arthur (modern Dalian) 1896 and of the Amur province 1900. Japan successfully besieged Port Arthur May 1904–Jan 1905, took Mukden (modern Shenyang) on 29 Feb–10 March, and on 27 May defeated the Russian Baltic fleet, which had sailed halfway around the world to Tsushima Strait. A peace was signed 23 Aug 1905. Russia surrendered its lease on Port Arthur, ceded S Sakhalin to Japan, evacuated Manchuria, and recognized Japan's interests in Korea.

Rutherford Ernest 1871–1937. New Zealand physicist, a pioneer of modern atomic science. His main research was in the field of radioactivity, and he discovered alpha, beta, and gamma rays. He named the nucleus, and was the first to recognize the nuclear nature of the atom. Nobel prize 1908.

Rwanda Republic of (*Republika y'u Rwanda*); *area* 26,338 sq km/10,173 sq mi; *capital* Kigali; *features* Mount Karisimbi 4,507 m/14,792 ft; Kagera River and National Park; *political system* transitional; *population* (1993 est) 7,700,000 (Hutu 90%, Tutsi 9%, Twa 1%); growth rate 3.3% p.a. During the 1993–94 civil war, several thousands were killed; *languages* Kinyarwanda, French (official); Kiswahili; *religions* Roman Catholic 54%, animist 23%, Protestant 12%, Muslim 9%.

rye cereal *Secale cereale* grown extensively in N Europe and other temperate regions. The flour is used to make dark-coloured ('black') breads. Rye is grown mainly as a forage crop, but the grain is also used to make whisky and breakfast cereals.

Ryukyu Islands southernmost island group of Japan, stretching towards Taiwan and including Okinawa, Miyako, and Ishigaki; *area* 2,254 sq km/870 sq mi; *capital* Naha, on Okinawa; *features* 73 islands, some uninhabited; *population* (1985) 1,179,000.

S

Sacramento industrial port and capital (since 1854) of California, USA, 130 km/80 mi NE of San Francisco; population (1990) 369,400, metropolitan area 1,481,100. It stands on the Sacramento River.

Sadat Anwar 1918–1981. Egyptian politician. Succeeding ◊Nasser as president 1970, he restored morale by his handling of the Egyptian campaign in the 1973 war against Israel. He was assassinated by Islamic fundamentalists. Nobel Peace Prize with Israeli prime minister Menachem Begin 1978.

Sade Donatien Alphonse François, Comte de, known as the *Marquis de Sade* 1740–1814. French author. He was imprisoned for sexual offences and finally committed to an asylum. He wrote plays and novels dealing explicitly with a variety of sexual practices, including sadism, deriving pleasure or sexual excitement from inflicting pain on others.

sage perennial herb *Salvia officinalis* with grey-green aromatic leaves used for flavouring. It grows up to 50 cm/20 in high and has bluish-lilac or pink flowers.

Sahara largest desert in the world, occupying 5,500,000 sq km/2,123,000 sq mi of N Africa from the Atlantic to the Nile, covering: W Egypt; part of W Sudan; large parts of Mauritania, Mali, Niger, and Chad; and southern parts of Morocco, Algeria, Tunisia, and Libya. Small areas in Algeria and Tunisia are below sea level, but it is mainly a plateau with a central mountain system, including the Ahaggar Mountains in Algeria, the Aïr Massif in Niger, and the Tibesti Massif in Chad, of which the highest peak is Emi Koussi, 3,415 m/11,208 ft. The area of the Sahara expanded by 650,000 sq km/251,000 sq mi 1940–90, but reafforestation is being attempted in certain areas.

Sahel marginal area to the S of the Sahara, from Senegal to Somalia, where the desert is gradually encroaching. The desertification is partly due to climatic change but has also been caused by the pressures of a rapidly expanding population, which have led to overgrazing and the destruction of trees and scrub for fuelwood. In recent years many famines have taken place in the area.

saint holy man or woman respected for his or her wisdom, spirituality, and dedication to their faith. Within the Roman Catholic church a saint is officially recognized through canonization by the pope after a thorough investigation of the lives and miracles attributed to them. In the Orthodox church saints are recognized by the patriarch and Holy Synod after recommendation by local churches. The term is also used in Buddhism for individuals who have led a virtuous and holy life.

St Christopher (St Kitts)–Nevis Federation of; *area* 269 sq km/104 sq mi (St Christopher 176 sq km/68 sq mi, Nevis 93 sq km/36 sq mi); *capital* Basseterre (on St Christopher); *features* fertile plains on coast; black beaches; *political system* federal constitutional monarchy; *population* (1993 est) 44,000; growth rate 0.2% p.a.; *language* English; *religion* Anglican 36%, Methodist 32%, other Protestant 8%, Roman Catholic 10% (1985 est).

St George's port and capital of Grenada, on the SW coast; population (1986) 7,500, urban area 29,000. It was founded 1650 by the French.

St John's port and capital of Antigua and Barbuda, on the NW coast of Antigua; population (1982) 30,000.

St Lucia *area* 617 sq km/238 sq mi; *capital* Castries; *features* volcanic peaks; Gros and Petit Pitons; *political system* constitutional monarchy; *population* (1993) 136,000; growth rate 2.8% p.a.; *languages* English; French patois; *religion* Roman Catholic 90%.

St Petersburg capital of the St Petersburg region, Russia, at the head of the Gulf of Finland; population (1989 est) 5,023,500. Its name was changed to *Petrograd* 1914 and was called *Leningrad* 1924–91, when its original name was restored. Built on a low and swampy site, St Petersburg is split up by the mouths of the river Neva, which connects it with Lake Ladoga. The climate is severe.

St Vincent and the Grenadines *area* 388 sq km/150 sq mi, including islets of the Northern Grenadines 43 sq km/17 sq mi; *capital* Kingstown; *features* Mustique, one of the Grenadines, a holiday resort; Soufrière volcano; *political system* constitutional monarchy; *population* (1993 est) 115,000; growth rate –4% p.a.; *languages* English; French patois; *religions* Anglican 47%, Methodist 28%, Roman Catholic 13%.

salamander any tailed amphibian of the order *Urodela*. They are sometimes confused with lizards, but unlike lizards they have no scales or claws. Salamanders have smooth or warty moist skin. The order includes some 300 species, arranged in nine families, found mainly in the northern hemisphere. Salamanders include hellbenders, mudpuppies, waterdogs, sirens, mole salamanders, newts, and lungless salamanders (dusky, woodland, and spring salamanders).

Salinger J(erome) D(avid) 1919– . US writer. He wrote the classic novel of mid-20th-century adolescence *The Catcher in the Rye* 1951. He developed his lyrical Zen themes in *Franny and Zooey* 1961 and *Raise High the Roof Beams, Carpenters and Seymour: An Introduction* 1963, short stories about a Jewish family named Glass, after which he stopped publishing.

salmon any of the various bony fishes of the family Salmonidae. More specifically the name is applied to several species of game fishes of the genera Salmo and Oncorhynchus of North America and Eurasia that mature in the ocean but, to spawn, return to the freshwater streams where they were born. Their normal colour is silvery with a few dark spots, but the colour changes at the spawning season.

Salmonella very varied group of bacteria that colonize the intestines of humans and some animals. Some strains cause typhoid and paratyphoid fevers, while others cause salmonella ▷food poisoning, which is characterized by stomach pains, vomiting, diarrhoea, and headache. It can be fatal in elderly people, but others usually recover in a few days without antibiotics. Most cases are caused by contaminated animal products, especially poultry meat.

salt in chemistry, any compound formed from an acid and a base through the replacement of all or part of the hydrogen in the acid by a metal or electropositive radical. *Common salt* is sodium chloride.

salt, common or *sodium chloride* NaCl white crystalline solid, found dissolved in sea water and as rock salt (halite) in large deposits and salt domes. Common salt is used extensively in the food industry as a preservative and for flavouring, and in the chemical industry in the making of chlorine and sodium.

Salvador port and naval base in Bahia state, NE Brazil, on the inner side of a peninsula separating Todos Santos Bay from the Atlantic Ocean; population (1991) 2,075,400.

Salzburg capital of the state of Salzburg, W Austria, on the river Salzach; population (1981) 139,400. The city is dominated by the Hohensalzburg fortress. It is the birthplace of the composer Wolfgang Amadeus Mozart and an annual music festival has been held here since 1920.

Samaritan member or descendant of the colonists forced to settle in Samaria (now N Israel) by the Assyrians after their occupation of the ancient kingdom of Israel 722 BC. Samaritans adopted a form of Judaism, but adopted only the Pentateuch, the five books of Moses of the Old Testament, and regarded their temple on Mount Gerizim as the true sanctuary.

Samoa, American group of islands 4,200 km/2,610 mi S of Hawaii, administered by the USA; *area* 200 sq km/77 sq mi; *capital* Fagatogo on Tutuila; *features* five volcanic islands, including Tutuila, Tau, and Swain's Island, and two coral atolls; *population* (1990) 46,800; *languages* Samoan and English; *religion* Christian.

Samoa, Western Independent State of (*Samoa i Sisifo*); *area* 2,830 sq km/1,093 sq mi; *capital* Apia (on Upolu island); *features* lava flows on Savai'i; *political system* liberal democracy; *population* (1993 est) 200,000; growth rate 1.1% p.a.; *languages* English, Samoan (official); *religions* Protestant 70%, Roman Catholic 20%.

Sampras Pete(r) 1971– . US tennis player, winner of Wimbledon 1993 and 1994. At the age of 19 years and 28 days, he became the youngest winner of the US Open 1990. A fine server and volleyer, Sampras also won the inaugural Grand Slam Cup in Munich 1990.

samurai member of the military caste in Japan from the mid-12th century until 1869, when the feudal system was abolished and all samurai pensioned off by the government. A samurai was an armed retainer of a *daimyō* (large landowner) with specific duties and privileges and a strict code of honour. A *rōnin* was a samurai without feudal allegiance.

Sana'a capital of Yemen, SW Arabia, 320 km/200 mi N of Aden; population (1986) 427,000. A walled city, with fine mosques and traditional architecture, it is rapidly being modernized.

San Andreas fault geological fault line stretching for 1,125 km/700 mi in a NW–SE direction through the state of California, USA.

sand loose grains of rock, sized 0.0625–2.00 mm/0.0025–0.08 in in diameter, consisting chiefly of ▷quartz, but owing their varying colour to mixtures of other minerals. Sand is used in cement-making, as an abrasive, in glassmaking, and for other purposes.

Sand George. Pen name of Amandine Aurore Lucie Dupin 1804–1876. French author. Her prolific literary output was often autobiographical. In 1831 she left her husband after nine years of marriage and, while living in Paris as a writer, had love affairs with Alfred de Musset, Chopin, and others. Her first novel *Indiana* 1832 was a plea for women's right to independence.

San Diego city and military and naval base in California, USA; population (1990) 1,110,500, metropolitan area 2,498,000. It is an important Pacific Ocean fishing port.

Sandinista member of a Nicaraguan left-wing organization (Sandinist National Liberation Front, FSLN) named after Augusto César Sandino, a guerrilla leader killed in 1934. It was formed 1962 and obtained widespread support from the trade unions, the church, and the middle classes, which enabled it to overthrow the regime of General Anastasio Somoza in July 1979. The FSLN dominated the Nicaraguan government and fought a civil war against US-backed Contra guerrillas until 1988. The FSLN was defeated in elections of 1990 but remained the party with the largest number of seats.

sandstone ▷sedimentary rocks formed from the consolidation of sand, with sand-sized grains (0.0625–2 mm/0.0025–0.08 in) in a matrix or cement. Their principal component is quartz. Sandstones are commonly permeable and porous, and may form freshwater ▷aquifers. They are mainly used as building materials.

San Francisco chief Pacific port of the USA, in California; population (1990) 724,000, metropolitan area of San Francisco and Oakland 3,686,600. The city stands on a peninsula, on the south side of the Golden Gate Strait, spanned 1937 by the world's second-ongest single-span bridge, 1,280 m/4,200 ft. The strait gives access to San Francisco Bay.

Sanger Frederick 1918– . English biochemist, the first person to win a Nobel Prize for Chemistry twice: the first in 1958 for determining the structure of insulin, and the second in 1980 for work on the chemical structure of genes.

San José capital of Costa Rica; population (1989) 284,600.

San Juan capital of Puerto Rico; population (1990) 437,750. It is a port and industrial city.

San Marino Republic of (*Repubblica di San Marino*); *area* 61 sq km/24 sq mi; *capital* San Marino; *features* surrounded by Italian territory; one of the world's smallest states; *political system* direct democracy; *population* (1993) 24,000; growth rate 0.1% p.a.; *language* Italian; *religion* Roman Catholic 95%.

San Salvador capital of El Salvador 48 km/30 mi from the Pacific Ocean, at the foot of San Salvador volcano (2,548 m/8,360 ft); population (1984) 453,000.

Sanskrit the dominant classical language of the Indian subcontinent, a member of the Indo-Iranian group of the Indo-European language family, and the sacred language of Hinduism. The oldest form of Sanskrit is *Vedic*, the variety used in the *Vedas* and *Upanishads* (about 1500–700 BC).

Santer Jacques 1937– . Luxembourg politician, prime minister from 1984. In July 1994 he was nominated to succeed Jacques Delors as president of the European Commission.

Santiago capital of Chile; population (1990) 4,385,500. It is famous for its broad avenues.

Santo Domingo capital and chief sea port of the Dominican Republic; population (1982) 1,600,000. Founded 1496 by Bartolomeo, brother of Christopher Columbus, it is the oldest colonial city in the Americas.

São Paulo city in Brazil, 72 km/45 mi NW of its port Santos; population (1991) 9,700,100, metropolitan area 15,280,000. It is 900 m/3,000 ft above sea level, and 2° S of the Tropic of Capricorn. It is South America's leading industrial city and is the centre of Brazil's coffee trade.

São Tomé e Principe Democratic Republic of; *area* 1,000 sq km/386 sq mi; *capital* São Tomé; *head of state* Miguel Trovoada from 1991; *population* (1993 est) 130,000; growth rate 2.5% p.a.; *languages* Portuguese (official), Fang (Bantu); *religions* Roman Catholic 80%, animist.

sapphire deep-blue, transparent gem variety of the mineral ▷corundum Al_2O_3, aluminium oxide. Small amounts of iron and titanium give it its colour. A corundum gem of any colour except red (which is a ruby) can be called a sapphire; for example, yellow sapphire.

Sappho *c.* 610–*c.* 580. Greek lyric poet. A native of Lesbos and contemporary of the poet Alcaeus, she was famed for her female eroticism (hence lesbianism). The surviving fragments of her poems express a keen sense of loss, and delight in the worship of the goddess ▷Aphrodite.

Saracen ancient Greek and Roman term for an Arab, used in the Middle Ages by Europeans for all Muslims. The equivalent term used in Spain was ▷Moor.

Sarajevo capital of Bosnia-Herzegovina; population (1991) 415,600. A Bosnian Gavrilo Princip, assassinated Archduke Franz Ferdinand here 1914, thereby precipitating World War I. From April 1992 the city was the target of a siege by Bosnian Serb forces in their fight to carve up the newly independent republic. A United Nations ultimatum and the threat of NATO bombing led to a cease-fire Feb 1994, although fighting continued.

sarcoma malignant ▷tumour arising from the fat, muscles, bones, cartilage, or blood and lymph vessels and connective tissues. Sarcomas are much less common than ▷carcinomas.

Sardinia (Italian *Sardegna*) mountainous island, special autonomous region of Italy; area 24,100 sq km/9,303 sq mi; population (1990) 1,664,400. Its capital is Cagliari. It is the second-largest Mediterranean island and includes Costa Smeralda (Emerald Coast) tourist area in the NE and *nuraghi* (fortified Bronze Age dwellings).

Sartre Jean-Paul 1905–1980. French author and philosopher, a leading proponent of ◊existentialism. He published his first novel, *La Nausée/Nausea* 1937, followed by the trilogy *Les Chemins de la Liberté/Roads to Freedom* 1944–45 and many plays, including *Huis Clos/In Camera* 1944. *L'Etre et le néant/Being and Nothingness* 1943, his first major philosophical work, sets out a radical doctrine of human freedom.

satellite any small body that orbits a larger one, either natural or artificial. Natural satellites that orbit planets are called moons. The first *artificial satellite*, *Sputnik 1*, was launched into orbit around the Earth by the USSR 1957. Artificial satellites are used for scientific purposes, communications, weather forecasting, and military applications. The largest artificial satellites can be seen by the naked eye.

satellite television transmission of broadcast signals through artificial communications satellites. Mainly positioned in geostationary orbit, satellites have been used since the 1960s to relay television pictures around the world. Higher-power satellites have more recently been developed to broadcast signals to cable systems or directly to people's homes.

Saturn in astronomy, the second-largest planet in the solar system, sixth from the Sun, and encircled by bright and easily visible equatorial rings. Viewed through a telescope it is ochre. Saturn orbits the Sun every 29.46 years at an average distance of 1,427,000,000 km/886,700,000 mi. Its equatorial diameter is 120,000 km/75,000 mi, but its polar diameter is 12,000 km/7,450 mi smaller, a result of its fast rotation and low density, the lowest of any planet.

Saturn in Roman mythology, the god of agriculture, identified by the Romans with the Greek god ◊Kronos. His period of rule was the ancient Golden Age. Saturn was dethroned by his sons Jupiter, Neptune, and Dis. At his festival, the Saturnalia in Dec, gifts were exchanged, and slaves were briefly treated as their masters' equals.

Saudi Arabia Kingdom of (*al-Mamlaka al-'Arabiya as-Sa'udiya*); *area* 2,200,518 sq km/849,400 sq mi; *capital* Riyadh; *environment* oil pollution caused by the Gulf War 1990–91 has damaged 460 km/285 mi of the Saudi coastline; *features* Nafud Desert in N and the Rub'al Khali (Empty Quarter) in S; with a ban on women drivers, there are an estimated 300,000 chauffeurs; *political system* absolute monarchy; *population* (1993 est) 17,500,000 (16% nomadic); growth rate 3.1% p.a.; *language* Arabic; *religion* Sunni Muslim; there is a Shi'ite minority.

Saul in the Old Testament, the first king of Israel. He was anointed by Samuel and warred successfully against the neighbouring Ammonites and Philistines, but fell from God's favour in his battle against the Amalekites. He became jealous and suspicious of ◊David and turned against him and Samuel. After being wounded in battle with the Philistines, in which his three sons died, he committed suicide.

savanna or *savannah* extensive open tropical grasslands, with scattered trees and shrubs. Savannas cover large areas of Africa, North and South America, and N Australia. The soil is acidic and sandy and generally considered suitable only as pasture for low-density grazing.

Savonarola Girolamo 1452–1498. Italian reformer, a Dominican friar and an eloquent preacher. His crusade against political and religious corruption won him popular support, and in 1494 he led a revolt in Florence that expelled the ruling Medici family and established a democratic republic. His denunciations of Pope Alexander VI led to his excommunication in 1497, and in 1498 he was arrested, tortured, hanged, and burned for heresy.

Saxon member of a Germanic tribe inhabiting the Danish peninsula and northern Germany. The Saxons migrated from their homelands, under pressure from the Franks, and spread into various parts of Europe, including Britain (see ◊Anglo- Saxon). They also undertook piracy in the North Sea and English Channel.

saxophone member of a hybrid brass instrument family of conical bore, with a single-reed woodwind mouthpiece and keyworks, invented about 1840 by Belgian Adolphe Sax (1814–1894). Soprano, alto, tenor, and baritone forms remain current. The soprano saxophone is usually straight; the others are characteristically curved back at the mouthpiece and have an upturned bell. The saxophone was incorporated into dance bands of the 1930s and 1940s, and assumed its modern guise as an abrasive solo jazz instrument after 1945.

scabies contagious infection of the skin caused by the parasitic itch mite *Sarcoptes scabiei*, which burrows under the skin to deposit eggs. Treatment is by antiparasitic creams and lotions.

Scandinavia peninsula in NW Europe, comprising Norway and Sweden; politically and culturally it also includes Denmark, Iceland, the Faroe Islands, and Finland.

scanning in medicine, the noninvasive examination of body organs to detect abnormalities of structure or function. Detectable waves – for example, ◊ultrasound, gamma or ◊X-rays – are passed through the part to be scanned. Their absorption pattern is recorded, analysed by computer, and displayed pictorially on a screen.

Scarlatti (Giuseppe) Domenico 1685–1757. Italian composer. The eldest son of Italian Baroque composer Alessandro Scarlatti (1660–1725), he lived most of his life in Portugal and Spain. He wrote over 500 sonatas for harpsichord.

scarlet fever or *scarlatina* acute infectious disease, especially of children, caused by the bacteria in the *Streptococcus pyogenes* group. It is marked by fever, vomiting, sore throat and a bright red rash spreading from the upper to the lower part of the body. The rash is followed by the skin peeling in flakes. It is treated with antibiotics.

scepticism ancient philosophical view that absolute knowledge of things is ultimately unobtainable, hence the only proper attitude is to suspend judgement. Its origins lay in the teachings of the Greek philosopher Pyrrho, who maintained that peace of mind lay in renouncing all claims to knowledge.

Schiele Egon 1890–1918. Austrian Expressionist artist. Originally a landscape painter, he was strongly influenced by Art Nouveau, in particular Gustav Klimt, and developed a contorted linear style, employing strong colours. His subject matter includes portraits and openly erotic nudes. In 1911 he was arrested for alleged obscenity.

Schiller Johann Christoph Friedrich von 1759–1805. German dramatist, poet, and historian. He wrote *Sturm und Drang* ('storm and stress') verse and plays, including the dramatic trilogy *Wallenstein* 1798–99. Much of his work concerns the aspirations for political freedom and the avoidance of mediocrity.

schizophrenia mental disorder, a psychosis of unknown origin, which can lead to profound changes in personality, behaviour, and perception, including delusions and hallucinations. It is more common in males and the early onset form is more severe than when the illness develops in later life. Modern treatment approaches include drugs, family therapy, stress reduction, and rehabilitation. It is now recognized as an organic disease, associated with structural anomalies in the brain.

Schliemann Heinrich 1822–1890. German archaeologist. In 1871 he began excavating at Hissarlik, Turkey, a site which yielded the ruins of nine consecutive cities and discovered the site of Troy. His later excavations were at Mycenae 1874–76, where he discovered the ruins of the ▷Mycenaean civilization.

Schlüter Poul Holmskov 1929– . Danish right-wing politician, leader of the Conservative People's Party (KF) from 1974 and prime minister 1982–93. In Jan 1993 Schlüter resigned, accused of dishonesty over his role in an incident involving Tamil refugees. He was succeeded by Poul Nyrup Rasmussen.

Schoenberg Arnold (Franz Walter) 1874–1951. Austro-Hungarian composer. He was a US citizen from 1941. After Romantic early works such as *Verklärte Nacht/Transfigured Night* 1899 and the *Gurrelieder/Songs of Gurra* 1900–11, he experimented with atonality (absence of key), producing works such as *Pierrot lunaire/Moonstruck Pierrot* 1912 for chamber ensemble and voice, before developing the twelve-tone system of musical composition.

scholasticism the theological and philosophical systems that were studied in both Christian and Judaic schools in Europe in the medieval period. It sought to integrate biblical teaching with Platonic and Aristotelian philosophy.

Schrödinger Erwin 1887–1961. Austrian physicist who advanced the study of wave mechanics (see ▷quantum theory). Born in Vienna, he became senior professor at the Dublin Institute for Advanced Studies 1940. He shared (with Paul Dirac) a Nobel prize 1933.

Schubert Franz (Peter) 1797–1828. Austrian composer. His ten symphonies include the incomplete eighth in B minor (the 'Unfinished') and the 'Great' in C major. He wrote chamber and piano music, including the 'Trout Quintet', and over 600 lieder (songs) combining the Romantic expression of emotion with pure melody. They include the cycles *Die schöne Müllerin/The Beautiful Maid of the Mill* 1823 and *Die Winterreise/The Winter Journey* 1827.

Schumacher Fritz (Ernst Friedrich) 1911–1977. German economist who believed that the increasing size of institutions, coupled with unchecked economic growth, created a range of social and environmental problems. He argued his case in books like *Small is Beautiful* 1973, and tested it practically through establishing the Intermediate Technology Development Group.

Schumann Robert Alexander 1810–1856. German composer and writer. His songs and short piano pieces portray states of emotion with great economy. Among his compositions are four symphonies, a violin concerto, a piano concerto, sonatas, and song cycles, such as *Dichterliebe/Poet's Love* 1840. Mendelssohn championed many of his works.

science any systematic field of study or body of knowledge that aims, through experiment, observation, and deduction, to produce reliable explanation of phenomena, with reference to the material and physical world.

Scientology 'applied religious philosophy' founded in California in 1954 by L Ron Hubbard (1911–86) as the *Church of Scientology*. It claims to 'increase man's spiritual awareness', but its methods of recruiting and retaining converts have been criticized.

Scilly, Isles of or *Scilly Isles/Islands*, or *Scillies* group of 140 islands and islets lying 40 km/25 mi SW of Land's End, England; administered by the Duchy of Cornwall; area 16 sq km/6.3 sq mi; population (1991) 2,050. The five inhabited islands are *St Mary's*, the largest, on which is Hugh Town, capital of the Scillies; *Tresco*, the second largest, with subtropical gardens; *St Martin's*, noted for beautiful shells; *St Agnes*; and *Bryher*.

scorpion any arachnid of the order Scorpiones. Common in the tropics and subtropics, scorpions have large pincers and long tails ending in upcurved poisonous stings, though the venom is not usually fatal to a healthy adult human. Some species reach 25 cm/10 in. They produce live young rather than eggs, and hunt chiefly by night.

Scot inhabitant of Scotland, part of Britain; or person of Scottish descent. Originally the Scots were a Celtic (Gaelic) people of N Ireland who migrated to Scotland in the 5th century.

Scotland the northernmost part of Britain, formerly an independent country, now part of the UK; *area* 78,470 sq km/ 30,297 sq mi; *capital* Edinburgh; *features* the Highlands in the N with the Grampian Mountains; Southern Uplands (including the Lammermuir Hills; islands of the Orkneys, Shetlands, and Western Isles; the world's greatest concentration of nuclear weapons are at the UK and US bases on the Clyde, near Glasgow; *government* Scotland sends 72 members to the UK Parliament at Westminster. Local government is on similar lines to that of England, but there is a differing legal system; *population* (1988 est) 5,094,000; *languages* English; Scots, a lowland dialect (derived from Northumbrian Anglo-Saxon); Gaelic spoken by 1.3%, mainly in the Highlands; *religions* Presbyterian (Church of Scotland), Roman Catholic.

Scots English language as traditionally spoken and written in Scotland, regarded by some scholars as a distinct language. Scots derives from the Northumbrian dialect of Anglo-Saxon or Old English, and has been a literary language since the 14th century.

Scott (George) Gilbert 1811–1878. English architect. As the leading practical architect of the mid-19th-century Gothic Revival in England, Scott was responsible for the building or restoration of many public buildings and monuments, including the Albert Memorial, London, 1863–72.

Scott Robert Falcon (known as *Scott of the Antarctic*) 1868–1912. English explorer who commanded two Antarctic expeditions, 1901–04 and 1910–12. On 18 Jan 1912 he reached the South Pole, shortly after Norwegian Roald ▷Amundsen, but on the return journey he and his companions died in a blizzard only a few miles from their base camp. His journal was recovered and published in 1913.

Scott Walter 1771–1832. Scottish novelist and poet. His first works were translations of German ballads, followed by poems such as *The Lady of the Lake* 1810 and *Lord of the Isles* 1815. He gained a European reputation for his historical novels such as *The Heart of Midlothian* 1818, *Ivanhoe* 1819, and *The Fair Maid of Perth* 1828. His last years were marked by frantic writing to pay off his debts, after the bankruptcy of his publishing company 1826.

Scottish law the legal system of Scotland. Owing to its separate development, Scotland has a system differing from the rest of the UK, being based on ▷civil law. Its continued separate existence was guaranteed by the Act of Union with England in 1707.

Scout member of a worldwide youth organization that emphasizes character, citizenship, and outdoor life. It was founded (as the Boy Scouts) in England 1908 by Robert ▷Baden- Powell.

scuba acronym for *self-contained underwater breathing apparatus*, another name for ▷aqualung.

scurvy disease caused by deficiency of vitamin C (ascorbic acid), which is contained in fresh vegetables and fruit. The signs are weakness and aching joints and muscles, progressing to bleeding of the gums and other spontaneous haemorrhage, and drying-up of the skin and hair. It is reversed by giving the vitamin.

Scythia region north of the Black Sea between the Carpathian mountains and the river Don, inhabited by the Scythians 7th–1st centuries BC. From the middle of the 4th century, they were slowly superseded by the Sarmatians. The Scythians produced ornaments and vases in gold and electrum with animal decoration. Although there is no surviving written work, there are spectacular archaeological remains, including vast royal burial mounds which often contain horse skeletons.

seafloor spreading growth of the ocean crust outwards (sideways) from ocean ridges. The concept of seafloor spreading has been combined with that of continental drift and incorporated into ▷plate tectonics.

seal aquatic carnivorous mammal of the families Otariidae and Phocidae (sometimes placed in a separate order, the Pinnipedia). The eared seals or sea lions (Otariidae) have small external ears, unlike the true seals (Phocidae). Seals have a streamlined body with thick blubber for insulation, and front and hind flippers. They feed on fish, squid, or crustaceans, and are commonly found in Arctic and Antarctic seas, but also in Mediterranean, Caribbean, and Hawaiian waters.

Sea Peoples unidentified seafaring warriors who may have been Achaeans, Etruscans, or ▷Philistines, who ravaged and settled the Mediterranean coasts in the 12th–13th centuries BC. They were defeated by Ramses III of Egypt 1191 BC.

sea urchin any of various orders of the class Echinoidea among the ◊echinoderms. They all have a globular body enclosed with plates of lime and covered with spines. Sometimes the spines are anchoring organs, and they also assist in locomotion. Sea urchins feed on seaweed and the animals frequenting them, and some are edible.

seaweed any of a vast collection of marine and freshwater, simple, multicellular plant forms belonging to the ◊algae and found growing from about highwater mark to depths of 100–200 m/300–600 ft. Some have holdfasts, stalks, and fronds, sometimes with air bladders to keep them afloat, and are green, blue-green, red, or brown.

Sebastiano del Piombo (Sebastiano Veneziano) *c.* 1485–1547. Italian painter of the High Renaissance. Born in Venice, he was a pupil of ◊Giorgione and developed a similar style of painting. In 1511 he moved to Rome, where his friendship with Michelangelo (and rivalry with Raphael) inspired him to his greatest works, such as *The Raising of Lazarus* 1517–19 (National Gallery, London).

Sebastian, St Roman soldier, traditionally a member of Emperor Diocletian's bodyguard until his Christian faith was discovered. He was martyred by being shot with arrows. Feast day 20 Jan.

Second World War alternative name for ◊World War II, 1939–45.

sedative any drug that has a calming effect, reducing anxiety and tension. Sedatives will induce sleep in larger doses. Examples are ◊barbiturates, ◊narcotics, and ◊benzodiazepines.

sediment any loose material that has 'settled' – deposited from suspension in water, ice, or air, generally as the water current or wind speed decreases. Typical sediments are, in order of increasing coarseness, clay, mud, silt, sand, gravel, pebbles, cobbles, and boulders.

sedimentary rock rock formed by the accumulation and cementation of deposits that have been laid down by water, wind, ice, or gravity. Sedimentary rocks cover more than two-thirds of the Earth's surface and comprise three major categories: clastic, chemically precipitated, and organic (or biogenic). Clastic sediments are the largest group and are composed of fragments of pre-existing rocks; they include clays, sands, and gravels. Chemical precipitates include some limestones and evaporated deposits such as gypsum and halite (rock salt). Coal, oil shale, and limestone made of fossil material are examples of organic sedimentary rocks.

seed the reproductive structure of higher plants (◊angiosperms and ◊gymnosperms). It develops from a fertilized ovule and consists of an embryo and a food store, surrounded and protected by an outer seed coat, called the testa. The food store is contained either in a specialized nutritive tissue, the endosperm, or in the ◊cotyledons of the embryo itself. In angiosperms the seed is enclosed within a ◊fruit, whereas in gymnosperms it is usually naked and unprotected, once shed from the female cone. Following ◊germination the seed develops into a new plant.

seed plant any seed-bearing plant; also known as a *spermatophyte*. The seed plants are subdivided into two classes: the ◊angiosperms, or flowering plants, and the ◊gymnosperms, principally the cycads and conifers.

Seine French river rising on the Langres plateau NW of Dijon, and flowing 774 km/472 mi NW to join the English Channel near Le Havre, passing through Paris and Rouen.

seismology study of earthquakes and how their shock waves travel through the Earth. By examining the global pattern of waves produced by an earthquake, seismologists can deduce the nature of the materials through which they have passed. This leads to an understanding of the Earth's internal structure.

selenium grey, nonmetallic element, symbol Se, atomic number 34, relative atomic mass 78.96. It belongs to the sulphur group and occurs in several allotropic forms that differ in their physical and chemical properties. It is an essential trace element in human nutrition. Obtained from many sulphide ores and selenides, it is used as a red colouring for glass and enamel.

Sellers Peter 1925–1980. English comedian and film actor. He was noted for his skill at mimicry. He made his name in the madcap British radio programme *The Goon Show* 1949–60. His films include *The Ladykillers* 1955, *I'm All Right Jack* 1960, *Dr Strangelove* 1964, five *Pink Panther* films 1964–78 (as the bumbling Inspector Clouseau), and *Being There* 1979.

semaphore visual signalling code in which the relative positions of two moveable pointers or hand-held flags stand for different letters or numbers. The system is used by ships at sea and for railway signals.

semiconductor crystalline material with an electrical conductivity between that of metals (good) and insulators (poor). The conductivity of semiconductors can usually be improved by minute additions of different substances or by other factors. Silicon, for example, has poor conductivity at low temperatures, but this is improved by the application of light, heat, or voltage; hence silicon is used in ◊transistors, rectifiers, and ◊integrated circuits (silicon chips).

Semite member of any of the peoples of the Middle East originally speaking a Semitic language, and traditionally said to be descended from Shem, a son of Noah in the Bible. Ancient Semitic peoples include the Hebrews, Ammonites, Moabites, Edomites, Babylonians, Assyrians, Chaldaeans, Phoenicians, and Canaanites. The Semitic peoples founded the monotheistic religions of Judaism, Christianity, and Islam.

Senate in ancient Rome, the 'council of elders'. Originally consisting of the heads of patrician families, it was recruited from ex-magistrates and persons who had rendered notable public service, but was periodically purged by the censors. Although nominally advisory, it controlled finance and foreign policy.

Seneca Lucius Annaeus *c.* 4 BC– AD 65. Roman Stoic playwright, author of essays and nine tragedies. He was tutor to the future emperor Nero but lost favour after the latter's accession to the throne and was ordered to commit suicide. His tragedies were accepted as classical models by 16th-century dramatists.

Senegal Republic of (*République du Sénégal*); *area* 196,200 sq km/75,753 sq mi; *capital* (and chief port) Dakar; *features* river Senegal; the Gambia forms an enclave within Senegal; *political system* emergent socialist democratic republic;

population (1993) 7,970,000; growth rate 3.1% p.a.; *languages* French (official); African dialects are spoken; *religions* Muslim 80%, Roman Catholic 10%, animist.

Seoul or *Sŏul* capital of South ▷Korea (Republic of Korea), near the Han River, and with its chief port at Inchon; population (1985) 10,627,800.

sepal part of a flower, usually green, that surrounds and protects the flower in bud. The sepals are derived from modified leaves, and are collectively known as the ▷calyx.

Sephardi (plural *Sephardim*) Jew descended from those expelled from Spain and Portugal in the 15th century, or from those forcibly converted during the Inquisition to Christianity (Marranos). Many settled in N Africa and in the Mediterranean countries, as well as in the Netherlands, England, and Dutch colonies in the New World. Sephardim speak Ladino, a 15th-century Romance dialect, as well as the language of their nation.

sequencing in biochemistry, determining the sequence of chemical subunits within a large molecule. Techniques for sequencing amino acids in proteins were established in the 1950s, insulin being the first for which the sequence was completed. Efforts are now being made to determine the sequence of base pairs within ▷DNA.

sequoia two species of conifer in the redwood family Taxodiaceae, native to W USA. The redwood *Sequoia sempervirens* is a long-lived timber tree, and one specimen, the Howard Libbey Redwood, is the world's tallest tree at 110 m/361 ft, with a circumference of 13.4 m/44 ft. The giant sequoia *Sequoiadendron giganteum* reaches up to 30 m/100 ft in circumference at the base, and grows almost as tall as the redwood. It is also (except for the bristlecone pine) the oldest living tree, some specimens being estimated at over 3,500 years of age.

Serb member of Yugoslavia's largest ethnic group, found mainly in Serbia, but also in neighbouring Bosnia- Herzegovina and Croatia. Their language, generally recognized to be the same as Croat and hence known as *Serbo- Croatian* (or *Serbo-Croat*) belongs to the Slavic branch of the Indo-European family. The different dialects of Serbo-Croatian tend to be written by the Greek Orthodox Serbs in the Cyrillic script, and by the Roman Catholic Croats in the Latin script.

Serbia (Serbo-Croatian *Srbija*) constituent republic of Yugoslavia, which includes Kosovo and Vojvodina; *area* 88,400 sq km/34,122 sq mi; *capital* Belgrade; *population* (1991) 9,791,400; *language* the Serbian variant of Serbo-Croatian; *religion* Serbian Orthodox.

serum clear fluid that separates out from clotted blood. It is blood plasma with the anticoagulant proteins removed, and contains ▷antibodies and other proteins, as well as the fats and sugars of the blood. It can be produced synthetically, and is used to protect against disease.

set or *class* in mathematics, any collection of defined things (elements), provided the elements are distinct and that there is a rule to decide whether an element is a member of a set. It is usually denoted by a capital letter and indicated by curly brackets {}.

Settlement, Act of in Britain, a law passed 1701 during the reign of King William III, designed to ensure a Protestant succession to the throne by excluding the Roman Catholic descendants of James II in favour of the Protestant House of Hanover. Elizabeth II still reigns under this act.

Seurat Georges 1859–1891. French artist. He originated, with Paul Signac, the Neo-Impressionist technique of Pointillism (painting with small dabs rather than long brushstrokes). Examples of his work are *Bathers at Asnières* 1884 (National Gallery, London) and *Sunday on the Island of La Grande Jatte* 1886 (Art Institute of Chicago).

Seven Wonders of the World in antiquity, the ▷pyramids of Egypt, the Hanging Gardens of Babylon, the temple of Artemis at Ephesus, the statue of Zeus at Olympia, the Mausoleum at Halicarnassus, the Colossus of Rhodes, and the Pharos (lighthouse) at Alexandria.

Severn river of Wales and England, rising on the NE side of Plynlimmon, N Wales, and flowing 338 km/210 mi through Shrewsbury, Worcester, and Gloucester to the Bristol Channel. It is the longest river in Great Britain.

sex determination process by which the sex of an organism is determined. In many species, the sex of an individual is dictated by the two sex chromosomes (X and Y) it receives from its parents. In mammals, some plants, and a few insects, males are XY, and females XX; in birds, reptiles, some amphibians, and butterflies the reverse is the case. In bees and wasps, males are produced from unfertilized eggs, females from fertilized eggs.

sexism belief in (or set of implicit assumptions about) the superiority of one's own sex, often accompanied by a stereotype or preconceived idea about the opposite sex. Sexism may also be accompanied by ▷discrimination on the basis of sex, generally as practised by men against women.

sexually transmitted disease (STD) any disease transmitted by sexual contact, involving transfer of body fluids. STDs include not only traditional ▷venereal disease, but also a growing list of conditions, such as ▷AIDS and scabies, which are known to be spread primarily by sexual contact. Other diseases that are transmitted sexually include viral ▷hepatitis.

sexual reproduction reproductive process in organisms that requires the union, or ▷fertilization, of gametes (such as eggs and sperm). These are usually produced by two different individuals, although self-fertilization occurs in a few ▷hermaphrodites such as tapeworms. Most organisms other than bacteria and cyanobacteria (▷blue- green algae) show some sort of sexual process. Except in some lower organisms, the gametes are of two distinct types called eggs and sperm. The organisms producing the eggs are called females, and those producing the sperm, males. The fusion of a male and female gamete produces a *zygote*, from which a new individual develops.

Seychelles Republic of; *area* 453 sq km/175 sq mi; *capital* Victoria (on Mahé island); *features* Aldabra atoll, containing world's largest tropical lagoon; the unique 'double coconut' (*coco de mer*); *political system* emergent democracy; *population* (1993 est) 80,000; growth rate 2.2% p.a.; *languages* creole (Asian, African, European mixture)

95%, English, French (all official); *religion* Roman Catholic 90%.

Seymour Jane *c.* 1509–1537. Third wife of Henry VIII, whom she married in 1536. She died soon after the birth of her son Edward VI.

Shackleton Ernest 1874–1922. Irish Antarctic explorer. In 1907–09, he commanded an expedition that reached 88° 23′ S latitude, located the magnetic South Pole, and climbed Mount Erebus.

Shaftesbury Anthony Ashley Cooper, 1st Earl of Shaftesbury 1621–1683. English politician, a supporter of the Restoration of the monarchy. He became Lord Chancellor in 1672, but went into opposition in 1673 and began to organize the ◊Whig Party. He headed the Whigs' demand for the exclusion of the future James II from the succession, secured the passing of the Habeas Corpus Act 1679, then, when accused of treason 1681, fled to Holland.

Shakespeare William 1564–1616. English dramatist and poet. He is considered the greatest English dramatist. His plays, written in blank verse with some prose, can be broadly divided into *lyric plays*, including *Romeo and Juliet* and *A Midsummer Night's Dream*; *comedies*, including *The Comedy of Errors*, *Much Ado About Nothing*, and *Measure For Measure*; *historical plays*, such as *Henry VI*, *Richard III*, and *Henry IV*; and *tragedies*, such as *Hamlet* and *Macbeth*. He also wrote numerous sonnets.

shale fine-grained and finely layered ◊sedimentary rock composed of silt and clay. It is a weak rock, splitting easily along bedding planes to form thin, even slabs (by contrast, mudstone splits into irregular flakes). Oil shale contains kerogen, a solid bituminous material that yields ◊petroleum when heated.

Shanghai port on the Huang-pu and Wusong rivers, Jiangsu province, China, 24 km/15 mi from the Chang Jiang estuary; population (1986) 6,980,000, the largest city in China. The municipality of Shanghai has an area of 5,800 sq km/2,239 sq mi and a population of 13,342,000. It handles about 50% of China's imports and exports.

Shannon longest river in Ireland, rising in County Cavan and flowing 386 km/240 mi through loughs Allen and Ree and past Athlone, to reach the Atlantic Ocean through a wide estuary below Limerick. It is also the greatest source of electric power in the republic, with hydroelectric installations at and above Ardnacrusha, 5 km/3 mi N of Limerick.

Shari'a the law of ◊Islam believed by Muslims to be based on divine revelation, and drawn from a number of sources, including the Koran, the Hadith, and the consensus of the Muslim community. Under this law, *qisās*, or retribution, allows a family to exact equal punishment on an accused; *diyat*, or blood money, is payable to a dead person's family as compensation.

shark any member of various orders of cartilaginous fishes (class Chondrichthyes), found throughout the oceans of the world. There are about 400 known species of shark. They have tough, usually grey, skin covered in denticles (small toothlike scales). A shark's streamlined body has side pectoral fins, a high dorsal fin, and a forked tail with a large upper lobe. Five open gill slits are visible on each side of the generally pointed head. Most sharks are fish- eaters, and a few will attack humans. They range from several feet in length to the great *white shark Carcharodon carcharias*, 9 m/ 30 ft long, and the harmless plankton-feeding *whale shark Rhincodon typus*, over 15 m/50 ft in length.

Shaw George Bernard 1856–1950. Irish dramatist. He was also a critic and novelist, and an early member of the socialist ◊Fabian Society. His plays combine comedy with political, philosophical, and polemic aspects, aiming to make an impact on his audience's social conscience as well as their emotions. They include *Arms and the Man* 1894, *Devil's Disciple* 1897, *Man and Superman* 1903, *Pygmalion* 1913, and *St Joan* 1923. Nobel prize 1925.

sheep any of several ruminant, even-toed, hoofed mammals of the family Bovidae. Wild species survive in the uplands of central and E Asia, N Africa, S Europe and North America. The domesticated breeds are all classified as *Ovis aries*. Various breeds of sheep are reared worldwide for meat, wool, milk, and cheese, and for rotation on arable land to maintain its fertility.

Sheffield industrial city on the river Don, South Yorkshire, England; population (1991) 501,200. It is famous for its steelware, including cutlery.

Shelley Mary Wollstonecraft 1797–1851. English writer. She was the daughter of Mary Wollstonecraft and William Godwin. In 1814 she eloped with the poet Percy Bysshe Shelley, whom she married 1816. Her novels include *Frankenstein* 1818, *The Last Man* 1826, and *Valperga* 1823.

Shelley Percy Bysshe 1792–1822. English lyric poet. He was a leading figure in the Romantic movement. Expelled from Oxford University for atheism, he fought all his life against religion and for political freedom. This is reflected in his early poems such as *Queen Mab* 1813. He later wrote tragedies including *The Cenci* 1818, lyric dramas such as *Prometheus Unbound* 1820, and lyrical poems such as 'Ode to the West Wind'. He drowned while sailing in Italy.

Sheridan Richard Brinsley 1751–1816. Irish dramatist and politician. His social comedies include *The Rivals* 1775, celebrated for the character of Mrs Malaprop, and *The School for Scandal* 1777. He also wrote a burlesque, *The Critic* 1779. In 1776 he became lessee of the Drury Lane Theatre. He became a member of Parliament 1780.

sheriff in England and Wales, the crown's chief executive officer in a county for ceremonial purposes; in Scotland, the equivalent of the English county-court judge, but also dealing with criminal cases; and in the USA the popularly elected head law-enforcement officer of a county, combining judicial authority with administrative duties.

Sherpa member of a people in NE Nepal related to the Tibetans and renowned for their mountaineering skill. They frequently work as support staff and guides for climbing expeditions. A Sherpa, Tensing Norgay, was one of the first two people to climb to the summit of Everest.

Shetland Islands islands off the N coast of Scotland, beyond the Orkney Islands; *area* 1,400 sq km/541 sq mi; *features* over 100 islands including Muckle Flugga (latitude 60° 51′ N) the northernmost of the British Isles; *population* (1991) 22,500; *language* dialect derived from Norse, the islands having been a Norse dependency from the 9th century until 1472 when they were annexed by Scotland.

Shi'ite or *Shiah* member of a sect of Islam that believes that ◊Ali was ◊Muhammad's first true successor. The Shi'ites are doctrinally opposed to the Sunni Muslims. They developed their own law differing only in minor directions, such as inheritance and the status of women. In Shi'ism, the clergy are empowered to intervene between God and humans, whereas among the Sunni, the relationship with God is direct and the clergy serve as advisers. The Shi'ites are prominent in Iran, the Lebanon, and Indo-Pakistan, and are also found in Iraq and Bahrain.

shingles common name for ◊herpes zoster, a disease characterized by infection of sensory nerves, with pain and eruption of blisters along the course of the affected nerves.

Shinto the indigenous religion of Japan. It combines an empathetic oneness with natural forces and loyalty to the reigning dynasty as descendants of the Sun goddess, Amaterasu-Omikami. Traditional Shinto followers stressed obedience and devotion to the emperor, and an aggressive nationalistic aspect was developed by the Meiji rulers. Today Shinto has discarded these aspects.

ship large seagoing vessel. The Greeks, Phoenicians, Romans, and Vikings used ships extensively for trade, exploration, and warfare. The 14th century was the era of European exploration by sailing ship, largely aided by the invention of the compass. In the 15th century Britain's Royal Navy was first formed, but in the 16th–19th centuries Spanish and Dutch fleets dominated the shipping lanes of both the Atlantic and Pacific. The ultimate sailing ships, the fast US and British tea clippers, were built in the 19th century. Also in the 19th century, iron was first used for some shipbuilding instead of wood. Steam-propelled ships of the late 19th century were followed by compound engine and turbine-propelled vessels from the early 20th century.

shock in medicine, circulatory failure marked by a sudden fall of blood pressure and resulting in pallor, sweating, fast (but weak) pulse, and sometimes complete collapse. Causes include disease, injury, and psychological trauma.

shogun in Japanese history, title of a series of military strongmen 1192–1868 who relegated the emperor's role to that of figurehead. Technically an imperial appointment, the office was treated as hereditary and was held by the Minamoto clan 1192–1219, by the Ashikaga 1336–1573, and by the Tokugawa 1603–1868. The shogun held legislative, judicial, and executive power.

Shona member of a Bantu-speaking people of S Africa, comprising approximately 80% of the population of Zimbabwe. They also occupy the land between the Save and Pungure rivers in Mozambique, and smaller groups are found in South Africa, Botswana, and Zambia. The Shona are mainly farmers, living in scattered villages. The Shona language belongs to the Niger-Congo family.

Short Parliament the English Parliament that was summoned by Charles I on 13 April 1640 to raise funds for his war against the Scots. It was succeeded later in the year by the ◊Long Parliament.

Shostakovich Dmitry (Dmitriyevich) 1906–1975. Soviet composer. His music is tonal, expressive, and sometimes highly dramatic; it was not always to official Soviet taste. He wrote 15 symphonies, chamber and film music, ballets, and operas, the latter including *Lady Macbeth of Mtsensk* 1934, which was suppressed as 'too divorced from the proletariat', but revived as *Katerina Izmaylova* 1963.

shot put or *putting the shot* in athletics, the sport of throwing (or putting) overhand from the shoulder a metal ball (or shot). Standard shot weights are 7.26 kg/16 lb for men and 4 kg/8.8 lb for women.

Shropshire (sometimes abbreviated to *Salop*) county of W England; *area* 3,490 sq km/1,347 sq mi; *towns* Shrewsbury (administrative headquarters), Telford, Oswestry, Ludlow; *features* bisected, on the Welsh border, NW–SE by the river Severn; Ironbridge Gorge open-air museum of industrial archaeology, with the Iron Bridge (1779), the world's first cast-iron bridge; *population* (1991) 406,400.

SI abbreviation for *Système International [d'Unités]* (French 'International System [of Metric Units]'); see ◊SI units.

Sibelius Jean (Christian) 1865–1957. Finnish composer. His works include nationalistic symphonic poems such as *En saga* 1893 and *Finlandia* 1900, a violin concerto 1904, and seven symphonies.

Siberia Asian region of Russia, extending from the Ural Mountains to the Pacific Ocean; *area* 12,050,000 sq km/4,650,000 sq mi; *towns* Novosibirsk, Omsk, Krasnoyarsk, Irkutsk; *features* long and extremely cold winters; forests covering about 5,000,000 sq km/1,930,000 sq mi; the Siberian tiger, the world's largest cat, is an endangered species.

Sicily (Italian *Sicilia*) the largest Mediterranean island, an autonomous region of Italy; area 25,700 sq km/9,920 sq mi; population (1990) 5,196,800. Its capital is Palermo. The region also includes the islands of Lipari, Egadi, Ustica, and Pantelleria. Etna, 3,323 m/10,906 ft high, is the highest volcano in Europe; its last major eruption was in 1971.

Sickert Walter (Richard) 1860–1942. English artist. His Impressionist cityscapes of London and Venice, portraits, and domestic and music-hall interiors capture subtleties of tone and light, often with a melancholic atmosphere.

sickle-cell disease hereditary chronic blood disorder common among people of black African descent; also found in the E Mediterranean, parts of the Persian Gulf, and in NE India. It is characterized by distortion and fragility of the red blood cells, which are lost too rapidly from the circulation. This often results in ◊anaemia.

Sidney Philip 1554–1586. English poet and soldier. He wrote the sonnet sequence *Astrophel and Stella* 1591, *Arcadia* 1590, a prose romance, and *Apologie for Poetrie* 1595, the earliest work of English literary criticism.

Sierra Leone Republic of; *area* 71,740 sq km/27,710 sq mi; *capital* Freetown; *features* hot and humid climate (3,500 mm/138 in rainfall p.a.); *political system* transitional; *population* (1993 est) 4,400,000; growth rate 2.5% p.a.; *languages* English (official), local languages; *religions* animist 52%, Muslim 39%,

Protestant 6%, Roman Catholic 2% (1980 est).

sievert SI unit (symbol Sv) of radiation dose equivalent. It replaces the rem (1 Sv equals 100 rem). Some types of radiation do more damage than others for the same absorbed dose – for example, the same absorbed dose of alpha radiation causes 20 times as much biological damage as the same dose of beta radiation. The equivalent dose in sieverts is equal to the absorbed dose of radiation in rays multiplied by the relative biological effectiveness. Humans can absorb up to 0.25 Sv without immediate ill effects; 1 Sv may produce radiation sickness; and more than 8 Sv causes death.

Sigismund 1368–1437. Holy Roman emperor from 1411. He convened and presided over the Council of Constance 1414–18, where he promised protection to the religious reformer Huss, but imprisoned him after his condemnation for heresy and acquiesced in his burning. King of Bohemia from 1419, he led the military campaign against the ▷Hussites.

Sihanouk Norodom 1922– . Cambodian politician, king 1941–55 and from 1993. He was prime minister 1955–70 and 1975–76, when he was forced to resign by the Khmer Rouge. He returned from exile Nov 1991 under the auspices of a United Nations-brokered peace settlement to head a coalition government. He was re-elected king after the 1993 elections, in which the royalist party won a majority.

Sikhism religion professed by 14 million Indians, living mainly in the Punjab. Sikhism was founded by Nanak (1469– c. 1539). Sikhs believe in a single God who is the immortal creator of the universe and who has never been incarnate in any form, and in the equality of all human beings; Sikhism is strongly opposed to caste divisions. Their holy book is the *Guru Granth Sahib*. Guru Gobind Singh (1666–1708) instituted the *Khanda-di-Pahul*, the baptism of the sword, and established the Khalsa ('pure'), the company of the faithful. The Khalsa wear the five Ks: *kes*, long hair; *kangha*, a comb; *kirpan*, a sword; *kachh*, short trousers; and *kara*, a steel bracelet. Sikh men take the last name 'Singh' ('lion') and women 'Kaur' ('princess').

Silesia region of Europe, long disputed because of its geographical position, mineral resources, and industrial potential; now in Poland and the Czech Republic. It was seized by Prussia's Frederick the Great and this was finally recognized by Austria 1763, after the Seven Years' War. After World War I, it was divided among newly formed Czechoslovakia, revived Poland, and Germany, which retained the largest part. After World War II, all German Silesia east of the Oder-Neisse line was transferred to Polish administration.

silica silicon dioxide, SiO_2, the composition of the most common mineral group, of which the most familiar form is quartz. Other silica forms are chalcedony, chert, opal, tridymite, and cristobalite. Common sand consists largely of silica in the form of quartz.

silicon brittle, nonmetallic element, symbol Si, atomic number 14, relative atomic mass 28.086. It is the second-most abundant element (after oxygen) in the Earth's crust and occurs in amorphous and crystalline forms. In nature it is found only in combination with other elements, chiefly with oxygen in silica (silicon dioxide, SiO_2) and the silicates. These form the mineral ◊quartz, which makes up most sands, gravels, and beaches.

silicon chip ◊integrated circuit with microscopically small electrical components on a piece of silicon crystal only a few millimetres square.

silk fine soft thread produced by the larva of the ◊silkworm moth when making its cocoon. It is soaked, carefully unwrapped, and used in the manufacture of textiles. The introduction of synthetics originally harmed the silk industry, but rising standards of living have produced an increased demand for real silk. It is manufactured in China, India, Japan, and Thailand.

Silk Road ancient and medieval overland route of about 6,400 km/4,000 mi by which silk was brought from China to Europe in return for trade goods; it ran west via the Gobi Desert, Samarkand, and Antioch to Mediterranean ports in Greece, Italy, the Middle East, and Egypt. Buddhism came to China via this route, which was superseded from the 16th century by sea trade.

silkworm usually the larva of the *common silkworm moth Bombyx mori*. After hatching from the egg and maturing on the leaves of white mulberry trees (or a synthetic substitute), it spins a protective cocoon of fine silk thread 275 m/900 ft long. To keep the thread intact, the moth is killed before emerging from the cocoon, and several threads are combined to form the commercial silk thread woven into textiles.

Silurian period of geological time 439–409 million years ago, the third period of the Palaeozoic era. Silurian sediments are mostly marine and consist of shales and limestone. Luxuriant reefs were built by coral-like organisms. The first land plants began to evolve during this period, and there were many ostracoderms (armoured jawless fishes). The first jawed fishes (called acanthodians) also appeared.

silver white, lustrous, extremely malleable and ductile, metallic element, symbol Ag (from Latin *argentum*), atomic number 47, relative atomic mass 107.868. It occurs in nature in ores and as a free metal; the chief ores are sulphides, from which the metal is extracted by smelting with lead. It is one of the best metallic conductors of both heat and electricity; its most useful compounds are the chloride and bromide, which darken on exposure to light and are the basis of photographic emulsions.

Simenon Georges 1903–1989. Belgian crime writer. Initially a pulp fiction writer, in 1931 he created Inspector Maigret of the Paris Sûreté who appeared in a series of detective novels.

Simpson Wallis Warfield, Duchess of Windsor 1896–1986. US socialite, twice divorced. She married ◊Edward VIII 1937, who abdicated in order to marry her.

sin transgression of the will of God or the gods, as revealed in the moral code laid down by a particular religion. In Roman Catholic theology, a distinction is made between *mortal sins*, which, if unforgiven, result in damnation, and *venial sins*, which are less serious. In Islam, the one unforgivable sin is *shirk*, denial that Allah is the only god.

Sinatra Frank (Francis Albert) 1915– . US singer and film actor. Celebrated for his phrasing and emotion, especially on love ballads, he is particularly associated with the song 'My Way'. His films from 1941 include *From Here to Eternity* 1953 (Academy Award) and *Guys and Dolls* 1955.

sine in trigonometry, a function of an angle in a right-angled triangle which is defined as the ratio of the length of the side opposite the angle to the length of the hypotenuse (the longest side).

Singapore Republic of; *area* 622 sq km/240 sq mi; *capital* Singapore City; *features* Singapore Island is joined to the mainland by causeway across Strait of Johore; temperature range 21°–34°C/69°–93°F; *political system* liberal democracy with strict limits on dissent; *population* (1993 est) 2,800,000 (Chinese 75%, Malay 14%, Tamil 7%); growth rate 1.2% p.a.; *languages* Malay (national tongue), Chinese, Tamil, English (all official); *religions* Buddhist, Taoist, Muslim, Hindu, Christian.

Singapore City capital and port of Singapore, on the SE coast of the island of Singapore; population (1980) 2,413,945.

Singer Isaac Bashevis 1904–1991. Polish-born US novelist and short-story writer. He lived in the USA from 1935. His works, written in Yiddish, often portray traditional Jewish life in Poland and the USA, and the loneliness of old age. They include *The Family Moskat* 1950 and *Gimpel the Fool and Other Stories* 1957. Nobel prize 1978.

singularity in astrophysics, the point in ▷space–time at which the known laws of physics break down. Singularity is predicted to exist at the centre of a black hole, where infinite gravitational forces compress the infalling mass of a collapsing star to infinite density. It is also

thought, according to the Big Bang model of the origin of the universe, to be the point from which the expansion of the universe began.

Sinhalese member of the majority ethnic group of Sri Lanka (70% of the population). Sinhalese is the official language of Sri Lanka; it belongs to the Indo-Iranian branch of the Indo- European family, and is written in a script derived from the Indian Pali form. The Sinhalese are Buddhists. Since 1971 they have been involved in a violent struggle with the Tamil minority, who are seeking independence.

Sinn Féin Irish nationalist party. It was founded by Arthur Griffith (1872–1922) in 1905; in 1917 Eamon ▷de Valera became its president. It is the political wing of the Irish Republican Army (IRA), and is similarly split between comparative moderates and extremists. In 1985 it gained representation in 17 out of 26 district councils in Northern Ireland. Its president from 1978 is Gerry ▷Adams. In 1994, following the declaration of a cessation of military activities by the IRA, Sin Féin was poised to enter the political process aimed at securing lasting peace in Northern Ireland.

Sino-Japanese Wars two wars waged by Japan against China 1894–95 and 1931–45 to expand to the mainland. Territory gained in the First Sino-Japanese War (Korea) and in the 1930s (Manchuria, Shanghai) was returned at the end of World War II.

Sino-Tibetan languages group of languages spoken in SE Asia. This group covers a large area, and includes Chinese and Burmese, both of which have numerous dialects. Some classifications include the Tai group of languages (including Thai and Lao) in the Sino-Tibetan family.

sinusitis painful inflammation of one of the sinuses, or air spaces, that surround the nasal passages. Most cases clear with antibiotics and nasal decongestants, but some require surgical drainage.

siren in Greek mythology, a sea ▷nymph who lured sailors to their deaths along rocky coasts by her singing. ▷Odysseus, in order to hear the sirens safely, tied himself to the mast of his ship and stuffed his crew's ears with wax.

Sirius or *Dog Star* or *Alpha Canis Majoris* the brightest star in the sky, 8.6 light years from Earth in the constellation Canis Major. Sirius is a white star with a mass 2.3 times that of the Sun, a diameter 1.8 times that of the Sun, and a luminosity of 23 Suns. It is orbited every 50 years by a white dwarf, Sirius B, also known as the Pup.

sitar Indian stringed instrument, of the lute family. It has a pear-shaped body and long neck supported by an additional gourd resonator at the opposite end. A principal solo instrument, it has seven metal strings extending over movable frets and two concealed strings that provide a continuous drone.

Sitting Bull *c.* 1834–1893. North American Indian chief who agreed to ▷Sioux resettlement 1868. When the treaty was broken by the USA, he led the Sioux against Lieutenant Colonel Custer (1839–1876) at the Battle of the Little Bighorn 1876.

SI units (French *Système International d'Unités*) standard system of scientific units used by scientists worldwide. It was originally proposed in 1960, and it is based on seven basic units: the metre (m) for length, kilogram (kg) for mass, second (s) for time, ampere (A) for electrical current, kelvin (K) for temperature, mole (mol) for amount of substance, and candela (cd) for luminosity.

Siva or *Shiva* in Hinduism, the third chief god (with Brahma and Vishnu). As Mahadeva (great lord), he is the creator, symbolized by the phallic *lingam*, who restores what as Mahakala he destroys. He is often sculpted as Nataraja, performing his fruitful cosmic dance. His consort or female principle (*sakti*) is Parvati, otherwise known as Durga or Kali.

skating self-propulsion on ice by means of bladed skates, or on other surfaces by skates with small rollers (wheels of wood, metal, or plastic). The chief competitive ice-skating events are figure skating, for singles or pairs, ice-dancing, and simple speed skating. The first world ice-skating championships were held in 1896.

skeleton the rigid or semirigid framework that supports and gives form to an animal's body, protects its internal organs, and provides anchorage points for its muscles. The skeleton may be composed of bone and cartilage (vertebrates), chitin (arthropods), calcium carbonate (molluscs and other invertebrates), or silica (many protists). The human skeleton is composed of 206 bones.

skiing self-propulsion on snow by means of elongated runners (skis) for the feet, slightly bent upward at the tip. It is a popular recreational sport, as cross-country ski touring or as downhill runs on mountain trails; events include downhill; slalom, in which a series of turns between flags have to be negotiated; cross-country racing; and ski jumping, when jumps of over 150 m/490 ft are achieved from ramps up to 90 m/295 ft high.

skin the covering of the body of a vertebrate. In mammals, the outer layer (epidermis) is dead and its cells are constantly being rubbed away and replaced from below; it helps to protect the body from infection and to prevent dehydration. The lower layer (dermis) contains blood vessels, nerves, hair roots, and sweat and sebaceous glands, and is supported by a network of fibrous and elastic cells.

Skinner B(urrhus) F(rederic) 1903–1990. US psychologist, a radical behaviourist who rejected mental concepts, seeing the organism as a 'black box' where internal processes are not significant in predicting behaviour. He studied operant conditioning and maintained that behaviour is shaped and maintained by its consequences.

Skopje capital and industrial city of the Former Yugoslav Republic of Macedonia; population (1991) 563,300.

skull in vertebrates, the collection of flat and irregularly shaped bones (or cartilage) that enclose the brain and the organs of sight, hearing, and smell, and provide support for the jaws. In mammals, the skull consists of 22 bones joined by sutures. The floor of the skull is pierced by a large hole (foramen magnum) for the spinal cord and a number of smaller apertures through which other nerves and blood vessels pass.

skunk North American mammal of the weasel family. The common skunk *Mephitis mephitis* has a long, arched body, short legs, a bushy tail, and black fur with white streaks on the back. In self-defence, it discharges a foul-smelling fluid.

Skye largest island of the Inner Hebrides, off the W coast of Scotland; area 1,740 sq km/672 sq mi; population (1987) 8,100. It is separated from the mainland by the Sound of Sleat. The chief port is Portree. A privately financed toll bridge to the island is due to be completed 1995.

slash and burn simple agricultural method whereby natural vegetation is cut and burned, and the clearing then farmed for a few years until the soil loses its fertility, whereupon farmers move on and leave the area to regrow. Although this is possible with a small, widely dispersed population, it becomes unsustainable with more people and is now a form of ▷deforestation.

slate fine-grained, usually grey metamorphic rock that splits readily into thin slabs along its cleavage planes. It is the metamorphic equivalent of ▷shale.

Slav member of an Indo-European people in central and E Europe, the Balkans, and parts of N Asia, speaking closely related ▷Slavonic languages. The ancestors of the Slavs are believed to have included the Sarmatians and Scythians. Moving west from Central Asia, they settled in E and SE Europe during the 2nd and 3rd millennia BC.

slavery enforced servitude of one person (a slave) to another or one group to another. Slavery goes back to prehistoric times but declined in Europe after the fall of the Roman Empire. During the imperialism of Spain, Portugal, and Britain in the 16th–18th centuries and in the American South in the 17th–19th centuries, slavery became a mainstay of the economy, with millions of Africans sold to work on plantations in North and South America. Slavery was abolished in the British Empire 1833 and in the USA at the end of the Civil War 1863–65, but continues illegally in some countries.

Slavonic languages or *Slavic languages* branch of the Indo-European language family spoken in central and E Europe, the Balkans, and parts of N Asia. The family comprises the *southern group* (Slovene, Serbo-Croatian, Macedonian, and Bulgarian); the *western group* (Czech and Slovak, Sorbian in Germany, and Polish and its related dialects); and the *eastern group* (Russian, Ukrainian, and Belarusian).

sleep state of natural unconsciousness and activity that occurs at regular intervals in most mammals and birds, though there is considerable variation in the amount of time spent sleeping. Sleep differs from hibernation in that it occurs daily rather than seasonally, and involves less drastic reductions in metabolism. The function of sleep is unclear. People deprived of sleep become irritable, uncoordinated, forgetful, hallucinatory, and even psychotic.

sleeping sickness or *trypanosomiasis* infectious disease of tropical Africa, a form of ◊trypanosomiasis. Early symptoms include fever, headache, and chills, followed by ◊anaemia and joint pains. Later, the disease attacks the central nervous system, causing drowsiness, lethargy, and, if left untreated, death. Sleeping sickness is caused by either of two trypanosomes, *Trypanosoma gambiense* or *T. rhodesiense*. Control is by

eradication of the tsetse fly, which transmits the disease to humans.

Sligo county of the Republic of Ireland, in the province of Connacht, situated on the Atlantic coast of NW Ireland; area 1,800 sq km/695 sq mi; population (1991) 54,700.

slime mould or *myxomycete* extraordinary organism that shows some features of ◊fungus and some of ◊protozoa. Slime moulds are not closely related to any other group, although they are often classed, for convenience, with the fungi. There are two kinds, cellular slime moulds and plasmodial slime moulds, differing in their complex life cycles.

Slovak Republic Slovak Republic (*Slovenská Republika*); *area* 49,035 sq km/18,940 sq mi; *capital* Bratislava; *features* fine beech and oak forests with bears and wild boar; *political system* emergent democracy; *population* (1992) 5,300,000 (including 600,000 Hungarians and other minorities); growth rate 0.4% p.a.; *languages* Slovak (official); *religions* Roman Catholic (over 50%), Lutheran, Reformist, Orthodox.

Slovene member of the Slavic people of Slovenia and parts of the Austrian Alpine provinces of Styria and Carinthia. There are 1.5–2 million speakers of Slovene, a language belonging to the South Slavonic branch of the Indo- European family. The Slovenes use the Roman alphabet and the majority belong to the Roman Catholic Church.

Slovenia Republic of; *area* 20,251 sq km/7,817 sq mi; *capital* Ljubljana; *political system* emergent democracy; *population* (1993 est) 2,000,000 (Slovene 91%, Croat 3%, Serb 2%); *languages* Slovene, resembling Serbo-Croat, written

457

in Roman characters; *religion* Roman Catholic.

smallpox acute, highly contagious viral disease, marked by aches, fever, vomiting, and skin eruptions leaving pitted scars. Widespread vaccination programmes have eradicated this often fatal disease.

smart weapon programmable bomb or missile that can be guided to its target by laser technology, TV homing technology, or terrain-contour matching (TERCOM). A smart weapon relies on its pinpoint accuracy to destroy a target rather than on the size of its warhead.

smell sense that responds to chemical molecules in the air. It works by having receptors for particular chemical groups, into which the airborne chemicals must fit to trigger a message to the brain.

smelting processing a metallic ore in a furnace to produce the metal. Oxide ores such as iron ore are smelted with coke (carbon), which reduces the ore into metal and also provides fuel for the process.

Smetana Bedřich 1824–1884. Bohemian composer. He established a Czech nationalist style in, for example, the operas *Prodaná Nevěsta/The Bartered Bride* 1866 and *Dalibor* 1868, and the symphonic suite *Má Vlast/My Country* 1875–80. He conducted the National Theatre of Prague 1866–74.

Smith Adam 1723–1790. Scottish economist, often regarded as the founder of political economy. His *The Wealth of Nations* 1776 defined national wealth in terms of labour. The cause of wealth is explained by the division of labour – dividing a production process into several repetitive operations, each carried out by different workers. Smith advocated the free working of individual enterprise, and the necessity of 'free trade'.

Smith William 1769–1839. British geologist, the founder of stratigraphy. Working as a canal engineer, he observed while supervising excavations that different beds of rock could be identified by their fossils, and so established the basis of stratigraphy. He also produced the first geological maps of England and Wales.

smokeless fuel fuel that does not give off any smoke when burned, because all the carbon is fully oxidized to carbon dioxide (CO_2). Natural gas, oil, and coke are smokeless fuels.

smoking inhaling the fumes from burning substances, generally ▷tobacco in the form of cigarettes. The practice can be habit-forming and is dangerous to health, since carbon monoxide and other toxic materials result from the combustion process. A direct link between lung cancer and tobacco smoking was established 1950; the habit is also linked to respiratory and coronary heart diseases. In the West, smoking is now forbidden in many public places because even *passive smoking* – breathing in fumes from other people's cigarettes – can be harmful.

Smollett Tobias George 1721–1771. Scottish novelist. He wrote the picaresque novels *Roderick Random* 1748, *Peregrine Pickle* 1751, *Ferdinand Count Fathom* 1753, *Sir Launcelot Greaves* 1760–62, and *Humphrey Clinker* 1771. His novels are full of gusto and vivid characterization.

snail air-breathing gastropod mollusc with a spiral shell. There are thousands of species, on land and in water. The typical snails of the genus *Helix* have two species in Europe. The common garden snail *H. aspersa* is very destructive to plants.

snake reptile of the suborder Serpentes of the order Squamata, which also includes lizards. Snakes are characterized by an elongated limbless body, possibly evolved because of subterranean ancestors. One of the striking internal modifications is the absence or greatly reduced size of the left lung. The skin is covered in scales, which are markedly wider underneath where they form. There are 3,000 species found in the tropical and temperate zones, but none in New Zealand, Ireland, Iceland, and near the poles. Only three species are found in Britain: the adder, smooth snake, and grass snake.

snooker indoor game derived from ◊billiards (via pool). It is played with 22 balls: 15 red, one each of yellow, green, brown, blue, pink, and black, and one white cueball. Red balls are worth one point when sunk, while the coloured balls have ascending values from two points for the yellow to seven points for the black. The world professional championship was first held in 1927. The world amateur championship was first held 1963.

soap mixture of the sodium salts of various ◊fatty acids: palmitic, stearic, and oleic acid. It is made by the action of sodium hydroxide (caustic soda) or potassium hydroxide (caustic potash) on fats of animal or vegetable origin. Soap makes grease and dirt disperse in water in a similar manner to a ◊detergent.

Soares Mario 1924– . Portuguese socialist politician, president from 1986. Exiled 1970, he returned to Portugal 1974, and, as leader of the Portuguese Socialist Party, was prime minister 1976–78. He resigned as party leader 1980, but in 1986 he was elected Portugal's first socialist president.

Sobers Gary (Garfield St Aubrun) 1936– . West Indian test cricketer and arguably the world's finest ever all rounder. He held the world individual record for the highest test innings with 365 not out, until beaten by Brian Lara 1994.

Social and Liberal Democrats official name for the British political party formed 1988 from the former Liberal Party and most of the Social Democratic Party. The common name for the party is the *Liberal Democrats*.

social contract the idea that government authority derives originally from an agreement between ruler and ruled in which the former agrees to provide order in return for obedience from the latter. It has been used to support both absolutism (◊Hobbes) and democracy (◊Locke, ◊Rousseau).

Social Democratic Labour Party (SDLP) Northern Irish left-wing political party, formed 1970. Its aim is non-violent Irish unification, adopting a constitutional and conciliatory role. The SDLP, led by John Hume (1937–), was responsible for setting up the New Ireland Forum 1983, and for initiating talks with the leader of ◊Sinn Féin, Gerry Adams, 1993, which prompted a joint UK-Irish peace initiative and set in motion a Northern Ireland ceasefire 1994.

Social Democratic Party (SDP) British centrist political party 1981–90, formed by members of Parliament who resigned from the Labour Party. The

1983 and 1987 general elections were fought in alliance with the Liberal Party as the *Liberal/SDP Alliance*. A merger of the two parties was voted for by the SDP 1987, and the new party became the Social and Liberal Democrats, leaving a rump SDP that folded 1990.

socialism movement aiming to establish a classless society by substituting public for private ownership of the means of production, distribution, and exchange. The term has been used to describe positions as widely apart as anarchism and social democracy. Socialist ideas appeared in classical times; in early Christianity; among later Christian sects such as the ◊Anabaptists and Diggers; and, in the 18th and early 19th centuries, were put forward as systematic political aims by Jean-Jacques Rousseau, Claude Saint-Simon, François Fourier, and Robert Owen, among others. See also Karl ◊Marx and Friedrich ◊Engels.

Society Islands (French *Archipel de la Société*) archipelago in ◊French Polynesia, divided into the Windward Islands and the Leeward Islands; the administrative headquarters is Papeete on ◊Tahiti. The *Windward Islands* (French *Iles du Vent*) have an area of 1,200 sq km/460 sq mi and a population (1983) of 123,000. They comprise Tahiti, Moorea, Maio, and the smaller Tetiaroa and Mehetia. The *Leeward Islands* (French *Iles sous le Vent*) have an area of 404 sq km/156 sq mi and a population of 19,000. They comprise the volcanic islands of Raiatea, Huahine, Bora-Bora, Maupiti, Tahaa, and four small atolls.

sociobiology study of the biological basis of all social behaviour, including the application of ◊population genetics to the evolution of behaviour. It builds on the concept of inclusive fitness, contained in the notion of the 'selfish gene'. Contrary to some popular interpretations, it does not assume that all behaviour is genetically determined.

sociology systematic study of society, in particular of social order and social change, social conflict and social problems. It studies institutions such as the family, law, and the church, as well as concepts such as norm, role, and culture. Sociology attempts to study people in their social environment according to certain underlying moral, philosophical, and political codes of behaviour.

Socrates *c.* 469–399 BC. Athenian philosopher. He wrote nothing but was immortalized in the dialogues of his pupil Plato. In his desire to combat the scepticism of the ◊sophists, Socrates asserted the possibility of genuine knowledge. In ethics, he put forward the view that the good person never knowingly does wrong. True knowledge emerges through dialogue and systematic questioning and an abandoning of uncritical claims to knowledge.

sodium soft, waxlike, silver-white, metallic element, symbol Na (from Latin *natrium*), atomic number 11, relative atomic mass 22.898. It is one of the ◊alkali metals and has a very low density, being light enough to float on water. It is the sixth-most abundant element (the fourth-most abundant metal) in the Earth's crust. Sodium is highly reactive, oxidizing rapidly when exposed to air and reacting violently with water. Its most familiar compound is sodium chloride (common salt), which occurs naturally in the oceans and in salt deposits left by dried-up ancient seas.

sodium chloride or *common salt* or *table salt* NaCl white, crystalline compound found widely in nature. It is a a typical ionic solid with a high melting point (801°C/1,474°F); it is soluble in water, insoluble in organic solvents, and is a strong electrolyte when molten or in aqueous solution. Found in concentrated deposits, it is widely used in the food industry as a flavouring and preservative, and in the chemical industry in the manufacture of sodium, chlorine, and sodium carbonate.

Sofia or *Sofiya* capital of Bulgaria since 1878; population (1990) 1,220,900.

software in computing, a collection of programs and procedures for making a computer perform a specific task, as opposed to ▷hardware, the physical components of a computer system. Software is created by programmers and is either distributed on a suitable medium, such as the ▷floppy disc, or built into the computer in the form of firmware. Examples of software include ▷operating systems, compilers, and applications programs, such as payrolls. No computer can function without some form of software.

soil loose covering of broken rocky material and decaying organic matter overlying the bedrock of the Earth's surface. Various types of soil develop under different conditions: deep soils form in warm wet climates and in valleys; shallow soils form in cool dry areas and on slopes. *Pedology*, the study of soil, is significant because of the relative importance of different soil types to agriculture.

soil erosion the wearing away and redistribution of the Earth's soil layer. It is caused by the action of water, wind, and ice, and also by improper methods of ▷agriculture. If unchecked, soil erosion results in the formation of deserts (▷desertification). It has been estimated that 20% of the world's cultivated topsoil was lost between 1950 and 1990.

solar energy energy derived from the Sun's radiation. The amount of energy falling on just 1 sq km/0.3861 sq mi is about 4,000 megawatts, enough to heat and light a small town. In one second the Sun gives off 13 million times more energy than all the electricity used in the USA in one year. *Solar heaters* have industrial or domestic uses. They usually consist of a black (heat-absorbing) panel containing pipes through which air or water, heated by the Sun, is circulated, either by thermal ▷convection or by a pump. Solar energy may also be harnessed indirectly using *solar cells* (photovoltaic cells) made of panels of ▷semiconductor material (usually silicon), which generate electricity when illuminated by sunlight.

solar radiation radiation given off by the Sun, consisting mainly of visible light, ▷ultraviolet radiation, and ▷infrared radiation, although the whole spectrum of ▷electromagnetic waves is present, from radio waves to X-rays. High-energy charged particles such as electrons are also emitted, especially from solar ▷flares. When these reach the Earth, they cause magnetic storms (disruptions of the Earth's magnetic field), which interfere with radio communications.

Solar System the Sun (a star) and all the bodies orbiting it: the nine ▷planets (Mercury, Venus, Earth, Mars, Jupiter, Saturn, Uranus, Neptune, and Pluto), their moons, the asteroids, and the comets. It is thought to have formed from a cloud of gas and dust in space about 4.6 billion years ago. The Sun contains 99% of the mass of the Solar System.

solenoid coil of wire, usually cylindrical, in which a magnetic field is created by passing an electric current through it. This field can be used to move an iron rod placed on its axis. Mechanical valves attached to the rod can be operated by switching the current on or off, so converting electrical energy into mechanical energy. Solenoids are used to relay energy from the battery of a car to the starter motor by means of the ignition switch.

solicitor in the UK, a member of one of the two branches of the English legal profession, the other being a barrister. A solicitor is a lawyer who provides all-round legal services (making wills, winding up estates, conveyancing, divorce, and litigation). A solicitor cannot appear at High Court level, but must brief a barrister on behalf of his or her client. Solicitors may become circuit judges and recorders.

solid in physics, a state of matter that holds its own shape (as opposed to a liquid, which takes up the shape of its container, or a gas, which totally fills its container). According to ▷kinetic theory, the atoms or molecules in a solid are not free to move but merely vibrate about fixed positions, such as those in crystal lattices.

Solidarity (Polish *Solidarność*) national confederation of independent trade unions in Poland, formed under the leadership of Lech ▷Wałesa Sept 1980. An illegal organization from 1981 to 1989, it was then elected to head the Polish government. Divisions soon emerged in the leadership and in 1990 its political wing began to fragment (Wałesa resigned as chairman in Dec of

that year). In the Sept 1993 elections Solidarity gained less than 5% of the popular vote.

Solomon *c.* 974–*c.* 937 BC. In the Old Testament, third king of Israel, son of David by Bathsheba. During a peaceful reign, he was famed for his wisdom and his alliances with Egypt and Phoenicia. The much later biblical Proverbs, Ecclesiastes, and Song of Songs are attributed to him. He built the temple in Jerusalem with the aid of heavy taxation and forced labour, resulting in the revolt of N Israel.

Solomon Islands *area* 27,600 sq km/10,656 sq mi; *capital* Honiara (on Guadalcanal); *features* rivers ideal for hydroelectric power; *political system* constitutional monarchy; *population* (1993) 349,500 (Melanesian 95%, Polynesian 4%); growth rate 3.9% p.a.; *languages* English (official); there are some 120 Melanesian dialects; *religions* Anglican 34%, Roman Catholic 19%, South Sea Evangelical 17%.

solstice either of the days on which the Sun is farthest north or south of the celestial equator each year. The *summer solstice*, when the Sun is farthest north, occurs around June 21; the *winter solstice* around Dec 22.

solution two or more substances mixed to form a single, homogenous phase. One of the substances is the *solvent* and the others (*solutes*) are said to be dissolved in it.

solvent substance, usually a liquid, that will dissolve another substance (see ▷solution). Although the commonest solvent is water, in popular use the term refers to low-boiling-point organic liquids, which are harmful if used in a confined space. They can give rise to respiratory problems, liver damage, and neurological complaints.

Solzhenitsyn Alexander (Isayevich) 1918– . Soviet novelist. He was in prison and exile 1945–57 for anti- Stalinist comments. Much of his writing is semi-autobiographical and highly critical of the system, including *One Day in the Life of Ivan Denisovich* 1962, which deals with the labour camps under Stalin, and *The Gulag Archipelago* 1973, an exposé of the whole Soviet labour-camp network. This led to his expulsion from the USSR 1974. Nobel Prize for Literature 1970.

Somali member of a group of E African peoples from the Horn of Africa. Although the majority of Somalis live in the Somali Republic, there are minorities in Ethiopia and Kenya. Their Cushitic language belongs to the Hamitic branch of the Afro-Asiatic family.

Somalia Somali Democratic Republic (*Jamhuriyadda Dimugradiga Somaliya*); *area* 637,700 sq km/246,220 sq mi; *capital* Mogadishu; *environment* destruction of trees for fuel and by grazing livestock has led to an increase in desert area; *features* occupies a strategic location on the Horn of Africa; *political system* transitional; *population* (1993 est) 8,000,000 (including 350,000 refugees in Ethiopia and 50,000 in Djibouti); growth rate 3.1% p.a.; *languages* Somali, Arabic (both official), Italian, English; *religion* Sunni Muslim 99%.

Somerset county of SW England; *area* 3,460 sq km/1,336 sq mi; *towns* Taunton (administrative headquarters); Wells, Bridgwater, Glastonbury, Yeovil; *features* Mendip Hills, including Cheddar Gorge and Wookey Hole; Quantock Hills; Exmoor; Blackdown Hills; *population* (1991) 460,400.

Somme, Battle of the Allied offensive in World War I July–Nov 1916 at Beaumont-Hamel-Chaulnes, on the river Somme in N France, during which severe losses were suffered by both sides. It was planned by the Marshal of France, Joseph Joffre, and UK commander in chief Douglas Haig; the Allies lost over 600,000 soldiers and advanced 13 km/8 mi. It was the first battle in which tanks were used.

sonar (acronym for *sound navigation and ranging*) method of locating underwater objects by the reflection of ultrasonic waves. The time taken for an acoustic beam to travel to the object and back to the source enables the distance to be found since the velocity of sound in water is known. Sonar devices, or *echo sounders*, were developed 1920.

Sondheim Stephen (Joshua) 1930– . US composer and lyricist. He wrote the lyrics of Leonard Bernstein's *West Side Story* 1957 and composed witty and sophisticated musicals, including *A Little Night Music* 1973, *Pacific Overtures* 1976, *Sweeney Todd* 1979, *Into the Woods* 1987, and *Sunday in the Park with George* 1989.

sonnet fourteen-line poem of Italian origin introduced to England by Thomas Wyatt (1503–1542) in the form used by Petrarch (rhyming *abba abba cdcdcd* or *cdecde*) and followed by Milton and Wordsworth; Shakespeare used the form *abab cdcd efef gg*.

sophist one of a group of 5th-century BC itinerant lecturers on culture, rhetoric, and politics. Sceptical about the possibility of achieving genuine knowledge, they applied bogus reasoning and were concerned with winning arguments rather than establishing the truth. ▷Plato regarded them as dishonest and *sophistry* came to mean fallacious reasoning.

Sophocles *c.* 496–406 BC. Athenian dramatist. He is attributed with having developed tragedy by introducing a third actor and scene-painting, and ranked with ▷Aeschylus and ▷Euripides as one of the three great tragedians. He wrote some 120 plays, of which seven tragedies survive. These are *Antigone* 443 BC, *Oedipus the King* 429, *Electra* 410, *Ajax, Trachiniae, Philoctetes* 409 BC, and *Oedipus at Colonus* 401 (produced after his death).

Sotho member of a large ethnic group in southern Africa, numbering about 7 million and living mainly in Botswana, Lesotho, and South Africa. The Sotho are predominantly farmers, living in small village groups. They speak a variety of closely related languages belonging to the Bantu branch of the Niger-Congo family. With English, Sotho is the official language of Lesotho.

sound physiological sensation received by the ear, originating in a vibration that communicates itself as a pressure variation in the air and travels in every direction, spreading out as an expanding sphere. All sound waves in air travel with a speed dependent on the temperature; under ordinary conditions, this is about 330 m/1,070 ft per second. The pitch of the sound depends on the number of vibrations imposed on the air per second, but the speed is unaffected. The loudness of a sound is dependent primarily on the amplitude of the vibration of the air.

sound barrier concept that the speed of sound, or sonic speed (about 1,220 kph/760 mph at sea level), constitutes a speed limit to flight through the atmosphere, since a badly designed aircraft suffers severe buffeting at near sonic speed owing to the formation of shock waves. US test pilot Chuck Yeager first flew through the 'barrier' in 1947 in a Bell X-1 rocket plane. Now, by careful design, such aircraft as Concorde can fly at supersonic speed with ease, though they create in their wake a sonic boom.

South Africa Republic of (*Republiek van Suid-Afrika*); *area* 1,222,081 sq km/471,723 sq mi; *capital* and port Cape Town (legislative), Pretoria (administrative), Bloemfontein (judicial); *features* Drakensberg Mountains, Table Mountain; Limpopo and Orange rivers; the Veld and the Karoo; part of Kalahari Desert; Kruger National Park; *head of state and government* Nelson Mandela from 1994; *political system* liberal democracy; *population* (1993) 32,590,000 (73% black: Zulu, Xhosa, Sotho, Tswana; 18% white: 3% mixed, 3% Asian); growth rate 2.5% p.a.; *languages* English and Afrikaans; main African languages: Xhosa, Zulu, and Sesotho (all official); *religions* Dutch Reformed Church 40%, Anglican 11%, Roman Catholic 8%, other Christian 25%, Hindu, Muslim.

South African Wars two wars between the Boers (settlers of Dutch origin) and the British; essentially fought for the gold and diamonds of the Transvaal. In the *War of 1881* the Boers defeated the British, and the Transvaal regained its independence. The *War of 1899–1902*, also known as the *Boer War*, was a failed attempt, inspired by the Cape Colony prime minister Rhodes, to precipitate a revolt against Kruger, the Transvaal president. The war ended with the Peace of Vereeniging following the Boer defeat.

South America fourth largest of the continents, nearly twice as large as

Europe (13% of the world's land surface), extending S from ◊Central America; *area* 17,864,000 sq km/ 6,900,000 sq mi; *largest cities* (population over 3.5 million) Buenos Aires, São Paulo, Rio de Janeiro, Bogotá, Santiago, Lima, Caracas; *features* Lake Titicaca (the world's highest navigable lake); La Paz (highest capital city in the world); Atacama Desert; Inca ruins at Machu Picchu; rivers include the Amazon (world's largest and second longest), Parana, Madeira, São Francisco, Purus, Paraguay, Orinoco, Araguaia, Negro, Uruguay; *population* (1988) 285 million, rising to 550 million (est) by 2000.

South Australia state of the Commonwealth of Australia; *area* 984,000 sq km/ 379,824 sq mi; *capital* Adelaide (chief port); *towns* Whyalla, Mount Gambier; *features* Murray Valley irrigated area, including wine-growing Barossa Valley; mountains: Mount Lofty, Musgrave, Flinders; parts of the Nullarbor Plain, and Great Victoria and Simpson deserts; *population* (1987) 1,388,000; 1% Aborigines.

South Carolina state in SE USA; *area* 80,600 sq km/31,112 sq mi; *capital* Columbia; *population* (1990) 3,486,700; *features* subtropical climate in coastal areas; Myrtle Beach and Hilton Head Island ocean resorts.

South Dakota state in W USA; *area* 199,800 sq km/77,123 sq mi; *capital* Pierre; *population* (1990) 696,000.

South Glamorgan (Welsh *De Morgannwg*) county of S Wales, created 1974; *area* 416 sq km/161 sq mi; *towns* Cardiff (administrative headquarters), Barry, Penarth; *features* mixed farming in the fertile Vale of Glamorgan; Welsh Folk Museum at St Fagans, near Cardiff;

population (1991) 392,800; *languages* English, 6.5% Welsh-speaking.

South, the historically, the states of the USA bounded on the N by the ◊Mason–Dixon Line, the Ohio River, and the E and N borders of Missouri, with an agrarian economy based on plantations worked by slaves, and which seceded from the Union 1861, beginning the American Civil War, as the ◊Confederacy. The term is now loosely applied in a geographical and cultural sense, with Texas often regarded as part of the Southwest rather than the South.

South Yorkshire metropolitan county of NE England, created 1974; in 1986, most of the functions of the former county council were transferred to the metropolitan district councils; *area* 1,560 sq km/602 sq mi; *towns* Barnsley, Sheffield, Doncaster; *features* river Don; part of Peak District National Park; *population* (1991) 1,262,600.

Soviet Union alternative name for the former ◊Union of Soviet Socialist Republics (USSR).

soya bean leguminous plant *Glycine max*, native to E Asia, in particular Japan and China. Originally grown as a forage crop, it is increasingly used for human consumption in cooking oils and margarine, as a flour, soya milk, soy sauce, or processed into tofu, miso, or textured vegetable protein.

Soyinka Wole 1934– . Nigerian author. He was a political prisoner in Nigeria 1967–69. His works include the play *The Lion and the Jewel* 1963; his prison memoirs *The Man Died* 1972; *Aké, The Years of Childhood* 1982, an autobiography, and *Isara*, a fictionalized memoir 1989. Nobel Prize for Literature in 1986.

Soyuz Soviet series of spacecraft, capable of carrying up to three cosmonauts. Soyuz spacecraft consist of three parts: a rear section containing engines; the central crew compartment; and a forward compartment that gives additional room for working and living space. They are now used for ferrying crews up to space stations, though they were originally used for independent space flight.

space shuttle reusable crewed spacecraft. The first was launched 12 April 1981 by the USA. It was developed by NASA to reduce the cost of using space for commercial, scientific, and military purposes. After leaving its payload in space, the space- shuttle orbiter can be flown back to Earth to land on a runway, and is then available for reuse.

space station any large structure designed for human occupation in space for extended periods of time. Space stations are used for carrying out astronomical observations and surveys of Earth, as well as for biological studies and the processing of materials in weightlessness. The first space station was *Salyut 1*, and the USA has launched *Skylab*.

space–time in physics, combination of space and time used in the theory of ▷relativity. When developing relativity, Albert Einstein showed that time was in many respects like an extra dimension (or direction) to space. Space and time can thus be considered as entwined into a single entity, rather than two separate things.

Spain (*España*); *area* 504,750 sq km/ 194,960 sq mi; *capital* Madrid; *features* rivers Ebro, Douro, Tagus, Guadiana, Guadalquivir; Iberian Plateau (Meseta); Pyrenees, Cantabrian Mountains, Andalusian Mountains, Sierra Nevada; *political system* constitutional monarchy; *population* (1993 est) 39,200,000; growth rate 0.2% p.a.; *languages* Spanish (Castilian, official), Basque, Catalan, Galician, Valencian, Majorcan; *religion* Roman Catholic 99%.

Spanish Armada fleet sent by Philip II of Spain against England in 1588. Consisting of 130 ships, it sailed from Lisbon and carried on a running fight up the Channel with the English fleet of 197 small ships under Howard of Effingham and Francis ▷Drake. The Armada anchored off Calais but fireships forced it to put to sea, and a general action followed off Gravelines. What remained of the Armada escaped around the N of Scotland and W of Ireland, suffering many losses by storm and shipwreck on the way. Only about half the original fleet returned to Spain.

Spanish member of the Romance branch of the Indo- European language family, traditionally known as Castilian and originally spoken only in NE Spain. As the language of the court, it has been the standard and literary language of the Spanish state since the 13th century. It is now a world language, spoken in Mexico and all South and Central American countries (except Brazil, Guyana, Surinam, and French Guiana) as well as in the Philippines, Cuba, Puerto Rico, and much of the USA.

Spanish Succession, War of the war 1701–14 of Britain, Austria, the Netherlands, Portugal, and Denmark (the Allies) against France, Spain, and Bavaria. It was caused by Louis XIV's acceptance of the Spanish throne on behalf of his grandson, Philip, in defiance of the Partition Treaty of 1700, under which it would have passed to

Archduke Charles of Austria (later Holy Roman emperor Charles VI).

spark plug plug that produces an electric spark in the cylinder of a petrol engine to ignite the fuel mixture. It consists essentially of two electrodes insulated from one another. High-voltage (18,000 V) electricity is fed to a central electrode via the distributor. At the base of the electrode, inside the cylinder, the electricity jumps to another electrode earthed to the engine body, creating a spark.

sparrow any of a family (Passeridae) of small Old World birds of the order Passeriformes with short, thick bills, including the now worldwide house or English sparrow *Passer domesticus*.

Sparta ancient Greek city-state in the S Peloponnese (near Sparte), developed from Dorian settlements in the 10th century BC. The Spartans, known for their military discipline and austerity, took part in the ◊Persian and ◊Peloponnesian Wars.

species in biology, a distinguishable group of organisms that resemble each other or consist of a few distinctive types (as in polymorphism), and that can all interbreed to produce fertile offspring. Species are the lowest level in the system of biological classification.

spectroscopy study of spectra (see ◊spectrum) associated with atoms or molecules in solid, liquid, or gaseous phase. Spectroscopy can be used to identify unknown compounds and is an invaluable tool in science, medicine, and industry (for example, in checking the purity of drugs).

spectrum (plural *spectra*) in physics, an arrangement of frequencies or wavelengths when electromagnetic radiations are separated into their constituent parts. Visible light is part of the electromagnetic spectrum and most sources emit waves over a range of wavelengths that can be broken up or 'dispersed'; white light can be separated into red, orange, yellow, green, blue, indigo, and violet. The visible spectrum was first studied by Isaac ◊Newton, who showed in 1672 how white light could be broken up into different colours.

speed of light speed at which light and other ◊electromagnetic waves travel through empty space. Its value is 299,792,458 m/186,281 mi per second. The speed of light is the highest speed possible, according to the theory of ◊relativity, and its value is independent of the motion of its source and of the observer. It is impossible to accelerate any material body to this speed because it would require an infinite amount of energy.

speed of sound speed at which sound travels through a medium, such as air or water. In air at a temperature of 0°C/32°F, the speed of sound is 331 m/1,087 ft per second. At higher temperatures, the speed of sound is greater; at 18°C/64°F it is 342 m/ 1,123 ft per second. It is greater in liquids and solids; for example, in water it is around 1,440 m/4,724 ft per second, depending on the temperature.

Spender Stephen (Harold) 1909– . English poet and critic. His earlier poetry has a left-wing political content, as in *Twenty Poems* 1930, *Vienna* 1934, *The Still Centre* 1939, and *Poems of Dedication* 1946. Other works include the verse drama *Trial of a Judge* 1938, the autobiography *World within World* 1951, and translations. His *Journals 1939–83* were published 1985.

Spenser Edmund *c.* 1552–1599. English poet. He has been called the 'poet's poet' because of his rich imagery and command of versification. His major work is the moral allegory *The Faerie Queene*, of which six books survive (three published 1590 and three 1596). Other books include *The Shepheard's Calendar* 1579, *Astrophel* 1586, the love sonnets *Amoretti* and the *Epithalamion* 1595.

sperm or *spermatozoon* in biology, the male ▷gamete of animals. Each sperm cell has a head capsule containing a nucleus, a middle portion containing mitochondria (which provide energy), and a long tail (flagellum). See ▷sexual reproduction.

Sphinx mythological creature, represented in Egyptian, Assyrian, and Greek art as a lion with a human head. In Greek myth the Sphinx killed all those who came to her and failed to answer her riddle about what animal went firstly on four legs, then on two, and lastly on three: the answer is humanity (baby, adult, and old person with stick). She committed suicide when ▷Oedipus gave the right answer.

spice any aromatic vegetable substance used as a condiment and for flavouring food. Spices are mostly obtained from tropical plants, and include pepper, nutmeg, ginger, and cinnamon. They have little food value but increase the appetite and may facilitate digestion.

spider any arachnid (eight-legged animal) of the order Araneae. There are about 30,000 known species. Unlike insects, the head and breast are merged to form the cephalothorax, connected to the abdomen by a characteristic narrow waist. There are eight legs, and usually eight simple eyes. On the undersurface of the abdomen are spinnerets, usually six, which exude a viscid fluid. This hardens on exposure to the air to form silky threads, used to make silken egg cases, silk-lined tunnels, or various kinds of webs and snares for catching prey that is then wrapped. The fangs of spiders inject substances to subdue and digest prey, the juices of which are then sucked into the stomach by the spider.

Spielberg Steven 1947– . US film director, writer, and producer. His credits include such phenomenal box-office successes as *Jaws* 1975, *Close Encounters of the Third Kind* 1977, *Raiders of the Lost Ark* 1981, *ET* 1982, and *Jurassic Park* 1993 (three Academy Awards), and *Schindler's List* (seven Academy Awards), based on Thomas Keneally's novel 1993.

spin in physics, the intrinsic angular momentum of a subatomic particle, nucleus, atom, or molecule, which continues to exist even when the particle comes to rest. A particle in a specific energy state has a particular spin, just as it has a particular electric charge and mass. According to ▷quantum theory, this is restricted to discrete and indivisible values, specified by a spin quantum number. Because of its spin, a charged particle acts as a small magnet and is affected by magnetic fields.

spina bifida congenital defect in which part of the spinal cord and its membranes are exposed, due to incomplete development of the spine (vertebral column). It is a neural tube defect.

spinach annual plant *Spinacia oleracea* of the goosefoot family Chenopodiaceae. It is native to Asia and widely cultivated for its leaves, which are eaten as a vegetable.

spine backbone of vertebrates. In most mammals, it contains 26 small bones called vertebrae, which enclose and protect the spinal cord (which links the peripheral nervous system to the brain). The spine articulates with the skull, ribs, and hip bones, and provides attachment for the back muscles.

spinning art of drawing out and twisting fibres (originally wool or flax) into a long thread, or yarn, by hand or machine. Synthetic fibres are extruded as a liquid through the holes of a spinneret. Spinning was originally done by hand, then with the spinning wheel, and in about 1767 in England the inventor James Hargreaves built the machine called *spinning jenny* (patented 1770).

Spinoza Benedict or Baruch 1632–1677. Dutch philosopher who believed in a rationalistic pantheism that owed much to Descartes' mathematical appreciation of the universe. Mind and matter are two modes of an infinite substance that he called God or Nature, good and evil being relative. He was a determinist, believing that human action was motivated by self-preservation.

spleen organ in vertebrates, part of the reticuloendothelial system, which helps to process ♦lymphocytes. It also regulates the number of red blood cells in circulation by destroying old cells, and stores iron. It is situated on the left side of the body, behind the stomach.

sponge any saclike simple invertebrate of the phylum Porifera, usually marine. A sponge has a hollow body, its cavity lined by cells bearing flagellae, whose whiplike movements keep water circulating, bringing in a stream of food particles. The body walls are strengthened with protein (as in the bath sponge) or small spikes of silica, or a framework of calcium carbonate.

spore small reproductive or resting body, usually consisting of just one cell. Unlike a ♦gamete, it does not need to fuse with another cell in order to develop into a new organism. Spores are produced by the lower plants, most fungi, some bacteria, and certain protozoa. They are generally light and easily dispersed by wind movements. Plant spores are haploid and are produced by the sporophyte, following ♦meiosis.

spreadsheet in computing, a program that mimics a sheet of ruled paper, divided into columns and rows. The user enters values in the sheet, then instructs the program to perform some operation on them, such as totalling a column or finding the average of a series of numbers.

spring device, usually a metal coil, that returns to its original shape after being stretched or compressed. Springs are used in some machines (such as clocks) to store energy, which can be released at a controlled rate. In other machines (such as engines) they are used to close valves.

Sputnik series of ten Soviet Earth-orbiting satellites. *Sputnik 1* was the first artificial satellite, launched 4 Oct 1957. It weighed 84 kg/185 lb, with a 58 cm/23 in diameter, and carried only a simple radio transmitter which allowed scientists to track it as it orbited Earth. It burned up in the atmosphere 92 days later. Sputniks were superseded in the early 1960s by the Cosmos series.

square root in mathematics, a number that when squared (multiplied by itself) equals a given number. For example, the square root of 25 (written $\sqrt{25}$) is

$\pm$ 5, because 5 x 5 = 25, and (−5) x (−5) = 25. As an exponent, a square root is represented by ½, for example, $16^{\frac{1}{2}} = 4$.

squash or *squash rackets* racket-and-ball game usually played by two people on an enclosed court, derived from rackets. Squash became a popular sport in the 1970s and later gained competitive status. There are two forms of squash: the American form, which is played in North and some South American countries, and the English, which is played mainly in Europe and Commonwealth countries such as Pakistan, Australia, and New Zealand.

squirrel rodent of the family Sciuridae. Squirrels are found worldwide except for Australia, Madagascar, and polar regions. Some are tree dwellers; these generally have bushy tails, and some, with membranes between their legs, are called ◊flying squirrels. Others are terrestrial, generally burrowing forms called ground squirrels; these include chipmunks, gophers, marmots, and prairie dogs.

Sri Lanka Democratic Socialist Republic of (*Prajathanrika Samajawadi Janarajaya Sri Lanka*) (until 1972 *Ceylon*); *area* 65,600 sq km/25,328 sq mi; *capital* (and chief port) Colombo; *features* Adam's Peak (2,243 m/7,538 ft); ruined cities of Anuradhapura, Polonnaruwa; *political system* liberal democratic republic; *population* (1993 est) 17,800,000 (Sinhalese 74%, Tamils 17%, Moors 7%); growth rate 1.8% p.a.; *languages* Sinhala, Tamil, English; *religions* Buddhist 69%, Hindu 15%, Muslim 8%, Christian 7%.

SS German *S*chutz-*S*taffel 'protective squadron' Nazi elite corps established 1925. Under ◊Himmler its 500,000

membership included the full-time *Waffen-SS* (armed SS), which fought in World War II, and spare-time members. The SS performed state police duties and was brutal in its treatment of the Jews and others in the concentration camps and occupied territories. It was condemned as an illegal organization at the Nuremberg Trials of war criminals.

Staffordshire county of W central England; *area* 2,720 sq km/1,050 sq mi; *towns* Stafford (administrative headquarters), Stoke-on-Trent, Newcastle-under-Lyme; *features* Cannock Chase; Keele University 1962; Staffordshire bull terriers; *population* (1991) 1,031,100.

stalactite and stalagmite cave structures formed by the deposition of calcite dissolved in ground water. *Stalactites* grow downwards from the roofs or walls and can be icicle-shaped, straw-shaped, curtain-shaped, or formed as terraces. *Stalagmites* grow upwards from the cave floor and can be conical, fir- cone-shaped, or resemble a stack of saucers. Growing stalactites and stalagmites may meet to form a continuous column from floor to ceiling.

Stalin Joseph. Adopted name (Russian 'steel') of Joseph Vissarionovich Djugashvili 1879–1953. Soviet politician. A member of the October Revolution Committee 1917, Stalin became general secretary of the Communist Party 1922. Clashing with ◊Trotsky after ◊Lenin's death 1924, Stalin emerged as dictator after launching a series of five-year plans to collectivize industry and agriculture from 1928. All opposition was eliminated in the Great Purge 1936–38. After World War II, the USSR emerged as a superpower and Stalin quickly turned E Europe into a series of Soviet satellites while maintaining autocracy at home.

He was posthumously denounced by leaders of the Soviet regime.

stamen male reproductive organ of a flower. The stamens are collectively referred to as the androecium. A typical stamen consists of a stalk, or filament, with an anther, the pollen-bearing organ, at its apex, but in some primitive plants, such as *Magnolia*, the stamen may not be markedly differentiated.

Stamp Act UK act of Parliament in 1765 that sought to raise enough money from the American colonies to cover the cost of their defence. Refusal to use the required tax stamps and a blockade of British merchant shipping in the colonies forced repeal of the act the following year. It helped to precipitate the ◊American Revolution.

Stanislavsky Konstantin Sergeivich 1863–1938. Russian actor, director, and teacher of acting. He rejected the declamatory style of acting in favour of a more realistic approach, concentrating on the psychological basis for the development of character. As a director, he is acclaimed for his productions of the great plays of ◊Chekhov.

star luminous globe of gas, mainly hydrogen and helium, which produces its own heat and light by nuclear reactions. Although stars shine for a very long time – many billions of years – they are not eternal, and have been found to change in appearance at different stages in their lives.

starch widely distributed, high-molecular-mass ◊carbohydrate, produced by plants as a food store; main dietary sources are cereals, legumes, and tubers, including potatoes. It consists of varying proportions of two ◊glucose polymers (◊polysaccharides):   straight-chain

(amylose) and branched (amylopectin) molecules.

Star Chamber in English history, a civil and criminal court, named after the star-shaped ceiling decoration of the room in the Palace of Westminster, London, where its first meetings were held. Created in 1487 by Henry VII, the Star Chamber comprised some 20 or 30 judges. It was abolished 1641 by the ◊Long Parliament.

starfish or *seastar* any ◊echinoderm of the subclass Asteroidea with arms radiating from a central body. Usually there are five arms, but some species have more. They are covered with spines and small pincerlike organs. There are also a number of small tubular processes on the skin surface that assist in locomotion and respiration. Starfish are predators, and vary in size from 1.2 cm/0.5 in to 90 cm/3 ft.

States General former French parliament that consisted of three estates: nobility, clergy, and commons. First summoned 1302, it declined in importance as the power of the crown grew. It was not called at all 1614–1789 when the crown needed to institute fiscal reforms to avoid financial collapse. Once called, the demands made by the States General formed the first phase in the ◊French Revolution. States General is also the name of the Dutch parliament.

static electricity ◊electric charge that is stationary, usually acquired by a body by means of electrostatic induction or friction. Rubbing different materials can produce static electricity, as seen in the sparks produced on combing one's hair or removing a nylon shirt. In some processes static electricity is useful, as in paint spraying where the parts to be sprayed are charged with electricity of opposite polarity to that on the paint droplets, and in ◊xerography.

statistics branch of mathematics concerned with the collection and interpretation of data. For example, to determine the ◊mean age of the children in a school, a statistically acceptable answer might be obtained by calculating an average based on the ages of a representative sample, consisting, for example, of a random tenth of the pupils from each class. Probability is the branch of statistics dealing with predictions of events.

steady-state theory in astronomy, a rival theory to that of the ◊Big Bang, which claims that the universe has no origin but is expanding because new matter is being created continuously throughout the universe. The theory was proposed 1948 by Hermann Bondi (1919–), Thomas Gold (1920–), and Fred ◊Hoyle, but was dealt a severe blow in 1965 by the discovery of ◊cosmic background radiation (radiation left over from the formation of the universe) and is now largely rejected.

steam engine engine that uses the power of steam to produce useful work. It was the principal power source during the British Industrial Revolution in the 18th century. The first successful steam engine was built 1712 by English inventor Thomas Newcomen at Dudley, West Midalnds, and it was developed further by Scottish mining engineer James Watt from 1769 and by English mining engineer Richard Trevithick, whose high-pressure steam engine 1802 led to the development of the steam locomotive.

steel alloy or mixture of iron and up to 1.7% carbon, sometimes with other elements, such as manganese, phosphorus, sulphur, and silicon. The USA, Russia, Ukraine, and Japan are the main steel producers. Steel has innumerable uses, including ship and automobile manufacture, skyscraper frames, and machinery of all kinds.

Stein Gertrude 1874–1946. US writer. She influenced authors Ernest ◊Hemingway, Sherwood ◊Anderson, and F Scott ◊Fitzgerald with her radical prose style. Drawing on the stream-of-consciousness psychology of William James and on the geometry of Cezanne andthe Cubist painters in Paris, she evolved a 'continuous present' style made up of constant repetition and variation of simple phrases. Her work includes the self- portrait *The Autobiography of Alice B Toklas* 1933.

Steinbeck John (Ernst) 1902–1968. US novelist. His realist novels, such as *In Dubious Battle* 1936, *Of Mice and Men* 1937, and *The Grapes of Wrath* 1939 (Pulitzer Prize) (filmed 1940), portray agricultural life in his native California, where migrant farm labourers from the Oklahoma dust bowl struggled to survive. Nobel prize 1962.

Steiner Rudolf 1861–1925. Austrian philosopher, originally a theosophist, who developed his own mystic and spiritual teaching, anthroposophy, designed to develop the whole human being. A number of Steiner schools follow a curriculum laid down by him with a strong emphasis on the arts.

Stendhal pen name of Marie Henri Beyle 1783–1842. French novelist. His novels *Le Rouge et le noir/The Red and the Black* 1830 and *La Chartreuse de Parme/The Charterhouse of Parma*

1839 were pioneering works in their treatment of disguise and hypocrisy; a review of the latter by fellow novelist ◊Balzac in 1840 furthered Stendhal's reputation.

Stephen, St the first Christian martyr; he was stoned to death. Feast day 26 Dec.

Stephenson George 1781–1848. English engineer who built the first successful steam locomotive, and who also invented a safety lamp in 1815. He was appointed engineer of the Stockton and Darlington Railway, the world's first public railway, in 1821, and of the Liverpool and Manchester Railway in 1826. In 1829 he won a £500 prize with his locomotive *Rocket.*

Stephenson Robert 1803–1859. English civil engineer who constructed railway bridges such as the high-level bridge at Newcastle upon Tyne, England, and the Menai and Conway tubular bridges in Wales. He was the son of George Stephenson.

steppe the temperate grasslands of Europe and Asia. Sometimes the term refers to other temperate grasslands and semi-arid desert edges.

sterilization any surgical operation to terminate the possibility of reproduction. In women, this is normally achieved by sealing or tying off the ◊Fallopian tubes (tubal ligation) so that fertilization can no longer take place. In men, the transmission of sperm is blocked by ◊vasectomy.

Sterne Laurence 1713–1768. Irish writer. He created the comic anti-hero Tristram Shandy in *The Life and Opinions of Tristram Shandy, Gent* 1759–67, an eccentrically whimsical and bawdy novel which foreshadowed many of the techniques and devices of 20th-century novelists, including James Joyce. His other works include *A Sentimental Journey through France and Italy* 1768.

steroid in biology, any of a group of cyclic, unsaturated alcohols (lipids without fatty acid components), which, like sterols, have a complex molecular structure consisting of four carbon rings. Steroids include the sex hormones, such as ◊testosterone, the corticosteroid hormones produced by the ◊adrenal gland, bile acids, and ◊cholesterol. The term is commonly used to refer to ◊anabolic steroid. In medicine, synthetic steroids are used to treat a wide range of conditions.

Stevenson Robert Louis 1850–1894. Scottish novelist and poet. He wrote the adventure novel ◊*Treasure Island* 1883. Later works included the novels *Kidnapped* 1886, *The Master of Ballantrae* 1889, *The Strange Case of Dr Jekyll and Mr Hyde* 1886, and the anthology *A Child's Garden of Verses* 1885.

Stijl, De group of 20th-century Dutch artists and architects led by Piet ◊Mondrian from 1917. The group promoted Mondrian's 'Neo-Plasticism', an abstract style that sought to establish universal principles of design based on horizontal and vertical lines, the three primary colours, and black, white, and grey. They had a strong influence on the ◊Bauhaus school.

stimulant any substance that acts on the brain to increase alertness and activity; for example, ◊amphetamine. When given to children, stimulants may have a paradoxical, calming effect. Stimulants cause liver damage, are habit-forming, have limited therapeutic value, and are now prescribed only to treat narcolepsy and severe obesity.

Stirling James 1926–1992. Scottish architect. He was possibly the most influential of his generation. While in partnership with James Gowan (1924–   ), he designed the Leicester University Engineering Building 1959–63 in a Constructivist vein. His design for the Staatsgalerie, Stuttgart, Germany 1977–82, showed a blend of Constructivism, Modernism, and several strands of Classicism.

stock exchange institution for the buying and selling of stocks and shares (securities). The world's largest stock exchanges are London, New York (Wall Street), and Tokyo. The oldest stock exchanges are Antwerp 1460, Hamburg 1558, Amsterdam 1602, New York 1790, and London 1801. The former division on the London Stock Exchange between brokers (who bought shares from jobbers to sell to the public) and jobbers (who sold them only to brokers on commission, the 'jobbers' turn') was abolished in 1986.

Stockhausen Karlheinz 1928–   . German composer of avant-garde music. He has continued to explore new musical sounds and compositional techniques since the 1950s. His major works include *Gesang der Jünglinge* 1956, *Kontakte* 1960 (electronic music), and *Sirius* 1977.

Stockholm capital and industrial port of Sweden; population (1990) 674,500. It is built on a number of islands.

stocks and shares investment holdings (securities) in private or public undertakings. Although distinctions have become blurred, in the UK stock usually means fixed-interest securities – for example, those issued by central and local government – while shares represent a stake in the ownership of a trading company which, if they are ordinary shares, yield to the owner dividends reflecting the success of the company. In the USA the term stock generally signifies what in the UK is an ordinary share.

stoicism Greek school of philosophy, founded about 300 BC by Zeno of Citium. The stoics were pantheistic materialists who believed that happiness lay in accepting the law of the universe. They emphasized human brotherhood, denounced slavery, and were internationalist. The name is derived from the porch on which Zeno taught.

stomach the first cavity in the digestive system of animals. In mammals it is a bag of muscle situated just below the diaphragm. Food enters it from the oesophagus, is digested by the acid and ▷enzymes secreted by the stomach lining, and then passes into the duodenum. Some plant-eating mammals have multichambered stomachs that harbour bacteria in one of the chambers to assist in the digestion of ▷cellulose. The gizzard is part of the stomach in birds.

Stone Age the developmental stage of humans in ▷prehistory before the use of metals, when tools and weapons were made chiefly of stone, especially flint. The Stone Age is subdivided into the Old or Palaeolithic, the Middle or Mesolithic, and the New or Neolithic. The people of the Old Stone Age were hunters and gatherers, whereas the Neolithic people took the first steps in agriculture, the domestication of animals, weaving, and pottery.

Stonehenge megalithic monument dating from about 2000 BC on Salisbury Plain, Wiltshire, England. It consisted originally of a circle of 30 upright stones, their tops linked by lintel stones to form a continuous circle about 30 m/100 ft across. Within the circle was a horseshoe arrangement of five trilithons (two uprights plus a lintel, set as five separate entities), and a so-called 'altar stone' – an upright pillar – on the axis of the horseshoe at the open, NE end, which faces in the direction of the rising sun.

Stoppard Tom 1937– . Czechoslovak-born British dramatist. His works use wit and wordplay to explore logical and philosophical ideas. His play *Rosencrantz and Guildenstern are Dead* 1967 was followed by comedies including *The Real Inspector Hound* 1968, *Jumpers* 1972, *Travesties* 1974, *Dirty Linen* 1976, *The Real Thing* 1982, *Hapgood* 1988, and *Arcadia* 1993. He has also written for radio, television, and the cinema.

Strachey (Giles) Lytton 1880–1932. English critic and biographer. He was a member of the ◊Bloomsbury Group of writers and artists. His *Landmarks in French Literature* was written 1912. The mocking and witty treatment of Cardinal Manning, Florence Nightingale, Thomas Arnold, and General Gordon in *Eminent Victorians* 1918 won him recognition. His biography of *Queen Victoria* 1921 was more affectionate.

Stradivari Antonio (Latin form *Stradivarius*) 1644–1737. Italian stringed instrumentmaker, generally considered the greatest of all violinmakers. He was born in Cremona and studied there with Niccolò Amati. He produced more than 1,100 instruments from his family workshops, over 600 of which survive.

Strasbourg city on the river Ill, in Bas-Rhin *département*, capital of Alsace, France; population (1990) 255,900. The ◊Council of Europe meets here, and sessions of the European Parliament alternate between Strasbourg and Luxembourg.

Stratford-upon-Avon market town on the river Avon, in Warwickshire, England; population (1986 est) 20,900. It is the birthplace of William ◊Shakespeare and has the Royal Shakespeare Theatre 1932.

Strathclyde region of Scotland; *area* 13,900 sq km/5,367 sq mi; *towns* Glasgow (administrative headquarters), Paisley, Greenock, Kilmarnock, Clydebank, Hamilton, Coatbridge, Prestwick; *features* includes some of Inner Hebrides; Glencoe, site of the massacre of the Macdonald clan; Breadalbane; islands: Arran, Bute, Mull; *population* (1991) 2,248,700, half the population of Scotland.

stratosphere that part of the atmosphere 10–40 km/6–25 mi from the Earth's surface, where the temperature slowly rises from a low of –55°C/–67°F to around 0°C/32°F. The air is rarefied and at around 25 km/15 mi much ◊ozone is concentrated.

Strauss Johann (Baptist) 1825–1899. Austrian conductor and composer. He was the son of composer Johann Strauss (1804–1849). In 1872 he gave up conducting and wrote operettas, such as *Die Fledermaus/The Flittermouse* 1874, and numerous waltzes, such as *The Blue Danube* and *Tales from the Vienna Woods*, which gained him the title 'the Waltz King'.

Strauss Richard (Georg) 1864–1949. German composer and conductor. He followed the German Romantic tradition but had a strongly personal style, characterized by his bold, colourful orchestration. He first wrote tone poems such as *Don Juan* 1889, *Till Eulenspiegel's Merry Pranks* 1895, and *Also sprach Zarathustra/Thus Spake Zarathustra* 1896. He then moved on to opera with *Salome* 1905 and *Elektra* 1909. He reverted to a more traditional style with *Der Rosenkavalier/The Knight of the Rose* 1909–10.

Stravinsky Igor 1882–1971. Russian composer. He later adopted French (1934) and US (1945) nationalities. He studied under ◊Rimsky-Korsakov and wrote the music for the Diaghilev ballets *The Firebird* 1910, *Petrushka* 1911, and *The Rite of Spring* 1913 (controversial at the time for their unorthodox rhythms and harmonies). His versatile work ranges from his Neo-Classical ballet *Pulcinella* 1920 to the choral-orchestral *Symphony of Psalms* 1930. He later made use of serial techniques in such works as the *Canticum Sacrum* 1955 and the ballet *Agon* 1953–57.

stress in psychology, any event or situation that makes heightened demands on a person's mental or emotional resources. Stress can be caused by overwork, anxiety about exams, money, or job security, unemployment, bereavement, poor relationships, marriage breakdown, sexual difficulties, poor living or working conditions, and constant exposure to loud noise.

strike stoppage of work by employees, often as members of a trade union, to obtain or resist change in wages, hours, or conditions. A *lockout* is a weapon of an employer to thwart or enforce such change by preventing employees from working. Another measure is *work to rule*, when production is virtually brought to a halt by strict observance of union rules.

Strindberg August 1849–1912. Swedish dramatist and novelist. His plays are in a variety of styles including historical dramas, symbolic dramas (the two-part *Dödsdansen/The Dance of Death* 1901) and 'chamber plays' such as *Spöksonaten/The Ghost [Spook] Sonata* 1907. *Fadren/The Father* 1887 and *Fröken Julie/Miss Julie* 1888 are among his best-known works.

stroke or *cerebrovascular accident* or *apoplexy* interruption of the blood supply to part of the brain due to a sudden bleed in the brain (cerebral haemorrhage) or embolism or ◊thrombosis. Strokes vary in severity from producing almost no symptoms to proving rapidly fatal. In between are those (often recurring) that leave a wide range of impaired function, depending on the size and location of the event.

strong nuclear force one of the four fundamental ◊forces of nature, the other three being the electromagnetic force, gravity, and the weak nuclear force. The strong nuclear force was first described by Japanese physicist Hideki Yukawa 1935. It is the strongest of all the forces, acts only over very small distances (within the nucleus of the atom), and is responsible for binding together ◊quarks to form ◊hadrons, and for binding together protons and neutrons in the atomic nucleus. The particle that is the carrier of the strong nuclear force is the ◊gluon, of which there are eight kinds, each with zero mass and zero charge.

structuralism 20th-century philosophical movement that has influenced such areas as linguistics, anthropology, and literary criticism. Inspired by the work of the Swiss linguist Ferdinand de Saussure (1857–1913), structuralists believe that objects should be analysed as systems of relations, rather than as positive entities. Saussure proposed that language is a system of arbitrary signs, meaning that there is no intrinsic link between the 'signifier' (the sound or mark) and the 'signified' (the concept it represents). His ideas were extended into a general method for the social sciences by Claude ◊Lévi-Strauss. The French writer Roland Barthes (1915–1980) took the lead in applying the ideas of structuralism to literary criticism, arguing that the critic should identify the structures within a text that determine its possible meanings, independently of any reference to the real.

Stuart or *Stewart* royal family who inherited the Scottish throne in 1371 and the English throne in 1603, holding it until 1714, when Queen Anne died without heirs and the house of Stuart was replaced by the house of ◊Hanover.

Stuttgart capital of Baden-Württemberg, on the river Neckar, Germany; population (1988) 565,000. It is a fruit-growing and wine-producing centre; it was founded in the 10th century.

subatomic particle in physics, a particle that is smaller than an atom. Such particles may be indivisible ◊elementary particles, such as the ◊electron and ◊quark, or they may be composites, such as the ◊proton, ◊neutron, and alpha particle. See also ◊particle physics.

sublimation in chemistry, the conversion of a solid to vapour without passing through the liquid phase.

submarine underwater warship. The first underwater boat was constructed for James I of England by the Dutch scientist Cornelius van Drebbel (1572–1633) in 1620. A naval submarine, or submersible torpedo boat, the *Gymnote*, was launched by France 1888. The conventional submarine of World War I was driven by diesel engine on the surface and by battery-powered electric motors underwater. The diesel engine also drove a generator that produced electricity to charge the batteries.

sucrose or *cane sugar* or *beet sugar* $C_{12}H_{22}O_{10}$ a sugar found in the pith of sugar cane and in sugar beets. It is popularly known as ◊sugar.

Sudan Democratic Republic of (*Jamhuryat es-Sudan*); *area* 2,505,800 sq km/967,489 sq mi; *capital* Khartoum; *environment* the building of the Jonglei Canal to supply water to N Sudan and Egypt threatens the grasslands of S Sudan; *features* Sudd swamp; largest country in Africa; *political system* military republic; *population* (1993) 30,830,000; growth rate 2.9% p.a.; *languages* Arabic 51% (official), local languages; *religions* Sunni Muslim 73%, animist 18%, Christian 9% (in south).

Suez Canal artificial waterway, 160 km/100 mi long, from Port Said to Suez, linking the Mediterranean and Red seas, separating Africa from Asia, and providing the shortest eastwards sea route from Europe. It was opened 1869, nationalized 1956, blocked by Egypt during the Arab-Israeli War 1967, and not reopened until 1975.

Suez Crisis military confrontation Oct–Dec 1956 following the nationalization of the Suez Canal by President Nasser of Egypt. In an attempt to reassert international control of the canal, Israel launched an attack, after which British and French troops landed. Widespread international censure forced the withdrawal of the British and French. The crisis resulted in the resignation of British prime minister Eden.

Suffolk county of E England; *area* 3,800 sq km/1,467 sq mi; *towns* Ipswich (administrative headquarters), Bury St Edmunds, Lowestoft, Felixstowe; *features* undulating lowlands and flat coastline; Minsmere marshland bird reserve; site of Sizewell B, Britain's first pressurized-water nuclear reactor plant; *population* (1991) 636,300.

suffragette or *suffragist* woman fighting for the right to vote. In the UK, women's suffrage bills were repeatedly introduced and defeated in Parliament between 1886 and 1911, and a militant campaign was launched 1906 by Emmeline Pankhurst (1858–1928) and her daughters. In 1918 women were granted limited franchise; in 1928 it was extended to all women over 21. In the USA the 19th amendment to the constitution 1920 gave women the vote in federal and state elections.

Sufism mystical movement of ◊Islam that originated in the 8th century. Sufis believe that deep intuition is the only real guide to knowledge. The movement has a strong strain of asceticism. The name derives from Arabic *suf*, a rough woollen robe worn as an indication of disregard for material things. There are a number of groups or brotherhoods within Sufism, each with its own method of meditative practice, one of which is the whirling dance of the dervishes.

sugar or *sucrose* sweet, soluble crystalline carbohydrate found in the pith of sugar cane and in sugar beet. It is a *disaccharide* sugar, each of its molecules being made up of two simple-sugar (*monosaccharide*) units: glucose and fructose. Sugar is easily digested and forms a major source of energy in humans. A high consumption is associated with obesity and tooth decay.

Suleiman or *Solyman* 1494–1566. Ottoman sultan from 1520, known as *the Magnificent* and *the Lawgiver*. Under his rule, the Ottoman Empire flourished and reached its largest extent. He made conquests in the Balkans, the Mediterranean, Persia, and N Africa, but was defeated at Vienna in 1529 and Valletta (on Malta) in 1565. He was a patron of the arts, a poet, and an administrator.

Sullivan Arthur (Seymour) 1842–1900. English composer. He wrote operettas in collaboration with William Gilbert, including *HMS Pinafore* 1878, *The Pirates of Penzance* 1879, and *The Mikado* 1885. Their partnership broke down 1896. Sullivan also composed serious instrumental, choral, and operatic works – for example, the opera *Ivanhoe* 1890 – which he valued more highly than the operettas.

sulphate SO_4^{2-} salt or ester derived from sulphuric acid. Most sulphates are water soluble (the exceptions are lead, calcium, strontium, and barium sulphates), and require a very high temperature to decompose them.

sulphur brittle, pale-yellow, nonmetallic element, symbol S, atomic number 16, relative atomic mass 32.064. It occurs in three allotropic forms: two crystalline (called rhombic and monoclinic, following the arrangements of the atoms within the crystals) and one amorphous. It burns in air with a blue flame and a stifling odour. Insoluble in water but soluble in carbon disulphide, it is a good electrical insulator. Sulphur is widely used in the manufacture of sulphuric acid (used to treat phosphate rock to make fertilizers) and in making paper, matches, gunpowder and fireworks, in vulcanizing rubber, and in medicines and insecticides.

sulphur dioxide SO_2 pungent gas produced by burning sulphur in air or oxygen. It is widely used for disinfecting food vessels and equipment, and as a preservative in some food products. It occurs in industrial flue gases and is a major cause of ◊acid rain.

sulphuric acid or *oil of vitriol* H_2SO_4 a dense, viscous, colourless liquid that is extremely corrosive. It gives out heat when added to water and can cause severe burns. Sulphuric acid is used extensively in the chemical industry, in the refining of petrol, and in the manufacture of fertilizers, detergents, explosives, and dyes. It forms the acid component of car batteries.

Sumatra or *Sumatera* second-largest island of Indonesia, one of the Sunda Islands; area 473,600 sq km/182,800 sq mi; population (1989) 36,882,000. East of a longitudinal volcanic mountain range is a wide plain; both are heavily forested.

Sumerian civilization the world's earliest civilization, dating from about 3500 BC and located at the confluence of the Tigris and Euphrates rivers in lower Mesopotamia (present-day Iraq). It was a city-state with priests as secular rulers. After 2300 BC, Sumer declined.

Sun the ◊star at the centre of the solar system. Its diameter is 1,392,000 km/865,000 mi; its temperature at the surface is about 5,530°C/9,980°F) and at the centre 15,000,000°C/27,000,000°F). It is composed of about 70% hydrogen

and 30% helium, with other elements making up less than 1%. The Sun's energy is generated by nuclear fusion reactions that turn hydrogen into helium at its centre. The gas core is far denser than mercury or lead on Earth. The Sun is about 4.7 billion years old, with a predicted lifetime of 10 billion years.

Sundanese member of the second-largest ethnic group in the Republic of Indonesia. There are more than 20 million speakers of Sundanese, a member of the western branch of the Austronesian family. Like their neighbours, the Javanese, the Sundanese are predominantly Muslim. They are known for their performing arts, especially *jaipongan* dance traditions, and distinctive batik fabrics.

Sunni member of the larger of the two main sects of ◊Islam, with about 680 million adherents. Sunni Muslims believe that the first three caliphs were all legitimate successors of the prophet Muhammad, and that guidance on belief and life should come from the Koran and the Hadith, and from the Shari'a, not from a human authority or spiritual leader. Imams in Sunni Islam are educated lay teachers of the faith and prayer leaders. The name derives from the *Sunna*, Arabic 'code of behaviour', the body of traditional law evolved from the teaching and acts of Muhammad.

sunspot dark patch on the surface of the Sun, actually an area of cooler gas, thought to be caused by strong magnetic fields that block the outward flow of heat to the Sun's surface. Sunspots consist of a dark central *umbra*, about 4,000K (3,700°C/6,700°F), and a lighter surrounding *penumbra*, about 5,500K (5,200°C/9,400°F). They last from several days to over a month, ranging in size from 2,000 km/1,250 mi to groups stretching for over 100,000 km/62,000 mi.

superconductivity in physics, increase in electrical conductivity at low temperatures. The resistance of some metals and metallic compounds decreases uniformly with decreasing temperature until at a critical temperature (the superconducting point), within a few degrees of absolute zero (0 K/−273.16°C/−459.67°F), the resistance suddenly falls to zero. The phenomenon was discovered by Dutch scientist Heike Kamerlingh-Onnes (1853–1926) in 1911.

supergiant the largest and most luminous type of star known, with a diameter of up to 1,000 times that of the Sun and absolute magnitudes of between −5 and −9. Supergiants are likely to become ▷supernovae.

Superior, Lake largest and deepest of the ▷Great Lakes of North America, and the second largest lake in the world; area 83,300 sq km/32,200 sq mi.

supernova the explosive death of a star, which temporarily attains a brightness of 100 million Suns or more, so that it can shine as brilliantly as a small galaxy for a few days or weeks. Very approximately, it is thought that a supernova explodes in a large galaxy about once every 100 years. Many supernovae remain undetected because of obscuring by interstellar dust – astronomers estimate some 50%.

supersonic speed speed greater than that at which sound travels, measured in ▷Mach numbers. In dry air at 0°C/32°F, sound travels at about 1,170 kph/727 mph, but decreases its speed with altitude until, at 12,000 m/39,000 ft, it is only 1,060 kph/658 mph.

superstring theory in physics, a mathematical theory developed in the 1980s to explain the properties of ▷elementary particles and the forces between them (in particular, gravity and the nuclear forces) in a way that combines ▷relativity and ▷quantum theory. In string theory, the fundamental objects in the universe are not pointlike particles but extremely small stringlike objects. These objects exist in a universe of ten dimensions, although, for reasons not yet understood, only three space dimensions and one dimension of time are discernible.

Supreme Court highest US judicial tribunal, composed since 1869 of a chief justice (William Rehnquist from 1986) and eight associate justices. Appointments are made for life by the president, with the advice and consent of the Senate, and justices can be removed only by impeachment.

surface tension in physics, the property that causes the surface of a liquid to behave as if it were covered with a weak elastic skin; this is why a needle can float on water. It is caused by the exposed surface's tendency to contract to the smallest possible area because of unequal cohesive forces between ▷molecules at the surface. Allied phenomena include the formation of droplets, the concave profile of a meniscus, and the capillary action by which water soaks into a sponge.

surfing sport of riding on the crest of large waves while standing on a narrow, keeled surfboard, usually of light synthetic material such as fibreglass, about 1.8 m/6 ft long (or about 2.4–7 m/8–9 ft known as the Malibu), as first developed in Hawaii and Australia. Windsurfing is a recent development.

Surinam Republic of (*Republiek Suriname*); *area* 163,820 sq km/63,243 sq mi; *capital* Paramaribo; *features* Suriname River; *political system* emergent democratic republic; *population* (1991) 404,300 (Hindu 37%, Creole 31%, Javanese 15%); growth rate 1.1% p.a.; *languages* Dutch (official), Sranan (creole), English, others; *religions* Christian 30%, Hindu 27%, Muslim 20%.

Surrealism movement in art, literature, and film that developed out of ▷Dada around 1922. Led by André ▷Breton, who produced the *Surrealist Manifesto* 1924, the Surrealists were inspired by the thoughts and visions of the subconscious mind. They explored varied styles and techniques, and the movement became the dominant force in Western art between world wars I and II.

Surrey county of S England; *area* 1,660 sq km/641 sq mi; *towns* Kingston upon Thames (administrative headquarters), Guildford, Woking, Reigate, Leatherhead; *features* North Downs; Runnymede, Thameside, site of the signing of Magna Carta; Yehudi Menuhin School; Kew Palace and Royal Botanic; *population* (1991) 1,018,000.

suspension mixture consisting of small solid particles dispersed in a liquid or gas, which will settle on standing. An example is milk of magnesia, which is a suspension of magnesium hydroxide in water.

Suu Kyi Aung San 1945– . Myanmar (Burmese) politician and human rights campaigner, leader of the National League for Democracy (NLD), the main opposition to the military junta. When the NLD won the 1990 elections, the junta refused to surrender power, and placed Suu Kyi under house arrest. She is the daughter of former Burmese premier Aung San. Nobel Prize for Peace 1991

Suva capital and industrial port of Fiji, on Viti Levu; population (1981) 68,000.

Swahili language belonging to the Bantu branch of the Niger-Congo family, widely used in east and central Africa. Swahili originated on the E African coast as a *lingua franca* used among traders, and contains many Arabic loan words. It is an official language in Kenya and Tanzania.

Swaziland Kingdom of (*Umbuso weSwatini*); *area* 17,400 sq km/6,716 sq mi; *capital* Mbabane; *features* landlocked enclave between South Africa and Mozambique; *political system* transitional absolute monarchy; *population* (1993 est) 835,000; growth rate 3% p.a.; *languages* Swazi 90%, English (both official); *religions* Christian 57%, animist.

Sweden Kingdom of (*Konungariket Sverige*); *area* 450,000 sq km/173,745 sq mi; *capital* Stockholm; *environment* of the country's 90,000 lakes, 20,000 are affected by acid rain; 4,000 so severely that no fish are thought to survive in them; *features* lakes, including Vänern, Vättern, Mälaren, Hjälmaren; islands of Öland and Gotland; wild elk; *head of state* King Carl XVI Gustaf from 1973; *head of government* Ingvar Carlsson from 1994; *political system* constitutional monarchy; *population* (1993 est) 8,700,000 (including 17,000 Saami [Lapps] and 1.2 million immigrants from Turkey, Yugoslavia, Greece, Iran, Finland and other Nordic countries); growth rate 0.1% p.a.; *languages* Swedish; there are Finnish- and Saami-speaking minorities; *religion* Lutheran (official) 95%.

Swift Jonathan 1667–1745. Irish satirist and Anglican cleric. He wrote *Gulliver's Travels* 1726, an allegory describing travel to lands inhabited by giants, miniature people, and intelligent horses. Other works include *The Tale of a Tub* 1704.

swimming self-propulsion of the body through water. There are four strokes in competitive swimming: freestyle, breaststroke, backstroke, and butterfly. Distances of races vary between 50 and 1,500 m. Olympic-size pools are 50 m/55 yd long and have eight lanes.

Switzerland Swiss Confederation (German *Schweiz*, French *Suisse*, Romansch *Svizzera*); *area* 41,300 sq km/ 15,946 sq mi *capital* Bern; *environment* an estimated 43% of coniferous trees, particularly in the central Alpine region, have been killed by acid rain, 90% of which comes from other countries. Over 50% of bird species are classified as threatened; *features* winter sports area of the upper valley of the river Inn (Engadine); lakes Maggiore, Lucerne, Geneva, Constance; *head of state and government* Otto Stich from 1994; *government* federal democratic republic; *population* (1993) 6,900,000; growth rate 0.2% p.a.; *languages* German 65%, French 18%, Italian 12%, Romansch 1% (all official); *religions* Roman Catholic 50%, Protestant 48%.

Sydney capital and port of New South Wales, Australia; population (1990) 3,656,900. It is a financial centre, and has three universities. The 19th-century Museum of Applied Arts and Sciences is the most popular museum in Australia.

symbiosis any close relationship between two organisms of different species, and one where both partners benefit from the association. A well-known example is the pollination relationship between insects and flowers, where the insects feed on nectar and carry pollen from one flower to another. This is sometimes known as mutualism.

Symbolism late 19th-century movement in French poetry, which inspired a similar trend in French painting. The Symbolist poets used words for their symbolic rather than concrete meaning. Leading exponents were Paul Verlaine, Stéphane Mallarmé, and Arthur Rimbaud. The Symbolist painters rejected Realism and Impressionism, seeking expression through colour, line, and form. Their subjects were often mythological, mystical, or fantastic. Gustave Moreau was a leading Symbolist painter.

symmetry exact likeness in shape about a given line (axis), point, or plane. A figure has symmetry if one half can be rotated and/or reflected onto the other. (Symmetry preserves length, angle, but not necessarily orientation.) In a wider sense, symmetry exits if a change in the system leaves the essential features of the system unchanged; for example, reversing the sign of electric charges does not change the electrical behaviour of an arrangement of charges.

symphony abstract musical composition for orchestra, traditionally in four separate but closely related movements. It developed from the smaller sonata form, the Italian overture, and the concerto grosso.

synagogue in Judaism, a place of worship, also (in the USA) called a temple. As an institution it dates from the destruction of the Temple in Jerusalem AD 70, though it had been developing from the time of the Babylonian exile as a substitute for the Temple. In antiquity it was a public meeting hall where the Torah was also read, but today it is used primarily for prayer and services. A service requires a quorum (*minyan*) of ten adult Jewish men.

synapse junction between two ⟩nerve cells, or between a nerve cell and a muscle (a neuromuscular junction), across which a nerve impulse is transmitted. The two cells are separated by a narrow gap called the *synaptic cleft*. The gap is bridged by a chemical ⟩neurotransmitter, released by the nerve impulse.

syndicalism political movement in 19th-century Europe that rejected parliamentary activity in favour of direct action, culminating in a revolutionary general strike to secure worker ownership and control of industry. The idea originated in the 1830's. After 1918 syndicalism was absorbed in communism, although it continued to have an independent existence in Spain until the late 1930s.

Synge J(ohn) M(illington) 1871–1909. Irish dramatist. He was a leading figure in the Irish dramatic revival of the early 20th century. His six plays reflect the speech patterns of the Aran Islands and W Ireland. They include *In the Shadow of the Glen* 1903, *Riders to the Sea* 1904, and *The Playboy of the Western World* 1907, which caused riots at the Abbey Theatre, Dublin, when first performed.

synthesizer device that uses electrical components to produce sounds. In *preset synthesizers*, the sound of various instruments is produced by a built-in computer-type memory. In *programmable synthesizers* any number of new instrumental or other sounds may be produced

at the will of the performer. *Speech synthesizers* can break down speech into 128 basic elements (allophones), which are then combined into words and sentences, as in the voices of electronic teaching aids.

syphilis sexually transmitted disease caused by the spiral-shaped bacterium (spirochete) *Treponema pallidum*. Untreated, it runs its course in three stages over many years, often starting with a painless hard sore, or chancre, developing within a month on the area of infection (usually the genitals). The second stage, months later, is a rash with arthritis, hepatitis, and/or meningitis. The third stage, years later, leads eventually to paralysis, blindness, insanity, and death.

Syria Syrian Arab Republic (*al-Jamhuriya al-Arabya as-Suriya*); *area* 185,200 sq km/71,506 sq mi; *capital* Damascus; *features* Mount Hermon, Golan Heights; crusader castles (including Krak des Chevaliers); Phoenician city sites (Ugarit), ruins of ancient Palmyra; *political system* socialist republic; *population* (1993) 13,400,000; growth rate 3.5% p.a.; *languages* Arabic 89% (official), Kurdish 6%, Armenian 3%; *religions* Sunni Muslim 74%; ruling minority Alawite, and other Islamic sects 16%; Christian 10%.

systems analysis in computing, the investigation of a business activity or clerical procedure, with a view to deciding if and how it can be computerized. The analyst discusses the existing procedures with the people involved, observes the flow of data through the business, and draws up an outline specification of the required computer system.

T

table tennis or *ping pong* indoor game played on a rectangular table by two or four players. It was developed in Britain about 1880 and derived from lawn tennis. World championships were first held 1926.

Tacitus Publius Cornelius *c.* AD 55–*c.* 120. Roman historian. A public orator in Rome, he was consul under Nerva 97–98 and proconsul of Asia 112–113. He wrote histories of the Roman Empire, *Annales* and *Historiae*, covering the years AD 14–68 and 69–97 respectively. He also wrote a *Life of Agricola* 97 (he married Agricola's daughter 77) and a description of the Germanic tribes, *Germania* 98.

Tagore Rabindranath 1861–1941. Bengali Indian writer. He translated into English his own verse *Gitanjali* ('song offerings') 1912 and his verse play *Chitra* 1896. Nobel Prize for Literature 1913.

Tahiti largest of the ◊Society Islands, in ◊French Polynesia; area 1,042 sq km/ 402 sq mi; population (1983) 116,000. Its capital is Papeete. Tahiti was visited by Capt James ◊Cook 1769 and by Admiral ◊Bligh of the *Bounty* 1788. It came under French control 1843 and became a colony 1880.

Tai member of any of the groups of SE Asian peoples who speak Tai languages, all of which belong to the Sino-Tibetan language family. There are over 60 million speakers, the majority of whom live in Thailand. Tai peoples are also found in SW China, NW Myanmar (Burma), Laos, and N Vietnam.

taiga or *boreal forest* Russian name for the forest zone south of the ◊tundra, found across the northern hemisphere. Here, dense forests of conifers (spruces and hemlocks), birches, and poplars occupy glaciated regions punctuated with cold lakes, streams, bogs, and marshes. Winters are prolonged and very cold, but the summer is warm enough to promote dense growth.

Taipei or *Taibei* capital and commercial centre of Taiwan; population (1990) 2,719,700. The National Palace Museum 1965 houses the world's greatest collection of Chinese art, brought here from the mainland 1948.

Taiwan Republic of China (*Chung Hua Min Kuo*); *area* 36,179 sq km/13,965 sq mi; *capital* Taipei; *environment* industrial pollution has caused contamination of 30% of the annual rice crop with mercury, cadmium, and other heavy metals; *features* Penghu (Pescadores), Jinmen (Quemoy), Mazu (Matsu) islands; *political system* emergent democracy; *population* (1993 est) 21,000,000 (Taiwanese 84%, mainlanders 14%); growth rate 1.4% p.a.; *languages* Mandarin Chinese (official); Taiwan, Hakka dialects; *religions* officially atheist; Taoist, Confucian, Buddhist, Christian.

Tajik or *Tadzhik* member of the majority ethnic group living in Tajikistan; Tajiks also live in Afghanistan and parts of Pakistan and W China. Long associated with neighbouring Turkic peoples, the majority are Sunni Muslims; there is a Shi'ite minority in Afghanistan. The *Tajiki language* belongs to the West Iranian subbranch of the Indo-European family. It is written in the Cyrillic script.

Tajikistan Republic of; *area* 143,100 sq km/55,251 sq mi; *capital* Dushanbe; *features* Pik Kommunizma (Communism Peak); health resorts and mineral springs; *political system* emergent democracy; *population* (1993 est) 5,700,000 (Tajik 63%, Uzbek 24%, Russian 8%, Tatar 1%, Kyrgyz 1%, Ukrainian 1%); *language* Tajik, similar to Farsi (Persian); *religion* Sunni Muslim.

Taj Mahal white marble mausoleum built 1630–53 on the river Jumna near Agra, India. Erected by Shah Jahan to the memory of his favourite wife, it is a celebrated example of Indo-Islamic architecture, the fusion of Muslim and Hindu styles.

talc $Mg_3Si_4O_{10}(OH)_2$, mineral, hydrous magnesium silicate. It occurs in tabular crystals, but the massive impure form, known as *steatite* or *soapstone*, is more common. It is formed by the alteration of magnesium compounds and usually found in metamorphic rocks. Talc is very soft, ranked 1 on the Mohs' scale of hardness. It is used in powdered form in cosmetics, lubricants, and as an additive in paper manufacture.

Tallinn (German *Reval*) naval port and capital of Estonia; population (1987) 478,000. Vyshgorod castle (13th century) and other medieval buildings remain. It is a yachting centre.

Tallis Thomas *c.* 1505–1585. English composer. He was a master of counterpoint. His works include *Tallis's Canon* ('Glory to thee my God this night') 1567, the antiphonal *Spem in alium non habui* (about 1573) for 40 voices in various groupings, and a collection of 34 motets, *Cantiones sacrae*, 1575 (of which 16 are by Tallis and 18 by Byrd).

Talmud the two most important works of post-Biblical Jewish literature. The Babylonian and the Palestinian (or Jerusalem) Talmud provide a compilation of ancient Jewish law and tradition. The Babylonian Talmud was edited at the end of the 5th century AD and is the more authoritative version for later Judaism; both Talmuds are written in a mix of Hebrew and Aramaic.

Tamil member of the majority ethnic group living in the Indian state of Tamil Nadu (formerly Madras). Tamils also live in S India, N Sri Lanka, Malaysia, Singapore, and South Africa, totalling 35–55 million worldwide. Tamil belongs to the Dravidian family of languages; written records in Tamil date from the 3rd century BC. The 3 million Tamils in Sri Lanka are predominantly Hindu, unlike the Sinhalese, the majority group in Sri Lanka, who are mainly Buddhist.

Tamil Nadu formerly (until 1968) *Madras State* state of SE India; *area* 130,100 sq km/50,219 sq mi; *capital* Madras; *population* (1991) 55,638,300; *language* Tamil.

Tanganyika, Lake lake 772 m/2,534 ft above sea level in the Great Rift

Valley, E Africa, with Zaire to the W, Zambia to the S, and Tanzania and Burundi to the E. It is about 645 km/400 mi long, with an area of about 31,000 sq km/12,000 sq mi, and is the deepest lake (1,435 m/4,710 ft) in Africa. The mountains around its shores rise to about 2,700 m/8,860 ft.

Tang dynasty the greatest of China's imperial dynasties, which ruled 618–907. Founded by Li Yuan (566–635), it extended Chinese authority into central Asia, Tibet, Korea, and Annam, establishing what was then the world's largest empire. The dynasty's peak was reached during the reign (712–56) of Emperor Minghuang (Hsuan-tsung).

tangent in geometry, a straight line that touches a curve and gives the gradient of the curve at the point of contact. At a maximum, minimum, or point of inflection, the tangent to a curve has zero gradient. Also, in trigonometry, a function of an acute angle in a right-angled triangle, defined as the ratio of the length of the side opposite the angle to the length of the side adjacent to it; a way of expressing the gradient of a line.

tank armoured fighting vehicle that runs on tracks and is fitted with weapons systems capable of defeating other tanks and destroying life and property. The term was originally a code name for the first effective tracked and armoured fighting vehicle, invented by the British soldier and scholar Ernest Swinton, and first used in the Battle of the Somme 1916.

Tantrism forms of Hinduism and Buddhism that emphasize the division of the universe into male and female forces that maintain its unity by their interaction. Tantric Hinduism is associated with magical and sexual yoga practices that imitate the union of Siva and Sakti, as described in scriptures known as the *Tantras*. In Buddhism, the *Tantras* are texts attributed to the Buddha, describing methods of attaining enlightenment.

Tanzania United Republic of (*Jamhuri ya Muungano wa Tanzania*);*area* 945,000 sq km/364,865 sq mi; *capital* Dodoma (since 1983); *environment* the black rhino faces extinction as a result of poaching; *features* Mount Kilimanjaro, 5,895 m/19,340 ft, the highest peak in Africa; Serengeti National Park, Olduvai Gorge; Ngorongoro Crater, 14.5 km/9 mi across, 762 m/2,500 ft deep; *political system* transitional; *population* (1993 est) 28,200,000; growth rate 3.5% p.a.; *languages* Kiswahili, English (both official).

Taoism Chinese philosophical system, traditionally founded by the Chinese philosopher Lao Zi 6th century BC. The 'tao' or 'way' denotes the hidden principle of the universe, and less stress is laid on good deeds than on harmonious interaction with the environment, which automatically ensures right behaviour.

tape recording, magnetic method of recording electric signals on a layer of iron oxide, or other magnetic material, coating a thin plastic tape. The electrical signals from the microphone are fed to the electromagnetic recording head, which magnetizes the tape in accordance with the frequency and amplitude of the original signal The impulses may be audio (for sound recording), video (for television), or data (for computer). For playback, the tape is passed over the same, or another, head to convert magnetic into electrical signals, which are then amplified for reproduction. Tapes are easily demagnetized (erased) for reuse, and come in cassette, cartridge, or reel form.

tapeworm any of various parasitic flatworms of the class Cestoda. They lack digestive and sense organs, can reach 15 m/50 ft in length, and attach themselves to the host's intestines by means of hooks and suckers. Tapeworms are made up of hundreds of individual segments, each of which develops into a functional hermaphroditic reproductive unit capable of producing numerous eggs. The larvae of tapeworms usually reach humans in imperfectly cooked meat or fish, causing anaemia and intestinal disorders.

tar dark brown or black viscous liquid obtained by the destructive distillation of coal, shale, and wood. Tars consist of a mixture of hydrocarbons, acids, and bases. Creosote and ◊paraffin are produced from wood tar.

tarantula wolf spider *Lycosa tarantula* with a 2.5 cm/1 in body. It spins no web, relying on its speed in hunting to catch its prey. The name 'tarantula' is also used for any of the numerous large, hairy spiders of the family Theraphosidae, with large poison fangs, native to the SW USA and tropical America.

tarot cards fortune-telling aid consisting of 78 cards: the *minor arcana* in four suits (resembling playing cards) and the *major arcana*, 22 cards with densely symbolic illustrations that have links with astrology and the ◊kabbala.

Tarquinius Superbus (Tarquin the Proud) lived 6th century BC. Last king of Rome 534–510 BC. He abolished certain rights of Romans, and made the city powerful. According to legend, he was deposed when his son Sextus raped a Roman woman, Lucretia.

tartan woollen cloth woven in specific chequered patterns individual to Scottish clans, with stripes of different widths and colours crisscrossing on a coloured background; it is used in making skirts, kilts, trousers, and other articles of clothing.

tartrazine (E102) yellow food colouring produced synthetically from petroleum. Many people are allergic to foods containing it. Typical effects are skin disorders and respiratory problems. It has been shown to have an adverse effect on hyperactive children.

Tashkent capital of Uzbekistan; population (1990) 2,100,000. It was severely damaged by an earthquake 1966.

Tasmania formerly (1642–1856) *Van Diemen's Land* island off the south coast of Australia; a state of the Commonwealth of Australia; *area* 67,800 sq km/ 26,171 sq mi; *capital* Hobart; *features* Franklin River, a wilderness area saved from a hydroelectric scheme 1983, which also has a prehistoric site; unique fauna including the Tasmanian devil; *population* (1987) 448,000.

taste sense that detects some of the chemical constituents of food. The human tongue can distinguish only four basic tastes (sweet, sour, bitter, and salty) but it is supplemented by the sense of smell. What we refer to as taste is really a composite sense made up of both taste and smell.

Tatar or *Tartar* member of a Turkic people, the descendants of the mixed Mongol and Turkic followers of ◊Genghis Khan. The vast and wealthy Tatar state was conquered by Russia 1552. The Tatars now live mainly in the Russian autonomous republic of Tatarstan, W Siberia, Turkmenistan, and

Uzbekistan; they are mainly Muslim. The *Tatar language*, belongs to the Turkic branch of the Altaic family.

tau ◊elementary particle with the same electric charge as the electron but a mass nearly double that of a proton. It has a lifetime of around 3×10^{-13} seconds and belongs to the ◊lepton family of particles – those that interact via the electromagnetic, weak nuclear, and gravitational forces, but not the strong nuclear force.

taxation raising of money from individuals and organizations by the state in order to pay for the goods and services it provides. Taxation can be *direct* (a deduction from income) or *indirect* (added to the purchase price of goods or services) The standard form of indirect taxation in Europe is *value-added tax (VAT)*. *Income tax* is the most common form of direct taxation.

taxonomy another name for the ◊classification of living organisms.

Tayside region of Scotland; *area* 7,700 sq km/2,973 sq mi; *towns and cities* Dundee (administrative headquarters), Perth, Arbroath, Forfar *features* river Tay, the longest river in Scotland; Grampian Mountains; Lochs Tay and Rannoch; *population* (1991) 383,800.

Tbilisi formerly *Tiflis* capital of Georgia; population (1987) 1,194,000. It is a centre of Georgian culture, with fine medieval churches.

Tchaikovsky Pyotr Il'yich 1840–1893. Russian composer. His strong sense of melody, personal expression, and brilliant orchestration are clear throughout his many Romantic works, which include six symphonies, three piano concertos, a violin concerto, operas (for example, *Eugene Onegin*

1879), ballets (for example, *The Nutcracker* 1891–92), orchestral fantasies (for example, *Romeo and Juliet* 1870), and chamber and vocal music.

tea evergreen shrub *Camellia sinensis*, family Theaceae, of which the fermented, dried leaves are infused to make a beverage of the same name. Known in China as early as 2737 BC, tea was first brought to Europe AD 1610 and rapidly became a popular drink. In 1823 it was found growing wild in N India, and plantations were later established in Assam and Sri Lanka; producers today include Africa, South America, Georgia, Azerbaijan, Indonesia, and Iran.

technology the use of tools, power, and materials, generally for the purposes of production. Almost every human process for getting food and shelter depends on complex technological systems, which have been developed over a 3-million-year period. Significant milestones include the advent of the ◊steam engine 1712, the introduction of ◊electricity and the ◊internal combustion engine in the mid-1870s, and recent developments in communications, ◊electronics, and the nuclear and space industries. The *advanced technology* (highly automated and specialized) on which modern industrialized society depends is frequently contrasted with the *low technology* (labour-intensive and unspecialized) that characterizes some developing countries. *Intermediate technology* is an attempt to adapt scientifically advanced inventions to less developed areas by using local materials and methods of manufacture.

Tehran capital of Iran; population (1986) 6,043,000. Much of the city was rebuilt in the 1920s and 1930s. Tehran is the site of the Gulistan Palace (the former royal residence). The Shahyad Tower is a symbol of modern Iran.

tektite small, rounded glassy stone, found in certain regions of the Earth, such as Australasia. Tektites are probably the scattered drops of molten rock thrown out by the impact of a large ◊meteorite.

Tel Aviv officially *Tel Aviv-Jaffa* city in Israel, on the Mediterranean coast; population (1987) 320,000. It was founded 1909 as a Jewish residential area in the Arab town of Jaffa, with which it was combined 1949. During the ◊Gulf War 1991, Tel Aviv became a target for Iraqi missiles as part of Saddam Hussein's strategy to break up the Arab alliance against him.

telecommunications communications over a distance, generally by electronic means. Long-distance voice communication was pioneered 1876 by US inventor Alexander Graham ◊Bell when he invented the telephone. Today it is possible to communicate with most countries by telephone cable, or by satellite or microwave link, with over 100,000 simultaneous conversations and several television channels being carried by the latest satellites. Integrated-Services Digital Network (ISDN) makes videophones and high-quality fax possible; the world's first large-scale centre of ISDN began operating in Japan 1988. ISDN is a system that transmits voice and image data on a single transmission line by changing them into digital signals. The chief method of relaying long- distance calls on land is microwave radio transmission.

Telemann Georg Philipp 1681–1767. German Baroque composer, organist, and conductor. He conducted at the Johanneum, Hamburg, from 1721. His prolific output included concertos for both new and old instruments, such as violin, viola da gamba, flute, oboe, trumpet, and bassoon. Other works include 25 operas, numerous sacred cantatas, and instrumental fantasias.

telephone instrument for communicating by voice over long distances, invented by US inventor Alexander Graham ◊Bell 1876. The transmitter (mouthpiece) consists of a carbon microphone, with a diaphragm that vibrates when a person speaks into it. The diaphragm vibrations compress grains of carbon to a greater or lesser extent, altering their resistance to an electric current passing through them. This sets up variable electrical signals, which travel along the telephone lines to the receiver of the person being called. There they cause the magnetism of an electromagnet to vary, making a diaphragm above the electromagnet vibrate and give out sound waves, which mirror those that entered the mouthpiece originally.

telescope optical instrument that magnifies images of faint and distant objects; any device for collecting and focusing light and other forms of electromagnetic radiation. It is a major research tool in astronomy and is used to sight over land and sea; small telescopes can be attached to cameras and rifles. A telescope with a large aperture, or opening, can distinguish finer detail and fainter objects than one with a small aperture. The *refracting telescope* uses lenses, and the *reflecting telescope* uses mirrors. A third type, the *catadioptric telescope*, is a combination of lenses and mirrors.

teletext broadcast system of displaying information on a television screen. The information – typically about news items, entertainment, sport, and finance – is constantly updated. Teletext is a form of ▷videotext, pioneered in Britain by the British Broadcasting Corporation (BBC) with Ceefax and by Independent Television with Teletext.

television (TV) reproduction at a distance by radio waves of visual images. For transmission, a television camera converts the pattern of light it takes in into a pattern of electrical charges. This is scanned line by line by a beam of electrons from an electron gun, resulting in variable electrical signals that represent the picture. These signals are combined with a radio carrier wave and broadcast as electromagnetic waves. The TV aerial picks up the wave and feeds it to the receiver (TV set). This separates out the vision signals, which pass to a cathode-ray tube where a beam of electrons is made to scan across the screen line by line, mirroring the action of the electron gun in the TV camera. The result is a recreation of the pattern of light that entered the camera. Twenty-five pictures are built up each second with interlaced scanning in Europe (30 in North America), with a total of 625 lines in Europe (525 lines in North America and Japan).

Telford Thomas 1757–1834. Scottish civil engineer who opened up N Scotland by building roads and waterways. He constructed many aqueducts and canals, including the Caledonian canal 1802–23, and erected the Menai road suspension bridge 1819–26, a type of structure scarcely tried previously in England. In Scotland he constructed over 1,600 km/1,000 mi of road and 1,200 bridges, churches, and harbours.

temperature degree or intensity of heat of a body, and the condition that determines whether or not it will transfer heat to, or receive heat from, another body according to the laws of ▷thermodynamics. It is measured in degrees Celsius (before 1948 called centigrade), kelvin, or Fahrenheit.

Templars or *Knights Templar* or *Order of Poor Knights of Christ and of the Temple of Solomon* military religious order founded in Jerusalem 1119–20. They played an important part in the ▷Crusades of the 12th and 13th centuries. Through their international links, they became Europe's bankers and their resultant power and wealth, rather than their alleged heresy, probably motivated Philip IV of France, helped by the Avignon Pope Clement V, to suppress the order 1307–14.

Temple site of Jewish national worship in Jerusalem in both ancient and modern days. The Western or *Wailing Wall* is the surviving part of the western wall of the enclosure of Herod's Temple. Since the destruction of the Temple AD 70, Jews have gone there to pray and to mourn their dispersion and the loss of their homeland.

Ten Commandments in the Old Testament, the laws given by God to the Hebrew leader Moses on Mount Sinai, engraved on two tablets of stone. They are: to have no other gods besides Jehovah; to make no idols; not to misuse the name of God; to keep the sabbath holy; to honour one's parents; not to commit murder, adultery, or theft; not to give false evidence; not to be covetous. They form the basis of Jewish and Christian moral codes.

tendon or *sinew* cord of tough, fibrous connective tissue that joins muscle to bone in vertebrates. Tendons are largely composed of the protein collagen, and because of their inelasticity are very efficient at transforming muscle power into movement.

tendril in botany, a slender, threadlike structure that supports a climbing plant by coiling around suitable supports, such as the stems and branches of other plants. It may be a modified stem, leaf, leaflet, flower, leaf stalk, or stipule (a small appendage on either side of the leaf stalk), and may be simple or branched. The tendrils of Virginia creeper *Parthenocissus quinquefolia* are modified flower heads with suckerlike pads at the end that stick to walls, while those of the grapevine *Vitis* grow away from the light and thus enter dark crevices where they expand to anchor the plant firmly.

Tenerife largest of the ▷Canary Islands, Spain; area 2,060 sq km/795 sq mi; population (1981) 557,000. *Santa Cruz* is the main town, and *Pico de Teide* is an active volcano.

Tennessee state in E central USA; *area* 109,200 sq km/42,151 sq mi; *capital* Nashville; *features* Tennessee Valley Authority; Great Smoky Mountains National Park; Beale Street Historic District and Graceland, estate of Elvis Presley, Memphis; *population* (1990) 4,877,200.

tennis or *lawn tennis* racket-and-ball game invented towards the end of the 19th century, derived from real tennis. Although played on different surfaces (grass, wood, shale, clay, concrete), it is also called 'lawn tennis'. The aim of the two or four players is to strike the ball into the prescribed area of the court, with oval-headed rackets (strung with gut or nylon), in such a way that it cannot be returned. Major events include the *Davis Cup* first contested 1900 for international men's competition, and the annual All England Tennis Club championships (from 1877), an open event for players of both sexes at Wimbledon.

Tennyson Alfred, 1st Baron Tennyson 1809–1892. English poet. He was poet laureate 1850–92. His verse has a majestic, musical quality. His works include 'The Lady of Shalott', 'The Lotus Eaters', 'Ulysses', 'Break, Break, Break', 'The Charge of the Light Brigade'; the longer narratives *Locksley Hall* 1832 and *Maud* 1855; the elegy *In Memoriam* 1850; and a long series of poems on the Arthurian legends *The Idylls of the King* 1857–85.

Teresa Mother. Born Agnes Bojaxhiu 1910– . Roman Catholic nun. She was born in Skopje, Macedonia, and at 18 entered a Calcutta convent and became a teacher. In 1948 she became an Indian citizen and founded the Missionaries of Charity, based in Calcutta to help abandoned children and the dying. Nobel Peace Prize 1979.

terminal in computing, a device consisting of a keyboard and display screen (▷VDU) – or, in older systems, a teleprinter – to enable the operator to communicate with the computer. The terminal may be physically attached to the computer or linked to it by a telephone line (remote terminal). A 'dumb' terminal has no processor of its own, whereas an 'intelligent' terminal has its own processor and takes some of the processing load away from the main computer.

termite any member of the insect order Isoptera. Termites are soft-bodied social insects living in large colonies which include one or more queens (of relatively enormous size and producing an egg every two seconds), much smaller kings, and still smaller soldiers, workers, and immature forms. Termites build galleried nests of soil particles that may be 6 m/20 ft high.

terracotta brownish-red baked clay, usually unglazed, used in building, sculpture, and pottery. The term is specifically applied to small figures or figurines, such as those found at Tanagra in central Greece. Excavations at Xian, China, have revealed life-size terracotta figures of the army of the Emperor Shi Huangdi dating from the 3rd century BC.

terra firma (Latin) dry land; solid ground.

Tertiary period of geological time 65–1.64 million years ago, divided into five epochs: Palaeocene, Eocene, Oligocene, Miocene, and Pliocene. During the Tertiary, mammals took over all the ecological niches left vacant by the extinction of the dinosaurs, and became the prevalent land animals. The continents took on their present positions, and climatic and vegetation zones as we know them became established. Within the geological time column the Tertiary follows the Cretaceous period and is succeeded by the Quaternary period.

testis (plural *testes*) the organ that produces ◊sperm in male (and hermaphrodite) animals. In vertebrates it is one of a pair of oval structures that are usually internal, but in mammals (other than elephants and marine mammals), the paired testes (or testicles) descend from the body cavity during development, to hang outside the abdomen in a scrotal sac. The testes also secrete the male sex hormone androgen.

testosterone in vertebrates, hormone secreted chiefly by the testes, but also by the ovaries and the cortex of the adrenal glands. It promotes the development of secondary sexual characteristics in males. In animals with a breeding season, the onset of breeding behaviour is accompanied by a rise in the level of testosterone in the blood.

tetanus or *lockjaw* acute disease caused by the toxin of the bacillus *Clostridium tetani*, which usually enters the body through a wound. The bacterium is chiefly found in richly manured soil. Untreated, in seven to ten days tetanus produces muscular spasm and rigidity of the jaw spreading to other parts of the body, convulsions, and death. There is a vaccine, and the disease may be treatable with tetanus antitoxin and antibiotics.

tetracycline one of a group of antibiotic compounds having in common the four- ring structure of chlortetracycline, the first member of the group to be isolated. They are prepared synthetically or obtained from certain bacteria of the genus *Streptomyces*. They are broad-spectrum antibiotics, effective against a wide range of disease-causing bacteria.

tetrahedron (plural *tetrahedra*) in geometry, a solid figure (polyhedron) with four triangular faces; that is, a ◊pyramid on a triangular base. A regular tetrahedron has equilateral triangles as its faces.

Texas state in southwestern USA; *area* 691,200 sq km/266,803 sq mi; *capital* Austin; *features* Rio Grande River, Red River; arid Staked Plains, reclaimed by irrigation; Great Plains; Lyndon B Johnson Space Center, Houston; *population* (1990) 16,986,500.

Thackeray William Makepeace 1811–1863. English novelist and essayist. He was a regular contributor to *Fraser's Magazine* and *Punch*. His first novel was *Vanity Fair* 1847–48, followed by *Pendennis* 1848, *Henry Esmond* 1852 (and its sequel *The Virginians* 1857–59), and *The Newcomes* 1853–55, in which Thackeray's tendency to sentimentality is most marked.

Thai member of the majority ethnic group living in Thailand and N Myanmar (Burma). Thai peoples also live in SW China, Laos, and N Vietnam. They speak Tai languages, all of which belong to the Sino-Tibetan language family. There are over 60 million speakers, the majority of whom live in Thailand. Most Thais are Buddhists, but the traditional belief in spirits, *phi*, remains.

Thailand Kingdom of (*Prathet Thai* or *Muang Thai*); *area* 513,115 sq km/ 198,108 sq mi; *capital* and chief port Bangkok; *environment* tropical rainforest was reduced to 18% of the land area 1988 (from 93% in 1961); logging was banned by the government 1988; *features* rivers Chao Phraya, Mekong, Salween; ancient ruins of Sukhothai and Ayurrhaya; *political system* military-controlled emergent democracy; *population* (1993) 57,800,000 (Thai 75%, Chinese 14%); growth rate 2% p.a.; *languages* Thai and Chinese (both official); regional dialects; *religions* Buddhist 95%, Muslim 4%.

thalassaemia or *Cooley's anaemia* any of a group of chronic hereditary blood disorders that are widespread in the Mediterranean countries, Africa, the Far East, and the Middle East. They are characterized by an abnormality of the red blood cells and bone marrow, with enlargement of the spleen. The genes responsible are carried by about 100 million people worldwide. The diseases can be diagnosed prenatally.

Thames river in S England; length 338 km/210 mi. The longest river in England, it rises in the Cotswold Hills above Cirencester and is tidal as far as Teddington. Below London there is protection from flooding by means of the Thames Barrier (1982). The headstreams unite at Lechlade.

Thanksgiving (Day) national holiday in the US (fourth Thursday in Nov) and Canada (second Monday in Oct), first celebrated by the Pilgrim settlers in Massachusetts after their first harvest 1621.

Thatcher Margaret Hilda (born Roberts), Baroness Thatcher of Kesteven 1925– . British Conservative politician, Conservative Party leader 1975–90, prime minister 1979–90. In 1982 she sent British troops to recapture the Falkland Islands from Argentina. She confronted trade-union power during the miners' strike 1984–85, sold off majority stakes in many public utilities to the private sector, and introduced the unpopular community charge, or poll tax. A divided cabinet forced her to resign 1990.

Thebes capital of Boeotia in ancient Greece. In the Peloponnesian War it was allied with Sparta against Athens. For a short time after 371 BC when Thebes defeated Sparta at Leuctra, it was the most powerful state in Greece. Alexander the Great destroyed it 336 BC.

Thebes Greek name of an ancient city (*Niut-Ammon*) in Upper Egypt, on the Nile. It was the Egyptian capital under the New Kingdom from about 1600 BC. In the nearby *Valley of the Kings* are buried the 18th–20th dynasty kings, including Tutankhamen and Amenhotep III.

theorem mathematical proposition that can be deduced by logic from a set of axioms (basic facts that are taken to be true without proof). Advanced mathematics consists almost entirely of theorems and proofs, but even at a simple level theorems are important.

theory in science, a set of ideas, concepts, principles, or methods used to explain a wide set of observed facts. Among the major theories of science are ▷relativity, ▷quantum theory, ▷evolution, and ▷plate tectonics.

thermal conductivity in physics, the ability of a substance to conduct heat. Good thermal conductors, like good electrical conductors, are generally materials with many free electrons (such as metals).

thermocouple electric temperature-measuring device consisting of a circuit having two wires made of different metals welded together at their ends. A current flows in the circuit when the two junctions are maintained at different temperatures (Seebeck effect). The electromotive force generated – measured by a millivoltmeter – is proportional to the temperature difference.

thermodynamics branch of physics dealing with the transformation of heat into and from other forms of energy. It is the basis of the study of the efficient working of engines, such as the steam and internal-combustion engines. The three laws of thermodynamics are (1) energy can be neither created nor destroyed, heat and mechanical work being mutually convertible; (2) it is impossible for an unaided self-acting machine to convey heat from one body

to another at a higher temperature; and (3) it is impossible by any procedure, no matter how idealized, to reduce any system to the absolute zero of temperature (0K/–273°C) in a finite number of operations. Put into mathematical form, these laws have widespread applications in physics and chemistry.

thermometer instrument for measuring temperature. There are many types, designed to measure different temperature ranges to varying degrees of accuracy. Each makes use of a different physical effect of temperature. Expansion of a liquid is employed in common *liquid-in- glass thermometers*, such as those containing mercury or alcohol. The more accurate *gas thermometer* uses the effect of temperature on the pressure of a gas held at constant volume. A *resistance thermometer* takes advantage of the change in resistance of a conductor (such as a platinum wire) with variation in temperature. Another electrical thermometer is the ▷*thermocouple*. Mechanically, temperature change can be indicated by the change in curvature of a *bimetallic strip* (as commonly used in a ▷thermostat).

thermosphere layer in the Earth's ▷atmosphere above the mesosphere and below the exosphere. Its lower level is about 80 km/50 mi above the ground, but its upper level is undefined. The ionosphere is located in the thermosphere. In the thermosphere the temperature rises with increasing height to several thousand degrees Celsius. However, because of the thinness of the air, very little heat is actually present.

thermostat temperature-controlling device that makes use of feedback. It employs a temperature sensor (often a bimetallic strip) to operate a switch or valve to control electricity or fuel supply. Thermostats are used in central heating, ovens, and car engines.

Theseus in Greek mythology, a hero of ◊Attica, supposed to have united the states of the area under a constitutional government in Athens. Ariadne, whom he later abandoned on Naxos, helped him find his way through the Labyrinth to kill the ◊Minotaur. He also fought the Amazons and was one of the ◊Argonauts.

Thessaloniki (English *Salonika*) port in Macedonia, NE Greece, at the head of the Gulf of Thessaloniki; the second-largest city in Greece; population (1981) 706,200.

thiamine or *vitamin B₁* a water-soluble vitamin of the B complex. It is found in seeds and grain. Its absence from the diet causes the disease beriberi.

Thimbu or *Thimphu* capital since 1962 of the Himalayan state of Bhutan; population (1987) 15,000. There is a 13th-century fortified monastery, Tashich-oedzong, and the Memorial Charter to the Third King (1974).

Thirty Years' War major war 1618–48 in central Europe. Beginning as a German conflict between Protestants and Catholics, it was gradually transformed into a struggle to determine whether the ruling Austrian Habsburg family could gain control of all Germany. The war caused serious economic and demographic problems in central Europe. Under the *Peace of Westphalia* the German states were granted their sovereignty and the emperor retained only nominal control.

Thomas Dylan (Marlais) 1914–1953. Welsh poet. His poems, characterized by complex imagery and a strong musicality, include his 'play for voices' *Under Milk Wood* 1954, describing with humour and compassion a day in the life of the residents of a small Welsh fishing village. The short stories of *Portrait of the Artist as a Young Dog* 1940 are autobiographical.

Thomas à Kempis 1380–1471. German Augustinian monk who lived at the monastery of Zwolle. He took his name from his birthplace Kempen; his real surname was Hammerken. His *De Imitatio Christi/Imitation of Christ* is probably the most widely known devotional work ever written.

Thomson J(oseph) J(ohn) 1856–1940. English physicist who discovered the ◊electron. He was responsible for organizing the Cavendish atomic research laboratory at Cambridge University, UK. His work inaugurated the electrical theory of the atom and piloted English physicist Francis Aston's discovery of ◊isotopes. He was awarded the Nobel Prize for Physics 1906 for his research into the electrical conductivity of gases.

Thor in Norse mythology, the god of thunder (his hammer), and represented as a man of enormous strength defending humanity against demons. He was the son of Odin and Freya, and Thursday is named after him.

thorax in tetrapod vertebrates, the part of the body containing the heart and lungs, and protected by the rib cage; in arthropods, the middle part of the body, between the head and abdomen.

Thoreau Henry David 1817–1862. US author. One of the most influential figures of 19th-century US literature, he is best known for his vigorous defence of individualism and the simple life. His work *Walden, or Life in the Woods* 1854 stimulated the back-to-nature movement, and his widely influential essay Civil Disobedience 1849, advocated peaceful resistance to unjust laws.

Thrace (Greek *Thráki*) ancient region of the Balkans, SE Europe, formed by parts of modern Greece and Bulgaria. It was held successively by the Greeks, Persians, Macedonians, and Romans.

Three Mile Island island in the Shenandoah River near Harrisburg, Pennsylvania, USA, site of a nuclear power station which was put out of action following a major accident March 1979. Opposition to nuclear power in the USA was reinforced after this accident and safety standards reassessed.

throat in human anatomy, the passage that leads from the back of the nose and mouth to the ◊trachea and oesophagus. It includes the pharynx and the larynx, the latter being at the top of the trachea. The word 'throat' is also used to mean the front part of the neck, both in humans and other vertebrates; for example, in describing the plumage of birds. In engineering, it is any narrowing entry, such as the throat of a carburettor.

thrombosis condition in which a blood clot forms in a vein or artery, causing loss of circulation to the area served by the vessel. If it breaks away, it often travels to the lungs, causing pulmonary embolism.

thrush any bird of the large family Turdidae, order Passeriformes, found worldwide and known for their song. Thrushes are usually brown with speckles of other colours. They are 12–30 cm/5–12 in long.

thrush infection usually of the mouth (particularly in infants), but also sometimes of the vagina, caused by a yeastlike

fungus (*Candida*). It is seen as white patches on the mucous membranes.

thyme herb, genus *Thymus*, of the mint family Labiatae. Garden thyme *T. vulgaris*, native to the Mediterranean, grows to 30 cm/1 ft high, and has pinkish flowers. Its aromatic leaves are used for seasoning.

thymus organ in vertebrates, situated in the upper chest cavity in humans. The thymus processes ◊lymphocyte cells to produce T lymphocytes (T denotes 'thymus-derived'), which are responsible for binding to specific invading organisms and killing them or rendering them harmless.

thyroid ◊endocrine gland of vertebrates, situated in the neck in front of the trachea. It secretes several hormones, principally thyroxine, an iodine-containing hormone that stimulates growth, metabolism, and other functions of the body. The thyroid gland may be thought of as the regulator gland of the body's metabolic rate. If it is overactive, as in hyperthyroidism, the sufferer feels hot and sweaty, has an increased heart rate, diarrhoea, and weight loss. Conversely, an underactive thyroid leads to *myxoedema*, a condition characterized by sensitivity to the cold, constipation, and weight gain. In infants, an underactive thyroid leads to *cretinism*, a form of mental retardation.

Tibet autonomous region of SW China (Pinyin form *Xizang*); *area* 1,221,600 sq km/471,538 sq mi; *capital* Lhasa; *features* occupies a barren plateau bounded S and SW by the Himalayas and N by the Kunlun Mountains, traversed W to E by the Bukamagna, Karakoram, and other mountain ranges, and having an average elevation of 4,000–4,500 m/13,000–15,000 ft; the ◊yak is the main domestic animal; *population* (1991) 2,190,000 including 2,090,000 Tibetan nationalists (95.4%); many Chinese have settled in Tibet; 2 million Tibetans live in China outside Tibet; *religion* traditionally Lamaist (a form of Mahāyāna Buddhism).

Tibetan member of a Mongolian people inhabiting Tibet who practise a form of Mahāyāna Buddhism, introduced in the 7th century. Since China's Cultural Revolution 1966–68, refugee communities have formed in India and Nepal. The Tibetan language belongs to the Sino-Tibetan language family.

tibia the anterior of the pair of bones found between the ankle and the knee. In humans, the tibia is the shinbone.

tick any of an arachnid group (Ixodoidea) of large bloodsucking mites. Many carry and transmit diseases to mammals (including humans) and birds.

tide rise and fall of sea level due to the gravitational forces of the Moon and Sun. High tide occurs at an average interval of 12 hr 24 min 30 sec. The highest or *spring tides* are at or near new and full Moon; the lowest or *neap tides* when the Moon is in its first or third quarter. Some seas, such as the Mediterranean, have very small tides.

tiger largest of the great cats *Panthera tigris*, formerly found in much of central and S Asia but nearing extinction because of hunting and the destruction of its natural habitat. The tiger can grow to 3.6 m/12 ft long and weigh 300 kg/660 lbs; it has a yellow-orange coat with black stripes. It is solitary, and feeds on large ruminants. It is a good swimmer.

Tigré or *Tigray* region in the northern highlands of Ethiopia; area 65,900 sq km/25,444 sq mi. The chief town is Mekele. The region had an estimated population of 2.4 million in 1984, at a time when drought and famine were driving large numbers of people to fertile land in the S or into neighbouring Sudan. Since 1978 a guerrilla group known as the Tigré People's Liberation Front (TPLF) has been fighting for regional autonomy. The Tigré language is spoken by about 2.5 million people; it belongs to the SE Semitic branch of the Afro-Asiatic family.

timber wood used in construction, furniture, and paper pulp. *Hardwoods* include tropical mahogany, teak, ebony, rosewood, temperate oak, elm, beech, and eucalyptus. All except eucalyptus are slow-growing, and world supplies are almost exhausted. *Softwoods* comprise the ◊conifers (pine, fir, spruce, and larch), which are quick to grow and easy to work but inferior in quality of grain. *White woods* include ash, birch, and sycamore; all have light-coloured timber, are fast-growing, and can be used as veneers on cheaper timber.

Timişoara capital of Timiş county, W Romania; population (1985) 319,000. The revolt which overthrow the the Ceauşescu regime began here Dec 1989.

Timor largest and most easterly of the Lesser Sunda Islands, part of Indonesia; area 33,610 sq km/12,973 sq mi. Its indigenous people were the Atoni; successive migrants have included the Malay, Melanesian, Chinese, Arab, and Gujerati. In 1913, Timor was divided into *West Timor* (capital Kupang) and *East Timor* (capital Dili).

tin soft, silver-white, malleable and somewhat ductile, metallic element, symbol Sn (from Latin *stannum*), atomic number 50, relative atomic mass

118.69. Tin exhibits ▷allotropy, having three forms: the familiar lustrous metallic form above 55.8°F/13.2°C; a brittle form above 321.8°F/161°C; and a grey powder form below 55.8°F/13.2°C (commonly called tin pest or tin disease). The metal is quite soft (slightly harder than lead) and can be rolled, pressed, or hammered into extremely thin sheets; it has a low melting point. In nature it occurs rarely as a free metal. It resists corrosion and is therefore used for coating and plating other metals.

Tinbergen Niko(laas) 1907–1988. Dutch zoologist. He was one of the founders of ethology, the scientific study of animal behaviour in natural surroundings. Specializing in the study of instinctive behaviour, he shared a Nobel prize with Konrad ▷Lorenz and Karl von Frisch 1973. He is the brother of Jan Tinbergen.

tinnitus in medicine, constant buzzing or ringing in the ears. The phenomenon may originate from prolonged exposure to noisy conditions (drilling, machinery, or loud music) or from damage to or disease of the middle or inner ear. The victim may become overwhelmed by the relentless noise in the head.

Tintoretto adopted name of Jacopo Robusti 1518–1594. Italian painter. He was active in Venice. His dramatic religious paintings are spectacularly lit and full of movement, such as his huge canvases of the lives of Christ and the Virgin in the Scuola di San Rocco, Venice, 1564–88.

Tipperary county of the Republic of Ireland, in the province of Munster, divided into North and South Ridings; county town Clonmel; area 4,255 sq km/1,643 sq mi; population (1991) 132,600. It includes part of the Golden Vale, a dairy-farming region. There is horse and greyhound breeding.

Tirana or *Tiranë* capital (since 1920) of Albania; population (1990) 210,000. It was founded in the early 17th century by Turks when part of the Ottoman Empire. Although the city is now largely composed of recent buildings, some older districts and mosques have been preserved.

Tirol federal province of Austria; area 12,600 sq km/4,864 sq mi; population (1989) 619,600. Its capital is Innsbruck.

tissue in biology, any kind of cellular fabric that occurs in an organism's body. Several kinds of tissue can usually be distinguished, each consisting of cells of a particular kind bound together by cell walls (in plants) or extracellular matrix (in animals). Thus, nerve and muscle are different kinds of tissue in animals, as are parenchyma and sclerenchyma in plants.

tissue culture process by which cells from a plant or animal are removed from the organism and grown under controlled conditions in a sterile medium containing all the necessary nutrients. Tissue culture can provide information on cell growth and differentiation, and is also used in plant propagation and drug production.

Titan in astronomy, largest moon of the planet Saturn, with a diameter of 5,150 km/3,200 mi and a mean distance from Saturn of 1,222,000 km/759,000 mi. It was discovered 1655 by Dutch mathematician and astronomer Christiaan ▷Huygens, and is the second largest moon in the Solar System (Ganymede, of Jupiter, is larger).

Titanic British passenger liner, supposedly unsinkable, that struck an iceberg and sank off the Grand Banks of New-foundland on its first voyage 14–15 April 1912; 1,513 lives were lost. In 1985 it was located by robot submarine 4 km/2.5 mi down in an ocean canyon, preserved by the cold environment. In 1987 salvage operations began.

titanium strong, lightweight, silver-grey, metallic element, symbol Ti, atomic number 22, relative atomic mass 47.90. The ninth-most abundant element in the Earth's crust, its compounds occur in practically all igneous rocks and their sedimentary deposits. It is very strong and resistant to corrosion, so it is used in building high-speed aircraft and spacecraft; it is also widely used in making alloys, as it unites with almost every metal except copper and aluminium. Titanium oxide is used in high-grade white pigments.

Titian anglicized form of Tiziano Vecellio c. 1487–1576. Italian painter. One of the greatest artists of the High Renaissance. In 1533 he became court painter to Charles V, Holy Roman emperor, whose son Philip II of Spain later became his patron. Titian's work is richly coloured, with inventive composition. His portraits, religious paintings, and mythological scenes include *Bacchus and Ariadne* 1520–23 (National Gallery, London), *Venus and Adonis* 1554 (Prado, Madrid), and the *Pièta* about 1575 (Accademia, Venice).

Titicaca lake in the Andes, 3,810 m/12,500 ft above sea level and 1,220 m/4,000 ft above the tree line; area 8,300 sq km/3,200 sq mi, the largest lake in South America. It is divided between Bolivia (port at Guaqui) and Peru (ports at Puno and Huancane).

TNT (abbreviation for *trinitrotoluene*) $CH_3C_6H_2(NO_2)_3$, a powerful high explosive. It is a yellow solid, prepared in several isomeric forms from toluene by using sulphuric and nitric acids.

toad any of the more terrestrial warty-skinned members of the tailless amphibians (order Anura). The name commonly refers to members of the genus *Bufo*, family Bufonidae, which are found worldwide, except for the Australian and polar regions.

toadstool common name for many umbrella-shaped fruiting bodies of fungi. The term is normally applied to those that are inedible or poisonous.

tobacco any large-leaved plant of the genus *Nicotiana* of the nightshade family Solanaceae, native to tropical parts of the Americas. *N. tabacum* is widely cultivated in warm, dry climates for use in cigars and cigarettes, and in powdered form as snuff.

Togo Republic of (*République Togolaise*); *area* 56,800 sq km/21,930 sq mi; *capital* Lomé; *environment* the homes of thousands of people in Keto were destroyed by coastal erosion as a result of the building of the Volta dam; *features* Mono Tableland, Oti Plateau, Oti River; *political system* emergent democracy; *population* (1993 est) 4,100,000; growth rate 3% p.a.; *languages* French (official), Ewe, Kabre; *religions* animist 46%, Catholic 28%, Muslim 17%, Protestant 9%.

Tokyo capital of Japan, on Honshu Island; population (1990) 8,163,100, metropolitan area over 12 million. The Sumida River delta separates the city from its suburb of Honjo. It is Japan's main cultural and industrial centre. It suffered major destruction in World War II, when 60% of Tokyo's housing was destroyed. Subsequent rebuilding has made it into one of the world's most modern cities.

Tolpuddle Martyrs six farm labourers of Tolpuddle, a village in Dorset, SW England, who were transported to Australia in 1834 after being sentenced for 'administering unlawful oaths' – as a 'union', they had threatened to withdraw their labour unless their pay was guaranteed, and had been prepared to put this in writing. They were pardoned two years later, after nationwide agitation. They returned to England and all but one migrated to Canada.

Tolstoy Leo Nikolaievich 1828–1910. Russian novelist. He wrote *War and Peace* 1863–69 and *Anna Karenina* 1873–77. From 1880 Tolstoy underwent a profound spiritual crisis and took up various moral positions, including passive resistance to evil, rejection of authority (religious or civil) and private ownership, and a return to basic mystical Christianity. He was excommunicated by the Orthodox Church, and his later works were banned.

Toltec member of an ancient American Indian people who ruled much of Mexico in the 10th–12th centuries, with their capital and religious centre at Tula, NE of Mexico City. They also constructed a similar city at Chichén Itzá in Yucatán. After the Toltecs' fall the Aztecs took over much of their former territory, except for the regions regained by the Maya.

tonsils in higher vertebrates, masses of lymphoid tissue situated at the back of the mouth and throat (palatine tonsils), and on the rear surface of the tongue (lingual tonsils). The tonsils contain many ◊lymphocytes and are part of the body's defence system against infection.

tooth in vertebrates, one of a set of hard, bonelike structures in the mouth, used for biting and chewing food, and in defence and aggression. In humans, the first set (20 milk teeth) appear from age six months to two and a half years. The permanent ◊dentition replaces these from the sixth year onwards, the wisdom teeth (third molars) sometimes not appearing until the age of 25 or 30. Adults have 32 teeth: two incisors, one canine (eye tooth), two premolars, and three molars on each side of each jaw. Each tooth consists of an enamel coat (hardened calcium deposits), dentine (a thick, bonelike layer), and an inner pulp cavity, housing nerves and blood vessels. Mammalian teeth have roots surrounded by cementum, which fuses them into their sockets in the jawbones. The neck of the tooth is covered by the ◊gum, while the enamel- covered crown protrudes above the gum line.

topaz mineral, aluminium fluosilicate, $Al_2(F_2SiO_4)$. It is usually yellow, but pink if it has been heated, and is used as a gemstone when transparent. It ranks 8 on the Mohs' scale of hardness.

topography the surface shape and composition of the landscape, comprising both natural and artificial features, and its study. Topographical features include the relief and contours of the land; the distribution of mountains, valleys, and human settlements; and the patterns of rivers, roads, and railways.

topology branch of geometry that deals with those properties of a figure that remain unchanged even when the figure is transformed (bent, stretched) – for example, when a square painted on a rubber sheet is deformed by distorting the sheet. Topology has scientific applications, as in the study of turbulence in flowing fluids.

Torah in ◊Judaism, the first five books of the Hebrew Bible (Christian Old Testament). It contains a traditional history of the world from the Creation to the death of Moses; it also includes the Hebrew people's covenant with their one God, rules for religious observance, and guidelines for social conduct, including the Ten Commandments.

tornado extremely violent revolving storm with swirling, funnel-shaped clouds, caused by a rising column of warm air propelled by strong wind. A tornado can rise to a great height, but with a diameter of only a few hundred metres or less. Tornadoes move with wind speeds of 160–480 kph/100–300 mph, destroying everything in their path. They are common in central USA and Australia.

Toronto (North American Indian 'place of meeting') known until 1834 as *York* port and capital of Ontario, Canada, on Lake Ontario; metropolitan population (1985) 3,427,000. It is Canada's main industrial and commercial centre as well as an important cultural centre.

torpedo self-propelled underwater missile, invented 1866 by the British engineer Robert Whitehead (1823–1905). Modern torpedoes are homing missiles; some resemble mines in that they lie on the seabed until activated by the acoustic signal of a passing ship. A television camera enables them to be remotely controlled, and in the final stage of attack they lock on to the radar or sonar signals of the target ship.

torque the turning effect of force on an object. A turbine produces a torque that turns an electricity generator in a power station. Torque is measured by multiplying the force by its perpendicular distance from the turning point.

torsion in physics, the state of strain set up in a twisted material; for example, when a thread, wire, or rod is twisted, the torsion set up in the material tends to return the material to its original state. The *torsion balance*, a sensitive device for measuring small gravitational or magnetic forces, or electric charges, balances these against the restoring force set up by them in a torsion suspension.

tortoise reptile of the order Chelonia, family Testudinidae, with the body enclosed in a hard shell. Tortoises are related to the terrapins and ◊turtles, and range in length from 10 cm/4 in to 150 cm/5 ft. The shell consists of a curved upper carapace and flattened lower plastron joined at the sides. The head and limbs is withdrawn into it when the tortoise is in danger. Most land tortoises are herbivorous, feeding on plant material, and have no teeth. The mouth forms a sharp-edged beak. Tortoises have been known to live for 150 years.

touch sensation produced by specialized nerve endings in the skin. Some respond to light pressure, others to heavy pressure. Temperature detection may also contribute to the overall sensation of touch. Many animals, such as nocturnal ones, rely on touch more than humans do. Some have specialized organs of touch that project from the body, such as whiskers or antennae.

Toulouse-Lautrec Henri Marie Raymond de 1864–1901. French artist. Associated with the Impressionists, he was active in Paris where he painted entertainers and prostitutes in a style characterized by strong colours, bold design, and brilliant draughtsmanship. From 1891 his lithographic posters were a great success, skilfully executed and yet retaining the spontaneous character of sketches. His later work was to prove vital to the development of poster art.

Tour de France French road race for professional cyclists held annually over approximately 4,800 km/3,000 mi of primarily French roads. The race takes about three weeks to complete and the route varies each year, often taking in adjoining countries, but always ending in Paris. A separate stage is held every day, and the overall leader at the end of each stage wears the coveted 'yellow jersey' (French *maillot jaune*).

toxin any poison produced by another living organism (usually a bacterium) that can damage the living body. In vertebrates, toxins are broken down by ▷enzyme action, mainly in the liver.

trace element chemical element necessary in minute quantities for the health of a plant or animal. For example, magnesium, which occurs in chlorophyll, is essential to photosynthesis, and iodine is needed by the thyroid gland of mammals for making hormones that control growth and body chemistry.

trachea tube that forms an airway in air-breathing animals. In land-living ▷vertebrates, including humans, it is also known as the *windpipe* and runs from the larynx to the upper part of the chest. Its diameter is about 1.5 cm/0.6 in and its length 10 cm/4 in. It is strong and flexible, and reinforced by rings of ▷cartilage. In the upper chest, the trachea branches into two tubes: the left and right bronchi, which enter the lungs. Insects have a branching network of

tubes called tracheae, which conduct air from holes (spiracles) in the body surface to all the body tissues. The finest branches of the tracheae are called tracheoles.

tracheotomy or *tracheostomy* surgical opening in the windpipe (trachea), usually created for the insertion of a tube to enable the patient to breathe. It is done either to bypass an airway impaired by disease or injury, or to safeguard it during surgery or a prolonged period of mechanical ventilation.

trachoma chronic eye infection, resembling severe ▷conjunctivitis. The conjunctiva becomes inflamed, with scarring and formation of pus, and there may be damage to the cornea. It is caused by a viruslike organism (chlamydia), and is a disease of dry tropical regions. Although it responds well to antibiotics, numerically it remains the biggest single cause of blindness worldwide.

trade wind prevailing wind that blows towards the equator from the northeast and southeast. Trade winds are caused by hot air rising at the equator and the consequent movement of air from north and south to take its place. The winds are deflected towards the west because of the Earth's west-to-east rotation. The unpredictable calms known as the ▷doldrums lie at their convergence.

Trafalgar, Battle of battle 21 Oct 1805 in the Napoleonic Wars. The British fleet under Admiral Nelson defeated a Franco-Spanish fleet; Nelson was mortally wounded. The victory laid the foundation for British naval supremacy throughout the 19th century. It is named after Cape Trafalgar, a low headland in SW Spain, near the western entrance to the Straits of Gibraltar.

tranquillizer common name for any drug for reducing anxiety or tension, such as ◊benzodiazepines, barbiturates, antidepressants, and beta-blockers. The use of drugs to control anxiety is becoming much less popular, because most of the drugs available are capable of inducing dependence.

transactinide element any of a series of nine radioactive, metallic elements with atomic numbers that extend beyond the ◊actinide series, those from 104 (rutherfordium) to 112 (unnamed). They are grouped because of their expected chemical similarities (they are all bivalent), the properties differing only slightly with atomic number. All have ◊half-lives that measure less than two minutes.

transformer device in which, by electromagnetic induction, an alternating current (AC) of one voltage is transformed to another voltage, without change of ◊frequency. Transformers are widely used in electrical apparatus of all kinds, and in particular in power transmission where high voltages and low currents are utilized.

transfusion intravenous delivery of blood or blood products (plasma, red cells) into a patient's circulation to make up for deficiencies due to disease, injury, or surgical intervention. Cross-matching is carried out to ensure the patient receives the right blood group. Because of worries about blood-borne disease, there is a growing interest in autologous transfusion with units of the patient's own blood 'donated' over the weeks before an operation.

transistor solid-state electronic component, made of ◊semiconductor material, with three or more ◊electrodes, that can regulate a current passing through it. A transistor can act as an amplifier, oscillator, photocell, or switch, and (unlike earlier electron tubes) usually operates on a very small amount of power. Transistors commonly consist of a tiny sandwich of germanium or ◊silicon, alternate layers having different electrical properties because they are impregnated with minute amounts of different impurities. A crystal of pure germanium or silicon would act as an insulator (nonconductor).

transpiration the loss of water from a plant by evaporation. Most water is lost from the leaves through pores known as stomata, whose primary function is to allow ◊gas exchange between the plant's internal tissues and the atmosphere. Transpiration from the leaf surfaces causes a continuous upward flow of water from the roots via the ◊xylem, which is known as the transpiration stream.

transplant in medicine, the transfer of a tissue or organ from one human being to another or from one part of the body to another (skin grafting). In most organ transplants, the operation is for life-saving purposes, though the immune system tends to reject foreign tissue. Careful matching and immunosuppressive drugs must be used, but these are not always successful.

transubstantiation in Christian theology, the doctrine that the whole substance of the bread and wine changes into the substance of the body and blood of Jesus when consecrated in the ◊Eucharist.

transuranic element or *transuranium element* chemical element with an atomic number of 93 or more – that is, with a greater number of protons in the nucleus than has uranium. All transuranic elements are radioactive. Neptunium and plutonium are found in nature; the others are synthesized in nuclear reactions.

Transylvania mountainous area of central and NW Romania, bounded to the S by the Transylvanian Alps (an extension of the ◊Carpathian Mountains). It was part of Hungary from about 1000 until it voted to unite with Romania 1918. It is the home of the vampire legends.

tree perennial plant with a woody stem, usually a single stem or 'trunk', made up of ◊wood and protected by an outer layer of ◊bark. It absorbs water through a ◊root system. There is no clear dividing line between shrubs and trees, but sometimes a minimum achievable height of 6 m/20 ft is used to define a tree.

Trent, Council of conference held 1545–63 by the Roman Catholic Church at Trento, N Italy, initiating the ◊Counter-Reformation; see also ◊Reformation.

triangle in geometry, a three-sided plane figure, the sum of whose interior angles is 180°. Triangles can be classified by the relative lengths of their sides. A *scalene triangle* has three sides of unequal length; an *isosceles triangle* has at least two equal sides; an *equilateral triangle* has three equal sides (and three equal angles of 60°).

Triassic period of geological time 245–208 million years ago, the first period of the Mesozoic era. The continents were fused together to form the world continent Pangaea. Triassic sediments contain remains of early dinosaurs and other reptiles now extinct. By late Triassic times, the first mammals had evolved.

Trident nuclear missile deployed on certain US nuclear-powered submarines and in the 1990s also being installed on four UK submarines. Each missile has eight warheads and each of the four submarines will have 16 Trident D-5 missiles. The Trident replaced the earlier Polaris and Poseidon missiles.

trigonometry branch of mathematics that solves problems relating to plane and spherical triangles. Its principles are based on the fixed proportions of sides for a particular angle in a right- angled triangle, the simplest of which are known as the ◊sine, ◊cosine, and ◊tangent (so-called trigonometrical ratios). It is of practical importance in navigation, surveying, and simple harmonic motion in physics.

Trinidad and Tobago Republic of; *area* Trinidad 4,828 sq km/1,864 sq mi and Tobago 300 sq km/116 sq mi; *capital* Port-of-Spain; *features* Pitch Lake, a self-renewing source of asphalt used by 16th-century explorer Walter Raleigh to repair his ships; *political system* democratic republic'; *population* (1993 est) 1,300,000 (African descent 40%, Indian 40%, European 16%, Chinese and others 2%), 1.2 million on Trinidad; growth rate 1.6% p.a.; *languages* English (official), Hindi, French, Spanish; *religions* Roman Catholic 32%, Protestant 29%, Hindu 25%, Muslim 6%.

Trinity in Christianity, the union of three persons – Father, Son, and Holy Ghost/Spirit – in one godhead. The precise meaning of the doctrine has been the cause of unending dispute, and was the chief cause of the split between the

Eastern Orthodox and Roman Catholic churches. *Trinity Sunday* occurs on the Sunday after Pentecost (Whitsun).

Triple Alliance pact from 1882 between Germany, Austria-Hungary, and Italy to offset the power of Russia and France. It was last renewed 1912, but during World War I Italy's initial neutrality gradually changed and it denounced the alliance 1915. The term also refers to other alliances: 1668 – England, Holland, and Sweden; 1717 – Britain, Holland, and France (joined 1718 by Austria); 1788 – Britain, Prussia, and Holland; 1795 – Britain, Russia, and Austria.

Triple Entente alliance of Britain, France, and Russia 1907–17. In 1911 this became a military alliance and formed the basis of the Allied powers in World War I against the Central Powers, Germany and Austria-Hungary.

Tristan legendary Celtic hero who fell in love with Isolde, the bride he was sent to win for his uncle King Mark of Cornwall. The story became part of the Arthurian cycle and is the subject of Wagner's opera *Tristan und Isolde* 1865.

Trojan horse seemingly innocuous but treacherous gift from an enemy. In Greek mythology, during the siege of Troy, an enormous wooden horse left by the Greek army outside the gates of the city. When the Greeks had retreated, the Trojans, believing it to be a religious offering, brought the horse in. Greek soldiers then emerged from within the hollow horse and opened the city gates to enable Troy to be captured.

trombone brass wind instrument of mainly cylindrical bore, incorporating a movable slide which allows a continuous glissando (slide) in pitch over a span of half an octave. The tenor and bass trombones are staple instruments of the orchestra and brass band, also of Dixieland and jazz bands, either separately or as a tenor-bass hybrid.

tropics the area between the tropics of Cancer and Capricorn, defined by the parallels of latitude approximately 23°30' N and S of the equator. They are the limits of the area of Earth's surface in which the Sun can be directly overhead. The mean monthly temperature is over 20°C/68°F.

tropism or *tropic movement* the directional growth of a plant, or part of a plant, in response to an external stimulus such as gravity or light. If the movement is directed towards the stimulus it is described as positive; if away from it, it is negative. *Geotropism* for example, the response of plants to gravity, causes the root (positively geotropic) to grow downwards, and the stem (negatively geotropic) to grow upwards.

troposphere lower part of the Earth's ◊atmosphere extending about 10.5 km/6.5 mi from the Earth's surface, in which temperature decreases with height to about –60°C/–76°F except in local layers of temperature inversion. The *tropopause* is the upper boundary of the troposphere, above which the temperature increases slowly with height within the atmosphere. All of the Earth's weather takes place within the troposphere.

Trotsky Leon. Adopted name of Lev Davidovitch Bronstein 1879–1940. Russian revolutionary. He joined the Bolshevik party, taking a leading part in the seizure of power 1917 and raising the Red Army that fought the Civil War 1918–20. In the struggle for power that followed ◊Lenin's death 1924, Trotsky was defeated by his rival ◊Stalin. Exiled from 1929, he settled in Mexico, where he was assassinated with an ice pick at Stalin's instigation. Trotsky believed in world revolution and in permanent revolution, and was an uncompromising idealist.

trout any of various bony fishes in the salmon family, popular for sport and food, usually speckled and found mainly in fresh water. They are native to the northern hemisphere. Trout have thick bodies and blunt heads, and vary in colour. The common trout *Salmo trutta* is widely distributed in Europe, occurring in British fresh and coastal waters. Sea trout are generally silvery and river trout olive-brown, both with spotted fins and sides.

Troy (Latin *Ilium*) ancient city (now Hissarlik in Turkey) of Asia Minor, just S of the Dardanelles, besieged in the legendary ten-year Trojan War (mid-13th century BC), as described in Homer's *Iliad*. According to the legend, the city fell to the Greeks, who first used the stratagem of leaving behind, in a feigned retreat, a large wooden horse containing armed infiltrators to open the city's gates. Believing it to be a religious offering, the Trojans took it within the walls.

trumpet member of an ancient family of lip-reed instruments existing worldwide in a variety of forms and materials, and forming part of the brass section in a modern orchestra. Its distinguishing features are a generally cylindrical bore and straight or coiled shape, producing a penetrating tone of stable pitch for signalling and ceremonial use. Valve trumpets were introduced around 1820, giving access to the full range of chromatic pitches.

trypanosomiasis any of several debilitating long-term diseases caused by a trypanosome (protozoan of the genus *Trypanosoma*). They include sleeping sickness (nagana) in Africa, transmitted by the bites of ◊tsetse flies, and Chagas's disease in Central and South America, spread by assassin bugs.

tsetse fly any of a number of blood-feeding African flies of the genus *Glossina*, some of which transmit the disease nagana to cattle and sleeping sickness to human beings. Tsetse flies may grow up to 1.5 cm/0.6 in long.

tsunami (Japanese 'harbour wave') wave generated by an undersea ◊earthquake or volcanic eruption. In the open ocean it may take the form of several successive waves, rarely in excess of a metre/3ft in height, but known to reach more than 30 metres/100 ft high, and travelling at speeds of 650–800 kph/400–500 mph. In the coastal shallows tsunamis slow down and build up, producing towering waves that can sweep inland and cause great loss of life and property. In 1983 an earthquake in the Pacific caused tsunamis up to 3 m/10 ft high, which killed more than 100 people in Akita, Northern Japan.

tuba member of a family of valved lip-reed brass instruments of conical bore and deep, mellow tone, introduced around 1830 as bass members of the orchestra brass section and the brass band. The tuba is surprisingly agile and delicate for its size and pitch, qualities exploited by Berlioz, Ravel, and Vaughan Williams.

tuber swollen region of an underground stem or root, usually modified for storing food. The potato is a *stem tuber*, as shown by the presence of terminal and lateral buds, the 'eyes' of the potato.

Root tubers, for example dahlias, developed from adventitious roots (growing from the stem, not from other roots) lack these. Both types of tuber can give rise to new individuals and so provide a means of ▷vegetative reproduction.

tuberculosis (TB) formerly known as *consumption* or *phthisis* infectious disease caused by the bacillus *Mycobacterium tuberculosis*. It takes several forms, of which pulmonary tuberculosis is by far the most common. A vaccine, BCG, was developed around 1920 and the first antituberculosis drug, streptomycin, in 1944. The bacterium is mostly kept in check by the body's immune system; about 5% of those infected develop the disease.

Tudor dynasty English dynasty 1485–1603, descended from the Welsh Owen Tudor (*c.* 1400–1461), second husband of Catherine of Valois (widow of Henry V of England). Their son Edmund married Margaret Beaufort (1443–1509), the great-granddaughter of ▷John of Gaunt, and was the father of Henry VII, who became king by overthrowing Richard III 1485. The dynasty ended with the death of Elizabeth I 1603.

tumour overproduction of cells in a specific area of the body, often leading to a swelling or lump. Tumours are classified as *benign* or *malignant* (see ▷cancer). Benign tumours grow more slowly, do not invade surrounding tissues, do not spread to other parts of the body, and do not usually recur after removal. However, benign tumours can be dangerous in areas such as the brain. The most familiar types of benign tumour are warts on the skin. In some cases, there is no sharp dividing line between benign and malignant tumours.

tuna any of various large marine bony fishes of the mackerel family, especially the genus *Thunnus*, popular as food and game. Albacore *T. alalunga*, bluefin tuna *T. thynnus*, and yellowfin tuna *T. albacares* are commercially important.

tundra region of high latitude almost devoid of trees, resulting from the presence of permafrost. The vegetation consists mostly of grasses, sedges, heather, mosses, and lichens. Tundra stretches in a continuous belt across N North America and Eurasia.

tungsten hard, heavy, grey-white, metallic element, symbol W (from German *Wolfram*), atomic number 74, relative atomic mass 183.85. It occurs in the minerals wolframite, scheelite, and hubertite. It has the highest melting point of any metal (6,170°F/3,410°C) and is added to steel to make it harder, stronger, and more elastic; its other uses include high-speed cutting tools, electrical elements, and thermionic couplings. Its salts are used in the paint and tanning industries.

tunicate any marine ▷chordate of the subphylum Tunicata (Urochordata), for example the sea squirt. Tunicates have transparent or translucent tunics made of cellulose. They vary in size from a few millimetres to 30 cm/1 ft in length, and are cylindrical, circular, or irregular in shape. There are more than a thousand species.

Tunis capital and chief port of Tunisia; population (1984) 597,000. The ruins of ancient ▷Carthage are to the NE.

Tunisia Tunisian Republic (*al-Jumhuriya at-Tunisiya*); *area* 164,150 sq km/ 63,378 sq mi; *capital* and chief port Tunis; *features* fertile island of Jerba, linked to mainland by causeway (identified with island of lotus-eaters); Shott el Jerid salt lakes; holy city of Kairouan, ruins of Carthage; *political system* emergent democratic republic; *population* (1993 est) 8,600,000; growth rate 2% p.a.; *languages* Arabic (official), French; *religion* Sunni Muslim 95%; Jewish, Christian.

turbine engine in which steam, water, gas, or air is made to spin a rotating shaft by pushing on angled blades, like a fan. Turbines are among the most powerful machines. Steam turbines are used to drive generators in power stations and ships' propellers; water turbines spin the generators in hydroelectric power plants; and gas turbines power most aircraft and drive machines in industry.

Turin (Italian *Torino*) capital of Piedmont, NW Italy, on the river Po; population (1988) 1,025,000. There is a university, established 1404, and a 15th-century cathedral. Features include the Palazzo Reale (Royal Palace) 1646–58 and several gates to the city. It was the first capital of united Italy 1861– 64.

Turk member of any of the Turkic-speaking peoples of Asia and Europe, especially the principal ethnic group of Turkey. *Turkic languages* belong to the Altaic family and include Uzbek, Ottoman, Azeri, Turkoman, Tatar, Kirghiz, and Yakut, as well as Turkish, the national language of Turkey. From 1928 Turkish has been written in a variant of the Roman alphabet.

turkey any of several large game birds of the pheasant family, native to the Americas. The wild turkey *Meleagris galloparvo* reaches a length of 1.3 m/4.3 ft, and is native to North and Central American woodlands. The domesticated turkey derives from the wild species. The ocellated turkey *Agriocharis ocellata* is found in Central America; it has eyespots on the tail.

Turkey Republic of (*Türkiye Cumhuriyeti*); *area* 779,500 sq km/300,965 sq mi; *capital* Ankara; *environment* only 0.3% of the country is protected by national parks and reserves compared with a global average of 7% per country; *features* Bosporus and Dardanelles; Mount Ararat; archaeological sites include Çatal Hüyük, Ephesus, and rock villages of Cappadocia; *political system* democratic republic; *population* (1993) 58,870,000 (Turkish 85%, Kurdish 12%); growth rate 2.1% p.a.; *languages* Turkish (official), Kurdish, Arabic; *religion* Sunni Muslim 98%.

Turkmenistan Republic of; *area* 488,100 sq km/188,406 sq mi; *capital* Ashkhabad; *features* on the edge of the Kara Kum desert is the Altyn Depe, 'golden hill', site of a ruined city with a ziggurat, or stepped pyramid; *political system* socialist pluralist; *population* (1993 est) 4,000,000 (Turkmen 72%, Russian 10%, Uzbek 9%, Kazakh 3%, Ukrainian 1%); *language* West Turkic, closely related to Turkish; *religion* Sunni Muslim.

Turkoman or *Turkman* member of the majority ethnic group in Turkmenistan. They live to the E of the Caspian Sea, around the Kara Kum desert, and along the borders of Afghanistan and Iran. Their language belongs to the Turkic branch of the Altaic family.

Turks and Caicos Islands British crown colony in the West Indies, the southeastern archipelago of the Bahamas; *area* 430 sq km/166 sq mi; *capital* Cockburn Town on Grand Turk; *features* a group of some 30 islands, of which six are inhabited. The largest is the uninhabited *Grand Caicos*; others include *Grand Turk* (population 3,100), *South Caicos* (1,400), and *Middle Caicos* (400); *population* (1980) 7,500, 90% of African descent; *languages* English, French Creole; *religion* Christian.

turmeric perennial plant *Curcuma longa* of the ginger family, native to India and the East Indies; also the ground powder from its tuberous rhizomes, used in curries to give a yellow colour, and as a dyestuff.

Turner Joseph Mallord William 1775–1851. English landscape painter. He was one of the most original artists of his day. He travelled widely in Europe, and his landscapes became increasingly Romantic, with the subject often transformed in scale and flooded with brilliant, hazy light. Many later works anticipate Impressionism; for example, *Rain, Steam and Speed* 1844 (National Gallery, London).

Turpin Dick 1706–1739. English highwayman. The son of an innkeeper, he turned to highway robbery, cattle-thieving, and smuggling, and was hanged at York, England.

turquoise mineral, hydrous basic copper aluminium phosphate. Blue-green, blue, or green, it is a gemstone. Turquoise is found in Australia, Egypt, Ethiopia, France, Germany, Iran, Turkestan, Mexico, and southwestern USA. It was originally introduced into Europe through Turkey, from which its name is derived.

turtle freshwater or marine reptile whose body is protected by a shell. Turtles are related to tortoises, and some species can grow to a length of up to 2.5 m/8 ft. Turtles often travel long distances to lay their eggs on the beaches where they were born. Many species have suffered through destruction of their breeding sites as well as being hunted for food and their shell.

Tuscany (Italian *Toscana*) region of N central Italy, on the west coast; area 23,000 sq km/8,878 sq mi; population (1990) 3,562,500. Its capital is Florence. There are many vineyards, such as in the Chianti hills; it also has lignite and iron mines and marble quarries (Carrara marble is from here). The Tuscan dialect has been adopted as the standard form of Italian.

Tutankhamen king (pharaoh) of ancient Egypt of the 18th dynasty, about 1360–1350 BC. A son of Ikhnaton (also called Amenhotep IV), he was about 11 at his accession. In 1922 his tomb was discovered by the British archaeologists Lord Carnarvon and Howard Carter in the Valley of the Kings at Luxor, almost untouched by tomb robbers. The contents revealed many works of art and Tutankhamen's coffin of solid gold.

Tutsi minority ethnic group living in Rwanda and Burundi. Although fewer in number, they have traditionally been politically dominant over the Hutu majority and the Twa (or Pygmies). In Burundi, positions of power were monopolized by the Tutsis, who carried out massacres in response to Hutu rebellions, notably in 1972 and 1988. In Rwanda, where the balance of power is more even, Tutsis were massacred in their thousands by Hutu militia during the 1994 civil war.

Tutu Desmond (Mpilo) 1931– . South African priest, Anglican archbishop of Cape Town and general secretary of the South African Council of Churches 1979–84. He was one of the leading figures in the struggle against apartheid in the Republic of South Africa. Nobel Peace Prize 1984.

Tuvalu South West Pacific State of (formerly *Ellice Islands*); *area* 25 sq km/9.5 sq mi; *capital* Funafuti; *features* maximum height above sea level 6 m/20 ft; coconut palms are main vegetation; *political system* liberal democracy; *population* (1993 est) 10,000 (Polynesian 96%); growth rate 3.4% p.a.; *languages* Tuvaluan, English; *religion* Christian (Protestant).

Twain Mark. Pen name of Samuel Langhorne Clemens 1835–1910. US writer. He established his reputation with the comic masterpiece *The Innocents Abroad* 1869 and two classic American novels, in dialect, *The Adventures of Tom Sawyer* 1876 and *The Adventures of Huckleberry Finn* 1885. He also wrote satire, as in *A Connecticut Yankee at King Arthur's Court* 1889.

twin one of two young produced from a single pregnancy. Human twins may be genetically identical (monozygotic), having been formed from a single fertilized egg that splits into two cells, both of which became implanted. Nonidentical (fraternal or dizygotic) twins are formed when two eggs are fertilized at the same time.

two-stroke cycle operating cycle for internal combustion piston engines. The engine cycle is completed after just two strokes (movement up or down) of the piston, which distinguishes it from the more common ◊four-stroke cycle. Power mowers and lightweight motorcycles use two-stroke petrol engines, which are cheaper and simpler than four-strokes.

Tyler Wat. English leader of the ◊Peasants' Revolt of 1381. He was probably born in Kent or Essex, and may have served in the French wars. After taking Canterbury, he led the peasant army to Blackheath, outside London, and went on to invade the city. At Mile End King Richard II met the rebels and promised to redress their grievances, which included the imposition of a poll tax. At a further conference at Smithfield, London, Tyler was murdered.

Tyndale William 1492–1536. English translator of the Bible. The printing of his New Testament (the basis of the Authorized Version) was begun in Cologne 1525 and, after he had been forced to flee, completed in Worms. He was strangled and burned as a heretic at Vilvorde in Belgium.

typhoid fever acute infectious disease of the digestive tract, caused by the bacterium *Salmonella typhi*, and usually contracted through a contaminated water supply. It is characterized by bowel haemorrhage and damage to the spleen. Treatment is with antibiotics.

typhus any one of a group of infectious diseases caused by bacteria transmitted by lice, fleas, mites, and ticks. Symptoms include fever, headache, and rash. The most serious form is epidemic typhus, which also affects the brain heart, lungs, and kidneys and is associated with insanitary overcrowded conditions. Treatment is by antibiotics.

Tyrone county of Northern Ireland; *area* 3,160 sq km/1,220 sq mi; *towns and cities* Omagh (county town), Dungannon, Strabane, Cookstown; *features* Lough Neagh and Dreg rivers; Sperrin Mountains; *population* (1991) 158,500.

U

Uccello Paolo. Adopted name of Paolo di Dono 1397–1475. Italian painter. Active in Florence, he was one of the first to experiment with perspective. His surviving paintings date from the 1430s onwards. Decorative colour and detail dominate his later pictures. His works include *St George and the Dragon* about 1460 (National Gallery, London).

Uganda Republic of; *area* 236,600 sq km/91,351 sq mi; *capital* Kampala; *features* Ruwenzori Range (Mount Margherita, 5,110 m/16,765 ft); Lake Albert in W; *political system* emergent democratic republic; *population* (1993 est) 19,000,000 (largely the Baganda, after whom the country is named; also Langi and Acholi, some surviving Pygmies); growth rate 3.3% p.a.; *languages* English (official), Kiswahili, Luganda, and other African languages; *religions* Roman Catholic 33%, Protestant 33%, Muslim 16%, animist.

UK abbreviation for the ▷*United Kingdom.*

Ukraine *area* 603,700 sq km/233,089 sq mi; *capital* Kiev; *features* Askaniya-Nova Nature Reserve (established 1921); health spas with mineral springs; *political system* emergent democracy; *population* (1993 est) 52,000,000 (Ukrainian 73%, Russian 22%, Byelorussian 1%, Russian-speaking Jews 1%); *language* Ukrainian (Slavonic); *religions*
traditionally Ukrainian Orthodox; also Ukrainian Catholic.

Ukrainian member of the majority ethnic group living in Ukraine; there are minorities in Siberian Russia, Kazakhstan, Poland, Slovakia, and Romania. There are 40–45 million speakers of Ukrainian, a member of the East Slavonic branch of the Indo-European family, closely related to Russian. Ukrainian-speaking communities are also found in Canada and the USA.

Ulaanbaatar or *Ulan Bator* (formerly until 1924 *Urga*) capital and trading centre of the Mongolian Republic; population (1991) 575,000.

ulcer any persistent breach in a body surface (skin or mucous membrane). It may be caused by infection, irritation, or tumour and is often inflamed. Common ulcers include aphthous (mouth), gastric (stomach), duodenal, decubitus ulcers (pressure sores), and those complicating varicose veins.

Ulster former kingdom in Northern Ireland, annexed by England 1461, from Jacobean times a centre of English, and later Scottish, settlement on land confiscated from its owners; divided 1921 into Northern Ireland (counties Antrim, Armagh, Down, Fermanagh, Londonderry [now Derry], and Tyrone) and the Republic of Ireland (counties Cavan, Donegal, and Monaghan).

Ulster Defence Association (UDA) Northern Ireland Protestant paramilitary organization responsible for a number of sectarian killings. Fanatically loyalist, it established a paramilitary wing (the Ulster Freedom Fighters) to combat the ◊Irish Republican Army (IRA) on its own terms and by its own methods. No political party has acknowledged any links with the UDA. In 1994, following a cessation of military activities by the IRA, the UDA, along with other Protestant paramilitary organisations, declared a cease-fire.

Ulster Freedom Fighters (UFF) paramilitary wing of the Ulster Defence Association.

ultrasonics study and application of the sound and vibrations produced by ultrasonic pressure waves (see ◊ultrasound).

ultrasound pressure waves similar in nature to sound waves but occurring at frequencies above 20,000 Hz (cycles per second), the approximate upper limit of human hearing (15–16 Hz is the lower limit). Ultrasonics is concerned with the study and practical application of these phenomena.

ultrasound scanning or *ultrasonography* in medicine, the use of ultrasonic pressure waves to create a diagnostic image. It is a safe, noninvasive technique that often eliminates the need for exploratory surgery.

ultraviolet radiation electromagnetic radiation invisible to the human eye, of wavelengths from about 400 to 4 nm (where the ◊X-ray range begins). Physiologically, ultraviolet radiation is extremely powerful, producing sunburn and causing the formation of vitamin D in the skin.

Ulysses Roman name for ◊Odysseus, the Greek mythological hero.

UN abbreviation for the ◊*United Nations.*

ungulate general name for any hoofed mammal. Included are the odd-toed ungulates (perissodactyls) and the even-toed ungulates (artiodactyls), along with subungulates such as elephants.

Uniate Church any of the ◊Orthodox Churches that accept the Catholic faith and the supremacy of the pope and are in full communion with the Roman Catholic Church, but retain their own liturgy and separate organization.

unicellular organism animal or plant consisting of a single cell. Most are invisible without a microscope but a few, such as the giant ◊amoeba, may be visible to the naked eye. The main groups of unicellular organisms are bacteria, protozoa, unicellular algae, and unicellular fungi or yeasts. Some become disease-causing agents, ◊pathogens.

Unification Church or *Moonies* church founded in Korea 1954 by the Reverend Sun Myung ◊Moon. The number of members (often called 'moonies') is about 200,000 worldwide. The theology unites Christian and Taoist ideas and is based on Moon's book *Divine Principle*, which teaches that the original purpose of creation was to set up a perfect family, in a perfect relationship with God.

unified field theory in physics, the theory that attempts to explain the four fundamental forces (strong nuclear, weak nuclear, electromagnetic, and gravity) in terms of a single unified force (see ◊particle physics).

Union, Act of 1707 act of Parliament that brought about the union of England and Scotland; that of 1801 united England and Ireland. The latter was revoked when the Irish Free State was constituted 1922.

Union of Soviet Socialist Republics (USSR) communist former country in N Asia and E Europe, formed 1922 and broke up into independent states 1991; see Armenia, Azerbaijan, Belarus, Estonia, Georgia, Kazakhstan, Kyrgyzstan, Latvia, Lithuania, Moldova, Russian Federation, Tajikstan, Turkmenistan, Ukraine, and Uzbekistan.

United Arab Emirates (UAE) (*Ittihad al-Imarat al-Arabiyah*) federation of the emirates of Abu Dhabi, Ajman, Dubai, Fujairah, Ras al Khaimah, Sharjah, Umm al Qaiwain; *total area* 83,657 sq km/32,292 sq mi; *capital* Abu Dhabi; *features* linked by dependence on oil revenues; *political system* absolutism; *population* (1993) 2,100,000 (10% nomadic); growth rate 6.1% p.a.; *languages* Arabic (official), Farsi, Hindi, Urdu, English; *religions* Muslim 96%, Christian, Hindu.

United Kingdom of Great Britain and Northern Ireland (UK); *area* 244,100 sq km/94,247 sq m.i; *capital* London; *environment* an estimated 67% (the highest percentage in Europe) of forests have been damaged by acid rain; *features* milder climate than N Europe because of Gulf Stream; considerable rainfall. Nowhere more than 120 km/74.5 mi from sea; indented coastline, various small islands; *head of state* Queen Elizabeth II from 1952; *head of government* John Major from 1990; *political system* liberal democracy; *population* (1993 est) 58,000,000 (81.5% English, 9.6% Scottish, 1.9% Welsh, 2.4% Irish, 1.8% Ulster); growth rate 0.1% p.a.; *religion* Christian (55% Protestant, 10% Roman Catholic); Muslim, Jewish, Hindu, Sikh; *languages* English, Welsh, Gaelic.

United Nations (UN) association of states for international peace, security, and cooperation, with its headquarters in New York. The UN was established 1945 as a successor to the ◊League of Nations, and has played a role in many areas, such as refugees, development assistance, disaster relief, and cultural cooperation. Its membership in 1994 stood at 184 states. Boutros ◊Boutros-Ghali became secretary general 1992.

United States of America *area* 9,368,900 sq km/3,618,770 sq mi; *capital* Washington DC; *environment* almost 40% of rivers (by length) and 45% of lake area surveyed 1992 was impaired or in poor condition; the leading polluter was runoff of agricultural chemicals; *features* topography and vegetation ranges from tropical (Hawaii) to arctic (Alaska); *head of state and government* Bill Clinton from 1993; *political system* liberal democracy; *population* (1993 est) 257,000,000 (white 80%, black 12%, Asian/Pacific islander 3%, American Indian, Inuit, and Aleut 1%, Hispanic [included in above percentages] 9%); growth rate 0.9% p.a.; *languages* English, Spanish; *religions* Christian 86.5% (Roman Catholic 26%, Baptist 19%, Methodist 8%, Lutheran 5%), Jewish 1.8%, Muslim 0.5%, Buddhist and Hindu less than 0.5%.

universe all of space and its contents, the study of which is called cosmology. The universe is thought to be between 10 billion and 20 billion years old, and is mostly empty space, dotted with ◊galaxies for as far as telescopes can see. The most distant detected galaxies and ◊quasars lie 10 billion light years or more from Earth, and are moving farther apart as the universe expands. Several theories attempt to explain how the universe came into being and evolved, for example, the ⏵Big Bang theory of an expanding universe originating in a single explosive event, and the contradictory ⏵steady-state theory.

Unix multiuser ⏵operating system designed for minicomputers but becoming increasingly popular on large microcomputers, workstations, mainframes, and supercomputers. It was developed by AT&T's Bell Laboratories in the USA during the late 1960s, using the programming language C. It could therefore run on any machine with a C compiler, so ensuring its wide portability. Its wide range of functions and flexibility have made it widely used by universities and in commercial software.

unleaded petrol petrol manufactured without the addition of antiknock. It has a slightly lower octane rating than leaded petrol, but has the advantage of not polluting the atmosphere with lead compounds. Many cars can be converted to running on unleaded petrol by altering the timing of the engine, and most new cars are designed to do so. Cars fitted with a ⏵catalytic converter must use unleaded fuel.

unsaturated compound chemical compound in which two adjacent atoms are bonded by a double or triple covalent bond.

Upanishad one of a collection of Hindu sacred treatises, written in Sanskrit, connected with the ⏵Vedas but composed later, about 800–200 BC. Metaphysical and ethical, their doctrine equated the atman (self) with the Brahman (supreme spirit) – '*Tat tvam*

asi' ('Thou art that') – and developed the theory of the transmigration of souls.

Updike John (Hoyer) 1932– . US writer. Associated with the *New Yorker* magazine from 1955, he soon established a reputation for polished prose, poetry, and criticism. His novels include *The Poorhouse Fair* 1959, *The Centaur* 1963, *Couples* 1968, *The Witches of Eastwick* 1984, *Roger's Version* 1986, and *S.* 1988, and deal with the tensions and frustrations of contemporary US middle-class life and their effects on love and marriage.

Ur ancient city of the ⏵Sumerian civilization, in modern Iraq. Excavations by the British archaeologist Leonard Woolley show that it was inhabited from about 3500 BC. He discovered evidence of a flood that may have inspired the *Epic of Gilgamesh* as well as the biblical account, and remains of ziggurats, or step pyramids.

Ural Mountains (Russian *Ural'skiy Khrebet*) mountain system running from the Arctic Ocean to the Caspian Sea, traditionally separating Europe from Asia. The highest peak is Naradnaya, 1,894 m/6,214 ft. It has vast mineral wealth.

uranium hard, lustrous, silver-white, malleable and ductile, radioactive, metallic element of the ⏵actinide series, symbol U, atomic number 92, relative atomic mass 238.029. It is the most abundant radioactive element in the Earth's crust, its decay giving rise to essentially all radioactive elements in nature; its final decay product is the stable element lead. Uranium combines readily with most elements to form compounds that are extremely poisonous. The chief ore is ⏵pitchblende, in which the element was discovered by German chemist Martin Klaproth 1789; he named it after the planet Uranus, which had been discovered 1781.

Uranus in Greek mythology, the primeval sky god, whose name means 'Heaven'. He was responsible for both the sunshine and the rain, and was the son and husband of ◊Gaia, the goddess of the Earth. Uranus and Gaia were the parents of ◊Kronos and the ◊Titans.

Uranus the seventh planet from the Sun, discovered by William ◊Herschel 1781. It is twice as far out as the sixth planet, Saturn. Uranus has a diameter of 50,800 km/31,600 mi and a mass 14.5 times that of Earth. It orbits the Sun in 84 years at an average distance of 2.9 billion km/1.8 billion mi. The spin axis of Uranus is tilted at 98°, so that one pole points towards the Sun, giving extreme seasons. It has 15 moons, and in 1977 was discovered to have thin rings around its equator.

Urdu member of the Indo-Iranian branch of the Indo-European language family, related to Hindi and written not in Devanagari but in Arabic script. Urdu is strongly influenced by Farsi (Persian) and Arabic. It is the official language of Pakistan and is used by Muslims in India.

urea $CO(NH_2)_2$ waste product formed in the mammalian liver when nitrogen compounds are broken down. It is excreted in urine. When purified, it is a white, crystalline solid. In industry it is used to make urea-formaldehyde plastics (or resins), pharmaceuticals, and fertilizers.

urinary system system of organs that removes nitrogenous waste products and excess water from the bodies of animals. In vertebrates, it consists of a pair of kidneys, which produce urine; ureters, which drain the kidneys; and (in bony fishes, amphibians, some reptiles, and mammals) a bladder that stores the urine before its discharge. In mammals, the urine is expelled through the urethra; in other vertebrates, the urine drains into a common excretory chamber called a cloaca, and the urine is not discharged separately.

Ursa Major the third largest constellation in the sky, in the north polar region. Its seven brightest stars make up the familiar shape of the *Big Dipper* or *Plough*. The second star of the 'handle' of the dipper, called Mizar, has a companion star, Alcor. Two stars forming the far side of the 'bowl' (one of them, Dubhe, being the constellation's brightest star) act as pointers to the north pole star, Polaris.

Ursa Minor constellation in the northern sky. It is shaped like a dipper, with the north pole star Polaris at the end of the handle.

Uruguay Oriental Republic of (*República Oriental del Uruguay*); *area* 176,200 sq km/68,031 sq mi; *capital* Montevideo; *features* rivers Negro, Uruguay, Rio de la Plata; *political system* democratic republic; *population* (1993 est) 3,200,000 (Spanish, Italian; mestizo, mulatto, black); growth rate 0.7% p.a.; *language* Spanish; *religion* Roman Catholic 66%.

USA abbreviation for the ◊*United States of America.*

USSR abbreviation for the former ◊*Union of Soviet Socialist Republics.*

Utah state in western USA; *area* 219,900 sq km/84,881 sq mi; *capital* Salt Lake City; *features* Great American

Desert; Colorado river system; Dinosaur and Rainbow Bridge national monuments; national parks including Capitol Reef and Zion; Mormon temple and tabernacle, Salt Lake City: ***population*** (1990) 1,722,850.

uterus hollow muscular organ of female mammals, located between the bladder and rectum, and connected to the Fallopian tubes above and the vagina below. The embryo develops within the uterus, and in placental mammals is attached to it after implantation via the ▷placenta and umbilical cord. The lining of the uterus changes during the ▷menstrual cycle. In humans and other higher primates, it is a single structure, but in other mammals it is paired.

utilitarianism philosophical theory of ethics outlined by the philosopher Jeremy ▷Bentham and developed by John Stuart Mill. According to utilitarianism, an action is morally right if it has consequences that lead to happiness, and wrong if it brings about the reverse. Thus society should aim for the greatest happiness of the greatest number.

Utopia any ideal state in literature, named after philosopher Thomas More's ideal commonwealth in his book *Utopia* 1516. Other versions include Plato's *Republic*, Francis Bacon's *New Atlantis*, and *City of the Sun* by the Italian Tommaso Campanella (1568–1639).

Utrecht province of the Netherlands lying SE of Amsterdam, on the Kromme Rijn (Crooked Rhine); ***area*** 1,330 sq km/513 sq mi; ***capital*** Utrecht; ***population*** (1991) 1,026,800.

Uttar Pradesh state of N India; ***area*** 294,400 sq km/113,638 sq mi; ***capital*** Lucknow; ***features*** most populous state; Himalayan peak Nanda Devi 7,817 m/25,655 ft; ***population*** (1991) 138,760,400. ***language*** Hindi; ***religions*** 80% Hindu, 15% Muslim.

Uzbek member of the majority ethnic group (almost 70%) living in Uzbekistan; minorities live in Turkmenistan, Tajikistan, Kazakhstan, and Afghanistan. There are 10–14 million speakers of the ***Uzbek language***, which belongs to the Turkic branch of the Altaic family. Uzbeks are predominantly Sunni Muslims.

Uzbekistan Republic of; ***area*** 447,400 sq km/172,741 sq mi; ***capital*** Tashkent; ***environment*** in 1993 around 75% of the population living round the Aral Sea were suffering from illness, with alarming increases in typhoid and hepatitis A; local fruit and vegetables contained dangerous levels of pesticides and nitrates, and infant mortality was three times the national average; in the former fishing town of Muynak 70% of the population of 2,000 had precancerous conditions; ***features*** more than 20 hydroelectric plants; three natural gas pipelines; ***political system*** socialist pluralist; ***population*** (1993 est) 21,700,000 (Uzbek 71%, Russian 8%, Tajik 5%, Kazakh 4%); ***language*** Uzbek, a Turkic language; ***religion*** Sunni Muslim.

V

vaccine any preparation of modified pathogens (viruses or bacteria) that is introduced into the body, usually either orally or by a hypodermic syringe, to induce the specific ◊antibody reaction that produces ◊immunity against a particular disease.

vacuum in general, a region completely empty of matter; in physics, any enclosure in which the gas pressure is considerably less than atmospheric pressure (101,325 pascals).

vacuum flask or *Dewar flask* or *Thermos flask* container for keeping things either hot or cold. It has two silvered glass walls with a vacuum between them, in a metal or plastic outer case. This design reduces the three forms of heat transfer: radiation (prevented by the silvering), conduction, and convection (both prevented by the vacuum). A vacuum flask is therefore equally efficient at keeping cold liquids cold, or hot liquids hot.

Vaduz capital of the European principality of Liechtenstein; population (1984) 5,000.

vagina the lower part of the reproductive tract in female mammals, linking the uterus to the exterior. It admits the penis during sexual intercourse, and is the birth canal down which the baby passes during delivery.

Valencia industrial city in Valencia region, E Spain; population (1991) 777,400. The Community of Valencia, consisting of Alicante, Castellón, and Valencia, has an area of 23,300 sq km/ 8,994 sq mi and a population of 3,772,000.

valency in chemistry, the measure of an element's ability to combine with other elements, expressed as the number of atoms of hydrogen (or any other standard univalent element) capable of uniting with (or replacing) its atoms. The number of electrons in the outermost shell of the atom dictates the combining ability of an element.

Valentine, St according to tradition, a bishop of Terni martyred at Rome, now omitted from the calendar of saints' days as probably nonexistent. His festival was 14 Feb, but the custom of sending 'valentines' to a loved one on that day seems to have arisen because the day accidentally coincided with the Roman mid-February festival of Lupercalia.

Valentino Rudolph. Adopted name of Rodolfo Alfonso Guglielmi di Valentina d'Antonguolla 1895–1926. Italian-born US film actor and dancer. He was the archetypal romantic lover of the Hollywood silent era. His screen debut was 1919, but his first starring role was in *The Four Horsemen of the Apocalypse* 1921. His subsequent films include *The Sheik* 1921 and *Blood and Sand* 1922.

Valletta capital and port of Malta; population (1987) 9,000, urban area 101,000.

Valley of the Kings burial place of ancient kings opposite ◊Thebes, Egypt, on the left bank of the Nile.

value-added tax (VAT) tax on goods and services. VAT is imposed by the European Community – now European Union (EU) – on member states. The tax varies from state to state. An agreed proportion of the tax money is used to fund the EU.

valve in animals, a structure for controlling the direction of the blood flow. In humans and other vertebrates, the contractions of the beating heart cause the correct blood flow into the arteries because a series of valves prevent back flow. Diseased valves, detected as 'heart murmurs', have decreased efficiency. The tendency for low-pressure venous blood to collect at the base of limbs under the influence of gravity is counteracted by a series of small valves within the veins. It was the existence of these valves that prompted the 17th-century physician William Harvey to suggest that the blood circulated around the body.

vampire bat any South and Central American bat of the family Desmodontidae, of which there are three species. The *common vampire Desmodus rotundus* is found from N Mexico to central Argentina; its head and body grow to 9 cm/3.5 in. Vampires feed on the blood of birds and mammals; they slice a piece of skin from a sleeping animal with their sharp incisor teeth and lap up the flowing blood.

Van Allen radiation belts two zones of charged particles around the Earth's magnetosphere, discovered 1958 by US physicist James Van Allen. The atomic particles come from the Earth's upper atmosphere and the ◊solar wind, and are trapped by the Earth's magnetic field. The inner belt lies 1,000–5,000 km/620–3,100 mi above the equator, and contains ◊protons and ◊electrons. The outer belt lies 15,000–25,000 km/9,300–15,500 mi above the equator, but is lower around the magnetic poles. It contains mostly electrons from the solar wind.

Vanbrugh John 1664–1726. English Baroque architect and dramatist. He designed Blenheim Palace, Oxfordshire, and Castle Howard, Yorkshire, and wrote the comic dramas *The Relapse* 1696 and *The Provok'd Wife* 1697.

Vancouver industrial city in Canada, its chief Pacific seaport, on the mainland of British Columbia; population (1986) 1,381,000.

Vandal member of a Germanic people related to the ◊Goths. In the 5th century AD the Vandals invaded Roman ◊Gaul and Spain, many settling in Andalusia (formerly Vandalitia) and others reaching N Africa 429. They sacked Rome 455 but were defeated by Belisarius, general of the emperor Justinian, in the 6th century.

van Gogh Vincent. Dutch painter; see ◊Gogh, Vincent van.

vanilla any climbing orchid of the genus *Vanilla*, native to tropical America but cultivated elsewhere, with fragrant, large, white or yellow flowers. The dried and fermented fruit, or podlike capsules, of *V. planifolia* are the source of the vanilla flavouring used in cookery and baking.

Vanuatu Republic of (*Ripablik Blong Vanuatu*); *area* 14,800 sq km/5,714 sq mi; *capital* Vila (on Efate); *features* three active volcanoes; *political system* democratic republic; *population* (1993 est) 200,000 (90% Melanesian); growth rate 3.3% p.a.; *religions* Presbyterian 40%, Roman Catholic 16%, Anglican 14%, animist 15%.

Varanasi or *Benares* holy city of the Hindus in Uttar Pradesh, India, on the river Ganges; population (1981) 794,000. There are 1,500 golden shrines, and a 5 km/3 mi frontage to the Ganges with sacred stairways (ghats) for purification by bathing.

variable in mathematics, a changing quantity (one that can take various values), as opposed to a constant. For example, in the algebraic expression $y = 4x^3 + 2$, the variables are x and y, whereas 4 and 2 are constants.

varicose veins or *varicosis* condition where the veins become swollen and twisted. The veins of the legs are most often affected; other vulnerable sites include the rectum (haemorrhoids) and testes.

vasectomy male sterilization; an operation to cut and tie the ducts (the vas deferens) that carry sperm from the testes to the penis. Vasectomy does not affect sexual performance, but the semen produced at ejaculation no longer contains sperm.

VAT abbreviation for ▷value-added tax.

Vatican City State (*Stato della Città del Vaticano*); *area* 0.4 sq km/109 acres; *features* an enclave in the heart of Rome, Italy; the world's smallest state; Vatican Palace, official residence of the Pope John Paul II, who is head of state; basilica and square of St Peter's; churches in and near Rome, the pope's summer villa at Castel Gandolfo; *political system* absolute Catholicism; *population* (1985) approx. 1,000; *languages* Latin (official), Italian; *religion* Roman Catholic.

Vaughan Williams Ralph 1872–1958. English composer. His style was tonal and often evocative of the English countryside through the use of folk themes. Among his works are the orchestral *Fantasia on a Theme by Thomas Tallis* 1910; the opera *Sir John in Love* 1929, featuring the Elizabethan song 'Greensleeves'; and nine symphonies 1909–57.

Veda the most sacred of the Hindu scriptures, hymns written in an old form of Sanskrit; the oldest may date from 1500 or 2000 BC. The four main collections are: the *Rig-veda* (hymns and praises); *Yajur-Veda* (prayers and sacrificial formulae); *Sâma-Veda* (tunes and chants); and *Atharva-Veda*, or Veda of the Atharvans, the officiating priests at the sacrifices.

Vega or *Alpha Lyrae* brightest star in the constellation Lyra and the fifth-brightest star in the sky. It is a blue-white star, 25 light years from Earth, with a luminosity 50 times that of the Sun.

vegetative reproduction type of ▷asexual reproduction in plants that relies not on spores, but on multicellular structures formed by the parent plant. Some of the main types are stolons and runners, gemmae, bulbils, sucker shoots produced from roots (such as in the creeping thistle *Cirsium arvense*) , ▷tubers, ▷bulbs, ▷corms, and rhizomes. Vegetative reproduction has long been exploited in horticulture and agriculture, with various methods employed to multiply stocks of plants.

vein in animals with a circulatory system, any vessel that carries blood from the body to the heart. Veins contain valves that prevent the blood from running back when moving against gravity. They always carry deoxygenated blood, with the exception of the veins leading from the lungs to the heart in birds and mammals, which carry newly oxygenated blood.

Velázquez Diego Rodriguez de Silva y 1599–1660. Spanish painter. The outstanding Spanish artist of the 17th century, in 1623 he became court painter to Philip IV in Madrid. Notable among his portraits is *Las Meninas/The Maids of Honour* 1656 (Prado, Madrid). He also painted occasional religious paintings and genre scenes.

veldt subtropical grassland in South Africa, equivalent to the Pampas of South America.

velocity speed of an object in a given direction. Velocity is a ◊vector quantity, since its direction is important as well as its magnitude (or speed).

vena cava either of the two great veins of the trunk, returning deoxygenated blood to the right atrium of the ◊heart. The *superior vena cava*, beginning where the arches of the two innominate veins join high in the chest, receives blood from the head, neck, chest, and arms; the *inferior vena cava*, arising from the junction of the right and left common iliac veins, receives blood from all parts of the body below the diaphragm.

venereal disease (VD) any disease mainly transmitted by sexual contact, although commonly the term is used specifically for gonorrhoea and syphilis, both occurring worldwide, and chancroid ('soft sore') and lymphogranuloma venerum, seen mostly in the tropics. The term ◊sexually transmitted disease (STD) is more often used to encompass a growing list of conditions passed on primarily, but not exclusively, by sexual contact.

Veneto region of NE Italy, comprising the provinces of Belluno, Padova (Padua), Treviso, Rovigo, Venezia (Venice), and Vicenza; area 18,400 sq km/7,102 sq mi; population (1990) 4,398,100. Its capital is Venice. Veneto forms part of the N Italian plain, with the delta of the river Po; it includes part of the Alps and Dolomites, and Lake Garda.

Venezuela Republic of (*República de Venezuela*); *area* 912,100 sq km/352,162 sq mi; *capital* Caracas; *features* Angel Falls, world's highest waterfall; *government* federal democratic republic; *population* (1993) 20,410,000 (mestizos 70%, white (Spanish, Portuguese, Italian) 20%, black 9%, American Indian 2%); growth rate 2.8% p.a.; *languages* Spanish (official), Indian languages 2%; *religions* Roman Catholic 96%, Protestant 2%.

Venice (Italian *Venezia*) city, port, and naval base on the NE coast of Italy; population (1990) 79,000. It is the capital of Veneto region. The old city is built on piles on low-lying islands in a salt-water lagoon, sheltered from the Adriatic Sea by the Lido and other small strips of land. There are about 150 canals crossed by some 400 bridges. Venice was one of the centres of the Italian Renaissance.

Venn diagram in mathematics, a diagram representing a ◊set or sets and the logical relationships between them. The sets are drawn as circles. An area of overlap between two circles (sets) contains elements that are common to both sets, and thus represents a third set. Circles that do not overlap represent sets with no elements in common (disjoint sets). The method is named after the British logician John Venn (1834–1923).

ventricle in zoology, either of the two lower chambers of the heart that force blood into the circulation by contraction of their muscular walls. The term also refers to any of four cavities within the brain in which cerebrospinal fluid is produced.

Venus in Roman mythology, the goddess of love and beauty, equivalent to the Greek ◊Aphrodite. The patrician Romans believed that they were descended from Aeneas, who was the son of the goddess and Anchises, a Trojan noble. She was venerated as the godess of military victory and patroness of spring.

Venus second planet from the Sun. It orbits the Sun every 225 days at an average distance of 108.2 million km/67.2 million mi and can approach the Earth to within 38 million km/24 million mi, closer than any other planet. Its diameter is 12,100 km/7,500 mi and its mass is 0.82 that of Earth. Venus rotates on its axis more slowly than any other planet, once every 243 days and from east to west, the opposite direction to the other planets (except Uranus and possibly Pluto). Venus is shrouded by clouds of sulphuric acid droplets that sweep across the planet from east to west every four days. The atmosphere is almost entirely carbon dioxide, which traps the Sun's heat by the ◊greenhouse effect and raises the planet's surface

temperature to 480°C/900°F, with an atmospheric pressure of 90 times that at the surface of the Earth.

Verdi Giuseppe (Fortunino Francesco) 1813–1901. Italian opera composer of the Romantic period. He took his native operatic style to new heights of dramatic expression. In 1842 he wrote the opera *Nabucco*, followed by *Ernani* 1844 and *Rigoletto* 1851. Other works include *Il Trovatore* and *La Traviata* both 1853, *Aïda* 1871, and the masterpieces of his old age, *Otello* 1887 and *Falstaff* 1893. His *Requiem* 1874 commemorates Italian poet and novelist Alessandro Manzoni (1775–1873).

Verlaine Paul 1844–1896. French lyric poet. He was acknowledged as the leader of the Symbolist poets (see ◊Symbolism. His volumes of verse, strongly influenced by the poets Charles Baudelaire and Arthur ◊Rimbaud, include *Poèmes saturniens/ Saturnine Poems* 1866, *Fêtes galantes/ Amorous Entertainments* 1869, and *Romances sans paroles/Songs without Words* 1874. In 1873 he was imprisoned for shooting and wounding Rimbaud. His later works reflect his attempts to lead a reformed life.

Vermeer Jan 1632–1675. Dutch painter. Most of his pictures are genre scenes, characterized by a limpid clarity, a distinct air of stillness, and colour harmonies often based on yellow and blue. He frequently depicted solitary women in domestic settings, as in *The Lacemaker* about 1655 (Louvre, Paris).

Vermont state in NE USA; *area* 24,900 sq km/9,611 sq mi; *capital* Montpelier; *features* brilliant autumn foliage and winter sports; Green Mountains; Lake Champlain; *population* (1990) 562,800.

Verne Jules 1828–1905. French author. He wrote tales of adventure that anticipated future scientific developments: *Five Weeks in a Balloon* 1862, *Journey to the Centre of the Earth* 1864, *Twenty Thousand Leagues under the Sea* 1870, and *Around the World in Eighty Days* 1873.

Veronese Paolo (Paolo Caliari) *c.* 1528–1588. Italian painter. He specialized in grand decorative schemes, such as his ceilings in the Doge's Palace in Venice, with their *trompe l'oeil* effects and inventive detail. Whether religious, mythological, historical, or allegorical, his paintings celebrate the power and splendour of Venice.

Versailles, Treaty of peace treaty after World War I between the Allies (except the USA) and Germany, signed 28 June 1919. It established the ◊League of Nations. Germany surrendered Alsace-Lorraine to France, and large areas in the east to Poland, and made smaller cessions to Czechoslovakia, Lithuania, Belgium, and Denmark and Germany agreed to pay reparations for war damage.

vertebral column the backbone, giving support to an animal and protecting the spinal cord. It is made up of a series of bones or vertebrae running from the skull to the tail with a central canal containing the nerve fibres of the spinal cord. In tetrapods the vertebrae show some specialization with the shape of the bones varying according to position. In the chest region the upper or thoracic vertebrae are shaped to form connections to the ribs. The backbone is only slightly flexible to give adequate rigidity to the animal structure.

vertebrate any animal with a backbone. The 41,000 species of vertebrates

include mammals, birds, reptiles, amphibians, and fishes. They include most of the larger animals, but in terms of numbers of species are only a tiny proportion of the world's animals. The zoological taxonomic group Vertebrata is a subgroup of the ◊phylum Chordata.

Vesalius Andreas 1514–1564. Belgian physician who revolutionized anatomy. His great innovations were to perform postmortem dissections and to make use of illustrations in teaching anatomy.

Vesuvius (Italian *Vesuvio*) active volcano SE of Naples, Italy; height 1,277 m/4,190 ft. In 79 BC it destroyed the cities of Pompeii, Herculaneum, and Stabiae.

VHF (abbreviation for *very high frequency*) referring to radio waves that have very short wavelengths (10 m–1 m). They are used for interference-free FM transmissions. VHF transmitters have a relatively short range because the waves cannot be reflected over the horizon like longer radio waves.

Vichy government in World War II, the right-wing government of unoccupied France after the country's defeat by the Germans June 1940, named after the spa town of Vichy, France, where the national assembly was based under Prime Minister Pétain until the liberation 1944. Authoritarian and collaborationist, the Vichy regime cooperated with the Germans even after they had moved to the unoccupied zone Nov 1942.

Victoria state of SE Australia; *area* 227,600 sq km/87,854 sq mi; *capital* Melbourne; *population* (1987) 4,184,000; 70% in the Melbourne area.

Victoria 1819–1901. Queen of the UK from 1837, when she succeeded her uncle William IV, and empress of India from 1876. In 1840 she married Prince ◊Albert of Saxe-Coburg and Gotha. Her relations with her prime ministers ranged from the affectionate (Melbourne and Disraeli) to the stormy (Peel, Palmerston, and Gladstone).

Victoria, Lake or *Victoria Nyanza* largest lake in Africa; area over 69,400 sq km/26,800 sq mi; length 410 km/255 mi. It lies on the equator at an altitude of 1,136 m/3,728 ft, bounded by Uganda, Kenya, and Tanzania. It is a source of the river Nile.

vicuna ◊ruminant mammal *Lama vicugna* of the camel family that lives in herds on the Andean plateau. It can run at speeds of 50 kph/30 mph. It has good eyesight, fair hearing, and a poor sense of smell. It was hunted close to extinction for its meat and soft brown fur, which was used in textile manufacture, but the vicuna is now a protected species; populations are increasing thanks to strict conservation measures. It is related to the alpaca, the guanaco, and the llama.

video camera or *camcorder* portable television camera that takes moving pictures electronically on magnetic tape. It produces an electrical output signal corresponding to rapid line-by-line scanning of the field of view. The output is recorded on video cassette and is played back on a television screen via a video cassette recorder.

video cassette recorder (VCR) device for recording on and playing back video cassettes; see ◊videotape recorder.

video disc disc with pictures and sounds recorded on it, played back by laser. The video disc is a type of ◊compact disc.

videotape recorder (VTR) device for recording pictures and sound on cassettes or spools of magnetic tape. The first commercial VTR was launched 1956 for the television broadcasting industry, but from the late 1970s cheaper models developed for home use, to record broadcast programmes for future viewing and to view rented or owned video cassettes of commercial films.

videotext system in which information (text and simple pictures) is displayed on a television (video) screen. There are two basic systems, known as ◊teletext and ◊viewdata. In the teletext system information is broadcast with the ordinary television signals, whereas in the viewdata system information is relayed to the screen from a central data bank via the telephone network. Both systems require the use of a television receiver (or a connected VTR) with special decoder.

Vienna (German *Wien*) capital of Austria, on the river Danube at the foot of the Wiener Wald (Vienna Woods); population (1986) 1,481,000.

Vientiane (Lao *Vieng Chan*) capital and chief port of Laos on the Mekong River; population (1985) 377,000. It is noted for its pagodas, canals, and houses on stilts. The Temple of the Heavy Buddha, the Pratuxai triumphal arch, and the Black Stupa are here. The Great Sacred Stupa to the NE of the city is the most important national monument in Laos.

Vietnam Socialist Republic of (*Công Hòa Xã Hôi Chu Nghĩa Viêt Nam*); *area* 329,600 sq km/127,259 sq mi; *capital* Hanoi; *environment* during the Vietnam War an estimated 2.2 million hectares/ 5.4 million acres of forest were destroyed. The country's National Conservation Strategy is trying to replant 500 million trees each year; *features* Karst hills of Halong Bay, Cham Towers; *political system* communism; *population* (1993 est) 70,400,000 (750,000 refugees, majority ethnic Chinese left 1975–79, some settled in SW China, others fled by sea – the 'boat people' – to Hong Kong and elsewhere); growth rate 2.4% p.a.; *languages* Vietnamese (official), French, English, Khmer, Chinese, local languages; *religions* Buddhist, Taoist, Confucian, Christian.

Vietnam War 1954–1975 war between communist North Vietnam and US-backed South Vietnam. Following the division of French Indochina into North and South Vietnam and the Vietnamese defeat of the French 1954, US involvement in Southeast Asia grew. Noncommunist South Vietnam was viewed, in the context of the 1950s and the ⊳cold war, as a bulwark against the spread of communism throughout SE Asia. Advisers and military aid were dispatched to the region at increasing levels because of the so-called domino theory, which contended that the fall of South Vietnam would precipitate the collapse of neighboring states. The USA spent $141 bn in aid to the South Vietnamese government. Corruption and inefficiency within the South Vietnamese government led the US to assume ever greater responsibility for the war effort, until 1 million US combat troops were engaged. 200,000 South Vietnamese soldiers, 1 million North Vietnamese soldiers, and 500,000 civilians were killed. 56,555 US soldiers were killed 1961–75, a fifth of them by their own troops. The war destroyed 50% of the country's forest cover and 20% of agricultural land. Cambodia, a neutral neighbour,

was bombed by the US 1969–75, with 1 million killed or wounded.

Viking or *Norseman* medieval Scandinavian sea warrior. The Vikings traded with and raided Europe in the 8th–11th centuries. They were given ⊳Normandy by France, conquered England 1013, and in the east established the first Russian state and founded Novgorod. The Vikings reached the Byzantine Empire in the south, and in the west sailed the seas to Ireland, Iceland, Greenland, and North America.

villus plural *villi* small fingerlike projection extending into the interior of the small intestine and increasing the absorptive area of the intestinal wall. Digested nutrients, including sugars and amino acids, pass into the villi and are carried away by the circulating blood.

Vilnius capital of Lithuania; population (1987) 566,000.

vine or *grapevine* any of various climbing woody plants of the genus *Vitis*, family Vitaceae, especially *V. vinifera*, native to Asia Minor and cultivated from antiquity. Its fruit is eaten or made into wine or other fermented drinks; dried fruits of certain varieties are known as raisins and currants. Many other species of climbing plant are also termed vines.

viola bowed, stringed musical instrument, the alto member of the violin family. With its dark, vibrant tone, it is suitable for music of reflective character, as in Stravinsky's *Elegy* 1944. Its principal function is supportive in string quartets and orchestras.

violet any plant of the genus *Viola*, family Violaceae, with toothed leaves and mauve, blue, or white flowers, such as the heath dog violet *V. canina* and sweet violet *V. odorata.* A pansy is a kind of violet.

violin bowed, four-stringed musical instrument, the smallest and highest pitched (treble) of the violin family. The strings are tuned in fifths (G3, D4, A4, and E5).

Virgil (Publius Vergilius Maro) 70–19 BC. Roman poet. He wrote the *Eclogues* 37 BC, a series of pastoral poems; the *Georgics* 30 BC, four books on the art of farming; and his epic masterpiece, the *Aeneid* 30–19 BC. He was patronized by Maecenas on behalf of Octavian (later the emperor Augustus).

Virginia state in E USA; ***area*** 105,600 sq km/40,762 sq mi; ***capital*** Richmond; ***features*** Blue Ridge Mountains; Mount Vernon (home of George Washington 1752–99); Jamestown and Yorktown historic sites; ***population*** (1990) 6,187,400.

Virgin Islands group of about 100 small islands, northernmost of the Leeward Islands in the Antilles, West Indies. They comprise the ***US Virgin Islands*** St Thomas (with the capital, Charlotte Amalie), St Croix, St John, and about 50 small islets; area 350 sq km/135 sq mi; population (1990) 101,800; and the ***British Virgin Islands*** Tortola (with the capital, Road Town), Virgin Gorda, Anegada, and Jost van Dykes, and about 40 islets; area 150 sq km/58 sq mi; population (1987) 13,250.

virtual reality advanced form of computer simulation, in which a participant has the illusion of being part of an artificial environment. The participant views the environment through two tiny television screens (one for each eye) built into a visor. Sensors detect movements of the participant's head or body, causing the apparent viewing position to change. Gloves (datagloves) fitted with sensors may be worn, which allow the participant seemingly to pick up and move objects in the environment.

virus infectious particle consisting of a core of nucleic acid (DNA or RNA) enclosed in a protein shell. Viruses are acellular and able to function and reproduce only if they can invade a living cell to use the cell's system to replicate themselves. In the process they may disrupt or alter the host cell's own DNA. The healthy human body reacts by producing an antiviral protein, ▷interferon, which prevents the infection spreading to adjacent cells.

viscose yellowish, syrupy solution made by treating cellulose with sodium hydroxide and carbon disulphide. The solution is then regenerated as continuous filament for the making of ▷rayon and as cellophane.

Vishnu in Hinduism, the second in the triad of gods (with Brahma and Siva) representing three aspects of the supreme spirit. He is the ***Preserver***, and is believed to have assumed human appearance in nine *avatāras*, or incarnations, in such forms as Rama and Krishna. His worshippers are the Vaishnavas.

visual display unit (VDU) computer terminal consisting of a keyboard for input data and a screen for displaying output. The oldest and the most popular type of VDU screen is the ▷cathode-ray tube (CRT), which uses essentially the same technology as a television screen. Other types use plasma display technology and ▷liquid-crystal displays.

vitamin any of various chemically unrelated organic compounds that are necessary in small quantities for the normal functioning of the human body. Many act as coenzymes, small molecules that enable ◊enzymes to function effectively. They are normally present in adequate amounts in a balanced diet. Deficiency of a vitamin may lead to a metabolic disorder ('deficiency disease'), which can be remedied by sufficient intake of the vitamin. They are generally classified as *water-soluble* (B and C) or *fat-soluble* (A, D, E, and K). See separate entries for individual vitamins.

Vivaldi Antonio (Lucio) 1678–1741. Italian Baroque composer, violinist, and conductor. He wrote 23 symphonies; 75 sonatas; over 400 concertos, including *The Four Seasons* 1725 for violin and orchestra; over 40 operas; and much sacred music. His work was largely neglected until the 1930s.

vivisection literally, cutting into a living animal. Used originally to mean experimental surgery or dissection practised on a live subject, the term is often used by antivivisection campaigners to include any experiment on animals, surgical or otherwise.

Vladivostok port (naval and commercial) in E Siberian Russia, at the Amur Bay on the Pacific coast; population (1987) 615,000. It is kept open by icebreakers during winter.

vocal cords the paired folds, ridges, or cords of tissue within a mammal's larynx, and a bird's syrinx. Air constricted between the folds or membranes makes them vibrate, producing sounds. Muscles in the larynx change the pitch of the sounds produced, by adjusting the tension of the vocal cords.

volatile in chemistry, term describing a substance that readily passes from the liquid to the vapour phase. Volatile substances have a high vapour pressure.

volcano crack in the Earth's crust through which hot magma (molten rock) and gases well up. The magma becomes known as lava when it reaches the surface. A volcanic mountain, usually cone shaped with a crater on top, is formed around the opening, or vent, by the build-up of solidified lava and ashes (rock fragments). Most volcanoes arise on plate margins (see ◊plate tectonics), where the movements of plates generate magma or allow it to rise from the mantle beneath. However, a number are found far from plate-margin activity, on 'hot spots' where the Earth's crust is thin.

Volga longest river in Europe; 3,685 km/2,290 mi, 3,540 km/2,200 mi of which are navigable. It drains most of the central and eastern parts of European Russia, rises in the Valdai plateau, and flows into the Caspian Sea 88 km/55 mi below the city of Astrakhan.

volt SI unit of electromotive force or electric potential, symbol V. A small battery has a potential of 1.5 volts; the domestic electricity supply in the UK is 240 volts (110 volts in the USA); and a high-tension transmission line may carry up to 765,000 volts.

Voltaire Pen name of François-Marie Arouet 1694–1778. French writer. He was the embodiment of the 18th-century ◊Enlightenment. A trenchant satirist of social and political evils, his many works include *Lettres philosophiques sur les Anglais/Philosophical Letters on the English* 1733; *Le Siècle de Louis XIV/The Age of Louis XIV* 1751; the satirical fable *Candide* 1759, his best-known work; and *Dictionnaire philosophique* 1764.

voodoo set of magical beliefs and practices, followed in some parts of Africa, South America, and the West Indies, especially Haiti. It arose in the 17th century on slave plantations as a combination of Roman Catholicism and W African religious traditions; believers retain membership in the Roman Catholic church. Beliefs include the existence of *loa*, spirits who closely involve themselves in human affairs, and some of whose identities mesh with those of Christian saints.

vote expression of opinion by ▷ballot, show of hands, or other means. In systems that employ direct vote, the ▷plebiscite and ▷referendum are fundamental mechanisms. In parliamentary elections the results can be calculated in a number of ways. The main electoral systems are *simple plurality* or *first past the post*, with single- member constituencies (USA, UK, India, Canada); *absolute majority*, achieved for example by the *alternative vote*, where the voter, in single-member constituencies, chooses a candidate by marking preferences (Australia), or by the *second ballot*, where, if a clear decision is not reached immediately, a second ballot is held (France, Egypt); *proportional representation*, achieved for example by the *party list* system (Israel, most countries of Western Europe, and several in South America), the *additional member* system (Germany), the *single transferable vote* (Ireland and Malta), and the *limited vote* (Japan).

vulture any of various carrion-eating birds of prey with naked heads and necks and with keen senses of sight and smell. Vultures are up to 1 m/3.3 ft long, with wingspans of up to 3.5 m/11.5 ft. The plumage is usually dark, and the head brightly coloured.

W

Wagner Richard 1813–1883. German opera composer. He revolutionized the 19th-century conception of opera, envisaging it as a wholly new art form unifying musical, poetic, and scenic elements. His works include *Tannhäuser* 1845, *Lohengrin* 1848, and *Tristan und Isolde* 1865. In 1872 he founded the Festival Theatre in Bayreuth; his masterpiece *Der Ring des Nibelungen/The Ring of the Nibelung*, a sequence of four operas, was first performed there 1876.

Wales (Welsh *Cymru*) Principality of; constituent part of the UK, in the W between the British Channel and the Irish Sea; *area* 20,780 sq km/8,021 sq mi; *capital* Cardiff; *features* Snowdonia Mountains (Snowdon 1,085 m/3,561 ft, the highest point in England and Wales) in the NW; in the SE the Black Mountains, Brecon Beacons, and Black Forest ranges; rivers Severn, Wye, Usk, and Dee; *population* (1991) 2,835,100; *languages* English, 19% Welsh-speaking; *religions* Nonconformist Protestant denominations; Roman Catholic minority.

Wałesa Lech 1943– . Polish trade-union leader, president of Poland from 1990. He founded ◊Solidarity (Solidarność) in 1980, an organization, independent of the Communist Party, which forced substantial political and economic concessions from the Polish government 1980–81 until being outlawed. Nobel Prize for Peace 1983.

Wales, Prince of title conferred on the eldest son of the UK's sovereign. Prince ◊Charles was invested as 21st prince of Wales at Caernarvon 1969 by his mother, Elizabeth II.

Walker Alice 1944– . US poet, novelist, critic, and essay writer. Active in the US civil-rights movement since the 1960s, she wrote about the double burden of racist and sexist oppression, about colonialism, and the quest for political and spiritual recovery. Her novel *The Color Purple* 1982 told in the form of letters, was filmed 1985.

Walpole Robert, 1st Earl of Orford 1676–1745. British Whig politician, the first 'prime minister' as First Lord of the Treasury and chancellor of the Exchequer 1715–17 and 1721–42. He encouraged trade and tried to avoid foreign disputes (until forced into the War of Jenkins's Ear with Spain 1739).

walrus Arctic marine carnivorous mammal *Odobenus rosmarus* of the same family (Otaridae) as the eared ◊seals. It can reach 4 m/13 ft in length, and weigh up to 1,400 kg/3,000 lb. It has webbed flippers, a bristly moustache, and large tusks. It is gregarious except at breeding time and feeds mainly on molluscs. It has been hunted close to extinction for its ivory tusks, hide, and blubber. The Alaskan walrus is close to extinction.

Wankel engine rotary petrol engine developed by the German engineer Felix Wankel (1902–1988) in the 1950s. It operates according to the same stages as the ◊four- stroke petrol engine cycle, but these stages take place in different sectors of a figure- eight chamber in the space between the chamber walls and a triangular rotor. Power is produced once on every turn of the rotor. The Wankel engine is simpler in construction than the four-stroke piston petrol engine, and produces rotary power directly (instead of via a crankshaft). Problems with rotor seals have prevented its widespread use.

Warhol Andy. Adopted name of Andrew Warhola 1928–1987. US Pop artist and filmmaker. He made his name in 1962 with paintings of Campbell's soup cans, Coca-Cola bottles, and film stars. In his New York studio, the Factory, he and his assistants produced series of garish silk-screen prints. His films include the semidocumentary *Chelsea Girls* 1966 and *Trash* 1970.

Warsaw (Polish *Warszawa*) capital of Poland, on the river Vistula; population (1990) 1,655,700.

wart protuberance composed of a local overgrowth of skin. The common wart (*verruca vulgaris*) is due to a virus infection. It usually disappears spontaneously within two years, but can be treated with peeling applications, burning away (cautery), or freezing (cryosurgery).

Warwickshire county of central England; *area* 1,980 sq km/764 sq mi; *towns and cities* Warwick (administrative headquarters), Royal Leamington Spa,

Nuneaton, Rugby, Stratford-upon-Avon; *features* Kenilworth and Warwick castles; site of the Battle of Edgehill; *population* (1991) 484,200.

Wash, the bay of the North Sea between Norfolk and Lincolnshire, England. The rivers Nene, Ouse, Welland, and Witham drain into the Wash.

Washington state in northwestern USA; *area* 176,700 sq km/68,206 sq mi; *capital* Olympia; *features* Columbia River; national parks: Olympic (Olympic Mountains), Mount Rainier (Cascade Range), North Cascades; 90 dams; *population* (1990) 4,866,700 (including 1.4% Indians, mainly of the Yakima people).

Washington George 1732–1799. First president of the USA 1789–97. He was a strong opponent of the British government's policy, and on the outbreak of the ◊American Revolution was chosen as commander in chief. His aristocratic outlook alienated his secretary of state, Thomas Jefferson, who resigned in 1793, thus creating the two-party system.

Washington DC (District of Columbia) national capital of the US, on the Potomac River; *area* 69 sq mi/180 sq km; *population* (1983) 606,900 (metropolitan area, extending outside the District of Columbia, 3 million); *features* Buildings of architectural note: the Capitol, the Pentagon, the White House, the Washington Monument, and the Jefferson and Lincoln memorials; the National Gallery; Library of Congress; National Archives; Folger Shakespeare Library; Smithsonian Institution.

water H_2O liquid without colour, taste, or odour. It is an oxide of hydrogen. Water begins to freeze at

0°C or 32°F, and to boil at 100°C or 212°F. When liquid, it is virtually incompressible; frozen, it expands by $\frac{1}{11}$ of its volume. At 39.2°F/4°C, one cubic centimetre of water has a mass of one gram; this is its maximum density, forming the unit of specific gravity. It has the highest known specific heat, and acts as an efficient solvent, particularly when hot. Most of the world's water is in the sea; less than 0.01% is fresh water.

Watergate US political scandal, named after the building in Washington DC that housed the Democrats' campaign headquarters in the 1972 presidential election. Five men, hired by the Republican Committee to Re-elect the President (CREEP), were caught after breaking into the Watergate building. Investigations revealed White House involvement and in Aug 1974, President ◊Nixon was forced by the Supreme Court to surrender to Congress tape recordings of conversations with administration officials, which indicated his complicity in a cover-up. Nixon resigned rather than face impeachment for obstruction of justice and other crimes.

Waterloo, Battle of battle on 18 June 1815 in which British forces commanded by Wellington defeated the French army of Emperor Napoleon near the village of Waterloo, 13 km/8 mi S of Brussels, Belgium. Napoleon found Wellington's army isolated from his allies and began a direct offensive to smash them, but the British held on until joined by the Prussians under General Blücher. Four days later Napoleon abdicated for the second and final time.

water pollution any addition to fresh or sea water that disrupts biological processes or causes a health hazard. Common pollutants include nitrate, pesticides, and sewage, though a huge range of industrial contaminants, such as chemical byproducts and residues created in the manufacture of various goods, also enter water – legally, accidentally, and through illegal dumping.

water table the upper level of ground water (water collected underground in porous rocks). Water that is above the water table will drain downwards; a spring forms where the water table cuts the surface of the ground. The water table rises and falls in response to rainfall and the rate at which water is extracted, for example, for irrigation and industry.

Watson James Dewey 1928– . US biologist whose research on the molecular structure of DNA and the genetic code, in collaboration with Francis ◊Crick, earned him a shared Nobel prize in 1962. Based on earlier works, they were able to show that DNA formed a double helix of two spiral strands held together by base pairs. Watson resigned as head of the US government's ◊human genome project in April 1992.

watt SI unit (symbol W) of power (the rate of expenditure or consumption of energy). A light bulb, for example, may use 40, 100, or 150 watts of power; an electric heater will use several kilowatts (thousands of watts). The watt is named after the Scottish engineer James Watt.

Watt James 1736–1819. Scottish engineer who developed the steam engine. He made Thomas Newcomen's steam engine vastly more efficient by cooling the used steam in a condenser separate from the main cylinder.

Waugh Evelyn (Arthur St John) 1903–1966. English novelist. His social satires include *Decline and Fall* 1928, *Vile Bodies* 1930, and *The Loved One* 1948. A Roman Catholic convert from 1930, he developed a serious concern with religious issues in *Brideshead Revisited* 1945. *The Ordeal of Gilbert Pinfold* 1957 is largely autobiographical.

wave in physics, a disturbance travelling through a medium (or space). There are two types: in a *longitudinal wave* (such as a ▷sound wave) the disturbance is parallel to the wave's direction of travel; in a *transverse wave* (such as an ▷electromagnetic wave) it is perpendicular. The medium (for example the Earth, for seismic waves) is not permanently displaced by the passage of a wave.

wave in the oceans, a ridge or swell formed by wind or other causes. The power of a wave is determined by the strength of the wind and the distance of open water over which the wind blows (the fetch). Waves are the main agents of coastal erosion and deposition: sweeping away or building up beaches, creating spits and berms, and wearing down cliffs by their hydraulic action and by the corrasion of the sand and shingle that they carry. A ▷tsunami (misleadingly called a 'tidal wave') is formed after a submarine earthquake.

wavelength the distance between successive crests of a ▷wave. The wavelength of a light wave determines its colour; red light has a wavelength of about 700 nanometres, for example. The complete range of wavelengths of electromagnetic waves is called the electromagnetic ▷spectrum.

wax solid fatty substance of animal, vegetable, or mineral origin. Waxes are composed variously of ▷esters, ▷fatty acids, free ▷alcohols, and solid hydrocarbons.

weakon or *intermediate vector boson* in physics, a ▷gauge boson that carries the weak nuclear force, one of the fundamental forces of nature. There are three types of weakon, the positive and negative W particle and the neutral Z particle.

weaving the production of textile fabric by means of a loom. The basic process is the interlacing at right angles of longitudinal threads (the warp) and horizontal threads (the weft), the latter being carried across from one side of the loom to the other by a type of bobbin called a shuttle.

Weber Carl Maria Friedrich Ernst von 1786–1826. German composer. He established the Romantic school of opera with *Der Freischütz/The Marksman* 1821 and *Euryanthe* 1823. He was kapellmeister (chief conductor) at Breslau 1804–06, Prague 1813–16, and Dresden 1816. He died during a visit to London where he produced his opera *Oberon* 1826, written for the Covent Garden Theatre.

Webster John *c.* 1580–1634. English dramatist. He ranks after Shakespeare as the greatest tragedian of his time, and is the Jacobean whose plays are most frequently performed today. His two great plays *The White Devil* 1612 and *The Duchess of Malfi* 1614 are dark, violent tragedies obsessed with death and decay.

Wedgwood Josiah 1730–1795. English pottery manufacturer. He set up business in Staffordshire in the early 1760s to produce his agateware as well as unglazed blue or green stoneware (jasper) decorated with white Neo-Classical designs, using pigments of his own invention.

weight the force exerted on an object by ◊gravity. The weight of an object depends on its mass – the amount of material in it – and the strength of the Earth's gravitational pull, which decreases with height. Consequently, an object weighs less at the top of a mountain than at sea level. On the Moon, an object has only one-sixth of its weight on Earth, because the pull of the Moon's gravity is one- sixth that of the Earth.

Weill Kurt (Julian) 1900–1950. German composer. He wrote chamber and orchestral music and collaborated with Bertolt Brecht on operas such as *Die Dreigroschenoper/The Threepenny Opera* 1928 and *Aufsteig und Fall der Stadt Mahagonny/The Rise and Fall of the City of Mahagonny* 1930, all attacking social corruption. In 1935 he went to the USA where he wrote a number of successful scores for Broadway, among them the antiwar musical *Johnny Johnson* 1936 and *Street Scene* 1947.

Weimar Republic the constitutional republic in Germany 1919–33, which was crippled by the election of antidemocratic parties to the Reichstag (parliament), and then subverted by the Nazi leader Hitler after his appointment as chancellor 1933. It took its name from the city where in Feb 1919 a constituent assembly met to draw up a democratic constitution.

welding joining pieces of metal (or nonmetal) at faces rendered plastic or liquid by heat or pressure (or both). The principal processes today are gas and arc welding, in which the heat from a gas flame or an electric arc melts the faces to be joined. Additional 'filler metal' is usually added to the joint.

Welles (George) Orson 1915–1985. US actor and film and theatre director. His first film was *Citizen Kane* 1941, which he produced, directed, and starred in. Using innovative lighting, camera angles and movements, it is a landmark in the history of cinema, yet he subsequently directed very few films in Hollywood. His performances as an actor include the character of Harry Lime in *The Third Man* 1949.

Wellington capital and industrial port of New Zealand on North Island on the Cook Strait; population (1991) 149,600, urban area 324,800.

Wellington Arthur Wellesley, 1st Duke of Wellington 1769–1852. British soldier and Tory politician. As commander in the Peninsular War, he expelled the French from Spain 1814. He defeated Napoleon Bonaparte at Quatre-Bas and Waterloo 1815, and was a member of the Congress of Vienna. As prime minister 1828–30, he was forced to concede Roman Catholic emancipation.

Wells H(erbert) G(eorge) 1866–1946. English writer. He is best remembered for his 'scientific romances' such as *The Time Machine* 1895 and *The War of the Worlds* 1898. His later novels had an anti-establishment, anti-conventional humour remarkable in its day, for example *Kipps* 1905 and *Tono-Bungay* 1909. His many other books include the prophetic *The Shape of Things to Come* 1933.

Welsh people of ◊Wales; see also ◊Celts. The term is thought to be derived from an old Germanic term for 'foreigner', and so linked to Walloon (Belgium) and Wallachian (Romania).

It may also derive from the Latin *Volcae*, the name of a Celtic people of France. The *Welsh language* (Welsh: *Cymraeg*) is a member of the Celtic branch of the Indo-European language family, spoken chiefly in the rural north and west of Wales; it is the strongest of the surviving Celtic languages.

Wenceslas, St 907–929. Duke of Bohemia who attempted to Christianize his people and was murdered by his brother. He is patron saint of the Czech Republic and 'good King Wenceslas' of the popular carol. Feast day 28 Sept.

Wesley John 1703–1791. English founder of ⊳Methodism. When the pulpits of the Church of England were closed to him and his followers, he took the gospel to the people. For 50 years he rode about the country on horseback, preaching daily, largely in the open air. His sermons became the doctrinal standard of the Wesleyan Methodist Church.

West Rebecca. Pen name of Cicely Isabel Fairfield 1892–1983. Irish journalist and novelist, an active feminist from 1911. *The Meaning of Treason* 1959 deals with the spies Burgess and Maclean. Her novels have political themes and include *The Fountain Overflows* 1956 and *The Birds Fall Down* 1966.

West Bank Israeli-occupied area (5,879 sq km/2,270 sq mi) on the west bank of the river Jordan; population (1988) 866,000. In 1993 an Israeli-PLO preliminary accord was signed, promising partial autonomy for Palestinians and phased withdrawal of Israeli troops from occupied territories.

West Bengal state of NE India; *area* 87,900 sq km/33,929 sq mi; *capital* Calcutta; *population* (1991) 67,982,700.

Western Australia state of Australia; *area* 2,525,500 sq km/974,843 sq mi; *capital* Perth; *features* Monte Bello Islands; NW coast subject to hurricanes (willy-willies); Lasseter's Reef; *population* (1987) 1,478,000.

Western Isles island area of Scotland, comprising the Outer Hebrides (Lewis, Harris, North and South Uist, and Barra); *area* 2,900 sq km/1,120 sq mi; *towns and cities* Stornoway on Lewis (administrative headquarters); *features* divided from the mainland by the Minch channel; Callanish monolithic circles of the Stone Age on Lewis; *population* (1991) 29,100.

Western Sahara formerly *Spanish Sahara* disputed territory in NW Africa bounded to the N by Morocco, to the W and S by Mauritania, and to the E by the Atlantic Ocean; *area* 266,800 sq km/103,011 sq mi; *capital* Laâyoune (Arabic *El Aaiún*); *features* electrically monitored fortified wall enclosing the phosphate area; *population* (1988) 181,400; another estimated 165,000 live in refugee camps near Tindouf, SW Algeria; *language* Arabic; *religion* Sunni Muslim.

West Glamorgan (Welsh *Gorllewin Morgannwg*) county of SW Wales; *area* 817 sq km/315 sq mi; *features* Gower Peninsula; *population* (1991) 361,400; *languages* English, 15% Welsh-speaking.

West Indian inhabitant of or native to the West Indies, or person of West Indian descent. The West Indies are culturally heterogeneous; in addition to the indigenous Carib and Arawak Indians, there are peoples of African, European, and Asian descent, as well as peoples of mixed descent.

West Indies archipelago of about 1,200 islands, dividing the Atlantic Ocean from the Gulf of Mexico and the Caribbean Sea. The islands are divided into: *Bahamas*; *Greater Antilles* Cuba, Hispaniola (Haiti, Dominican Republic), Jamaica, and Puerto Rico; *Lesser Antilles* Aruba, Netherlands Antilles, Trinidad and Tobago, the Windward Islands (Grenada, Barbados, St Vincent, St Lucia, Martinique, Dominica, Guadeloupe), the Leeward Islands (Montserrat, Antigua, St Christopher (St Kitts)–Nevis, Barbuda, Anguilla, St Martin, British and US Virgin Islands), and many smaller islands.

West Midlands metropolitan county of central England, created 1974; in 1986, most of the functions of the former county council were transferred to the metropolitan district councils; *area* 900 sq km/347 sq mi; *towns and cities* Birmingham, Wolverhampton, Coventry; *population* (1991) 2,551,700.

Westphalia, Treaty of agreement 1648 ending the ◊Thirty Years' War. The peace marked the end of the supremacy of the Holy Roman Empire and the emergence of France as a dominant power. It recognized the sovereignty of the German states, Switzerland, and the Netherlands; Lutherans, Calvinists, and Roman Catholics were given equal rights.

West Sussex county of S England, created 1974, formerly part of Sussex; *area* 2,020 sq km/780 sq mi; *towns and cities* Chichester (administrative headquarters), Crawley, Horsham, Haywards Heath, Shoreham (port), Bognor Regis (coastal resort); *features* the Weald, South Downs; Arundel and Bramber castles; *population* (1991) 702,300.

West Virginia state in E central USA; *area* 62,900 sq km/24,279 sq mi; *capital* Charleston; *features* port of Harper's Ferry, restored as when John Brown seized the US armoury 1859; *population* (1990) 1,793,500.

West Yorkshire metropolitan county of NE England, created 1974; in 1986, most of the functions of the former county council were transferred to the metropolitan district councils; *area* 2,040 sq km/787 sq mi; *towns and cities* Wakefield, Leeds, Bradford, Halifax, Huddersfield; *features* Ilkley Moor, Haworth Moor, Haworth Parsonage; part of the Peak District National Park; *population* (1991) 2,013,700.

wetland permanently wet land area or habitat. Wetlands include areas of marsh, fen, ◊bog, flood plain, and shallow coastal areas. Wetlands are extremely fertile. They provide warm, sheltered waters for fisheries, lush vegetation for grazing livestock, and an abundance of wildlife. Estuaries and seaweed beds are more than 16 times as productive as the open ocean.

whale any marine mammal of the order Cetacea, with front limbs modified into flippers and with internal vestiges of hind limbs. The order is divided into the toothed whales (Odontoceti) and the baleen whales (Mysticeti). The toothed whales include ◊dolphins and porpoises, along with large forms such as sperm whales. The baleen whales, with plates of modified mucous membrane called baleen in the mouth, are all large in size and include finback and right whales. There were hundreds of thousands of whales at the beginning of the 20th century, but they have been hunted close to extinction (see ◊whaling).

whaling the hunting of whales, largely discontinued 1986. Whales are killed for whale oil (made from the thick layer of fat under the skin called 'blubber'), used for food and cosmetics; for the large reserve of oil in the head of the sperm whale, used in the leather industry; and for *ambergris*, a waxlike substance from the intestines, used in making perfumes. There are synthetic substitutes for all these products. Whales are also killed for their meat, which is eaten by the Japanese and was used as pet food in the USA and Europe.

wheat cereal plant derived from the wild *Triticum*, a grass native to the Middle East. It is the chief cereal used in breadmaking and is widely cultivated in temperate climates suited to its growth. Wheat is killed by frost, and damp renders the grain soft, so warm, dry regions produce the most valuable grain.

Whig Party in the UK, predecessor of the Liberal Party. The name was first used of rebel Covenanters and then of those who wished to exclude James II from the English succession (as a Roman Catholic). The party was in power continuously 1714–60. During the French Revolution, the Whigs demanded parliamentary reform in Britain, and from the passing of the Reform Bill in 1832 became known as Liberals.

Whistler James Abbott McNeill 1834–1903. US painter and etcher. He was active in London from 1859. Influenced by Japanese prints, he painted riverscapes and portraits that show subtle composition and colour harmonies: for example, *Arrangement in Grey and Black: Portrait of the Painter's Mother* 1871 (Louvre, Paris).

White Patrick (Victor Martindale) 1912–1990. Australian writer. He did more than any other to put Australian literature on the international map. His partly allegorical novels explore the lives of early settlers in Australia and often deal with misfits or inarticulate people. They include *The Aunt's Story* 1948, *The Tree of Man* 1955, and *Voss* 1957. Nobel Prize for Literature 1973.

white blood cell or *leucocyte* one of a number of different cells that play a part in the body's defences and give immunity against disease. Some (phagocytes and macrophages) engulf invading microorganisms, others kill infected cells, while ◊lymphocytes produce more specific immune responses. White blood cells are colourless, with clear or granulated cytoplasm, and are capable of independent amoeboid movement. They occur in the blood, ◊lymph and elsewhere in the body's tissues.

white dwarf small, hot ◊star, the last stage in the life of a star such as the Sun. White dwarfs have a mass similar to that of the Sun, but only 1% of the Sun's diameter, similar in size to the Earth. Most have surface temperatures of 8,000°C/14,400°F or more, hotter than the Sun. Yet, being so small, their overall luminosities may be less than 1% of that of the Sun. The Milky Way contains an estimated 50 billion white dwarfs.

Whitman Walt(er) 1819–1892. US poet. He published *Leaves of Grass* 1855, which contains the symbolic 'Song of Myself'. It used unconventional free verse (with no rhyme or regular rhythm) and scandalized the public by its frank celebration of sexuality.

Whit Sunday Christian church festival held seven weeks after Easter, commemorating the descent of the Holy Spirit on the Apostles. The name is probably derived from the white garments worn by candidates for baptism at the festival. Whit Sunday corresponds to the Jewish festival of Shavuot (Pentecost).

whooping cough or *pertussis* acute infectious disease, seen mainly in children, caused by colonization of the air passages by the bacterium *Bordetella pertussis.* The main symptom is violent and persistent coughing, associated with the sharp intake of breath that is the characteristic 'whoop', and often followed by vomiting and severe nose bleeds.

Wight, Isle of island and county of S England; *area* 380 sq km/147 sq mi; *towns and cities* Newport (administrative headquarters), resorts: Ryde, Sandown, Shanklin, Ventnor; *features* the *Needles*, pointed chalk rocks up to 30 m/100 ft high in the sea to the W; the *Solent*, sea channel between Hampshire and the island; *Cowes*, venue of Regatta Week and headquarters of the Royal Yacht Squadron; Farringford, home of poet Alfred Tennyson; *population* (1991) 124,600.

Wilberforce William 1759–1833. English reformer who was instrumental in abolishing slavery in the British Empire. He entered Parliament 1780; in 1807 his bill for the abolition of the slave trade was passed, and in 1833, largely through his efforts, slavery was abolished throughout the empire.

Wilde Oscar (Fingal O'Flahertie Wills) 1854–1900. Irish writer. With his flamboyant style and quotable conversation, he dazzled London society and, on his lecture tour 1882, the USA. He published his only novel, *The Picture of Dorian Gray*, 1891, followed by a series of sharp comedies, including *A Woman*

of No Importance 1893 and *The Importance of Being Earnest* 1895. In 1895 he was imprisoned for two years for homosexual offences; he died in exile.

William (I) the Conqueror *c.* 1027–1087. King of England from 1066. He was the illegitimate son of Duke Robert the Devil and succeeded his father as duke of Normandy 1035. Claiming that his relative King Edward the Confessor had bequeathed him the English throne, William invaded the country 1066, defeating ◊Harold II at Hastings, Sussex, and was crowned king of England.

William (III) of Orange 1650–1702. King of Great Britain and Ireland from 1688, the son of William II of Orange and Mary, daughter of Charles I. He was offered the English crown by the parliamentary opposition to James II. He invaded England 1688 and in 1689 became joint sovereign with his wife, ◊Mary II. He defeated James II at the battle of the Boyne 1690. He was succeeded by Mary's sister, Anne.

William (full name William Arthur Philip Louis) 1982– . Prince of the UK, first child of the Prince and Princess of Wales.

Williams Tennessee (Thomas Lanier) 1911–1983. US dramatist. His work is characterized by fluent dialogue and analysis of the psychological deficiencies of his characters. His plays, usually set in the Deep South against a background of decadence and degradation, include *The Glass Menagerie* 1945, *A Streetcar Named Desire* 1947, and *Cat on a Hot Tin Roof* 1955.

Wilson (James) Harold, Baron Wilson of Rievaulx 1916–1995. British Labour politician, party leader from 1963, prime minister 1964–70 and 1974–76. His premiership was dominated by the issue of UK admission to membership of the European Community (now the European Union), the social contract (unofficial agreement with the trade unions), and economic difficulties.

Wiltshire county of SW England; *area* 3,480 sq km/1,343 sq mi; *towns and cities* Trowbridge (administrative headquarters), Salisbury, Swindon, Wilton; *features* Marlborough Downs; Savernake Forest; Salisbury Plain, a military training area used since Napoleonic times; Neolithic Stonehenge, Avebury stone circle, Silbury Hill, West Kennet Long Barrow; *population* (1991) 564,500.

wind the lateral movement of the Earth's atmosphere from high-pressure areas (anticyclones) to low-pressure areas (depression). Its speed is measured using an anemometer or by studying its effects on, for example, trees by using the ▷Beaufort Scale. Although modified by features such as land and water, there is a basic worldwide system of ▷trade winds, ▷westerlies, and polar easterlies.

Windermere largest lake in England, in Cumbria, 17 km/10.5 mi long and 1.6 km/1 mi wide.

Windhoek capital of Namibia; population (1988) 115,000. It is just N of the Tropic of Capricorn, 290 km/180 mi from the W coast.

wind turbine windmill of advanced aerodynamic design connected to an electricity generator and used in wind-power installations. Wind turbines can be either large propeller-type rotors mounted on a tall tower, or flexible metal strips fixed to a vertical axle at top and bottom. In 1990, over 20,000 wind turbines were in use throughout the world, generating 1,600 megawatts of power.

wing in biology, the modified forelimb of birds and bats, or the membranous outgrowths of the exoskeleton of insects, which give the power of flight. Birds and bats have two wings. Bird wings have feathers attached to the fused digits ('fingers') and forearm bones, while bat wings consist of skin stretched between the digits. Most insects have four wings, which are strengthened by wing veins.

Winnipeg capital and industrial city in Manitoba, Canada, on the Red River, S of Lake Winnipeg; population (1986) 623,000.

Wisconsin state in N central USA; *area* 145,500 sq km/56,163 sq mi; *capital* Madison; *cities* Milwaukee, Green Bay, Racine; *features* lakes: Superior, Michigan; Mississippi River; Door peninsula; *population* (1990) 4,891,800.

Wittgenstein Ludwig 1889–1951. Austrian philosopher. His *Tractatus Logico- Philosophicus* 1922 postulated the 'picture theory' of language: that words represent things according to social agreement. He subsequently rejected this idea, and developed the idea that usage was more important than convention.

Wodehouse P(elham) G(renville) 1881–1975. English novelist. He became a US citizen 1955. His humorous novels portray the accident-prone world of such characters as the socialite Bertie Wooster and his invaluable and impeccable manservant Jeeves, and Lord Emsworth of Blandings Castle with his prize pig, the Empress of Blandings.

Woden or *Wodan* the foremost Anglo-Saxon god, whose Norse counterpart is ⬦Odin.

wolf any of two species of large wild dogs of the genus *Canis*. The grey or timber wolf *C. lupus*, of North America and Eurasia, is highly social, measures up to 90 cm/3 ft at the shoulder, and weighs up to 45 kg/100 lb. It has been greatly reduced in numbers except for isolated wilderness regions.

Wollstonecraft Mary 1759–1797. British feminist, member of a group of radical intellectuals called the English Jacobins, whose book *A Vindication of the Rights of Women* 1792 demanded equal educational opportunities for women. She married William Godwin and died giving birth to a daughter, Mary (later Mary ⬦Shelley).

Wolsey Thomas *c.* 1475–1530. English cleric and politician. In Henry VIII's service from 1509, he became archbishop of York 1514, cardinal and lord chancellor 1515, and began the dissolution of the monasteries. His reluctance to further Henry's divorce from Catherine of Aragon, partly because of his ambition to be pope, led to his downfall 1529. He was charged with high treason 1530 but died before being tried.

women's movement campaign for the rights of women. Once women's right to vote (see ⬦suffragette) was achieved in the 20th century, the movement strived towards equal social and economic opportunities, including employment. In industrialized societies, there remains a contradiction between the accepted principle of equality of women and the demonstrable inequalities that still exist.

wood the hard tissue beneath the bark of many perennial plants; it is composed of water-conducting cells, or secondary ⬦xylem, and gains its hardness and strength from deposits of lignin. *Hardwoods*, such as oak, and *softwoods*, such as pine, have commercial value as structural material and for furniture.

woodland area in which trees grow more or less thickly; generally smaller than a forest. Temperate climates, with four distinct seasons a year, tend to support a mixed woodland habitat, with some conifers but mostly broad-leaved and deciduous trees, shedding their leaves in autumn and regrowing them in spring. In the Mediterranean region and parts of the southern hemisphere, the trees are mostly evergreen.

woodlouse crustacean of the order Isopoda. Woodlice have segmented bodies and flattened undersides. The eggs are carried by the female in a pouch beneath the thorax.

Woolf Virginia (born Virginia Stephen) 1882–1941. English novelist and critic. In novels such as *Mrs Dalloway*, *To the Lighthouse* 1927, and *The Waves* 1931, she used a 'stream of consciousness' technique to render inner experience. In *A Room of One's Own* 1929, *Orlando* 1928, and *The Years* 1937, she examines the importance of economic independence for women and other feminist principles.

Wordsworth William 1770–1850. English Romantic poet. In 1797 he moved with his sister Dorothy to Somerset to be near ⬦Coleridge, collaborating with him on *Lyrical Ballads* 1798 (which included 'Tintern Abbey'). From 1799 he lived in the Lake District, and later works include *Poems* 1807 (including 'Intimations of Immortality') and *The Prelude* (written by 1805, published 1850). He was appointed poet laureate 1843.

World Bank popular name for the *International Bank for Reconstruction and Development* specialized agency of the United Nations that borrows in the commercial market and lends on commercial terms. It was established 1945 under the 1944 Bretton Woods agreement, which also created the International Monetary Fund.

World Cup the most prestigious competition in international soccer; World Cup events are also held in rugby union, cricket, and other sports.

World Health Organization (WHO) agency of the United Nations established 1946 to prevent the spread of diseases and to eradicate them. Its headquarters are in Geneva, Switzerland.

World War I 1914–1918. War between the Central European Powers (Germany, Austria-Hungary, and allies) on one side and the Triple Entente (Britain and the British Empire, France, and Russia) and their allies, including the USA (which entered 1917), on the other side. An estimated 10 million lives were lost and twice that number were wounded. It was fought on the eastern and western fronts, in the Middle East, in Africa, and at sea. Towards the end of the war Russia withdrew because of the Russian Revolution 1917. The peace treaty of Versailles 1919 was the formal end to the war.

World War II 1939–1945. War between Germany, Italy, and Japan (the Axis powers) on one side, and Britain, the Commonwealth, France, the USA, the USSR, and China (the Allied powers) on the other. An estimated 55 million lives were lost, 20 million of them citizens of the USSR. The war was fought in the Atlantic and Pacific theatres. In 1945, Germany surrendered (May) but Japan fought on until the USA dropped atomic bombs on Hiroshima and Nagasaki (Aug).

worm any of various elongated limbless invertebrates belonging to several phyla. Worms include the ◊flatworms, such as flukes and ◊tapeworms; the roundworms or ◊nematodes, such as the eelworm and the hookworm; the marine ribbon worms or nemerteans; and the segmented worms or ◊annelids.

Wren Christopher 1632–1723. English architect. His ingenious use of a refined and sober Baroque style can be seen in his best-known work, St Paul's Cathedral, London, 1675–1710, and in the many churches he built in London including St Mary-le-Bow, Cheapside, 1670–77 and St Bride's, Fleet Street, 1671–78. Other works include the Sheldonian Theatre, Oxford, 1664–69; Greenwich Hospital, London, begun 1694; and Marlborough House, London, 1709–10 (now much altered).

wrestling sport popular in ancient Egypt, Greece, and Rome, and included in the Olympics from 704 BC. The two main modern international styles are *Greco-Roman*, concentrating on above-waist holds, and *freestyle*, which allows the legs to be used to hold or trip; in both the aim is to throw the opponent to the ground.

Wright Frank Lloyd 1869–1959. US architect. He is known for 'organic architecture', in which buildings reflect their natural surroundings. From the 1890s, he developed his celebrated *prairie house* style, a series of low, spreading houses with projecting roofs. He later diversified, employing reinforced concrete to explore a variety of geometric forms. Among his buildings is the Guggenheim Museum, New York, 1959, a spiral ramp rising from a circular plan.

Wright Orville 1871–1948 and Wilbur 1867–1912. US inventors; brothers who pioneered piloted, powered flight. Inspired by Otto Lilienthal's gliding, they perfected their piloted glider 1902. In 1903 they built a powered machine, a 12–hp 341-kg/750-lb plane, and became the first to make a successful powered flight, near Kitty Hawk, North Carolina. Orville flew 36.6 m/120 ft in 12 sec; Wilbur, 260 m/852 ft in 59 sec.

Wycliffe John *c.* 1320–1384. English religious reformer. Allying himself with the party of John of Gaunt, which was opposed to ecclesiastical influence at court, he attacked abuses in the church, maintaining that the Bible rather than the church was the supreme authority. He criticized such fundamental doctrines as priestly absolution, confession, and indulgences, and set disciples to work on translating the Bible into English.

Wyoming state in westerm USA; *area* 253,400 sq km/97,812 sq mi; *capital* Cheyenne; *features* Rocky Mountains; national parks: Yellowstone (including the geyser Old Faithful), Grand Teton; *population* (1990) 453,600.

X

X chromosome larger of the two sex chromosomes, the smaller being the ▷Y chromosome. These two chromosomes are involved in sex determination. Females have two X chromosomes, males have an X and a Y.

xenon colourless, odourless, gaseous, non-metallic element, symbol Xe, atomic number 54, relative atomic mass 131.30. It is grouped with the ▷inert gases and was long believed not to enter into reactions, but is now known to form some compounds, mostly with fluorine. It is a heavy gas present in very small quantities in the air (about one part in 20 million).

Xenophon c. 430–354 BC. Greek historian, philosopher, and soldier. He was a disciple of ▷Socrates (described in Xenophon's *Symposium*). In 401 he joined a Greek mercenary army aiding the Persian prince Cyrus, and on the latter's death took command. His *Anabasis* describes how he led 10,000 Greeks on a 1,600-km/1,000-mile march home across enemy territory. His other works include *Memorabilia, Apology,* and *Hellenica/A History of My Times.*

xerography dry, electrostatic method of producing images, without the use of negatives or sensitized paper, invented in the USA by Chester Carlson 1938 and applied in the Xerox photocopier.

xerophyte plant adapted to live in dry conditions. Common adaptations to reduce the rate of ▷transpiration include a reduction of leaf size, sometimes to spines or scales; a dense covering of hairs over the leaf to trap a layer of moist air (as in edelweiss); water storage cells; sunken stomata; and permanently rolled leaves or leaves that roll up in dry weather (as in marram grass). Many desert cacti are xerophytes.

Xhosa member of a Bantu people of southern Africa, living mainly in the Black National State of Transkei. Traditionally, the Xhosa were farmers and pastoralists, with a social structure based on a monarchy. Many are now town-dwellers, and provide much of the unskilled labour in South African mines and factories. Their Bantu language belongs to the Niger-Congo family.

Xia dynasty or *Hsia dynasty* China's first legendary ruling family, c. 2200–c. 1500 BC, reputedly founded by the model emperor Yu the Great. He is believed to have controlled floods by constructing dykes. Archaeological evidence suggests that the Xia dynasty really did exist, as a Bronze Age civilization where writing was being developed, with its capital at Erlidou (Erh-li-t'ou) in Henan (Honan).

Xinjiang Uygur or *Sinkiang Uighur* autonomous region of NW China; *area* 1,646,800 sq km/635,665 sq mi; *capital*

Urumqi; *features* Junggar Pendi (Dzungarian Basin) and Tarim Pendi (Tarim Basin, which includes Lop Nor, China's nuclear testing ground, although the research centres were moved to the central province of Sichuan 1972) separated by the Tian Shan Mountains; *population* (1990) 15,156,000; the region has 13 recognized ethnic minorities, the largest being 6 million Uigurs (Muslim descendants of Turks); *religion* 50% Muslim.

X-ray band of electromagnetic radiation in the wavelength range 10^{-11} to 10^{-9} m (between gamma rays and ultraviolet radiation; see ▷electromagnetic waves). Applications of X-rays make use of their short wavelength or their penetrating power (as in medical X-rays of internal body tissues). X-rays are dangerous and can cause cancer.

xylem tissue found in vascular plants, whose main function is to conduct water and dissolved mineral nutrients from the roots to other parts of the plant. Xylem is composed of a number of different types of cell, and may include long, thin, usually dead cells known as tracheids; fibres (schlerenchyma); thin-walled parenchym cells; and conducting vessels.

xylophone musical ▷percussion instrument of African and Indonesian origin, consisting of a series of resonant hardwood bars of varying lengths, each with its own distinct pitch, arranged in sequence and played with hard sticks. It first appeared as an orchestral instrument in Saint-Saëns' *Danse macabre* 1874, illustrating dancing skeletons.

Y

yachting pleasure cruising or racing a small and light vessel, whether sailing or power-driven. At the Olympic Games, seven sail-driven categories exist: Soling, Flying Dutchman, Star, Finn, Tornado, 470, and Windglider or windsurfing (boardsailing). The Finn and Windglider are solo events; the Soling class is for three-person crews; all other classes are for crews of two.

yak species of cattle *Bos grunniens*, family Bovidae, which lives in wild herds at high altitudes in Tibet. It stands about 2 m/6 ft at the shoulder and has long shaggy hair on the underparts. It has large, upward-curving horns and humped shoulders. It is in danger of becoming extinct.

yam any climbing plant of the genus *Dioscorea*, family Dioscoreaceae, cultivated in tropical regions; its starchy tubers are eaten as a vegetable. The Mexican yam *D. composita* contains a chemical used in the manufacture of the contraceptive pill.

Yamoussoukro capital of ◊Ivory Coast; population (1986) 120,000. The economy is based on tourism and agricultural trade.

Yangon formerly (until 1989) *Rangoon* capital and chief port of Myanmar (Burma) on the Yangon River, 32 km/20 mi from the Indian Ocean; population (1983) 2,459,000. It was given the name Rangoon (meaning 'end of conflict') by King Alaungpaya 1755.

Yaoundé capital of Cameroon, 210 km/130 mi E of the port of Douala; population (1984) 552,000.

Y chromosome smaller of the two sex chromosomes. In male mammals it occurs paired with the other type of sex chromosome (X), which carries far more genes. The Y chromosome is the smallest of all the mammalian chromosomes and is considered to be largely inert (that is, without direct effect on the physical body). See also ◊sex determination.

yeast one of various single-celled fungi (especially the genus *Saccharomyces*) that form masses of minute circular or oval cells by budding. When placed in a sugar solution the cells multiply and convert the sugar into alcohol and carbon dioxide. Yeasts are used as fermenting agents in baking, brewing, and the making of wine and spirits. Brewer's yeast *S. cerevisiae* is a rich source of vitamin B.

Yeats W(illiam) B(utler) 1865–1939. Irish poet. He was a leader of the Celtic revival and a founder of the Abbey Theatre in Dublin. His early work was romantic and lyrical, as in the poem 'The Lake Isle of Innisfree' and the plays *The Countess Cathleen* 1892 and *The Land of Heart's Desire* 1894. His later books of poetry include *The Wild Swans* *at Coole* 1917 and *The Winding Stair* 1929. He was a senator of the Irish Free State 1922–28. Nobel Prize for Literature 1923.

yellow fever or *yellow jack* acute tropical viral disease, prevalent in the Caribbean area, Brazil, and on the west coast of Africa. It is transmitted by mosquitoes. Its symptoms include a high fever, headache, joint and muscle pains, vomiting and jaundice, possibly leading to liver failure; the heart and kidneys may also be affected. Mortality is high in serious cases.

Yeltsin Boris Nikolayevich 1931– . Russian politician, Soviet president 1990–91, and president of the newly independent Russian Federation from 1991. He directed the Federation's secession from the USSR and established a new, decentralized confederation, the ◊Commonwealth of Independent States, with himself as the most powerful leader. Despite severe economic problems and civil unrest, he survived a coup attempt 1993, but was forced to compromise on the pace and extent of his reforms after far-right gains in elections to a new bicameral parliament.

Yemen Republic of (*al Jamhuriya al Yamaniya*); formerly, until 1990, *North Yemen* and *South Yemen*; *area* 531,900 sq km/205,367 sq mi; *capital* San'ā; *features* once known as *Arabia felix* because of its fertility, includes islands of Perim (in strait of Bab-el-Mandeb, at S entrance to Red Sea), Socotra, and Kamaran; *political system* emergent democratic republic; *population* (1993) 13,000,000; growth rate 2.7% p.a.; *language* Arabic; *religions* Sunni Muslim 63%, Shi'ite Muslim 37%.

Yerevan industrial city and capital of Armenia, a few miles N of the Turkish border; population (1987) 1,168,000.

yew any evergreen coniferous tree of the genus *Taxus* of the family Taxaceae, native to the northern hemisphere. The leaves and bright red berrylike seeds are poisonous; the wood is hard and close-grained.

Yiddish member of the west Germanic branch of the Indo-European language family, deriving from 13th–14th-century Rhineland German and spoken by northern, central, and eastern European Jews, who have carried it to Israel, the USA, and many other parts of the world. Written in the Hebrew alphabet, it has many dialects as well as many borrowed words from Polish, Russian, Lithuanian, and other languages.

yin and yang the passive (characterized as feminine, negative, intuitive) and active (characterized as masculine, positive, intellectual) principles of nature. Their interaction is believed to maintain equilibrium and harmony in the universe and to be present in all things. In Taoism and Confucianism they are represented by two interlocked curved shapes within a circle, one white, one black, with a spot of the contrasting colour within the head of each.

yoga Hindu philosophical system attributed to Patanjali, who lived about 150 BC at Gonda, Uttar Pradesh, India. He preached mystical union with a personal deity through the practice of self-hypnosis and a rising above the senses by abstract meditation, adoption of special postures, and ascetic practices. As practised in the West, yoga is more a system of mental and physical exercise, and of induced relaxation as a means of relieving stress.

Yokohama Japanese port on Tokyo Bay; population (1990) 3,220,350.

Yom Kippur the Jewish Day of ⊳Atonement.

York cathedral and industrial city in North Yorkshire, N England; population (1991) 98,700. Attracting 3 million tourists a year, its features include the Gothic York Minster; the 14th-century city wall with four gates or 'bars'; medieval streets collectively known as the Shambles; the Jorvik Viking Centre, containing wooden remains of Viking houses. There are fine examples of 17th- to 18th-century domestic architecture; Theatre Royal, site of a theatre since 1765; Castle Museum; National Railway Museum.

yucca plant of the genus *Yucca*, family Liliaceae, with over 40 species found in Latin America and southwest USA. The leaves are stiff and sword-shaped and the flowers white and bell-shaped.

Yugoslavia *area* 58,300 sq km/22,503 sq mi; *capital* Belgrade; *political system* socialist pluralist republic; *population* (1992) 10,460,000; *languages* Serbian variant of Serbo-Croatian, Slovenian; *religion* Eastern Orthodox 41% (Serbs), Roman Catholic 12% (Croats), Muslim 3%.

Z

Zagreb industrial city and capital of Croatia, on the Sava River; population (1991) 706,800. Zagreb was a Roman city (*Aemona*) and has a Gothic cathedral. Its university was founded 1874. The city was damaged by bombing Oct 1991 during the Croatian civil war.

Zaire Republic of (*République du Zaïre*) (formerly *Congo*); *area* 2,344,900 sq km/905,366 sq mi; *capital* Kinshasa; *features* lakes Tanganyika, Mobutu Sese Seko, Edward; Ruwenzori mountains; *political system* transitional; *population* (1993 est) 40,256,000; growth rate 2.9% p.a.; *languages* French (official), Swahili, Lingala, other African languages; over 300 dialects; *religions* Christian 70%, Muslim 10%.

Zaïre River formerly (until 1971) *Congo* second-longest river in Africa, rising near the Zambia–Zaire border (and known as the *Lualaba River* in the upper reaches) and flowing 4,500 km/2,800 mi to the Atlantic Ocean, running in a great curve that crosses the equator twice, and discharging a volume of water second only to the Amazon. The chief tributaries are the Ubangi, Sangha, and Kasai.

Zambezi river in central and SE Africa; length 2,650 km/1,650 mi from NW Zambia through Mozambique to the Indian Ocean, with a wide delta near Chinde. Major tributaries include the Kafue in Zambia. It is interrupted by rapids, and includes on the Zimbabwe–Zambia border the Victoria Falls (Mosi-oa-tunya) and Kariba Dam, which forms the reservoir of Lake Kariba with large fisheries.

Zambia Republic of; *area* 752,600 sq km/290,579 sq mi; *capital* Lusaka; *features* Zambezi River, Victoria Falls, Kariba Dam; *political system* emergent democratic republic; *population* (1993 est) 9,000,000; growth rate 3.3% p.a.; *language* English (official); Bantu dialects; *religions* Christian 66%, animist, Hindu, Muslim.

Zanzibar island region of Tanzania; *area* 1,658 sq km/640 sq mi (80 km/50 mi long); *population* (1985) 571,000.

zebra black and white striped member of the horse genus *Equus* found in Africa; the stripes serve as camouflage or dazzle and confuse predators. It is about 1.5 m/5 ft high at the shoulder, with a stout body and a short, thick mane. Zebras live in family groups and herds on mountains and plains, and can run at up to 60 kph/40 mph. Males are usually solitary.

zebu any of a species of cattle *Bos indicus* found domesticated in E Asia, India, and Africa. It is usually light-coloured, with large horns and a large fatty hump near the shoulders. It is used for pulling loads, and is held by some

Hindus to be sacred. There are about 30 breeds.

Zen form of ◊Buddhism introduced from India to Japan via China in the 12th century. *Kōan* (paradoxical questions), tea-drinking, and sudden enlightenment are elements of Zen practice. Soto Zen was spread by the priest Dōgen (1200–1253), who emphasized work, practice, discipline, and philosophical questions to discover one's Buddha-nature in the 'realization of self'.

Zeno of Elea *c.* 490–430 BC. Greek philosopher who pointed out several paradoxes that raised 'modern' problems of space and time. For example, motion is an illusion, since an arrow in flight must occupy a determinate space at each instant, and therefore must be at rest.

Zeppelin Ferdinand, Count von Zeppelin 1838–1917. German airship pioneer. His first airship was built and tested 1900. During World War I a number of Zeppelin airships bombed England. They were also used for luxury passenger transport but the construction of hydrogen-filled airships with rigid keels was abandoned after several disasters in the 1920s and 1930s.

Zeus in Greek mythology, the chief of the gods (Roman Jupiter). He was the son of Kronos, whom he overthrew; his brothers included Pluto and Poseidon, his sisters Demeter and Hera. As the supreme god he dispensed good and evil and was the father and ruler of all humankind. His emblems are the thunderbolt and aegis (shield), representing the thundercloud. The colossal ivory and gold statue of the seated god, made by Phidias for the temple of Zeus in the Peloponnese, was one of the ◊Seven Wonders of the World.

Zhou Enlai or *Chou En-lai* 1898–1976 Chinese politician. Zhou, a member of the Chinese Communist Party (CCP) from the 1920s, was prime minister 1949–76 and foreign minister 1949–58. He was a moderate Maoist and weathered the Cultural Revolution. He played a key role in foreign affairs.

Zia Begum Khaleda 1945– . Bangladeshi conservative politician, prime minister from 1991. Leader of the Bangladesh Nationalist Party (BNP) from 1984, she has successfully overseen the transition from presidential to democratic parliamentary government.

zidovudine (formerly *AZT*) antiviral drug used in the treatment of ◊AIDS. It is not a cure for AIDS but is effective in prolonging life; it does not, however, delay the onset of AIDS in people carrying the virus.

ziggurat in ancient Babylonia and Assyria, a step pyramid of sun-baked brick faced with glazed bricks or tiles on which stood a shrine. The Tower of Babel as described in the Bible may have been a ziggurat.

Zimbabwe Republic of; *area* 390,300 sq km/150,695 sq mi; *capital* Harare; *features* Hwange National Park, part of Kalahari Desert; ruins of Great Zimbabwe; *political system* emergent democratic republic; *population* (1993 est) 10,700,000 (Shona 80%, Ndbele 19%; about 100,000 whites); growth rate 3.5% p.a.; *languages* English (official), Shona, Sindebele; *religions* Christian, Muslim, Hindu, animist.

zinc hard, brittle, bluish-white, metallic element, symbol Zn, atomic number 30, relative atomic mass 65.37. The principal ore is sphalerite or zinc blende (zinc sulphide, ZnS). Zinc is little affected by air or moisture at ordinary temperatures; its chief uses are in alloys such as brass and in coating metals (for example, galvanized iron). Its compounds include zinc oxide, used in ointments (as an astringent) and cosmetics, paints, glass, and printing ink.

Zion Jebusite (Amorites of Canaan) stronghold in Jerusalem captured by King David, and the hill on which he built the Temple, symbol of Jerusalem and of Jewish national life.

Zionism political movement advocating the re-establishment of a Jewish homeland in Palestine, the 'promised land' of the Bible, with its capital Jerusalem, the 'city of Zion'.

zither member of a family of musical instruments consisting of one or more strings stretched over a resonating frame. The modern concert zither has up to 45 strings of which five, passing over frets, are plucked with a plectrum for melody, and the remainder are plucked with the fingers for harmonic accompaniment.

zodiac zone of the heavens containing the paths of the Sun, Moon, and planets. When this was devised by the ancient Greeks, only five planets were known, making the zodiac about 16° wide. In astrology, the zodiac is divided into 12 signs, each 30° in extent: Aries, Taurus, Gemini, Cancer, Leo, Virgo, Libra, Scorpio, Sagittarius, Capricorn, Aquarius, and Pisces. These do not cover the same areas of sky as the astronomical constellations. *(See table at back.)*

Zola Émile Edouard Charles Antoine 1840–1902. French novelist and social reformer. *La Fortune des Rougon/The Fortune of the Rougons* 1867 began a series of some 20 naturalistic novels, portraying the fortunes of a French family under the Second Empire. They include *Le Ventre de Paris/The Underbelly of Paris* 1873, *Nana* 1880, and *La Débâcle/The Debacle* 1892. In 1898 he published *J'accuse/I Accuse*, a pamphlet indicting the persecutors of Alfred ◊Dreyfus, for which he was prosecuted for libel but later pardoned.

zoology branch of biology concerned with the study of animals. It includes description of present-day animals, the study of evolution of animal forms, anatomy, physiology, embryology, behaviour, and geographical distribution.

Zoroastrianism pre-Islamic Persian religion founded by the Persian prophet Zoroaster in the 6th century BC, and still practised by the Parsees in India. The *Zendavesta* are the sacred scriptures of the faith. The theology is dualistic, *Ahura Mazda* or *Ormuzd* (the good God) being perpetually in conflict with *Ahriman* (the evil God), but the former is assured of eventual victory.

Z particle in physics, an ◊elementary particle, one of the weakons responsible for carrying the weak nuclear force.

Zulu member of a group of southern African peoples mainly from Natal, South Africa. Their present homeland, KwaZulu, represents the nucleus of the once extensive and militaristic Zulu kingdom. Many Zulus, as supporters of the political organization Inkatha, violently opposed the nonracial constitution adopted in South Africa 1993, demanding greater autonomy. The *Zulu language*, closely related to Xhosa, belongs to the Bantu branch of the Niger-Congo family.

Zürich financial centre and industrial city on Lake Zürich; population (1990) 341,300. Situated at the foot of the Alps, it is the capital of Zürich canton and the largest city in Switzerland.

Zwingli Ulrich 1484–1531. Swiss Protestant, born in St Gallen. He was ordained a Roman Catholic priest 1506, but by 1519 was a Reformer and led the Reformation in Switzerland with his insistence on the sole authority of the Scriptures. He was killed in a skirmish at Kappel during a war against the cantons that had not accepted the Reformation.

zygote ▷ovum (egg) after ▷fertilization but before it undergoes cleavage to begin embryonic development.

Tables

England: sovereigns

reign	name	relationship
West Saxon kings		
901–25	Edward the Elder	son of Alfred the Great
925–40	Athelstan	son of Edward I
940–46	Edmund	half-brother of Athelstan
946–55	Edred	brother of Edmund
955–59	Edwy	son of Edmund
959–75	Edgar	brother of Edwy
975–78	Edward the Martyr	son of Edgar
978–1016	Ethelred II	son of Edgar
1016	Edmund Ironside	son of Ethelred
Danish kings		
1016–35	Canute	son of Sweyn I of Denmark, who conquered England in 1013
1035–40	Harold I	son of Canute
1040–42	Hardicanute	son of Canute
West Saxon kings (restored)		
1042–66	Edward the Confessor	son of Ethelred II
1066	Harold II	son of Godwin
Norman kings		
1066–87	William I	illegitimate son of Duke Robert the Devil
1087–1100	William II	son of William I
1100–35	Henry I	son of William I
1135–54	Stephen	grandson of William II
House of Plantagenet		
1154–89	Henry II	son of Matilda (daughter of Henry I)
1189–99	Richard I	son of Henry II
1199–1216	John	son of Henry II
1216–72	Henry III	son of John
1272–1307	Edward I	son of Henry III
1307–27	Edward II	son of Edward I
1327–77	Edward III	son of Edward II
1377–99	Richard II	son of the Black Prince

House of Lancaster

1399–1413	Henry IV	son of John of Gaunt
1413–22	Henry V	son of Henry IV
1422–61, 1470–71		Henry VI son of Henry V

House of York

1461–70, 1471–83		Edward IV son of Richard, Duke of York
1483	Edward V	son of Edward IV
1483–85	Richard III	brother of Edward IV

House of Tudor

1485–1509	Henry VII	son of Edmund Tudor, Earl of Richmond
1509–47	Henry VIII	son of Henry VII
1547–53	Edward VI	son of Henry VIII
1553–58	Mary I	daughter of Henry VIII
1558–1603	Elizabeth I	daughter of Henry VIII

House of Stuart

1603–25	James I	great-grandson of Margaret (daughter of Henry VII)
1625–49	Charles I	son of James I
1649–60	the Commonwealth	

House of Stuart (restored)

1660–85	Charles II	son of Charles I
1685–88	James II	son of Charles I
1689–1702	William III and Mary	son of Mary (daughter of Charles I); daughter of James II
1702–14	Anne	daughter of James II

House of Hanover

1714–27	George I	son of Sophia (grand-daughter of James 1)
1727–60	George II	son of George I
1760–1820	George III	son of Frederick (son of George II)
1820–30	George IV (regent 1811–20)	son of George III
1830–37	William IV	son of George III
1837–1901	Victoria	daughter of Edward (son of George III)

House of Saxe-Coburg

1901–10	Edward VII	son of Victoria

House of Windsor

1910–36	George V	son of Edward VII
1936	Edward VIII	son of George V
1936–52	George VI	son of George V
1952–	Elizabeth II	daughter of George VI

Scotland: kings and queens 1005–1603

(from the unification of Scotland to the union of the crowns of Scotland and England)

reign	name	reign	name
Celtic kings		**English domination**	
1005	Malcolm II	1292–96	John Baliol
1034	Duncan I	1296–1306	annexed to England
1040	Macbeth	**House of Bruce**	
1057	Malcolm III Canmore	1306	Robert the Bruce
1093	Donald II Donablane	1329	David II
1094	Duncan II		
1094	Donald II (restored)	**House of Stuart**	
1097	Edgar	1371	Robert II
1107	Alexander I	1390	Robert III
1124	David I	1406	James I
1153	Malcolm IV	1437	James II
1165	William the Lion	1460	James III
1214	Alexander II	1488	James IV
1249	Alexander III	1513	James V
1286–90	Margaret of Norway	1542	Mary
		1567	James V
		1603	union of crowns

United Kingdom: prime ministers from 1721

term	name	party
1721–42	Robert Walpole	Whig
1742–43	Earl of Wilmington	Whig
1743–54	Henry Pelham	Whig
1754–56	Duke of Newcastle	Whig
1756–57	Duke of Devonshire	Whig
1757–62	Duke of Newcastle	Whig
1762–63	Earl of Bute	Tory
1763–65	George Grenville	Whig
1765–66	Marquess of Rockingham	Whig
1767–70	Duke of Grafton	Whig
1770–82	Lord North	Tory
1782	Marquess of Rockingham	Whig
1782–83	Earl of Shelburne	Whig
1783	Duke of Portland	coalition
1783–1801	William Pitt the Younger	Tory
1801–04	Henry Addington	Tory
1804–06	William Pitt the Younger	Tory
1806–07	Lord Grenville	coalition
1807–09	Duke of Portland	Tory
1809–12	Spencer Perceval	Tory
1812–27	Earl of Liverpool	Tory
1827	George Canning	coalition
1827–28	Viscount Goderich	Tory
1828–30	Duke of Wellington	Tory
1830–34	Earl Grey	Tory
1834	Viscount Melbourne	Whig
1834–35	Robert Peel	Whig
1835–41	Viscount Melbourne	Whig
1841–46	Robert Peel	Conservative
1846–52	Lord Russell	Liberal
1852	Earl of Derby	Conservative
1852–55	Lord Aberdeen	Peelite
1855–58	Viscount Palmerston	Liberal
1858–59	Earl of Derby	Conservative
1859–65	Viscount Palmerston	Liberal
1865–66	Lord Russell	Liberal
1866–68	Earl of Derby	Conservative
1868	Benjamin Disraeli	Conservative
1868–74	W E Gladstone	Liberal
1874–80	Benjamin Disraeli	Conservative

1880–85	W E Gladstone	Liberal
1885–86	Marquess of Salisbury	Conservative
1886	W E Gladstone	Liberal
1886–92	Marquess of Salisbury	Conservative
1892–94	W E Gladstone	Liberal
1894–95	Earl of Rosebery	Liberal
1895–1902	Marquess of Salisbury	Conservative
1902–05	Arthur James Balfour	Conservative
1905–08	H Campbell-Bannerman	Liberal
1908–15	H H Asquith	Liberal
1915–16	H H Asquith	coalition
1916–22	David Lloyd George	coalition
1922–23	Andrew Bonar Law	Conservative
1923–24	Stanley Baldwin	Conservative
1924	Ramsay MacDonald	Labour
1924–29	Stanley Baldwin	Conservative
1929–31	Ramsay MacDonald	Labour
1931–35	Ramsay MacDonald	national coalition
1935–37	Stanley Baldwin	national coalition
1937–40	Neville Chamberlain	national coalition
1940–45	Winston Churchill	coalition
1945–51	Clement Attlee	Labour
1951–55	Winston Churchill	Conservative
1955–57	Anthony Eden	Conservative
1957–63	Harold Macmillan	Conservative
1963–64	Alec Douglas-Home	Conservative
1964–70	Harold Wilson	Labour
1970–74	Edward Heath	Conservative
1974–76	Harold Wilson	Labour
1976–79	James Callaghan	Labour
1979–90	Margaret Thatcher	Conservative
1990–	John Major	Conservative

United States of America: presidents and elections

year elected/ took office	president	party	losing candidate(s)	party
1789	1. George Washington	Federalist	no opponent	
1792	re-elected		no opponent	
1796	2. John Adams	Federalist	Thomas Jefferson	Democrat–Republican
1800	3. Thomas Jefferson	Democrat–Republican	Aaron Burr	Democrat–Republican
1804	re-elected		Charles Pinckney	Federalist
1808	4. James Madison	Democrat–Republican	Charles Pinckney	Federalist
1812	re-elected		DeWitt Clinton	Federalist
1816	5. James Monroe	Democrat–Republican	Rufus King	Federalist
1820	re-elected		John Quincy Adams	Democrat–Republican
1824	6. John Quincy Adams	Democrat Republican	Andrew Jackson	Democrat–Republican
	Henry Clay	Democrat–Republican	William H Crawford	Democrat–
1828	7. Andrew Jackson	Democrat	John Quincy Adams	National Republican
1832	re-elected		Henry Clay	National Republican
1836	8. Martin Van Buren	Democrat	William Henry Harrison	Whig
1840	9. William Henry Harrison	Whig	Martin Van Buren	Democrat
1841	10. John Tyler[1]	Whig		
1844	11. James K Polk	Democrat	Henry Clay	Whig
1848	12. Zachary Taylor	Whig	Lewis Cass	Democrat
1850	13. Millard Fillmore[2]	Whig		
1852	14. Franklin Pierce	Democrat	Winfield Scott	Whig
1856	15. James Buchanan	Democrat	John C Fremont	Republican
1860	16. Abraham Lincoln	Republican	Stephen Douglas	Democrat
			John Breckinridge	Democrat
			John Bell	Constitutional Union
1864	re-elected		George McClellan	Democrat
1865	17. Andrew Johnson[3]	Democrat		

1868	18. Ulysses S Grant	Republican	Horatio Seymour	Democrat
1872	re-elected		Horace Greeley	Democrat–Liberal
1876	19. Rutherford B Hayes	Republican	Samuel Tilden	Democrat
1880	20. James A Garfield	Republican	Winfield Hancock	Democrat
1881	21. Chester A Arthur[4]	Republican		
1884	22. Grover Cleveland	Democrat	James Blaine	Republican
1888	23. Benjamin Harrison	Republican	Grover Cleveland	Democrat
1892	24. Grover Cleveland	Democrat	Benjamin Harrison	Republican
			James Weaver	People's
1896	25. William McKinley	Republican	William J Bryan	Democrat–People's
1900	re-elected		William J Bryan	Democrat
1901	26. Theodore Roosevelt[5]	Republican		
1904	re-elected		Alton B Parker	Democrat
1908	27. William H Taft	Republican	William J Bryan	Democrat
1912	28. Woodrow Wilson	Democrat	Theodore Roosevelt	Progressive
			William H Taft	Republican
1916	re-elected		Charles E Hughes	Republican
1920	29. Warren G Harding	Republican	James M Cox	Democrat
1923	30. Calvin Coolidge[6]	Republican		
1924	re-elected		John W Davis	Democrat
	Robert M LaFollette	Progressive		
1928	31. Herbert Hoover	Republican	Alfred E Smith	Democrat
1932	32. Franklin D Roosevelt	Democrat	Herbert Hoover	Republican
			Norman Thomas	Socialist
1936	re-elected		Alfred Landon	Republican
1940	re-elected		Wendell Willkie	Republican
1944	re-elected		Thomas E Dewey	Republican
1945	33. Harry S Truman[7]	Democrat		
1948	re-elected		Thomas E Dewey	Republican
			J Strom Thurmond	States' Rights
			Henry A Wallace	Progressive
1952	34. Dwight D Eisenhower	Republican	Adlai E Stevenson	Democrat
1956	re-elected		Adlai E Stevenson	Democrat
1960	35. John F Kennedy	Democrat	Richard M Nixon	Republican
1963	36. Lyndon B Johnson[8]	Democrat		
1964	re-elected		Barry M Goldwater	Republican
1968	37. Richard M Nixon	Republican	Hubert H Humphrey	Democrat
			George C Wallace	
1972	re-elected		George S McGovern	Democrat
1974	38. Gerald R Ford[9]	Republican		

1976	39. Jimmy Carter	Democrat	Gerald R Ford	Republican
1980	40. Ronald Reagan	Republican	Jimmy Carter	Democrat
			John B Anderson	Independent
1984	re-elected		Walter Mondale	Democrat
1988	41. George Bush	Republican	Michael Dukakis	Democrat
1993	42. Bill Clinton	Democrat	George Bush	Republican

[1] *became president on death of Harrison*
[2] *became president on death of Taylor*
[3] *became president on assassination of Lincoln*
[4] *became president on assassination of Garfield*
[5] *became president on assassination of McKinley*
[6] *became president on death of Harding*
[7] *became president on death of F D Roosevelt*
[8] *became president on assassination of Kennedy*
[9] *became president on resignation of Nixon*

Nobel Prizes: recent winners

Peace

1985 International Physicians for the Prevention of Nuclear War
1986 Elie Wiesel (*USA*)
1987 President Oscar Arias Sanchez (*Costa Rica*)
1988 The United Nations peacekeeping forces
1989 The Dalai Lama (*Tibet*)
1990 President Mikhail Gorbachev (*USSR*)
1991 Aung San Suu Kyi (*Myanmar*)
1992 Rigoberta Menche (*Guatemala*)
1993 Nelson Mandela and Frederik Willem de Klerk (*South Africa*)
1994 Yassir Arafat (*Palestine*) and Yitzhak Rabin and Shimon Perez (*Israel*)

Literature

1985 Claude Simon (*France*)
1986 Wole Soyinka (*Nigeria*)
1987 Joseph Brodsky (*USSR/USA*)
1988 Naguib Mahfouz (*Egypt*)
1989 Camilo José Cela (*Spain*)
1990 Octavio Paz (*Mexico*)
1991 Nadine Gordimer (*South Africa*)
1992 Derek Walcott (*St Lucia*)
1993 Toni Morrison (*USA*)
1994 Kenzaburo Oe (*Japan*)

Economics

1985 Franco Modigliani (*USA*)
1986 James Buchanan (*USA*)
1987 Robert Solow (*USA*)
1988 Maurice Allais (*France*)
1989 Trygve Haavelmo (*Norway*)
1990 Harry M Markowitz (*USA*), Merton H Miller (*USA*), and William F Sharpe (*USA*)
1991 Ronald H Coase (*USA*)
1992 Gary S Becker (*USA*)
1993 Robert Fogel and Douglass North (*USA*)
1994 John F Nash (*USA*), John C Harsanyi (*USA*), and Reinhard Selten (*Germany*)

Chemistry

1985 Herbert A Hauptman (*USA*) and Jerome Karle (*USA*)
1986 Dudley Herschbach (*USA*), Yuan Lee (*USA*), and John Polanyi (*Canada*)
1987 Donald Cram (*USA*), Jean-Marie Lehn (*France*), and Charles Pedersen (*USA*)

1988	Johann Deisenhofer (*West Germany*), Robert Huber (*West Germany*), and Hartmut Michel (*West Germany*)
1989	Sydney Altman (*USA*) and Thomas Cech (*USA*)
1990	Elias James Corey (*USA*)
1991	Richard R Ernst (*Switzerland*)
1992	Rudolph A Marcus (*USA*)
1993	Kary Mullis (*USA*) and Michael Smith (*Canada*)
1994	George A Olah (*USA*)

Physics

1985	Klaus von Klitzing (*West Germany*)
1986	Ernst Ruska (*West Germany*), Gerd Binnig (*West Germany*), and Heinrich Rohrer (*Switzerland*)
1987	Georg Bednorz (*West Germany*) and Alex Müller (*Switzerland*)
1988	Leon Lederman, Melvin Schwartz, and Jack Steinberger (*USA*)
1989	Norman Ramsey (*USA*), Hans Dehmeit (*USA*), and Wolfgang Paul (*West Germany*)
1990	Richard E Taylor (*Canada*), Jerome I Friedman (*USA*), and Henry W Kendall (*USA*)
1991	Pierre-Gilles de Gennes (*France*)
1992	Georges Charpak (*France*)
1993	Joseph Taylor (*USA*) and Russell Hulse (*USA*)
1994	Clifford G Shull (*USA*) and Bertram N Brockhouse (*Canada*)

Physiology or medicine

1985	Michael Brown (*USA*) and Joseph L Goldstein (*USA*)
1986	Stanley Cohen (*USA*) and Rita Levi-Montalcini (*Italy*)
1987	Susumu Tonegawa (*Japan*)
1988	James Black (*UK*), Gertrude Elion (*USA*), and George Hitchings (*USA*)
1989	Michael Bishop (*USA*) and Harold Varmus (*USA*)
1990	Joseph Murray (*USA*) and Donnall Thomas (*USA*)
1991	Erwin Neher (*Germany*) and Bert Sakmann (*Germany*)
1992	Edmond Fisher (*USA*) and Edwin Krebs (*USA*)
1993	Phillip Sharp (*USA*) and Richard Roberts (*UK*)
1994	Alfred Gilman (*USA*) and Martin Rodbell (*USA*)

Academy Awards: recent winners

1979 Best Picture: *Kramer vs Kramer*, Best Director: Robert Benton *Kramer vs Kramer*; Best Actor: Dustin Hoffman *Kramer vs Kramer*, Best Actress: Sally Field *Norma Rae*

1980 Best Picture: *Ordinary People*; Best Director: Robert Redford *Ordinary People*; Best Actor: Robert De Niro *Raging Bull*; Best Actress: Sissy Spacek *Coal Miner's Daughter*

1981 Best Picture: *Chariots of Fire*; Best Director: Warren Beatty *Reds*; Best Actor: Henry Fonda *On Golden Pond*; Best Actress: Katharine Hepburn *On Golden Pond*

1982 Best Picture: *Gandhi*; Best Director: Richard Attenborough *Gandhi*; Best Actor: Ben Kingsley *Gandhi*; Best Actress: Meryl Streep *Sophie's Choice*

1983 Best Picture: *Terms of Endearment*; Best Director: James L Brooks *Terms of Endearment*; Best Actor: Robert Duvall *Tender Mercies*; Best Actress: Shirley MacLaine *Terms of Endearment*

1984 Best Picture: *Amadeus*; Best Director: Milos Forman *Amadeus*; Best Actor: F Murray Abraham *Amadeus*; Best Actress: Sally Field *Places in the Heart*

1985 Best Picture: *Out of Africa*; Best Director: Sidney Pollack *Out of Africa*; Best Actor: William Hurt *Kiss of the Spiderwoman*; Best Actress: Geraldine Page *The Trip to Bountiful*

1986 Best Picture: *Platoon*; Best Director: Oliver Stone *Platoon*; Best Actor: Paul Newman *The Color of Money*; Best Actress: Marlee Matlin *Children of a Lesser God*

1987 Best Picture: *The Last Emperor*; Best Director: Bernardo Bertolucci *The Last Emperor*; Best Actor: Michael Douglas *Wall Street*; Best Actress: Cher *Moonstruck*

1988 Best Picture: *Rain Man*; Best Director: Barry Levinson *Rain Man*; Best Actor: Dustin Hoffman *Rain Man*; Best Actress: Jodie Foster *The Accused*

1989 Best Picture: *Driving Miss Daisy*; Best Director: Oliver Stone *Born on the 4th of July*; Best Actor: Daniel Day-Lewis *My Left Foot*; Best Actress: Jessica Tandy *Driving Miss Daisy*

1990 Best Picture: *Dances with Wolves*; Best Director: Kevin Costner *Dances with Wolves*; Best Actor: Jeremy Irons *Reversal of Fortune*; Best Actress: Kathy Bates *Misery*

1991 Best Picture: *The Silence of the Lambs*; Best Director: Jonathan Demme *The Silence of the Lambs*; Best Actor: Anthony Hopkins *The Silence of the Lambs*; Best Actress: Jodie Foster *The Silence of the Lambs*

1992 Best Picture: *Unforgiven*; Best Director: Clint Eastwood *Unforgiven*; Best Actor: Al Pacino *Scent of a Woman*; Best Actress: Emma Thompson *Howards End*

1993 Best Picture: *Schindler's List*; Best Director: Steven Spielberg *Schindler's List*; Best Actor: Tom Hanks *Philadelphia*; Best Actress: Holly Hunter *The Piano*

1994 Best Picture: *Forrest Gump;* Best Director: Robert Zemeckis *Forrest Gump;* Best Actor: Tom Hanks *Forrest Gump;* Best Actress: Jessica Lange *Blue Sky*

Cinema awards: Best Film awards from four top film festivals (recent winners)

Cannes Film Festival Palme d'Or for Best Film
1985 When Father Was Away on Business (*Yug*)
1986 The Mission (*GB*)
1987 Under the Sun of Satan (*Fr*)
1988 Pelle the Conqueror (*Den*)
1989 Sex, Lies and Videotape (*USA*)
1990 Wild at Heart (*USA*)
1991 Barton Fink (*USA*)
1992 The Best Intentions (*Swe*)
1993 The Piano (*NZ/Australia*); Farewell My Concubine (*Hong Kong/China*)
1994 Pulp Fiction (*USA*)

Venice Film Festival Golden Lion for Best Film
1985 Sans toit ni loi aka Vagabonde (*Fr*)
1986 Le Rayon Vert (*Fr*)
1987 Au Revoir les Enfants (*Fr*)
1988 La Leggenda del Santo Bevitore (The Legend of the Holy Drinker) (*It*)
1989 Beiqing Chengshi (City of Sadness) (*Taiwan*)
1990 Rosencrantz and Guildenstern are Dead (*GB*)
1991 Urga (*Russia*)
1992 Story of Qiu Ju (*China*)
1993 Short Cuts (*USA*),Three Colours Blue (*Pol*)
1994 Vive l'Amour (*Taiwan*); Before the Rain (*Macedonia*)

Berlin Film Festival Golden Bear for Best Film
1985 Wetherby (*GB*); Die Frau und der Fremde (*FRG*)
1986 Stammheim (*FRG*)
1987 The Theme (*USSR*)
1988 Red Sorghum (*China*)
1989 Rain Man (*USA*)
1990 Skylarks on a String (*Czech*); Music Box (*USA*)
1991 La Casa del Sorriso (House of Smiles) (*It*)
1992 Grand Canyon (*USA*)
1993 Woman from the Lake of Centred Souls (*China*); Wedding Banquet (*Taiwan*)
1994 In the Name of the Father (*USA/Ireland*)

British Academy of Film and Television Arts (BAFTA) Best Film Awards
1985 The Killing Fields (*UK*)
1986 The Purple Rose of Cairo (*USA*)
1987 A Room with a View (*UK*)
1988 Jean de Florette (*Fr*)
1989 The Last Emperor (*USA*)
1990 Dead Poets Society (*USA*)
1991 Goodfellas (*USA*)
1992 The Commitments (*UK*)
1993 Howard's End (*UK*)
1994 Schindler's List (*USA*)
1995 Four Weddings and a Funeral (*UK*)

International book awards: recent winners

Booker Prize (*UK*)

1985	Keri Hulme *The Bone People*
1986	Kingsley Amis *The Old Devils*
1987	Penelope Lively *Moon Tiger*
1988	Peter Carey *Oscar and Lucinda*
1989	Kazuo Ishiguro *The Remains of the Day*
1990	A S Byatt *Possession*
1991	Ben Okri *The Famished Road*
1992	Barry Unsworth *Sacred Hunger*, Michael Ondaatje *The English Patient* (joint winners)
1993	Roddy Doyle *Paddy Clarke Ha Ha Ha*
1994	James Kelman *How Late It Was, How Late*

Whitbread Literary Award: Book of the Year (*UK*)

1985	Peter Ackroyd *Hawksmoor*
1986	Kazuo Ishiguro *An Artist of the Floating World*
1987	Ian McEwan *The Child in Time*
1988	Salman Rushdie *The Satanic Verses*
1989	Lindsay Clarke *The Chymical Wedding*
1990	Nicholas Mosley *Hopeful Monsters*
1991	Jane Gardam *The Queen of the Tambourine*
1992	Alasdair Gray *Poor Things*
1993	Joan Brady *Theory of War*
1994	William Trevor *Felicia's Journey*

Prix Goncourt (*France*)

1985	Yann Queffelec *Les Noces Barbares*
1986	Michel Host *Valet de Nuit*
1987	Tahir Ben Jelloun *La Nuit Sacrée*
1988	Erik Orsenna *L'Exposition Coloniale*
1989	Jean Vautrin *Un Grand Pas vers le Bon Dieu*
1990	Jean Rouault *Les Champs d'Honneur*
1991	Pierre Combescot *Les Filles du Calvaire*
1992	Patrick Chamoisean *Texaco*
1993	Amin Maalouf *Le Rocher de Tanios*
1994	Didier van Cauwelaert *Un Aller Simple*

Pulitzer Prize for Fiction (*USA*)

1985	Alison Lurie *Foreign Affairs*
1986	Larry McMurtry *Lonesome Dove*
1987	Peter Taylor *A Summons to Memphis*
1988	Toni Morrison *Beloved*
1989	Anne Tyler *Breathing Lessons*
1990	Oscar Hijuelos *The Mambo Kings Play Songs of Love*
1991	John Updike *Rabbit at Rest*
1992	Jane Simley *A Thousand Acres*
1993	Robert Olen Butler *A Good Scent from a Strange Mountain*
1994	E Annie Proulx *The Shipping News*

Tables

562

Wedding anniversaries

In many Western countries, different wedding anniversaries have become associated with gifts of different materials. There is variation between countries.

anniversary	material	anniversary	material
1st	cotton	14th	ivory
2nd	paper	15th	crystal
3rd	leather	20th	china
4th	fruit, flowers	25th	silver
5th	wood	30th	pearl
6th	sugar	35th	coral
7th	copper, wool	40th	ruby
8th	bronze, pottery	45th	sapphire
9th	pottery, willow	50th	gold
10th	tin	55th	emerald
11th	steel	60th	diamond
12th	silk, linen	70th	platinum
13th	lace		

Birthstones

month	stone	quality
January	garnet	constancy
February	amethyst	sincerity
March	bloodstone	courage
April	diamond	innocence and lasting love
May	emerald	success and hope
June	pearl	health and purity
July	ruby	love and contentment
August	agate	married happiness
September	sapphire	wisdom
October	opal	hope
November	topaz	fidelity
December	turquoise	harmony

Signs of the zodiac

Spring

Aries	The Ram	21 March-20 April
Taurus	The Bull	21 April-21 May
Gemini	The Twins	22 May-21 June

Summer

Cancer	The Crab	22 June-23 July
Leo	The Lion	24 July-23 August
Virgo	The Virgin	24 Aug-23 Sept

Autumn

Libra	The Balance	24 Sept-23 Oct
Scorpio	The Scorpion	24 Oct-22 Nov
Sagittarius	The Archer	23 Nov-21 Dec

Winter

Capricorn	The Goat	22 Dec-20 Jan
Aquarius	The Water Bearer	21 Jan-19 Feb
Pisces	The Fishes	20 Feb-20 March

Conversion tables

to convert from imperial to metric	multiply by	multiply by	to convert from metric to imperial
length			
inches	25.4	0.039,37	millimetres
feet	0.3048	3.2808	metres
yards	0.9144	1.0936	metres
furlongs	0.201	4.971	kilometres
miles	1.6093	0.6214	kilometres
area			
square inches	6.4516	0.1550	square centimetres
square feet	0.0929	10.7639	square metres
square yards	0.8361	1.1960	square metres
square miles	2.5900	0.3861	square kilometres
acres	4046.86	0.000,247	square metres
acres	0.4047	2.47105	hectares
hectares	0.001	1,000	square kilometres
mass			
ounces	28.3495	0.03527	grams
pounds	0.4536	2.2046	kilograms
stone (14 lb)	6.3503	0.1575	kilograms
tons (imperial)	1016.05	0.00098	kilograms
tons (US)	907.2	0.001	kilograms
tons (imperial)	0.9842	1.0161	tonnes
tons (US)	0.9072	1.102	tonnes
speed			
miles per hour	1.6093	0.6214	kilometres per hour
feet per second	0.3048	3.2808	metres per second
fuel consumption			
miles per gallon	0.3540	2.825	kilometres per litre
miles per US gallon	0.4251	2.3521	kilometres per litre
gallons per mile	2.8248	0.3540	litres per kilometre
US gallons per mile	2.3521	0.4251	litres per kilometre

Oceans and seas

	area		average depth	
	sq km	sq mi	m	ft
Pacific Ocean	166,242,000	64,186,300	3,939	12,925
Atlantic Ocean	86,557,000	33,420,000	3,575	11,730
Indian Ocean	73,427,500	28,350,500	3,840	12,598
Arctic Ocean	13,224,000	5,105,700	1,038	3,407
South China Sea	2,975,000	1,148,500	1,464	4,802
Caribbean Sea	2,516,000	971,400	2,575	8,448
Mediterranean Sea	2,510,000	969,100	1,501	4,926
Bering Sea	2,261,061	873,000	1,491	4,893
Gulf of Mexico	1,508,000	582,100	1,614	5,297
Sea of Okhotsk	1,392,000	537,500	973	3,192
Sea of Japan	1,013,000	391,100	1,667	5,468
Hudson Bay	730,000	281,900	93	305
East China Sea	665,000	256,600	189	620
Andaman Sea	565,000	218,100	1,118	3,667
Black Sea	508,000	196,100	1,190	3,906
Red Sea	453,000	174,900	538	1,764
North Sea	427,000	164,900	94	308
Baltic Sea	382,000	147,500	55	180
Yellow Sea	294,000	113,500	37	121
Persian Gulf	230,000	88,800	100	328
Gulf of St Lawrence	162,000	62,530	810	2,660
Gulf of California	153,000	59,100	724	2,375
English Channel	89,900	34,700	54	177
Irish Sea	88,550	34,200	60	197
Bass Strait	75,000	28,950	70	230